Lecture Notes in Computer Science 9579

Commenced Publication in 1973
Founding and Former Series Editors:
Gerhard Goos, Juris Hartmanis, and Jan van Leeuwen

Editorial Board

Fusheng Wang · Gang Luo
Chunhua Weng · Arijit Khan
Prasenjit Mitra · Cong Yu (Eds.)

Biomedical Data Management and Graph Online Querying

VLDB 2015 Workshops, Big-O(Q) and DMAH
Waikoloa, HI, USA, August 31 – September 4, 2015
Revised Selected Papers

 Springer

Editors
Fusheng Wang
Stony Brook University
Stony Brook, NY
USA

Gang Luo
University of Utah
Salt Lake City, UT
USA

Chunhua Weng
Columbia University
New York, NY
USA

Arijit Khan
Nanyang Technological University
Singapore
Singapore

Prasenjit Mitra
Qatar Computing Research Institute
Doha
Qatar

Cong Yu
Google Research
New York, NY
USA

ISSN 0302-9743   ISSN 1611-3349 (electronic)
Lecture Notes in Computer Science
ISBN 978-3-319-41575-8   ISBN 978-3-319-41576-5 (eBook)
DOI 10.1007/978-3-319-41576-5

Library of Congress Control Number: 2016943069

LNCS Sublibrary: SL3 – Information Systems and Applications, incl. Internet/Web, and HCI

Printed on acid-free paper

This Springer imprint is published by Springer Nature
The registered company is Springer International Publishing AG Switzerland

Preface

In this volume we present the contributions accepted for the First International Workshop on Data Management and Analytics for Medicine and Healthcare (DMAH 2015) and the Big-O(Q) VLDB 2015 Workshop on Big-Graphs Online Querying, held at the Big Island of Hawaii in conjunction with the 41st International Conference on Very Large Data Bases on August 31 – September 4, 2015.

The goal of DMAH workshop is to bring together people in the field cross-cutting information management and medical informatics to discuss innovative data management and analytics technologies highlighting end-to-end applications, systems, and methods to address problems in health care, public health, and everyday wellness, with clinical, physiological, imaging, behavioral, environmental, and omic-data, and data from social media and the Web. It provides a unique opportunity for interaction between information management researchers and biomedical researchers in an interdisciplinary field.

For the DMAH workshop, 13 papers were received. A rigorous, single-blind, peer-review selection process was adopted, resulting in six accepted papers and one accepted abstract presented at the workshop. Each paper was reviewed by three members of the Program Committee, who were carefully selected for their knowledge and competence. As far as possible, papers were matched with the reviewer's particular interests and special expertise. The result of this careful process can be seen in the high quality of the contributions published in this volume.

Graph data management has become a hot topic in the database community in recent years, because of an increasing realization that querying and reasoning about the interconnections between entities can lead to interesting and deep insights into a variety of phenomena. Despite much work in the area from the perspective of emerging applications, graph data management and online querying are still nascent topics in the database community with many open questions such as graph query optimization and benchmarking, declarative versus procedural graph query languages, graph data representation, optimal graph partitioning and dynamic workload balancing techniques, and the role of modern hardware in graph processing, among many others. The Big-O(Q) Workshop is an attempt to discuss some thoughts on these topics, and highlight which exciting and important research problems we think are still open.

For the Big-O(Q) Workshop, three papers were accepted from nine submissions. Each paper was peer reviewed by at least three reviewers from the Program Committee.

We would like to express our sincere thanks especially to the internationally renowned speakers who gave keynote talks at the workshop plenary sessions: Prof. Amar Das of Dartmouth College, USA, Prof. Ulf Leser of Humboldt-Universität in

Berlin, Germany, and Prof. Laks V.S. Lakshmanan of the University of British Columbia. We would like to thank the members of the Program Committee for their attentiveness, perseverance, and willingness to provide high-quality reviews.

September 2015

Fusheng Wang
Gang Luo
Chunhua Weng
Arijit Khan
Prasenjit Mitra
Cong Yu

Organization

DMAH 2015

Workshop Chairs

Fusheng Wang	Stony Brook University, USA
Gang Luo	University of Utah, USA
Chunhua Weng	Columbia University, USA

Program Committee

Syed Sibte Raza Abidi	Dalhousie University, Canada
Ümit Çatalyürek	The Ohio State University, USA
Carlo Combi	University of Verona, Italy
Amarendra Das	Dartmouth College, USA
Peter Elkin	University of Buffalo, USA
Kerstin Denecke	Universität Leipzig, Germany
Dejing Dou	University of Oregon, USA
Guoqian Jiang	Mayo Clinic, USA
Jun Kong	Emory University, USA
Tahsin Kurc	Stony Brook University, USA
Fernando Martin-Sanchez	University of Melbourne, Australia
Casey Overby	University of Maryland, USA
Jyotishman Pathak	Mayo Clinic, USA
Yuval Shahar	Ben-Gurion University, Israel
Jimeng Sun	Georgia Institute of Technology, USA
Nicholas Tatonetti	Columbia University, USA
Xiang Li	Fudan University, China
Li Xiong	Emory University, USA
Hua Xu	University of Texas Health Science Center, USA
Lin Yang	University of Florida, USA
Lixia Yao	University of North Carolina at Charlotte, USA
Mehlha Yetisgen	University of Washington, USA

Big-O(Q) 2015

Workshop Chairs

Arijit Khan   ETH Zurich, Switzerland
Prasenjit Mitra   Qatar Computing Research Institute, Qatar
Cong Yu   Google Research, USA

Program Committee

Jan Van den Bussche   Universiteit Hasselt, Belgium
Khuzaima Daudjee   University of Waterloo, Canada
Amol Deshpande   University of Maryland, USA
Gosta Grahne   Concordia University, USA
Yuxiong He   Microsoft Research, USA
Themis Palpanas   Paris Descartes University, France
Sherif Sakr   NICTA/UNSW, Australia
Hanghang Tong   Arizona State University, USA
Yi Zhang   Google, USA

Challenges of Reasoning with Multiple Knowledge Sources in the Context of Drug Induced Liver Injury

(Extended Abstract)

Casey L. Overby[2], Alejandro Flores[1], Guillermo Palma[1],
Maria-Esther Vidal[1], Elena Zotkina[2], and Louiqa Raschid[2]

[1] Universidad Simón Bolvar, Venezuela
[2] University of Maryland, USA
coverby@medicine.umaryland.edu,
{aflores,gpalma,mvidal}@ldc.usb.ve,
{ezotkina,louiqa}@umiacs.umd.edu

Many classes of drugs, their interaction pathways and gene targets are known to play a role in drug induced liver injury (DILI). Pharmacogenomics research to understand the impact of genetic variation on how patients respond to drugs may also help explain some of the variability, e.g., the onset or severity, of an observed occurrence of adverse drug reactions (ADR) such as DILI. The goal of this project is to combine rich genotype and phenotype data with data about drugs, genes, pathways, to better understand the drivers of scenarios such as DILI. We will define protocols to create datasets and develop methods to identify patterns (groups or clusters of drugs and genes) and to reason about temporal clinical events, for explanation and prediction of DILI.

This extended abstract presents the challenges of such efforts to benefit from combining datasets including knowledge of associations between genotypes and phenotypes relevant to drug treatment. The motivating example will be a case study around drugs known to lead to unpredictable ("idiosyncratic") adverse drug reactions (ADRs) in susceptible individuals. Identifying genetic risk factors associated with idiosyncratic ADRs has the potential to facilitate detection of "at risk" patients. Drug-induced liver injury (DILI) is one ADR for which the associated genetic factors have been studied since the 1980s. The drugs that lead to this toxicity are structurally diverse and belong to a number of different therapeutic classes. See [5,6] for a comprehensive review.

Figure 1 is a representation of the complex and heterogeneous knowledge that will be used to study DILI. The V-Model [4] represents temporal clinical events and provides a framework for clinical problem-action relationships. Temporal clinical events informed by the V-Model is illustrated in the bottom half of Figure 1. It will provide information for temporal reasoning in order to propose possible drugs (actions) causing an ADR (problems) (Figure 1, questions 1–3). The questions are as follows: 1. What problems indicate the ADR? 2. What encounter occurred prior to the ADR? 3. What actions could have caused the ADR?

Additional resources include DrugBank, PharmGKB, the Human Phenotype Ontology and the Disease Ontology. They capture semantic knowledge around the concepts of drugs, gene-targets, enzymes, diseases, and phenotypes, all interacting with biological pathways. This is represented in the knowledge graph in the upper half of Figure 1. They facilitate inferring potential causal relationships between drugs and ADRs (Figure 1, question 4), namely, *Is the ADR due to a drug?*

We briefly summarize the semantic knowledge that will be applied to our case study as follows: 1. We will consider similarities between pairs of drugs and between pairs of gene targets. 2. We will consider shared pathways and interactions between pairs of drugs; this may also lead to adverse drug reactions (ADRs). 3. We will consider more complex interactions in pathways of drug targets, metabolizing enzymes, transporters, etc. 4. For a drug in use, we will consider interactions between (a) phenotypes or diagnoses associated with an ADR exhibited by the patient and (b) gene targets involved in drug mechanisms. This will provide evidence for or against the drug in question being a causal factor of a given ADR.

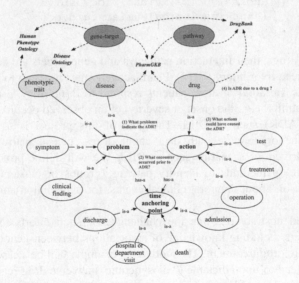

Fig. 1. V-Model Representation of clinical events and the PharmGKB Knowledge Graph for pharmacogenomic data.

An additional challenge is to map clinical data into our representation of temporal clinical events (Figure 1, solid lines). Relevant clinical data will be extracted for known DILI patients using previous approaches [2]. We will limit datasets to electronic health record systems (EHR) with computerized provider order entry (CPOE) in order to facilitate running queries of temporal data including patient encounters, e.g., visits, and medication orders. We also plan to explore use of ontologies such as the Ontology of Adverse Events (OAE)[1]. to represent the relationships between problems, time anchoring points and actions in order to infer causal ADRs. In addition, clinical notes may require Natural Language Processing (NLP) and Information Extraction (IE) techniques. Our methodology to find patterns in graphs clustered around biological pathways will rely on a semantics based edge partitioning (semEP) solution; semEP is a variant of community detection. Details of semEP are in [3].

To summarize, a DILI study will combine genotype, phenotype and pharmacogenomic knowledge and datasets. A simple representation of temporal clinical events informed by the V-Model[4] models temporal clinical events and provides a framework to connect clinical problem-action relationships. A methodology based on semEP - semantics based edge partitioning to create communities - will be extended to find patterns.

References

1. He, Y., Sarntivijai, S., Lin, Y., Xiang, Z., Guo, A., Zhang, S., Jagannathan, D., Toldo, L., Tao, C., Smith, B. et al.: OAE: The ontology of adverse events. Journal of Biomedical Semantics, **29**(5) (2014)
2. Overby, C.L., Pathak, J., Gottesman, O., Haerian, K., Perotte, A., Murphy, S., Bruce, K., Johnson, S., Talwalkar, J., Shen, Y. et al.: A collaborative approach to developing an electronic health record phenotyping algorithm for drug-induced liver injury. J. Am. Med. Inform. Assoc. pp. 243–252 (2013)
3. Palma, G., Vidal, M., Raschid, L.: Drug-target interaction prediction using semantic similarity and edge partitioning. In: Mika, P., Tudorache, T., Bernstein, A., Welty, C., Knoblock, C., Vrandečić, D., Groth, P., Noy, N., Janowicz, K., Goble, C. et al. (eds.) The Semantic Web - ISWC 2014 - 13th International Semantic Web Conference Proceedings, Part I. LNCS, vol. 8796, pp. 131–146. Springer, Heidelberg (2014)
4. Park, H., Choi, J.: V-model: a new perspective for ehr-phenotyping. BMC Med. Inform. Decis. Mak. **14**(90) (2014)
5. Russmann, S., Jetter, A., Kullak-Ublick, G.: Pharmacogenomics of drug-induced liver injury. Heptology, **52**(2) (2010)
6. Urban, T., Daly, A., Aithal, G.: Genetic basis of drug-induced liver injury: Present and future. Seminars in liver injury, **34**(2) (2014)

Contents

Medical Imaging Analytics

Big-Graphs Online Querying

Information Retrieval and Data Analytics for Electronic Medical Records

Vector Space Models
for Encoding and Retrieving Longitudinal
Medical Record Data

Haider Syed[1,2(✉)] and Amar K. Das[1,3]

[1] Social Computing & Health Informatics Lab, Hanover, USA
haider.syed@cs.dartmouth.edu, amar.das@dartmouth.edu
[2] Department of Computer Science, Dartmouth College, Hanover, USA
[3] Department of Biomedical Data Science,
Geisel School of Medicine at Dartmouth, Hanover, NH 03755, USA

Abstract. Vector space models (VSMs) are widely used as information retrieval methods and have been adapted to many applications. In this paper, we propose a novel use of VSMs for classification and retrieval of longitudinal electronic medical record data. These data contain sequences of clinical events that are based on treatment decisions, but the treatment plan is not recorded with the events. The goals of our VSM methods are (1) to identify which plan a specific patient treatment sequence best matches and (2) to find patients whose treatment histories most closely follow a specific plan. We first build a traditional VSM that uses standard terms corresponding to the events found in clinical plans and treatment histories. We also consider temporal terms that represent binary relationships of precedence between or co-occurrence of these events. We create four alternative VSMs that use different combinations of standard and temporal terms as dimensions, and we evaluate their performance using manually annotated data on chemotherapy plans and treatment histories for breast cancer patients. In classifying treatment histories, the best approach used temporal terms, which had 87 % accuracy in identifying the correct clinical plan. For information retrieval, our results showed that the traditional VSM performed best. Our results indicate that VSMs have good performance for classification and retrieval of longitudinal electronic medical records, but the results depend on how the model is constructed.

1 Introduction

The past decade has seen the widespread adoption of Electronic Medical Records (EMRs), which has resulted in data collection that better tracks healthcare quality and outcomes. EMR technologies, however, have a number of limitations in supporting healthcare analytics. EMRs capture clinical encounters that are based on treatment decisions; however, the treatment plan is usually not encoded. An unmet user need is ascertaining which patients are on a specific treatment plan. To address this challenge, we propose a *search* method based on information retrieval that ranks patient treatment histories in the EMR in order of similarity to the treatment events in a plan. Another challenge is that users have to manually abstract the plan from the treatment events,

F. Wang et al. (Eds.): Big-O(Q) and DMAH 2015, LNCS 9579, pp. 3–15, 2016.
DOI: 10.1007/978-3-319-41576-5_1

which can be laborious for large numbers of patients. To solve this challenge, we propose a *classification* method that matches the sequence of events to a patient treatment history to a defined clinical plan. The search and classification methods need to account for the fact that treatment histories may deviate from clinical plans, so the match is not likely to be exact.

To implement a common solution for both of these challenges, we use vector space models (VSMs), which are widely utilized for information retrieval and web search. For the VSM, we encode both treatment histories and clinical plans as vectors. We consider the use of a standard VSM approach in which individual events in treatment histories or clinical plans are vector terms. We also propose the novel use of terms that correspond to temporal relations between two events. To our knowledge, our work presents the first application of VSMs that uses coded data from EMRs and that includes temporal relations as terms. We evaluate standard and temporal terms from treatment data and plan information for breast cancer patients using five different VSMs. The authors had previously addressed the classification problem using a novel sequence alignment approach [1, 2]. The proposed VSM approaches, in contrast, assess the value of different temporal relations and also provide scalability and performance with Big Data collections extracted from EMRs.

2 Related Work

The first practical implementation of the VSM was developed for information retrieval of documents [3, 4]. A VSM traditionally represents each document as a term vector where the terms are the unique words found in the entire corpus. One advantage of VSMs compared to Boolean-term matching for document retrieval is their ability to rank the relevance of the search results based on the similarity between vectors. Since their inception, VSMs have been used for applications in a multitude of domains, including medical applications, and have been extended to other forms of data. There have been many efforts to use VSMs on unstructured medical documents [5–9]. Mao and Chu [10] create a phrase-based VSM to represent documents where the phrases consist of concepts and words. The method is developed and tested for medical document retrieval; the authors report a 16 % increase in retrieval accuracy compared to a basic VSM. Efforts by Hassanpour et al. [11, 12] have extended VSMs to incorporate semantically related terms from an ontology and use weights based on semantic similarity. Using this approach, a novel semantic search method is developed to find publications semantically similar to ontology-based definitions. The approach extends vector space models to incorporate the terms from the definitions as vectors in the same VSM representing the documents. Hassanpour et al. [12] then use the approach to rank which snippet of texts within the documents contain the definitions. In [13], Mondal et al. extend the VSM approach to support medical decision-making; they propose a ranking system that can recommend medications based on a set of diagnoses.

3   Temporal Model

EMRs consist of a wide variety of structured information, such as logs of clinical events. The logs consist of date-stamped codes of diagnostic or treatment information that occurred during a patient encounter (Fig. 1). The timing and ordering of the events are essential to clinical interpretation, such as identifying a clinical plan from the

Patient ID	Event Code	Encounter Date
1011	A	January 8, 2014
1011	B	January 8, 2014
1011	C	January 8, 2014
1011	D	January 15, 2014
1011	E	January 29, 2014

(a)

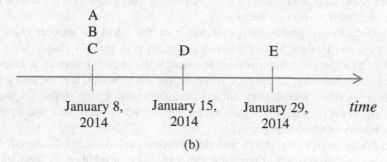

(b)

Fig. 1. (a) An example of a clinical event log for a single patient, represented as a table of longitudinal encounter data containing diagnostic or treatment event codes and the date stamp of the encounter. As shown, there are three concurrent codes that occurred on an encounter of January 8th, followed by two more encounters on January 15th and 29th. (b) The same information in the clinical event log represented as a timeline.

temporal pattern of treatment events. Building a traditional VSM, using only the set of coded terms from the events in patient's medical records, would lose the ordering information among the events shown in Fig. 1. Two patients who had the identical set of events in a different order would have identical vector representations in the model. This issue motivated our effort to pursue VSM approaches that capture ordering of the events as temporal terms. Specifically, we create terms that encode precedence between or co-occurrence of events. We specify the co-occurrence of events A and B as the term

'A-B' and the precedence of event D before event E as the term 'D→E'. A more complex set of thirteen temporal relations can exist between two intervals [20]; precedence and co-occurrence relations are sufficient, however, to capture temporality between single time stamps.

Many extensions have been developed for traditional VSMs. Some efforts have tried to incorporate correlations among the vector terms, and have explored the use of association rules to include correlations [14–16]. Another approach, called the Generalized VSM, extends VSMs to allow correlated terms as it supports non-orthogonal components [17, 18]; the approach represents the terms using vectors with binary weights that indicate the presence or absence of all possible permutations of terms that can co-occur. VSMs are particularly useful in Natural Language Processing and much work has been done in incorporating semantics in VSMs [19]. However, none of these prior extensions have used temporal information in the VSM.

4 Methods

A traditional VSM represents documents as terms vectors. Each dimension of the vector space represents a term that exists in the corpus. In the document representation as a term vector, the terms that appear in the document are assigned a non-zero value. The values given to the terms, called the term weights, depend on the choice of a weighting scheme. For information retrieval, a query's terms are represented as a vector, and documents are ranked by similarity to the query based on the cosine of the angle between their respective vectors.

Our approach incorporates temporal terms in the VSM to support (1) finding treatment histories that most closely match a clinical plan and (2) classifying a treatment history as a specific treatment plan. For search, the vectors represent a 'corpus' of patient treatment histories, where each vector represents a patient, and the query vector represents a specific clinical plan. In contrast, the classification approach uses the clinical plans as the corpus, where each vector represents a clinical plan, and a patient's treatment history is the query vector.

We consider the relative search and classification performance of different VSMs that include standard terms and temporal terms (Fig. 2). In addition to the traditional VSM, which has no temporal terms, we build four alternative VSMs using temporal terms. We build a VSM, called *sequential VSM* (sVSM), that includes precedence terms in the linear pairwise sequence the events occur longitudinally, and we create a separate VSM, called *temporal VSM* (tVSM), that includes all precedence relations between encounters. The precedence terms in the sVSM are a subset of the precedence terms in the tVSM. Both the sVSM and tVSM use all found co-occurrence terms. We present further details in Sect. 4.1.

The different VSMs are used to measure the similarity between term vectors representing patient treatment histories and clinical plans. Therefore, the models must present a way to compute levels of similarity between vectors. To this end, all VSMs present two degrees of freedom: a similarity measure that can compute relatedness between vectors, and a weighting scheme to affect the importance of the different vector terms in computing the similarity. In our experiments, a similarity metric called the cosine similarity

VSM Approach	Example Terms from Fig. 1
1. Traditional VSM	A, B, C, D, E
2. Sequential VSM (sVSM)	A-B, A-C, B-C, A→D, B→D, C→D, D→E
3. Temporal VSM (tVSM)	A-B, A-C, B-C, A→D, B→D, C→D, D→E, A→E, B→E, C→E
4. Traditional + sVSM	A, B, C, D, E A-B, A-C, B-C, A→D, B→D, C→D, D→E
5. Traditional + tVSM	A, B, C, D, E A-B, A-C, B-C, A→D, B→D, C→D, D→E, A→E, B→E, C→E

Fig. 2. A set of five different VSMs with terms derived from the clinical event log in Fig. 1. The traditional VSM consists of just the events found in the clinical event log. No temporal information is encoded. The sequential and temporal VSMs use temporal terms based on co-occurrence and precedence of events. The co-occurrence relations (shown in red), represent concomitant events and are specified as a term based on two event names separated by a hyphen. The precedence relations indicate the occurrence of one event before another event, and are represented by an arrow signifying the ordering of the two events. The sequential VSM uses precedence terms in the linear pairwise sequence the events occur longitudinally whereas the temporal VSM includes all possible precedence relations by creating terms pairing each event and any subsequent event. Both the sequential and temporal VSMs have the same set of co-occurrence relations. We consider two hybrid models that incorporate the traditional (non-temporal) terms with the terms for the sequential or temporal VSM. (Color figure online)

measure is used to evaluate the performance of the five approaches under two weighting schemes: term-frequency (tf) and term-frequency, inverse-document frequency (tf-idf), as described in Sect. 4.2.

4.1 Vector Space Models

There are five VSMs considered in this paper: a traditional VSM (VSM), a sequential VSM (sVSM), a temporal VSM (tVSM), a traditional + sVSM and a traditional + tVSM. Each of these models are discussed below. For the sake of simplicity, the example events discussed in this paper are represented as single letters, instead of complete event names. Using single letters as example terms is merely a design choice as the term labels are not involved in quantifying similarity between vectors. Figure 1 shows an example patient and the term vectors that would be needed to represent the patient in each of the VSMs described below. The terms shown for each model are the terms that would have non-zero weights in the respective models.

Traditional VSM. Each unique event that appears in the medical records or possible queries is represented as a single dimension of the vector space. For a set of patients that have undergone events A, B, C, D, E, F, G and H; the terms in the vectors would simply be A B C D E F G and H. To represent a patient in this vector space who has the event log shown in Fig. 1, the vector terms would simply have a non-zero weight for the terms A, B, C, D and E, and a zero for the terms F, G and H.

Sequential VSM (sVSM). The sequential VSM contains two types of temporal terms: precedence and co-occurrence terms. The precedence terms are created by pairing consecutive events. If a patient receives A followed by B and B is followed by C, the precedence terms that arise will be A→B and B→C. The co-occurrence terms represent encounters that occur at the same time. For concomitant events, EMRs do not specify relative ordering of the events. We this order the events lexicographically to maintain a consistent manner of creating terms for the VSM. For the example in Fig. 1, the patient undergoes the events A, B and C on the same day, followed by an event D a week later and another event E two weeks later. For this example, the co-occurrence relations in the sVSM model are A-B, A-C, and B-C. The precedence relations for this example are A→D, B→D, C→D, and C→E.

Temporal VSM (tVSM). The temporal VSM incorporates terms for co-occurrence relations in exactly the same way as the sVSM. The difference between the models is in their representation of precedence relations. The sVSM only models precedence relations between adjacent events; the tVSM creates precedence terms between each event and every event that occurs thereafter. In contrast, the tVSM creates all possible forward permutation pairs between an event and every subsequent event. For the example patient in Fig. 1, the precedence relations in this case are A→D, A→E, B→D, B→E, C→D, and C→E.

Traditional + sVSM. This model is simply the union of vector terms of the traditional VSM and the sVSM.

Traditional + tVSM. This hybrid model contains all the terms used in the traditional VSM and the tVSM.

4.2 Similarity Measure and Weighting Schemes

Given the vector space representations described in Sect. 4.1, we must choose a metric to quantify the similarity between vectors in the various models. Past work on VSMs has used a variety of similarity metrics. We employ the cosine similarity measure, *Sim*, which is widely used in information retrieval. Sim calculates the L2-normalized inner product of the two vectors in question. Length-normalizing the vectors projects them onto a unit sphere, so computing the dot product between the vectors results in the cosine of the angle that is distended between them, which is a measure of the similarity between the vectors. Specifically, the formula for the measure is given by Eq. 1, where x and y are two vectors.

$$Sim(x, y) = \frac{x.y}{\|x\|\|y\|} \tag{1}$$

If the input vectors are non-negative, the values of Sim(x, y) range from 0 to 1 whereby a score of 0 indicates orthogonal vectors or no similarity and a score of 1 represents a perfect match.

The term weights in a traditional VSM are binary and indicate presence or absence of terms, however, different weighting schemes have been evaluated in informational retrieval and have shown to improve results over a basic Boolean retrieval model. In our work, we evaluate the performance of two weighting schemes that are widely used for text documents: the term-frequency (tf) weighting and the term-frequency inverse-document frequency (tf-idf) weighting. tf weighs the terms in the VSM by the frequencies of their occurrence or by some function of their frequency of occurrence; tf captures the intuition that if a word appears frequently in a document, it is important and should have a stronger impact on the similarity level. Tf-idf schemes weigh the terms in a way that increases linearly with the number of terms and is offset by the frequency of the term in the complete corpus. Tf-idf schemes preserve the idea that a frequent word in a document is important; however, words that appear frequently across the corpus are not as important, as they do not help differentiate between documents and so are weighed less by the idf portion of the formula.

5 Experiments and Results

In this study, we evaluate the performance of the different VSMs for search and classification of treatment histories using EMR data on breast cancer chemotherapy. The administration of breast cancer chemotherapies are based on clinical plans, called regimens, and are specified in published guidelines [21]. Physicians use the guidelines to devise patient treatments, but EMRs often do not directly record the clinical plan with the treatment history. There is a need for an autonomous method to match a patient record to a pre-defined plan, since identifying the plan is the first step in studying its effectiveness. Furthermore, there is a need for a cohort retrieval tool that allows investigators to search the EMR data for patients whose treatment history is similar to a given plan. The patient data is described in Sect. 5.1, and the pre-defined patterns that shape the treatments are discussed in Sect. 5.2.

5.1   Patient Dataset

Our evaluation of the VSM models was done on events logs from the EMR system of Dartmouth-Hitchcock Medical Center. A new EMR system (Epic) was instituted on April 2, 2011, and our extraction was done on November 1, 2014. We retrieved data on 928 patients who had been diagnosed with invasive breast cancer, as confirmed by a tumor registry. Since chemotherapy treatments are typically initiated and completed within a year after diagnosis, we selected patients who had a diagnosis made between April 2, 2011 and November 1, 2013. We de-identified the data by removing all personal health information except encounter dates; a random offset of -60 to 60 days was added to each encounter to preserve relative timing. The Committee for the Protection of Human Subjects at Dartmouth College approved our study protocol. The resulting clinical event log consisted of over 50,000 events. We filtered treatment events associated with chemotherapy administration. We selected only chemotherapy treatments that were approved for invasive breast cancer, based on the National Comprehensive Care Network (NCCN) breast cancer guidelines [21–24]. We found 178 patients who received such medications.

5.2   Chemotherapy Regimens

The administration and timing of chemotherapy medications are based on regimens, which are plans shown in clinical studies to have efficacy and acceptable side effects. We reviewed the NCCN breast cancer guidelines published between 2011 through 2014, the time period of our data extraction, and encoded 41 unique chemotherapy regimens [21–24]. An example of a NCCN regimen is shown in Fig. 3. The author AD has experience encoding protocols, and reviewed the treatment histories of the patients who had received chemotherapy and determined the best matching regimen. We found that 115 patients had clearly identifiable NCCN regimens. The other patients had incomplete data or were given treatment combinations not found in NCCN guidelines (perhaps representing new clinical trial studies). Our results found that physicians used a subset of 13 out of the total of 41 regimens.

Chemotherapy Medication	Administration Schedule
Fluorouracil, Epirubicin, and Cyclophosphamide	Together every three weeks for three cycles, followed by
Paclitaxel	Every three weeks for three cycles
with Pertuzumab	on the same day as paclitaxel
and Trastuzumab	on the same day as paclitaxel and then every three weeks alone to complete 1 year

Fig. 3.   An example of a breast cancer chemotherapy regimen derived from the 2014 National Comprehensive Care Network guideline. The guidelines specify the administration of drugs, including their timing.

5.3   VSM Specification

Each chemotherapy medication used in treating breast cancer was assigned a single letter code, which is also commonly done clinically. For example, Docetaxel and Cyclophosphamide are denoted as T and C, respectively. The term vectors for the treatment histories and recommended regimens both used these codes. For each patient and regimen, we create a vector representation for the traditional VSM, sVSM and tVSM, and two hybrid models using the method described in Sect. 4.1. There are two ways in which the terms of the different models could have been created. The method used in this work only created the terms that would be necessary to represent the patients and regimens. An alternative approach is to create a term vector that captures all possible static and temporal relationships between the different events. In this way, no matter what the query might be, the vector space would be able to model it. The number of dimensions in each of the VSMs is shown in Table 1. We use the cosine similarity measure to compute the similarity between every regimen and each patient, and compare the tf and tf-idf weighting schemes.

Table 1. The number of dimensions in each of the vector space models for the breast cancer chemotherapy dataset

VSM approach	Number of dimensions
Traditional VSM	10
sVSM	110
tVSM	111
Traditional + sVSM	120
Traditional + tVSM	121

5.4 Evaluation Results for Classification

We compare similarity of the term vector for each patient's treatment history to the term vectors for possible treatment regimens using the cosine similarity measure, and match the patient's treatment history to the chemotherapy regimen that has the highest similarity score with the patient. The matched regimen for each patient is then compared to the regimen that was annotated manually to the patient. Ignoring patients for whom the regimen could not be identified manually, the accuracy of the different vector space models are presented in Table 2. It should be noted that for the tf-idf scheme, the idf weights are based on the corpus which for the classification problem is the set of 41 recommended regimens.

Table 2. The classification accuracy of five different VSM models

VSM approach	Classification accuracy	
	tf weighting	tf-idf weighting
Traditional VSM	82.9 %	82.9 %
sVSM	86.3 %	87.2 %
tVSM	85.5 %	83.8 %
Traditional + sVSM	86.3 %	87.1 %
Traditional + tVSM	86.3 %	84.6 %

5.5   Evaluation Results for Search

To search for patients who might be on a given chemotherapy regimen, we compute the similarity of the query vector against all patient's treatment history vectors derived from the data set. The results of the search are ranked in decreasing order of their similarity to the query. The position of each patient within the search results is the rank of the patient whereby patients that receive the same similarity score are assigned the same rank. In an ideal search engine, all the patients that are actually on the query regimen would have a rank of 1, which would signify that all the patients following the regimen appear at the top of the search results. However, since patient treatments may have some variation relative to the underlying treatment plan, it is likely that some patients who are on the query regimen will not receive the same similarity score compared to the query vector and therefore will have different ranks.

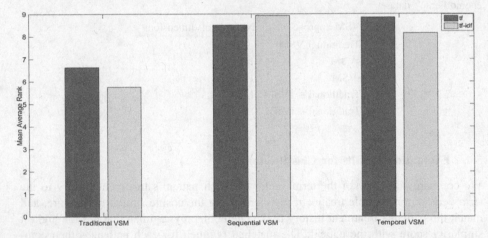

Fig. 4. Mean Average Rank for different vector space models using the tf weighted and tf-idf weighted cosine similarity measure. A traditional VSM, temporal VSM and hybrid VSM are considered. The best performance is seen in the case of a traditional VSM using a tf-idf weighted cosine similarity measure.

In our evaluation, we consider the performance across all of the 13 regimens known to be in the EMR data set. For each regimen, we query the VSM and rank the patients in decreasing order of similarity. In the resulting list, a subset of the patient treatment histories will have been manually annotated to be on the query regimen. For each result set, we average the rank of the patients who are known to be on the query regimen. This computed average rank is an indication of the average position in the search results of the patients that are on the particular query regimen; therefore, a lower average rank indicates a higher performing VSM whereby the relevant patients are clustered near the top of the results. The process of computing the average rank is repeated for each of the 13 regimens and the mean of the average ranks is computed to obtain a mean average rank for a given VSM model and weighting scheme. This process is performed for each of the 5 models considered using the tf and tf-idf weighting schemes. The results of this evaluation are shown in Fig. 4. The figure does not show the results for the hybrid models, for the sake of simplicity; the hybrid models did not outperform the other three models indicating that the hybrid do not provide any advantage over the simpler models.

6   Conclusions

The paper presents the application and evaluation of VSMs to modeling clinical event logs found in EMRs. In specifying the dimensions of the VSM, we consider including temporal terms representing co-occurrence and precedence relationships among clinical events. We provide two applications of the VSM for the tasks of (1) classification, to match a patient's treatment history to one of a set of pre-specified clinical plans, and (2) search, to retrieve patient treatment histories that are closest to a clinical plan. Based on literature review, we believe this work is the first use of VSMs for structured, longitudinal EMR data and the first use of VSMs with temporal terms.

We developed a set of five VSM approaches that differ in their choice of terms: a traditional VSM, which does not include temporal terms; two VSMs, which include co-occurrence and precedence terms; and two hybrid VSMs, which have standard and temporal terms. The evaluation results for the classification task show that use of temporal terms improves accuracy. The sequential VSM (sVSM) with the tf-idf weighting scheme, in particular, had the best accuracy of 87 %. The results for the search task found that the traditional VSM has the best performance in terms of the average rank of the search results; using a tf-idf weighting scheme was found to work better than the tf-weighting scheme. Our results suggest that using standard, non-temporal terms perform well for information retrieval compared to the use of temporal terms in the sVSM and tVSM models. The decreased performance with the use of temporal terms in the VSM could be related to several factors. Since the VSMs with temporal terms have about ten times more dimensions than the static model, it is possible that the increased dimensionality worsened the resulting ranking. The manner in which temporal information was represented also introduces redundancy in the VSMs. The findings of this study suggest that inclusion of temporal information provides improvement when classifying treatment histories but that inclusion of temporality worsens the performance of information retrieval compared to a traditional VSM approach.

7   Future Work

As there is no standard method for representing temporal information as terms of the VSMs, this work represents an exploration into an untapped domain. Other approaches to incorporate temporal information into VSMs and the use of different term-weighting schemes may have the potential to improve results. Another aspect of temporality in EMR data is the temporal distance between different events. The relative timing between events can be important; for example, in the administration of chemotherapy treatments, the cyclical timing is a central part of the definition of the treatment plans. Incorporating such information into the models could potentially allow further discrimination between different chemotherapy regimens. There are different possibilities for including such information in the vector terms, which we plan to consider in future work. The work presented in this paper shows that VSMs have many potential applications for handling large volumes of healthcare data.

References

1. Syed, H., Das, A.K.: Identifying chemotherapy regimens in electronic health record data using interval-encoded sequence alignment. In: Holmes, J.H., Bellazzi, R., Sacchi, L., Peek, N. (eds.) AIME 2015. LNCS, vol. 9105, pp. 143–147. Springer, Heidelberg (2015)
2. Syed, H., Das, A.K.: Temporal Needleman–Wunsch. In: Proceedings of 2015 IEEE/ACM International Conference on Data Science and Advanced Analytics (DSAA 2015) (2015)
3. Salton, G.: The SMART Retrieval System: Experiments in Automatic Document Processing. Prentice-Hall Inc., Upper Saddle River (1971)
4. Salton, G., Wong, A., Yang, C.S.: A vector space model for automatic indexing. Commun. ACM **18**(11), 613–620 (1975). doi:10.1145/361219.361220
5. Suzuki, T., Yokoi, H., Fujita, S., Takabayashi, K.: Automatic DPC code selection from electronic medical records: text mining trial of discharge summary. Methods Inf. Med. **47**(6), 541–548 (2008)
6. Prados-Suárez, B., Molina, C., Peña, Y.C., de Reyes, M.P.: Improving electronic health records retrieval using contexts. Expert Syst. Appl. **39**(10), 8522–8536 (2012)
7. Hauskrecht, M., Valko, M., Batal, I., Clermont, G., Visweswaran, S., Cooper, G.F.: Conditional outlier detection for clinical alerting. In: AMIA Annual Symposium Proceedings/AMIA Symposium 2010, pp. 286–290 (2010)
8. Jain, H., Thao, C., Zhao, H.: Enhancing electronic medical record retrieval through semantic query expansion. ISeB **10**(2), 165–181 (2012)
9. Mao, W., Chu, W.W.: The phrase-based vector space model for automatic retrieval of free-text medical documents. Data Knowl. Eng. **61**(1), 76–92 (2007)
10. Mao, W., Chu, W.W.: Free-text medical document retrieval via phrase-based vector space model. In: Proceedings/AMIA Annual Symposium, AMIA Symposium 2002, pp. 489–493 (2002)
11. Hassanpour, S., O'Connor, M.J., Das, A.K.: Evaluation of semantic-based information retrieval methods in the autism phenotype domain. In: AMIA Annual Symposium Proceedings/AMIA Symposium, pp. 569–577 (2011)
12. Hassanpour, S., O'Connor, M.J., Das, A.K.: A semantic-based method for extracting concept definitions from scientific publications: evaluation in the autism phenotype domain. J. Biomed. Semant. **4**(1), 14 (2013)
13. Mondal, D., Gangopadhyay, A., Russell, W.: Medical decision making using vector space model. In: Proceedings of the 1st ACM International Health Informatics Symposium (IHI 2010), pp. 386–390. ACM, New York (2010)
14. Pôssas, B., Ziviani, N., Meira, Jr. W.: Enhancing the set-based model using proximity information. In: Laender, A.H., Oliveir, A.L., (eds.) (SPIRE 2002). LNCS, vol. 2476, pp. 104–116. Springer, Heidelberg (2002)
15. Pôssas, B., Ziviani, N., Meira, W.J., Ribeiro-Neto, B.: Set-based model: a new approach for information retrieval. In: SIGIR 2002, pp. 230–237 (2002)

16. Silva, I.R., Souza, J.A.N., Santos, K.S.: Dependence among terms in vector space model. In: Proceedings of the International Database Engineering and Applications Symposium (IDEAS 2004), pp. 97–102 (2004)

17. Wong, S.K.M., Ziarko, W., Raghavan, V.V., Wong, P.C.N.: On modeling of information retrieval concepts in vector spaces. ACM Trans. Database Syst. **12**(2), 299–321 (1987)

18. Wong, S.K.M., Ziarko W., Wong, P.C.N.: Generalized vector space model in information retrieval. In: SIGIR 85 Proceedings of the 8th Annual International ACM SIGIR Conference on Research and Development in Information Retrieval, pp. 18–25 (1985)

19. Turney, P.D., Pantel, P.: From frequency to meaning: vector space models of semantics. J. Artif. Intell. Res. **37**, 141–188 (2010)

20. Allen, J.F.: Maintaining knowledge about temporal intervals. Commun. ACM **26**(11), 832–843 (1983)

21. Carlson, R.W., Allred, D.C., Anderson, B.O., et al.: Invasive breast cancer. J. Natl. Compr. Cancer Netw. **9**(2), 136–222 (2011)

22. National Comprehensive Cancer Network. Breast cancer. NCCN Clinical Practice Guidelines in Oncology, version 1.2012 (Accessed from the web) (2012)

23. National Comprehensive Cancer Network. Breast cancer. NCCN Clinical Practice Guidelines in Oncology, version 1.2013 (Accessed from the web) (2013)

24. Gradishar, W.J., Anderson, B.O., Blair, S.L., et al.: Breast cancer version 3.2014. J. Natl. Compr. Cancer Netw. **12**(4), 542–590 (2014)

The Study of the Compatibility Rules of Traditional Chinese Medicine Based on Apriori and HMETIS Hypergraph Partitioning Algorithm

Miao Wang[1], Jiayun Li[2], Li Chen[2], Yanjun Huang[2], Qiang Zhou[1], Lijuan Che[1], and Huiliang Shang[2(✉)]

[1] Shanghai University of T.C.M., No. 1200, Cailun Road,
Shanghai 201210, China
miawang2004@hotmail.com, john-zh@163.com,
chelijuan152003@yahoo.com.cn
[2] Department of Electronic Engineering, Fudan University,
No. 220, Handan Road, 200433 Shanghai, China
{jiayunli11,li_chen12,yjhuang12,shangh1}@fudan.edu.cn

Abstract. One of the major research contents carried by scholars of Traditional Chinese medical science (TCM) is to discover the compatibility rules of herbs to increase the efficacy in treating certain syndromes. However, up to now, most of the compatibility rules of herbs are based on empirical analyses, which make them hard to study. Since concepts of Big Data and machine learning have been popularized gradually, how to use data mining techniques to effectively figure out core herbs and compatibility rules becomes the main research aspect of TCM informatics. In this paper, the hypergraph partitioning algorithm HMETIS based on Apriori is applied to exploit and analyze clinical data about lung cancer. The result shows that all 15 Chinese herbs obtained by the algorithm accord with the core concepts of the treatment of lung cancer by experienced TCM doctors, namely replenishing nutrition, clearing heat-toxin, resolving phlegm and eliminating pathogenic factors.

Keywords: Data mining · Compatibility rules of herbs · Apriori algorithm · Hypergraph · Community partitioning · HMETIS

1 Introduction

1.1 The Value of the Study on the Compatibility of Chinese Herbs

The culture of traditional Chinese medical science (TCM) has a long history. In the lengthy course of the clinical medical practice, a large number of scholars of TCM gradually realize the intricacy of disease mechanism. As the therapeutic effect of one kind of Chinese herb to diseases with complicated pathogenic factors is often unsatisfactory, scholars have attempted to use several types of herbs in combination [1]. With the increasing popularity of herb combination in the field of TCM, it has been found out that some groups of combined Chinese herbs may strength treatment effects,

© Springer International Publishing Switzerland 2016
F. Wang et al. (Eds.): Big-O(Q) and DMAH 2015, LNCS 9579, pp. 16–31, 2016.
DOI: 10.1007/978-3-319-41576-5_2

while other groups may have counteractive or even side effects [1]. On the basis of the above facts, scholars through the ages have gathered rich clinical experience, and tracked out a relatively mature compatibility system of Chinese herbs [2, 3].

At the present stage, most compatibility rules, which are supported by partial TCM theories, are concluded by famous veteran doctors of TCM through practice. However, the substantive characteristics of these rules, such as unity, dialectic, objectivity, etc., are too abstract and subjective to be quantified and inherited [4, 5]. Since database, artificial intelligence, and mathematical statics are developing rapidly, data mining has become an important method to interdisciplinary research. Therefore, applying data mining techniques to the compatibility study of Chinese herbs, is a significant research direction which means TCM theories are able to be combined with data techniques. Through data mining, the core herbs of certain syndromes can be figured out from the TCM clinical database, subsequently disclosing the compatibility rules concealed in the data, and promoting the dissemination and popularization of these rules ultimately.

1.2 Basic Knowledge About Data Mining

Data mining is a crucial step in the discovery of database knowledge [6], which occurs in an electronic databank, and aims at discovering the hidden patterns in the data by statistics, machine learning, expert systems, etc. [7]. According to the knowledge types obtained by data mining algorithms, the data mining system can be classified into three categories: classification, clustering, and association rule. The analysis in this paper will be primarily based on the association rule, a kind of algorithm regularly used in shopping habits analysis to promote sales of commodities, or pointed advertising placement. The main idea of the association rule algorithm is to capture the relations among different data items from large amounts of data. The next paragraph explains the algorithm in detail.

Let I be a set $(I = \{I_1, I_2, \ldots, I_m\})$. Let T be the set of transactions $(T = \{T_1, T_2, \ldots, T_n\})$ where each transaction T_i is a non-empty subset of the set I. An association rule is an expression of the form $A \Rightarrow B$, where A and B are elements or element groups of I, and are called the antecedent as well as the consequent respectively. The support of a rule indicates the ratio of the occurrence numbers of A and B in the same transaction to the total transaction number n, and is defined as:

$$Support = \frac{|A \cup B|}{|T|} \tag{1}$$

The confidence measures the probability of the presence of B in the same transaction under the condition where A has appeared in a certain transaction. The confidence is defined as:

$$Confidence = \frac{|A \cup B|}{|A|} \tag{2}$$

The association rule algorithm aims to discover the rules satisfying the support and confidence thresholds [8] 327–404. Nevertheless, since a practical database contains an extremely large number of items, it is impossible to search for the required rules by traversal and enumeration [9, 10]. In order to reduce some unnecessary calculation of support and confidence, and to enhance the efficiency of the association rule algorithm, Agrawal and Srikant advanced the Apriori algorithm in 1994 [9, 10]. The algorithm finds out the frequent itemsets meeting the requirements, and then seeks for the association rules fulfilling the confidence threshold in these itemsets. The Apriori algorithm avoids needless calculation and judgment, and greatly elevates the efficiency, making the application of association rules in large-scale database possible.

1.3   Related Work on the Compatibility Rules of Chinese Herbs Using Data Mining

Jingsheng Shang, Lisheng Hu et al. [11] did research on the compatibility rules of Banxia Xiexin decoction using data mining. In their paper, they utilized the frequency statistics to analyze the rules, and found the distribution characteristics of the herbs in the decoction.

Liang Ye et al. [12] conducted research on the compatibility rules of Siwu decoction treating dysmenorrhea by the association rule algorithm, studied the involved herbs via the Hypothesis Testing approach, and then concluded the herbs closely related to the prescription.

As for using the complex network to study the compatibility rules, Xuezhong Zhou et al. [13] synthesized and modeled the clinical symptoms and diagnosis results. Complex network can integrate and visualize TCM information, as well as provide a platform for researchers to discover the compatibility rules of Chinese herbs.

Runshun Zhang et al. [14] also applied the complex network to the research on the compatibility rules of herbs treating the disharmony of liver and spleen. After studying the node centricity of various herbs and the side centricity of herb pairs, they gained the core herbs which could cure the disharmony.

Research on the compatibility rules of Chinese herbs based on the Apriori algorithm is mainly conducted by setting a support threshold as well as a confidence threshold, and finding association rules meet these requirements. However, when encountering a large database with huge numbers of herbs and clinical cases, we may obtain quite sophisticated association rules. Due to the fact that the Apriori algorithm only figures out frequent itemsets according to the support threshold, we cannot acquire some frequent itemsets when the threshold is relatively high. By lowering the support threshold, we may not lose these frequent itemsets, but at the same time, many disturbances are introduced.

The visualization of the compatibility of Chinese herbs is usually achieved by using network to express the relations between herbs, and analyzing the compatibility with the centricity of complex network and community detection algorithms. Generally, in a complex network, herbs are presented as vertices and the appearance number of two herbs in the same case represents the weight of edges, thus inevitably causing the loss of information about herbs and prescriptions [14].

1.4   Our Research

The paper applies a hypergraph partitioning algorithm based on the Apriori algorithm to the discovery of core herbs treating lung cancer. The experimental data come from 952 effective clinical lung cancer cases of Longhua Hospital Shanghai University of Traditional Chinese Medicine, and we obtain 15 kinds of core herbs, including Chinese Sage Herb, Coastal Glehnia Root, Radix Asparagi, Radix Asteris, etc. After the comparison with literature on TCM, it is shown that the core herbs accord with the main ideas, namely replenishing nutrition, clearing heat-toxin, and resolving phlegm, during the treatment of lung cancer.

The paper is divided into four parts. The first part is the introduction which presents the major research directions as well as the commonly-used algorithms in the domain of data mining, and analyzes the meaning and progress of the research on the compatibility of Chinese herbs. The second part applies the Apriori algorithm to the construction of the hypergraph. On the basis of the hypergraph, the HMETIS algorithm is utilized to partition it for the purpose of getting the compatibility rules of core herbs. The third part is the experimental process, including the introduction of the data set, the presentation of the experimental results, and the analyses of these results. The fourth part makes a conclusion, pointing out the remaining problems in the experiment and indicating the further research direction for enhancement in the future.

2   Data Mining on the Compatibility Rules of Core Herbs with Apriori and Hypergraph Partitioning Algorithm

2.1   Apriori Algorithm

Basic Ideas.   The Apriori property: Any subset of a frequent itemset is also frequent [6, p. 333].
k-itemset: A set with k elemental items is called a k-itemset [6, pp. 328–329]

Principle of the Apriori Algorithm.   In the first part *Introduction*, the paper preliminarily states the association rules and the concepts of support as well as confidence. However, if the association rules meeting the support and confidence thresholds are searched for by traversing the database, the time complexity will be extremely high. Therefore, this method is impractical in a large-scale database. Through calculation, as for a database containing d itemsets, the total number of association rules may be [6, p. 331]:

$$R = 3^d - 2^{d+1} + 1 \tag{3}$$

For example, there will be 3,484,687,250 association rules if an actual database has 20 transactions (itemsets). Generally, a databank of TCM includes hundreds of or thousands of medical cases, so that it is unfulfillable to calculate the support and confidence of all the possible association rules via directly traversing a huge database.

In order to lower the time complexity and avoid the unnecessary calculation of support and confidence, the mining of association rules is divided into two sub-problems [6, pp. 331–391]:

(1) The mining of frequent itemsets: Find out all the frequent itemsets having support greater than the threshold. According to the Apriori property, any subset of a frequent itemset is also a frequent itemset. Therefore, if any subset of an itemset is infrequent, the itemset is absolutely not a frequent itemset. The Apriori algorithm operates the data mining process by several steps: The algorithm firstly obtains all the frequent 1-itemsets. Then, it combines different frequent (k-1)-itemsets to get candidate k-itemsets by iteration. Finally, Apriori finds out frequent k-itemsets due to the support threshold from the candidates.

(2) The mining of association rules: As for each frequent itemset L, generate all the subsets of it. As for each subset S, calculate the corresponding confidence. If the confidence satisfies the confidence threshold, generate the association rule $S \Rightarrow L - S$, where $L - S$ represents a set made up of elemental items belonging to L, but not belonging to S.

Process of the Apriori Algorithm. The Apriori algorithm captures the frequent itemsets with support greater than the threshold, and then finds out the association rules meeting the confidence requirement. The algorithm separates the mining of the association rules into two steps, averting the calculation of unnecessary support and confidence, reducing the time complexity, and enormously enhancing the algorithm efficiency. Figure 1 is the flow chart of Apriori:

Illustration: freq 1itemset—frequent itemsets with one elemental item; freqKitemset—frequent itemsets with K elemental items.

2.2 Hypergraph and Hypergraph Community Partitioning

Basic Ideas of Hypergraph. Suppose V is a set of vertices and E is a set of hyperedges, any hyperedge e included in E is a subset of V.

$$\forall e_{e \in E} \subseteq V \tag{4}$$

Therefore, $G = \{V, E, W\}$ represents a hypergraph, and W is the weight of hyperedge. Generally speaking, a hypergraph consists of vertices and hyperedges which connect two or more vertices [15, 16].

A graph made up of vertices and edges can only represent relations between two vertices, but there are many complicated relations among multiple objects in real life, which are difficult to express with simple graphs, such as the cooperation between several authors and the classification of documents. In some cases where complicated relations other than pairwise relations exist, a hypergraph is useful in describing these relations.

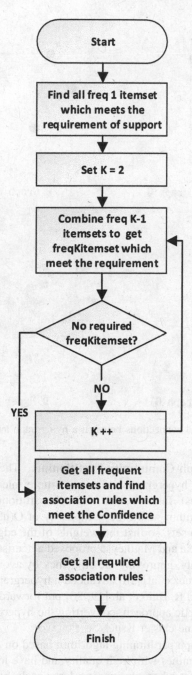

Fig. 1. Flow chart of the Apriori algorithm finding association rules

Figure 2 shows the differences and connections between a hypergraph and an ordinary graph.

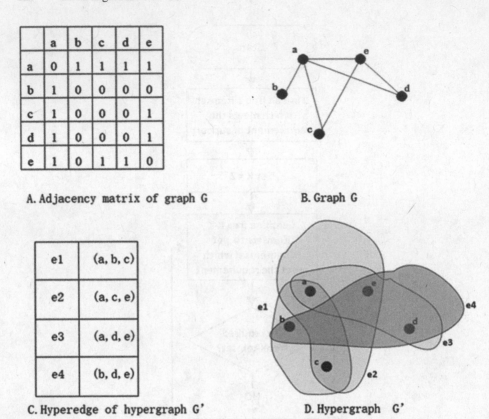

	a	b	c	d	e
a	0	1	1	1	1
b	1	0	0	0	0
c	1	0	0	0	1
d	1	0	0	0	1
e	1	0	1	1	0

A. Adjacency matrix of graph G   B. Graph G

e1	(a, b, c)
e2	(a, c, e)
e3	(a, d, e)
e4	(b, d, e)

C. Hyperedge of hypergraph G′   D. Hypergraph G′

Fig. 2. Differences and connections between a hypergraph and an ordinary graph

Basic Ideas of Hypergraph Community Partitioning. The hypergraph community partitioning is to divide a hypergraph into two or more internally closely connected subgraphs (or communities). In the realm of graph partitioning, Kernighan–Lin is a heuristic partitioning algorithm with time complexity of $O(n2 \log(n))$. The algorithm separates vertices into two sets, so that the weights of the edges connecting two parts are minimized [40]. Fiduccia and Mattheyse proposed a heuristic partitioning algorithm using linear time complexity, improving the efficiency by avoiding unnecessary search and calculation [17]. Vazquez et al. [18] advanced a hypergraph partitioning algorithm based on Bayesian. Samuel R. Bulò et al. [19, 20] put forward a hypergraph clustering algorithm in a game-theoretic approach, converting the hypergraph clustering problem into a non-cooperative game cluster issue.

HMETIS is a hypergraph partitioning algorithm based on a multilevel structure, so that it can produce communities with high quality and have low time complexity. The algorithm also operates fast when partitioning large-scale hypergraphs, so it can be used in a series of practical problems including Very Large-Scale Integration (VLSI). The core of the algorithm is to find hyperedge cuts with least weights, so that a hypergraph is divided into closely connected communities [21, 22]. In this paper, we apply the HMETIS algorithm to the partitioning of the hypergraph constructed from frequent itemsets so as to find core herbs treating lung cancer.

2.3   The Construction of Hypergraph and the Assessment of Hypergraph Community Partition

In this paper, we apply a hypergraph partitioning algorithm HMETIS based on Apriori to the discovery of core herbs in Traditional Chinese Medicine (TCM). Main processes of the algorithm include: inputting data to construct a hypergraph, partitioning the hypergraph, assessing the division results, choosing the closely connected communities, and acquiring core herbs.

Construction of Hypergraph.   According to the definition of hypergraph, each hyperedge consists of two or more vertices. The frequent itemsets found by the Apriori algorithm meet the support threshold and have certain relevance, so we choose these frequent itemsets to construct hyperedges. However, support alone cannot reflect the associations of two or more elemental items comprehensively. For example, some kinds of supplementary herbs usually appear in TCM prescriptions, so that pairs made up of these herbs and other herbs generally have high support. Nevertheless, it does not mean that the supplementary herbs have strong compatibility with others or are qualified to become core herbs in TCM prescriptions. To avoid the disturbance from quite frequent items, we set the average of confidence of association rules within a frequent itemset as the weight of a hyperedge. For instance, the average confidences of all frequent itemsets acquired by the Apriori algorithm are presented in Table 1.

Table 1. Average confidences of frequent itemsets acquired by the Apriori algorithm

Frequent itemset ID	Frequent itemset	Average confidence
e1	(A,B,C)	0.4
e2	(A,C,D,E)	0.6
e3	(B,C,D)	0.3
e4	(A,D,E)	0.8

According to the frequent itemsets and the average confidences, we construct the hypergraph model, shown in Fig. 3. If no association rules in one frequent itemset meet the confidence threshold, then delete the hyperedge.

Next, we use JAVA to read the TCM diagnosis data from Excel, apply Apriori to find frequent Itemsets which meet the requirements, present the frequent itemsets in the form of hyperedges, calculate the average of confidence in association rules as the weight of the hyperedges, and finally write the result of hypergraph in a txt file.

Hypergraph Community Partitioning and the Assessment.   When we invoke HMETIS command lines in JAVA, the main parameter we should set is the community number after the partition. By calculating the inner connectivity closeness index Fitness

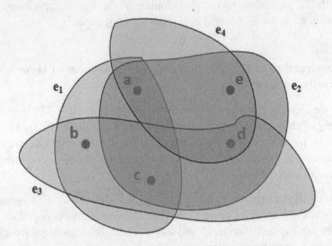

Fig. 3. Hypergraph constructed by frequent itemsets

of each partitioned community in the hypergraph, we constantly modify the parameter
to achieve better results. The index Fitness is calculated as [21]:

$$fitness = \frac{\sum_{e \subseteq C} Weight(e)}{\sum_{|e \cap C| > 0} Weight(e)} \tag{5}$$

Through the calculation of Fitness in every partitioned community, we can get an
average Fitness. By modifying the community number, we can get a partially optimized
partitioning solution. After determining the best community number, we use the
HMETIS algorithm to partition the hypergraph and output the community (or subgraph)
with the largest Fitness. The flow chart of the partitioning algorithm is shown in Fig. 4.

3 Data and Results

3.1 Data Source

The experimental data come from clinical lung cancer diagnosis records of Longhua
Hospital Shanghai University of Traditional Chinese Medicine. The original data have
1000 cases. After the deletion of duplicated and ineffective data, the total number of the
available cases is 952. Each case contains a patient ID, symptoms, and herbs. Table 2 is
the basic statistics results of the data.

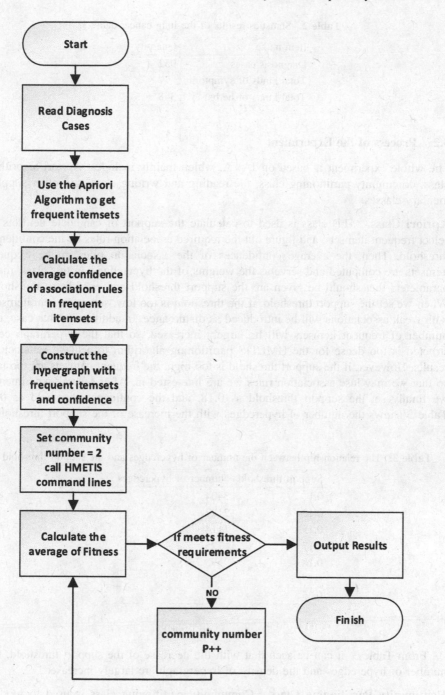

Fig. 4. Flow chart of the partitioning algorithm

Table 2. Statistics results of the lung cancer data

Item name	Quantity
Diagnosis cases	952
Total kinds of symptoms	77
Total kinds of herbs	348

3.2   Process of the Experiment

The whole experiment is based on JAVA, which mainly includes: Apriori algorithm class, community partitioning class, file reading and writing class, and other supplementary classes.

Apriori Class. This class is used to calculate the support of candidate itemsets to select frequent itemsets, and figure out the required association rules by the confidence threshold. Then, the average confidences of the association rules in the frequent itemsets are computed and serve as the weights of the hyperedges. In this class, main parameters that should be given are the support threshold and confidence threshold. When we set the support threshold, if the threshold is too low, some frequent itemsets with weak associations will be introduced as disturbance. In addition, in that case, the number of frequent itemsets will be largely increased, so that the hypergraph constructed is too dense for the HMETIS partitioning algorithm to achieve satisfactory results. However, if the support threshold is too high, the frequent itemsets are too few so that we may lose association rules we are interested in. After several experiments, we finally set the support threshold as 0.18, and the confidence threshold as 0.9. Table 3 shows the number of hyperedges with the increase of the support threshold.

Table 3. The relationship between the number of hyperedges and the support threshold

Support threshold	Number of hyperedges
0.1	3404
0.12	2177
0.15	1114
0.17	725
0.18	593
0.2	457
0.25	243

From Table 3, it can be seen that with the decrease of the support threshold, the number of hyperedges and the density of hypergraph are largely increased.

Community Partitioning Class. Community partitioning class is used to modify parameters and call the HMETIS command lines. The class partitions the hypergraph and selects the community with the finest connectivity as the output. As for determining parameters, we find it most satisfying when the support threshold is 0.18, the confidence threshold is 0.9, and the community (subgraph) number is 3. With these parameters, the HMETIS function is used to separate the hypergraph.

3.3 Results

After processing the lung cancer diagnosis records, we obtain 593 frequent itemsets (hyperedges), the maximum of which includes 7 kinds of herbs. Use the HMETIS algorithm to partition the hypergraph, and the biggest connectivity closeness index Fitness of the community is 0.470588. A total of 15 kinds of herbs treating lung cancer are found in this community, listed in Table 4.

Table 4. Core herbs treating lung cancer acquired by the hypergraph partitioning

Herb	Herb
Chinese Sage Herb	raw oysters
Coastal Glehnia Root	Raw Radix Astragali
Radix Asparagi	Fruit of Fiverleaf Akebia
Radix Asteris	Chickens Gizzard-membrane
Coix Seed	Bulb of Thunberg Fritillary
Spica Prunellae	Herba Selaginellae Doederleinii
Radix Ophiopogonis	Spreading Hedyotis Herb
almond	

3.4 Result Assessment

In order to evaluate the core herbs gained from the experiments, we refer to the medical records from Pro. Jiaxiang Liu and other prescriptions on treating lung cancer from famous veteran doctors of TCM.

According to the establishment mechanism of lung cancer, Liu considers the treatment should be focused on replenishing nutrition, clearing heat-toxin, and resolving phlegm.

Herbs that help to nourish stomach can replenish the patients' nutrition, and enhance their immunity. Herbs helping to eliminate pathogenic factors can remove pathogens away from the body, but such effects cannot be achieved when patients are rather weak. Hence, these two kinds of herbs may be combined to attain the ultimate goal [23].

The 15 kinds of herbs obtained by the hypergraph community partitioning algorithm are analyzed in the following paragraphs on the basis of our reference to the medical records from Liu.

Herba Selaginellae Doederleinii, Chinese Sage Herb, Spreading Hedyotis Herb.
Herba Selaginellae Doederleinii, Chinese Sage Herb, Spreading Hedyotis Herb have the effect of clearing heat-toxin. According to *National Herbs Compilation*, Herba Selaginellae Doederleinii can treat Inflammations and cancers [24]. *Ben Jing* describes

that Chinese Sage Herb also has the effect of removing blood stasis. Besides, experiments show Spreading Hedyotis Herb regulates immunity and resists malignant tumors [25, 26].

Research [25] also found that the combination of Chinese Sage Herb and Herba Selaginellae Doederleinii had a synergy, strengthening the effect of clearing heat-toxin, as both herbs targeted the lung.

Spica Prunellae, Raw Oysters, Fruit of Fiverleaf Akebia. Phlegm results from the obstruction in primary and collateral channels due to the invasion of pathogens and toxics [25].

In light of clinical diagnosis cases, Spica Prunellae is effective in preventing tumors from spreading [27]. Raw oysters are mainly used to dissipate phlegm and resolve masses [28]. Fruit of Fiverleaf Akebia nurtures liver, kidney, stomach, and spleen, mainly easing the pain caused by the stagnation of the vital energy circulation.

With the combination of these three herbs, their medical effect of dissipating phlegm is enhanced. In addition, treating heat as well as dampness stasis and nurturing body organs are beneficial to resolving phlegm, so these three herbs are widely applied together in curing phlegm accumulation and some kinds of tumors [25, 28] 62.

Coastal Glehnia Root, Radix Asparagi, Radix Ophiopogonis. Liu considers the physical weakness is the cause of lung cancer, so the key points should be the cultivation of immunity and the nurture of body. By replenishing nutrition, the tumors may be dissolved [25].

Coastal Glehnia Root, Radix Asparagi, and Radix Ophiopogonis belong to the herbs with nurturance. Radix Ophiopogonis can cure weakness and nurture the lung [28] 16, while Radix Asparagi can promote the production of body fluid and moisten the lung [28] 9.

The combined use of Radix Ophiopogonis, Radix Asparagi, and Coastal Glehnia Root can enhance the effect of building up health. Radix Asparagi and Radix Ophiopogonis are also usually used together when curing sore throat and cough. The combination of Coastal Glehnia Root and Radix Ophiopogonis is necessary when pulmonary functions are regulated [25, 29].

Raw Radix Astragali, Chickens Gizzard-membrane, Coix Seed. Raw Radix Astragali, Chickens Gizzard-membrane, and Coix Seed are usually utilized together to nurture spleen and stomach [28], strengthening the body, replenishing nutrition, and subsequently helping the treatment of lung cancer.

Radix Asteris, Bulb of Thunberg Fritillary, Almond. Radix Asteris, Bulb of Thunberg Fritillary, and almond all have the effect of arresting the cough and clearing the lung-heat [30].

However, according to *Ben Cao Jing Shu*, Radix Asteris is mild in medicine property, so it is not suitable to be applied alone. With the company of Radix Asparagi and Radix Ophiopogonis, which are cool in medical property, their properties are counteracted, so the ideal effects of herbs are achieved.

Generally speaking, the core herbs obtained through the algorithm basically accord with the conclusions on treating lung cancer of Pro. Jiaxiang Liu and other experienced

TCM experts. The purposes of replenishing nutrition, clearing heat-toxin, and resolving phlegm can also be seen in the literature on TCM, suggesting our results have a certain reference value.

4   Conclusion and Outlook

4.1   Conclusion

In this paper, the hypergraph community partitioning algorithm is used to exploit 952 cases of clinical lung cancer diagnosis records from Longhua Hospital Shanghai University of Traditional Chinese Medicine.

Firstly, frequent itemsets and association rules are obtained using the Apriori algorithm. These frequent itemsets meeting the support and confidence requirements serve as hyperedges; the average confidence of association rules in a frequent itemset serves as the weight of the corresponding hyperedge; those association rules which do not meet the confidence requirement are removed.

After the construction of the hypergraph, the HMETIS algorithm is used to partition it. The degree of internal connectivity closeness of one subgraph is evaluated by calculating the index Fitness, and higher average of the indexes of all the subgraphs is acquired by modifying the parameters in the HMETIS algorithm.

From data mining, we find compatibility rules with 15 kinds of core herbs: Chinese Sage Herb, Coastal Glehnia Root, Radix Asparagi, Radix Asteris, Coix Seed, raw oysters, Raw Radix Astragali, Fruit of Fiverleaf Akebia, Chickens Gizzard-membrane, Bulb of Thunberg Fritillary, Spica Prunellae, Herba Selaginellae Doederleinii, Radix Ophiopogonis, Spreading Hedyotis Herb, and almond.

By comparing the core herbs achieved from the algorithm with diagnosis records and academic materials of TCM, it proves that the herbs accord with the conclusions on treating lung cancer of Pro. Jiaxiang Liu and other experienced TCM experts. The purpose of replenishing nutrition, clearing heat-toxin, and resolving phlegm can also been seen in the literature on TCM, suggesting there is a certain reference value in our results.

4.2   Outlook

In our paper, 15 core herbs treating lung cancer are concluded through the hypergraph community partitioning algorithm, which are substantially consistent with the diagnosis results of Pro. Jiaxiang Liu and other well-known TCM experts. However, the support threshold, the partitioned community number, and other parameters in the algorithm are obtained by testing during several experiments, with subjectivity and uncertainty to some extent.

In addition, the paper only considers whether herbs appear in clinical diagnosis records, but do not consider how the dosage affects the efficacy and the compatibility rules of herbs. Besides that, the assessment of the herbs is largely dependent on the existing literature on TCM and the therapeutic experience from physicians, lacking objective and theoretical evaluation criteria.

Based on the above points, the directions of improvement are:

1. Exploring methods of adjusting parameters to avoid subjectivity and instability caused by the artificial setting; increasing training data sets, so that the optimal parameter combination is able to be summarized.
2. Gathering the information on the ratios of herbs; using the Apriori algorithm or other complex network algorithms to discover the relations between the efficacy and the ratios, and to find more accurate compatibility rules between Chinese herbs.

Acknowledgment. This work was supported by National Natural Science Foundation of China (Grant No. 61301028); Natural Science Foundation of Shanghai China (Grant No. 13ZR1402900); Doctoral Fund of Ministry of Education of China (Grant No. 20120071120016).

References

1. Yejun, C.: Data mining Technology and its application in Traditional Chinese Medicine. Zhejiang University (2003)
2. Zhou, X., Liu, Y., et al.: Research on compound drug compatibility of complex network. Chin. J. Inf. Tradit. Chin. Med. **15**(11), 98–100 (2008)
3. Meng, F., Li, M., et al.: Mining the medication law of ancient analgesic formulas based on complex network. J. Tradit. Chin. Med. **54**(2), 145–148 (2013)
4. Zhang, B.: Research on data-mining technology applied traditional Chinese prescription compatibility based on association rules. J. Gansu Lianhe Univ. (Nat. Sci.) **25**(1), 82–86 (2011)
5. Zhou, X., et al.: Development of traditional Chinese medicine clinical data warehouse for medical knowledge discovery and decision support. Artif. Intell. Med. **48**(2), 139–152 (2010)
6. Tan, P.-N., Steinbach, M., Kumar, V.: Introduction to Data Mining, vol. 1. Pearson Addison Wesley, Boston (2006)
7. Domingos, P.: A few useful things to know about machine learning. Commun. ACM **55**(10), 78–87 (2012)
8. Han, J., Kamber, M., Pei, J.: Data Mining, Southeast Asia Edition: Concepts and Techniques. Morgan kaufmann, San Francisco (2006)
9. Agrawal, R., Srikant, R.: Fast algorithms for mining association rules. In: Proceedings of 20th International Conference Very Large Data Bases VLDB, vol. 1215, pp. 487–499 (1994)
10. Tseng, V.S., et al.: Efficient algorithms for mining high utility itemsets from transactional databases. IEEE Trans. Knowl. Data Eng. **25**(8), 1772–1786 (2013)
11. Shang, J., Lisheng, H., et al.: Data mining of the law of compatibility of medicines and application of banxia xiexin decoction. J. China-Jpn. Friendship Hosp. **19**(4), 227–229 (2005)
12. Ye, L., Fan, X., et al.: Association among four-drug decoction and the like for dysmenorrhea at all times. J. Nanjing Univ. Tradit. Chin. Med. (Nat. Sci.) **24**(2), 94–96 (2008)
13. Zhou, X., Liu, B.: Network analysis system for traditional Chinese medicine clinical data. In: 2nd International Conference on Biomedical Engineering and Informatics, BMEI 2009, pp. 1–5. IEEE (2009)

14. Zhang, R., Zhou, X., et al.: Study on compounding rules of Chinese herb prescriptions for treating syndrome of liver and spleen disharmony by scale-free network. World Sci. Technol.-Modernization Tradit. Chin. Med. **12**(6), 882–887 (2010)
15. Yu, J., Tao, D., Wang, M.: Adaptive hypergraph learning and its application in image classification. IEEE Trans. Image Process. **21**(7), 3262–3272 (2012)
16. Kernighan, B.W., Lin, S.: An efficient heuristic procedure for partitioning graphs. Bell Syst. Tech. J. **49**(2), 291–307 (1970)
17. Fiduccia, C.M, Robert M.M.: A linear-time heuristic for improving network partitions. In: 19th Conference on Design Automation. IEEE (1982)
18. Vazquez, A.: Finding hypergraph communities: a bayesian approach and variational solution. J. Stat. Mech. Theor. Exp. (2009)
19. Chakraborty, A., Saptarshi, G.: Clustering hypergraphs for discovery of overlapping communities in folksonomies. In: Mukherjee, A., Choudhury, M., Peruani, F., Ganguly, N., Mitra, B. (eds.) Dynamics on and of Complex Networks, vol. 2, pp. 201–220. Springer, New York (2013)
20. Bulò, S.R., Marcello, P.: A game-theoretic approach to hypergraph clustering. Adv. Neural Inf. Process. Syst. **35**, 1571–1579 (2009)
21. Li, Y.: An entropy-based algorithm for detecting overlapping communities in hyper-networks. Sci. Technol. Eng. **13**(7), 1856–1859 (2013)
22. Han, E.-H., et al.: Clustering in a high-dimensional space using hypergraph models. In: Proceedings of Data Mining and Knowledge Discovery (1997)
23. Church, K.W., Patrick, H.: Word association norms, mutual information, and lexicography. Comput. linguist. **16**(1), 22–29 (1990)
24. Lin, X.: Experience of Professor Xixiang Liu in treating lung cancer. Inf. Tradit. Chin. Med. **12**(4), 36–37 (1995)
25. Liu, J., Pan, M., et al.: Clinical study of Jin Hu Kang oral liquid for treating non-small cell lung cancer. Tumor **21**(6), 463–465 (2001)
26. Ji, W.: Professor LIU Jia-xiang's experience in the treatment of lung cancer with Chinese drug pair. Chin. Arch. Tradit. Chin. Med. **28**(6), 1154–1156 (2010)
27. Shiyun, Z., Jinnan, Z.: Experimental study on treatment of compound hedyotic diffusa in tumor-burdened mice. Pract. Clin. J. Integr. Tradit. Chin. West. Med. **09**, 81–83 (2014)
28. Wang, P., Zhang, S.: Research advances of the anticancer mechanisms of prunella vulgaris. Shandong Sci. **23**(2), 38–41 (2010)
29. Yan, P.: Traditional Chinese Medicine Dispensing Technology. Chemical industry press (2006)
30. The State Administration of Traditional Chinese Medicine 《Zhonghua Bencao》 .Shanghai: Shanghai science and technology publishing house (1999)

Comparing Small Graph Retrieval Performance for Ontology Concepts in Medical Texts

Daniel R. Schlegel[✉], Jonathan P. Bona, and Peter L. Elkin

Department of Biomedical Informatics,
University at Buffalo, Buffalo, NY 14260, USA
{drschleg,jpbona,elkinp}@buffalo.edu

Abstract. Some terminologies and ontologies, such as SNOMED CT, allow for post–coordinated as well as pre-coordinated expressions. Post–coordinated expressions are, essentially, small segments of the terminology graphs. Compositional expressions add logical and linguistic relations to the standard technique of post-coordination. In indexing medical text, many instances of compositional expressions must be stored, and in performing retrieval on that index, entire compositional expressions and sub-parts of those expressions must be searched. The problem becomes a small graph query against a large collection of small graphs. This is further complicated by the need to also find sub-graphs from a collection of small graphs. In previous systems using compositional expressions, such as iNLP, the index was stored in a relational database. We compare retrieval characteristics of relational databases, triplestores, and general graph databases to determine which is most efficient for the task at hand.

1 Introduction

Some terminologies and ontologies, such as SNOMED CT, allow for concepts which are post-coordinated as well as those which are pre-coordinated. Post-coordinated concepts are, essentially, small segments of the terminology or ontology graph. Compositional expressions (CEs) extend the idea of post-coordination, adding logical and linguistic relations. The advantage of using CEs created from ontologies and terminologies is that multiple linguistic surface forms for the same concept are mapped to a single logical form (and hence, a graph structure). For example, the following three forms, all representing the idea of hypertension which is controlled, map to a logical form in which the SNOMED CT concept for "hypertension" is the first argument in a binary `hasModifier` relation with the SNOMED CT concept for "uncontrolled."

1. Uncontrolled hypertension
2. HT, uncontrolled
3. Uncontrolled hypertensive disorder

It's important to note that you cannot simply encode medical texts using SNOMED and get similar results without CEs. In fact, 41 % of clinical problems require CEs in order to be represented properly [5].

© Springer International Publishing Switzerland 2016
F. Wang et al. (Eds.): Big-O(Q) and DMAH 2015, LNCS 9579, pp. 32–44, 2016.
DOI: 10.1007/978-3-319-41576-5_3

Compositional expression graphs are quite small, generally including only a handful of nodes and relations. For information retrieval purposes, these nodes and relations are tagged with the document from which they are derived. We derive CEs from text automatically using a natural language processing system. A single document may lead to the creation of hundreds of compositional expressions, so a large corpus results in a very large collection of small graph CEs.

In performing information retrieval, a system must search this very large collection of small graphs for specific instances of the query graph. The query graph may be a subgraph of the one stored in the database and still be a match.

Previous work has measured the performance of graph databases on various graph operations [3,4], and traversal/retrieval of subgraphs of large graphs [13, 14,22], but no work has been done on the problem we encounter here (retrieving a small graph from a collection of such graphs).

In Sect. 2 we discuss the three types of database systems used in this study and the sample queries. We also discuss the CE representations used, and the formats of the queries for each database system. Our evaluation methodology is presented in Sect. 3, followed by Sect. 4, which presents the results of running each of the queries on each of the database systems. Finally we conclude with Sect. 5.

2   Methods

Three different types of database systems will be used in this study. Representing traditional relational databases we will use Microsoft SQL Server 2014 [8] and Oracle 11g R2 [12]. A general graph database (Neo4j 2.2.3 [10]) will be evaluated, along with an RDF triplestore (Ontotext's GraphDB 6.4 SE [11]). RDF triplestores are also a kind of graph database, but tailored to a specific representation, namely the use of RDF triples.

The information output of the NLP process which creates the CEs can be represented as instances of fifteen logical relations, four unary, and the rest binary (see Table 1). Some of these relations are adapted from SNOMED CT itself [18], while others are standard logical relations, and still others have been created in-house. The method by which these relations are represented as a graph is presented in the respective database subsection.

Three queries have been selected for evaluation (see Fig. 1). These queries were selected because of the prevalence of results in our dataset, the likelihood that these are real representative queries, and the ability of the queries to test various characteristics of the database systems. Queries one and two both have a single relation, but whereas nearly all CEs which contain the two codes in query one are answers to that query, this is the case for only about half of those for query two. Query three is more complex in that it uses multiple relations conjoined. Queries two and three also have many more results than query one.

In the following three subsections we discuss details of the CE representations used for each of the respective database systems, and the nature of the queries to be performed using each of those systems.

Table 1. Relations used in CEs. The relation name is given, along with labels for one or both arguments (dependent on whether the relation is unary or binary). The semantics of each relation are provided in the last column.

Relation	Argument 1	Argument 2	Semantics
and	and_1	and_2	and_1 and and_2 are True
or	or_1	or_2	Either or_1 or or_2 are True
not	not	–	not is False
non	non	–	non is False
possible	$possible$	–	$possible$ is Possible
exception	$exception$	–	$exception$ is an exception
exceptionTo	$clause$	$exception$	$exception$ is an exception to $clause$
accompaniedBy	$clause$	$with$	$clause$ is accompanied by $with$
hasModifier	$modified$	$modifier$	$modified$ is modified by $modifier$
hasQualifier	$qualified$	$qualifier$	$qualified$ is qualified by $qualifier$
hasLaterality	$concept$	$laterality$	$concept$ has laterality $laterality$
hasSpecimen	$measurement$	$specimen$	$measurement$ has specimen type $specimen$
hasFindingSite	$condition$	$bodysite$	$condition$ has finding site $bodysite$
hasProcedureSite	$procedure$	$bodysite$	$procedure$ has finding site $bodysite$
hasScaleType	$test$	$scale$	$test$ has scale type $scale$

1. Right cataract extraction

> hasLaterality(< Cataract extraction (54885007) >,
> < Right side (24028007) >)

2. Controlled hypertension

> hasModifier(< Hypertension (38341003) >,
> < Controlled (31509003) >)

3. Pack year smoking history

> and(hasModifier(< Finding of tobacco smoking behavior (365981007) >,
> < Pack years (315609007) >),
> hasQualifier(< Finding of tobacco smoking behavior (365981007) >,
> < History of (392521001) >))

Fig. 1. Queries used in evaluation of the databases.

2.1   Relational Database

The relational database format adopted for this study is that which was previously used in iNLP [6,7,9]. The table containing the CEs is made up of 10 columns, as seen in Table 2. Each row contains space for a relation and two

Table 2. Column descriptions of the relational database format.

Column Name	Description
docid	Document ID
secid	Record section ID
ceid	ID of the CE
senid	Sentence ID
cerowid	ID of the row within the CE
operand1	First operand of the relation
relation	The relation
operand2	Second operand of the relation
optype1	Type of thing in the operand1 cell
optype2	Type of thing in the operand2 cell

operands (*relation*, *operand1*, and *operand2*, respectively), along with pedigree data about where the source of the relation is in the text (*docid*, *secid*, and *senid*). Each relation from Table 1 is mapped to a numeric identifier for use in the *relation* column. The column *ceid* gives an identifier unique to the CE within the document, and *cerowid* provides a reference to a row within a CE. There are then two helper columns, *optype1* and *optype2*, which indicate the kind of thing in *operand1* and *operand2* respectively (either, a SNOMED CT code, a reference to a *cerowid*, or null).

Table 3. Relational database representation of a match for query three: pack year smoking history.

docid	secid	ceid	senid	cerowid	operand1	relation	operand2	optype1	optype2
102153	51	13	1	1	365981007	null	null	1	0
102153	51	13	1	3	315609007	null	null	1	0
102153	51	13	1	2	1	100	3	2	2
102153	51	13	1	5	392521001	null	null	1	0
102153	51	13	1	4	1	101	5	2	2
102153	51	13	1	6	2	0	4	2	2

Table 3 shows some of the rows for the CE with ID 13 in document 102153. In this snippet, there are three rows for SNOMED codes (*cerowids* 1, 3, and 5), representing a finding of tobacco smoking behavior, pack years, and history, respectively. The "1" in column *optype1* indicates that these are in fact SNOMED CT codes. The row with *cerowid* 3 connects the contents of *cerows* 1 and 3 with relation 100, which is `hasModifier`. The 2s in *optype1* and *optype2* indicate that the contents of *operand1* and *operand2* are both *cerow* IDs. The row with *cerowid* = 4 connects the contents of *cerow*s 1 and 4 with relation 101, which is `hasQualifier`. Finally, the `hasModifier` and `hasQualifier` relations are combined in the last row with the `and` relation (relation 0).

Performing a query using this representation is a two-step process. First, all CEs which contain the SNOMED CT codes for the concepts of interest are retrieved. This query is written as follows:

```
SELECT a.docid, a.ceid, cerowid, operand1,
       relation, operand2
FROM ce_codes as a
INNER JOIN (SELECT docid, ceid FROM ce_codes
           WHERE operand1 in (codes)
           GROUP BY docid, ceid
           HAVING count(distinct operand1) = codes.length) b
ON
  a.docid = b.docid
  AND a ceid = b.ceid
ORDER BY a.docid, a.ceid
```

where `codes` is the list of SNOMED CT codes of interest.[1] Then, each candidate CE structure must be verified against the query. We have written code to verify the structure of the retrieved CE in parallel with that of the user query.

As mentioned previously, the relational database systems used in this project are Microsoft SQL Server 2014 and Oracle 11g R2. These were chosen since they are large, enterprise-grade database systems, and previous experimentation by the iNLP group showed that queries of the type discussed here executed much more quickly on these than other database systems.

2.2   General Graph Database

There are many graph database solutions available, each with somewhat different capabilities [2]. We chose Neo4j because of its relatively recent rise in popularity, and benchmarks which show that it has both very good performance and scales well to large datasets. It's worth mentioning that Neo4j is also very good at some graph operations which may be useful in practice, such as path matching.

In order to store CEs in Neo4j, we use a directed graph in which nodes are used to represent both SNOMED CT concepts and the relations previously discussed. Nodes are annotated with the pedigree information discussed for the relational database. Edges are labeled with the roles played by each argument of the logical relation (given in columns 2 and 3 of Table 1), and are directed from each relation to its arguments.[2] One major advantage of this graph representation is that we can easily represent a relation being an argument of another

---

[1] Appropriate table indexes were created to speed execution as much as possible.

[2] This is a simplified, impure, version of a propositional graph, as used in the SNePS family [17] of knowledge representation and reasoning systems, and for which a formal mapping is defined between logical expressions and the graph structure [15,16].

relation without leaving the graph formalism, or relying on any "hacks". We use properties for many node attributes (such as pedigree information) instead of relations only because Neo4j indexes on properties. We use two such indexes, on relation names and code values.

In Fig. 2 the same example from Table 3 is presented using the graph formalism defined here. The three bottom nodes have the type `Code`, and represent the three SNOMED CT terms in the example. The four edges incident to those nodes indicate the roles played by those nodes in the relations represented by the sources of those edges. The nodes with type `Relation` represent relations, such as `hasModifier`.

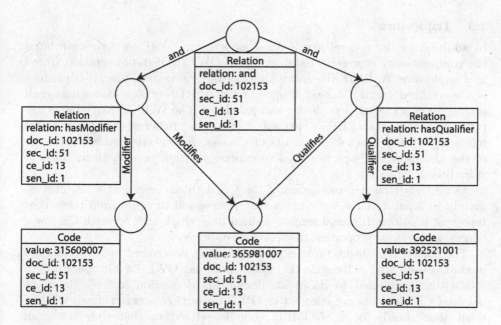

Fig. 2. Graph database representation of a match for query three: pack year smoking history.

Queries for Neo4j can be done in a single step — there is no need to verify the graph structure after the query is complete. The query for "controlled hypertension" (Query 2) is given below, where the relation node is given the label `rel`, which has two edges to nodes for codes (labeled `controlled` and `hypertension` for readability) – one with a `MODIFIER` label, and one with a `MODIFIES` label. The codes the edges point to are 38341003 and 31509003, respectively. These queries, using the Cypher query system, are created using a kind of ASCII art which is easy for users, and easy to generate programmatically.

```
MATCH (controlled:Code {value:38341003})
  <-[:MODIFIES]-(rel:Relation)-[:MODIFIER]->
    (hypertension:Code {value:31509003})
RETURN rel.docid
```

Neo4j also allows queries to be written entirely programmatically, using the Java API. This is a much more involved process. The user first accesses all nodes with a certain property value (*e.g.*, code value), and explores outward, first getting attached edges of a certain type, then nodes at the other end of those edges. This process continues as necessary, allowing the user to find and verify graph structures.

2.3 Triplestore

In addition to the general graph database system Neo4j, we have translated the compositional expression database to an OWL/RDF representation stored in a triplestore. An RDF (Resource Description Framework) [20,21] triplestore is a specialized graph database designed to store RDF triples: statements each consisting of a *subject*, a *predicate*, and an *object*. The Web Ontology Language (OWL) [19] is built on RDF and extends it to support richer modeling and logical inference. An OWL ontology consists of *Classes*, *Individuals* that are instances of the classes, and *Properties* used to express relations among them. *Literals* store literal data values.

Our OWL/RDF representation of the CE database uses just a few classes, mainly to separate CEs components that correspond to codes from those that represent relations. It contains many named individuals (one for each CE row / entry), and several properties, discussed more below.

For each CE element (uniquely identified by a *cerowid* in the relational model), we created a `NamedIndividual` and used OWL `DataProperties` to relate that individual to its ce id, document id, section id, etc. Relations between CE elements are encoded as OWL `ObjectProperties`. Each CE element that stands for a SNOMED code is related to that code using an `AnnotationProperty`.

OWL `DataProperties` are used to relate individuals to literals. We created a data property called *document id* to relate each CE element individual to its literal document identifier. We use similar data properties to relate each CE element to its section id, sentence id, etc.

`AnnotationProperties` are used to provide annotations for resources. For instance, the annotation property *rdfs:label* is commonly used to associate an individual with a readable label. We use *rdfs:label* and an annotation property of our own, *has code*, which is used to label each CE individual that represents a code with the corresponding code.

`ObjectProperties` are used to relate individuals to each other. The fact that one CE element indicates the negation of another CE element can be represented by relating the two with an object property – in this case one we've labeled *not-rel*:

```
{ce1 not-rel ce2 }
```

CE binary relations are represented in the OWL/RDF version in a similar manner to the Neo4j propositional graph. Each relation has an individual that stands for the relation CE element, and two data properties are used to connect it to its relata. The triples that encode the *has modifier* relation between two code CE elements, `cee1` and `cee2`, where that relation is expressed by a third (`cee3`), are as follows:

```
{cee3 modifier cee1 }
{cee3 modifies cee2 }
```

Here both `modifier` and `modifies` are object properties.

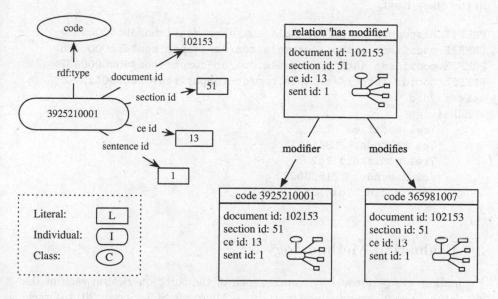

Fig. 3. OWL/RDF representation for compositional expressions

Figure 3 shows the basic representation scheme. The left side depicts a small RDF graph for a single code CE element. The individual that represents the entry is labeled with the corresponding code as an annotation property. That individual is an instance of the class `code`, which is used to easily distinguish entries for codes from those for relations (represented with the class `relation`). The edges from the individual to the rectangular boxes with literal values represent data properties that are used to connect this individual to the literal values of its document id, section id, etc.

The right side of Fig. 3 shows three boxes, each of which stands for a single CE element subgraph like the one just described. An edge between two boxes corresponds to a data property asserted between the two individuals at the center of those subgraphs (*i.e.*, the individuals for those CE elements). These three boxes taken together with the data properties between them represent the fact that in the document with id 102153, at the indicated section, sentence, and so on, the entry that corresponds to code 3925210001 modifies the CE element with code 365981007. The other CE relations, including unary relations, other binary relations, and logical relations (*and*, *or*, etc.) are represented similarly using object properties between individuals.

Our queries for the CE data triplestore are in the SPARQL query language, which works by specifying triple patterns that are matched against the contents of the RDF graph to retrieve results. The following is a SPARQL version of the query for "controlled hypertension" (Query 2). The first few lines are used to map the long identifiers for properties to shorter names used in the query. An alternative would be to include the properties' label assertions among the triples in the query itself.

```
PREFIX hascode: <http://example.com/db-comparison#dbc0000455>
PREFIX modifier: <http://example.com/db-comparison#dbc0000438>
PREFIX modifies: <http://example.com/db-comparison#dbc0000437>
PREFIX docid: <http://example.com/db-comparison#dbc0000412>
select ?did
WHERE {
        ?rel modifies: ?c1 .
        ?c1 hascode:"38341003" .
        ?rel modifier: ?c2 .
        ?c2 hascode: "31509003" .
        ?rel docid: ?did .
}
```

3   Evaluation Methodology

Evaluation was performed by running each of the three queries on each of the six database configurations under study — Microsoft SQL Server 2014, Oracle 11g R2, Neo4j with the Cypher query language, Neo4j using the Java API, and the triplestore GraphDB. Each test was run 10 times, restarting the database systems in between tests to remove any possibility of cached results.[3] We did use a "warmup query" for each system, using a query unrelated to this study, to ensure that the database was fully loaded before running our queries. Averages of the 10 runs are reported in the next section. Significance of the differences between the systems was ascertained using the Student's t-test.

4   Results

We used a collection of 41,585 medical records for this study. The result of running these records through our natural language processing system was 840,184

---

[3] All tests were run on a laptop with a Core i7 4600U CPU, 16GB of RAm, and an SSD. Evaluation code was run in a VirtualBox VM running Ubuntu 14.04.

compositional expressions. These compositional expressions were stored in each of the three types of database systems described above. Queries were written for each database system, designed to be fairly efficient. The relational databases and graph database contain slightly over 9 million rows and nodes, respectively. The triple store translation of the CE data consists of nearly 72 million triples. The average query times for each database on each query are presented in Table 4.

The average speed of each query using each database system and technique was compared with all others using a Student's t-test. We found that the differences between each system were extremely statistically significant for queries one and three with $p < .0001$. On query two, Neo4j's Cypher query engine was not significantly different from its Java API. Also on this query, Neo4j with Cypher was found to be faster than GraphDB with $p < .05$ and Neo4j with the Java API was faster with $p < .005$. All other differences were extremely significant, with $p < .0001$.

Table 4. Average execution time over 10 runs of each query on each of the database systems under consideration.

DB Type	DB Product	Query 1	Query 2	Query 3
Relational	SQL Server 2014	2434 ms	2517 ms	2471 ms
	Oracle 11g R2	1904 ms	2229 ms	3037 ms
Graph	Neo4j (Cypher)	287 ms	272 ms	729 ms
	Neo4j (Java API)	105 ms	263 ms	128 ms
Triplestore	Ontotext GraphDB	49 ms	339 ms	206 ms

It appears that the query time for Microsoft SQL Server is fairly stable, regardless of the number of results or number of codes used in the query. This suggests that the query time is largely dependent on the size of the database, and not on the number of query results. Oracle, on the other hand, seems more sensitive to the number of codes being queried (but, this is obviously a small sample). The complexity of the CE graph to be verified did not appear to play a big part – this is implemented as fairly efficient Java code and occupies an extremely small percentage of the processing time. In Table 5, the number of CEs returned by the query (column 2) is presented, along with the number of CEs which were verified (column 3), and the number of unique documents matched.

The time for execution of the queries using Neo4j's Cypher query engine do suggest that the query complexity (*i.e.*, the complexity of the graph being matched) has some effect on query time. The sample size is rather small here, so more investigation will be needed to determine the exact variables at fault for increased query time. What we can say here, though, is that queries of the complexity of those examined here execute much faster with Neo4j than with either relational database system.

Table 5. The number of CEs returned by each relational query, along with the number which were verified to be instances of the query graph, and the number of unique documents the CEs come from.

Query	Query CEs	Verified CEs	Unique Docs
1	13	12	10
2	107	58	54
3	107	76	74

We have also explored writing Neo4j queries programmatically using the Java API instead of using the Cypher query engine. As others have found (*e.g.*, [1]), this usually is even faster than using Cypher. The disadvantage to this approach is that there is a need to understand the data in great detail. Whereas Cypher is able to use cost analysis to determine which order to perform query segments, such facilities are not readily available from the Java API. It is possibly for this reason that query 2 is slower using the Java API than using Cypher.

As with Neo4j, the triplestore queries are fast enough that they are certainly acceptable for any imagined use of the system. Both Neo4j and GraphDB claim to scale to billions of entries, but we did not assess how well either would scale to handle much larger data sets for this application.

Both Neo4j and triplestores fare well in straightforward matching of sub-graphs in the query comparison, but it's worth noting that these systems have potential advantages, not realized here, which are dependent on the specific application. Neo4j allows for queries involving paths in the graph, allowing some types of reasoning to be performed very quickly. It also allows for graph operations such as shortest-path. With triplestores, the availability of logical reasoners for OWL — including the powerful inference capabilities built into Ontotext's GraphDB — creates the potential for much more interesting queries than examined here.

As a very simple example, we might want to query for CEs that are about not just one particular SNOMED code, but that code and all of its sub-concepts. Both Neo4j and GraphDB have ways of doing this. In GraphDB, one could load SNOMED into the triple store, establishing connections between SNOMED concepts and the CEs that use them, and testing queries that require reasoning about relations between concepts and between concepts and CEs. Such functionality could also be achieved using Neo4j's ability to efficiently follow paths in a graph, or by using a reasoner external to the CE data store.

None of the database systems here have been configured to any great extent for the fastest query processing possible. On the relational databases we created appropriate indexes, but didn't evaluate options such as alternate views of the data or stored procedures. With Neo4j we didn't attempt to use any of the available toolkits which lie atop the Java API to do fast querying. GraphDB provides a variety of configuration parameters that can be adjusted to affect performance for different kinds and amounts of data. We did not utilize these options in our comparison. The triplestore version of the CE data currently uses string literals to store values that could be stored as numeric literals. A slight performance increase might be obtained by a version that uses numeric literals for this instead.

With all of these systems, it is unknown how query speed scales as query size/complexity increases. While returning more data from a query could affect the performance of queries in RDBs and neo4j, it could be the case that this has a slightly larger effect on triplestore because it would be required to match more triples in order to retrieve additional properties associated with a particular resource. In the absence of tests with such queries, we have no reason to suspect that this would significantly affect the running time.

5 Conclusion

Fourty-one percent of clinical problems require post-coordinated CEs to represent their knowledge. For information retrieval purposes, medical texts which have been coded using CEs must be stored in some sort of database. Traditionally, relational databases would be used for this task. We have found that graph databases — both general and RDF triplestores — outperformed relational databases by a factor of up to fifty over the queries. On average, the graph database Neo4j was 5.7x faster than relational databases when using the Cypher query engine, and 16.1x faster when using the Java API. Our chosen triplestore, GraphDB, averaged 20.6x faster than relational databases. These performance issues can make the difference between a practical and an impractical solution.

References

1. Andrš, J.: Metadata repository benchmark: PostgreSQL vs. Neo4j (2014). http://mantatools.com/metadata-repository-benchmark-postgresql-vs-neo4j
2. Angles, R.: A comparison of current graph database models. In: 2012 IEEE 28th International Conference on Data Engineering Workshops (ICDEW), pp. 171–177. IEEE (2012)
3. Ciglan, M., Averbuch, A., Hluchy, L.: Benchmarking traversal operations over graph databases. In: 2012 IEEE 28th International Conference on Data Engineering Workshops (ICDEW), pp. 186–189. IEEE (2012)
4. Dominguez-Sal, D., Urbón-Bayes, P., Giménez-Vañó, A., Gómez-Villamor, S., Martínez-Bazán, N., Larriba-Pey, J.L.: Survey of graph database performance on the HPC scalable graph analysis benchmark. In: Shen, H.T. (ed.) WAIM 2010. LNCS, vol. 6185, pp. 37–48. Springer, Heidelberg (2010)
5. Elkin, P.L., Brown, S.H., Husser, C.S., Bauer, B.A., Wahner-Roedler, D., Rosenbloom, S.T., Speroff, T.: Evaluation of the content coverage of snomed ct: ability of SNOMED clinical terms to represent clinical problem lists. In: Mayo Clinic Proceedings. vol. 81, pp. 741–748. Elsevier (2006)
6. Elkin, P.L., Froehling, D.A., Wahner-Roedler, D.L., Brown, S.H., Bailey, K.R.: Comparison of natural language processing biosurveillance methods for identifying influenza from encounter notes. Ann. Intern. Med. 156(1_Part_1), 11–18 (2012)

7. Elkin, P.L., Trusko, B.E., Koppel, R., Speroff, T., Mohrer, D., Sakji, S., Gurewitz, I., Tuttle, M., Brown, S.H.: Secondary use of clinical data. Stud Health Technol. Inform. **155**, 14–29 (2010)

8. Microsoft: SQL server 2014 (2015). http://www.microsoft.com/en-us/server-cloud/products/sql-server/

9. Murff, H.J., FitzHenry, F., Matheny, M.E., Gentry, N., Kotter, K.L., Crimin, K., Dittus, R.S., Rosen, A.K., Elkin, P.L., Brown, S.H., et al.: Automated identification of postoperative complications within an electronic medical record using natural language processing. Jama **306**(8), 848–855 (2011)

10. Neo Technology Inc: Neo4j, the world's leading graph database. (2015). http://neo4j.com/

11. Ontotext: Ontotext GraphDB. (2015). http://ontotext.com/products/ontotext-graphdb/

12. Oracle: Database 11g R2 (2015). http://www.oracle.com/technetwork/database/index.html

13. Partner, J., Vukotic, A., Watt, N., Abedrabbo, T., Fox, D.: Neo4j in Action. Manning Publications Company, Greenwich (2014)

14. Rodriguez, M.: MySQL vs. Neo4j on a large-scale graph traversal (2011). https://dzone.com/articles/mysql-vs-neo4j-large-scale

15. Schlegel, D.R.: Concurrent Inference Graphs. Ph.D. thesis, State University of New York at Buffalo (2015)

16. Schlegel, D.R., Shapiro, S.C.: Visually interacting with a knowledge base using frames, logic, and propositional graphs. In: Croitoru, M., Rudolph, S., Wilson, N., Howse, J., Corby, O. (eds.) GKR 2011. LNCS, vol. 7205, pp. 188–207. Springer, Heidelberg (2012)

17. Shapiro, S.C., Rapaport, W.J.: The SNePS family. Comput. Math. Appl. **23**(2–5), 243–275 (1992)

18. The International Health Terminology Standards Development Organisation:SNOMED CT technical implementation guide (July 2014)

19. W3C OWL Working Group: Owl 2 web ontology language document overview (2nd edn.) (2012). http://www.w3.org/TR/owl2-overview/

20. W3C RDF Working Group: Rdf 1.1 semantics (2014). http://www.w3.org/TR/rdf11-mt/

21. W3C RDF Working Group: Rdf schema 1.1 (2014). http://www.w3.org/TR/rdf-schema/

22. Zhao, F., Tung, A.K.: Large scale cohesive subgraphs discovery for social network visual analysis. Proc. VLDB Endowment **6**(2), 85–96 (2012)

Data Management and Visualization of Medical Data

Maps of Human Disease: A Web-Based Framework for the Visualization of Human Disease Comorbidity and Clinical Profile Overlay

Naiyun Zhou[1(✉)], Joel Saltz[2], and Klaus Mueller[3]

[1] Biomedical Engineering, Stony Brook University, Stony Brook, NY 11794, USA
naiyun.zhou@stonybrook.edu
[2] Biomedical Informatics, Stony Brook University, Stony Brook, NY 11794, USA
joel.saltz@stonybrookmedicine.edu
[3] Computer Science, Stony Brook University, Stony Brook, NY 11794, USA
mueller@cs.stonybrook.edu

Abstract. We present a practical framework for visual exploration of co-morbidities between diseases. By utilizing high-quality multilevel layout and clustering algorithms, we have implemented an innovative two-layer multiplex network of human diseases. Specifically, we extract the International Classification of Diseases, Ninth Revision (ICD9) codes from an Electronic Medical Records (EMRs) database to build our map of human diseases. In the lower layer, the abbreviated disease terms of ICD9 codes in the irregular regions look like cities in geographical maps. The connections represent the disease pairs co-morbidities, calculated by using co-occurrence. In the upper layer, we visualize multi-object profile of clinical information. For practical application, we propose an interactive system for users to define parameters of representations of the map (see a map representation example in Fig. 1). The demonstrated visualization method offer an opportunity to visually uncover the significant information in clinical data.

Keywords: Human disease comorbidity · EMRs · Graph layout algorithm · Clinical information visualization

1 Introduction

EMRs contain insightful clinical information for assessing disease risk [5]. In the diagnosis table of an EMRs database, disease comorbidity refers to multiple diseases co-occurring in same patients more than chance alone [19]. Due to its implication for understanding human health, it is universally regarded as an important healthcare research topic. Many statistics and bioinformatics research have been conducted on comorbidity to invent computational inference tools [2,14]. In clinical informatics field, we hope to provide an efficient and effective visualization technique for EMRs data mining, especially comorbidity analysis. The main challenges for this interdisciplinary study lie in effective computation

© Springer International Publishing Switzerland 2016
F. Wang et al. (Eds.): Big-O(Q) and DMAH 2015, LNCS 9579, pp. 47–60, 2016.
DOI: 10.1007/978-3-319-41576-5_4

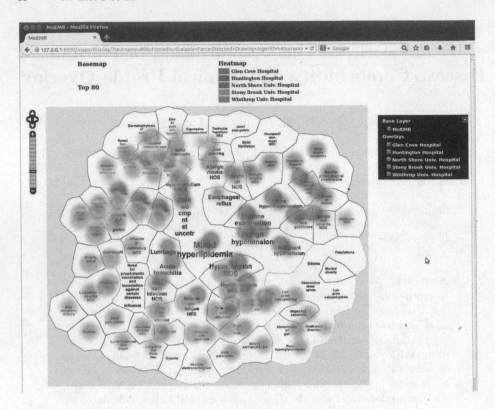

Fig. 1. A Map of Top 80 Human Disease rendered in the web browser. The base map specification: Force Directed Placement (FDP) drawing algorithm, load factor: 5, edges disabled, coloring disabled. The heat map specification: the patient number density distributions of 5 large hospitals on Long Island. (Color figure online)

of diagnosis data, embedding comorbidity network (represented as graph strings) and clinical information highlight as a heat map overlay.

A recent work [6] on visual exploration of research papers in computer science field has addressed most of our visual analytics issues. It is an open-source visualization system based on graph drawing and map representation for data co-occurrence in large-scale relational database. Thanks to their open source github repository, we leveraged their document processing codes on our EMRs data (Diagnosis Table) to calculate similarity matrix of disease pairs. The disease terms are represented as nodes and the connections of high comorbidity are represented as edges. We also use Graphviz [4] open source graph drawing library to visualize graphs in our approach. In the graph embedding and clustering part, we choose the scalable force directed algorithm and modularity based geometric clustering algorithm respectively. The two algorithms are highly related [17], because the spring model layout is consistent with clustering by optimal modularity. For clinical information overlay, we created multiple objects in our program to demonstrate categories in one type of clinical information (e.g. male and female in gender). At the same time, we manipulate the issue of heat spots overlap on single node by displacing heat spots in different directions by a small proportion. In the system, we nicely enable selections for top disease number, base map color representation, connection display and clinical information type.

In general, the main contributions of Maps of Human Disease are: First, we generate an esthetically symmetric layout of disease comorbidity by scalable force directed placement (SFDP), a graph drawing algorithm, which demonstrates relationships between prevalent diseases nicely. Second, differently from [6], we develop a multi-object heat map overlay solution to visualize multiple information profiles simultaneously on single base map. This is a very efficient mechanism for users to compare and discriminate clinical information via disease comorbidity within one visual space. Finally, we propose an interactive browser-based system for users to do parameter selection prior to the process of map generation.

2   Related Work

Analyzing and visualizing information in EMRs have been conducted to guide the diagnosis of future patients or to be used in studies of a certain disease. A number of researchers have explored visualization techniques for organizing the patient records in temporal event sequences [20], in which an outflow is proposed to summarize temporal event data that has been retrieved from EMRs. Other works focused on building an intuitive multi-faceted assessment of the patient overall information [21]. Interesting functionalities and hierarchies via body-centric data arrangement and standard health care coding support doctors or physician's review and analytical reasoning. Particularly, these EMRs representations typically operate without disease co-occurrence visualization, which enlightens us to apply the state-of-art graph-drawing methods on disease co-morbidity.

In the respect of research on human disease network, comprehensive approaches have been investigated on disease-related gene clusters detection [18], properties of the Disease Gene Network [9], and molecular relationships among distinct phenotypes [1]. Few of them discussed disease network layout algorithms in their research paper, except NodeXL (http://en.wikipedia.org/wiki/NodeXL), a free and open-source network analysis and visualization software package for Microsoft Excel. NodeXL provides well-known Force-directed graph drawing layout algorithms such as Fruchterman-Reingold [7] and Harel-Koren [10]. Another interesting work developed a phenotypic human disease network derived from two statistical measures quantifying associations between diseases [3]. In their two layer map, they used different colors to group nodes on the base map by first letter of the ICD 10 codes. The heat map shows significant group of related diseases over age and gender. However, their maps do not show any text information (eg. disease terms) on the nodes. Furthermore, they have not applied any geographic components to strengthen the map metaphor, which leads to poor vision effect.

3   Data and Methods

The raw data for this research is Practice Fusion De-Identified Data Set downloaded from https://www.kaggle.com/c/pf2012/data. We use records from two of the tables: the Diagnosis Table and the Patient Table. The Diagnosis Table consists of three columns: DiagnosisID (Primary Key), PatientID (Foreign Key) and ICD9Code. The Patient Table consists of three columns: PatientID (Primary Key), Gender and YearOfBirth. The total number of patient is 10,000. The hospital information in our system is fictitious.

The three main steps in our system is (1) generating comorbidity graph from comorbidity matrix, (2) generating base map via several graph related algorithms and finally, (3) generating clinical information heat map. Before the first step, we preprocess the raw data by merging the diagnoses (represented by ICD9 codes) belong to every patient together as an entity. In the process of map representation when disease terms needed, we create a look up table containing ICD9 codes and corresponding disease terms, which allow short access time.

3.1   Comorbidity Graph Generation

In this thread, we defined two variable parameters, 'top number' as the number of nodes in the final comorbidity graph, and 'load factor' as the number of emitting edges from each node. The top number is used in Sects. 3.1.1 and 3.1.2, and the load factor is used in Sect. 3.1.3 .

3.1.1   Disease Term Ranking

Once the entities are loaded into the memory, we rank the ICD9 codes according to their occurrence frequency. Each code's weight is assigned by the times it occurred within the Diagnosis Table. The ranking list is acquired by sorting the codes weights and slicing based on the 'top number'. In our maps, the font size of each node is proportional to its rank in this list, clinically expressed as prevalence rate.

3.1.2   Comorbidity Matrix Computation

Comorbidity matrix is the measurement to quantify edge lengths in the final comorbidity graph. Every element in comorbidity matrix is the pairwise similarity values between top diseases. We use Jaccard coefficient [16] to accommodate the Boolean nature of ICD9 codes in the entities. The Jaccard similarity coefficient is defined as the size of the intersection divided by the size of the union of the sample sets. In our study, pairwise comorbidity will be calculated within every pair of 'top' diseases:

$$J(S_i, S_j) = \frac{S_i \cap S_j}{S_i \cup S_j},$$

where S_i and S_j are the sets of patientID with disease i or j in the Diagnosis Table.

3.1.3   Edge Number Filtering and Edge Length Calculation

Considering the visual clarity of the map, we select most highly related diseases from S_j for each disease in S_i ('load factor' = 1). In the next stage, the pairwise comorbidity matrix is transformed into a matrix of edge lengths for graph drawing. Since the value of $J(S_i, S_j)$ is in range of 0 and 1, in order to get an appropriate distribution, we need as well normalize $J(S_i, S_j)$, by dividing $\max_{p,q}^{p=q} J(S_p, S_q)$, thus we get rescaled value $J'(S_i, S_j)$. Based on $J'(S_i, S_j)$, each edge length of two nodes, $D(S_i, S_j)$ in the graph, is calculated by logarithm scaling:

$$D(S_i, S_j) = -E \cdot log[(1 - \sigma) \cdot J'(S_i, S_j) + \sigma],$$

where E is a scaling factor, we set it to be 1, and σ is a smoothing value, set to be 0.05. Logarithm scaling provides a better map metaphor by enlarging comorbidity values within the small range [6].

3.2   Base Map Generation

Base map generation is the most important thread in our approach. We apply Scalable Force Directed Placement (SFDP) [12], a fast graph drawing algorithm that efficiently layout large graphs, on large map generation. In the following part, we use a modularity based clustering algorithm [15] to group vertices into clusters. Lastly, in order to uncover beautifully the underlying structural information and neighborhoods, we apply the mapping and the coloring algorithms described in GMap [8].

3.2.1   Embedding

In our system, we generate the positions of the nodes in two-dimensional plane by a spring-embedder [13], which relies on spring forces and mechanical energy based on Hooke's law. Basically, in the spring model, repulsive forces between all nodes and attractive forces between directly connected nodes are calculated iteratively to assign an energy state for each node, thus achieving a minimal energy state by moving each node based on the resultant force. In this basic model, the geometric layout is determined by the initial state and the structure of the graph itself, which shows independence. However, the lengths between pairs of nodes may not match the graph theoretic distances calculated in Sect. 3.1.3. Here, we adopted Kamada and Kawai's refined spring model [13], minimizing the difference between energy states corresponds to the geometric and graph distances. The graph distances in this model are computed by and All-Pairs-Shortest-Path computation (Floyd-Warshall algorithm or Johnson's algorithm).

Clinical researchers usually need a quite large map. So, we use SFDP, a multilevel force-directed placement algorithm offering good layouts for large graphs within reasonable running time. This algorithm uses a k-centers approximation to coarsen the original graph, followed by Kamada and Kawai's layout model. For implementation details in this algorithm, please refer [10]. We can compare the visual difference of FDP and SFDP on a top 800 diseases graph from Figs. 2, 3, 4 and 5. In Fig. 4, SFDP provides much clearer groups of nodes (like cities of countries in geographic maps) than that of FDP (Fig. 2). Obviously, SFDP algorithm makes it easy for doctors or physicians to understand the co-occurrence of prevalent diseases. In Fig. 3, the connection edges between pairs of diseases are so intricate that the layout is not informative for representation or research. In contrast, in Fig. 5, the diseases having high co-occurrence with Mixed Hyperlipidemia surround it without any edge intersection, which shows the relationship in a great way. Therefore, we recommend using SFDP for large map representation.

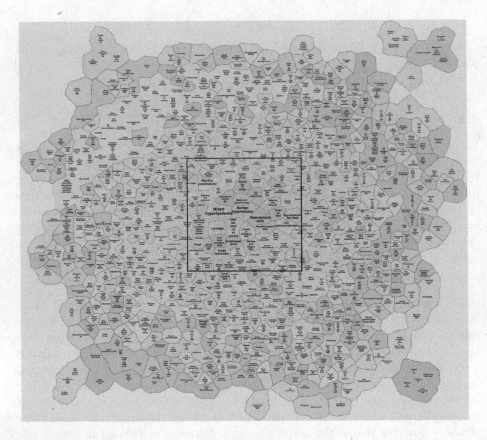

Fig. 2. A Map of Top 800 Human Disease. The base map specification: FDP drawing algorithm, load factor: 1, edges enabled, coloring enabled.

3.2.2   Clustering

Human diseases with high prevalence usually have dense connections among groups. We use a modularity based clustering method [17] to group nodes. It maximizes the modularity of the adjacent matrix of the graph via a spectral technique. The adjacent matrix modularity is defined as real edge numbers

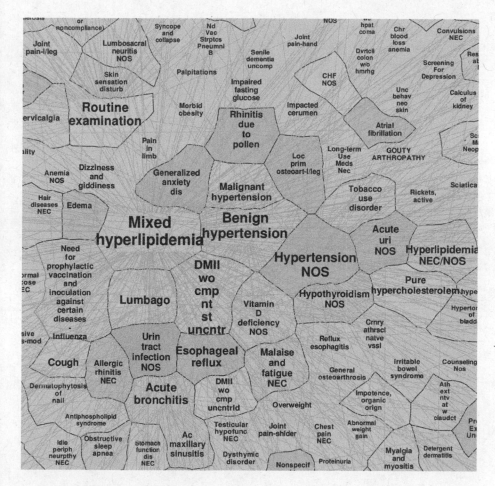

Fig. 3. The enlarged area within the black square in Fig. 2.

within groups minus the expected number of edges placed at random. Clusters can be detected based on computing the leading eigenvector of the adjacent matrix modularity and classifying nodes according to the signs in the eigenvector.

3.2.3 Geographic Mapping and Coloring

To make a visually pleasing geographical map, we adopt a modified Voronoi diagram of the nodes as the mapping algorithm, which is described in [8]. In this diagram, the boundaries of the clusters are more rounded than traditional Voronoi diagram, while some of the inner boundaries are kept artificially straight. In the last step, we color the countries (clusters) with ColorBrewer Theorem [11], which distinguishes adjacent clusters with two most different colors. For more

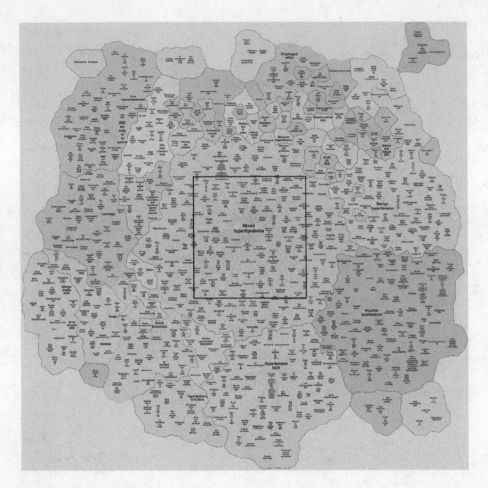

Fig. 4. A Map of Top 800 Human Disease. The base map specification: SFDP drawing algorithm, load factor: 1, edges enabled, coloring enabled.

information about the color distance function used in this method, please see details in [8].

3.3   Heat Map Generation

The heat map intensity in the overlay represents the significance of the information over certain nodes. There are three clinical information items: hospital, gender and age. The diameter of each heat spot is calculated by taking logarithm scale of normalized patient number density respective to the option within selected information type. Particularly, every node might have multiple highlight spots of information options, so we shift the heat spot centers by a little proportion in different directions to solve overlapping issue (as Fig. 1 shown). Solid semi-transparent circles are laid over the nodes as raster overlay.

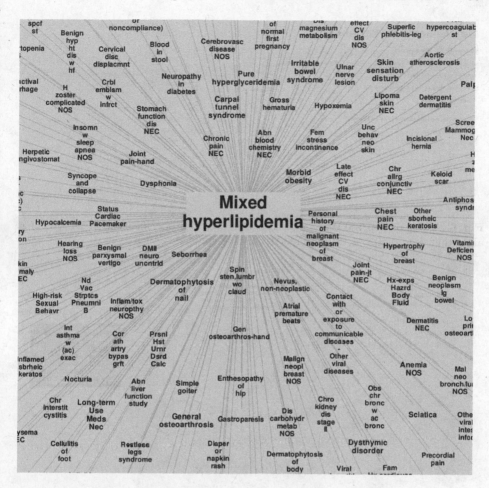

Fig. 5. The enlarged area within the black square in Fig. 4.

3.4   Implementation

The system is implemented using Django Web application framework with modular design in Ubuntu 12.04. The four main modules in our system are: comorbidity graph generation, base map generation, heat map generation and map rendering. We render our SVG formatted base maps in web browser using AT&T's GraphViz system [4]. For the heat maps, we utilize heat map modules, together with zooming and panning tools from the open source OpenLayers JavaScript library. The programming language used in the framework is Python 2.7.3.

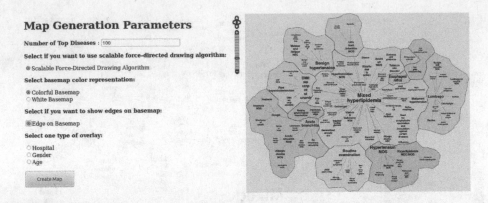

Fig. 6. A Map of Top 100 Human Disease. The base map specification: SFDP drawing algorithm, load factor: 1, edges enabled, coloring enabled.

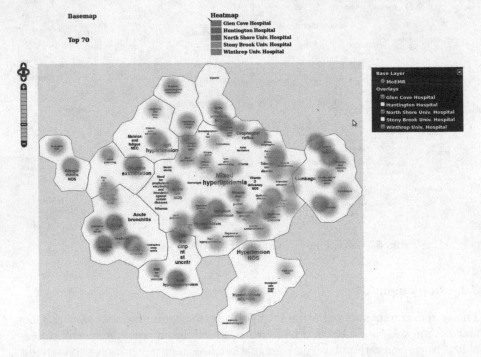

Fig. 7. Maps of Top 70 Human Disease. The base map specification: SFDP drawing algorithm, load factor: 1, edges disabled, coloring disabled. The heat map specification: the patient number density distributions of 5 large hospitals on Long Island, with Glen Cove Hospital, North Shore University Hospital and Winthrop University Hospital selected. (Color figure online)

4   Case Studies

Two case studies focused on the base map and the heat map were done respectively to demonstrate the layout of disease co-occurrence relationships and clinical information highlight. There is a 'Map Generation Parameters' input user interface in our system, which is rendered in the web browser before map representation, as shown in the left part of Fig. 6.

In the first case study, we intend to get a colorful map of 100 prevalent diseases. In order to illustrate the most important relationship between diseases occurred frequently, we set the load factor for each node to be 1, which means only one edge emitting from each node in the graph. For better clustering, we choose SFDP for graph drawing algorithm. Since no heat map is needed in this case, we just leave the 'overlay' selection part blank, as shown in the user interface (Fig. 6). The result shows a hierarchical structure of a hundred prevalent diseases (extracted from the data set) that are grouped into 11 clusters. We can tell from the map that 'Mixed Hyperlipidemia' is the Top 1 human disease and it is the center of 9 sub-prevalent diseases. Obviously, the hierarchical structure improves our understanding of these one hundred diseases. It does make sense that mixed hyperlipidemia, hypertension and diabetes mellitus are highly related. For another example, in the red region (in

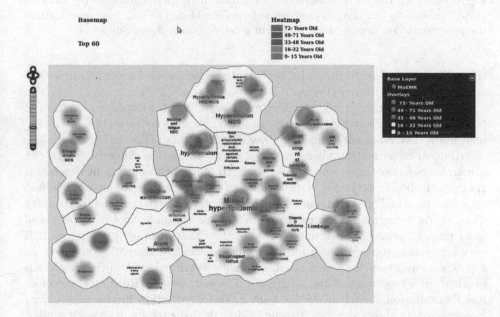

Fig. 8. Maps of Top 60 Human Disease. The base map specification: SFDP drawing algorithm, load factor: 1, edges disabled, coloring disabled. The heat map specification: the patient number density distributions of 5 age ranges, with >72 Years Old, 49–71 Years Old and 33–48 Years Old selected (Color figure online)

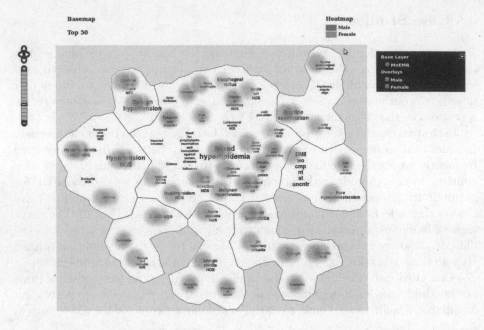

Fig. 9. Maps of Top 50 Human Disease. The base map specification: SFDP drawing algorithm, load factor: 1, edges disabled, coloring disabled. The heat map specification: the patient number density distributions of genders. (Color figure online)

the left bottom corner of the map), both acute bronchitis and acute sinusitis NOS are diseases of respiratory system.

In the second case study, the heat maps are clinical information overlays of hospital, age and gender respectively. In Fig. 7, we demonstrate three hospitals' heat maps (five hospitals altogether) over Top 70 Human Disease base map. The distribution of patient number density of every hospital is different, which can illustrate, to some degree, the clinical strength of hospitals or patient concentration near to hospitals. In Fig. 8, heat maps of three elder age ranges are overlaid on a base map of Top 60 Human Disease. In the map, the patient number density distribution is normalized in each age range. For example, in Fig. 8, people of elder than 72 years old cover more diseases than that of other age rangers. It is very interesting to do research on prevalent diseases in different age rangers. In Fig. 9, a comparison of patient number density distribution from two genders is overlaid on a base map of Top 50 Human Disease. Despite Routine Gynecological Examination is exclusively for women, the information in this map driven by gender data shows significant trend of prevalent diseases among each gender. This visualization approach provides an efficient way for researchers or doctors to filter or determine gender-exclusive diseases.

5 Conclusions and Future Work

Our work proposes a practical framework for visual exploration of comorbidity between diseases. Experimental results show the goodness of SFDP graph drawing algorithm on large-scale data set, which also provide clinical meaning and nice visualization for researchers. Clinical information (hospital, age, gender) profiles are visualized by heat map overlay. In this paper, we have shown clinically valuable case studies that evaluate our system.

Future works could be considered in many promising directions to help medical personnel to arrive at more accurate diagnoses and treatments. For example, we can incorporate database technique with our visualization to standardize data entry queries and clinical data management. This work might need to be cooperated with physicians who are professional at EMR database. In addition, the flexibility of our system should be improved in respect of more types of clinical information overlay, comparable data visualization among options in a heat map and further statistical analysis. For comparable data visualization, we can solve this issue by normalizing patient number density in different groups. While this processing may lead to poor visual effect due to large distribution bias among different groups, we can create an option button in the user interface to control this functionality.

Acknowledgements. We thank Dr. Stephen Kobourov's group for their great work on Maps of Computer Science. Without their generosity of sharing their original codes on github, we cannot implement our ideas on the clinical data. Particularly, we are most grateful for Daniel Fried's help in configuring and setting up the dependencies of their project on our client system, which laid a very solid foundation for our further development.

References

1. Barabási, A.-L., Gulbahce, N., Loscalzo, J.: Network medicine: a network-based approach to human disease. Nat. Rev. Genet. **12**(1), 56–68 (2011)
2. Capobianco, E., Liò, P.: Comorbidity networks: beyond disease correlations. J. Complex Netw. **3**(3), 319–332 (2015)
3. Chmiel, A., Klimek, P., Thurner, S.: Spreading of diseases through comorbidity networks across life and gender. New J. Phy. **16**(11), 115013 (2014)
4. Ellson, J., Gansner, E.R., Koutsofios, L., North, S.C., Woodhull, G.: Graphviz - open source graph drawing tools. In: Mutzel, P., Jünger, M., Leipert, S. (eds.) GD 2001. LNCS, vol. 2265, pp. 483–484. Springer, Heidelberg (2002)
5. Folino, F., Pizzuti, C., Ventura, M.: A comorbidity network approach to predict disease risk. In: Khuri, S., Lhotská, L., Pisanti, N. (eds.) ITBAM 2010. LNCS, vol. 6266, pp. 102–109. Springer, Heidelberg (2010)
6. Fried, D., Kobourov, S.G.: Maps of computer science. In: Pacific Visualization Symposium (PacificVis), 2014 IEEE, pp. 113–120. IEEE (2014)
7. Fruchterman, T.M., Reingold, E.M.: Graph drawing by force-directed placement. Softw. Pract. Experience **21**(11), 1129–1164 (1991)

8. Gansner, E.R., Yifan, H., Kobourov, S.: GMap: visualizing graphs and clusters as maps. In: Pacific Visualization Symposium (PacificVis), 2010 IEEE, pp. 201–208. IEEE (2010)
9. Goh, K.I., Cusick, M.E., Valle, D., Childs, B., Vidal, M., Barabási, A.L.: The human disease network. Proc. Nat. Acad. Sci. **104**(21), 8685–8690 (2007)
10. Harel, D., Koren, Y.: A fast multi-scale method for drawing large graphs. In: Marks, J. (ed.) GD 2000. LNCS, vol. 1984, pp. 183–196. Springer, Heidelberg (2001)
11. Harrower, M., Brewer, C.A.: Colorbrewer. org: an online tool for selecting colour schemes for maps. Cartographic J. **40**(1), 27–37 (2003)
12. Yifan, H.: Efficient, high-quality force-directed graph drawing. Math. J. **10**(1), 37–71 (2005)
13. Kamada, T., Kawai, S.: An algorithm for drawing general undirected graphs. Inform. Process. Lett. **31**(1), 7–15 (1989)
14. Moni, M.A., Lio, P.: comoR: a software for disease comorbidity risk assessment. J. Clin. Bioinformatics **4**(1), 8 (2014)
15. Newman, M.E.J.: Modularity and community structure in networks. Proc. Nat. Acad. Sci. **103**(23), 8577–8582 (2006)
16. Niwattanakul, S., Singthongchai, J., Naenudorn, E., Wanapu, S.: Using of jaccard coefficient for keywords similarity. In: Proceedings of the International MultiConference of Engineers and Computer Scientists, vol. 1, p. 6 (2013)
17. Noack, A.: Modularity clustering is force-directed layout. Phys. Rev. E **79**(2), 026102 (2009)
18. Sun, P.G., Gao, L., Han, S.: Prediction of human disease-related gene clusters by clustering analysis. Int. J. Biol. Sci. **7**(1), 61 (2011)
19. van Weel, C., Schellevis, F.G.: Comorbidity and guidelines: conflicting interests. Lancet **367**(9510), 550–551 (2006)
20. Wongsuphasawat, K., Gotz, D.: Outflow: visualizing patient flow by symptoms and outcome. In: IEEE VisWeek Workshop on Visual Analytics in Healthcare, Providence (2011)
21. Zhang, Z., Mittal, A., Garg, S., Dimitriyadi, A.E., Ramakrishnan, I.V., Zhao, R., Viccellio, A.: Mueller, K.: A visual analytics framework for emergency room clinical encounters, In: IEEE Workshop on Visual Analytics in Health Care (2010)

Secure Similarity Queries:
Enabling Precision Medicine with Privacy

Jinfei Liu[✉] and Li Xiong

Department of Mathematics and Computer Science,
Emory University, Atlanta, USA
{jinfei.liu,lxiong}@emory.edu

Abstract. Up till now, most medical treatments are designed for average patients. However, one size doesn't fit all, treatments that work well for some patients may not work for others. Precision medicine is an emerging approach for disease treatment and prevention that takes into account individual variability in people's genes, environments, lifestyles, etc. A critical component for precision medicine is to search existing treatments for a new patient by similarity queries. However, this also raises significant concerns about patient privacy, i.e., how such sensitive medical data would be managed and queried while ensuring patient privacy? In this paper, we (1) briefly introduce the background of the precision medicine initiative, (2) review existing secure kNN queries and introduce a new class of secure skyline queries, (3) summarize the challenges and investigate potential techniques for secure skyline queries.

Keywords: Secure queries · Precision medicine · Similarity queries · Privacy

1 Introduction

Earlier this year, the President announced the precision medicine initiative that aims to accelerate progress toward a new era of precision medicine. Precision medicine takes individual variability into account. For example, blood typing has been used to guide blood transfusions for more than one century [5]. The prospect of applying precision medicine broadly has been dramatically improved by (1) the recent development of large-scale biologic databases, e.g., human genome sequence, (2) powerful methods for characterizing patients, e.g., proteomics, genomics, and even mobile health technology, as well as (3) computational tools for analyzing large datasets.

With the increasing collections of patient data including the Electronic Health Record (EHR), genetic data, omics data, as well as individual health data collected from smart devices such as Apple watch and fitbit, we have the unprecedented opportunity to utilize such a wealth of information to personalize the treatment and prevention for individuals based on their unique genes, health record, environment, life style, etc. An important class of queries to support such an initiative is similarity based patient search queries, i.e., given an

F. Wang et al. (Eds.): Big-O(Q) and DMAH 2015, LNCS 9579, pp. 61–70, 2016.
DOI: 10.1007/978-3-319-41576-5_5

individual patient, a physician may wish to retrieve similar patients based on a variety of features or attributes, in order to design and customize an optimal and personalized treatment plan for the new patient.

Consider a simple example below. Let P denote a sample heart disease dataset with attributes ID, age, sex, cp (chest pain type), trestbps (resting blood pressure), chol (serum cholestoral), thalach (maximum heart rate achieved). We sampled five patient records from the heart disease dataset of UCI machine learning repository [16] as shown in Table 1.

Table 1. Sample of heart disease dataset.

ID	age	sex	cp	trestbps	chol	thalach	treatment
p_1	39	1	3	120	339	170	tm_1
p_2	40	0	2	130	237	170	tm_2
p_3	51	1	2	110	208	142	tm_3
p_4	42	1	3	130	215	138	tm_4
p_5	40	1	2	130	209	178	tm_5

Consider a physician who is treating a patient $Q = < 40, 0, 2, 125, 210, 160 >$. The physician can use similarity queries (e.g., kNN) to search the k most similar patients to study their treatments in order to enhance and personalize the treatment for patient Q.

In parallel with the precision medicine initiative, an emerging computing paradigm in recent years is cloud computing. More and more data owners (e.g., hospital, CDC) may wish to outsource their data to an external service provider which manages the data on behalf of the data owner. By outsourcing dataset to the cloud server, many security issues arise, such as *data privacy* (protecting the confidentiality of the dataset from the cloud server). To achieve data privacy, data owners are required to use data anonymization or cryptographic techniques over their datasets before outsourcing them to untrusted cloud server.

One direction is to anonymize the sensitive dataset before outsourcing them to cloud server. There are two main categories: traditional data de-identification or anonymization techniques [20,21,25,33] and differential privacy techniques [3,4,7,9,19,35] with more strict mathematical guarantees. For a classic and detailed survey, please see [10]. While these techniques provide a promising approach for privacy preserving data sharing, they typically require data generalization or data perturbation which limits the data utility of the resulting dataset. Another direction is cryptographic techniques [11,12,26], i.e., the data owner leverages some encryption techniques to encrypt the dataset before outsourcing them to cloud server, which can support certain kinds of query processing on the encrypted data. In addition, to preserve *query privacy* (protecting the confidentiality of the query from the cloud server), authorized clients are required to encrypt their queries before sending them to the cloud server.

Fig. 1. Secure similarity queries.

Figure 1 illustrates the processing of encrypted query over encrypted dataset. Clients (e.g., physician) encrypted their queries Q before sending to the cloud server, data owners (e.g., hospital, CDC) encrypted their sensitive data before outsourcing to the cloud server as well. At the end of the queries, the query output should be revealed only to clients. While this approach provides a strong data confidentiality guarantee and more accurate query support, the processing of encrypted query over encrypted dataset becomes challenging.

In this paper, we consider the problem of supporting similarity queries on encrypted data in the data outsourcing setting. We (1) review existing secure kNN queries and introduce a new problem of secure skyline queries, (2) summarize the challenges and investigate potential techniques for secure skyline queries.

The rest of the paper is organized as follows. Section 2 reviews the existing secure kNN queries and introduces another class of secure skyline queries. Challenges and potential techniques for secure skyline queries are discussed in Sect. 3. Section 4 concludes the paper.

2 Secure Similarity Queries

In this section, we first review the secure kNN queries and present the scenario that we think is the most practical. We then introduce the problem of secure skyline queries.

2.1 Secure kNN Queries

The k-Nearest Neighbor query is a classic and foundational problem that has been extensively studied in data management field [30,32]. Back to the example in Table 1. For simplicity, assume $k = 2$. If we leverage Euclidean distance as the similarity metric and each attribute takes the same weight, kNN queries returns p_4 and p_5. Therefore, the physician can study the specific treatments tm_4 and tm_5 to enhance the treatment for new patient Q.

The most related previous works on secure kNN queries are [8,14,15,28, 31,34,36,37]. Wong et al. [34] proposed a new encryption scheme called asymmetric scalar-product-preserving encryption In their work, data and query are

Table 2. Summary of existing works.

Literature	Data Privacy	Query Privacy	Techniques and vulnerabilities
[15, 34]	√	√	vulnerable to the CPA attacks
[36]	√	√	returns more than k results
[37]	√	√	oblivious transfer paradigm
[31]	N/A	N/A	SMC paradigm
[14]	N/A	√	group NN queries
[28]	N/A	√	based on specific hardware

encrypted using slightly different encryption schemes before being outsourced to the cloud server and all the clients know the private key. Hu et al. [15] proposed a method based on provably secure homomorphic encryption scheme. However, both schemes are vulnerable to the CPA attacks as illustrated by Yao et al. [36]. And then Yao et al. [36] proposed a new method based on secure Voronoi diagram. Instead of asking the cloud server to retrieve the exact kNN result, their method retrieves a relevant encrypted partition E(R) for E(Q) such that R is guaranteed to contain the kNN of Yi et al. [37] propose solutions for secure kNN queries based on oblivious transfer paradigm. Those four works consider data privacy and query privacy, but the clients need to be involved in some computation. Qi et al. [31] proposed efficient protocols with linear computation and communication complexity for secure kNN queries, when the data is distributed between two parties who want to cooperatively compute the answers without revealing to each other their private data. Hashem et al. [14] identified the challenges in preserving user privacy for group nearest neighbor queries and provided a comprehensive solution to this problem. Papadopoulos et al. [28] introduced methods that offer strong (query) location privacy, by integrating private information retrieval functionality. Specifically, they leveraged secure hardware-aided Private Information Retrieval (PIR), which has been proven very efficient. Those two works only satisfy query privacy. We summarize the existing works in Table 2.

Recently, Elmehdwi et al. [8] proposed a secure kNN queries protocol that meets the following requirements: data privacy, query privacy, low (or no) computation overhead on client, and hidden data access patterns. Suppose the data owner (e.g., hospital) owns a database P of n patient records, denoted by $p_1, ..., p_n$, and m attributes. Let $p_{i,j}$ denote the jth attribute value of patient p_i. We assume that hospital initially encrypts their database attribute with public key encryption system, i.e., hospital computes $E(p_{i,j})$ for $1 \leq i \leq n$ and $1 \leq j \leq m$. Let the encrypted database be denoted by $E(P)$. We assume that hospital outsources $E(P)$ as well as the future querying processing services to the cloud server. Consider an authorized physician who wants to ask the cloud server for kNN existing patients that are most similar to his/her new specific patient Q based on $E(P)$. During this process, physician's query Q and patient records of database P should not be revealed to the cloud server. Based on our understanding, this is the most practical scenario in real world. In order to protect query result not to be revealed to the cloud server, the protocol of [8] needs to be repeated k iterations because only the 1NN instead of kNN is returned by each iteration. Therefore, how to design efficient protocol for secure kNN queries is still challenging. Furthermore, in their protocol, the knowledge of whether two values are equal is revealed to the cloud server.

2.2   Skyline Queries

The indispensable assumption for kNN queries is that the clients' attribute weights are known in advance, so that a single aggregated similarity metric can be computed between a pair of patients aggregating the similarity between all attribute pairs. However, this assumption does not always hold in practical applications. Back to the example of Table 1, for each client, the criteria for retrieving similar patients may vary significantly and the relative importance of the attributes contributing to the overall similarity may not be clear. Therefore, clients have to retrieve similar patients considering all possible relative weights which is in spirit similar to skyline.

The skyline problem was firstly studied in computational geometry [18] which focused on worst-case time complexity. [17,23] proposed output-sensitive algorithms achieving $O(n \log v)$ in the worst-case where v is the number of skyline points which is far less than n in general. Since the introduction of the skyline queries by Borzsonyi et al. [2], skyline has been extensively studied in database field because the clients' attribute weights are not required. Many works studied extensions or variants of the classical skyline definition. Papadias et al. [27] studies group-by skyline which groups the objects based on their values in one dimension and then computes the skyline for each group. The group based skyline, called Gskyline, was proposed in [22]. [24,29] studied the skyline problem for uncertain data. We briefly show the skyline queries definition as follows.

Definition 1 (Skyline Queries [6]). *Given a dataset P of n points and a query point q in d-dimensional space. Let p and p' be two different points in P, we say p dynamically dominates p' with regard to the query point q, denoted by $p \prec_d p'$, if for all i, $|p[i] - q[i]| \leq |p'[i] - q[i]|$, and for at least one i, $|p[i] - q[i]| < |p'[i] - q[i]|$, where $p[i]$ is the ith dimension of p and $1 \leq i \leq d$. The skyline points are those points that are not dynamically dominated by any other point in P.*

Back to the example of Table 1. It is easy to see p_2 (p_5) dominates p_1 (p_3 and p_4) with regard to the query Q, respectively. Furthermore, no other patients can dominate p_2 and p_5. Therefore, the skyline queries with regard to Q returns p_2 and p_5.

2.3   Problem Statement

Based on the existing secure kNN queries and the definition of skyline queries, we state our problem as follows.

Secure Skyline Queries. Suppose the data owner Alice owns a dataset P of n tuples, denoted by $p_1, ..., p_n$. Each tuple has m attributes, we use $p_{i,j}$ denote the jth dimension of ith tuple, where $1 \leq i \leq n$ and $1 \leq j \leq m$. Before outsourcing the dataset to cloud server C_1, Alice encrypted $p_{i,j}$ by employing the Pailliar cryptosystem, we use pk and sk denote the public key and private key, respectively. Alice sends $E_{pk}(p_{i,j})$ for $1 \leq i \leq n$ and $1 \leq j \leq m$ to C_1 and the private key sk to C_2. From now on, Alice does not need to participant in any computation. An authorized client Bob who wants to know the skyline tuples corresponding to his query tuple $Q = <q_1, ..., q_m>$, is not willing to reveal his sensitive query tuple. Therefore, before sending his query tuple Q to the cloud server C_1, Bob uses the same public key pk to encrypt his query tuple Q. Therefore, Bob sends $E_{pk}(Q) = < E_{pk}(q_1), ..., E_{pk}(q_m) >$ to cloud server C_1. After that, Bob does not need to participant "any" computation to obtain the final queries result. Our ultimate goal for secure skyline queries is that (1) patient records of P should not be revealed to the cloud server, (2) physician's patient query Q should not be revealed to the could server, (3) which patient records correspond to the skyline queries should not be revealed to the cloud server.

In general, a "good" secure skyline queries protocol needs to satisfy the properties as follows.

- Preserve the confidentiality of sensitive dataset P and query Q in the protocol.
- Accurately compute the result of skyline queries.
- Incur low computation and communication cost between different parties, e.g., cloud server C_1 and C_2, data owner, and client.
- Hiding data access patterns from the cloud servers.

3   Challenges and Potential Techniques

In this section, we briefly discuss the challenges and some potential techniques for secure skyline queries.

3.1   Challenges

In secure kNN queries, we only need to securely compute the distance between each patient p_i and the query patient Q based on the given similarity metric, and then find the k nearest neighbors. However, in secure skyline queries, (1) we need to securely compute all the dominance relationship between $\binom{n}{2}$ patients pairs with regard to the query patient Q, (2) for each dominance relationship judgement, all the m attributes are considered simultaneously which leads to 3^m probabilities. Therefore, more intermediate information need to be computed by cloud server and more possibilities that P can be recovered. Furthermore, the output size of skyline can be varied based on the distribution of input dataset. Thus, the secure computation iterations can not be fixed.

3.2   Potential Techniques

Lots of cryptosystems are leveraged in secure similarity queries, in this subsection, we list some techniques that may be employed by secure skyline queries as follows.

Paillier's Homomorphic Cryptosystem [26]. Similar to secure kNN queries, we can use Paillier's homomorphic cryptosystem to do secure distance computation, secure comparison, and secure multiplication. Paillier's homomorphic cryptosystem is a partial homomorphic encryption system which satisfies homomorphic addition of ciphertexts and homomorphic multiplication to plaintexts. We list those two homomorphic properties as follows.

– **Homomorphic addition:**

$$D(E(m_1)E(m_2) \bmod n^2) = m_1 + m_2 \bmod n$$

– **Homomorphic multiplication:**

$$D(E(m_1)^k \bmod n^2) = km_1 \bmod n$$

Hidden Vector Encryption [1]. Hidden Vector Encryption (HVE) schemes are encryption schemes in which each ciphertext C is associated with a binary vector $X = (x_1, ..., x_n)$ (each element has value 0 or 1) and each key K is associated with binary vector $Y = (y_1, ..., y_n)$ with "don't care" entries (denoted by $\star$) (each element has value 0,1, or $\star$). Key K can decrypt ciphertext C iff X and Y agree for all i for which y_i is not $\star$. HVE schemes are an important type of predicate encryption schemes as they can be used to construct more sophisticated predicate encryption schemes, e.g., conjunctive, subset, and range queries.

HVE was used for searchable encryption in the context of processing location data [13]. To the best of our knowledge, HVE has never been used in secure kNN queries. However, in secure skyline queries, HVE may be a promising technique to determine the dominance relationship between two records while ensuring patient privacy.

4   Conclusion

In this paper, we introduced an important class of secure similarity based queries in the context of precision medicine. After reviewing the existing secure kNN queries, we proposed another important query, secure skyline queries which has not been studied. We investigated the challenges for secure skyline queries and discussed the potential techniques.

Acknowledgement. The authors would like to thank the anonymous reviewers for their helpful comments. This research was partially supported by the National Institute of General Medical Sciences of the National Institutes of Health under award number R01GM114612 and the Patient-Centered Outcomes Research Institute (PCORI) under award ME-1310-07058.

References

1. Boneh, D., Waters, B.: Conjunctive, subset, and range queries on encrypted data. In: Vadhan, S.P. (ed.) TCC 2007. LNCS, vol. 4392, pp. 535–554. Springer, Heidelberg (2007)
2. Börzsönyi, S., Kossmann, D., Stocker, K.: The skyline operator. In: Proceedings of the 17th International Conference on Data Engineering, 2–6 April 2001, Heidelberg, pp. 421–430 (2001)
3. Chawla, S., Dwork, C., McSherry, F., Smith, A., Wee, H.M.: Toward privacy in public databases. In: Kilian, J. (ed.) TCC 2005. LNCS, vol. 3378, pp. 363–385. Springer, Heidelberg (2005)
4. Chen, R., Mohammed, N., Fung, B.C.M., Desai, B.C., Xiong, L.: Publishing set-valued data via differential privacy. PVLDB 4(11), 1087–1098 (2011)
5. Collins, F.S., Varmus, H.: A new initiative on precision medicine. New Engl. J. Med. 1(1), 793–795 (2015)
6. Dellis, E., Seeger, B.: Efficient computation of reverse skyline queries. In: Proceedings of the 33rd International Conference on Very Large Data Bases, University of Vienna, Austria, 23–27 September 2007, pp. 291–302 (2007)
7. Dwork, C.: Differential privacy. In: Bugliesi, M., Preneel, B., Sassone, V., Wegener, I. (eds.) ICALP 2006. LNCS, vol. 4052, pp. 1–12. Springer, Heidelberg (2006)
8. Elmehdwi, Y., Samanthula, B.K., Jiang, W.: Secure k-nearest neighbor query over encrypted data in outsourced environments. In: IEEE 30th International Conference on Data Engineering, ICDE 2014, Chicago, March 31 - April 4 2014, pp. 664–675 (2014)
9. Fan, L., Bonomi, L., Xiong, L., Sunderam, V.S.: Monitoring web browsing behavior with differential privacy. In: 23rd International World Wide Web Conference, WWW 2014, Seoul, 7–11 April 2014, pp. 177–188 (2014)
10. Fung, B.C.M., Wang, K., Chen, R., Yu, P.S.: Privacy-preserving data publishing: a survey of recent developments. ACM Comput. Surv. 42(4), 14 (2010)
11. Gentry, C.: Fully homomorphic encryption using ideal lattices. In: Proceedings of the 41st Annual ACM Symposium on Theory of Computing, STOC 2009, Bethesda, May 31 - June 2, 2009, pp. 169–178 (2009)
12. Gentry, C.: Computing arbitrary functions of encrypted data. Commun. ACM 53(3), 97–105 (2010)
13. Ghinita, G., Rughinis, R.: An efficient privacy-preserving system for monitoring mobile users: making searchable encryption practical. In: Fourth ACM Conference on Data and Application Security and Privacy, CODASPY 2014, San Antonio, 03–05 March 2014, pp. 321–332 (2014)
14. Hashem, T., Kulik, L., Zhang, R.: Privacy preserving group nearest neighbor queries. In: Proceedings EDBT 2010, 13th International Conference on Extending Database Technology, Lausanne, 22–26 March 2010, pp. 489–500 (2010)
15. Hu, H., Xu, J., Ren, C., Choi, B.: Processing private queries over untrusted data cloud through privacy homomorphism. In: Proceedings of the 27th International Conference on Data Engineering, ICDE 11–16 April 2011, Hannover, pp. 601–612 (2011)
16. Janosi, A., Steinbrunn, W., Pfisterer, M., Detrano, R.: Heart disease datase. In: The UCI Archive (1998). https://archive.ics.uci.edu/ml/datasets/Heart+Disease
17. Kirkpatrick, D.G., Seidel, R.: Output-size sensitive algorithms for finding maximal vectors. In: Proceedings of the First Annual Symposium on Computational Geometry, Baltimore, 5–7 June 1985, pp. 89–96 (1985)

18. Kung, H.T., Luccio, F., Preparata, F.P.: On finding the maxima of a set of vectors. J. ACM **22**(4), 469–476 (1975)

19. Li, H., Xiong, L., Jiang, X.: Differentially private synthesization of multi-dimensional data using copula functions. In: Proceedings of the 17th International Conference on Extending Database Technology, EDBT 2014, Athens, 24–28 March 2014, pp. 475–486 (2014)

20. Li, N., Li, T., Venkatasubramanian, S.: t-closeness: privacy beyond k-anonymity and l-diversity. In: Proceedings of the 23rd International Conference on Data Engineering, ICDE 2007, The Marmara Hotel, Istanbul, 15–20 April 2007, pp. 106–115 (2007)

21. Liu, J., Luo, J., Huang, J.Z.: Rating: Privacy preservation for multiple attributes with different sensitivity requirements. In: IEEE 11th International Conference on Data Mining Workshops (ICDMW), Vancouver, 11 December 2011, pp. 666–673 (2011)

22. Liu, J., Xiong, L., Pei, J., Luo, J., Zhang, H.: Finding pareto optimal groups: group-based skyline. PVLDB **8**(13), 2086–2097 (2015)

23. Liu, J., Xiong, L., Xu, X.: Faster output-sensitive skyline computation algorithm. Inf. Process. Lett. **114**(12), 710–713 (2014)

24. Liu, J., Zhang, H., Xiong, L., Li, H., Luo, J.: Finding probabilistic k-skyline sets on uncertain data. In: Proceedings of the 24rd ACM International Conference on Conference on Information and Knowledge Management, CIKM 2015, Melbourne, 19–23 October 2015

25. Machanavajjhala, A., Gehrke, J., Kifer, D., Venkitasubramaniam, M.: l-diversity: privacy beyond k-anonymity. In: Proceedings of the 22nd International Conference on Data Engineering, ICDE 2006, 3–8 April 2006, Atlanta, p. 24 (2006)

26. Paillier, P.: Public-key cryptosystems based on composite degree residuosity classes. In: Stern, J. (ed.) EUROCRYPT 1999. LNCS, vol. 1592, p. 223. Springer, Heidelberg (1999)

27. Papadias, D., Tao, Y., Fu, G., Seeger, B.: Progressive skyline computation in database systems. ACM Trans. Database Syst. **30**(1), 41–82 (2005)

28. Papadopoulos, S., Bakiras, S., Papadias, D.: Nearest neighbor search with strong location privacy. PVLDB **3**(1), 619–629 (2010)

29. Pei, J., Jiang, B., Lin, X., Yuan, Y.: Probabilistic skylines on uncertain data. In: Proceedings of the 33rd International Conference on Very Large Data Bases, University of Vienna, Austria, 23–27 September 2007, pp. 15–26 (2007)

30. Pramanik, S., Li, J.: Fast approximate search algorithm for nearest neighbor queries in high dimensions. In: Proceedings of the 15th International Conference on Data Engineering, Sydney, 23–26 March 1999, p. 251 (1999)

31. Qi, Y., Atallah, M.J.: Efficient privacy-preserving k-nearest neighbor search. In: 28th IEEE International Conference on Distributed Computing Systems (ICDCS 2008), 17–20 June 2008, Beijing, pp. 311–319 (2008)

32. Shahabi, C., Tang, L.A., Xing, S.: Indexing land surface for efficient kNN query. PVLDB **1**(1), 1020–1031 (2008)

33. Sweeney, L.: k-anonymity: a model for protecting privacy. Int. J. Uncertainty Fuzziness Knowl. Based Syst. **10**(5), 557–570 (2002)

34. Wong, W.K., Cheung, D.W., Kao, B., Mamoulis, N.: Secure knn computation on encrypted databases. In: Proceedings of the ACM SIGMOD International Conference on Management of Data, SIGMOD 2009, Providence, June 29 - July 2 2009, pp. 139–152 (2009)

35. Xiao, Y., Xiong, L., Yuan, C.: Differentially private data release through multidimensional partitioning. In: Jonker, W., Petković, M. (eds.) SDM 2010. LNCS, vol. 6358, pp. 150–168. Springer, Heidelberg (2010)
36. Yao, B., Li, F., Xiao, X.: Secure nearest neighbor revisited. In: 29th IEEE International Conference on Data Engineering, ICDE 2013, Brisbane, 8–12 April 2013, pp. 733–744 (2013)
37. Yi, X., Paulet, R., Bertino, E., Varadharajan, V.: Practical k nearest neighbor queries with location privacy. In: IEEE 30th International Conference on Data Engineering, ICDE 2014, Chicago, March 31 - April 4 2014, pp. 640–651 (2014)

Time-, Energy-, and Monetary Cost-Aware Cache Design for a Mobile-Cloud Database System

Mikael Perrin[1](✉), Jonathan Mullen[1], Florian Helff[1],
Le Gruenwald[1], and Laurent d'Orazio[2]

[1] School of Computer Science, University of Oklahoma, Norman, OK, USA
{mikael.perrin, jonathan, fhelff, ggruenwald}@ou.edu
[2] CNRS, UMR 6158, LIMOS, Blaise Pascal University,
Clermont-Ferrand, France
laurent.dorazio@isima.fr

Abstract. Growing demand for mobile access to data is only outpaced by the growth of large and complex data, accentuating the constrained nature of mobile devices. The availability and scalability of cloud resources along with techniques for caching and distributed computation can be used to address these problems, but bring up new optimization challenges, often with competing concerns. A user wants a quick response using minimal device resources, while a cloud provider must weigh response time with the monetary cost of query execution. To address these issues we present a three-tier mobile cloud database model and a decisional semantic caching algorithm that formalizes the query planning and execution between mobile users, data owners and cloud providers, allowing stake holders to impose constraints on time, money and energy consumption while understanding the possible tradeoffs between them. We use a hospital application as a user case.

Keywords: Mobile · Cloud · Energy consumption · Monetary cost · Cache

1 Introduction

The main principle of mobile computing is the possibility to provide to the user resources independent of his/her location. A mobile device has the advantage of being light and easily transportable, but has constraints on its limited resources, such as memory, computing power, screen size, network connection and energy. Those constraints are even more important when they are compared to the resources available on a server, and even more with a computation service on the cloud with elastic resources [1]. When the mobile device's lack of resources becomes critical, using cloud services becomes necessary to answer to the user constraints.

On the cloud, the different pricing models used by the cloud service providers bring a new challenge for the management of the resources, which is to solve a two-dimensional

---

This work is partially supported by the National Science Foundation Award No. 1349285

F. Wang et al. (Eds.): Big-O(Q) and DMAH 2015, LNCS 9579, pp. 71–85, 2016.
DOI: 10.1007/978-3-319-41576-5_6

optimization problem concerning two constraints: query execution time and monetary cost that the cloud service tenants must pay to the cloud service providers. On the mobile device, one of the most important resources for its users is the remaining battery life. The remaining energy can be used either to evaluate queries or to check the results. Therefore, this adds up a third dimension to the optimization problem: the mobile device's energy consumption. Also, in order to reduce network communication between the user and the cloud, which consequently reduces the query processing time, we can use a cache system [2] called semantic caching. A cache system allows previously processed data to be stored. Those data can be computed or downloaded from a server. If they are to be requested again, the cache will return them in a transparent way in order to minimize the query processing time. At least two different event types can occur in the cache. When a looked up item is found within the cache, it is called a cache hit; otherwise, it is a cache miss. A semantic cache allows the cache to be used even though some of the data are not available in the cache. Therefore, the input query will be divided into two sub-queries: one to retrieve data from the cache and one to be sent to the server to retrieve the missing data. Therefore, using semantic caching allows the size of the data transferred between the cloud and the mobile device to be reduced.

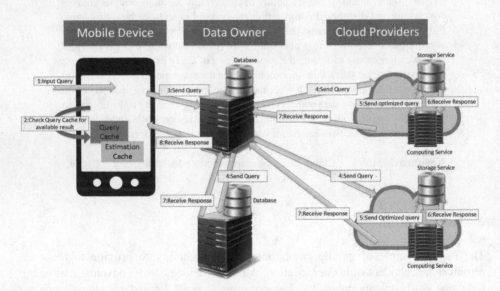

Fig. 1. 3-tier mobile cloud database architecture

To solve this optimization problem in an environment where data locality matters, we propose a 3-tier architecture (Fig. 1) and apply it to a user case of medical applications. Indeed, we can imagine that during a meeting, a hospital director wants to access some doctor information items and projects. To do this, he/she uses a tablet (**mobile device**) and builds the query with the user interface provided by the application installed on it. The hospital owns some private data, such as the doctor's identity, and stores it on a server infrastructure with physical limitations. This static infrastructure is called the **data owner**. Some of the information is not considered private, such as this meeting's date and time with the director, and can be stored on elastic infrastructures on the cloud called **cloud providers**. Those services can answer to the real need in computing resources or storage resources for the hospital. The data owner can access those services.

With the proposed architecture, our goal is to solve the following research question: How can we process fast queries from a mobile device while respecting the user constraints on query execution time, energy consumption and monetary cost? More particularly, how can we use the cache system to estimate whether it is more profitable to process the query on the mobile device or on the data owner/cloud servers? The key contribution of this work is the development of a second cache on the mobile device called estimation cache working with the semantic query cache. The rest of the paper is organized as follows: Sect. 2 discusses the background and related work; Sect. 3 presents the proposed algorithm, called MOCCAD-Cache; Sect. 4 presents the experimental results evaluating the performance of the proposed solution; and finally, Sect. 5 concludes the paper and suggests future work.

2 Background and Related Work

[3, 4] offered a formal definition of semantic caching which consists of three key ideas. Firstly, semantic caching contains a semantic description of the data contained in each cache entry such as the query relation, the projection attributes and the query predicates. This semantic description is used to designate the data items contained in the corresponding entry and to know quickly if the entry can be used to answer to the input query. Secondly, a value function is used for cache data replacement. For example, if the chosen value function is time, we can choose to replace the oldest entries. Finally, each cache entry is called a semantic region and is considered as the unit for replacement within the cache. It stores the information concerning the results of a query: a list of projection attributes, a list of query constraints (predicates), the number of tuples for this region, the maximum size of a tuple, the result tuples and additional data used to handle data replacement within the cache. When a query is processed, the semantic cache manager analyses the cache content and creates two sub-queries: a *probe query* to retrieve data in the cache; and a *remainder query* to retrieve the missing data from the database server.

In addition to the query optimization on the mobile device, it is mandatory to take into account the optimization made on the cloud. Several pricing models are proposed by different cloud providers for each of the cloud services they can sell. Also, several computation, transfer and storage models can be used regarding different cloud services. For example, Amazon Glacier [5] is a good solution in terms of monetary cost if most of the queries used on this storage service are insert operations and a few of them are read operations. Amazon S3 [6] is more relevant if the restriction on money is lower and if a quicker and more frequent access to the data is required. Map Reduce is a programming model that permits distributed and parallel computing on a cluster [7]. Map Reduce is the heart of Hadoop, a framework made of a file system (HDFS) and a resource management platform (YARN). Several platforms for data management have been built on top of Hadoop, like Hive [8] or Pig [9].

A common way to represent queries on the cloud is to define them under directed acyclic graphs (DAGs) [10, 11]. Each node corresponds to operations and each edge represents the data flow. Each operation can be a logical operation in a query plan (operator graph), or a concrete operation to process the corresponding data (concrete operator graph). For those concrete operator graphs, the query execution and the cost estimation is similar to what has been explained in the previous section and in a more general way, equivalent to the RDBMS case. The difference between cloud query processing and query processing on a RDBMS is that the different possibilities to process a query are infinite on the cloud due to the infinite number of configurations and query plans. Also, query optimization on the cloud takes into consideration the money in addition of the time, making it a two dimensional optimization problem. To solve this problem, [11] first minimizes the processing time with a budget constraint, then minimizes the monetary cost with a time constraint and finally finds the trade-off between the suggested solutions. The authors use a greedy algorithm to assign each concrete operation to an operator respecting the constraint and then build the schedule for query processing. This algorithm is executed several times to generate several schedules. A filter operation will then choose the best of those schedules corresponding to the parameter to optimize and the given constraints.

[4, 12] define the notion of *query trimming* which corresponds to the cache analysis, necessary to split the input query into a probe query and a remainder query. More recently, other contributions have been added to this area [13–15]. However, even though their contributions improve the performance of the query trimming algorithm, the version in [4] provides much more accuracy towards its implementation. During this query trimming algorithm, four types of event can occur: cache exact hit and cache miss as explained previously, as well as cache extended hit and cache partial hit added by the semantic caching definitions.

Cache Extended Hit. There are several types of cache extended hit: the result of the input query is included inside one of the regions in the cache (Fig. 2a); the result of the input query needs to be retrieved from several regions in the cache (Fig. 2b); and the input query and the semantic region's query are equivalent (Fig. 2c). Thus, if we retrieve the semantic region's query result, we also retrieve the input query result.

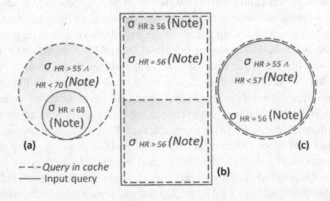

Fig. 2. Example: cache extended hit

Cache Partial Hit. Part of the query result can be retrieved from the cache with a probe query, but another part needs to be retrieved from the database server with the remainder query. For example, with the input query as $\sigma_{HR \geq 57}(NOTE)$ and our example's cache content shown in Fig. 3, query (3) can be used to retrieve only a part of the query result. Therefore, all the tuples corresponding to the remainder query $\sigma_{HR > 57}(NOTE)$ would be downloaded from the database server.

$$\sigma_{HR < 57}(NOTE) \qquad (1)$$

$$\sigma_{age > 28 \, \wedge \, age < 32}(DOCTOR) \qquad (2)$$

$$\sigma_{HR = 57}(NOTE) \qquad (3)$$

Fig. 3. Example: cache content for partial hit

In order to demonstrate the performance of semantic caching for a server in ideal conditions, [3, 16] compared this type of caching with page caching and tuple caching. For page caching, when a query is posed at the client side, if one of the pages (statically sized transfer unit) has not been found, then all the data corresponding to the page will be obtained from the server. For tuple caching, the unit is the tuple itself. This type of caching has good flexibility but a huge overhead in terms of performance. More recently, [17] showed the performance of semantic caching for types of applications requiring important workloads and using a limited bandwidth environment. Their results support our choice of semantic caching inside our Mobile-Cloud environment as a good way to reduce the overhead in query processing time. [18, 19] studied semantic caching performance in a mobile environment and mainly focuses on location dependent applications to emphasize how useful semantic caching can be in such an environment.

Semantic caching, however, can create some overhead in several cases. This overhead has not been considered, mainly due to the assumption made in the previous works that it is always more efficient to process a query on the mobile device's cache rather than on the cloud. For many years, the bandwidth and the resources provided by the server disallowed one to even think about using the server to process the query when the result is already close to the user. However the power of cloud computing changes the game's rules. Several estimations now need to be computed in order to determine where the query should be processed in order to meet the user's constraints.

3 Proposed Solution

This section describes the processing time, energy consumption and monetary cost estimation computations as well as the proposed caching algorithm, MOCCAD-Cache. We assume that only selection queries are posed without any join operations. We also assume that no network disconnection occurs and that the database on the cloud is not altered. From the mobile device, only the data owner can be accessed. However, since we do not assume any difference between the data owner and the cloud servers while focusing on caching, the data owner and the cloud servers will be considered as one in our algorithm.

3.1 Estimation Computation

To compute the time and energy needed to process a query on the cloud, it is necessary to consider the time and energy needed to transfer the data between the mobile device and the cloud. To do this, we need to estimate the size of the query result sent back from the cloud. Then, knowing the bandwidth, it is possible to determine the time to download the data. [20] provided a formula to compute this size. The total time to retrieve the data from the cloud can be computed by adding the time to send the query to the cloud (negligible due to the small amount of data transferred), the time to process the query on the cloud, and the time to download the result. The estimated time and money to process a given query on the cloud are posed to the cloud services.

From the query execution time, it is possible to estimate the corresponding energy consumption. Three different steps define query processing time on the mobile device. $t_{compute\_estimation}$ is the time to compute the estimation (i.e. time to process the cache to determine the probe and remainder queries and compute their respective estimations). $t_{process\_mobile}$ is the time to process a query on the mobile device. $t_{process\_cloud}$ is the time to process a query on the cloud. Also, different steps described in [21, 22] allow us to model the power consumption during the different activities and suspended states on the mobile device. Here we use the electric intensity I in Amperes. I_{idle} is the energy consumed when the mobile device is awake but no application is active (considered negligible). I_{CPU} is the energy consumed when the mobile device processes a query on its cache. $I_{network\_low}$ is the energy consumed when the mobile device waits while the query is processed on the cloud. $I_{network\_high}$ is the energy consumed when the mobile device retrieves the query results from the cloud. In order to know the amount of battery has been consumed, we need to determine the intensity of each component used in the previously defined states. The consumed energy amount allows us to quantify the amount of energy that we drain from the battery Q in Ampere Hours, which can be computed by multiplying I the current in Amps and t the processing time in hours. Therefore, we can simplify the computation of the energy consumption estimation by using only the electrical charge.

$$Q_{compute\_estimation} = I_{CPU} \times t_{compute\_estimation} \tag{1}$$

$$Q_{process\_mobile} = I_{CPU} \times t_{process\_mobile} \tag{2}$$

$$Q_{process\_cloud} = I_{network\_low} \times t_{exec\_query} + I_{network\_high} \times t_{send\_result} \tag{3}$$

$$Q_{total} = Q_{compute\_estimation} + Q_{process\_mobile} + Q_{process\_cloud} \tag{4}$$

These time and the energy consumption estimations depend mainly on the type of event that occurred during query trimming. If a cache hit occurs, we consider that retrieving the query result is negligible in terms of time and energy consumption. We consider also negligible the processing cost in the equivalent extended hit case (Fig. 2c). The cases where a semantic region has to be processed (i.e. included extended hit or partial hit) can be a little bit more complex. The complexity of this type of evaluation depends mainly on the data structure used to store the tuples within the cache [23], as well as on the presence or not of indexes for the attributes that belong to the input query predicates [20]. In our proposed algorithm, the tuples are stored randomly in a contiguous list. It will therefore be necessary to check serially each tuple to see if it satisfies the input query predicate. The time corresponding to those operations can be determined statistically by processing queries on several segments of different sizes before any evaluation.

3.2 Cache Managers

The organization of managers presented in [24] is used for cache management which consists of three independent parts. The Cache Content Manager is used to manage the results inside the cache. It is used for insertion, deletion and look up. The Cache Replacement Manager is used to handle cache data replacement by some more relevant items. The Cache Resolution Manager is used to retrieve the data in the cache as well as to invoke some external tool to load the missing data items, for example.

Also, we introduce three other types of managers to handle the computation of every estimation as well as the elaboration of a better solution. The Mobile Estimation Computation Manager is used to compute the execution time and the energy consumption while executing a query on the mobile device. The Cloud Estimation Computation Manager is used to compute the time, the mobile energy consumption and the monetary cost necessary to process a query on the cloud. Finally, the Optimization Manager takes care of the choice between the mobile query processing estimation and the cloud query processing estimation while respecting the user constraints, such as the remaining battery percentage, the maximum query response time and the money to be paid to the cloud service providers for the query evaluation. Three cache structures, query cache, mobile estimation cache, and cloud estimation cache described below, are used to provide a solution for the given problem. However, each cache owns its content manager, replacement manager and resolution manager.

Query Cache: This cache uses Semantic Caching [3] to store the results of the previously executed queries.

Mobile Estimation Cache: This cache contains all the estimations corresponding to the query eventually processed on the mobile device. More specifically, it contains the estimated execution time and the energy consumption for the query result retrieval within the query cache.

Cloud Estimation Cache: This cache contains all the estimations corresponding to the query if it is processed on the cloud. Even though an estimation is found in this cache, it does not mean that the corresponding query has been processed. For both estimation caches, only the events of cache hit and cache miss can occur.

3.3 The MOCCAD Cache Algorithm

The MOCCAD-Cache algorithm shown in Fig. 4 consists of 4 main steps corresponding to the different phases occurring during a query processing algorithm: query cache analysis, estimation computation, decision making, and query evaluation. First we need to analyze the query cache in order to know what is usable to answer the input query. Then, depending on the result of the previous step, we may need to estimate the cost to process a query on the mobile device (processing time and energy consumption) as well as the cost (processing time, energy consumption and monetary cost) to process a query on the cloud. If we have to compute a mobile query processing estimation and a cloud query processing estimation, then we will need to make a decision upon those estimations and the user constraints in order to finally execute the query.

First of all, in order to estimate a query processing cost, it is necessary to determine how much time and energy will be spent to analyze the query cache. The algorithm in [12] can be used to analyze two queries in order to know if they are equivalent or if one implies the other. This algorithm can be very expensive regarding the number of predicates contained in both the input query and the query in the cache. In order to estimate the time and energy necessary to process this algorithm, it is essential to compute some statistics for the execution time and the energy consumption regarding the number of predicates to be analyzed. This should be done only once when the application is started for the first time on the mobile device. We assume that the mobile device has a sufficient amount of energy to compute those statistics. Also, during the second phase of the estimation, we need some additional pre-processed data necessary to estimate the query processing cost on the mobile device. More specifically, we still need to download some metadata and information items from the database hosted on the cloud, which are required to estimate the size of the query result after we processed the query on it, such as relation name, number of tuples, average tuple size, etc. Those information items are downloaded once when the algorithm accesses the database. We assume that the database on the cloud is never altered.

This algorithm requires the query to be processed as an input. It needs three different caches: the query cache, the mobile estimation cache and the cloud estimation cache. It also uses the different managers for estimation computations and decisions.

First of all, we analyze the query cache (Line 4 in MOCCAD-Cache Algorithm). The query cache calls its content manager which will return 3 different items: the type of cache hit or miss, the probe query and the remainder query. Secondly, the estimation computation is made regarding the query analysis result (Line 5 to Line 20 in MOCCAD-Cache Algorithm). In the case of a query cache exact hit (*CACHE_HIT*), the query processing cost on the mobile device is considered negligible. Therefore, the query will be directly executed on the mobile device to retrieve the result. In the case of a partial hit (*PARTIAL_HIT*), it is necessary to estimate the processing time to process the probe query on the mobile device as well as the cost to process the remainder query on the cloud. Those two estimations need to be added to get the estimated cost to retrieve the complete result. Additionally, we need to compute the estimated cost to process the whole input query on the cloud. To acquire such estimations we use the acquireEstimation function. This function looks for those estimations in the cloud or mobile estimation caches (Line 1 in acquireEstimation Function). If they are not

MOCCAD Cache Algorithm: CacheManager::load
Input: **Query** inQuery, **QueryCache, MobileEstimationCache**
mobileEstiCache, **CloudEstimationCache** cloudEstiCache,
MobileEstimationComputationManager mobileECompM,
CloudEstimationComputationManager cloudECompM,
OptimizationManager oM.
Output: Query Result.

```
1:   mobileEstiResult ← ∞
2:   cloudEstiResult ← ∞
4:   queryLookup,pQuery,rQuery ← queryCache.lookup(inQuery)
5:   if queryLookup = CACHE_HIT then
6:       mobileEstiResult ← 0
8:   else if queryLookup = PARTIAL_HIT then
9:       estiRemainder ← acquireEstimation(rQuery, cloudEstiCache,
cloudECompM)
10:      estiProbe ← acquireEstimation(pQuery, mobileEstiCache,
mobileECompM)
11:      mobileEstiResult ← estiRemainder + estiProbe
12:      cloudEstiCache ← acquireEstimation(inQuery,
cloudEstiCache, cloudECompM)
14:  else if queryLookup = EXTENDED_HIT then
15:      mobileEstiResult ← acquireEstimation(inQuery,
mobileEstiCache, mobileECompM)
16:      cloudEstiResult ← acquireEstimation(inQuery,
cloudEstiCache, cloudECompM)
18:  else if queryLookup = CACHE_MISS then
19:      cloudEstiResult ← acquireEstimation( inQuery,
cloudEstiCache, cloudECompM)
20:  end if
22:  bestEstimation, queryPlan ← oM.optimize(queryLookup,
mobileEstiResult, cloudEstiResult)
23:  if bestEstimation != NIL then
24:      queryResult ← queryCache.process(queryPlan)
25:      queryCache.replace(queryResult, queryPlan)
26:  end if
```

acquireEstimation Function:
Input: **Query** query, **EstimationCache** estimationCache,
EstimationComputationManager estimationCompManager
Output: **Estimation** estiResult.

```
1:   estiLookup ← estiCache.lookup(query)
2:   if estiLookup = CACHE_HIT then
3:       estiResult ← estiCache.process(query)
4:   else
5:       estiResult ← estimationCompManager.compute(query)
6:       estiCache.replace(query, estiResult)
7:   end if
8:   return estiResult
```

Fig. 4. MOCCAD-Cache Algorithm and acquireEstimation Function

available in those caches, then the estimation is computed by the estimation computation manager. Then, the estimation cache calls its replacement manager to insert the new estimation into the cache (Line 4 to Line 6 in the acquireEstimation function). This way, even though the query is not executed, the estimation still belongs to the cache. This works the same way for both the cloud estimation cache and the mobile estimation cache. In the case of a cache extended hit (*EXTENDED_HIT*), it can be very expensive to process the query on the mobile device; it is therefore important to compute the estimation before this execution. Additionally, we estimate the costs regarding the execution of the query on the cloud in order to decide whether the query should be executed on the mobile device or on the cloud. Finally, in the case of a cache miss (*CACHE_MISS*), the algorithm computes the costs to process the query on the cloud to be sure they respect the user constraints.

Once the estimations have been computed, it is now possible to make a decision on where the query should be processed and then build the query plan (Line 22 in MOCCAD-Cache Algorithm). If it is possible to process the query while respecting the execution time, energy consumption and monetary cost constraints, then the query cache (*QueryCache*) calls its resolution manager to process the generated query plan and returns the result (Lines 23 to 26 in MOCCAD-Cache Algorithm). The execution time, the estimated energy and the money spent will be updated in the estimation caches to contain the real values. Then, we use the query cache's replacement manager to replace the data within the query cache. If some segment should be removed from the query cache, the corresponding estimation will be removed from the mobile estimation cache. We cannot keep this estimation since it is based on the current segment on which the result can be retrieved. If this segment is replaced by another one requiring less processing cost than the first one to retrieve the result, then the estimation is not accurate anymore. However, another possible solution could be to store this estimation elsewhere for replacement purposes. Finally, after the replacement, the query result is sent to the user.

4 Experiments and Results

The MOCCAD-Cache algorithm and all the associated algorithms [4, 12] have been implemented on Android Kit Kat 4.4.3. The experiments have been run on a HTC One M7ul embedding a Qualcomm Snapdragon 600 with a 1.728 GHz CPU, 2 GB of RAM and a battery capacity of 2300 mAh. On the cloud side, a private cloud from the University of Oklahoma has been used. It uses one node with the following configuration: 16 GB of RAM, Intel Xeon CPU E5-2670 at 2.60 GHz. A Hadoop framework (Version 2.4.0) as well as the data warehouse infrastructure, Hive, have been used for this experimentation. This cloud infrastructure can be accessed through a RESTful web service running on a tomcat server (Version 7.0). The web service can ask the cloud to estimate the cost of a query and to process a query on the cloud infrastructure using HiveQL. It can also return the metadata items related to the stored relation(s) using Hive Metastore. This Hive Metastore uses a MySQL Server (Version 5.1.73) to store the metadata. A 200,000 tuples relation is stored on HDFS and gathers 6 uniformly distributed attributes: ExpTable(bigint Id [200,000 values], string Name, string Info, int IntAttr1 [10,000 values], int IntAttr2 [50,000 values], int IntAttr3 [100,000 values]).

In order to study the performance of the MOCCAD-Cache in each case where we can use some results from the cache, the different experiments aim to measure the total query processing time, the total monetary cost and the total energy consumption for each percentage of exact hits, extended hits and partial hits on the query cache. This experiment is made on a query processor without cache, a query processor with a semantic cache, and a decisional semantic cache (MOCCAD-Cache). For each experiment, three runs have been done in order to minimize the environment noises such as Wi-Fi throughput variations, cloud computation time variation, and mobile processing time variation. Each run gathers 50 queries. The cache is warmed up with 10 segments storing from one tuple to 100,000 tuples. No cache replacement is used.

The experiment results show that the query processing time, the energy consumption and the monetary cost regarding the percentage of exact hits are similar between semantic caching and MOCCAD-Cache. This shows that our estimation cache prevents any overhead that could be caused by the estimation computation. Regarding the percentage of extended hits, when no cache is used, the query processing time (Fig. 5) decreases regarding the total result size of the used query sets. When MOCCAD-Cache is used, more queries are processed on the cloud compared to semantic caching. Therefore, the different estimations and decisions occurring when using the MOCCAD-Cache determine that it is more efficient to process a query on the cloud rather than on the mobile device. Thus, our MOCCAD-Cache algorithm is faster than semantic caching. However, more money is spent on the cloud since more queries are processed on it (Fig. 6). When a money constraint is added, our algorithm can prevent too expensive queries from being processed. Therefore, the number of queries

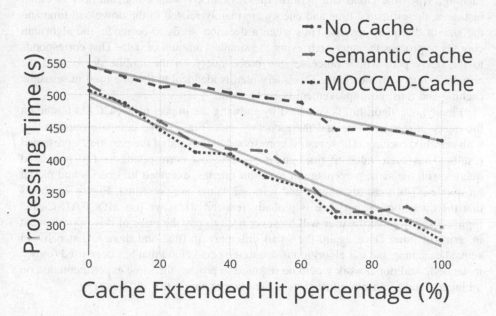

Fig. 5. Processing time for fifty queries regarding cache extended hit percentage (Color figure online)

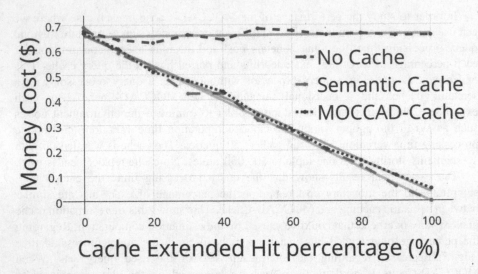

Fig. 6. Monetary cost for fifty queries regarding cache extended hit percentage (Color figure online)

not meeting the constraints is reduced with our algorithm compared to semantic caching which does not take into account any of the user constraints.

Regarding the partial hit percentage, our algorithm performs similarly to semantic caching. When the cloud can perform queries quickly with a high number of cloud instances, the estimated time and energy are mainly related to the download time and the size of the query results. Thus when a decision needs to be made, the algorithm chooses to process the query retrieving the smallest amount of data. This corresponds to the query plan which processes the probe query on the mobile device and the remainder query on the cloud. This query plan is identical to the one used in semantic caching and thus, no improvement is being made.

Finally, our algorithm is validated by showing the impact of MOCCAD-Cache on the query processing time and the monetary cost (Fig. 7). We compare our solution with semantic caching. Those results correspond to the total of the previously presented results. Thus each value of time and monetary cost corresponds to 150 processed queries with the same percentage of exact hit queries, extended hit queries and partial hit queries. The most significant and relevant values are presented. Figure 7a shows that the query processing time is globally reduced when we use MOCCAD-Cache. Figure 7b shows that the user will however need to pay the price of this improvement in terms of time. Once again, the small difference in time and money cost between semantic caching and our algorithm is due to the small cloud that has been used (only 5 instances). Additional work would be required to process the same experimentation on a bigger cloud (with more instances) to really emphasize this difference.

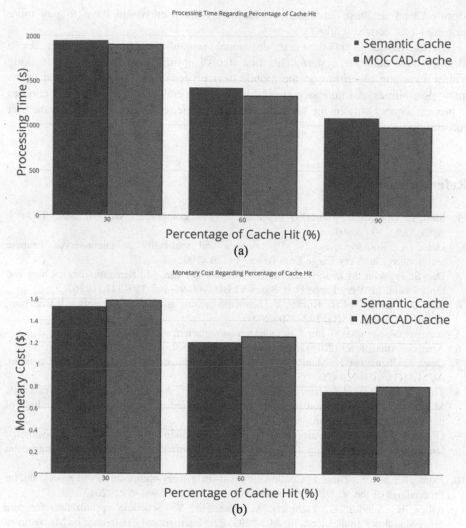

Fig. 7. Global impact of cache hit percentage on the query cost (Color figure online)

5 Conclusion and Future Work

In this research, we have proposed a time, energy and money cost-aware semantic caching algorithm called MOCCAD-Cache for a 3-tier mobile cloud database architecture. MOCCAD-Cache can estimate the time, energy and money to be spent for a given query when it is processed on the cloud or when it is processed on the mobile device. This way, it can decide which query plan is the best considering the user constraints in terms of query processing time, energy consumption and monetary costs, and is an improvement over semantic caching because it can perform queries faster in a

Mobile-Cloud database environment. However, the user would have to pay more monetary cost consequently.

MOCCAD-Cache is the first decisional semantic caching algorithm for a Mobile-Cloud database system. This first step of optimization and decision making within a caching algorithm on the mobile device needs many expansions and opens many possibilities. A future step aims at handling several cloud providers and chooses to process a query only on the services where it is the least expensive regarding the user constraints.

References

1. Mell, P., Grance, T.: The NIST definition of cloud computing. Nat. Inst. Stan. Technol. NIST **53**(6), 50 (2009)
2. Delis, A., Roussopoulos, N.: Performance and scalability of client-server database architectures. In: Very Large Data Bases, VLDB (1992)
3. Dar, S., Franklin, M.J., Jonsson, B.T., Srivastava, D., Tan, M.: Semantic data caching and replacement. In: Very Large Data Bases VLDB, vol. 96, pp. 330–341 (1996)
4. Ren, Q., Dunham, M.H., Kumar, V.: Semantic caching and query processing. IEEE Trans. Knowl. Data Eng. **15**(1), 192–210 (2003)
5. Amazon Glacier (2015). http://aws.amazon.com/glacier/. Accessed 2015
6. Amazon, Amazon S3 (2015). http://aws.amazon.com/s3/. Accessed 2015
7. Dean, J., Ghemawat, S.: MapReduce: simplified data processing on large clusters. Commun. ACM **51**(1), 107–113 (2008)
8. Thusoo, A., Sarma, J.S., Jain, N., Shao, Z., Chakka, P., Anthony, S., Liu, H., Wyckoff, P., Murthy, R.: Hive: a warehousing solution over a map-reduce framework. In: Proceedings of the VLDB Endowment, pp. 1626–1629 (2009)
9. Olston, C., Reed, B., Srivastava, U., Kumar, R., Tomkins, A.: Pig latin: a not-so-foreign language for data processing. In: ACM SIGMOD International Conference on Management of Data (2008)
10. Bruno, N., Jain, S., Zhou, J.: Continuous cloud-scale query optimization and processing. In: Proceedings of the VLDB Endowment, vol. 6, no. 11, pp. 961–972 (2013)
11. Kllapi, H., Sitaridi, E., Tsangaris, M., Ioannidis, Y.: Schedule optimization for data processing flows on the cloud. In: ACM SIGMOD International Conference on Management of Data (2011)
12. Guo, S., Sun, W., Weiss, M.A.: Solving satisfiability and implication problems in database systems. ACM Trans. Database Syst. (TODS) **21**(2), 270–293 (1996)
13. Abbas, M.A., Qadir, M.A., Ahmad, M., Ali, T., Sajid, N.A.: Graph based query trimming of conjunctive queries in semantic caching. In: 2011 7th International Conference on Emerging Technologies (ICET). IEEE (2011)
14. Ahmad, M., Asghar, S., Qadir, M.A., Ali, T.: Graph based query trimming algorithm for relational data semantic cache. In: Proceedings of the International Conference on Management of Emergent Digital EcoSystems. ACM (2010)
15. Ahmad, M., Qadir, M., Sanaullah, M., Bashir, M.F.: An efficient query matching algorithm for relational data semantic cache. In: 2nd International Conference on Computer, Control and Communication, IC4 2009. IEEE (2009)
16. Chidlovskii, B., Borghoff, U.M.: Semantic caching of Web queries. VLDBJ **9**(1), 2–17 (2000)

17. Jónsson, B.Þ., Arinbjarnar, M., Þórsson, B., Franklin, M.J., Srivastava, D.: Performance and overhead of semantic cache management. ACM Trans. Internet Technol. (TOIT) **6**(3), 302–331 (2006)
18. Ren, Q., Dunham, M.H.: Using semantic caching to manage location dependent data in mobile computing. In: Proceedings of the 6th Annual International Conference on Mobile Computing and Networking (2000)
19. Lee, K.C., Leong, H.V., Si, A.: Semantic query caching in a mobile environment. ACM SIGMOBILE Mobile Comput. Commun. Rev. **3**(2), 28–36 (1999)
20. Silberschatz, A., Korth, H.F., Sudarshan, S.: Database System Concepts. McGraw-Hill, New York (1997)
21. Carroll, A., Heiser, G.: An analysis of power consumption in a smartphone. In: USENIX Annual Technical Conference (2010)
22. Gordon, M., Zhang, L., Tiwana, B., Dick, R., Mao, Z., Yang, L.: Power Tutor, A Power Monitor for Android-Based Mobile Platforms (2009)
23. Cormen, T.H., Leiserson, C.E., Rivest, R.L., Stein, C.: Introduction to Algorithms. MIT press, Cambridge (2011)
24. d'Orazio, L.: Caches adaptables et applications aux systèmes de gestion de données reparties a grande échelle. Dissertations Ph.D. Thesis, Institut National Polytechnique de Grenoble (2007)

Biomedical Data Sharing and Integration

BiobankCloud: A Platform for the Secure Storage, Sharing, and Processing of Large Biomedical Data Sets

Alysson Bessani[5], Jörgen Brandt[2], Marc Bux[2], Vinicius Cogo[5],
Lora Dimitrova[4], Jim Dowling[1], Ali Gholami[1], Kamal Hakimzadeh[1],
Micheal Hummel[4], Mahmoud Ismail[1], Erwin Laure[1], Ulf Leser[2(✉)],
Jan-Eric Litton[3], Roxanna Martinez[3], Salman Niazi[1],
Jane Reichel[6], and Karin Zimmermann[4]

[1] KTH - Royal Institute of Technology, Stockholm, Sweden
`{jdowling,gholami,mahh,maism,erwinl,smkniazi}@kth.se`
[2] Humboldt-Universität zu Berlin, Berlin, Germany
`{joergen.brandt,bux,leser}@informatik.hu-berlin.de`
[3] Karolinska Institute, Solna, Sweden
`{Jan-Eric.Litton,Roxanna.Martinez}@ki.se`
[4] Charite, Berlin, Germany
`{Lora.Dimitrova,Michael.Hummel,Karin.Zimmermann}@charite.de`
[5] LaSIGE, Faculdade de Ciências, Universidade de Lisboa, Lisbon, Portugal
`{bessani,vielmo}@lasige.di.fc.ul.pt`
[6] Uppsala University, Uppsala, Sweden
`jane.reichel@jur.uu.se`

Abstract. Biobanks store and catalog human biological material that is increasingly being digitized using next-generation sequencing (NGS). There is, however, a computational bottleneck, as existing software systems are not scalable and secure enough to store and process the incoming wave of genomic data from NGS machines. In the BiobankCloud project, we are building a Hadoop-based platform for the secure storage, sharing, and parallel processing of genomic data. We extended Hadoop to include support for multi-tenant studies, reduced storage requirements with erasure coding, and added support for extensible and consistent metadata. On top of Hadoop, we built a scalable scientific workflow engine featuring a proper workflow definition language focusing on simple integration and chaining of existing tools, adaptive scheduling on Apache Yarn, and support for iterative dataflows. Our platform also supports the secure sharing of data across different, distributed Hadoop clusters. The software is easily installed and comes with a user-friendly web interface for running, managing, and accessing data sets behind a secure 2-factor authentication. Initial tests have shown that the engine scales well to dozens of nodes. The entire system is open-source and includes pre-defined workflows for popular tasks in biomedical data analysis, such as variant identification, differential transcriptome analysis using RNA-Seq, and analysis of miRNA-Seq and ChIP-Seq data.

© Springer International Publishing Switzerland 2016
F. Wang et al. (Eds.): Big-O(Q) and DMAH 2015, LNCS 9579, pp. 89–105, 2016.
DOI: 10.1007/978-3-319-41576-5_7

1   Introduction

Biobanks store and catalog human biological material from identifiable individuals for both clinical and research purposes. Recent initiatives in personalized medicine created a steeply increasing demand to sequence the human biological material stored in biobanks. As of 2015, such large-scale sequencing is under way in hundreds of projects around the world, with the largest single project sequencing up to 100.000 genomes[1]. Furthermore, sequencing also is becoming more and more routine in a clinical setting for improving diagnosis and therapy especially in cancer [1]. However, software systems for biobanks traditionally managed only metadata associated with samples, such as pseudo-identifiers for patients, sample collection information, or study information. Such systems cannot cope with the current requirement to, alongside such metadata, also store and analyze genomic data, which might mean everything from a few Megabytes (e.g., genotype information from a SNP array) to hundreds of Gigabytes per sample (for whole genome sequencing with high coverage).

For a long time, such high-throughput sequencing and analysis was only available to large research centers that (a) could afford enough modern sequencing devices and (b) had the budget and IT expertise to manage high performance computing clusters. This situation is changing. The cost of sequencing is falling rapidly, and more and more labs and hospitals depend on sequencing information for daily research and diagnosis/treatment. However, there is still a pressing need for flexible and open software systems to enable the computational analysis of large biomedical data sets at a reasonable price. Note that this trend is not restricted to genome sequencing; very similar developments are also happening in other medical areas, such as molecular imaging [2], drug discovery [3], or data generated from patient-attached sensors [4].

In this paper, we present the BiobankCloud platform, a collaborative project bringing together computer scientists, bioinformaticians, pathologists, and biobankers. The system is designed as a "platform-as-a-service", i.e., it can be easily installed on a local cluster (or, equally well, in a public cloud) using Karamel and Chef[2]. Primary design goals are flexibility in terms of the analysis being performed, scalability up to very large data sets and very large cluster set-ups, ease of use and low maintenance cost, strong support for data security and data privacy, and direct usability for users. To this end, it encompasses (a) a scientific workflow engine running on top of the popular Hadoop platform for distributed computing, (b) a scientific workflow language focusing on easy integration of existing tools and simple rebuilding of existing pipelines, (c) support for automated installation, and (d) role-based access control. It also features (e) HopsFS, a new version of Hadoop's Distributed Filesystem (HDFS) with improved throughput, supported for extended metadata, and reduced storage requirements compared to HDFS, (f) Charon, which enables the federation of clouds at the file system level, and (g) a simple Laboratory Information

---

[1] See http://www.genomicsengland.co.uk/
[2] http://www.karamel.io/

Management Service with an integrated web interface for authenticating/authorizing users, managing data, designing and searching for metadata, and support for running workflows and analysis jobs on Hadoop. This web interface hides much of the complexity of the Hadoop backend, and supports multi-tenancy through first-class support for *Studies*, *SampleCollections* (DataSets), *Samples*, and *Users*.

In this paper, we give an overview on the architecture of the BiobankCloud platform and describe each component in more detail. The system is currently under development; while a number of components already have been released for immediate usage (e.g., Hops, SAASFEE), a first overall platform release is planned for the near future. The system is essentially agnostic to the type of data being managed and the types of analysis being performed, but developed with genome sequencing as most important application area. Therefore, throughout this paper we will use examples from this domain.

2   Related Work

Our platform covers a broad set of technologies providing components that solve problems in the areas of security in Hadoop, sharing data, parallel data processing, and data management. Here, we focus on related work in the area of parallel data analytics and discuss some general and some domain-specific solutions. In general, research in platforms for large-scale data analysis is flourishing over the last years. General purpose data parallel processing systems like Spark [5] or Flink [6] support efficient and distributed data analysis, but focus on providing SQL support for querying data. This leads to some design choices that make supporting scientific analysis pipelines (or scientific workflows) rather cumbersome. In contrast, specialized scientific workflow management systems like Taverna, Kepler, or Galaxy, typically neglect the Big Data aspect, i.e., they are not able to scale workflow executions efficiently over large clusters [7].

The lack of a flexible and open platform for running complex analysis pipelines over large data sets led to the development of a number of highly specialized systems. For instance, tools like Crossbow [8] perform one specific operation (sequence alignment) in a distributed manner, but cannot be used for any other type of analysis. Also for the most important types of complex analysis, like sequence assembly or mutation detection and evaluation, specialized systems exist. Some very popular systems, like GATK [9], only support parallelism on a single machine and cannot scale-out to make use of additional computational resources. Technically more advanced solutions like Adam [10], Halvade [11], Seal [12], and PigSeq [13] show much better scaling, but are not general purpose solutions but specifically developed for one type of analysis. Appropriate models of data security and privacy are not supported in any of the systems we are aware of. There are frameworks that enhance Hadoop with access control, such as Apache Ranger that supports attribute-based access control and is general and expressive enough to be applied to most Hadoop services. However, attribute-based access control does not have high enough throughput

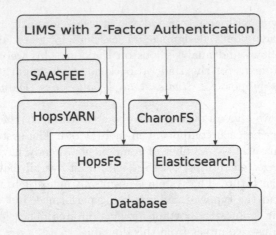

Fig. 1. BiobankCloud architecture

to support authorization of all HDFS operations at the NameNode or all application requests at the ResourceManager. Overall, we see a clear lack of a flexible, open, secure, and scalable platform for scientific data analysis on large data sets.

3   Architecture

Our platform has a layered architecture (see Fig. 1). In a typical installation, users will access the system through the web interface with 2-factor authentication. From there, she can access all services, such as the enhanced file system HopsFS (see Sect. 5), the workflow execution engine SAASFEE (see Sect. 6), the federated cloud service CharonFS (see Sect. 8), and an Elasticsearch instance to search through an entire installation. SAASFEE is built over YARN, while CharonFS can use HopsFS as a backing store. HopsFS and Elasticsearch use a distributed, in-memory database for metadata management. Note that all services can also be accessed directly through command-line interfaces.

Data Sets for Hadoop

The web interface has integrated a LIMS to manage the typical data items inside a biobank, and to provide fine-grained access control to these items. These items are also reflected in the Hadoop installation. Specifically, BiobankCloud introduces **DataSets** as a new abstraction, where a DataSet consists of a related group of directories, files, and extended metadata. DataSets can be indexed and searched (through Elasticsearch) and are the basic unit of data management in BiobankCloud; all user-generated files or directories belong to a single DataSet. In biobanking, a sample collection would be a typical example of a DataSet. To allow for access control of users to DataSets, which is not inherent in the DataSet concept, we introduce the notion of **Studies**. A Study is a grouping of researchers and DataSets (see Fig. 2) and the basic unit of privacy protection (see below).

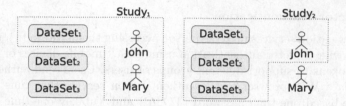

Fig. 2. Study1 has John and Mary as users and includes DataSet1, while Study2 has only John as a user and includes DataSet1, DataSet2, and DataSet3.

4   Security Model

The BiobankCloud environment deploys strong security features for concerns such as confidentiality, integrity, and non-repudiation [14] of data access. This includes authentication, authorization, and auditing. The system allows defining different roles with different access privileges. In designing the system, we applied the Cloud Privacy Threat Modeling [15] approach to identify the privacy requirements of processing sensitive biomedical data. This model implements a data management policy that aligns with the European data protection directive. The project further implements tools to ensure the correct allocation of legal responsibilities for the data processed within the platform.

Figure 3 shows the different components of the employed security mechanisms. All BiobankCloud services are protected behind the firewall and only accessible through the secure interfaces over HTTPS channels.

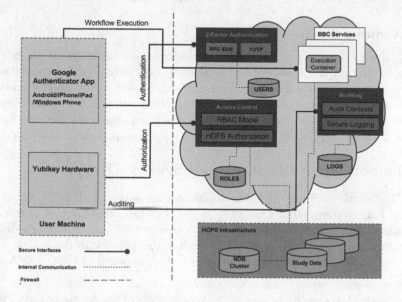

Fig. 3. Secure access to the BiobankCloud via a web front-end.

4.1   2-Factor Authentication

The authentication services map the person accessing the platform to a user identity. We provide 2-factor authentication using smart mobile devices or Yubikey[3] hardware tokens to support different groups of users. Users send authentication requests via a Web browser to the authentication service that runs instances of the time-based one-time password (TOTP) and Yubikey one-time password (YOTP) protocols.

In a mobile scenario, a user supplies an one-time generated password by a commercial authenticator in addition to a simple password that was decided during the account registration. The login page authenticates the user to the platform using the TOTP module (Time-Based One-Time Password) as an implementation of the RFC 6238. In contrast, a Yubikey user would enter the Yubikey device into a USB port. The user enters the simple password that was decided during the account registration and pushes the Yubikey button. The Yubikey login page authenticates the user to the platform via the YOTP module.

4.2   Role-Based Access Control

The access control component ensures authorized access to all data and services within a platform installation. Therefore, the system defines several roles[4] which are granted certain access rights to certain studies. Examples are a DataOwner (users who may create new data sets), a DataScientist (users who can run workflows on the data), or an auditor (users with access to audit trails for auditing). DataSets technically can be shared between studies, and users may have different roles in different studies. We use the access control mechanism of HopsFS to implement the Study- and DataSet-based authorization model.

4.3   Auditing Service

Finally, the auditing service enables the platform administrator or an external auditor to discover the history of accessing the platform to detect any violation to a policy. It includes several contexts such as role, account, study, and login audits. The secure login service assures that actions that are taken by the users are registered for tracing and auditing purposes. Each log event contains information such as initiator, target, IP/MAC addresses, timestamp, action, and outcome.

5   Hadoop Open Platform-as-a-Service (Hops)

A full installation of our platform builds on an adapted distribution of the Hadoop File System (HDFS), called HopsFS, which builds on a new metadata management architecture based on a shared-nothing, in-memory distributed database (see Fig. 4). Provided enough main memory in the nodes, metadata can grow to TBs in size with our approach (compared to 100 GB in Apache

---

[3] Yubikey Manual, http://www.yubico.com/
[4] The concrete roles should be seen as implementations of the European Data Protection Directive.

HDFS [16]), which allows HopsFS to store 100 s of millions of files. The HopsFS architecture includes multiple stateless NameNodes that manage the namespace metadata stored in the database (see Fig. 4a). HopsFS' clients and DataNodes are aware of all NameNodes in the system. HopsFS is highly available: whenever a NameNode fails the failed operations are automatically retried by clients and the DataNodes by forwarding the failed requests to a different live NameNode. We use MySQL Cluster [17] as the database, as it has high throughput and is also highly available, although any distributed in-memory database that supports transactions and row level locking could be used. On database node failures, failed transactions are re-scheduled by NameNodes on surviving database nodes.

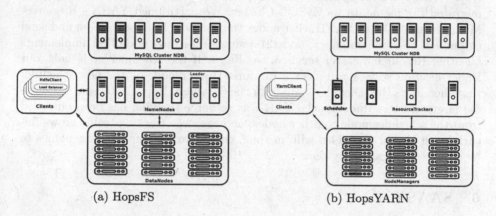

(a) HopsFS   (b) HopsYARN

Fig. 4. HopsFS and HopsYARN architectures.

We ensure the consistency of the file system metadata by implementing serialized transactions on well-ordered operations on metadata [18]. A leader NameNode is responsible for file system maintenance tasks, and leader failure triggers our own leader-election service based on the database [19]. HopsFS can reduce the amount of storage space required to store genomic data, while maintaining high availability by storing files using Reed-Solomon erasure coding, instead of the traditional three-way replication used in HDFS. Erasure-coding can reduce disk space consumption by 44 % compared to three-way replication. In HopsFS, an ErasureCodingManager runs on the leader NameNode, managing file encoding and file repair operations, as well as implementing a policy that places file blocks on DataNodes in such a way that ensures that, in the event of a DataNode failure, affected files can still be repaired.

Designing, Indexing, and Searching Extended Metadata

We store genomes in HopsFS. However, biobanks require much more extensive metadata for genomes than is available for HDFS files. The limited metadata available in HDFS files includes file size, time last modified, and owner. We also need information such as the sample and sample collection the genome belongs to, the type of sample, and donor information. Our LIMS provides a UI tool for biobankers who are not programmers to design their own extended metadata that is linked to genomes, sample collections, DataSets, or Studies. This extended metadata is stored in the same database as the file system metadata and the integrity of the extended metadata is guaranteed using foreign keys to the file or directory the metadata refers to. To make this extended metadata searchable, we asynchronously and transparently replicate it to Elasticsearch. This indexing of extended metadata enables free-text searching for samples.

HopsYARN

HopsYARN is our implementation of Apache YARN, in which we have (again) migrated the metadata to MySQL Cluster. We partitioned YARN's Resource-Manager into (1) ResourceTracker nodes that process heartbeats from and send commands to NodeManagers, and (2) a single scheduler node that implements all other ResourceManager services, see Fig. 4. If the scheduler node fails, our leader election service will elect a ResourceTracker node as the new scheduler that then loads the scheduler state from the database. HopsYARN scales to handle larger clusters than Apache YARN as resource tracking has been offloaded from the scheduler node to other nodes, and resource tracking traffic grows linearly with cluster size. This will, in time, enable larger numbers of genomes to be analyzed in a single system.

6   SAASFEE

To process the vast amounts of genomic data stored in today's biobanks, researchers have a diverse ecosystem of tools at their disposal [20]. Depending on the research question at hand, these tools are often used in conjunction with one another, resulting in complex and intertwined analysis pipelines. Scientific workflow management systems (SWfMSs) facilitate the design, refinement, execution, monitoring, sharing, and maintenance of such analysis pipelines. SAASFEE [21] is a SWfMS that supports the scalable execution of arbitrarily complex workflows. It encompasses the functional workflow language Cuneiform as well as Hi-WAY, a higher-level scheduler for both Hadoop YARN and HopsYARN. See Fig. 5 for the complete software stack of SAASFEE.

Analysis pipelines for large-scale genomic data employ many different software tools and libraries with diverse Application Programming Interfaces (APIs). At the same time the growing amounts of data to be analyzed necessitate parallel and distributed execution of these analysis pipelines. Thus, the methods for specifying such analysis pipelines need to meet both concerns – integration and parallelism equally. The functional workflow Language Cuneiform has been designed to meet these requirements [22]. Cuneiform allows the integration of software tools and libraries with APIs in many different programming languages. This way, command-line tools (e.g., Bowtie [23]) can be integrated with similar ease as, for instance, R libraries (e.g., CummeRbund [24]). By partitioning large

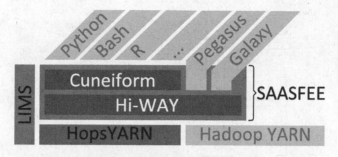

Fig. 5. The software stack of the scientific workflow management system SAASFEE, which comprises the functional workflow language Cuneiform as well as the Hi-WAY workflow scheduler for Hadoop. Cuneiform can execute foreign code written in languages like Python, Bash, and R. Besides Cuneiform, Hi-WAY can also interpret the workflow languages of the SWfMSs Pegasus and Galaxy. SAASFEE can be run both on Hops as well as Apache Hadoop. SAASFEE and HopsYARN can be interfaced and configured via the web interface provided by the LIMS.

data sets and processing these partitions in parallel, data parallelism can be exploited in addition to task parallelism to speed up computation. Cuneiform automatically detects and exploits data and task parallelism in a workflow specification. Editing and debugging workflows is supported by the tools and visualization features provided with the Cuneiform interpreter.

Hi-WAY is a higher-level scheduler that enables the execution of scientific workflows on top of YARN. Hi-WAY executes each of the tasks comprising the workflow in a separate container, which is the basic unit of computation in YARN. Input, output, and intermediate files created during a workflow execution are stored in Hadoop's distributed file system HDFS. Consequently, Hi-WAY benefits form the fault-tolerance and scalability of the Hadoop ecosystem. It has been evaluated to scale to more than 600 concurrent tasks.

Hi-WAY provides a selection of established scheduling policies conducting task placement based on (a) the locality of a task's input data to diminish network load and (b) task runtime estimation based on past measurements to utilize resources efficiently. To enable repeatability of experiments, Hi-WAY generates exhaustive provenance traces during workflow execution, which can be shared and re-executed or archived in a database. One of the major distinctive features of SAASFEE is its strong emphasis on integration of external software. This is true for both Cuneiform, which is able to integrate foreign code and command-line tools, and Hi-WAY, which is capable of running not only Cuneiform workflows, but also workflows designed in the SWfMSs Pegasus [25] and Galaxy [26].

We demonstrate the applicability of SAASFEE for large-scale biobank use cases by discussing an example workflow for variant calling. In this use case we try to discover differences in the genome of an organism in comparison to a reference genome. Furthermore, the discovered differences are annotated with database information to ease their interpretation by a specialist. Figure 6 shows the static call graph for this workflow which was automatically derived from the

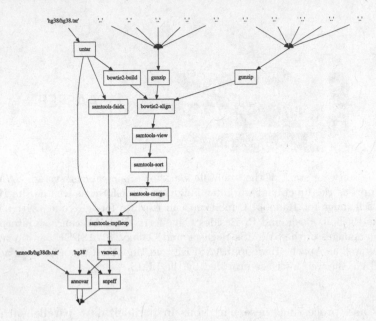

Fig. 6. Static call graph of variant calling workflow. Box-shaped nodes represent distinct tasks, edges represent data dependencies.

workflow script written in Cuneiform. It enumerates the different data processing steps and gives a coarse overview of task dependencies. Each of these tasks integrates a different command-line tool which is wrapped in Cuneiform and called like a function. The workflow is extensible in the way that each intermediate result can serve as the input to a new sub-workflow and tools can be differently parametrized and, if file formats are standardized, exchanged with different tools.

As a first step to test the scalability of SAASFEE for large-scale use cases which are relevant for biobanks, we ran this variant calling pipeline on 10 GB of compressed whole genome sequencing reads from the 1000 Genomes Project. These reads were aligned against a reference genome, variants were called, and the resulting sets of variants were annotated using publicly available databases. Figure 7 shows the scalability of this workflow. Within the limits of the setup chosen, linear scaling behavior could be achieved for the variant calling workflow.

7   Workflows Implemented in BiobankCloud

Next generation sequencing, a technology first introduced to the market in 2005, has revolutionized biological research during the last ten years [27]. This technology allows scientist to study not only the genome of any species, but also the transcriptome and the epigenome. We have implemented several pipelines for the analysis of the most common types of next generation sequencing data into the BiobankCloud.

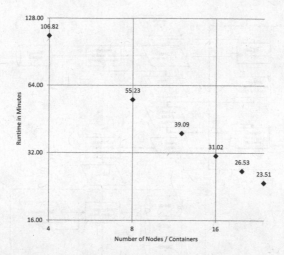

Fig. 7. Scalability experiment for the SAASFEE software stack. A variant calling workflow has been scaled out on up to 24 nodes. Both axes, the runtime in minutes and the number of nodes are on a logarithmic scale (published in Brandt et al. 2015 [22]).

Variant Calling pipeline: Genetic variations represent changes in the order of the bases in a DNA sequence and variations in the human genome play a decisive role in human disease. The most common variations in the genome are the single nucleotide variations and short insertions and deletions. For this pipeline, whole genome sequencing and/or whole exome sequencing data can be chosen as input data and the workflow was derived from Thalheim [28]. Figure 8 shows a schematic overview on this Variant Calling pipeline built in BiobankCloud.

Gene Expression pipeline: This pipeline uses RNA-Seq data as input and enables the user to study differential expression on different levels such as genes and transcripts. Furthermore, it detects differential splicing and promoter use between two or more groups of interest. The pipeline was implemented according to Trapnell et al. [29,30].

ChIP-Seq pipeline: ChIP-Seq (Chromatin immunoprecipitation coupled with high-throughput sequencing) is the standard technique for studying the genome-wide binding profiles of DNA-binding proteins, e.g. transcription factors, as well as the distribution of histone modifications. ChIP-Seq NGS data are the input data for this pipeline and the workflow is described by Dimitrova et al. [31] was used

microRNA pipeline: microRNAs are short expressed RNAs that play a key role in many biological processes and in different diseases. Our pipeline for analysis of the expression profiles of microRNAs is based on the publication of Kozubek et al. [32] and is using small RNA-Seq data as input.

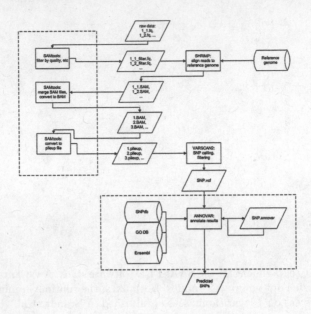

Fig. 8. Subsequent processing steps in BiobankCloud's Variant Calling pipeline.

8   Sharing Data Between Clusters with CHARON

An innovative aspect of the BiobankCloud PaaS is the capability to interconnect several PaaS deployments in a self-managed federation [33], which enables data sharing between biobanks and other BiobankCloud users. These federations can also include public storage clouds, allowing biobanks to extrapolate the capacity of their private resources to the virtually infinite capacity of clouds without endangering the individuals' privacy. These capabilities are implemented through a novel distributed storage system called CHARON.

CHARON is a cloud-backed file system capable of storing and sharing big data in a secure and reliable way using multiple cloud providers and storage repositories. It is secure and reliable because it does not require trust on any single provider, and it supports the storage of different data sets in distinct locations to comply with required privacy premises and regulations. Three types of data locations are supported in CHARON: cloud-of-clouds, single (public) storage cloud, and private repository (e.g., a private cloud). Furthermore, the private repository can be a disk in the client's machine running the CHARON file system client, a disk in a remote machine (e.g., a private data center), or any other distributed storage system (e.g., HopsFS).

Private repositories have variable dependability and are subject to local infrastructure restrictions. CHARON transfers data from one private repository to another securely through encrypted channels. The single-cloud scenario allows the controlled data sharing between two biobanks, but its dependability directly depends on a single entity – the chosen public cloud provider. The multi-cloud (or cloud-of-clouds) data replication is a possible location to store data, and is where CHARON stores all its metadata securely. It avoids having any cloud service provider as a single point of failure, operating correctly even if a fraction of the providers are unavailable or misbehave (due to bugs, intrusions, or even malicious insiders) [34]. Independently from the chosen data location, the data stored in CHARON can be shared among mutually-trusted system users.

Figure 9 illustrates a deployment scenario where two biobanks store their data in diverse storage locations—private repositories, single public cloud providers, and a resilient cloud-of-clouds. In this scenario, the namespace tree has six nodes: directories d1 and d2, and files A, B, C, and D. The namespace is maintained in the cloud-of-clouds, together with file B. File D, less critical, is kept in a single public cloud. File A is stored locally because it cannot leave biobank 2 (e.g., due to legal constraints). File C is shared between the two sites (e.g., in the same legal framework), thus being stored in both of them.

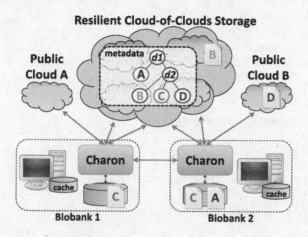

Fig. 9. CHARON overview.

Two distinguishing features of CHARON are its *serverless design* and its *efficient management of large files.* The former means that no client-managed server is required in the cloud for CHARON, which incurs in reduced maintenance costs. The latter is achieved by employing state-of-the-art techniques for data management such as: working with data blocks instead of whole files, prefetching data blocks, multi-level cache, data compression, and background writes.

9 Automated Installation

BiobankCloud supports automated installation. It can easily be installed by non-technical users who can click-through an installation using only a file that defines a BiobankCloud cluster and account credentials for a cloud computing platform. Our solution is based on the configuration management platform Chef [35].

Listing 1.1. Karamel Cluster Definition for BiobankCloud

```
name: BiobankCloud ec2:
    type: m3.medium
    region: eu-west-1

cookbooks:
  ndb:
    github:"hopshadoop/ndb-chef"
  hops:
    github:"hopshadoop/hops-hadoop-chef"
  hopsworks:
    github:"hopshadoop/hopsworks-chef"
  hiway:
    github:"biobankcloud/hiway-chef"

attrs:
  hopsworks:
    user: bbc

groups:
  ui:
    size: 4
    recipes:
        - hopsworks, hiway::client
  mgmtnodes:
    size: 4
    recipes:
        - hops::nn, hops::rm, ndb::mgmd, ndb::mysqld
  datanodes:
    size: 2
    recipes:
        - ndb::ndbd
  workers:
    size: 100
    recipes:
        - hops::dn, hops::nm, hiway::worker
```

The main reason we adopted Chef is that it provides support for both upgrading long-lived stateful software and parametrized installations. This contrasts with container-based approaches, such as Docker, that are not yet suitable for online upgrading of stateful systems and also have limited support for parametrization and orchestration. Chef has, however, no support for orchestrating installations. For distributed systems with many services, such as BiobankCloud, there is often a need to start and initialize services in a well-defined order, that is, to orchestrate the installation and starting of services. To this end, we developed an orchestration engine for Chef called Karamel.

In Chef, the basic unit of installation is a recipe, a program written in a domain-specific language for Ruby. In keeping with best practice, in BiobankCloud, each recipe corresponds to a single distributed system service. Recipes are grouped together into software artifacts called cookbooks. We have written Chef cookbooks and services for all our software components. Our Hadoop platform stores its single cookbook in a repository on GitHub called *hops-hadoop-chef*. For each Hadoop service, our hops cookbook has a recipe that both installs and starts it. The recipes include the NameNode (hops::nn), the DataNode (hops::dn), ResourceManager (hops::rm), and Node-Manager (hops::nm). Hops also uses a database called NDB, with its cookbook stored in ndb-chef. Similarly, our LIMS (hopsworks) and SAASFEE (hiway) have their own repositories. Karamel augments cookbooks with orchestration rules for recipes defined in a file called *Karamelfile*. The Karamelfile defines what services need to be running within the cluster (and locally) before a given recipe is executed.

Provided the set of all recipes that need to be installed on all nodes, as well as the orchestration rules for the cookbooks, Karamel can take a declarative cluster definition and execute it to install the BiobankCloud platform. In Listing 1.1, we can see a definition of a large BiobankCloud cluster, consisting of 110 nodes. The cluster is defined for Amazon Web Services (*ec2*), but that section of the file can be modified to deploy the same cluster in a different cloud platform, such as OpenStack. The *cookbooks* section defines where the cookbook software artifacts are located. Karamel uses this information to download orchestration rules for the cookbooks and metadata, thus enabling smaller cluster definition files, since they do not need their own orchestration rules. The *attrs* section defines a single parameter for the user that will run the LIMS. In production installations, the *attrs* section typically contains more extensive configuration parameters. Finally the *groups* section defines groups of nodes that install the same software stack. The software stack for each group is defined as a list of recipes. Here, we have four different groups: one for the front-end LIMS (ui), one for the Hadoop and database management services (mgmtnodes), one for the database (datanodes), and one for the storage and processing nodes (workers).

10 Conclusions

In this paper, we introduced the BiobankCloud platform, which provides many features necessary for biobanks to adopt Hadoop-based solutions for managing NGS data. Critical security features that we have introduced for managing sensitive data include multi-tenancy to isolate Studies and 2-factor authentication. Next-generation data management systems for NGS data must be massively scalable. We introduced our scalable storage service, HopsFS, our processing framework, HopsYARN, and our framework for scalable bioinformatics workflows, SAASFEE. We also provide metadata design and search services, while ensuring the integrity of metadata. Finally, in Charon, we showed how we can leverage public clouds to share data securely between clusters. BiobankCloud's secure and scalable open platform software is helping to remove the biobank bottleneck and enabling population-level genomics.

Acknowledgements. This work is funded by the EU FP7 project "Scalable, Secure Storage and Analysis of Biobank Data" under Grant Agreement no. 317871.

References

1. Janitz, M. (ed.): Next-generation genome sequencing: towards personalized medicine. Wiley, Chichester (2011)
2. Weissleder, R., Pittet, M.Y.: Imaging in the era of molecular oncology. Nature **452**(7187), 580–589 (2008)
3. Costa, F.F.: Big data in biomedicine. Drug Discov. Today **19**(4), 433–440 (2014)
4. Swan, M.: The quantified self: fundamental disruption in big data science and biological discovery. Big Data **1**(2), 85–99 (2013)
5. Zaharia, M., Chowdhury, M., Franklin, M.J., Shenker, S., Stoica, I.: Spark: Cluster computing with working sets. HotCloud (2010)
6. Dudoladov, S., Xu, C., Schelter, S., Katsifodimos, A., Ewen, S., Tzoumas, K., Markl, V.: Optimistic recovery for iterative dataflows in action. SIGMOD, Melbourne, Australia (2015)
7. Bux, M., Leser, U.: Parallelization in Scientific Workflow Management Systems. CoRR/abs:1303.7195 U (2013)
8. Langmead, B., Schatz, M.C., Lin, J., Pop, M., Salzberg, S.L.: Searching for SNPs with cloud computing. Genome Biol. **10**(11), R134 (2009)
9. McKenna, A., Hanna, M., Banks, E., Sivachenko, A., Cibulskis, K., Kernytsky, A., Garimella, K., Altshuler, D., Gabriel, S., Daly, M., et al.: The genome analysis toolkit: a mapreduce framework for analyzing next-generation DNA sequencing data. Genome Res. **20**(9), 1297–1303 (2010)
10. Nothaft, F.A., Massie, M., Danford, T., Zhang, Z., Laserson, U., Yeksigian, C., Kottalam, J., Ahuja, A., Hammerbacher, J., Linderman, M., Franklin, M.J., Joseph, A.D., Patterson, D.A.: Rethinking data-intensive science using scalable analytics systems. SIGMOD, Melbourne, Australia (2015)
11. Decap, D., Reumers, J., Herzeel, C., Costanza, P., Fostier, J.: Halvade: scalable sequence analysis with MapReduce. Bioinformatics, btv179+ (2015)
12. Pireddu, L., Leo, S., Zanetti, G.: SEAL: a distributed short read mapping and duplicate removal tool. Bioinformatics **27**(15), 2159–2160 (2011)
13. Schumacher, A., Pireddu, L., Niemenmaa, M., Kallio, A., Korpelainen, E., Zanetti, G., Heljanko, K.: SeqPig: simple and scalable scripting for large sequencing data sets in Hadoop. Bioinformatics **30**(1), 119–120 (2014)
14. Gholami, A., Dowling, J., Laure, E.: A security framework for population-scale genomics analysis. The International Conference on High Performance Computing and Simulation (2015)
15. Gholami, A., Lind, A.-S., Reichel, J., Litton, J.-E., Edlund, A., Laure, E.: Privacy threat modeling for emerging BiobankClouds. Procedia Comput. Sci. **37**, 489–496 (2014). EUSPN-2014/ICTH
16. Shvachko, K., Kuang, H., Radia, S., Chansler, R.: The hadoop distributed file system. In: IEEE Symposium on Mass Storage Systems and Technologies (2010)

17. Ronström, M., Oreland, J.: Recovery principles of MySQL Cluster 5.1. PVLDB (2005)
18. Hakimzadeh, K., Sajjad, H.P., Dowling, J.: Scaling HDFS with a strongly consistent relational model for metadata. In: Magoutis, K., Pietzuch, P. (eds.) DAIS 2014. LNCS, vol. 8460, pp. 38–51. Springer, Heidelberg (2014)
19. Niazi, S., Ismail, M., Berthou, G., Dowling, J.: Leader election using NewSQL database systems. In: Bessani, A., Bouchenak, S. (eds.) DAIS. LNCS, vol. 9038, pp. 158–172. Springer, Heidelberg (2015)
20. Pabinger, S., Dander, A., Fischer, M., Snajder, R., Sperk, M., Efremova, M., Krabichler, B., Speicher, M.R., Zschocke, J., Trajanoski, Z.: A survey of tools for variant analysis of next-generation genome sequencing data. Briefings Bioinform. 15, 256–278 (2014)
21. Bux, M., Brandt, J., Lipka, C., Hakimzadeh, K., Dowling, J., Leser, U.: SAASFEE: scalable scientific workflow execution engine. PVLDB (2015)
22. Brandt, J., Bux, M., Leser, U.: Cuneiform: A functional language for large scale scientific data analysis. In: Workshops of the EDBT/ICDT, Brussels, Belgium (2015)
23. Langmead, B., Trapnell, C., Pop, M., Salzberg, S.L., et al.: Ultrafast and memory-efficient alignment of short dna sequences to the human genome. Genome Biol. 10(3), R25 (2009)
24. Goff, L.A., Trapnell, C., Kelley, D.: Cummerbund: visualization and exploration of cufflinks high-throughput sequencing data. R Package Version 2.2 (2012)
25. Deelman, E., Vahi, K., Juve, G., Rynge, M., Callaghan, S., Maechling, P.J., Mayani, R., Chen, W., da Silva, R.F., Livny, M., Wenger, K.: Pegasus: A workflow management system for science automation. Future Gener. Comput. Syst. 46, 17–35 (2015)
26. Goecks, J., Nckrutenko, A., Taylor, J.: Galaxy: a comprehensive approach for supporting accessible, reproducible, and transparent computational research in the life sciences. Genome Biol. 11, R86 (2010)
27. Shendure, J., Ji, H.: Next-generation dna sequencing. Nature Biotechnol. 26(10), 1135–1145 (2008)
28. Thalheim, L.: Point mutation analysis of four human colorectal cancer exomes. Master thesis, Humboldt Universität zu Berlin, Germany (2013)
29. Trapnell, C., Roberts, A., Goff, L., Pertea, G., Kim, D., Kelley, D.R., Pimentel, H., Salzberg, S.L., Rinn, J.L., Pachter, L.: Differential gene and transcript expression analysis of rna-seq experiments with tophat and cufflinks. Nature Protoc. 7(3), 562–578 (2012)
30. Trapnell, C., Hendrickson, D.G., Sauvageau, M., Goff, L., Rinn, J.L., Pachter, L.: Differential analysis of gene regulation at transcript resolution with rna-seq. Nature Biotechnol. 31(1), 46–53 (2013)
31. Dimitrova, L., Seitz, V., Hecht, J., Lenze, D., Hansen, P., Szczepanowski, M., Ma, L., Oker, E., Sommerfeld, A., Jundt, F., et al.: Pax5 overexpression is not enough to reestablish the mature b-cell phenotype in classical hodgkin lymphoma. Leukemia 28(1), 213 (2014)
32. Kozubek, J., Ma, Z., Fleming, E., Duggan, T., Wu, R., Shin, D.-G.: In-depth characterization of microrna transcriptome in melanoma. PloS One 8(9), e72699 (2013)
33. Verissimo, P.E., Bessani, A.: E-biobanking: What have you done to my cell samples? IEEE Secur. Priv. 11(6), 62–65 (2013)
34. Bessani, A., Correia, M., Quaresma, B., Andre, F., Sousa, P.: DepSky: Dependable and secure storage in cloud-of-clouds. ACM Trans. Storage 9(4), 382–401 (2013)
35. Nelson-Smith, S.: Test-Driven Infrastructure with Chef: Bring Behavior-Driven Development to Infrastructure as Code. O'Reilly Media Inc (2013)

Medical Imaging Analytics

Three-Dimensional Data Analytics
for Pathology Imaging

Yanhui Liang[1], Jun Kong[1], Yangyang Zhu[2], and Fusheng Wang[2]($\boxtimes$)

[1] Emory University, Atlanta, GA, USA
[2] Stony Brook University, Stony Brook, NY, USA
`fusheng.wang@stonybrook.edu`

Abstract. Three-dimensional (3D) structural changes and spatial relationships of micro-anatomic objects in whole-slide digital pathology
images encode a large wealth of information on normal tissue development and disease progression. In this paper, we present a complete framework for quantitative spatial analytics of 3D micro-anatomic objects with
pathology image volumes, with special focus on vessels and nuclei. Reconstructing 3D vessel structures from a sequence of whole-slide images,
we simulate 3D biological systems by generating 3D nuclei uniformly
distributed around 3D vessels. Given nuclei are distributed around vessels, intersection detection with 3D nuclei and vessels is conducted by
a heuristic algorithm with data structure Axis-Aligned Bounding-Box
($AABB$). Motivated by real-world use case, we also travel the $AABB$
tree constructed from 3D vessel structures to perform the distance-
based query between 3D nuclei and vessels. We quantitatively evaluate
the performance of 3D intersection detection by the heuristic algorithm
and distance-based query based on $AABB$ tree traversal. Experimental results demonstrate the efficiency of our framework for 3D spatial
analytics with whole-slide serial pathology image dataset.

Keywords: Pathology imaging · 3D data simulation · Spatial
analytics · Distance-base query · $AABB$ Tree

1 Introduction

High-throughput digital scanning technologies have turned pathology image data
as an emerging imaging modality to facilitate basic scientific research and diagnosis at cellular level by clinicians and researchers. With quantitative analysis
of pathology imaging data, clinicians and researchers are able to explore the
morphological and functional characteristics of biological systems as well as to
gain insights on the underlying mechanisms of normal tissue development and
pathological evolutions of distinct diseases. Numerous quantitative analyses of
micro-anatomic objects in pathology images have been proposed, such as tumor
and cancer grading based on nuclei analysis [1–5] and spatial query of large-
scale nuclei objects [6–8]. However, these approaches are bounded by 2D biological structure analysis and limited for processing 3D micro-anatomic objects
presented in pathology imaging volumes.

© Springer International Publishing Switzerland 2016
F. Wang et al. (Eds.): Big-O(Q) and DMAH 2015, LNCS 9579, pp. 109–125, 2016.
DOI: 10.1007/978-3-319-41576-5_8

As 2D micro-anatomic objects in pathology images are only approximate representations of their true 3D structures, information of 3D spatial relationships and morphological features is substantially lost when 3D structures are projected to a 2D image focal plane. This could pose serious problems for those analyses where an accurate description of spatial relationships of biological objects is required. In liver disease diagnosis, for instance, 3D structural changes of liver vessels and the spatial relationships between nuclei and vessels in 3D space are essential for better understanding of liver disease progression [10]. By contrast, 2D profiles of nuclei, vessels and their spatial relationships in liver tissue microscopy images highly depend on the location and angle of the cutting plane during tissue slide preparation. Therefore, they are substantially different from their true 3D shapes and represent erroneous spatial relationships in most cases. This results in a high demand for efficient methods on large-scale analytics of 3D histopathologic objects from volumes of sequential pathology images.

Modeling and analysis of functional structures of human, such as blood vessels, have been studied in a large set of investigations, ranging from vessel segmentation, structure tracking, to 3D visualization of vascular structures [11–13]. However, these studies mainly focus on either radiology images (such as Computed Tomography, and Magnetic Resonance Imaging), or 3D contrast-enhanced imaging modalities (including Computed Tomography Angiography and Magnetic Resonance Angiography). Compared with radiology image modalities, digital pathology images have much higher resolutions and contain more information on the cellular level. Therefore, a direct application of analytics methods for radiology images to pathology images is not feasible.

In this paper, we present a complete framework for spatial analytics of 3D nuclei and vessels with pathology image volumes. Given a set of histological whole-slide images of liver sequential tissue sections, we first reconstruct 3D vessels by an efficient approach. Next, we represent 3D nuclei by mesh models and make them uniformly distributed in vicinity of 3D vessels in a 3D space for biological system simulation. As 3D nuclei and vessels of interest in biological systems are separable, we perform 3D intersection detection in parallel to production of 3D nuclei around vessel structures by a heuristic algorithm with Axis-Aligned Bounding-Box ($AABB$) data structure. Those 3D nuclei intersecting with vessels are then removed for further analysis. With the remaining nuclei and reconstructed 3D vessels, we compute the shortest distance between each 3D nucleus and its closest vessel by distance-based query. Based on geometric primitives in the 3D mesh model, we build an $AABB$ tree to store each 3D vessel structure and achieve the shortest distance by a recursive $AABB$ tree traversal. In experiments, we quantitatively evaluate the performance of algorithms for 3D intersection detection and distance-based query with 3D nuclei and vessels. Experimental results demonstrate the efficiency of our workflow for 3D data analytics with pathology image volumes.

The remainder of the paper is organized as follows. Generation and analytics of 3D pathology imaging data are described in Sect. 2. To evaluate our system performance, we present results of 3D intersection detection by heuristic algorithm and distance-based query by $AABB$ tree traversal in Sect. 3. In Sect. 4, we conclude our paper by offering discussions on the potential and future development directions of our framework for 3D objects integrative analytics with large-scale pathology image volumes.

2   3D Data Generation and Analytics

We present the overall working schema of 3D pathology data analytics in Fig. 1. Given a sequence of pathology images, we first perform 3D vessel reconstruction to recover the 3D vessel structures. We then simulate 3D nuclei by mesh models and make them uniformly distributed around the vessel structures in the 3D space. Nuclei intersecting with vessels are detected by 3D intersection detection module and removed from further analysis. We conduct 3D pathology data analytics, with its application to a real-world use case: distance-based query with 3D vessels and nuclei. We demonstrate each component in detail as follows.

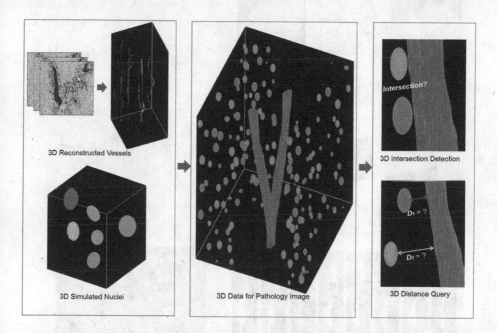

Fig. 1. The framework of 3D data generation and analytics for pathology images.

2.1   3D Vessel Reconstruction

Micro-anatomic objects in digital pathology images provide rich information about morphological and functional characteristics of biological systems, especially in the 3D space. Compared to 2D pathology imaging, modeling and analysis of 3D micro-anatomic objects significantly enhance studies on the underlying mechanisms of disease progression and pathological evolutions of distinct cancers. In our previous work [14,15], we proposed complete frameworks for modeling and analyzing 3D vessel structures with whole-slide pathology images of adjacent liver tissue sections. These liver sections are separated by 50 μm. After resections, human liver samples are paraffin embedded and formalin fixed [10]. Then the embedded samples are cut into slices with thin thickness. The resulting slices are dyed with dual chromogen immunohistochemistry (IHC) [9]. Specifically, DAB IHC is directed against CD34 antigen as a blood vessel marker. Haemotoxylin nuclear counterstain is also used. Finally, these slides are scanned with ScanScope AT scanner (Aperio, http://www.leicabiosystems.com/) at 40x magnification and converted into digital images compressed with JPEG2000 and Matrox Imaging Library (MIL 8.0, http://www.matrox.com/).

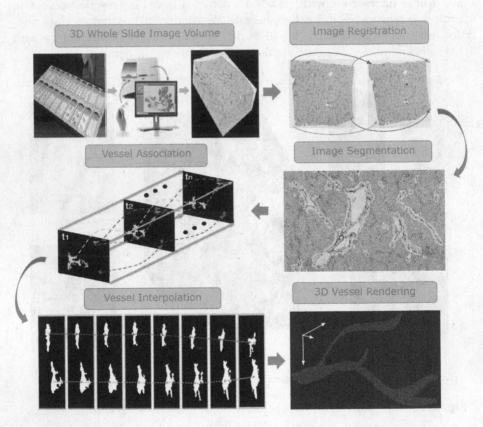

Fig. 2. The framework of 3D vessel reconstruction with serial whole-slide microscopy imaging data.

The workflow includes image registration, image segmentation, vessel cross-section association, vessel objects interpolation and 3D vessel structure reconstruction, as shown in Fig. 2. First, all slides in the same series are registered with a two-stage process. Initially, images are rigidly registered using phase correlation [16]. For non-rigid registration, the whole image is partitioned into a set of evenly spaced patches that are aligned separately with phase correlation. Then, B-Spline transformation is applied to the rigidly transformed image patches to estimate the global non-rigid pixel spatial change by a set of 64 control points [10].

After registering all the slides to a reference image, we identify vessels with an improved variational level set framework [15]. To achieve accurate segmentation results, we apply a Vessel Directed Fitting Energy (VDFE) with prior information on vessel tube probability to the energy minimization paradigm. The proposed VDFE uses joint information derived from image regions, vessel edges, and prior vessel tube probability map, leading to a fast convergence to the optimal segmented vessel objects with the minimization process.

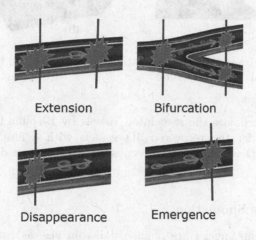

Extension   Bifurcation

Disappearance   Emergence

Fig. 3. Four vessel association cases.

Next, we associate the segmented vessel objects across all slides by local bi-slide vessel mapping and global vessel structure association. Bi-slide vessel mapping generates sub-vessel structures between adjacent slides considering vessel shape descriptors and spatial features with pre-defined one-to-one, one-to-two, one-to-none and none-to-one association cases, shown as in Fig. 3.

– one-to-one (extension): the main vessel still continues to extend to the next frame;
– one-to-two (bifurcation): bifurcation occurs and the vessel grows into two small branches;
– one-to-none (disappearance): the vessel stops growing;
– none-to-one (emergence): new vessel appears.

In the global association, a Bayesian Maximum A Posteriori (MAP) framework is adopted to recover the global vessel structures across all images with the posterior probability modeled as a Markov chain. We recover associated vessel structures by solving the MAP problem with Linear Programming technique [17].

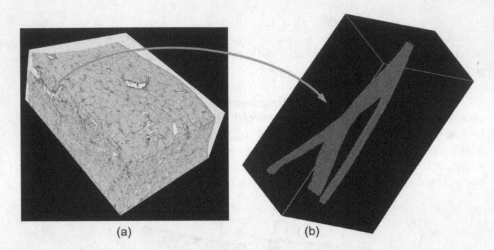

(a)   (b)

Fig. 4. 3D vessel reconstruction. (a) 3D pathology image volume; (b) Reconstruction of a representative 3D vessel structure.

Finally, we interpolate the associated vessels by B-spline interpolation and volumetrically render the recovered 3D vessels with a mesh representation. A representative 3D vessel structure reconstructed from our data in illustrated in Fig. 4.

2.2   3D Nucleus Simulation

In biological systems, nuclei are much smaller in size as compared to vessel structures [18]. As a result, it is challenging to generate 3D pathology image datasets with z-axis resolution high enough to support 3D nuclei reconstruction in practice. In our whole-slide pathology image dataset, for instance, the resolution in z-axis is $50\,\mu m$ while the diameters of nuclei are usually less than $10\,\mu m$ [15]. When biopsy samples are sectioned into slices, each nucleus only appears in no more than one slice. Therefore, reconstruction of 3D nuclei is not feasible given the dataset with large "gap" between adjacent image pairs. In order to study 3D spatial relationships involving nuclei, we perform nuclei simulation by sphere and ellipsoid models with mesh representation in this study [19]. We denote a simulated unit sphere with mesh representation as $M_s = (V_s, E_s, T_s)$ where V_s denotes the vertices, E_s the edges and T_s the triangles (facets) of M_s. We generate an ellipsoid model $M_e = (V_e, E_e, T_e)$ by applying the following transformation to M_s:

$$\mathbf{v_e} = \mathbf{v_s} * Diag(\mathbf{r_e}) * \mathcal{R}_x^T(\alpha) * \mathcal{R}_y^T(\beta) * \mathcal{R}_z^T(\gamma) + \mathbf{c_e} \qquad (1)$$

where $\mathbf{v_e} = [x_e, y_e, z_e]^T \in V_e$ is a vertex in the ellipsoid model M_e; $\mathbf{v_s} = (x_s, y_s, z_s)^T$ is a node in the sphere model M_s and $\mathbf{v_s} \in V_s$; $\mathbf{r_e} = [r_x, r_y, r_z]^T$ and $\mathbf{c_e} = [c_x, c_y, c_z]^T$ are the radii and center of M_e, respectively; $Diag(\mathbf{r_e})$ is a square diagonal matrix with the elements of $\mathbf{r_e}$ on the main diagonal; α, β and γ are the rotation angles along x, y and z axis; $\mathcal{R}^T(\cdot)$ is rotation matrix and defined as follows:

$$\mathcal{R}_x(\alpha) = \begin{pmatrix} 1 & 0 & 0 \\ 0 & \cos(\alpha) & \sin(\alpha) \\ 0 & -\sin(\alpha) & \cos(\alpha) \end{pmatrix} \tag{2}$$

$$\mathcal{R}_y(\beta) = \begin{pmatrix} \cos(\beta) & 0 & \sin(\beta) \\ 0 & 1 & 0 \\ -\sin(\beta) & 0 & \cos(\beta) \end{pmatrix} \tag{3}$$

$$\mathcal{R}_z(\gamma) = \begin{pmatrix} \cos(\gamma) & \sin(\gamma) & 0 \\ -\sin(\gamma) & \cos(\gamma) & 0 \\ 0 & 0 & 1 \end{pmatrix} \tag{4}$$

We propagate the same relationships between vertices in the sphere model M_s to the ellipsoid model M_e by setting the edges $E_e = E_s$ and triangles $T_e = T_s$. By this approach, we can simulate 3D nuclei in a 3D space. We present a representative simulation result in Fig. 5.

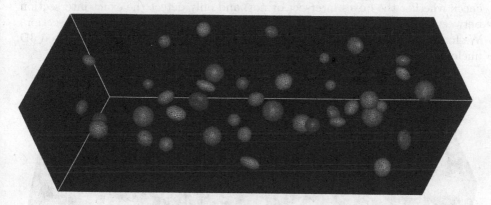

Fig. 5. Simulated 3D nuclei with mesh representation (best viewed in color)(Color figure online).

As nuclei are assumed to be uniformly distributed in certain local region in biological systems, we randomly generate points in 3D space by uniform distribution and use them as centers for 3D nuclei. As nuclei and vessel structures of interest in 3D pathology images are separable to each other, we check and guarantee there is no intersection between 3D nuclei and vessels when generating nuclei centers. Due to the large amount of geometric primitives in 3D objects, detection of intersections between 3D triangles (facets) of mesh surface is expensive in practice. To address this problem, we employ a heuristic algorithm for 3D intersection detection [20]. Assuming we have two mesh objects $M_n = (V_n, E_n, T_n)$ and $M_v = (V_v, E_v, T_v)$ indicating a 3D nucleus and a 3D vessel, respectively, we approximate the vertices T_n and T_v of the 3D nucleus and

---

Algorithm 1. Detection of Intersection between two 3D mesh objects [20].

---

1 Compute the $AABB$ $b_n \in B_n$ for each $t_n \in T_n$ of a 3D nucleus M_n;
2 Compute the $AABB$ $b_v \in B_v$ for each $t_v \in T_v$ of a 3D vessel M_v;
3 **for** $\forall b_n \in B_n$ & $\forall b_v \in B_v$ **do**
4   Detect if b_n and b_v intersect each other: $IB_{nv} = intersection(b_n, b_v)$;
5   **if** $IB_{nv} == \boldsymbol{TRUE}$ **then**
6   Detect if t_n and t_v intersect each other: $IT_{nv} = intersection(t_n, t_v)$;
7   **if** $IT_{nv} == \boldsymbol{TRUE}$ **then**
8   **return TRUE**;
9   **end**
10   **end**
11 **end**
12 **return FALSE**;
    `/* function `$res = intersection(a, b)$` detects if two objects intersect`
    `and returns a bool value.`   `*/`

3D vessel with their Axis-Aligned Bounding Box ($AABB$) B_n and B_v. We first check whether the boxes intersect or not, and only detect the exact intersection between the triangles contained in the boxes if a pair of boxes has intersection. We formulate the above procedure in Algorithm 1 and present the generated 3D nuclei and vessels in Fig. 6.

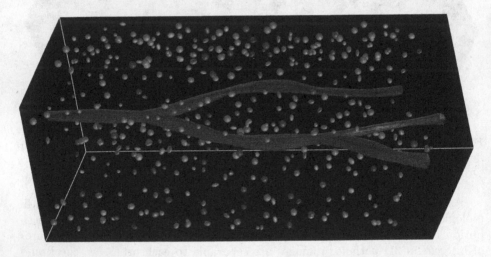

Fig. 6. A 3D reconstructed vessel with simulated 3D nuclei (best viewed in color).

2.3 Distance-Based Query for 3D Vessel and Nucleus

Given the reconstructed 3D vessels and simulated 3D nuclei, we explore their spatial relationships by a distance-based query. Due to the smaller nuclear size

---

Algorithm 2. Distance-based query for 3D nucleus and 3D vessel [22].

Input : An $AABB$ tree ABT_v from axis-aligned bounding-boxes B_v of mesh facets generated for 3D vessel M_v;

A ball $Ball_N$ centered at 3D nucleus $N(\mathbf{c_n})$ with initial radius r_N;

Output: The shortest distance d between $N(\mathbf{c_n})$ and M_v;

1 $p = \text{get\_closest\_point}(ABT_v, r_N, N(\mathbf{c_n}))$;
2 **return** $||p, N(\mathbf{c_n})||_2$;

/* $|| \cdot ||_2$ is L_2 norm distance. */

3 **Function** get_closest_point$(ABT_v, r_N, N(\mathbf{c_n}))$

/* it returns the closest point from a ball query. */

4 | $d = ||p, N(\mathbf{c_n})||_2$;
5 | **if** $d \geq r_N$ **then**
6 | | **return** p;
7 | **else**
8 | | **if** $p \in ABTL_v$ **then**

/* p is from the left chid $ABTL_v$ of tree ABT_v. */

9 | | | $r_N^* = $ d;
10 | | | **return** get_closest_point$(ABTL_v, r_N^*, N(\mathbf{c_n}))$;
11 | | **else**

/* p is from the right chid $ABTR_v$ of tree ABT_v. */

12 | | | $r_N^* = $ d;
13 | | | **return** get_closest_point$(ABTR_v, r_N^*, N(\mathbf{c_n}))$;
14 | | **end**
15 | **end**
16 **end**

---

in reference to vessel structures [18], we simply represent each 3D nucleus by its center in 3D space in our study. We denote a 3D nucleus as $N(\mathbf{c_n})$ where $\mathbf{c_n} = (x_n, y_n, z_n)$ is the center of $N(\mathbf{c_n})$. The distance query problem is then formulated as follows:

Distance-based query problem: Given a 3D nucleus $N(\mathbf{c_n})$ and a 3D vessel $M_v = (V_v, E_v, T_v)$, we compute the distance between the nucleus $N(\mathbf{c_n})$ and the triangles (facets) T_v of M_v, and take the shortest one as the distance between the nucleus and the 3D vessel.

To address the above issue, one intuitive approach is to calculate the distance between $N(\mathbf{c_n})$ and each triangle $t_v \in T_v$ in the vessel surface, and choose the smallest value as the final result. In practice, however, it is computationally expensive as the number of facets in a 3D object may be large. Take our 3D vessels as examples, one basic model we build for a vessel structure contains 14,150 facets. If we try to refine the vessel surface for better visualization, the number of facets can increase to 10,865,664, which makes it infeasible for distance computation by brute force way. As a result, we need a better method to solve the problem.

Table 1. Total amount of detected intersections in 3D nuclei and 3D vessels.

# of Triangles	24250	34250	44250	54250	64250	74250	84250	94250
# of Intersections	70	158	231	259	274	332	436	474

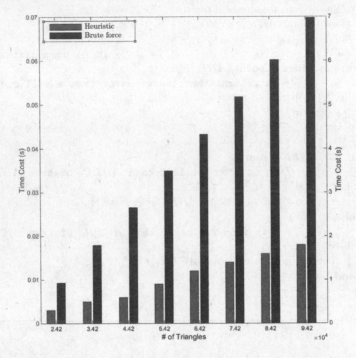

Fig. 7. The time cost of detecting the first 3D intersection by heuristic algorithm and brute force approach (best viewed in color)(Color figure online).

As suggested in [21,22], one potential solution is to build Axis-Aligned Bounding Box ($AABB$) tree with the geometric primitives (triangles) on 3D vessel surface. In this study, we adopt a top-down way to construct the $AABB$ tree. First the $AABB$ of the whole set of triangles T_v is computed and taken as the root node of the tree. Next we sort all triangles in T_v based on the axis aligned with the longest side of the $AABB$ box. The sorted triangles are equally separated into two sets and the $AABBs$ of the two separated sets are computed as the left and right child of the root node. This process is repeated recursively until there is only a single triangle contained in an $AABB$ box. Given the constructed $AABB$ tree, we compute the distance from a 3D nucleus to a 3D vessel by distance-based query.

Assuming the query nucleus is $N(\mathbf{c_n})$ and ABT_v is the $AABB$ tree constructed from the 3D vessel M_v, computation of the distance between $N(\mathbf{c_n})$ and M_v is processed as a ball query with $N(\mathbf{c_n})$ as the center [22]. We represent the ball as $Ball_N = (N(\mathbf{c_n}), r_N)$ where r_N is the radius. With $Ball_N$, we first

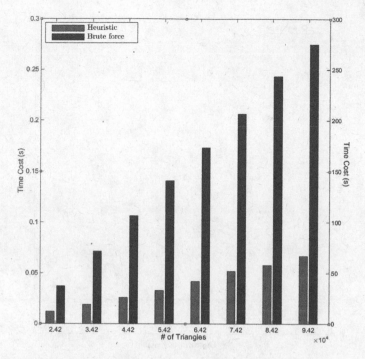

Fig. 8. The time cost of detecting all the 3D intersections by heuristic algorithm and brute force approach (best viewed in color).

traverse ABT_v with recursive intersection query. For all intersections, the closest point p is found by the shortest distance from the query nucleus $N(\mathbf{c_n})$ to the axis-aligned bounding-boxes B_v of 3D vessel triangles; r_N is updated with the distance between p and $N(\mathbf{c_n})$. The resulting r_N is then used for the remaining recursive traversals of ABT_v. The shortest distance is achieved by recursively applying the above procedure until r_N cannot be further reduced. We present the whole procedure in Algorithm 2.

3 Experimental Results

We quantitatively evaluate the performance of algorithms for two modules: 3D nuclei simulation and distance-based query between 3D nuclei and vessels. The computing environment in our study is CentOS 6.6 (64 bit) with Intel(R) Xeon(R) CPU E5-2650 at 2.30GHz. The data in the experiments include 9 reconstructed vessel structures and more than 1 million 3D nuclei, both with different number of triangles (facets) in their mesh models.

For 3D nuclei simulation, we evaluate the performance of the heuristic algorithm compared to brute force method. In this component, we simulate different number of 3D nuclei uniformly distributed in vicinity of the 3D vessel structures in the 3D space. We detect the intersections between 3D nuclei and vessels, and

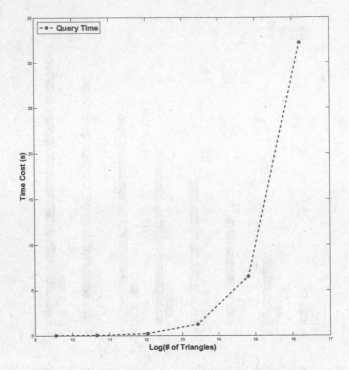

Fig. 9. The query time cost of distance-based query.

remove all nuclei that intersect with any of the 3D vessels. Table 1 shows the number of triangles in the 3D mesh models of our dataset and the total number of intersections between 3D nuclei and vessels. We estimate the time cost of 3D intersection detection by heuristic algorithm and brute force approach. Figures 7 and 8 present the time cost of detecting the first intersection and all intersections between 3D nuclei and vessels, respectively. Both comparison results demonstrate the efficiency of the heuristic algorithm with $AABB$ structures is superior to that of naive brute force approach for different number of triangles (facets) in 3D mesh models. For distances computation between 3D nuclei and vessels by distance-based query, we use an efficient data structure $AABB$ tree to store the geometric primitives of mesh models. Given a 3D nucleus, we compute its distance to a 3D vessel by travelling the $AABB$ tree built from the 3D vessel. We present experimental results of distance query between a 3D nucleus and vessel structures with different number of triangles (facets) in Table 2. Values in the first column are the number of triangles in each 3D vessel. The second column shows the distance query time and the third column represents the total time cost of both $AABB$ tree creation and distance query. As shown in Figs. 9 and 10, the difference between the total time cost and its corresponding query time is small, suggesting the efficiency of $AABB$ tree construction.

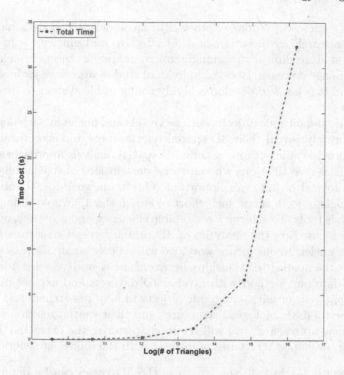

Fig. 10. The total time cost of distance-based query.

Table 2. Time cost for distance-based query between 3D nuclei and vessels (Mean ± Standard Deviation).

# of Triangles	Query Time (s)	Total Time (s)
14,148	0.0116 ± 0.0009	0.0118 ± 0.0008
42,444	0.0382 ± 0.0025	0.0388 ± 0.0022
169,776	0.2322 ± 0.0145	0.2404 ± 0.0130
679,104	1.2434 ± 0.1090	1.2800 ± 0.1054
2,716,416	6.5342 ± 0.5300	6.6823 ± 0.5183
10,865,664	32.2006 ± 2.8225	32.3485 ± 2.8634

4   Discussion and Conclusion

Recently, the development of commercial whole slide imaging scanners prompts the generation of high-magnification, high-resolution images from whole slide tissues in an efficient manner. This makes it increasingly feasible to routinely produce sequential whole slide images of tissue sections even for a medium-scale study. The resulting high-resolution digital pathology image data provides a rich source of tissue phenotypic information on clinical relevant histological features and spatial relationships across histopathology hallmarks in specimen architectures.

However, 3D microscopy image data is still an underutilized data modality in biomedical research as there is a lack of effective and efficient approaches to extract and analyze clinically meaningful micro-anatomic objects from large-scale whole slide image datasets. Besides, individual studies may have various research demands and it is hard to develop a highly configurable system to meet diverse requirements.

As 2D micro-anatomic objects, such as vessels and nuclei in pathology images cannot accurately reveal their 3D spatial relationships and structural changes, we aim to provide efficient and generic 3D spatial analysis approaches to facilitate biomedical investigations where precise descriptions of spatial relationships between biological objects are important. Our framework for 3D analytics of histopathologic objects is one such effort to enrich the 3D whole-slide pathology image analysis tools. To achieve a reasonable efficiency and accuracy, our current approach is focused on the analytics of 3D primary vessel structures and their surrounding nuclei. In our future work, we will recover small 3D vessels to globally explore the spatial relationships between nuclei and vessels. Additionally, we will validate our method with diverse 3D datasets and extract informative 3D spatial patterns of micro-anatomic objects to help researchers and clinicians better understand 3D biological structures and their spatial relationships.

As a follow-up research, we will try to characterize the extracted 3D vessels and other tube-shaped structures of interest with the following generic features:

- Vessel length. As in [23], the length of the 3D vessel can be determined by the medial axis with the hamonic skeletonization technique;
- Thickness of vessel wall. The vessel wall thickness can be used to measure blood flow volume and to indicate the degree of vascular integrity closely related to oncogenesis;
- 3D vessel bifurcations. The number of bifurcations along the artery could be a clinically relevant parameter that determines the complexity of the vessel structures;
- Angles at bifurcations. The angles at bifurcations of the vessels could affect volume of blood flow;
- Local cross-sectional area. Cross-sectional areas at different locations along a vessel can characterize vessel structures.

For 3D nuclei and other spherical - or ellipsoidal - shaped objects, we are interested in following characteristics:

- Centroid. The (x, y, z) coordinate determines the position of the nucleus in space;
- Length of semi-principle axes. Semi-principle axis in all dimensions determine an object shape and are important feature to distinguish normal nuclei from tumor nuclei;
- Volume. Volume determines the size of nucleus;
- Global pattern. Nuclei density can be used to identify specific classes of tissue areas.

We are also interested in the spatial relationships between these 3D objects:

- Spatial distance. What is the distance between vessels and nuclei? Which nucleus is closest to a vessel structure? What is the distance between two vessels?
- Spatial join. Given the extracted 3D nuclei and ground truth, what are the overlapped volumes?
- Spatial pattern discovery. What are the specific disease-related vessel structure spatial distributions? Are there any nuclear clusters clinically meaningful?

With these 3D structure features and their geometry spatial-relationships quantitatively characterized, we expect to establish better clinically relevant patient stratification protocols and explore molecularly correlated phenotypic information.

In a typical study, a 3D pathology image set may consist of thousands of adjacent tissue slices and contain millions of 3D micro-anatomic objects of interest. As a result, these 3D data can take several Terabytes (TB) storage and their 3D mesh models contains huge number of geometric primitives. This poses numerous challenging problems to perform spatial analytics on these "3D big data". Recently, a large suite of high performance spatial data analytics frameworks [24,25] have been proposed for large-scale 2D dataset. In [25], a scalable and high performance spatial data warehousing system for running large scale spatial queries on "Hadoop-GIS" is proposed. The whole system includes query language, query translation and query engine. The query engine consists of index building, query processing and boundary handling on top of Hadoop. In future, we will use "Hadoop-GIS" as a solid foundation and try to extend it for spatial analysis of large-scale 3D datasets.

We present in this paper a complete analysis workflow for spatial relationships between 3D nuclei and 3D vessels derived from serial pathology images. The proposed framework includes 3D nuclei simulation, 3D intersection detection and 3D distance computation. To detect 3D intersection between nuclei and vessels, we create $AABB$ for each triangle (facet) of 3D mesh models and utilize a heuristic algorithm to perform intersection detection. We construct an $AABB$ tree with the $AABBs$ of a 3D vessel and compute the distance between a given 3D nucleus to the 3D vessel by $AABB$ tree traversal. We quantitatively evaluate the performance of the heuristic algorithm for 3D intersection detection and distance-based query by $AABB$ tree traversal. Experimental results demonstrate the promise of our framework for 3D micro-anatomic objects analytics in pathology image volumes.

Acknowledgement. This research is supported in part by grants from National Science Foundation ACI 1443054 and IIS 1350885, and National Institute of Health K25CA181503.

References

1. Petushi, S., Garcia, F.U., Habe, M., Katsinis, C., Tozeren, A.: Large-scale computations on histology images reveal grade-differentiating parameters for breast cancer. BMC Med. Lmaging **6**(14), 1070–1075 (2006)
2. Kong, J., Sertel, O., Shimada, H., Boyer, K.L., Saltz, J.H., Gurcan, M.: Computer-aided evaluation of neuroblastoma on whole-slide histology images: classifying grade of neuroblastic differentiation. Pattern Recogn. **42**(6), 1080–1092 (2009)
3. Foran, D.J., Chen, W., Yang, L.: Automated image interpretation computer-assisted diagnosis. Anal. Cell. Pathol. **34**(6), 279–300 (2011)
4. Han, J., Chang, H., Loss, L., Zhang, K., Baehner, F.L., Gray, J.W., Spellman, P., Parvin, B.: Comparison of sparse coding and kernel methods for histopathological classification of gliobastoma multiforme. IEEE Int. Symp. Biomed. Imaging **6**, 711–714 (2011)
5. Kong, J., Cooper, L.D., Wang, F.S., Gao, J., Teodoro, G., Scarpace, L., Mikkelsen, T., Moreno, C.S., Saltz, J.H., Brat, D.J.: Generic, computer-based morphometric human disease classification using large pathology images uncovers signature molecular correlates. PLoS One **8**(11), e81049 (2013)
6. Aji, A., Wang, F.S., Saltz, J.H.: Towards building a high performance spatial query system for large scale medical imaging data. In: Proceedings of the 20th ACM SIGSPATIAL International Conference on Advances in Geographic Information Systems (ACM SIGSPATIAL GIS), pp. 309–318 (2012)
7. Aji, A., Liu, Q.L., Wang, F.S., Kurc, T., Saltz, J.H.: MIGIS: High Performance Spatial Query System for Analytical Pathology Imaging. Pathology Informatics Conference (2012)
8. Wang, K.B., Huai, Y., Lee, R.B., Wang, F.S., Zhang, X.D., Saltz, J.H.: Accelerating pathology image data cross-comparison on CPU-GPU hybrid systems. In: Proceedings of the 38th International Conference on Very Large Databases (VLDB), vol. 5, no. 11, pp. 1543–1554 (2012)
9. Ismail, A., Gray, S., Jackson, P., Shires, M., Crellin, D.M., Magee, D., Quirke, P., Treanor, D.: 3D Histopathology of the liver using dual chromogen histochemistry. reAgents, 20–22 (2010)
10. Roberts, N., Magee, D., Song, Y., Brabazon, K., Shires, M., Crellin, D., Orsi, N.M., Quirke, R., Quirke, P., Treanor, D.: Toward routine Use of 3D histopathology as a research tool. Am. J. of Path **180**(5), 1835–1842 (2012)
11. Lesage, D., Angelini, E.D., Bloch, I., Funka-Lea, G.: A review of 3D vessel lumen segmentation techniques: models, features and extraction schemes. Med. Image Anal. **13**(6), 819–845 (2009)
12. Friman, O., Hindennach, M., Kühnel, C., Peitgen, H.O.: Multiple hypothesis template tracking of small 3D vessel structures. Med. Image Anal. **14**(2), 160–171 (2009)
13. Kubisch, C., Glaer, S., Neugebauer, M., Preim, B.: Vessel visualization with volume rendering. In: Linsen, L., Hagen, H., Hamann, B., Hege, H.-C. (eds.) Visualization in Medicine and Life Sciences II. Mathematics and Visualization, pp. 109–134. Springer, Heidelberg (2012)
14. Liang, Y.H., Wang, F.S., Treanor, D., Magee, D., Teodoro, G., Zhu, Y.Y., Kong, J.: Liver whole slide image analysis for 3D vessel reconstruction. In: IEEE International Symposium on Biomedical Imaging (2015)

15. Liang, Y.H., Wang, F.S., Treanor, D., Magee, D., Teodoro, G., Zhu, Y.Y., Kong, J.: Whole-slide histological image analysis for 3D primary vessel reconstruction. In: The 18th International Conference on Medical Image Computing and Computer Assisted Intervention (MICCAI) (2015)

16. Decastro, E., Morandi, C.: Registration of translated and rotated images using. IEEE Trans. Pattern Anal. **9**, 700–703 (1987)

17. Dantzig, G.B.: Linear Programming and Extensions. Princeton University Press, Princeton, NJ (1963)

18. Lodish, H., Berk, A., Zipursky, S.Z., Matsudaira, P., Baltimore, D., Darnell, J.: Molecular Cell Biology, 4th edn. W. H. Freeman, New York (1999)

19. Fang, Q.Q., Boas, D.: Tetrahedral mesh generation from volumetric binary and gray-scale images. In: Proceedings in IEEE International Symposium on Biomedical Imaging, pp. 1142–1145 (2009)

20. Zomorodian, A., Edelsbrunner, H.: Fast software for box intersection. Int. J. Comput. Geom. Appl. **12**, 143–172 (2002)

21. Terdiman, P.: OPCODE 3D Collision Detection library (2005)

22. Alliez, P., Tayeb, S., Wormser, C.: 3D fast intersection and distance computation. In: CGAL User and Reference Manual. CGAL Editorial Board, 4.6th edn (2015)

23. Yang, Y., Zhu, L., Haker, S., Tannenbaum, A.R., Giddens, D.P.: Harmonic skeleton guided evaluation of stenoses in human coronary arteries. In: International Conference Medical Image Compututer Assisted Intervention (MICCAI), pp. 490–497 (2005)

24. Gates, A., Natkovich, O., Chopra, S., Kamath, P., Narayanam, S., Olston, C., Reed, B., Srinivasan, S., Srivastava, U.: Building a high level dataflow system on top of MapReduce: The Pig experience. In: Proceedings of the International Conference on Very Large Databases (VLDB), vol. 2, no. 2, pp. 1414–1425 (2009)

25. Aji, A., Wang, F.S., Vo, H., Lee, R.B., Liu, Q.L., Zhang, X.D., Saltz, J.H.: Hadoop-GIS: a spatial data warehousing system over mapreduce. In: Proceedings of the 39th International Conference on Very Large Databases (VLDB), pp. 26 30 (2013)

Automated Analysis of Muscle X-ray Diffraction Imaging with MCMC

C. David Williams$^{(\boxtimes)}$, Magdalena Balazinska, and Thomas L. Daniel

University of Washington, Seattle, WA 98195, USA
cdave@uw.edu

Abstract. High-speed X-ray diffraction is the state-of-the-art approach to understanding protein structure and dynamics in living tissues, especially muscles. Existing analytic approaches, however, require expert hand-digitization to extract parameters of interest. This produces repeatable measurements, but remains subjective and does not offer information on the precision of the measured parameters or strict reproducibility of analyzed data. We developed a processing tool chain, which first segments the diffraction image into regions of interest using highly conserved features and then samples the possible parameter values with a Markov chain Monte Carlo approach. Our approach produces an automated, reproducible, objective estimate of relevant image parameters.

Keywords: Image analysis · X-ray diffraction · Muscle structure · MCMC modeling

1 Motivation

The molecular regulation of force generating protein systems remains a fundamental open problem in biology. Muscle uses a highly organized lattice of interacting elastic and force generating molecules to create controlled macroscale movement [8,9]. The advent of advanced X-ray diffraction imaging lets us analyze protein motions at spatial and temporal scales never previously realized, giving novel insight into the molecular basis of motion in living systems.

Exploring the dynamics of protein interactions in muscle requires imaging that provides information at the nanometer to Angstrom scale. X-ray diffraction provides that information and is unique in its ability to image live muscle during movement, where other techniques (e.g. solution biochemistry or cryo electron microscopy) are only able to resolve properties of isolated individual molecular motors or anatomic features of static, dried muscle. This ability to image *in vivo* makes X-ray diffraction the only direct means of measuring the structural changes that generate force; all other techniques that permit some level of molecular motor activity require the removal of those motors from the regulating structure of the thick/thin filament lattice and are thus less informative about the processes that actually control activation. This is a key advantage of X-ray diffraction: changes in muscle microstructure are highly correlated with changes

© Springer International Publishing Switzerland 2016
F. Wang et al. (Eds.): Big-O(Q) and DMAH 2015, LNCS 9579, pp. 126–133, 2016.
DOI: 10.1007/978-3-319-41576-5_9

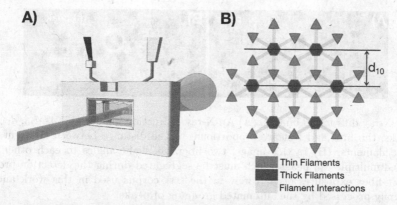

Fig. 1. Data collection and interpretation. (A) Diffractive imaging of an isolated muscle sample requires a physiological solution bath with top entry for mounting to force/length controllers (arms) and front and rear cut outs to allow the X-ray beam to pass through and scatter off the muscle sample. (B) Muscle's contractile lattice is composed of thick and thin filaments. When viewed down the long axis, these filaments form a hexagonal array. The d_{10} spacing is the distance between adjacent lines of thick filaments, and is proportional to the distance molecular motors (gray links) must diffuse across in order to bind. (Color figure online)

in force production and any attempt to separate the two removes significant aspects of the system's response to real-world stimuli [1,3].

Surprisingly, we still use human experts to manually extract structural parameters from X-ray images with NIH ImageJ via manual selection of peaks and rock-of-eye parameter fitting. This produces repeatable measurements but is subjective, fails to provide confidence intervals for the measured values, and is not reproducible by naive digitizers. Additionally hand digitization is a time-intensive analytic technique, with a single digitizer able to process only a few hundreds of images a day. Historically this rate has been sufficient, but new high-speed imaging systems let us investigate short-timescale components of muscle contraction and generate data sets with many thousands of images. The need for an automated and reproducible image analysis tool chain is clear.

We seek to build a service for the automated analysis of muscle structure X-ray images. Users should specify the analysis they need using a declarative query interface and the system should automatically process the user's image database. In this work, we present the first components of the processing tool chain at the heart of this service. The toolchain first segments the diffraction image into regions of interest using conserved features and then samples the possible parameter values with a Markov chain Monte Carlo approach.

2   Prototype

We focus initially on measuring the d_{10} parameter, a crucial spacing in muscle shown in Figs. 1 and 2. The d_{10} spacing determines the distance which muscle's

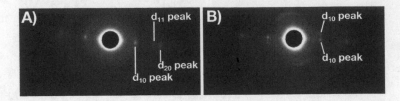

Fig. 2. X-ray diffraction images. (A) An X-ray diffraction image exhibits d_{10}, d_{11}, and d_{20} peaks; the first and last are proportional to the distance between adjacent rows of thick filaments. (B) In this image, two fibers at slight angles to each other have generated multiple d_{10} peaks which must be segregated during the detection process. Such two-fiber exposures occur rarely in the test corpus used in this work and are successfully processed by the automated grouping of peaks.

molecular motors must bridge in order to bind and generate force [10]. This distance changes during contraction and thus regulates the force produced [5].

Images generated during experiments share several key features, which serve as challenges or fiduciary marks during analysis. As seen in Fig. 2, the brightest part of the image background is occluded by a circular stop. This physical block prevents damage to the detector from the high photon flux at the center of the X-ray beam. Surrounding the blocked region, the remainder of the image displays an exponentially decaying background. We must locate and model the symmetric pairs of diffraction peaks interrupting the exponential background. Our core data analysis pipeline includes two steps: image segmentation and image modeling with MCMC processes.

2.1   Image Segmentation

The system first identifies the dark central circular blocked region to act as a relative landmark for subsequent operations. Consistent with experimental design, we assume it contains the center of the diffraction pattern. The edge of the background surrounding the block is the brightest region, so the system first splits the image between areas with values less than and greater than two standard deviations above the mean. This partitioning yields a binary image where the center blocked region is surrounded by a halo of the upper end of the pattern background and occasional dots where diffraction peaks rise more than two standard deviations above background. We convert this binary image to a hierarchical contour set with OpenCV, an open source library of standard image processing techniques [2]. We then take the blocked region to be the inner-most contour and model it as the smallest enclosing circle, shown as light green in Fig. 3B.

With the central blocked region located, we identify local maxima in three by three groups after Gaussian smoothing with kernel having a three pixel standard deviation. We reject resulting maxima in regions unlikely to provide peaks of interest before attempting to match peak pairs. Masked rejection-regions consist of: (1) a circular zone around the central blocked region where the blocking

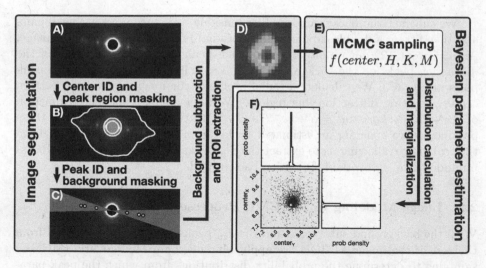

Fig. 3. Analysis workflow. (A) An X-ray diffraction image is read in. (B) The blocked center region (in green) is detected and used as a landmark. Low signal regions, the central blocked region, and image edges are masked off, leaving only the foreground outlined in white. (C) The image is smoothed and peaks are detected, paired, and classified. To remove the exponentially decaying background from the peaks we mask off the area around the diffraction lines, shown in gray. The remaining background is then collapsed into a radial profile centered at the mean peak position. A double exponential fit to this profile is computed and subtracted from the regions of interest surrounding the d_{10} peaks, leaving just the peak signal shown in (D). (E) We use an MCMC sampler to calculate the parameters generating the distributions these peaks are sampled from. (F) We marginalize across peak parameters other than those of interest, extracting peak positions and the error in those position estimations. (Color figure online)

generates non-peak local maxima, (2) areas below the 80th percentile where detector noise dominates, (3) areas near the image edge where peaks are partially cropped. The resulting unmasked area from which we keep maxima is bounded by a white border in Fig. 3B.

Next, we cluster maxima into peak pairs based on their distance and angle from the center of the blocked region. Starting with those maxima nearest the blocked region, a corresponding maximum is sought an equal distance away from the blocked region and located so that the angle formed by the two maxima and the center of the blocked region is 180°. In cases where the matching maxima is clipped by the image frame or fails to be distinguished from background the initial maximum is discarded. For a maxima to be considered a match its distance and angle must match those of the initial maxima within 10 %. With peak pairs now identified (shown as color matched dots in Fig. 3C), the diffraction center is identified by taking the mean location between peak pairs and the background is removed.

We subtract the background by first masking arcs encompassing peak pairs and then fitting a double exponential to a radial profile of the remaining image. An arc swept 12° out on either side of each peak pair masks the effect of the diffraction peaks on the background (shown as a light gray arc under the peak pairs in Fig. 3C). We calculate a radial profile of the image around the pattern center, omitting diffraction line regions. We fit a double exponential function of the form $background = a + be^{-xc} + de^{-xe}$ to the radial profile. From these parameters we generate an estimated background image and subtract it from the real image, allowing us to extract the d_{10} peaks as regions of interest (ROIs) unhindered by an overlaid diffraction background.

2.2   Image Modeling with MCMC Processes

With the background subtracted and the d_{10} peaks identified and isolated from the rest of the image as ROIs, we apply Markov chain Monte Carlo (MCMC) sampling to determine the probability distributions from which the peak parameters could be drawn. We treat the peaks as being drawn from an underlying Pearson VII distribution, commonly used to fit X-ray diffraction peaks [7]. This process allows us to generate possible peak matches using five parameters: peak center x-location, peak center y-location, peak height, peak spread, and peak decay rate. We perform an initial peak fitting by residual minimization between a generated peak and the extracted ROI. This gives a set of starting parameters that we use, with random variation, to initialize the positions of the MCMC agents that will explore the model space.

Before MCMC sampling we must define our query's likelihood and prior. We choose a flat prior as our initial information about the model is minimal. To calculate the likelihood we represent each pixel's photon count as a Poisson process in the form $P(d|m) = e^{-m}\left(m^d/d!\right)$ where m is the model value and d is the experimental data value. These functions are fed into *emcee*, an efficient MCMC analysis Python library [4]. After a burn in period of 100 steps, the sampler histories are erased and a further 1000 steps are run to generate the posterior probability distributions of our peak parameters.

One of MCMC modeling's convenient features is that extracting only a subset of parameters marginalizes across those we discard. That is, when we are interested in only the x- and y-locations of the peak center to precisely calculate d_{10} spacing (as in Fig. 3F), we automatically integrate our uncertainty about peak height, spread, and decay.

3   Preliminary Evaluation

We apply our workflow to a test corpus of 1,220 images generated using X-ray diffraction during insect flight muscle research at the Argonne National Laboratory BioCAT Beamline. Sample high-quality and challenging images are shown in Figs. 2A and B [6]. We tested the output of our automated system against the results from a domain expert manually digitizing peak locations. Our initial image segmentation step, described in Sect. 2.1, successfully identifies the center blocked region of each image in greater than 99 % of images in our test corpus. The overall process allows us to calculate peak-to-peak distances to sub-pixel accuracy with a confidence interval of 90 %, with residuals between expectation values and manually digitized peak positions shown in Fig. 4. MCMC sampling combined with image segmentation allows us to precisely, accurately, and automatically locate the d_{10} peak centers and thus calculate the lattice spacing measured by a diffraction image to within 0.03 nm.

Because the images in our corpus are a standard sample of those produced by high-speed X-ray diffraction, our positive preliminary results are a strong indication for the potential of this approach.

4   Challenges and Next Steps

Our initial data processing pipeline produces an automated, reproducible, objective estimate of relevant image parameters but the following challenges remain:

- Development of a declarative language to describe processing steps will speed use of this technique and ease reproducibility. The key question is to define the types of operations that users should be able to specify and how to specify them. Our goal is to generalize to a broad set of analysis needs for X-ray images of muscle structure.
- Packaging of this tool chain into a cloud deployable containerized image will enable trivial scaling to work with larger datasets. Furthermore, the ability to access to tool chain directly through a web browser with automatic back-end deployment of the analysis pipeline will facilitate adoption.
- This toolchain works best when applied to sharp and well defined images produced by isolated fibers. When working with images produced by *in vivo*

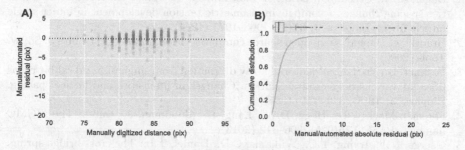

Fig. 4. Validation against hand-measurement. (A) The majority of residuals (between the manually and automatically measured d_{10} peak distances) are within a single pixel of the manually digitized validation values. In a handful of outliers the automated method mis-identifies a closer structure as the d_{10} pair. (B) The cumulative distribution of the residuals shows that half of the automated measurements agree within 0.8 pixels and over 90 % agree within 3 pixels. A quartile box plot above shows the heavily left-weighted asymmetry of the residual distribution.

samples, such as those taken through a fly thorax, diffraction from multiple muscles in different orientations is common. These multiple-muscle images produce a more extreme version of the image shown in Fig. 2B, where twin rotated peaks that are twisted and blurred about the center of the diffraction pattern and may have substantially divergent d_{10} distances. Twin rotated peaks must be classified by diffraction line/muscle and treated independently during analysis.

– Application of these techniques to coming ultra-high temporal-resolution images with far lower signal:noise will strain autosegmentation and peak-fitting techniques.

The increasing prevalence of advanced diffractive imaging techniques demands data analytic methods that can handle, objectively and reproducible, significant increases in the volume of data generated and analyzed. This toolchain is a first step in a process that will greatly increase the power and capabilities of a widely used approach to understanding protein structure in living tissue.

Acknowledgments. This work was supported in part by NSF grant IIS-1110370, the Intel Science and Technology Center for Big Data, the Army Research Office through ARO Grants W911NF-13-1-0435 and W911NF-14-1-0396, an award from the Gordon and Betty Moore Foundation and the Alfred P Sloan Foundation, the Washington Research Foundation Fund for Innovation in Data-Intensive Discovery, and the UW eScience Institute.

We thank Jake VanderPlas for helpful discussions of statistical techniques, Tom Irving for advice on X-ray imaging, Gideon Dunster for digitization of diffraction images, and Simon Sponberg for the sharing of diffraction images.

References

1. Bagni, M.A., Cecchi, G., Griffiths, P.J., Maeda, Y., Rapp, G., Ashley, C.C.: Lattice spacing changes accompanying isometric tension development in intact single muscle fibers. Biophys. J. **67**(5), 1965–1975 (1994)
2. Bradski, G.: OpenCV: an open source computer vision library. Dr. Dobb's J. Softw. Tools (2000)
3. Brenner, B., Yu, L.C.: Equatorial x-ray diffraction from single skinned rabbit psoas fibers at various degrees of activation. Changes in intensities and lattice spacing. Biophys. J. **48**(5), 829–834 (1985)
4. Foreman-Mackey, D., Hogg, D.W., Lang, D., Goodman, J.: emcee: The MCMC hammer. PASP **125**(925), 306–312 (2013)
5. George, N.T., Irving, T.C., Williams, C.D., Daniel, T.L.: The cross-bridge spring: can cool muscles store elastic energy? Science **340**(6137), 1217–1220 (2013)
6. Irving, T.C.: X-ray diffraction of indirect flight muscle from drosophila in vivo. In: Vigoreaux, J.O. (ed.) Nature's Versatile Engine: Insect Flight Muscle Inside and Out, Landes Bioscience, Georgetown, TX, pp. 197–213 (2006)
7. Jnr, M.M.H., Veeraraghavan, V.G., Rubin, H., Winchell, P.G.: The approximation of symmetric x-ray peaks by pearson type vii distributions. J. Appl. Cryst. **10**, 66–68 (1977)

8. Millman, B.M.: The filament lattice of striated muscle. Physiol Rev. **78**(2), 359–391 (1998)

9. Reedy, M.K., Holmes, K.C., Tregear, R.T.: Induced changes in orientation of the cross-bridges of glycerinated insect flight muscle. Nature **207**(5003), 1276–1280 (1965)

10. Williams, C.D., Salcedo, M.K., Irving, T.C., Regnier, M., Daniel, T.L.: The length-tension curve in muscle depends on lattice spacing. Proc. Biol. Sci. **280**(1766), 20130697 (2013)

SparkGIS: Efficient Comparison and Evaluation of Algorithm Results in Tissue Image Analysis Studies

Furqan Baig[1]([✉]), Mudit Mehrotra[1], Hoang Vo[1],
Fusheng Wang[1,2], Joel Saltz[1,2], and Tahsin Kurc[2]

[1] Department of Computer Science, Stony Brook University, New York, USA
fbaig@cs.stonybrook.edu
[2] Department of Biomedical Informatics, Stony Brook University, New York, USA

Abstract. Algorithm evaluation provides a means to characterize variability across image analysis algorithms, validate algorithms by comparison of multiple results, and facilitate algorithm sensitivity studies. The sizes of images and analysis results in pathology image analysis pose significant challenges in algorithm evaluation. We present SparkGIS, a distributed, in-memory spatial data processing framework to query, retrieve, and compare large volumes of analytical image result data for algorithm evaluation. Our approach combines the in-memory distributed processing capabilities of Apache Spark and the efficient spatial query processing of Hadoop-GIS. The experimental evaluation of SparkGIS for heatmap computations used to compare nucleus segmentation results from multiple images and analysis runs shows that SparkGIS is efficient and scalable, enabling algorithm evaluation and algorithm sensitivity studies on large datasets.

1 Introduction

Tissue specimens obtained from patients contain rich and biologically meaningful morphologic information that can be linked to molecular alterations and clinical outcome, providing a complementary methodology to genomic data analysis for clinical investigations [3,4,12,13,16]. Manual histopathology using high-power microscopes has been the de facto standard in clinical settings for health care delivery. However, this process corresponds to a qualitative analysis of the tissue, is labor-intensive, and is not feasible in research studies involving thousands of tissue specimens. Advances in tissue imaging technologies have made it possible for investigators and research teams to collect high-resolution images of whole slide tissue specimens. Hence, quantitative analysis of tissue specimens is increasingly becoming a key component of clinical research in Pathology and in many clinical imaging studies targeting complex diseases such as cancer [9,13].

While a quantitative analysis of tissue data can provide new insights into disease mechanisms and facilitate greater reproducibility, image analysis pipelines are not immune to inter-method and inter-analysis variability. Most image analysis methods are sensitive to input parameters and input data. It is not uncommon

F. Wang et al. (Eds.): Big-O(Q) and DMAH 2015, LNCS 9579, pp. 134–146, 2016.
DOI: 10.1007/978-3-319-41576-5_10

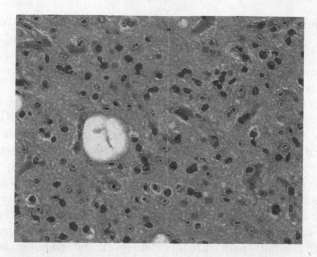

Fig. 1. Nucleus segmentation results from two analysis runs. Each segmented nucleus is represented by a polygon. The color of a polygon overlaid on the original image indicates whether it was generated by the first run (dark blue) or the second (lime). (Color figure online)

that an analysis pipeline optimized for a particular set of images will not do so well when it is applied to another set of images. Consider object segmentation which is a common step in image analysis. A nucleus segmentation pipeline for tissue image analysis will detect and delineate the boundaries of nuclei in an image. Input parameters, such as intensity thresholds and the choice of algorithms for seed detection and for separation of clumped nuclei, will impact the results (the number and locations of detected nuclei, the shape of boundaries of a nucleus, etc.). Figure 1 shows nuclear segmentation results from two analysis runs. As is seen in the figure, the two analysis pipelines have good agreement in some regions (i.e., the boundaries of the polygons overlap closely) and large disagreement in other regions, where either one algorithm has not segmented nuclei while the other has or there are large differences between the boundaries of a nucleus segmented by the two algorithms. Both algorithm developers and biomedical researchers require methods and tools for detecting, studying, and quantifying variability in results from multiple analyses. We refer to this process as *uncertainty and sensitivity quantification*. A systematic approach for algorithm sensitivity study can facilitate the development of refined algorithms. It can also substantially help the development of large repositories of curated analysis results.

The uncertainty/sensitivity quantification process is a data intensive and computationally expensive process when thousands of whole slide tissue images are analyzed by multiple analysis runs. State-of-the-art scanners are capable of capturing tissue images at very high resolutions, typically in the range of $50,000 \times 50,000$ to $100,000 \times 100,000$ pixels. A nuclear segmentation pipeline may segment hundreds of thousands to millions of nuclei in an image. A common metric for comparing results from two analysis runs is the Jaccard index [10]. Computation of the Jaccard index involves spatial joins between the two sets of results and calculations of how much segmented nuclei overlap. This is an expensive operation that can take hours on a single machine for a single image and a pair of result sets.

In this work, we propose, develop and evaluate SparkGIS; a high performance, in-memory, distributed framework to support comparison of image analysis algorithms targeting high-resolution microscopy images. The important features of SparkGIS are: (1) It combines the in-memory distributed processing capabilities of Apache Spark with the high performance spatial query capabilities of Hadoop-GIS; (2) It provides an I/O abstraction layer to support non-HDFS data sources (e.g., databases) and parallelizes I/O operations for such sources; (3) It employs data pipelining and multi-task execution optimizations for algorithm comparison jobs involving many images and algorithms. We implement *Heatmap* computations with this framework and evaluate the implementation using real data generated by analyses of whole slide tissue images. The Heatmap implementation is used to compare results from nucleus segmentation pipelines. We describe how SparkGIS combines the capabilities of Spark and Hadoop-GIS to efficiently support spatial data operations and execute Heatmap computations.

2   Related Work

Spatial data processing systems built on cloud computing frameworks have been the focus of recent research works [2,7,8,14,15]. SpatialHadoop [7] is an extension to Apache Hadoop for spatial data processing on the MapReduce framework [5]. It extends core hadoop classes to support spatial data types and functions. Hadoop-GIS [2] presents a scalable MapReduce framework for spatial query processing with a specialized pathology image analysis add-on. It implements optimizations for spatial partitioning, partitioned based parallel processing over MapReduce using the Real-time Spatial Query Engine (RESQUE) and multi-level spatial indexing. Hadoop-GIS supports a spatial bucketing algorithm that utilizes R*-Tree based global and on-demand local indexing for efficient spatial query processing. SparkGIS's query processing model is extended from Hadoop-GIS's MapReduce based spatial query work flow. MD-HBase [14] leverages a multi-dimensional K-d and Quad-Tree based index over key-value store to efficiently execute range and nearest neighbor queries in real time. It is built on HBase, a column oriented NoSQL distributed database that runs on top of Hadoop. Although all of these systems exhibit comprehensive distributed functionality, they inherently have high inter-job data movement cost. Hadoop requires disk reads and writes for any data passing between interdependent jobs. This can prove to be a major performance bottleneck for spatial processing which heavily relies on iterating over data through multiple map-reduce jobs.

Distributed in-memory data processing systems aim to keep data in memory to facilitate multiple iterations over it by multiple dependent jobs. Apache Spark

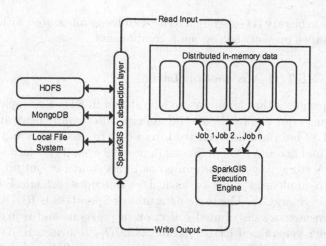

Fig. 2. SparkGIS architecture. IO abstraction layer is decoupled from query processing engine. Data is read in distributed workers' memory. SparkGIS execution engine spawns multiple jobs on this data to efficiently compute spatial query results. Results are provided back to IO abstraction layer for storage.

[17,18] presents a Directed Acyclic Graph (DAG) execution engine that supports in-memory map reduce style processing. Spark's architecture is built around an in-memory data abstraction termed as "Resilient Distributed Dataset" (RDD). An RDD represents an immutable, distributed data elements that can be processed in parallel. Spark allows multiple operations to be executed on the same dataset; examples of operations include parallelize, map, reduce, filter, and groupByKey. GeoSpark [11] extends Spark with a spatial processing layer that provides support for spatial data types and functionality. Although GeoSpark uses a similar query processing approach to ours, it solely relies on Apache Spark as its data accessing layer. SparkGIS, decouples data access layer from actual query processing allowing it to be extended to other types of data sources. It employs spatial query and data processing operations implemented by Hadoop-GIS along with data pipelining and multi concurrent task execution optimizations to reduce execution time.

3 SparkGIS Framework

The main goal of SparkGIS is to provide a high performance, scalable distributed spatial query processing framework tailored to processing of large volumes of results generated by tissue image analysis runs. To this end, the design of SparkGIS combines the advantages of Apache Spark's in-memory distributed computing capability [17,18] with Hadoop-GIS's spatial query processing capability [2]. Figure 2 illustrates the high-level SparkGIS framework. The framework consists of two main components: an I/O abstraction layer and an execution engine. The main purpose of this design is to decouple IO from execution which allows for any arbitrary IO subsystem to be seamlessly integrated with SparkGIS. In this section we present the two main components.

3.1   SparkGIS I/O Abstraction Layer

Hadoop-GIS requires that input datasets be stored in HDFS or copied to HDFS for spatial query processing. SparkGIS relaxes this requirement and provides an abstract I/O interface that can read from or write to HDFS and non-HDFS data sources and execute I/O operations in parallel even if the data source is not distributed. A storage system to be used as input source or output destination only needs to implement a set of basic I/O functions *getDataAsRDD()* and *writeRDD()* in SparkGIS. The basic data unit of SparkGIS is RDD<Polygon>, which is an in-memory distributed collection of polygons and is extended from Apache Spark's generalized RDD. *getDataAsRDD()* returns a RDD<Polygon> instance populated with data from an input source; *writeRDD()* writes an output RDD to a destination.

SparkGIS inherits all data sources supported by Apache Spark. These include local file system, HDFS and any storage source supported by Hadoop. Distributed IO for all such storage sources are internal to Apache Spark and their details are beyond the scope of this study. In addition to inherited data sources, the current implementation of SparkGIS supports MongoDB as a data source and destination. There is an open source MongoDB connector for Apache Spark, referred to here as the Mongo-Hadoop connector [1], but it has some drawbacks. The Mongo-Hadoop connector distributes queries on the basis of MongoDB collections. To process a query on a given collection, it first copies the whole collection in memory as RDD and then compute the query on it. This copying makes it inefficient, and in some cases infeasible, to process queries on large collections – in our case, data from a collection may not fit in memory. SparkGIS's *getDataAsRDD()* implementation for MongoDB executes the following steps:

1. Query the MongoDB server for the total count of documents matching given criteria, e.g. image ID and algorithm name in our case.
2. Create an appropriate number of splits of documents. The split size is based on several variable including *number of nodes in cluster* and *total number of documents*.
3. Distribute the splits among cluster nodes. Each cluster node reads its own range of documents from the MongoDB server and appends them to a RDD for processing.

3.2   SparkGIS Execution Engine

The execution engine of SparkGIS uses the Apache Spark runtime environment as the underlying distributed execution platform and Hadoop-GIS spatial query functions for queries. SparkGIS leverages the in-memory processing of Apache Spark. Keeping data in-memory for iterative processing greatly reduces the processing time. In addition, and more specifically for spatial query processing in our case, in-memory data also removes inter-job I/O costs. SparkGIS's query execution model is based on the Hadoop-GIS RESQUE and uses optimized spatial operators and indexing methods implemented in RESQUE. SparkGIS uses RESQUE functions as a shared library which can easily be shipped to cluster nodes and whose methods can be invoked from SparkGIS to process distributed in-memory spatial data. SparkGIS supports several common spatial query types essential to comparison of analysis results in tissue image analysis. The first type of query, which is our main focus in this work, is the spatial join query, i.e. spatial operations used to combine two or more datasets with respect to a spatial relationship. Four steps are performed for this query type: combine input datasets into a single collection; partition the combined spatial data space into tiles; map all polygons to appropriate tiles; and process the tiles in parallel. Other query types include spatial containment and finding objects contained in subregions and computing density of those objects. These query types can leverage a similar work flow with little or no modification.

In the next section, we present how the analysis results evaluation work flow is supported and how the heatmap computations are implemented in SparkGIS.

3.3 SparkGIS Based Analysis Results Evaluation Workflow and Heatmap Computations

The SparkGIS data processing work flow for comparison of result sets from two analysis runs consists of the following steps: (1) Data retrieval for a given image and analysis runs A and B; (2) Data preparation for both result sets; and (3) Execution of spatial operations and computation of output. Figure 3 shows the core Spark functions used in implementing these three stages. We describe in this section the work flow stages for computation of heatmaps to compare and evaluate results from two nucleus segmentation runs.

For a given image and a pair of analysis runs, the implementation of the heatmap computations partitions the image regularly into KxK-pixel tiles, where

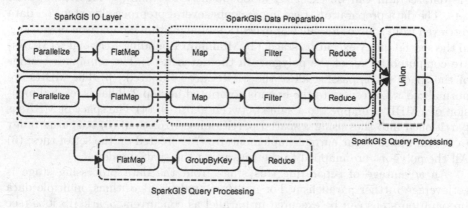

Fig. 3. This figure illustrates the stages involved in SparkGIS spatial join query in terms of Apache Spark's functions

K is a user-defined value. It then computes a Jaccard index [10] or a Dice coefficient [6] for each tile. The coefficient computation for a tile involves (1) finding all the segmented nuclei (represented as polygons) that intersect or are contained in the tile, (2) performing a spatial join between the sets of polygons from the two analysis runs, and (3) computing the coefficients based on the amount of overlap between intersecting polygons.

Data Retrieval. Segmented objects in a tissue image are typically represented by polygons; each polygon represents the boundaries of a segmented nucleus, for example. The data retrieval step is responsible for retrieving these polygons from storage sources. Each image can have hundreds of thousands to millions of polygons from a single analysis run. Therefore, data retrieval for multiple analysis runs can easily scale up to tens of millions of polygons for a single image. If results from an analysis run are stored in files in HDFS, each row of a data file stores a polygon representing a segmented nucleus. The result set may be stored by the analysis application in one or more files for each (image id, analysis run name/id) pair. When HDFS is a data source, the SparkGIS I/O layer calls Spark I/O functions to retrieve the data. If input data is, for example, stored in MongoDB, the Spark I/O layer composes a MongoDB query to retrieve polygon data and executes the steps described in Sect. 3. A master node creates splits and distributes them among worker nodes by invoking the *parallelize()* function. Each worker node implements a *flatMap* function which reads its own split of data from the data source and returns a list of polygons. This list is appended to the RDD returned to the master node. The RDD is cached in memory for further processing. Upon return of *getDataAsRDD()* function, an RDD will be ready for processing. Figure 3 illustrates the use of Spark functions and execution engine in the SparkGIS I/O layer.

Data Preparation. Data preparation separates tasks that are specific to single dataset and can be executed independently for multiple algorithm result sets. The data preparation stage implements several preprocessing steps on data retrieved from sources for efficient execution of algorithm comparison operations in the spatial query execution stage: (1) Minimum Bounding Rectangles (MBRs) are computed for all of the polygons in the dataset; (2) The minimum bounds of the space encompassing all of the MBRs are computed; (3) The MBRs are normalized with respect to the bounds computed in step 2. That is, each dimension of a MBR is mapped to a value between $[0.0, 1.0]$; (4) The space of MBRs is partitioned into tiles using a spatial partitioning algorithm; (5) A spatial index (a R-tree index in our current implementation) is created on the set of tiles; (6) All the polygons are mapped to the tiles using the spatial index.

An advantage of separating this stage from the data processing stage is to leverage further parallelism. For multiple analysis algorithms, multiple data preparation steps can be executed in parallel as concurrent SparkGIS jobs (see Fig. 4). Consequently this improves the overall system performance along with better resource utilization.

Figure 3 shows the Spark functions that are executed to prepare the retrieved data for processing. The *Map* function is executed in parallel on the RDD prepared by the IO layer. Each worker extracts Minimum Bounding Rectangles (MBRs) for each polygon in its data split. The next step *filters* out any invalid MBRs. The last step in the data preparation stage implements a *reduce* phase which calculate the space dimensions for the whole dataset from the MBRs. A data configuration object is generated by the data preparation step which contains the space dimensions along with a pointer to the cached polygon data RDD.

Query and Data Processing. Once the data preparation step is finished, the data processing stage is invoked. SparkGIS ships the RESQUE shared library to all workers and invoke its functions. To combine all the cached RDD's from generated configurations SparkGIS uses Apache Spark's *Union* operator. The *FlatMap* function partitions the combined data into tiles covering the whole combined spatial space. Once all polygons are mapped to appropriate tiles, they are grouped by tile IDs by calling the *groupByKey* function. *GroupByKey* is an expensive operation involving *shuffle* operation which requires a lot of data movement among cluster nodes. Prior to this step, all processing was done on local distributed in-memory data partitions with minimum cross nodes data transfer. Once grouped by tile IDs, all tiles are processed in parallel using RESQUE to generate results for spatial join query.

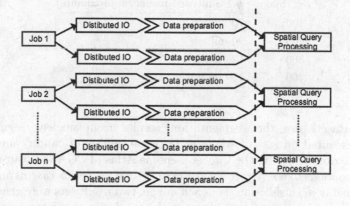

Fig. 4. Multiple concurrent jobs can be submitted to SparkGIS framework. The stages of these jobs as described in Sect. 3.3 are pipelined for efficient batch processing.

The final result of comparing multiple algorithm analysis results is a heatmap based on the spatial join query. The heatmap signifies the most agreed upon regions by all the compared algorithm analyses for a given image. From spatial join results, heatmaps are generated by calculating an average similarity index per tile. SparkGIS currently supports heatmaps based on Jaccard and Dice metrics.

Multiple Concurrent Task/Job Execution. Each job in SparkGIS goes through these stages to process data from a pair of analysis result sets. Executing a single job at a time when a large number of datasets needs to be processed will result in low overall performance and underutilized cluster resources. Multiple stages of the work flow can be overlapped in a batch for further performance gain when processing multiple images. Each work flow as described in Sect. 3.3 has its own context. This allows for multiple contexts to be active simultaneously in the system. Figure 4 illustrates the execution strategy for processing results from multiple algorithms and multiple datasets by pipelining the multiple stages of each work flow.

4   Experimental Performance Evaluation

We have used a CentoOS 6.5 cluster with 5 nodes with 120 total cores. Each node has 24 logical cores with hyper-threading (Intel (R) Xeon (R) CPU E5-2660 v2 at 2.20 GHz) and 128 GB memory. We employed Apache Spark-1.4.1 as our cluster computing framework. For Hadoop-GIS we used the same environment with default configurations. For a fair comparison between Hadoop-GIS and SparkGIS, datasets were uploaded to HDFS with replication factor set to 3 on each data node.

Table 1. Number of segmented nuclei for different sets of images (caseids).

# Images	# Segmented nuclei (approximate)
100	70 million
200	90 million
300	125 million
400	150 million

The datasets are the segmentation results from nucleus segmentation pipelines executed on sets of whole slide tissue images of cancer tumors. The images were obtained from the Cancer Genome Atlas (TCGA) repository[1]. Each image corresponds to a separate TCGA case id – we use terms *caseids* and *images* interchangeably in this section. For each image, two result sets were generated by two different analysis pipelines. The spatial boundaries of the segmented nuclei were converted into polygons and normalized. The number of polygons in the datasets used in the evaluation is shown in Table 1.

4.1   Batch Factor

The batch factor is the number of concurrent tasks submitted to SparkGIS. We experimented with several batch sizes to come up with a good value for efficient execution. SparkGIS uses Java's default *ExecutorService* to submit multiple

---

[1] http://cancergenome.nih.gov.

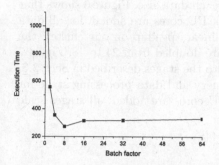

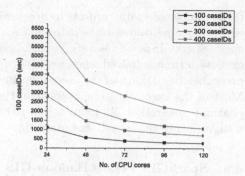

Fig. 5. SparkGIS Batch factor. Our experimental evaluations indicates 8 to be the optimal batch factor for our setup.

Fig. 6. SparkGIS scalability with varying number of images. (Color figure online)

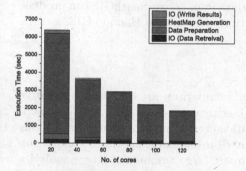

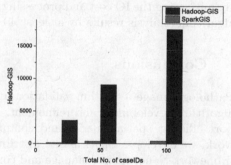

Fig. 7. Breakdown of execution time into the I/O, data preparation, and data processing stages (Sect. 3.3). (Color figure online)

Fig. 8. A comparison of HadoopGIS and SparkGIS for heatmap computation. SparkGIS outperforms HadoopGIS due to lower I/O overheads through efficient in-memory processing. (Color figure online)

concurrent jobs to the Spark cluster. Our results on 120 CPU cores show that SparkGIS can handle up to 8 algorithm evaluation jobs simultaneously. Figure 5 shows that increasing the batch factor to greater than 8 leads to diminishing performance results in our setup. This is mainly due to the limit on the number of jobs that can be scheduled on available nodes and CPU cores.

4.2 Execution Performance and Scalability

In this evaluation we fixed the batch factor to 8 (optimal from Sect. 4.1) and varied the total number of CPU cores across different data sizes. Data size was determined from the number of images. Each caseID corresponds to a pathology image having two separate algorithm analysis results. Table 1 summarizes the total number of spatial objects to process for each data size. Figure 6 shows that execution time decreases as more nodes and CPU cores are added, for all data sizes. SparkGIS achieves very good, almost linear speedup on our cluster; the execution time is halved when worker cores are doubled from 24 to 48. Figure 7 presents a breakdown of the execution time into the stages described in Sect. 3.3. Most of the execution time is spent in the query and data processing stage for heatmap generation. As more nodes and CPU cores are added, all stages scale well, reducing the overall execution time.

4.3   SparkGIS Versus Hadoop-GIS

We compared the results of SparkGIS with Hadoop-GIS to generate heatmaps for results from two analysis runs. The total number of images processed in these algorithms were varied across several experiments. Figure 8 shows the performance comparison for the two distributed spatial query processing frameworks. By mitigating the IO cost and processing data in memory, SparkGIS can produce algorithm analysis results by at least 40 times faster than Hadoop-GIS.

5   Conclusions

Pathology image algorithm validation and comparison are essential to iterative algorithm development and refinement. A critical component for this is to support efficient spatial queries and computation of comparison metrics. In this work, we develop a Spark based distributed, in-memory algorithm comparison framework to normalize, manage and compare large amounts of image analytics result data. Our approach is based on spatial query processing principles in the Hadoop-GIS framework but takes advantage of in-memory and pipelined data processing. Our experiments on real datasets show that SparkGIS is efficient and scalable. The experiments demonstrate that by reducing the IO costs associated with data staging and inter-job data movement spatial query processing performance can be improved by orders of magnitude. The actual query processing can be decomposed in multiple stages to leverage further performance gain through parallelization and multiple concurrent task processing. In future work, we plan to focus on further evaluation of the spatial query pipeline in SparkGIS using more datasets and on extending SparkGIS to support a larger set of analytical operations, in addition to current heatmap generation functions.

Acknowledgments. This work was funded in part by HHSN261200800001E from the NCI, 1U24CA180924-01A1 from the NCI, 5R01LM011119-05 and 5R01LM009239-07 from the NLM.

References

1. Mongo hadoop. https://github.com/mongodb/mongo-hadoop
2. Aji, A., Wang, F., Vo, H., Lee, R., Liu, Q., Zhang, X., Saltz, J.: Hadoop gis: a high performance spatial data warehousing system over mapreduce. Proc. VLDB Endow. **6**(11), 1009–1020 (2013)
3. Beck, A.H., Sangoi, A.R., Leung, S., Marinelli, R.J., Nielsen, T.O., van de Vijver, M.J., West, R.B., van de Rijn, M., Koller, D.: Systematic analysis of breast cancer morphology uncovers stromal features associated with survival. Sci. Transl. Med. **3**(108), 108ra113 (2011)
4. Cooper, L.A.D., Kong, J., Gutman, D.A., Wang, F., Gao, J., Appin, C., Cholleti, S.R., Pan, T., Sharma, A., Scarpace, L., Mikkelsen, T., Kur, T.M., Moreno, C.S., Brat, D.J., Saltz, J.H.: Integrated morphologic analysis for the identification and characterization of disease subtypes. JAMIA **19**(2), 317–323 (2012)
5. Dean, J., Ghemawat, S.: Mapreduce: simplified data processing on large clusters. Commun. ACM **51**(1), 107–113 (2008)
6. Dice, L.R.: Measures of the amount of ecologic association between species. Ecology **26**(3), 297–302 (1945)
7. Eldawy, A.: Spatialhadoop: towards flexible and scalable spatial processing using mapreduce. In: Proceedings of the 2014 SIGMOD PhD Symposium, pp. 46–50. ACM, New York (2014)
8. Frye, R., McKenney, M.: Big data storage techniques for spatial databases: implications of big data architecture on spatial query processing. In: Information Granularity, Big Data, and Computational Intelligence, pp. 297–323. Springer, Switzerland (2015)
9. Fuchs, T.J., Buhmann, J.M.: Computational pathology: challenges and promises for tissue analysis. Comput. Med. Imaging Graph. **35**(7), 515–530 (2011)
10. Jaccard, P.: Etude comparative de la distribution florale dans une portion des Alpes et du Jura. Impr. Corbaz (1901)
11. Jia Yu, J.W., Sarwat, M.: Geospark: a cluster computing framework for processing large-scale spatial data. In: Proceedings of the 2015 International Conference on Advances in Geographic Information Systems, ACM SIGSPATIAL 2015 (2015)
12. Kong, J., Cooper, L.A.D., Wang, F., Chisolm, C., Moreno, C.S., Kur, T.M., Widener, P.M., Brat, D.J., Saltz, J.H.: A comprehensive framework for classification of nuclei in digital microscopy imaging: an application to diffuse gliomas. In: ISBI, pp. 2128–2131. IEEE (2011)
13. Louis, D.N., Feldman, M., Carter, A.B., Dighe, A.S., Pfeifer, J.D., Bry, L., Almeida, J.S., Saltz, J., Braun, J., Tomaszewski, J.E., et al.: Computational pathology: a path ahead. Archives of Pathology and Laboratory Medicine (2015)
14. Nishimura, S., Das, S., Agrawal, D., Abbadim A.E.: Md-hbase: a scalable multidimensional data infrastructure for location aware services. In: Proceedings of the 2011 IEEE 12th International Conference on Mobile Data Management, MDM 2011, vol. 01, pp. 7–16. IEEE Computer Society, Washington, DC (2011)
15. You, S., Zhang, J., Gruenwald, L.: Large-scale spatial join query processing in cloud. In: IEEE CloudDM Workshop, to appear 2015. http://www-cs.ccny.cuny.edu/~jzhang/papers/spatial_cc_tr.pdf

16. Yuan, Y., Failmezger, H., Rueda, O.M., Ali, H.R., Gräf, S., Chin, S.-F., Schwarz, R.F., Curtis, C., Dunning, M.J., Bardwell, H., Johnson, N., Doyle, S., Turashvili, G., Provenzano, E., Aparicio, S., Caldas, C., Markowetz, F.: Quantitative image analysis of cellular heterogeneity in breast tumors complements genomic profiling. Sci. Transl. Med. 4(157), 157ra143 (2012)
17. Zaharia, M., Chowdhury, M., Das, T., Dave, A., Ma, J., McCauley, M., Franklin, M.J., Shenker, S., Stoica, I.: Resilient distributed datasets: a fault-tolerant abstraction for in-memory cluster computing. In: Proceedings of the 9th USENIX Conference on Networked Systems Design and Implementation, NSDI 2012, p. 2. USENIX Association, Berkeley (2012)
18. Zaharia, M., Chowdhury, M., Franklin, M.J., Shenker, S., Stoica, I.: Spark: cluster computing with working sets. In: Proceedings of the 2nd USENIX Conference on Hot Topics in Cloud Computing, HotCloud 2010, p. 10. USENIX Association, Berkeley (2010)

Big-Graphs Online Querying

Social Network Analytics: Beyond the Obvious

Laks V.S. Lakshmanan[✉]

University of British Columbia, Vancouver, BC, Canada
laks@cs.ubc.ca

1 The Background

Over the last decade and a half, there has been an explosion of interest in the analysis and mining of very large networks, including those arising in social and information networks, biological networks such as protein-protein interaction networks, web graph, collaboration networks, customer-product interaction networks, and road networks, to name a few. The interest has been fueled by driving applications as well as by the unprecedented availability of real network data. Of particular note among the driving applications are the study of spread of infections and innovations, word-of-mouth marketing or the so-called viral marketing, and tracking of events and stories in social media. In this talk, I will use viral marketing and event and story evolution tracking as concrete settings with which to describe some exciting research that has been done over the past several years. In the process, I will briefly discuss some less obvious applications of mining large graphs.

2 Viral Marketing

Many processes over networks propagate in a stochastic manner. For example, diseases or infections spread from people to their contacts. Adoption of products, technology, or rumors propagate from people to their friends. These phenomena can potentially propagate transitively, that is, adoption can propagate from an initial adoptor to any user connected to her by one or more links. Ideas and innovation within organizations have also been known to propagate from individuals to their coworkers or collaborators and so forth in a similar manner. In mathematical sociology, there are well-known diffusion models to capture such phenomena, including SIR, SIRS, independent cascade, linear threshold, triggering model, and so forth (e.g., see [8, 12, 13, 15, 19, 23]). Initially, all nodes in a network are inactive, i.e., they are not infected or have not adopted an item. Given a network and a (stochastic) diffusion model, the model defines a random process which, given an initial set of active nodes of the network, $S := S_0$, specifies the sets of active nodes S_t, at successive time steps $t \geq 0$. This corresponds to the view of diffusion as a discrete time process, a primary focus of this talk. The model may be progressive or non-progressive: in progressive models, a node once becoming active, can never become inactive again, whereas in non-progressive models, there is no such restriction. The majority of the literature has focused

© Springer International Publishing Switzerland 2016
F. Wang et al. (Eds.): Big-O(Q) and DMAH 2015, LNCS 9579, pp. 149–154, 2016.
DOI: 10.1007/978-3-319-41576-5_11

on progressive models, although a small stream of papers on non-progressive models is starting to appear. For the most part, we will focus on progressive models.

We refer to the initial set of active nodes as *seeds*. A key computational problem in the study of random propagation phenomena is called *influence maximization*. Using viral marketing as an example, this problem can be phrased as follows. We can regard initial adopters as nodes which are incentivized by the viral campaign runner to adopt the item, e.g., by being given free or price-discounted samples of the item being marketed. For a network, diffusion model M, and seeds S, we denote by $\sigma_M(S)$ the expected number of nodes that are activated at the end of the diffusion process, a quantity referred to as *spread*. The influence maximization problem can be formalized as follows [15]: *Given a network $G = (V, E)$, a stochastic diffusion model M, and a number k, find a set of at most k seeds S that maximizes the spread $\sigma_M(S)$.*

We drop the subscript M whenever the model is clear from the context. Influence maximization is typically an NP-hard problem [15], and even computing the exact spread for a given seed set is #P-hard under major propagation models [4,5]. For several popular models such as independent cascade, linear threshold, and their generalized variants, the spread function $\sigma : 2^V \rightarrow [\|V\|]$ is known to satisfy the nice properties of monotonicity and submodularity. A function σ is monotone, provided more seeds cannot hurt the diffusion spread, that is, $\sigma(S) \leq \sigma(S')$, whenever $S \subseteq S'$. Furthermore, it is submodular, provided the marginal gain of a new node diminishes as the seed set grows, that is $\sigma(S \cup \{u\}) - \sigma(S) \geq \sigma(S' \cup \{u\}) - \sigma(S')$, whenever $S \subseteq S'$ and $u \in V \setminus S'$. A natural algorithm for influence maximization is a simple greedy algorithm, which repeatedly adds the node with the maximum marginal gain to the current seed set, initially empty. When σ is monotone and submodular, the greedy algorithm yields a $(1 - 1/e)$-approximation to the optimum [21]. However, computing marginal gain is #P-hard (see above) and we can use Monte-Carlo (MC) simulation to estimate the spread to a desired level of accuracy. Factoring this in leads to a $(1 - 1/e - \epsilon)$-approximation to the optimum solution [15].

The basic greedy algorithm above along with MC simulation for spread estimation has been found to be extremely slow. Thus, there have been numerous efforts at improving upon it, some directly improving the efficiency of the greedy algorithm [10,18], some using heuristics [4,5,11,14], alternative models of spread [9], and more efficient approximation algorithms [7,24,25]. Impressive strides have been made in improving the efficiency of influence maximization. There are several critical questions concerned with the functionality or expressiveness of the basic viral marketing paradigm. The first part of this talk will address these questions.

Influence maximization is just one kind of an optimization problem that naturally arises in viral marketing. Can we optimize other resources such as the number (or cost) of seeds selected or the time needed for the campaign to bear fruit, i.e., propagation time? There can be the proverbial slip between merely being influenced enough to consider adopting a product seriously and the actual adoption. E.g., a customer may gather additional information about the product from her social network or other sources and then decide whether to adopt the product. Or the customer may have her own valuation for a product and may make an adoption decision based on the offer price. In practice, viral marketing or more generally propagation of information rarely happens in isolation. What are appropriate models for capturing competition and what are some natural optimization problems for the competitive setting? While there have been several works on competitive influence maximization, most of them ignore the fundamental role played by the network owner, who acts as a host providing viral markering services to its clients. In a marketplace, some products may compete with each other while others may complement a given product. How can we account for such complex interactions between products? Most prior art is based on a discrete time propagation model such as independent cascade or linear threshold and assumes that the pairwise influence probabilities between nodes are known beforehand. In practice, real network datasets do not come accompanied by influence probabilities. Can we learn these probabilities from propagations observed in the past? What if no such past propagation data is available? Social advertising constitutes one of the most significant sectors of digital advertising, whereby a host of a social platform makes money from promoted posts. This paradigm has failed to take advantage of viral propagation of promoted posts, until recently. What are the benefits and challenges arising from the integration of social advertising with viral marketing?

3 Event and Story Detection and Tracking

User generated content in social media can serve as a promising source for timely recognition of new and emerging events, often more effective than mainstream media. An example is the event related to the "Stop Online Piracy Act" (SOPA) movement. On January 16, 2012, SOPA was emerging as a prominent event and Wikipedia, among many other sites, announced that it was going to protest against it on January 18. On January 17, an event related to Apple's announcement of new product versions (e.g., iBooks 2) was emerging and on January 19, the "Apple event" was intertwined with the SOPA event since Apple threw its support behind the protest. By the time Apple unveiled iBooks 2 on January 21, much of the buzz related to it did not also mention SOPA so the two events effectively split. This case study underscores several important points. Firstly, mainstream media are too slow to pick up and react to new and emerging events which surge quickly in social media. On the other hand, posts in social media are riddled with considerable noise, are of considerable volume, and evolve quickly. At the same time, these very factors make it overwhelming for users to manually track and pick out interesting emerging events by themselves. There is thus an urgent need for tools which can automatically extract and summarize significant information from social streams, e.g., report emerging bursty events, or track the evolution of one or more specific events in a given time span.

There are several previous studies [17,22] on detecting new emerging events from text streams. However, in many scenarios, users are dissatisfied with just a static view of emerging events. Instead, they may want to know the history of an event and may like to issue advanced queries like *"how're things going?"* (in the context of a specific event). The ideal answer of such a query would be a "panoramic view" of the event, showing the whole evolution life cycle of an event, namely how new events emerge, grow, and decay, as well as how different events merge and an event splits into different events, as demonstrated in the example above.

We can model social streams as dynamically evolving post networks, defined as follows: *The post network corresponding to a social stream Q at a specific moment is a graph $G(V, E)$, where each node $p \in V$ is a post in Q, and each edge $(p_i, p_j) \in E$ indicates that the similarity between p_i and p_j is above a threshold, where the similarity may take both content and temporal proximity into account.*

We can then model events as clusters over these post networks. Social streams are typically of very large scale, evolve quickly, and contain a significant amount of noise. The algorithms employed for detecting event clusters and for tracking their evolution thus face the following challenges:

- Traditional approaches (e.g., [16]) based on decomposing a dynamic network into snapshots and processing each snapshot independently from scratch are prohibitively expensive. An efficient single-pass incremental computation framework is essential for event evolution tracking over social streams that exhibit very large throughput rates.
- The second challenge is the formalization and tracking of event evolution operations under an incremental computation framework, as the network evolves. Most related work reports event activity just based on burst volume over time [17]. While certainly useful, this is just not capable of showing the composite evolution behaviors about how events split or merge, for instance.
- The third challenge is the handling of bulk updates. Since dynamic post networks may change rapidly, a node-by-node approach to incremental updating will lead to poor performance. A subgraph-by-subgraph approach to incremental updating is critical for achieving good performance over very large, fast-evolving dynamic networks such as post networks.

At a high level, event evolution tracking bears resemblance to previous work on density-based clustering over streaming data, e.g., DenStream [3], DStream [6] and cluster maintenance in [1,2]. However, there are several major differences with this body of work. First, the existing work can only handle addition of nodes/edges one by one, while event evolution tracking calls for addition of *subgraphs*. Second, the focus of event evolution tracking is analyzing the event evolution dynamics in the whole life cycle, in contrast with previous works on clustering over streaming data. Topic tracking approaches are usually formulated as a classification problem: when a new story arrives, compare it with topic features in the training set using decision trees or k-NN, and if it matches sufficiently, declare it to be on a topic. These approaches assume that topics are *predefined before tracking*, which just doesn't work for event evolution tracking in social streams. Comparing with existing event detection and tracking approaches [17,20], event evolution tracking needs to trace the whole life cycle and capture composite evolution behaviors such as merging and splitting of events.

Transient stories embedded in social posts can be interesting and informative and thus their extraction and tracking is an important problem. For example, the loss of and subsequent search for Malaysia Airlines flight MH 370 has associated with it several transient, fast changing, and related stories, beginning first with the disappearance of the flight, Australian authorities suggesting possible sighting of objects from that flight in the Indian ocean, Malaysian authorities updating their search, followed by Australian authorieis following suit, etc. These constitute a series of transient and related stories. How can we effectively and efficiently extract these stories from social media and how can find stories that are related to given stories? These are some interesting challenges we will discuss.

4 Conclusions

In sum, social and information networks and social media present unprecedented sources of rich graph structured real datasets, offering a wealth of possibilities for analysis and mining. Applications of mining such datasets are manifold. In this talk, I will confine our attention to viral marketing and event and story detection and tracking, and describe work that has been done in our research group in recent years. I will conclude with several interesting open problems worthy of future research. The bibliography below is necessarily incomplete and most notably does not include most of our own work, in collaboration with several students, postocs, and colleagues. These works as well as the collaborators will be highlighted in the talk.

References

1. Agarwal, M.K., Ramamritham, K., Bhide, M.: Real time discovery of dense clusters in highly dynamic graphs: identifying real world events in highly dynamic environments. PVLDB 5(10), 980–991 (2012)
2. Angel, A., Koudas, N., Sarkas, N., Srivastava, D.: Dense subgraph maintenance under streaming edge weight updates for real-time story identification. PVLDB 5(6), 574–585 (2012)
3. Cao, F., Ester, M., Qian, W., Zhou, A.: Density-based clustering over an evolving data stream with noise. In: SDM (2006)
4. Chen, W., Wang, C., Wang, Y.: Scalable influence maximization for prevalent viral marketing in large-scale social networks. In: KDD, pp. 1029–1038 (2010)
5. Chen, W., Yuan, Y., Zhang, L.: Scalable influence maximization in social networks under the linear threshold model. In: ICDM, pp. 88–97 (2010)
6. Chen, Y., Tu, L.: Density-based clustering for real-time stream data. In: KDD, pp. 133–142 (2007)
7. Cohen, E., Delling, D., Pajor, T., Werneck, R.F.: Sketch-based influence maximization and computation: scaling up with guarantees. In: CIKM (2014)

8. Durrett, R.: Lecture Notes on Particle Systems and Percolation. Wadsworth Publishing, California (1988)
9. Goyal, A., Bonchi, F., Lakshmanan, L.V.S.: A data-based approach to social influence maximization. PVLDB **5**(1), 73–84 (2011)
10. Goyal, A., Lu, W., Lakshmanan, L.V.S.: Celf++: optimizing the greedy algorithm for influence maximization in social networks. In: WWW (Companion Volume), pp. 47–48 (2011)
11. Goyal, A., Lu, W., Lakshmanan, L.V.S.: Simpath: an efficient algorithm for influence maximization under the linear threshold model. In: ICDM, pp. 211–220 (2011)
12. Granovetter, M.: Threshold models of collective behavior. Am. J. Sociol. **83**(6), 1420–1443 (1978)
13. Gruhl, D., Guha, R.V., Liben-Nowell, D., Tomkins, A.: Information diffusion through blogspace. In: Proceedings of the 13th International Conference on World Wide Web (WWW 2004) (2004)
14. Jung, K., Heo, W., Chen, W.: IRIE: scalable and robust influence maximization in social networks. In: ICDM, pp. 918–923 (2012)
15. Kempe, D., Kleinberg, J.M., Tardos, É.: Maximizing the spread of influence through a social network. In: KDD, pp. 137–146 (2003)
16. Kim, M.-S., Han, J.: A particle-and-density based evolutionary clustering method for dynamic networks. PVLDB **2**(1), 622–633 (2009)
17. Leskovec, J., Backstrom, L., Kleinberg, J.M.: Meme-tracking and the dynamics of the news cycle. In: KDD, pp. 497–506 (2009)
18. Leskovec, J., Krause, A., Guestrin, C., Faloutsos, C., VanBriesen, J., Glance, N.: Cost-effective outbreak detection in networks. In: Proceedings of the 13th ACM SIGKDD International Conference on Knowledge Discovery and Data Mining, pp. 420–429. ACM (2007)
19. Liggett, T.: Interacting Particle Systems. Springer, New York (1985)
20. Marcus, A., Bernstein, M.S., Badar, O., Karger, D.R., Madden, S., Miller, R.C.: Tweets as data: demonstration of tweeql and twitinfo. In: SIGMOD Conference, pp. 1259–1262 (2011)
21. Nemhauser, G.L., Wolsey, L.A., Fisher, M.L.: An analysis of approximations for maximizing submodular set functions - i. Math. Program. **14**(1), 265–294 (1978)
22. Sakaki, T., Okazaki, M., Matsuo, Y.: Earthquake shakes twitter users: real-time event detection by social sensors. In: WWW, pp. 851–860 (2010)
23. Schelling, T.: Micromotives and Macrobehavior. Norton (1978)
24. Tang, Y., Shi, Y., Xiao, X.: Influence maximization in near-linear time: a martingale approach. In: Proceedings of the 2015 ACM SIGMOD International Conference on Management of Data, SIGMOD 2015, pp. 1539–1554. ACM, New York (2015)
25. Tang, Y., Xiao, X., Shi, Y.: Influence maximization: near-optimal time complexity meets practical efficiency. In: SIGMOD (2014)

S2X: Graph-Parallel Querying
of RDF with GraphX

Alexander Schätzle[(✉)], Martin Przyjaciel-Zablocki,
Thorsten Berberich, and Georg Lausen

Department of Computer Science, University of Freiburg,
Georges-Köhler-Allee 051, 79110 Freiburg, Germany
{schaetzle,zablocki,lausen}@informatik.uni-freiburg.de

Abstract. RDF has constantly gained attention for data publishing due to its flexible data model, raising the need for distributed querying. However, existing approaches using general-purpose cluster frameworks employ a record-oriented perception of RDF ignoring its inherent graph-like structure. Recently, GraphX was published as a graph abstraction on top of Spark, an in-memory cluster computing system. It allows to seamlessly combine graph-parallel and data-parallel computation in a single system, an unique feature not available in other systems. In this paper we introduce S2X, a SPARQL query processor for Hadoop where we leverage this unified abstraction by implementing basic graph pattern matching of SPARQL as a graph-parallel task while other operators are implemented in a data-parallel manner. To the best of our knowledge, this is the first approach to combine graph-parallel and data-parallel computation for SPARQL querying of RDF data based on Hadoop.

Keywords: RDF · SPARQL · Hadoop · Spark · GraphX

1 Introduction

Driven by initiatives like Schema.org, one can expect the amount of RDF [8] data to grow steadily towards massive scale, requiring distributed solutions to store and query it. Likewise, the Hadoop ecosystem has become the de facto standard in the area of large-scale distributed processing and has been applied to many diverse application fields. The recent development and integration of in-memory frameworks (e.g. *Spark, Impala*) facilitates even further application fields covering not only classical ETL-like but also more interactive workloads.

In addition, storing RDF data in a common data pool (e.g. *HDFS*) among various Hadoop-based applications enables manifold synergy benefits compared with dedicated infrastructures, where interoperability between different systems comes along with high integration costs. Consequently, there already exists some work on querying RDF with Hadoop, e.g. [6,7,9,11,12], but they all follow a relational-style model to manage RDF data. However, the RDF data model can also be interpreted as a graph and query processing (in terms of SPARQL) as a

© Springer International Publishing Switzerland 2016
F. Wang et al. (Eds.): Big-O(Q) and DMAH 2015, LNCS 9579, pp. 155–168, 2016.
DOI: 10.1007/978-3-319-41576-5_12

task to identify subgraphs that match a query pattern. Implementing such graph computations using *data-parallel* frameworks like MapReduce or Spark can be challenging and inefficient as they do not provide any graph abstraction and do not exploit their inherent graph structure. Specialized parallel graph processing systems like *Pregel, Giraph* and *GraphLab* (see [5] for comparison) are tailored towards such iterative graph algorithms but they are either not integrated in the Hadoop ecosystem or come with their own programming abstraction that cannot be combined with existing data-parallel frameworks. Thus, in order to compose graph-parallel and data-parallel operations, the data has to be moved or copied from one system to the other.

Recently, an abstraction for graph-parallel computation was added to Spark, called *GraphX* [3]. It is implemented on top of Spark but complements it with graph-specific optimizations similar to those in specialized graph processing systems. This bridges the gap between the record-centric view of data-parallel frameworks and the graph-parallel computation of specialized systems, paving the way for new applications that seamlessly combine the best of both worlds. Moreover, it fits to our concept of having a common data pool as it uses HDFS for permanent storage.

In this paper we introduce S2X (SPARQL on Spark with GraphX). It combines graph-parallel abstraction of GraphX to implement the graph pattern matching part of SPARQL with data-parallel computation of Spark to build the results of other SPARQL operators. There is not much other work yet on querying RDF with SPARQL using a parallel graph processing framework. In [4] the authors present an implementation on top of GraphLab while Trinity.RDF [15] is an RDF implementation on top of the Trinity graph engine which uses a distributed key-value store. However, both approaches use their own dedicated data storage which conceptually differs from our approach to use a common data pool for synergy reasons. To the best of our knowledge, there is currently no other work on SPARQL querying on Hadoop using a native graph abstraction for RDF due to the lack of suitable graph processing frameworks for Hadoop. We think that GraphX is a promising step to bridge this gap.

Our major contributions are as follows: (1) We define a mapping from RDF to the property graph model of GraphX. (2) Based on this model we introduce S2X, a SPARQL implementation on top of GraphX and Spark. (3) Finally, we provide some preliminary experiments to compare S2X with a state of the art SPARQL engine that uses MapReduce as execution layer.

2   Graph-Parallel Computation with GraphX

Spark [13] is a general-purpose in-memory cluster computing system that can run on Hadoop. The central data structure is a so-called *Resilient Distributed Dataset* (RDD) [14] which is a fault-tolerant collection of elements that can be operated on in parallel. Spark attempts to keep an RDD in memory and partitions it across all machines in the cluster. Conceptually, Spark adopts a *data-parallel* computation model that builds upon a record-centric view of data, similar to *MapReduce* and *Apache Tez*. A job is modeled as a directed acyclic graph (DAG) of tasks where each task runs on a horizontal partition of the data.

Spark also comes with a rich stack of high-level tools, including an API for graphs and *graph-parallel* computation called *GraphX* [3]. It adds an abstraction to the API of Spark to ease the usage of graph data and provides a set of typical graph operators. It is meant to bridge the gap between data-parallel and graph-parallel computation in a single system such that data can be seamlessly viewed both as a graph and as collections of items without data movement or duplication. Graph-parallel abstraction builds upon a vertex-centric view of graphs where parallelism is achieved by graph partitioning and computation is expressed in the form of user-defined vertex programs that are instantiated concurrently for each vertex and can interact with adjacent vertex programs. Like many other graph-parallel systems, GraphX adopts the *bulk-synchronous parallel* (BSP) execution model where all vertex programs run concurrently in a sequence of so-called *supersteps*. In every superstep a vertex program performs its local transformations and can exchange information with adjacent vertices which is then available to them in the following superstep.

GraphX uses a *vertex-cut* partitioning strategy that evenly assigns edges to machines and allows vertices to span multiple machines in a way that the number of machines spanned by each vertex is minimized. Internally, a graph is represented by two separate collections for edges (EdgeRDD) and vertices (VertexRDD). The graph operators of GraphX are likewise expressed as a combination of data-parallel operations on these collections in Spark with additional graph-specific optimizations inspired from specialized graph processing systems. For example, as many graph computations need to join the edge and vertex collection, GraphX maintains a routing table co-partitioned with the vertex collection such that each vertex is sent only to the edge partitions that contain adjacent edges. This way, GraphX achieves performance parity with specialized graph processing systems (e.g. *Giraph* and *GraphLab*) [3].

3   RDF Property Graph Model in S2X

The property graph data model of GraphX combines the graph structure with vertex and edge properties. Formally, a *property graph* is a directed multigraph and can be defined as $PG(P) = (V, E, P)$ where V is a set of vertices and $E = \{(i, j) \mid i, j \in V\}$ a set of directed edges from i (*source*) to j (*target*). Every vertex $i \in V$ is represented by an unique identifier. $P_V(i)$ denotes the properties of vertex $i \in V$ and $P_E(i, j)$ the properties of edge $(i, j) \in E$. $P = (P_V, P_E)$ is the collection of all properties. In the following we use the notation $i.x = P_V(i).x$ for property x of vertex $i \in V$ and $(i, j).y = P_E(i, j).y$ for property y of edge $(i, j) \in E$, respectively. The separation of structure and properties is an important design aspect of GraphX as many applications preserve the structure of the graph while changing its properties, as we also do in S2X.

In RDF [8] the basic notion of data modeling is a so-called *triple* $t = (s, p, o)$ where s is called *subject*, p *predicate* and o *object*, respectively. It can be interpreted as an edge from s to o labeled with p, $s \xrightarrow{p} o$. An RDF dataset is a set

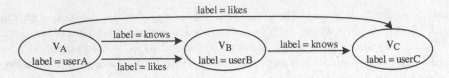

Fig. 1. Property graph representation of RDF graph G_1

of triples and hence forms a directed labeled graph. The simplicity and flexibility of RDF allows to model any kind of knowledge about arbitrary resources, represented by global identifiers (*IRIs*), e.g. the IRI for Leonardo da Vinci in DBpedia is http://dbpedia.org/resource/Leonardo_da_Vinci.

We now define how to represent an RDF graph $G = \{t_1, \ldots, t_n\}$ in the property graph data model of GraphX. Let $S(G) = \{s \mid \exists p, o : t = (s, p, o) \in G\}$ be the set of all subjects in G. The sets of all predicates $P(G)$ and all objects $O(G)$ are defined accordingly. Then $PG(P) = (V, E, P)$ is the corresponding property graph for G with $V = S(G) \cup O(G)$, $E = \{(s, o) \mid \exists t = (s, p, o) \in G\}$, $P_V.label : V \to S(G) \cup O(G)$ and $P_E.label : E \to P(G)$. IRIs cannot be used as vertex identifiers in GraphX as it requires 64-bit integers for efficiency reasons. We use the provided `zipWithUniqueID` function of Spark to derive unique integer IDs for all subjects and objects in G and preserve the original terms in the *label* property. Hence, every triple $t = (s, p, o) \in G$ is represented by two vertices $v_s, v_o \in V$, an edge $(v_s, v_o) \in E$ and properties $v_s.label = s$, $v_o.label = o$, $(v_s, v_o).label = p$.

For example, the corresponding property graph representation of an RDF graph $G_1 = \{(userA, knows, userB), (userA, likes, userB), (userA, likes, userC), (userB, knows, userC)\}$ is illustrated in Fig. 1. For brevity, we use a simplified notation of RDF without IRIs.

4 Query Processing in S2X

SPARQL [10] is the W3C recommended query language for RDF. It combines graph pattern matching with additional more relational-style operators like OPTIONAL and FILTER to produce a set of so-called *solution mappings*, i.e. it does not produce triples and hence is not closed. For example, the SPARQL query Q in Listing 1.1 retrieves a single result (or solution mapping) for the RDF graph G_1 in Sect. 3: $\{(?A \to userA, ?B \to userB, ?C \to userC)\}$

Listing 1.1. SPARQL query Q

```
SELECT * WHERE {
  ?A knows ?B . ?A likes ?B . ?B knows ?C
}
```

More formally, the basic notion in SPARQL is a so-called *triple pattern* $tp = (s', p', o')$ with $s' = \{s, ?s\}$, $p' = \{p, ?p\}$ and $o' = \{o, ?o\}$, i.e. a triple where every part is either an RDF term (called *bound*) or a variable (indicated by ? and called *unbound*). A set of triple patterns forms a *basic graph pattern* (BGP). Consequently, the query in Listing 1.1 contains a single BGP $bgp_Q = \{tp_1, tp_2, tp_3\}$ with $tp_1 = (?A, knows, ?B)$, $tp_2 = (?A, likes, ?B)$ and $tp_3 = (?B, knows, ?C)$.

Let V be the infinite set of query variables and T be the set of valid RDF terms. A *(solution) mapping* μ is a partial function $\mu : V \to T$. We call $\mu(?v)$ the variable binding of μ for $?v$ and $vars(tp)$ the set of variables contained in triple pattern tp. Abusing notation, for a triple pattern tp we call $\mu(tp)$ the triple that is obtained by substituting the variables in tp according to μ. The *domain* of μ, $dom(\mu)$, is the subset of V where μ is defined. Two mappings μ_1, μ_2 are called *compatible*, $\mu_1 \sim \mu_2$, iff for every variable $?v \in dom(\mu_1) \cap dom(\mu_2)$ it holds that $\mu_1(?v) = \mu_2(?v)$. It follows that mappings with disjoint domains are always compatible and the set-union (merge) of two compatible mappings, $\mu_1 \cup \mu_2$, is also a mapping. The answer to a triple pattern tp for an RDF graph G is a bag of mappings $\Omega_{tp} = \{\mu \mid dom(\mu) = vars(tp), \mu(tp) \in G\}$. The merge of two bags of mappings, $\Omega_1 \bowtie \Omega_2$, is defined as the merge of all compatible mappings in Ω_1 and Ω_2, $\Omega_1 \bowtie \Omega_2 = \{(\mu_1 \cup \mu_2) \mid \mu_1 \in \Omega_1, \mu_2 \in \Omega_2, \mu_1 \sim \mu_2\}$. Finally, the answer to a basic graph pattern $bgp = \{tp_1, \ldots, tp_m\}$ is then defined as the merge of all bags of mappings for $tp_1, \ldots, tp_m$, $\Omega_{bgp} = \Omega_{tp_1} \bowtie \ldots \bowtie \Omega_{tp_m}$.

All other SPARQL operators use a bag of mappings as input, i.e. they are not evaluated on the underlying RDF graph directly but on the result of one or more BGPs or other operators. Thus, the actual graph pattern matching part of SPARQL is defined by BGPs whereas the other operators are defined in a more relational fashion. In S2X we take advantage of the fact that GraphX is not a standalone specialized graph processing system but a graph abstraction library on top of Spark. BGP matching in S2X is realized in a graph-parallel manner using the GraphX API and the other operators and modifiers (OPTIONAL, FILTER, ORDER BY, PROJECTION, LIMIT and OFFSET) are realized in a more data-parallel manner using the API of Spark. Relying on Spark as the back-end of S2X, graph-parallel and data-parallel computation can be combined smoothly without the need for data movement or duplication.

Fard et al. [2] present an approach for distributed vertex-centric pattern matching on directed graphs with labeled vertices. In contrast to RDF, there are no edge labels and at most one edge between two vertices. In S2X we follow the idea of the *dual simulation* algorithm from [2] but adapt it to our property graph representation of RDF (cf. Sect. 3) and SPARQL BGP matching.

4.1   Match Candidates and Match Sets

The basic idea of our BGP matching algorithm is that every vertex in the graph stores the variables of a query where it is a possible candidate for. We start with matching all triple patterns of a BGP independently and then exchange messages between adjacent vertices to validate the match candidates until they do not change anymore.

A *match candidate* of vertex v is a 4-tuple $matchC = (v, ?var, \mu, tp)$. $?var \in vars(tp)$ is the variable of tp where v is a candidate for and μ is the corresponding mapping for tp with $dom(\mu) = vars(tp)$ and $\mu(?var) = v.label$. The set of all candidate matches of a vertex v is called *match set* of v, $matchS(v)$.

The match set of a vertex is also called its *local* match set whereas the match sets of adjacent vertices are called *remote* match sets. We store the local match set of a vertex v as a property of this vertex, $v.matchS$. Conceptually, the whole process can be summarized as follows:

1. All possibly relevant vertices (i.e. *match candidates*) are determined by matching each edge with all triple patterns from the BGP (Superstep 1 in Algorithm 1).
2. Match candidates are validated using local (Algorithm 2) and remote match sets (Algorithm 3) and invalid ones get discarded.
3. Locally changed match sets are sent to their neighbors in the graph for validation in next superstep.
4. Process continues with step 2 until no changes occur.
5. The determined subgraph(s) are collected and merged to produce the final SPARQL compliant output (Algorithm 4).

4.2 BGP Matching

Let $G = \{t_1, \ldots, t_n\}$ be an RDF graph, $PG(P)$ the corresponding property graph and $bgp = \{tp_1, \ldots, tp_m\}$ a BGP. The algorithm for BGP matching is depicted in Algorithm 1.

Initially (Superstep 1), we iterate over all edges from PG and check whether it matches any of the triple patterns from bgp, i.e. $\exists t_i \in G, tp_j \in bgp, \mu : \mu(tp_j) = t_i$. Recap that every edge of PG corresponds to a triple in G. If there is a match, we generate a *match candidate* for every variable in subject or object position of the triple pattern and store it in the corresponding vertex of PG. For example, consider a triple $t = (userA, knows, userB)$ and a triple pattern $tp = (?A, knows, ?B)$. t matches tp and hence we derive the following two match candidates:

$$matchC_1 = (v_A, ?A, (?A \rightarrow userA, ?B \rightarrow userB), tp)$$

$$matchC_2 = (v_B, ?B, (?A \rightarrow userA, ?B \rightarrow userB), tp)$$

$matchC_1$ is stored in the match set of v_A (line 7) and $matchC_2$ in the match set of v_B (line 10), respectively. Recap that v_A is the vertex for $userA$ in the corresponding property graph and v_B the vertex for $userB$, respectively (cf. Fig. 1). If there is a triple pattern from bgp that does not find any match, the algorithm terminates as bgp cannot be fulfilled (line 12). After this initialization, the match sets of all vertices yield an overestimation of the result for bgp as they do not take into account that the generated mappings of the match candidates have to be compatible. For example, consider again G_1 from Sect. 3 and bgp_Q from query Q in Listing 1.1. Table 1 lists the match sets of vertices v_A, v_B and v_C after the first superstep of Algorithm 1.

Algorithm 1. BGPMATCHING

---

input: $PG(P) : (V, E, P)$
$\qquad BGP : Set\langle TriplePattern : (s, p, o)\rangle$
output: $matchVertices : Set\langle v : V \rangle$

1 $matchTp : Set\langle TriplePattern\rangle \leftarrow \emptyset, matchVertices \leftarrow \emptyset$
   // Superstep 1
2 **foreach** $(v_s, v_o) \in E$ **do**
3 $\quad$ **foreach** $tp : TriplePattern \in BGP$ **do**
4 $\quad\quad$ **if** $\exists \mu : \mu(tp) = (v_s.label, (v_s, v_o).label, v_o.label)$ **then**
5 $\quad\quad\quad$ $matchTP \leftarrow matchTP \cup tp$
6 $\quad\quad\quad$ **if** $isVar(tp.s)$ **then**
7 $\quad\quad\quad\quad$ $v_s.matchS \leftarrow v_s.matchS \cup (v_s, tp.s, \mu, tp)$
8 $\quad\quad\quad\quad$ $matchVertices \leftarrow matchVertices \cup v_s$
9 $\quad\quad\quad$ **if** $isVar(tp.o)$ **then**
10 $\quad\quad\quad\quad$ $v_o.matchS \leftarrow v_o.matchS \cup (v_o, tp.o, \mu, tp)$
11 $\quad\quad\quad\quad$ $matchVertices \leftarrow matchVertices \cup v_o$
12 **if** $matchTP \neq BGP$ **then return** $\emptyset$
13 **else** $activeVertices \leftarrow matchVertices$

   // Superstep 2...n
14 **while** $activeVertives \neq \emptyset$ **do**
15 $\quad$ $tmpVertices \leftarrow \emptyset$
16 $\quad$ **foreach** $v : V \in activeVertices$ **do**
17 $\quad\quad$ $old \leftarrow v.matchS$
18 $\quad\quad$ **if** $\#superstep > 2$ **then**
19 $\quad\quad\quad$ validateRemoteMatchSet(v, BGP)
20 $\quad\quad$ validateLocalMatchSet(v, BGP)
21 $\quad\quad$ **if** $v.matchS = \emptyset$ **then**
22 $\quad\quad\quad$ $matchVertices \leftarrow matchVertices \setminus \{v\}$
23 $\quad\quad$ **if** $v.matchS \neq old \parallel \#superstep = 2$ **then**
24 $\quad\quad\quad$ $tmpVertices \leftarrow tmpVertices \cup v.neighbors$
25 $\quad\quad\quad$ sendToAllNeighbors$(v, v.matchS)$
26 $\quad$ $activeVertices \leftarrow tmpVertices$
27 **return** $matchVertices$

Algorithm 2. VALIDATELOCALMATCHSET

---

input: $v : V, BGP : Set\langle TriplePattern : (s, p, o)\rangle$

1 **foreach** $matchC_1 : (v, ?var, \mu, tp) \in v.matchS$ **do**
2 $\quad$ **foreach** $tp \in BGP \neq matchC_1.tp$ **do**
3 $\quad\quad$ **if** $matchC_1.?var \in vars(tp)$ **then**
4 $\quad\quad\quad$ **if** $\nexists matchC_2 : (v, ?var, \mu, tp) \in v.matchS :$
5 $\quad\quad\quad$ $tp = matchC_2.tp$ &
6 $\quad\quad\quad$ $matchC_1.?var = matchC_2.?var$ &
7 $\quad\quad\quad$ $matchC_1.\mu \sim matchC_2.\mu$ **then**
8 $\quad\quad\quad\quad$ $v.matchS \leftarrow v.matchS \setminus \{matchC_1\}$
9 $\quad\quad\quad\quad$ **break**

Algorithm 3. VALIDATEREMOTEMATCHSET

---

input: $v : V$, $remoteMS : Set\langle matchC : (v, ?var, \mu, tp)\rangle$

1 **foreach** $matchC_1 : (v, ?var, \mu, tp) \in v.matchS$ **do**
2      $?var2 \leftarrow vars(matchC_1.tp) \setminus \{matchC_1.?var\}$
3   **if** $?var2 \neq \emptyset$ **then**
4   **if** $\nexists\ matchC_2 : (v, ?var, \mu, tp) \in remoteMS :$
5              $?var2 = matchC_2.?var$ &
6              $matchC_1.tp = matchC_2.tp$ &
7              $matchC_1.\mu \sim matchC_2.\mu$ **then**
8                  $v.matchS \leftarrow v.matchS \setminus \{matchC_1\}$

Table 1. Match candidates & sets in every Superstep of BGP matching (G_1, bgp_Q) with $tp_1 = (?A, knows, ?B)$, $tp_2 = (?A, likes, ?B)$, and $tp_3 = (?B, knows, ?C)$

	Superstep 1			Superstep 2		
v	$?var$	μ	tp	$?var$	μ	tp
v_A	$?A$	$(?A \rightarrow userA, ?B \rightarrow userB)$	tp_1	$?A$	$(?A \rightarrow userA, ?B \rightarrow userB)$	tp_1
	$?B$	$(?B \rightarrow userA, ?C \rightarrow userB)$	tp_3	—		
	$?A$	$(?A \rightarrow userA, ?B \rightarrow userB)$	tp_2	$?A$	$(?A \rightarrow userA, ?B \rightarrow userB)$	tp_2
	$?A$	$(?A \rightarrow userA, ?B \rightarrow userC)$	tp_2	—		
v_B	$?B$	$(?A \rightarrow userA, ?B \rightarrow userB)$	tp_1	$?B$	$(?A \rightarrow userA, ?B \rightarrow userB)$	tp_1
	$?C$	$(?B \rightarrow userA, ?C \rightarrow userB)$	tp_3	$?C$	$(?B \rightarrow userA, ?C \rightarrow userB)$	tp_3
	$?B$	$(?A \rightarrow userA, ?B \rightarrow userB)$	tp_2	$?B$	$(?A \rightarrow userA, ?B \rightarrow userB)$	tp_2
	$?A$	$(?A \rightarrow userB, ?B \rightarrow userC)$	tp_1	—		
	$?B$	$(?B \rightarrow userB, ?C \rightarrow userC)$	tp_3	$?B$	$(?B \rightarrow userB, ?C \rightarrow userC)$	tp_3
v_C	$?B$	$(?A \rightarrow userA, ?B \rightarrow userC)$	tp_2	—		
	$?B$	$(?A \rightarrow userB, ?B \rightarrow userC)$	tp_1	—		
	$?C$	$(?B \rightarrow userB, ?C \rightarrow userC)$	tp_3	$?C$	$(?B \rightarrow userB, ?C \rightarrow userC)$	tp_3

	Superstep 3			Superstep 4		
v	$?var$	μ	tp	$?var$	μ	tp
v_A	$?A$	$(?A \rightarrow userA, ?B \rightarrow userB)$	tp_1	$?A$	$(?A \rightarrow userA, ?B \rightarrow userB)$	tp_1
	—			—		
	$?A$	$(?A \rightarrow userA, ?B \rightarrow userB)$	tp_2	$?A$	$(?A \rightarrow userA, ?B \rightarrow userB)$	tp_2
	—			—		
v_B	$?B$	$(?A \rightarrow userA, ?B \rightarrow userB)$	tp_1	$?B$	$(?A \rightarrow userA, ?B \rightarrow userB)$	tp_1
	—			—		
	$?B$	$(?A \rightarrow userA, ?B \rightarrow userB)$	tp_2	$?B$	$(?A \rightarrow userA, ?B \rightarrow userB)$	tp_2
	—			—		
	$?B$	$(?B \rightarrow userB, ?C \rightarrow userC)$	tp_3	$?B$	$(?B \rightarrow userB, ?C \rightarrow userC)$	tp_3
v_C	—			—		
	—			—		
	$?C$	$(?B \rightarrow userB, ?C \rightarrow userC)$	tp_3	$?C$	$(?B \rightarrow userB, ?C \rightarrow userC)$	tp_3

In every following superstep $(2\ldots n)$, each vertex checks the validity of its local match set and sends it to its neighbors in the graph (both edge directions), if there are any changes. That is, in superstep i a vertex has access to the remote match sets of its neighbors from superstep $i-1$. The validation process can be grouped in two subtasks:

(1) If a vertex v is a candidate for variable $?var$, witnessed by a match candidate $matchC$ for $?var$, it must have a match candidate regarding $?var$ for all triple patterns $tp \in bgp$ that contain $?var$, i.e. $?var \in vars(tp)$. Furthermore, the mappings of all these match candidates must be compatible. Otherwise, $matchC$ is removed from the match set of v. This validation task only needs to consider the local match set of v and thus can already be executed in superstep 2 where remote match sets are not yet available. The validation of local match sets is depicted in Algorithm 2.

(2) Consider match candidate $matchC_1 = (v, ?var, \mu, tp)$ for vertex v where triple pattern tp contains another variable $?var2 \neq ?var$. Then there must be a neighbor of v connected by $tp.p$ which is a candidate for $?var2$. That is, there must exist a corresponding match candidate $matchC_2$ for $?var2$ in the remote match sets of v where the mappings of $matchC_1$ and $matchC_2$ are compatible. If not, $matchC_1$ is removed from the match set of v. The validation of remote match sets is depicted in Algorithm 3.

Continuing the example, in superstep 2 vertices v_A, v_B and v_C validate their local match sets without knowing the remote match sets of their neighbors, respectively. For example, v_A removes $(v_A, ?B, (?B \to uscrA, ?C \to userB), tp_3)$ from its local match set because in order to be a candidate for $?B$ it must also have match candidates for $?B$ with triple patterns tp_1 and tp_2. These do not exist as v_A has no incoming $knows$ and $likes$ edges. In addition, v_A also removes $(v_A, ?A, (?A \to userA, ?B \to userC), tp_2)$ as there is no match candidate for $?A$ with triple pattern tp_1 which is compatible to it. After superstep 2, v_A is not a candidate for $?B$ anymore as its match set contains no match candidate for $?B$ (cf. Superstep 2 in Table 1).

In superstep 3 v_B removes $(v_B, ?C, (?B \to userA, ?C \to userB), tp_3)$ from its local match set as v_A removed the corresponding match candidate for $?B$ in superstep 2 and hence it is not contained in the remote match sets at v_B in superstep 3. In superstep 4 the match sets do not change anymore and hence the algorithm terminates yielding v_A as a match for $?A$, v_B for $?B$ and v_C for $?C$, respectively.

4.3   From Graph-Parallel to Data-Parallel

The BGP matching algorithm determines the subgraph(s) of G (resp. PG) that match bgp, represented by the set of vertices that match some part of bgp ($matchVertices$) and the mappings for triple patterns stored in the match sets of each of these vertices. However, in SPARQL the result of a BGP is defined as a bag of mappings. To produce this final bag of mappings we have to merge the partial mappings of all matching vertices. This is depicted in Algorithm 4. For every triple pattern from bgp we collect the corresponding mappings from the match sets of all vertices (line 6), which gives us m bags of mappings $(\Omega_{tp_1}, \ldots, \Omega_{tp_m})$. These bags are incrementally merged to produce the final result (line 7). A merge of two bags of mappings, $\Omega_1 \bowtie \Omega_2$, can be implemented as a join between the mappings from Ω_1 and Ω_2 where the join attributes are the variables that occur in both sides, i.e. $dom(\Omega_1) \cap dom(\Omega_2)$. This is a data-parallel operation using the API of Spark which result is a collection (RDD) of mappings for bgp. Concluding the example, Algorithm 4 outputs a single solution mapping for bgp_Q: $\{(?A \rightarrow userA, ?B \rightarrow userB, ?C \rightarrow userC)\}$.

Algorithm 4. GENERATESOLUTIONMAPPINGS

---

input: $matchVertices : Set\langle v : V \rangle$,
      $BGP : Set\langle TriplePattern : (s, p, o) \rangle$
output: $\Omega_{bgp} : Set\langle \mu : SolutionMapping \rangle$

1 $\Omega_{bgp} \leftarrow \emptyset$
2 **foreach** $tp : TriplePattern \in BGP$ **do**
3    $\quad \Omega_{tp} \leftarrow \emptyset$
4    $\quad$ **foreach** $v : V \in matchVertices$ **do**
5    $\quad\quad$ **if** $\exists\ matchC : (v, ?var, \mu, tp) \in v.matchS : matchC.tp = tp$ **then**
6    $\quad\quad\quad \Omega_{tp} \leftarrow \Omega_{tp} \cup matchC.\mu$
7    $\quad \Omega_{bgp} \leftarrow \Omega_{bgp} \bowtie \Omega_{tp}$
8 **return** Ω_{bgp}

The remaining SPARQL operators are implemented using data-parallel operators from the Spark API, e.g. OPTIONAL is implemented by a left-outer join and FILTER as a filter function applied to a collection (RDD) of mappings.

5   Experiments

The experiments were performed on a small cluster with ten machines, each equipped with a six core Xeon E5-2420 1.9 GHz CPU, 2×2 TB disks and 32 GB RAM. We used the Hadoop distribution of Cloudera CDH 5.3.0 with Spark 1.2.0 and Pig 0.12. The machines were connected via Gigabit network. This is actually a low-end configuration as typical Hadoop nodes have 256 GB RAM, 12 disks or more and are connected via 10 Gigabit network or faster. We assigned 24 GB RAM for Spark where 60 % was used to cache the graph in memory. Spark has manifold configuration parameters that can have severe impact on performance. In our tests, adjusting these parameters improved the execution time of certain queries up to an order of magnitude while revealing a significant slowdown for others. Hence, we decided to use the default configuration of Spark and GraphX for comparability reasons, although some queries could be significantly improved this way. GraphX is in a very early stage of development and not yet recommended for production usage, so one can expect substantial progress in this area with future versions.

The main goal of this preliminary evaluation was to confirm the overall feasibility of our approach and identify possible flaws that we should address for future revisions of S2X. To this end, we compare the current version of S2X with PigSPARQL [11], a SPARQL query engine on top of *Apache Pig*, which has proven to be a competitive baseline for SPARQL query processing on Hadoop. We decided to use the Waterloo SPARQL Diversity Test Suite (WatDiv) [1] as, in contrast to other existing benchmarks, its focus is to benchmark systems against varying query shapes to identify their strengths and weaknesses. The WatDiv data model combines an e-commerce scenario with a kind of social network. We generated datasets with scale factors 10, 100 and 1000 which corresponds to 10 K, 100 K and 1 M users, respectively. In total, the graph of the largest dataset (SF1000) contained more than 10 M vertices. The generation of the GraphX property graph for this dataset took 12 min. The graph is loaded in the memory cache of Spark once and used for all queries. Match sets of vertices are cleared after every query execution. For PigSPARQL, the generation of its vertical partitioned data model took 90 s.

WatDiv comes with a set of 20 predefined query templates which can be grouped in four categories according to their shape: *star* (S), *linear* (L), *snowflake* (F) and *complex* (C). For every template we instantiated five queries, yielding 100 queries per dataset. The average runtime for each query template is listed in Table 2. For S2X, we split the overall runtime in two parts: BGP matching (cf. Algorithm 1) and generation of solution mappings (cf. Algorithm 4). This way, we can separate these two parts as the output format is merely a matter of choice and we could output the matching subgraph(s) just as well. For PigSPARQL, this separation is not applicable as it is purely data-parallel without a graph abstraction.

Overall, S2X outperforms PigSPARQL by up to an order of magnitude, especially for smaller graphs. Figure 2 illustrates the geometric mean per query group, demonstrating that S2X performs best for star and linear queries. The runtimes get more closer with larger graphs which demonstrates the excellent scalability of PigSPARQL due to its underlying MapReduce framework. For star queries, we can observe that S2X computes the BGP matching pretty fast and generation of mappings consumes a considerable amount of the overall runtime, especially for S1. This can be attributed to the fact that the generation of mappings depends on the number of triple patterns in the query and S1 is the largest of the star queries. The more patterns, the more joins are needed to compute the final output. This also applies in similar manner to PigSPARQL where the general idea is to incrementally join the results of every triple pattern. It is interesting to notice that this is not true for the BGP matching part of S2X where the runtime is not primarily attributed to the size of the query but rather to its shape and the size of the matching subgraph. In S2X we match all triple patterns in one initial superstep and subsequent supersteps are used to discard invalid match candidates. This is also the reason why star queries exhibit a good performance in S2X, since in every superstep a vertex sends its match set to its neighbors which adapt their own match sets accordingly. That means, if a query defines a path of length i, it takes i supersteps to propagate this information from one

Table 2. Runtimes (in s) for S2X (separated by BGP matching and generation of solution mappings) and PigSPARQL, GM = geometric mean

Q	SF10		SF100		SF1000	
	S2X	PS	S2X	PS	S2X	PS
S1	3.56, 1.78	42	7.87, 3.39	43	40.1, 23.1	57
S2	1.85, 0.63	41	3.47, 1.55	41	23.2, 5.34	46
S3	1.54, 0.42	41	3.05, 0.97	42	19.7, 2.77	44
S4	1.50, 0.54	41	3.17, 1.65	42	23.6, 10.4	46
S5	1.37, 0.38	41	2.68, 0.81	42	21.3, 2.47	44
S6	2.43, 0.94	41	3.68, 2.23	42	23.5, 9.09	46
S7	1.97, 0.92	41	3.87, 1.76	41	25.4, 9.03	46
L1	2.13, 1.16	77	5.12, 3.41	80	80.1, 122.4	87
L2	1.75, 0.73	78	4.46, 3.21	80	119.5, 215.4	83
L3	1.39, 0.35	41	2.85, 0.74	42	19.3, 2.64	46
L4	1.42, 0.23	41	2.17, 0.45	42	13.4, 0.99	44
L5	1.68, 0.75	79	4.18, 3.28	81	124.1, 224.4	82
F1	2.34, 3.04	110	4.53, 8.22	110	33.0, 19.9	115
F2	2.53, 1.16	80	5.02, 2.45	81	27.0, 9.73	83
F3	10.2, 13.5	80	57.1, 101	80	4571, 10837	92
F4	3.27, 2.70	80	7.83, 5.31	81	56.9, 58	85
F5	5.85, 4.66	80	11.9, 13	81	75.4, 97.5	99
C1	15.4, 51.5	157	34.95, 118	158	199.9, 389.6	170
C2	28.9, 49.8	237	124.7, 222	241	1217, 2652	272
C3	5.7, 1.27	42	11.6, 3.7	51	82.6, 14.9	64
GM	3.01, 1.57	64	6.73, 4.30	64.4	41.0, 18.6	71

vertex to the other (and another i for propagating any changes back). For star queries the path length is only one, thus less supersteps are needed.

In general, most queries scale well in S2X but for the largest graph with more than 10M vertices the runtimes of some queries increase disproportionately, especially for F3 and C2. This can be attributed to the low cluster configuration and the very large size of intermediate results of these queries which exceeded the available memory forcing Spark to spill to disk. For some other queries (e.g. L2, L5) we have noticed that a lot of time was spent for Java garbage collection which also significantly slow downs execution.

Through this comprehensive pre-evaluation, we identified some shortcomings in S2X that we should address in future work: (1) Match set sizes of vertices can be very skewed, especially for graphs with power-law degree distribution. This is also true for WatDiv where some vertices (users) can have hundreds of edges with same label (predicate) and others only a very few. Currently, we send the whole

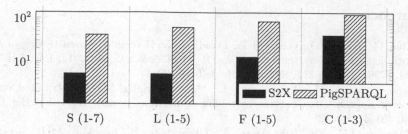

Fig. 2. GM (in s) per query group for S2X (BGP matching + generation of solution mappings) and PigSPARQL (WatDiv SF100, log scale)

match set of a vertex to its neighbors which can lead to very high network I/O. To save network bandwidth, we could cache the match sets of neighbor vertices and only send the changes from one superstep to the next. However, this will increase memory consumption of the property graph. Furthermore, the validation of large match sets (cf. Algorithms 2 and 3) gets expensive and stragglers can slow down the overall progress. More efficient data structures can mitigate this effect. (2) Graph partitioning in GraphX is optimized to distribute the workload for applications that are performed on the whole graph like PageRank. However, a typical SPARQL query defines a small connected subgraph pattern which can lead to highly unbalanced workloads. While this is a common problem in distributed systems, one way to address it is to adjust the partitioning to the actual task. (3) As we match all triple patterns at once in the first superstep, we generate a large overestimation of the final result. For queries that consist of many unselective (unbound subject and object) and one selective triple pattern (bound subject or object), this leads to many and large intermediate match sets where most match candidates are discarded later on. Most WatDiv queries reveal this kind of structure. In these cases, we could order the triple patterns by selectivity estimation and match only one (or some) in a superstep and send the match sets along the edges that are defined in the next triple pattern.

6   Conclusion

In this paper we introduced S2X, an RDF engine for Hadoop that combines graph-parallel with data-parallel computation to answer SPARQL queries. We defined a property graph representation of RDF for GraphX and designed a vertex-centric algorithm for BGP matching. Our experiments using a state of the art benchmark covering various query shapes illustrate that the combination of both graph-parallel and data-parallel abstraction can be beneficial compared to a purely data-parallel execution. For future work, we will address the current shortcomings of S2X that we have identified in our experiments to improve the scalability for graphs with power-law degree distribution and provide an extended evaluation including a comparison with other distributed in-memory frameworks for Hadoop.

References

1. Aluç, G., Hartig, O., Özsu, M.T., Daudjee, K.: Diversified stress testing of RDF data management systems. In: Mika, P., et al. (eds.) ISWC 2014, Part I. LNCS, vol. 8796, pp. 197–212. Springer, Heidelberg (2014)
2. Fard, A., Nisar, M., Ramaswamy, L., Miller, J., Saltz, M.: A distributed vertex-centric approach for pattern matching in massive graphs. In: IEEE Big Data, pp. 403–411 (2013)
3. Gonzalez, J.E., Xin, R.S., Dave, A., Crankshaw, D., Franklin, M.J., Stoica, I.: GraphX: graph processing in a distributed dataflow framework. In: 11th USENIX OSDI 2014, pp. 599–613 (2014)
4. Goodman, E.L., Grunwald, D.: Using vertex-centric programming platforms to implement SPARQL queries on large graphs. In: IA3 (2014)
5. Han, M., Daudjee, K., Ammar, K., Özsu, M.T., Wang, X., Jin, T.: An experimental comparison of pregel-like graph processing systems. PVLDB 7(12), 1047–1058 (2014)
6. Huang, J., Abadi, D.J., Ren, K.: Scalable SPARQL querying of large RDF graphs. PVLDB 4(11), 1123–1134 (2011)
7. Husain, M.F., McGlothlin, J.P., Masud, M.M., Khan, L.R., Thuraisingham, B.M.: Heuristics-based query processing for large RDF graphs using cloud computing. IEEE TKDE 23(9), 1312–1327 (2011)
8. Manola, F., Miller, E., McBride, B.: RDF Primer (2004). http://www.w3.org/TR/rdf-primer/
9. Papailiou, N., Konstantinou, I., Tsoumakos, D., Karras, P., Koziris, N.: H2RDF+: High-performance distributed joins over large-scale RDF graphs. In: IEEE Big Data, pp. 255–263 (2013)
10. Prud'hommeaux, E., Seaborne, A.: SPARQL query language for RDF (2008). http://www.w3.org/TR/rdf-sparql-query/
11. Schätzle, A., Przyjaciel-Zablocki, M., Hornung, T., Lausen, G.: PigSPARQL: A SPARQL query processing baseline for big data. In: Proceedings of the ISWC 2013 Posters & Demonstrations Track, pp. 241–244 (2013)
12. Schätzle, A., Przyjaciel-Zablocki, M., Neu, A., Lausen, G.: Sempala: interactive SPARQL query processing on hadoop. In: Mika, P., et al. (eds.) ISWC 2014, Part I. LNCS, vol. 8796, pp. 164–179. Springer, Heidelberg (2014)
13. Zaharia, M., Chowdhury, M., Das, T., Dave, A., Ma, J., McCauly, M., Franklin, M.J., Shenker, S., Stoica, I.: Fast and interactive analytics over hadoop data with spark. USENIX; Login 34(4), 45–51 (2012)
14. Zaharia, M., Chowdhury, M., Das, T., Dave, A., Ma, J., McCauly, M., Franklin, M.J., Shenker, S., Stoica, I.: Resilient distributed datasets: a fault-tolerant abstraction for in-memory cluster computing. In: Proceedings of the 9th USENIX Symposium on Networked Systems Design and Implementation, NSDI, pp. 15–28 (2012)
15. Zeng, K., Yang, J., Wang, H., Shao, B., Wang, Z.: A distributed graph engine for web scale RDF data. In: PVLDB 2013, pp. 265–276 (2013)

The Time Has Come: Traversal and Reachability in Time-Varying Graphs

Max Wildemann[1], Michael Rudolf[1,2]([⊠]), and Marcus Paradies[1,2]

[1] SAP SE, 69190 Walldorf, Germany
{max.wildemann,michael.rudolf01,m.paradies}@sap.com
[2] Database Technology Group, TU Dresden, 01187 Dresden, Germany

Abstract. Increasingly, enterprises require efficient graph processing capabilities to store and analyze the evolution of the graph topology over time. While a static graph captures information about the connectedness of vertices at a certain point in time, a *time-varying graph* keeps track of every data manipulation—insertion and removal of a vertex or an edge—performed on the graph and allows detecting topological changes, such as cluster growth and subgraph densification, and discovering behavioral patterns of the connected entities in the graph. Although temporal graph processing has been an active research area in the past decade, most well-known graph algorithms are defined on static graphs only.

In this paper we study the problem of graph traversals and reachability in the presence of a temporal dimension and derive three classes of temporal traversals from a set of realistic use cases. We validate our prototypical implementations against two graph processing systems, a columnar graph execution engine and a native graph database management system. Our experimental evaluation on a large real-world graph dataset demonstrates the generality and applicability of our solution and shows the scalability of our proposed temporal traversal operators to different graph sizes.

1 Introduction

In recent years, there has been an abundance of network data from various domains, such as social networks, communication networks, biological networks, and transportation networks. A large body of research has been conducted on identifying and computing properties of the graph topology—betweenness centrality measures, sizes of strongly connected components, and graph clustering, to name a few. Decreasing hardware prices for volatile and non-volatile storage and the increased demand to gather deep insights about the dynamics of evolving graphs are the key drivers to analyze not only a single and static graph snapshot containing the most recent data, but also to consider historical data and periods of time. The addition of a temporal dimension is a natural extension of the property graph data model and allows modelling the temporal validity of certain facts—vertices and edges—in the graph. Conceptually a *time-varying graph* [3] can be thought of as a sequence of graph snapshots, each one corresponding to a single discrete point in time and containing a set of vertices

© Springer International Publishing Switzerland 2016
F. Wang et al. (Eds.): Big-O(Q) and DMAH 2015, LNCS 9579, pp. 169–183, 2016.
DOI: 10.1007/978-3-319-41576-5_13

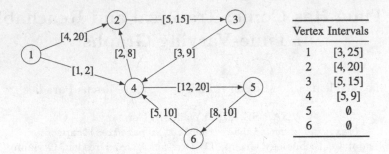

Fig. 1. Traversal on a graph with temporal edge attribute, start vertices $S = \{1\}$, and query interval $Q = [3, 25]$.

and edges that were valid at that instant. Figure 1 depicts an example of such a graph and the result of a temporal graph query with a start vertex $S = \{1\}$ and a query interval $Q = [3, 25]$. It traverses the graph starting at vertex 1 and returns each reachable vertex together with the time interval during which it is reachable. A typical application scenario for this type of query is a graph modeling power suppliers, consumers, and their interconnections. Given a vertex—a power station—an example query is: find all households that were affected by a power link failure in a given time interval.

Although temporal graph processing is a rather new field with many unexplored research directions, *relational-temporal* processing has been in the focus since the 1980s. Naturally, the most basic concepts of temporal data processing are based upon *system time (transaction time)* and *business time (valid time)*. System time denotes the time interval when the corresponding fact is stored in the database, whereas business time refers to the time validity of the fact in the real world. Based on these orthogonal temporal concepts, a variety of temporal operators are defined, including *time travel, temporal join,* and *temporal aggregation*. For temporal graph processing, however, no such operators exist yet.

Graph processing on web-scale graphs attracted many researchers to design, implement, and evaluate various distributed graph processing systems running on large clusters of machines with commodity hardware. Although offline graph analysis is an important field of research and a growing demand also from large business companies, there is also an increased need to store, manipulate, and process web-scale graphs in a transactional context within a database management system. Specialized graph database management systems (GDBMS) provide a clear graph abstraction and a native storage and retrieval of graph data. Although there have been initial studies on supporting temporal graphs in GDBMS, there is no native support yet either on the execution layer or on the query layer [4].

In this paper we take a deeper look at graph traversals—a fundamental building block for graph processing—and discuss their semantics in time-varying graphs. Our goal is not to provide a single algorithm that solves a specific temporal graph problem, but instead to generalize typical query patterns over time-varying graphs in the form of graph operator specifications. This follows the approach of traditional temporal data management, which reconsidered relational operators in the presence of a temporal dimension. Our operators are not system-specific and can be integrated into any GDBMS or RDBMS that supports graph processing. We summarize our contributions as follows:

- We describe a set of realistic use cases combining graph data with a temporal dimension and outline typical traversal patterns on temporal graphs.
- Based on these representative use cases, we derive three different classes of temporal graph traversals, describe how they can be formulated as native temporal traversal operators, and provide efficient algorithms for their implementation.
- We implemented all three traversal classes in two systems—GRAPHITE, a graph-aware columnar query execution engine and Sparksee, a popular native GDBMS—and evaluate them against real-world datasets of varying size.

The remainder of the paper is structured as follows. In Sect. 2 we describe realistic use cases that can benefit from a graph traversal operation that is able to handle dynamic graphs. We introduce a set of three novel traversal type classes that we derived from our use cases in Sect. 3 and discuss implementation details in Sect. 4. We evaluate our temporal traversal algorithms on two different database systems and present the results in Sect. 5. Section 6 discusses related work before we summarize our findings in Sect. 7.

2   Use Cases

Before going into the details of temporal graph traversal, we describe two motivational use cases that benefit from such a functionality.

2.1   Power Grid

A power distribution network (or simply power grid) is often modeled as a graph with one or more power plants, various energy consuming households, and infrastructure nodes in between forming the set of vertices. The edges represent the power lines connecting some of the above nodes. In this scenario there is the necessity for periodical maintenance of the infrastructure components in order to prevent a failure disconnecting households from all power sources. Potentially problematic is that the maintenance itself causes a downtime of one or more lines. Thus, the challenge is to create a maintenance schedule that does not partition the network by disconnecting all paths between power plants and one or more households. Temporal graph traversal can be used to validate those schedules by augmenting each vertex and edge with a validity interval expressing when it is available. Starting from the power plant, the traversal returns all reachable vertices along with an interval for each of them expressing when the vertex is reachable. Temporarily disconnected vertices have a gap in their reachability interval, while completely unreachable vertices do not show up at all.

2.2   Spread of Information

The analysis of information propagation has a variety of practical applications, from communication networks to the spreading of diseases. Consider a group of people talking via phone or writing emails to each other. At first sight, these two scenarios seem to be very similar but the topology of the modeling graph is not. Obviously, persons are the vertices of the graph, while each call or sent email is represented by an edge between the two communication partners. Emails with more than one receiver can be modeled as multiple edges. Note that the two considered communication types differ in the way information are exchanged: while an email is sent at a specific point in time, a phone call lasts some time. Therefore, edges representing emails are only valid at that one point in time whereas the validity of an edge representing a phone call is modeled by an interval. Additionally, the flow of information during a call is bidirectional in contrast to an email, which is why a phone call should be modeled as two opposing edges.

Both graphs are rather different, but the question concerning possible flows of information is the same. Temporal graph traversal can be used to calculate all possible flows during a given period of time. Starting at the vertex where the information has its origin, the result will be a set of vertices along with their reachability intervals. All returned persons possibly know the information and the beginning of their reachability interval is the earliest point in time at which they could have received it. However, it is not guaranteed that they are informed since it is not known which pieces of information are really passed during a communication. If no other communication channels exist, all persons that are not part of the result are definitely unaware of the information.

3   Temporal Graph Traversals

In this section we develop three types of temporal graph traversal, starting with an explanation of a non-temporal graph traversal and extending it accordingly.

The input of a graph traversal is a traversal configuration: let $G = (V, E)$ be a directed graph where V is the set of vertices and $E = V \times V$ the set of edges, a traversal configuration is a tuple $\tau := (S, p_v, p_e)$ consisting of a set of start vertices $S \subseteq V$, a vertex predicate p_v, and an edge predicate p_e.

Both predicates, p_v and p_e, consist of several atomic conditions combined with $\wedge$ or $\vee$. They are used to filter vertices or edges by their type or to enforce that an attribute value is in a specified range. Applying both filters results in a set of effective vertices $V_e \subseteq V$ and effective edges $E_e \subseteq E$. Given a traversal configuration τ, a traversal algorithm returns the set $R \subseteq V$ of reachable vertices. Well known example algorithms working that way are *breadth-first search* (BFS) and *depth-first search* (DFS).

In this paper we consider *time-varying graphs*, which means that each edge has two additional integer attributes expressing the lower and upper bound of its validity interval. This interval can be queried with the function *validity* : $E \to \mathbb{N} \times \mathbb{N}$. For the sake of convenience, we introduce the two functions *lower* : $\mathbb{N} \times \mathbb{N} \to \mathbb{N}$ and *upper* : $\mathbb{N} \times \mathbb{N} \to \mathbb{N}$, which return the lower or upper bound of a

---

Algorithm 1. TRAVERSAL

Input: A graph G and a temporal traversal configuration τ^T
Output: Set of vertices and their reachability intervals

1   $V_e \leftarrow p_v(V)$
2   $E_e \leftarrow \{(v,w) \in p_e(E) | v, w \in V_e\}$
3   $R \leftarrow S$
4   $W \leftarrow S$
5   **for** $v \in S$ **do**
6   $\quad$ $current_v = Q$
7   **repeat**
8   $\quad$ $W' \leftarrow \emptyset$
9   $\quad$ **for** $v \in W$ **do**
10 $\quad\quad$ **for** $(v,w) \in E_e$ **do**
11 $\quad\quad\quad$ $calcOutstanding(Q, (v,w))$
12 $\quad\quad\quad$ **if** $outstanding_w \neq \emptyset$ **then**
13 $\quad\quad\quad\quad$ $W' \leftarrow W' \cup \{w\}$
14 $\quad$ **for** $v \in W \cup W'$ **do**
15 $\quad\quad$ $finished_v \leftarrow finished_v \cup current_v$
16 $\quad\quad$ $current_v \leftarrow outstanding_v$
17 $\quad\quad$ $outstanding_v \leftarrow \emptyset$
18 $\quad$ $W \leftarrow W'$
19 $\quad$ $R \leftarrow R \cup W$
20 **until** $W = \emptyset$
21 **return** $(R, finished)$

---

given interval. Note that the validity of a vertex can also be expressed using the intervals assigned to its incoming and outgoing edges. If a vertex is not valid, none of these edges can be either. Therefore, the validity interval of an edge is always within the intersection of the validity intervals of its vertices.

To meaningfully traverse this type of graph, τ is extended to a temporal traversal configuration $\tau^T := (S, p_v, p_e, Q)$ with $Q \in \mathbb{N} \times \mathbb{N}$ denoting a query interval. The decision, whether or not an edge can be traversed, depends not only on the provided filter but also on the relation between the validity interval of the edge and the query interval. Along with the reachable vertices R, the temporal traversal returns a list of reachability intervals for each of them. As described by Allen [1], there are multiple relations between two intervals, which poses the question if those relations are equally useful for the traversal of a graph. While some of them would express travel back in time and therefore in general are not suitable, others can be used to achieve different traversal semantics. Without claiming to be exhaustive, we derived three different traversal types from the aforementioned use cases and present them in the following.

But before detailing the three types, we present a base algorithm that is common to all of them. Algorithm 1 is an abstract description of such a general temporal traversal operator. It works in a BFS fashion but uses three additional interval lists for each vertex of the graph. The list $current_v$ states for which points in time the vertex v is traversed during the current step. Therefore, at line 6, it is initialized with the query interval as its only element for all start vertices. In case a vertex v is discovered, it has to be traversed in the next step with the intervals contained in $outstanding_v$, the calculation of which depends on the traversal type. The remaining list, $finished_v$, states for which intervals all outgoing edges of v have already been traversed—thereby it serves two purposes. First of all, it is part of the result because it also represents the intervals for which a vertex is reachable after the traversal is finished. In addition to that, it is also used to ensure that no edge is traversed twice for the same point in time, which is not only crucial for the performance but also for the correctness (it replaces the cycle detection).

After the initialization, in line 7 the actual algorithm starts a loop until an iteration does not reveal new information, such as finding a so far undiscovered vertex or reaching an already known one at a new point in time. At first, the *outstanding* list for each outgoing edge of the current working set is calculated at line 11 in a traversal-specific way. If it is not empty, the target vertex of the edge is added to the working set of the next iteration. Thereafter, lines 14 to 17 update the intervals of all involved vertices. Afterwards the content of *current* can be added to the *finished* intervals and be replaced by *outstanding* for the next iteration. At the end of the loop, the working set is switched and the discovered vertices are added to the result. If the working set for the next step is empty at this point, the loop is aborted and the algorithm returns the results.

3.1   Time Stable Traversal

As the basis for the following definitions, we introduce the term *path*. Considering that edges consist of a source and target vertex, which can be queried by either $source : E \rightarrow V$ or $target : E \rightarrow V$, a path p is defined as follows:

$$p = (e_1, e_2, \ldots, e_n) \in E^n : \bigvee_{i=1}^{n-1} target(e_i) = source(e_{i+1})$$

The time stable (or just stable) traversal visits vertices that are reachable from the start vertex using an invariant path p, which entirely consists of edges valid for the whole query interval. Therefore, the following holds for each reachable vertex v, where $source(e_1) = s$ and $target(e_n) = v$:

$$\exists p = (e_1, e_2, \ldots, e_n) \in E^n : \bigvee_{i=1}^{n} Q \subseteq validity(e_i)$$

In Algorithm 1 the function $calcOutstanding()$ acts as a placeholder, and its implementation for the time stable traversal is shown in Algorithm 2. If the target vertex is not visited yet and the edge is valid for the whole query interval, Q is added to the *outstanding* list of the target vertex. By providing a query interval consisting of a single point in time, this traversal type can operate on

---

Algorithm 2. CALCOUTSTANDING (Stable Traversal)

Input: Query interval Q, edge $e = (v, w)$
Output: The new *outstanding* intervals of w
1 **if** $(current_w = \emptyset) \wedge (finished_w = \emptyset) \wedge (Q \cap validity(e) = Q)$ **then**
2 $\quad | \quad outstanding_w \leftarrow Q$

Table 1. Query results for $S = \{1\}$ and $Q = [5, 15]$ on the graph from Fig. 1.

Vertex	Time Stable	Reachability Interval Immediate	Delayed
1	$[5, 15]$	$[5, 15]$	$[5, 15]$
2	$[5, 15]$	$[5, 15]$	$[5, 15]$
3	$[5, 15]$	$[5, 15]$	$[5, 15]$
4	$\emptyset$	$[5, 9]$	$[5, 15]$
5	$\emptyset$	$\emptyset$	$[12, 15]$
6	$\emptyset$	$\emptyset$	$\emptyset$

a specific snapshot of the graph. In this particular case the result would be the same for all types, but the stable traversal is the most efficient type to calculate this kind of query. The output is illustrated in Table 1 for the start vertices $S = \{1\}$ and the query interval $Q = [5, 15]$.

3.2 Immediate Traversal

The immediate traversal considers a vertex v reachable from the start vertex s if a path between them exists for at least one instant during the query interval. Edges only valid outside the query interval can be removed before the traversal starts in order to improve the performance. In contrast to the previous type, it is not guaranteed that all remaining edges can be used during the traversal. The reason is that the decision whether or not an edge is usable depends not only on the query interval and the validity interval of the edge but also on the so far traversed path leading to it. Two requirements have to be met in order to traverse an edge: (1) the intervals of the edges along a path have to overlap or the path will not exist in its entirety for any point in time as demanded before, and (2) this overlap has to be during the query interval. By calculating the intersection between the query interval and all edge intervals along the path, both conditions can be checked. The intersection is empty *iff* at least one condition is violated and therefore the following holds for each reachable vertex v, where p is a path, $source(e_1) = s$, and $target(e_n) = v$:

$$\exists p = (e_1, e_2, \ldots, e_n) \in E^n : \left(\bigcap_{i=1}^{n} validity(e_i) \right) \cap Q \neq \emptyset$$

Algorithm 3. CALCOUTSTANDING (Immediate Traversal)

Input: Query interval Q, edge $e = (v, w)$
Output: The new *outstanding* intervals of w

1 $outstanding_w \leftarrow outstanding_w \cup \Big[(current_v \cap validity(e)) \setminus$

$(current_w \cup finished_w) \Big]$

Algorithm 4. CALCOUTSTANDING (Delayed Traversal)

Input: Query interval Q, edge $e = (v, w)$
Output: The new *outstanding* intervals of w

1 **if** $upper(validity(e)) \geq lower(outstanding_v) \wedge lower(validity(e)) \leq upper(Q)$
then

2      $outstanding_w \leftarrow$
    $\Big(\max\big(lower(validity(e)), lower(outstanding_v)\big), upper(Q) \Big)$

3      $outstanding_w \leftarrow outstanding_w \setminus \Big[current_w \cup finished_w \Big]$

The version of *calcOutstanding()* for the immediate traversal is shown in Algorithm 3. It basically extends the *outstanding* list of a vertex by the intersection as described before. Important to note is that the function also removes the elements of *finished* and *current* of the target vertex to ensure that a vertex is never traversed twice for the same point in time. As mentioned earlier, this is crucial for the correctness of the algorithm, since otherwise it would never terminate in the presence of cycles. Table 1 shows an example parameterized just like before with $S = \{1\}$ and $Q = [5, 15]$.

This traversal type can be used to solve the first use case of Sect. 2, because the result will contain all reachable vertices and their reachability information. The reachability interval of each vertex v stores all points in time at which a complete path from the power plant to v exists. Therefore, a gap specifies exactly when this vertex is disconnected from the power source. Vertices not present in the result are disconnected for the entire considered period of time. Note that a vertex might be reached via different paths at different points in time, even if neither of those paths exists for the whole query interval. As long as for each point in time at least one path exists, the reachability interval does not contain any gaps.

3.3 Delayed Traversal

The delayed traversal is even less restrictive regarding the traversable edges. In contrast to the preceding types, a vertex v is considered reachable from the start vertex s even if at no instant a complete path between them exists. This means that it is allowed to wait for edges to appear as long as the query interval is not exceeded. As before, all edges invalid during the query interval do not have to be considered. To prevent traveling back in time, the upper bound of an edge along the path always has to be at least as big as the lower bound of its preceding edge. Formally, for each reachable vertex v there exists a path p, with $source(e_1) = s$ and $target(e_n) = v$, as follows:

$$\exists p = (e_1, e_2, \ldots, e_n) \in E^n : \bigvee_{i=1}^{n} validity(e_i) \cap Q \neq \emptyset$$

$$\wedge \max_{j \in 1, \ldots, i} \left(lower(Q), lower(validity(e_j)) \right) \leq upper(validity(e_i))$$

The function to calculate the *outstanding* intervals for the delayed traversal is shown in Algorithm 3. If the considered edge exists at the same time or after the currently traversed interval, then the *outstanding* interval (it is always a single interval for this type) of the target vertex is calculated as follows. The lower bound is the maximum of the lower bound of the considered edge and the currently traversed interval to prevent traveling back in time. Since waiting is allowed, the upper bound is defined by the upper bound of the query interval. To ensure the algorithm terminates, the already finished interval is removed in this type as well. Table 1 shows an example result with $S = \{1\}$ and $Q = [5, 15]$.

This traversal is suitable for the second use case, the analysis of information propagation. In contrast to the power grid scenario, it is unnecessary that a complete path exists at any time. Since once obtained pieces of information are not forgotten, it is possible that some time passes between two calls or emails. The reachablity interval therefore starts at the earliest point in time at which a vertex is possibly informed and ends with the query interval.

4   Implementation Details

In this section we discuss implementation choices we made during the design and integration of the three traversal operators into GRAPHITE [9], a prototypical hybrid relational/graph processing system. We describe the internal data structures used in GRAPHITE and compare them with the data structures present in Sparksee, a popular graph database management system [6].

4.1   GRAPHITE

GRAPHITE stores a graph in two columnar tables, one for vertices and one for edges, and represents each attribute in the graph as a separate column (see Fig. 2 for an example). The graph topology is maintained as an edge list with two columns for the source and the target vertex of an edge, respectively. GRAPHITE allows storing a time-varying graph by adding two additional, numerical attributes to represent the validity interval, namely `validfrom` and `validto`.

In GRAPHITE we leverage the dictionary encoding, which produces a dense value domain, and store the data structures `current`, `finished`, and `outstanding` as vectors of interval lists. We rely on lists of intervals since interval operations (e.g., union) can lead to non-contiguous sets of points in time.

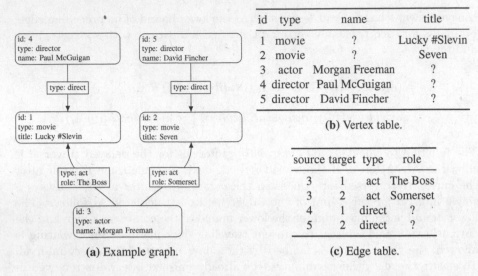

(b) Vertex table.

id	type	name	title
1	movie	?	Lucky #Slevin
2	movie	?	Seven
3	actor	Morgan Freeman	?
4	director	Paul McGuigan	?
5	director	David Fincher	?

(c) Edge table.

source	target	type	role
3	1	act	The Boss
3	2	act	Somerset
4	1	direct	?
5	2	direct	?

(a) Example graph.

Fig. 2. Example graph and internal graph representation in GRAPHITE.

We use simple double-linked lists to allow fast deletions and insertions at arbitrary positions, since we store intervals in the list ordered by their lower bound. This ordering is beneficial in two ways: (1) touching or overlapping intervals are easy to identify and can therefore be merged efficiently to keep the lists small, and (2) operations, such as intersections, can be computed by using sort/merge-based algorithms.

4.2 Sparksee

Sparksee is an in-memory graph database management system tailored to the processing of property graphs and with out-of-core processing capabilities. Each vertex/edge is identified by a system-generated *object identifier* (oid) and can have an abitrary set of attributes assigned to it. Sparksee stores a graph based on *value sets*, which group all pairs of the original set with the same value as a pair between value and the set of objects with such a value. Internally, a value set is represented by two maps implemented as B+-trees and a collection of compressed bitvectors to represent vertex/edge sets. The first map stores assignments of object identifiers to a corresponding value. The second map assigns to each value a set of object identifiers. Returning an attribute value for a given *oid* has a time complexity $\mathcal{O}(\log n)$ in Sparksee, which is considerably slower than a value lookup in constant time of $\mathcal{O}(1)$ in GRAPHITE.

Since *oids* cannot be used directly as indices for the `current`, `outstanding`, and `finished` data structures, we implement them as a hash map storing for an *oid* the list of intervals. Apart from this detail, we use for both evaluated systems the same traversal operator implementations.

4.3   Traversal Types

For the implementation of the three traversal types presented in Sect. 3 we came up with the following optimizations.

Stable Traversal. Since each edge has to be valid during the complete query interval, we can transform the generic implementation into a static filter condition that can be evaluated before the actual traversal starts. We extend the edge predicate p_e by two additional predicate conditions: (1) an edge has to be valid at the beginning of the query interval, and (2) it has to be still valid at the end of the query interval. All active edges that pass the filter predicate form a materialized subgraph that can be used by the traversal operator instead of performing expensive interval operations during the traversal.

Delayed Traversal. As mentioned before, *current*, *outstanding*, and *finished* are vectors of interval lists, but this is unnecessarily complex. Once a vertex is reached, the traversal will continue in the next step for all subsequent points in time. This vertex has to be traversed again only if it is reached earlier than before. Instead of storing a list of intervals, this behavior can also be achieved by just storing a single integer. For example, for *finished* this integer represents the instant from which on all subsequent points in time are already traversed. Then the rather complex interval operations are not needed and can be replaced by a comparison of two integers.

5   Experimental Evaluation

In this section we discuss the experimental evaluation of our prototypical implementation of the three traversal types in GRAPHITE and Sparksee.

5.1   Environmental Setup and Datasets

We conducted all experiments on a single machine operating SUSE Linux Enterprise Server 11 SP3 (64 bit) with two Intel Xeon X5550 processors running at 2.67 GHz and with 24 GB of main memory. We used a real-world telecommunication graph dataset (*Telecommunications - MI to MI 2013-11-01*)[1], describing temporally and spatially aggregated phone call information between households. The region is overlaid by a 100×100 grid to perform the spatial aggregation, and each cell in the grid contains a signal strength value that is proportional to the number of calls to all other cells. Each signal strength value is computed over ten minute intervals during the day. For our experiments we removed the edge attribute *signal strength* and transformed each start timestamp and time duration into an explicit time interval represented as integer pair.

---

[1] https://dandelion.eu/datagems/SpazioDati/telecom-mi-to-mi/.

Table 2. Average runtimes per edge for immediate and delayed traversals on different datasets.

	Small	Medium	Large
immediate	418 ns	351 ns	328 ns
delayed	195 ns	190 ns	186 ns

To test our approach for scalability, we derived three datasets from the original dataset with scales 1.0 (*large*), 0.5 (*medium*), and 0.25 (*small*). The *large* dataset has about 100 million edges while the other two datasets are generated by keeping each edge with a probability of 50% and 25%, respectively. For all experiments, we generated 100 queries with a randomly chosen start vertex and query interval—chosen between the earliest appearance and the latest disappearance of an edge in the dataset.

We focus in the experiments on the performance of the immediate traversal algorithm for the following two reasons: (1) after applying the optimization on the stable traversal, the implementation is a simple edge filter followed by a standard BFS algorithm, and (2) initial experiments evaluating the runtime per considered edge (cf. Table 2) show that the immediate traversal is computationally more challenging than the delayed traversal.

5.2 Experiments

The first experiment evaluates the scalability of our approach for different scales of the telecommunication dataset and the results are depicted in Fig. 3. For each query, we measure the total elapsed time of the query, count the number of considered edges, and derive a relative measure of runtime/edge. The runtime per edge for all dataset scales is nearly constant in Sparksee, indicating a good scaling behavior. In contrast, for GRAPHITE the runtime per edge even decreases for larger (and denser) graphs. To explain this, we selected the slowest query and provide a detailed runtime analysis—separated into key components of the algorithm—in Fig. 4, where (1) edge expansion refers to the actual traversal operation, (2) interval operations implement the logic to decide whether an edge is to be traversed (see function *calcOutstanding()* in Sect. 3 for details), and (3) the attribute access denotes the lookup of the attributes `validfrom` and `validto` to a given edge.

On both systems we can see that the runtime share of the interval operations decreases the denser the graph gets, which is caused by the fact that more edges will likely result in more overlapping intervals, which can be compressed into a single larger interval. In contrast to the amount of disjoint intervals, the size of a single interval has no negative impact on the runtime. While on GRAPHITE the runtimes for the remaining parts are similar for all three datasets, the attribute access costs increase for larger graphs in Sparksee, thus compensating for the gain of the interval operations.

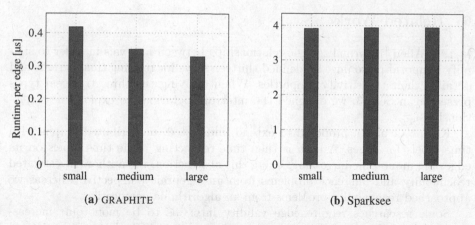

Fig. 3. Runtime per edge for the whole query set.

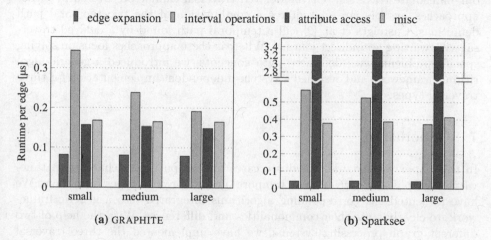

Fig. 4. Runtime share of key components for the query with the highest runtime.

Figure 4b indicates that the query processing time in Sparksee is dominated by the attribute access costs. To quantify the effect of attribute access we performed a microbenchmark and measured the elapsed time for retrieving a single attribute value (a time interval) for a randomly chosen edge on the medium-sized dataset. Sparksee achieves about 0.85×10^6 lookups per second, while GRAPHITE reaches about 10.13×10^6 lookups per second, resulting in an order of magnitude faster attribute access times. This is caused by Sparksee's internal data structures, which are based on B+-trees with logarithmic access time (in contrast to constant attribute access time in GRAPHITE). Due to the importance of attribute lookups for temporal graph traversal and the need to quickly access attributes during the traversal, this has a large impact on the overall performance.

6   Related Work

In 1983 Allen [1] formalized the relationships between intervals in order to simplify temporal reasoning. He defined thirteen ways for relating time periods and detailed their transitivity properties. When deriving the three traversal types presented in Sect. 3, we designed the interval operations to exploit these relationships.

Kempe et al. [5] proposed to extend undirected, unattributed graphs with time labels for edges. A path is then time-respecting if the time labels on its edges are monotonic increasing. Using this abstraction, the authors investigated reachability and inference problems from an algebraic perspective whereas we approached reachability problems from an algorithmic perspective.

Some researches require edge validity intervals to be monotonic increasing [8,10], while others allow them to overlap [3,7]. The latter is similar to our immediate traversal, but the delayed traversal cannot be covered by either approaches in isolation—it requires a combination of the two temporal path definitions. Casteigts et al. [2] call a temporal path found by a delayed traversal with waiting an indirect journey. Whereas these approaches focus on solving specific problems with dedicated path concepts, we introduced a generic algorithmic framework and designed a system-independent implementation for three traversal types.

7   Conclusion

In this paper we have described use cases for computing reachability in time-varying graphs and derived three temporal graph traversal types from them. We have presented the corresponding algorithms integrated into a generic framework, to clearly state their commonalities and differences. With the help of two different graph processing systems, we have implemented the three traversal operators and evaluated our implementations on a real-world graph dataset. An important observation is the influence of attribute access time on the overall traversal performance. Since graph traversals are a foundation for many complex graph algorithms, any graph processing system should place emphasis on efficient attribute access.

Acknowledgments. We would like to express our gratitude to Martin Kaufmann, who assisted in carving out the ideas presented in this paper and has given insightful feedback on previous versions of it. Also, Christof Bornhövd has encouraged us in pursuing this research direction and supported us in various ways.

References

1. Allen, J.F.: Maintaining knowledge about temporal intervals. Commun. ACM **26**(11), 832–843 (1983)
2. Casteigts, A., Flocchini, P., Mans, B., Santoro, N.: Measuring temporal lags in delay-tolerant networks. In: Proceedings of the IPDPS, pp. 209–218. IEEE (2011)
3. Casteigts, A., Flocchini, P., Quattrociocchi, W., Santoro, N.: Time-varying graphs and dynamic networks. Int. J. Parallel Emerg. Distrib. Syst. **27**(5), 387–408 (2012)
4. Cattuto, C., Quaggiotto, M., Panisson, A., Averbuch, A.: Time-varying Social Networks in a graph database: A Neo4j use case. In: Proceedings of the GRADES 2013, pp. 1–6 (2013)
5. Kempe, D., Kleinberg, J., Kumar, A.: Connectivity and inference problems for temporal networks. J. Comput. System Sci. **64**(4), 820–842 (2002)
6. Martínez-Bazan, N., Águila Lorente, M.A., Muntés-Mulero, V., Dominguez-Sal, D., Gómez-Villamor, S., Larriba-Pey, J.L.: Efficient graph management based on bitmap indices. In: Proceedings of the IDEAS, pp. 110–119 (2012)
7. Nicosia, V., Tang, J., Mascolo, C., Musolesi, M., Russo, G., Latora, V.: Graph metrics for temporal networks. In: Holme, P., Saramäki, J. (eds.) Temporal Networks. UCS, pp. 15–40. Springer, Heidelberg (2013)
8. Pan, R.K., Saramäki, J.: Path lengths, correlations, and centrality in temporal networks. Phys. Rev. E **84**(1), 197–206 (2011)
9. Paradies, M., Lehner, W., Bornhövd, C.: GRAPHITE: an extensible graph traversal framework for relational database management systems. In: Proceedings of the SSDBM, pp. 29: 1–29: 12 (2015)
10. Wu, H., Cheng, J., Huang, S., Ke, Y., Lu, Y., Xu, Y.: Path problems in temporal graphs. Proc. VLDB Endow. **7**(9), 721–732 (2014)

Robust Cardinality Estimation for Subgraph Isomorphism Queries on Property Graphs

Marcus Paradies[1,2(✉)], Elena Vasilyeva[1,2], Adrian Mocan[2],
and Wolfgang Lehner[1]

[1] Database Systems Group, TU Dresden, Dresden, Germany
{m.paradies,elena.vasilyeva}@sap.com, wolfgang.lehner@tu-dresden.de
[2] SAP SE, Walldorf, Germany
adrian.mocan@sap.com

Abstract. With an increasing popularity of graph data and graph processing systems, the need of efficient graph processing and graph query optimization becomes more important. Subgraph isomorphism queries, one of the fundamental graph query types, rely on an accurate cardinality estimation of a single edge of a pattern for efficient query processing. State of the art approaches do not consider two important aspects for cardinality estimation of graph queries on property graphs: the existence of nodes with a high outdegree and functional dependencies between attributes. In this paper we focus on these two challenges and integrate the detection of high-outdegree nodes and functional dependency analysis into the cardinality estimation. We evaluate our approach on two real data sets and compare it against a state-of-the-art query optimizer for property graphs as implemented in NEO4J.

1 Introduction

The recent advent of graph-structured data and the ever-growing need to process graph data led to the development of a plethora of graph processing systems and frameworks [5]. While some of them target long-running offline, analytic graph queries like PageRank calculation and community detection, others focus on online transactional queries. A subgraph isomorphism query is one of the most fundamental graph query types represented in both graph query paradigms. It is supported in most commercial GDBMS either through a specific language such as NEO4J's declarative query language CYPHER or can be emulated through a programming interface, such as in SPARKSEE [6]. A subgraph isomorphism query discovers all data subgraphs matching a query graph and belongs to queries with high computational costs [4]. To decrease the processing efforts, usually such queries rely on statistics about the underlying data graph and a cardinality estimation of each edge in a query graph. Therefore, to estimate a cardinality of a graph pattern, it is necessary to estimate precisely the cardinality of each single edge in a query. Query optimization based on the cardinality estimation of an edge(graph) becomes crucial for efficient subgraph isomorphism queries and adaptation of the online query processing.

© Springer International Publishing Switzerland 2016
F. Wang et al. (Eds.): Big-O(Q) and DMAH 2015, LNCS 9579, pp. 184–198, 2016.
DOI: 10.1007/978-3-319-41576-5_14

Figure 1 shows the result of a micro benchmark evaluating the cardinality estimation quality of NEO4J[1] for the LDBC data set at scale factor 1. We conduct evaluation for simple filter operations on nodes—a predicate on *firstname* and a conjunctive predicate on the correlated attributes *firstname* and *gender*—and for 1-hop traversals based on the *knows* subgraph describing relationships between forum users. NEO4J assumes a uniform distribution of selectivities for both, attributes and neighborhoods, respectively. This results in a dramatic cardinality underestimation with a q-error of about 1000 and more for the predicate evaluation on correlated attributes and for neighborhood queries on high-outdegree nodes. It is not our intention to belittle NEO4J and its query optimizer, but instead to raise fundamental problems in dealing with real-world graphs that are prevalent in most graph database management systems.

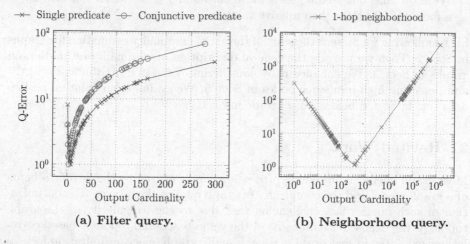

(a) **Filter query.**   (b) **Neighborhood query.**

Fig. 1. Output cardinality estimation with Q-error of filter evaluation on nodes and simple 1-hop neighborhood queries in Neo4j.

Although cardinality estimation for graph pattern matching on property graphs is a rather new research field, there have been extensive studies on graph pattern matching in SPARQL—the declarative query language of the RDF data model—and cardinality estimation techniques in RDFDBMS [7,8,16]. While some techniques can be directly applied to the graph pattern matching on property graphs, there are some fundamental differences caused by the different underlying data models like the RDF data model does not provide natural support for attributes on edges. Moreover, these techniques focus only on cardinality estimation of a star topology, which is a typical pattern in the RDF graphs. In opposite, property graphs can include arbitrary topologies and nodes and edges can be described by multiple attributes.

---

[1] We use the latest available version: Neo4j 2.3.0-M2.

As a single edge estimation is crucial for estimating the cardinality of a graph query, we improve it by addressing two important challenges—handling of correlated attributes with a skewed value distribution and cardinality estimation for neighborhood queries in the presence of high-outdegree nodes. We summarize our contributions as follows:

- We reuse a technique well-known from the relational world to detect soft functional dependencies between attributes and apply it to the property graph model.
- We propose *degree histograms*, a concise representation of the degree distribution with a dedicated handling of vertices with a large in/outdegree.
- We evaluate our approach on two realistic graph data sets with a rich set of attributes, correlations between attributes, and a skewed degree distribution. We show that our techniques achieve cardinality estimations that are up to a factor of 50 better than a naive solution.

In the following we present the state of the art of cardinality estimation for graphs in Sect. 2. Then we provide the general description of cardinality estimation on graphs in Sect. 3. We enhance it by considering correlated attributes in Sect. 4 and detecting high-outdegree nodes in Sect. 5. We evaluate our solution on two data sets in Sect. 6 before we conclude in Sect. 7.

2   Related Work

Most graph queries require high processing efforts caused by the flexible schema of a graph model and the complexity of graph queries themselves. The optimization of such queries is a challenging task due to the irregularity of the graph topology, the exposed attributes, and the value-based and topology-based correlations exhibited in real-world graphs. Usually graph query optimization focuses on establishing a traversal path through the query and answers the question: 'Which edge has to be processed next?' by estimating the cardinality of each candidate edge. In this section we discuss the state of the art work on cardinality estimation with the focus on graph data.

2.1   RDF Cardinality Estimation

In the graph database research community, cardinality estimation of patterns [7,8,16] is critical for RDF (Resource Description Framework) graphs, where each query can be represented as a join of several stars describing specific entities. The RDF data representation enables storing and processing of schema-free structured information. A typical pattern for RDF data is a star, therefore, it is taken as the base for query optimization.

Basic Graph Pattern (BGP) in a form of (un)bounded triples are used as a static optimization [16] to determine a join order for pattern calculation. The proposed system constructs a query plan by traversing edges according to the minimum estimated selectivity principle by passing first visiting triples to prevent a system from having to compute the Cartesian product of two intermediate result sets. To increase the estimation quality, cardinality for a bounded object is calculated deterministically, while an upper bound of the size of joined triples for unbounded objects is supported by domain/range information. In comparison to our approach, the cardinality estimation of BGP does not support the reduction of intermediate results based on the neighboring relations. Moreover, the underlying model differs from the property graph model and therefore does not support modeling of attributes on edges.

Cardinality estimation for the schema-free representation is provided by frequent path calculation [8] and characteristic sets identification [7]. In both cases these statistics are precomputed and they describe two kinds of patterns specific for the RDF data representation: chains and stars. In comparison to these solutions, we work with entities and calculate their cardinalities based on the estimated schema information and additional graph-specific characteristics like in - and outdegrees and their modifications for particular edge types. In addition, we provide more precise cardinality estimation by overcoming the independence assumption.

2.2 Cardinality Estimation in DBMS

Query optimization in DBMS is a long-term established research field. Leveraging statistics about data distributions, correlations, and selectivities have been around in the DBMS market since the very beginning. Cardinality estimation is used for example for establishing an optimal join order. For this purpose, the join selectivity and selectivity of a selection operator are calculated based on the data distribution and multidimensional histograms. To increase the performance of estimation, sampling techniques are used. We refer an interesting reader to the survey [2]. In our work we focus on eliminating predicates based on functional dependencies between them [10,12]. This allows us discarding dependent predicates from the cardinality estimation and thereby increasing the quality of the estimation.

2.3 Graph Cardinality Estimation

The property graph model is a natural graph data model where vertices represent entities and edges describe relationships between them. This data model is used in modern graph processing systems, e.g. NEO4J. By estimating a graph pattern of a property graph, we need to consider statistics from DBMS and graph databases. However, for the property graph data model, only a few works [1,9,15] exist that try to apply relational/RDF results to property graphs.

In graph databases statistics natural for graphs can be based on neighborhood relationships [1,9]. In this case, as statistics we can use the complete "neighborhood" function of a graph. The exact calculation of a neighborhood function is expensive, which is why multiple approximation methods are considered.

These statistics can be used to determine the similarity between two graphs or to calculate the diameter of a graph.

For pattern detection, to reduce the complexity of matching, nodes and edges are filtered based on the label similarity [15]. For this purpose, the algorithm Quick-SI pre-processes a data graph and computes frequencies of vertex labels and frequencies of triples (source, edge, and target labels). The algorithm joins edges starting with the low-frequency edges.

3   Graph Data Model and Cardinality Estimation

Our system uses the property graph model [13] as an underlying data model. It represents a graph as a directed multigraph, where nodes are entities and edges are relationships between them. Each edge and node can be described by multiple types of attributes that can differ among edges and nodes—even if they have the same semantic type.

Definition 1 (Property Graph). *We define a property graph as a directed graph $G = (V, E, u, f, g)$ over an attribute space $A = A_V \dot\cup A_E$, where: (1) V, E are finite sets of nodes and edges; (2) $u : E \to V^2$ is a mapping between edges and nodes; (3) $f : V \to A_V$ and $g : E \to A_E$ are attribute functions for nodes and edges; and (4) A_V and A_E are their attribute spaces.*

Typical queries supported by graph databases include subgraph isomorphism queries, reachability queries, etc. Graph databases rely on accurate cardinality estimation to process such queries efficiently and usually support multiple indices specific for each query type. Before estimating the cardinality for any graph query, we must take into account the specifics of property graphs expressed by notation and topology.

3.1   Notation: Attribute Histograms

A property graph can have attributes on nodes and on edges. For each attribute we construct a frequency histogram, where the x-axis represents values of the attribute domain and the y-axis shows the number of occurrences for the specific value in the data graph. We support numerical as well as categorical attributes. An important parameter of an attribute histogram is the bucket width, which allows controlling the size of the histogram and consequently the quality of the cardinality estimation. Dividing a one-dimensional histrogram into equi-width buckets can be easily applied to numerical value domains, but is not meaningful for categorical attribute domains. To tackle this problem we apply the creation of buckets not directly on the values, but instead on the value codes that stem from a dictionary encoding. Dictionary encoding is frequently used for compressing categorical values by replacing the variable-length value with a fixed-length value code. For one-dimensional histograms with a bucket size larger than one, the value frequency describes the number of occurences of values from an interval of value codes. While increasing the interval width allows reducing the memory consumption of the histogram, it also decreases the precision of the cardinality estimation.

3.2 Topology: Degree Histograms

The graph topology is a unique property of a graph model. It can be represented by an in - or outdegree of a node and its neighbors, typical graph topologies like triangles, stars etc.

General node in - or outdegree describes the maximum number of its direct neighbors. For cardinality estimation we define the in- and outdegree separately for each edge type. An edge type is a special kind of edge attributes allowing to extract subgraphs like a friend-of-friend network. An edge can have only a single edge type. Typically, there is only a small number of different edge types in a data graph ($N(types) << N(edges)$). For example, LDBC data set with scale factor 1 has 16 edge types, while the total number of edges exceeds 21Mio. We specialize a degree histogram for each available edge type and thereby increase the quality of the cardinality estimation. For each kind of degree and edge type we construct degree histograms that map node identifiers (or intervals) to the number of adjacent edges with a specific edge type.

3.3 Cardinality Estimation

To estimate the cardinality of a query graph, we have to estimate the cardinality of each node and edge in the query graph, and combine them together into a single query graph.

Vertex Cardinality Estimation. To estimate the cardinality of a single node in a query graph, we have to consider selectivities of the predicates.

For a data graph with N nodes the selectivity of a node without any predicate is $sel(v_i) = 1$. If a node v_i has predicate p_k then its selectivity is determined by the selectivity of its predicate

$$sel(v_i|p_k) = sel(p_k) = \frac{N(p_k)}{N} \tag{1}$$

The number of nodes matching a predicate p_k can be taken from the corresponding attribute histogram. The selectivity of a node v_i is defined as the selectivity over an attribute space $A = A_V$, where attributes are assumed to be independent:

$$sel(v_i|p_k, p_l) = sel(p_k) * sel(p_l) \tag{2}$$

Edge and Path Cardinality Estimation. The cardinality estimation of an edge is similar to the cardinality estimation of a node: we use predicate selectivities to estimate the number of edges matching the edge description as in Eq. 2. This estimation is node-irrespective. To estimate the cardinality of a path(1) $C(s-e-t)$ that represents *source(s)-edge(e)-target(t)*, we have to consider source and target nodes of an edge as follows. First, we estimate the selectivity and cardinality of a source and then we multiply it with the average outdegree for an edge. Finally, we multiply it by the selectivity of the target:

$$C(s - e - t) = sel(s) * N * avg.outdeg(e(type)) * sel(e) * sel(t) \tag{3}$$

The estimation of a path cardinality is commonly used in graph queries, for example: subgraph isomorphism queries for establishing the join order [15]. The estimation is crucial for enabling efficient graph processing. In the following we improve the above presented standard estimation by focusing on two challenges, namely: (1) notation: considering functional dependencies between attributes and (2) topology: handling nodes with a high outdegree.

4   Considering Functional Dependencies Between Attributes

Considering dependency between attributes of the same query edge or node can increase the quality of cardinality estimation. Inspiring by work on determining functional dependencies between columns [12], we detect soft functional dependencies between attributes of nodes or edges as follows. The dependency between attributes can be expressed by the uncertainty coefficient, also called entropy coefficient as

$$U(Y|X) = \frac{I_{XY}}{H_X} \tag{4}$$

where Y, X are two attributes, $I_{XY} = H_X + H_Y - H(XY)$ is their dependence information, $H(X), H(Y), H(XY)$ are the entropy values of attributes X, Y, and the coentropy of a joint distribution XY, respectively. The uncertainty coefficient $U(Y|X)$ shows how well an attribute value from X defines an attribute value from Y and varies between $[0; 1]$. While $U(Y|X) = 0$ indicates value independence of the two attributes, $U(Y|X) = 1$ expresses a strong dependency. The measure is not symmetric: $U(Y|X) \neq U(X|Y)$.

Example. Assume a data graph represents a social network, where some typical attributes for persons are a firstname and a gender. The functional dependency $U(gender|firstname)$ will be high, while $U(firstname|gender)$ is rather small. In practice we can almost always derive a gender of a person from his firstname. For example, Bob should be a male, while Alice is a female. The converse is not true: if a gender is a female, the firstname cannot be easily derived.

Functional dependencies are static statistics and are calculated offline. To reduce the overhead of determining functional dependencies between all pairs of attributes, we group attributes into several sets and calculate functional dependencies only between attributes of the same set. We create sets based on semantical relatedness between attributes. In many scenarios, for example, social networks, such sets are already defined in the form of an attribute *type* for nodes like a person, a web page, or a city. If the nodes do not have any attribute type, we create characteristic sets [7]. Originally, a characteristic set describes a typical star relationship for the RDF data.

In Fig. 2 we show the transformation of a characteristic set from RDF into the property graph model. As we can see, a characteristic set in the property graph represents only the typical schema of a node. To describe typical outgoing connections for a specific characteristic set in a property graph, we can create an edge characteristic set. It allows describing the topology and the notation

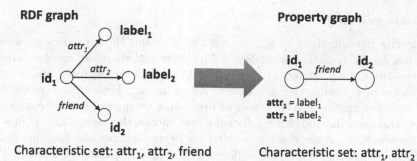

Fig. 2. Characteristic set for a property graph.

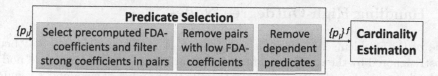

Fig. 3. Predicate selection for cardinality estimation.

Algorithm 1. Predicate Selection.

1: **function** SELECTPREDICATES($p[]$)
2:     $predicateMap$
3:     **for all** $p_i \in p[]$ **do**
4:         **for all** $p_i.next \in p[]$ **do**
5:             **if** $FDA(p_i, p_i.next) \geq FDA(p_i.next, p_i)$ **then**   ▷ select precomputed
FDA-coefficients and filter the strongest ones in pairs
6:                 $predicateMap \leftarrow FDA(p_i, p_i.next)$
7:             **else if** $FDA(p_i.next, p_i) > FDA(p_i, p_i.next)$ **then**
8:                 $predicateMap \leftarrow FDA(p_i.next, p_i)$
9:         **for all** $FDA \in predicateMap$ **do**
10:             **if** $FDA < threshold$ **then**   ▷ remove pairs with low FDA-coefficients
11:                 remove FDA
12:     $startPredicate \leftarrow max(predicateMap)$
13:     remove $startPredicate$ from $p[]$
14:     **for all** $pair \in predicateMap$ **do**
15:         **if** $pair[2] \in p$ **then**   ▷ remove dependent predicates
16:             remove $pair[2]$ from p
17:     $p[] \leftarrow startPredicate$ **return** $p[]$

---

of a graph more precisely and in such a way we can separate edges from the
analyzing attribute dependencies for nodes.

Predicate Selection

To calculate the selectivity of a node, we first filter out those predicates, whose attributes are functionally dependent from others and therefore can be derived from the already considered attributes. In Fig. 3 and Algorithm 1 we present the process of selecting the predicates. As an input, Algorithm 1 receives a set of node predicates. For each pair of predicates we query their precomputed pair of functional dependency coefficients and choose the largest one (Lines 5-8). Afterwards, we remove all dependencies below a threshold in Lines 9-11, dependent predicates, which can be derived by their pair partners (Lines 14-17), and return filtered predicates.

5   Handling High-Outdegree Nodes

One of the problems in cardinality estimation of graph queries that has been mostly ignored by the research community so far is the special handling of nodes with a large number of outgoing edges. Usually the number of such nodes is much smaller than the total number of nodes in a data graph and ignoring them can lead to dramatic cardinality underestimations.

In Fig. 4 we present the outdegree distributions for the DBPEDIA and LDBC data sets for a single edge type that we use later in the experimental evaluation in Sect. 6. The tail on the right-hand side of each figure represents nodes with a high outdegree. If we do not treat them separately, the cardinality estimation can produce an estimation error of several orders of magnitude.

For a correct handling of nodes with a high outdegree, we need to answer two questions: (1) how to discover such nodes and (2) how to efficiently store and process them.

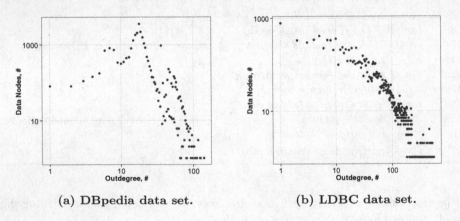

(a) DBpedia data set.   (b) LDBC data set.

Fig. 4. Outdegree diagrams.

5.1 Discovery of Nodes with a High Outdegree

Nodes with a high outdegree can be interpreted as outliers. To detect them, we have to study the degree distribution of nodes in a data graph and define a node v_i as an outlier, whose degree is much larger than the average degree ($avg.degree << degree_{v_i}$). For this purpose, we use the algorithm based on the calculation of the modified z-score for a univariate data set [3]. The calculation requires two components: the median and the median of the absolute deviation of the median that is calculated as

$$MAD = median|x_i - \widetilde{x}|, \tag{5}$$

where $\widetilde{x}$ is the sample median. As a consequence, the modified z-score can be computed as

$$M_i = \frac{0.6745 * (x_i - \widetilde{x})}{MAD}, \tag{6}$$

where $E(MAD) = 0.675\sigma$ for large normal data. The authors suggested $M_i >$ |3.5| to be outliers. In our case x_i is an outdegree of node v_i, which has at least one edge of a specific *type*. Therefore, we call a node an outlier, if its modified z-score is $M > |3.5|$. We refer the interested user to the survey of existing outlier detection methods [14].

5.2 Processing of High-Outdegree Nodes

Based on the selectivity estimation of the predicates on nodes, we distinguish between nodes with an average outdegree and those with a high outdegree. To identify efficiently, whether a given graph pattern matches one or multiple high-outdegree nodes, we use a lightweight data structure to partially index attributes for high-outdegree nodes. For each attribute, we use an ordered tree structure to map attribute values to high-outdegree nodes. The value of a node in the tree structure provides a reference to the corresponding cardinality of the node in the degree histogram. In a final step, we union the general cardinality estimation of nodes with the cardinality estimation of matched high-outdegree nodes.

6 Experimental Evaluation

In this section we provide an experimental evaluation of our techniques for detecting and leveraging functional dependencies during cardinality estimation and for detecting nodes with a high outdegree. We implemented the proposed techniques in GRAPHITE [11]—a columnar graph processing system—and conducted all experiments on a two socket Linux based system with Intel Xeon X5650 CPUs equipped with 6 cores @2.67 GHz and 48 GB RAM. We use two data sets in our experiments—LDBC scale factor 1 (3.7 Mio. vertices with 17 attributes, 21.7 Mio. edges with 16 types and 4 attributes) and DBPEDIA (0.2 Mio. vertices with 1543 attributes, 0.8 Mio. edges with 829 types)—and initially

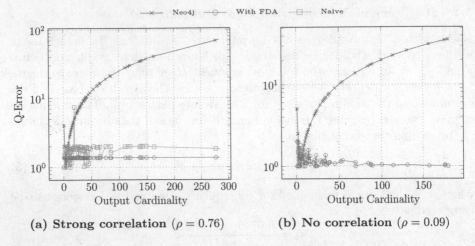

(a) **Strong correlation** $(\rho = 0.76)$ (b) **No correlation** $(\rho = 0.09)$

Fig. 5. Cardinality estimation quality of conjunctive queries on correlated and uncorrelated attributes.

populate them into GRAPHITE and NEO4J. For NEO4J, we created secondary indices on each vertex attribute to allow the system collecting additional statistics about the attributes.

6.1   Correlated Attributes

In this experiment we evaluate the influence of (soft) functional dependencies between vertex attributes on the quality of the cardinality estimation and present our results in Fig. 5. We use the LDBC data set at scale factor 1 and selected two representative conjunctive predicates (cf. Table 1). We evaluate the estimation quality for NEO4J, a naive cardinality estimation (using equi-width histograms with bucket size 1 and attribute independence assumption), and our cardinality estimation that automatically detects functional dependencies between attributes and takes them into account during the estimation process. For a strong functional dependency (see Fig. 5a), our cardinality estimation outperforms the cardinality estimation quality of NEO4J by up to factor 53 and a naive cardinality estimation (under the independence assumption) by up to 50 % for large output cardinalities. For uncorrelated attributes (see Fig. 5b) we decide, based on the estimated functional dependency and a threshold, whether we estimate the conjunctive cardinality under the independence assumption or by exploiting the knowledge about functional dependencies. For a weak functional dependency we estimate the cardinality under the independence assumption and represent both, the naive and our solution with functional dependency analysis by the same blue plot line.

6.2 High-Outdegree Vertices

In this set of experiments we evaluate the automatic detection of high-outdegree vertices and compare it with manually chosen numbers of nodes with a high outdegree based on the top-k principle. We conducted our evaluation on two data sets, DBPEDIA and LDBC, and generated different query templates instantiated with different predicate values (cf. Table 1).

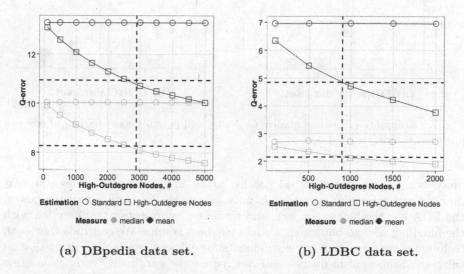

(a) DBpedia data set.   (b) LDBC data set.

Fig. 6. Evaluating functional dependency analysis.

While for the DBPEDIA data set (cf. Fig. 6a) the system automatically detected the kink at around 2886, it determined a value of around 900 for the LDBC data set. For both data sets, we observed that by increasing the number of considered high-outdegree nodes, the q-error decreases more slowly than before the kink.

6.3 End-to-End Cardinality Estimation

In this test we evaluate the influence of functional dependencies between attributes and the presence of high-outdegree nodes on the quality of the estimation (cf. Fig. 7). We consider four different configurations combined from two features: with or without functional dependency analysis (FDA) and with or without automatic selection of high-outdegree nodes (SN). NEO4J provides a good estimation quality for the LDBC data set but fails estimating the cardinality of queries for the DBPEDIA data set which requires an estimation of selective predicates. Most queries match at most a single source vertex and NEO4J estimates these high-selective vertices to 0. Since the q-error cannot be computed for a cardinality (exact and estimated) of 0, we omit the results for NEO4J for the DBPEDIA data set in Fig. 7a.

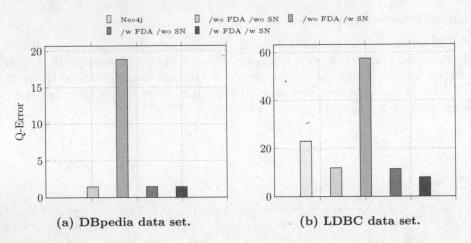

Fig. 7. Cardinality estimation quality for Neo4j and possible combinations of our two proposed techniques.

Since both query templates do not hit many high-outdegree nodes, the cardinality estimation improvement is only marginal. For both query templates, the FDA has the highest impact, and therefore, represents in conjunction with the handling of high-outdegree vertices the best results. We conclude that both techniques are important key components for efficient cardinality estimation on subgraph isomorphism queries and can reduce the cardinality estimation error significantly.

7   Conclusion

We tackled two important challenges that arise in graph pattern cardinality estimation caused by the skewedness of the degree distribution and the irregularity of exposed attributes in vertices and edges present in real-world graphs, namely: detection of functional dependencies between node attributes and consideration of nodes with a high outdegree. By analyzing two real-world graph data sets with a rich set of attributes and a power-law vertex degree distribution, we identified that these two aspects are important for the cardinality estimation of subgraph isomorphism queries over property graphs. With our solution for the cardinality estimation considering both aspects, we outperform a naive approach relying on average outdegree measures and the independence assumption in conjunctive predicates by up to 50 % and the cost-based query optimizer of NEO4J by up to a factor of 50.

A   Evaluated Queries

Table 1. Query templates used in the evaluation.

Figure	Data Set	Query Template
5a	LDBC	`MATCH (m:person)` `WHERE m.firstname=(?) AND m.gender=(?) RETURN m;`
5b	LDBC	`MATCH (m:person)` `WHERE m.lastname=(?) AND m.gender=(?) RETURN m;`
6a	DBpedia	`MATCH (m:)-[:type]->(n:)` `WHERE m.type=(?) RETURN n;`
6b	LDBC	`MATCH (m:person)-[:knows]->(n:person)` `WHERE m.id=(?) RETURN n;`
7b	LDBC	`MATCH (m:person)-[:knows]->(n:person)` `WHERE m.firstname=(?) AND m.gender=(?) RETURN n;`
7a	DBpedia	`MATCH (m:)-[:type]->(n:)` `WHERE m.airport=(?) AND m.short_name=(?) RETURN n;`

References

1. Boldi, P., Rosa, M., Vigna, S.: HyperANF: approximating the neighbourhood function of very large graphs on a budget. In: Proceedings of the WWW 2011, pp. 625–634 (2011)
2. Cormode, G., Garofalakis, M., Haas, P.J., Jermaine, C.: Synopses for massive data: samples, histograms, wavelets, sketches. Found. Trends Databases **4**(1–3), 1–294 (2012)
3. Iglewicz, B., Hoaglin, D.C.: How to Detect, Handle Outliers. ASQC Quality Press, Milwaukee (1993)
4. Lee, J., Han, W.-S., Kasperovics, R., Lee, J.-H.: An in-depth comparison of subgraph isomorphism algorithms in graph databases. In: Proceedings of the VLDB Endowment, vol. 6, pp. 133–144 (2012)
5. Lu, Y., Cheng, J., Yan, D., Wu, H.: Large-scale distributed graph computing systems: An experimental evaluation. Proc. VLDB Endow. **8**(3), 281–292 (2014)
6. Martínez-Bazan, N., Águila Lorente, M.A., Muntés-Mulero, V., Dominguez-Sal, D., Gómez-Villamor, S., Larriba-Pey, J.-L.: Efficient graph management based on bitmap indices. In: Proceedings of the IDEAS 2012, pp. 110–119 (2012)
7. Neumann, T., Moerkotte, G., Sets, C.: Accurate cardinality estimation for RDF queries with multiple joins. In: Proceedings of the ICDE 2011, pp. 984–994 (2011)
8. Neumann, T., Weikum, G.: RDF-3X: A RISC-style engine for RDF. Proc. VLDB Endow. **1**(1), 647–659 (2008)
9. Palmer, C.R., Gibbons, P.B., Faloutsos, C., ANF: a fast and scalable tool for data mining in massive graphs. In: Proceedings of the SIGKDD 2002, pp. 81–90 (2002)

10. Papenbrock, T., Ehrlich, J., Marten, J., Neubert, T., Rudolph, J.-P., Schönberg, M., Zwiener, J., Naumann, F.: Functional dependency discovery: an experimental evaluation of seven algorithms. Proc. VLDB Endow. **8**(10), 217–228 (2015)
11. Paradies, M., Lehner, W., Bornhövd, C.: GRAPHITE: an extensible graph traversal framework for relational database management systems. In: Proceedings of the SSDBM 2015, pp. 29: 1–29: 12 (2015)
12. Paradies, M., Lemke, C., Plattner, H., Lehner, W., Sattler, K.-U., Zeier, A., Krueger, J.: How to juggle columns: an entropy-based approach for table compression. In: Proceedings of the IDEAS 2010, pp. 205–215 (2010)
13. Rodriguez, M.A., Neubauer, P.: Constructions from dots and lines. Bull. Am. Soc. Inf. Sci. Technol. **36**(6), 35–41 (2010)
14. Seo, S.: A review and comparison of methods for detecting outliers in univariate data sets. Master's thesis, Faculty of Graduate School of Public Health, University of Pittsburgh (2006)
15. Shang, H., Zhang, Y., Lin, X., Yu, J.X.: Taming verification hardness: an efficient algorithm for testing subgraph isomorphism. Proc. VLDB Endow. **1**(1), 364–375 (2008)
16. Stocker, M., Seaborne, A., Bernstein, A., Kiefer, C., Reynolds, D.: SPARQL basic graph pattern optimization using selectivity estimation. In: Proceedings of the WWW 2008, pp. 595–604 (2008)

Author Index

Printed in the United States
By Bookmasters

Blackwell's
Concise Encyclopedia of
ENVIRONMENTAL
MANAGEMENT

Blackwell's
Concise Encyclopedia of

Environmental
Management

EDITED BY
PETER CALOW

**Blackwell
Science**

© 1999 by
Blackwell Science Ltd
Editorial Offices:
Osney Mead, Oxford OX2 0EL
25 John Street, London WC1N 2BL
23 Ainslie Place, Edinburgh EH3 6AJ
350 Main Street, Malden
  MA 02148 5018, USA
54 University Street, Carlton
  Victoria 3053, Australia
10, rue Casimir Delavigne
  75006 Paris, France

Other Editorial Offices:
Blackwell Wissenschafts-Verlag GmbH
Kurfürstendamm 57
10707 Berlin, Germany

Blackwell Science KK
MG Kodenmacho Building
7–10 Kodenmacho Nihombashi
Chuo-ku, Tokyo 104, Japan

First published 1999

Set by Excel Typesetters Co., Hong
Kong

A catalogue record for this title
is available from the British Library

ISBN 0-632-04951-0

Library of Congress
Cataloging-in-publication Data

Blackwell's concise encyclopedia of
environmental management/
edited by Peter Calow.
        p.   cm.
    ISBN 0-632-04951-0
    1. Environmental management—
Dictionaries.   2. Environmental
sciences—Dictionaries.   I. Calow,
Peter.
GE300.B54   1999
363.7'003—dc21   99-12178
                            CIP
                            Rev.

DISTRIBUTORS
Marston Book Services Ltd
PO Box 269
Abingdon, Oxon OX14 4YN
(*Orders*: Tel: 01235 465500
          Fax: 01235 465555)

USA
Blackwell Science, Inc.
Commerce Place
350 Main Street
Malden, MA 02148 5018
(*Orders*: Tel: 800 759 6102
                781 388 8250
          Fax: 781 388 8255)

Canada
Login Brothers Book Company
324 Saulteaux Crescent
Winnipeg, Manitoba R3J 3T2
(*Orders*: Tel: 204 837 2987)

Australia·
Blackwell Science Pty Ltd
54 University Street
Carlton, Victoria 3053
(*Orders*: Tel: 3 9347 0300
          Fax: 3 9347 5001)

For further information on
Blackwell Science, visit our website:
www.blackwell-science.com

Contents

List of Contributors

W.N.A. W.N. ADGER *CSERGE, School of Environmental Sciences, University of East Anglia, Norwich NR4 7TJ, UK*

J.K.A. J.K. AGEE *Division of Ecosystem Science and Conservation, University of Washington, Box 352100, Seattle, WA 98195, USA*

P.M.S.A. P.M.S. ASHTON *School of Forestry and Environmental Studies, Yale University, 360 Prospect Street, New Haven, CT 06511, USA*

J.A. J. AUSTIN *UK Meteorological Office, London Road, Bracknell RG12 2SZ, UK*

D.D.B. D.D. BALDOCCHI *Atmospheric Turbulence and Diffusion Division, US Department of Commerce, 456 South Illinois Avenue, PO Box 2456, Oak Ridge, TN 37831, USA*

J.S.B. J.S. BALE *School of Biological Sciences, University of Birmingham, Edgbaston, Birmingham B15 2TT, UK*

C.J.B. C.J. BARNARD *School of Biological Sciences, University of Nottingham, University Park, Nottingham NG7 2RD, UK*

R.S.K.B. R.S.K. BARNES *Department of Zoology, University of Cambridge, Downing Street, Cambridge CB2 3EJ, UK*

R.W.B. R.W. BATTARBEE *Environmental Change Research Centre, University College London, University of London, 26 Bedford Way, London WC1H 0AP, UK*

C.W.B. C.W. BEAN *Institute of Aquaculture, University of Stirling, Stirling FK9 4LA, UK*

J.B. J. BEDDINGTON *T.H. Huxley School of Environment, Earth Sciences and Engineering, Royal School of Mines, Prince Consort Road, London SW7 2BP, UK*

M.B. M. BERAN *OB Research Services, 1 The Croft, East Hagbourne, Didcot OX11 9LS, UK*

G.P.B. G.P. BERLYN *School of Forestry and Environmental Studies, Yale University, 370 Prospect Street, New Haven, CT 06511, USA*

D.A.B. D.A. BERRIGAN *Department of Zoology, Box 351800, University of Washington, Seattle, WA 98195, USA*

M.C.M.B. M.C.M. BEVERIDGE *Institute of Aquaculture, University of Stirling, Stirling FK9 4LA, UK*

I.J.B. I.J. BEVERLAND *Department of Public Health Sciences, University of Edinburgh, Medical School, Teviot Place, Edinburgh EH8 9AG, UK*

D.E.B. D.E. BIGNELL *Tropical Biology and Conservation Unit, Universiti Malaysia Sabah, 88999 Kota Kinabalu, Sabah, Malaysia*

S.J.B. S.J. BISSELL *Colorado Division of Wildlife, Denver, CO 80216, USA*

L.O.B. L.O. BJÖRN *Section of Plant Physiology, Lund University, Box 117, 221 00 Lund, Sweden*

J.F.B. J.F. BLYTH *Institute of Ecology and Resource Management, University of Edinburgh, Mayfield Road, Edinburgh EH9 3JU, UK*

P.B. P. BORRELL *EUROTRAC ISS, GSF-Forschungszenturm für Umwelt und Gesundheit, Kühbachstraße 11, D-81543 München, Germany*

A.D.B. A.D. BRADSHAW *58 Knowsley Road, Liverpool L19 0PG, UK*

P.M.B. P.M. BRAKEFIELD *Institute of Evolutionary and Ecological Sciences, University of Leiden, PO Box 9516, NL-2300 RA Leiden, The Netherlands*

D.R.B. D.R. BROOKS *Department of Zoology, University of Toronto, Toronto, Ontario M5S 3G5, Canada*

M.A.B.   M.A. BURGMAN *School of Forestry, University of Melbourne, Creswick, Victoria 3363, Australia*

F.W.B.   F.W. BURLEY *2400 NW 80th Street, Box 160, Seattle, WA 98117, USA*

J.C.   J. CAIRNS Jr *Department of Biology, Virginia Polytechnic Institute and State University, Blacksburg, VA 24061, USA*

T.V.C.   T.V. CALLAGHAN *Sheffield Centre for Arctic Ecology, Department of Animal and Plant Sciences, University of Sheffield, Tapton Experimental Gardens, 26 Taptonville Road, Sheffield S10 5BR, UK*

P.C.   P. CALOW *Department of Animal and Plant Sciences, University of Sheffield, Sheffield S10 2TN, UK*

J.N.C.   J.N. CAPE *Institute of Terrestrial Ecology, Bush Estate, Penicuik EH26 0QB, UK*

H.C.   H. CASWELL *Biology Department, Woods Hole Oceanographic Institution, Woods Hole, MA 02543, USA*

R.C.   R. CATCHPOLE *English Nature, Over Haddon, Derbyshire DE45 1JE, UK*

W.G.C.   W.G. CHALONER *Department of Geology, Royal Holloway, University of London, Egham Hill, Egham TW20 0EX, UK*

J.A.C.   J.A. CLARK *Department of Physiology and Environmental Science, University of Nottingham, Sutton Bonnington Campus, Loughborough LE12 5RD, UK*

S.G.C.   S.G. COMPTON *Ecology and Evolution Research Group, School of Biology, University of Leeds, Leeds LS2 9JT, UK*

L.M.C.   L.M. COOK *The Manchester Museum, University of Manchester, Oxford Road, Manchester M13 9PL, UK*

J.G.C.   J.G. COOKE *Centre for Ecosystem Management Studies, Mooshof, 79297 Winden, Germany*

R.M.M.C.   R.M.M. CRAWFORD *Plant Sciences Laboratory, Sir Harold Mitchell Building, University of St Andrews, St Andrews KY16 9AL, UK*

M.J.C.   M.J. CRAWLEY *Department of Biology, Imperial College of Science, Technology and Medicine, Silwood Park, Ascot SL5 7PY, UK*

J.Cr.   J. CRESSWELL *Department of Biological Sciences, University of Exeter, Hatherby Laboratories, Exeter EX4 4PS, UK*

P.J.C.   P.J. CURRAN *Department of Geography, University of Southampton, Highfield, Southampton, SO17 1BJ, UK*

K.D.   K. DAVIES *SAC, Crops Division, Bush Estate, Penicuik EH26 0PH, UK*

R.W.D.   R.W. DAVIES *Faculty of Science, Monash University, Wellington Road, Clayton 3168, Victoria, Australia*

A.J.D.   A.J. DAVIS *Ecology and Evolution Research Group, School of Biology, University of Leeds, Leeds LS2 9JT, UK*

J.C.D.   J.C. DEUTSCH *Crusade, 73 Collier Street, London N1 9BE, UK*

M.D.   M. DICKE *Department of Entomology, Wageningen Agricultural University, PO Box 8031, NL-6700 EH Wageningen, The Netherlands*

A.D.   A. DRIZO *Institute of Ecology and Resource Management, University of Edinburgh, Mayfield Road, Edinburgh EH9 3JU, UK*

C.D.   C. DYTHAM *Department of Biology, University of York, PO Box 373, Heslington, York YO1 5YW, UK*

P.E.   P. EGGLETON *Department of Entomology, The Natural History Museum, Cromwell Road, London SW7 5BD, UK*

J.R.E.   J.R. ETHERINGTON *Parc-y-Bont, Llanhowell, Solva, Haverfordwest SA62 6XX, UK*

D.A.F.   D.A. FALK *Society for Ecological Restoration, Department of Ecology and Evolutionary Biology, Biological Sciences West, University of Arizona, Tuscon, AZ 85721, USA*

J.G.F.   J.G. FARMER *Department of Chemistry, University of Edinburgh, West Mains Road, Edinburgh EH9 3JJ, UK*

B.W.F.   B.W. FERRY *School of Biological Sciences, Royal Holloway, University of London, Egham Hill, Egham TW20 0EX, UK*

E.A.F.　　E.A. FITZPATRICK *Department of Plant and Soil Science, University of Aberdeen, Cruickshank Building, St Machar Drive, Aberdeen AB24 3UU, UK*

T.L.F.　　T.L. FLEISCHNER *Environmental Studies Program, Prescott College, 220 Grove Avenue, Prescott, AZ 86301, USA*

V.F.　　V. FORBES *Department of Life Sciences and Chemistry, Roskilde University, PO Box 260, DK-4000 Roskilde, Denmark*

N.R.F.　　N.R. FRANKS *Department of Biology and Biochemistry, University of Bath, Claverton Down, Bath BA2 7AY, UK*

R.P.F.　　R.P. FRECKLETON *Schools of Environmental and Biological Sciences, University of East Anglia, Norwich NR4 7TJ, UK*

J.H.C.G.　　J.H.C. GASH *Institute of Hydrology, Crowmarsh Gifford, Wallingford OX10 8BB, UK*

O.L.G.　　O.L. GILBERT *Department of Landscape, University of Sheffield, Sheffield S10 2TN, UK*

P.S.G.　　P.S. GILLER *Department of Zoology and Animal Ecology, University College Cork, Lee Maltings, Prospect Row, Ireland*

H.C.J.G.　　H.C.J. GODFRAY *Department of Biology, Imperial College of Science, Technology and Medicine, Silwood Park, Ascot SL5 7PY, UK*

F.B.G.　　F.B. GOLDSMITH *Department of Biology, University College London, University of London, Gower Street, London WC1 6BT, UK*

J.G.　　J. GRACE *Institute of Ecology and Resource Management, University of Edinburgh, Mayfield Road, Edinburgh EH9 3JU, UK*

M.C.G.　　M.C. GRAHAM *Department of Chemistry, University of Edinburgh, West Mains Road, Edinburgh EH9 3JJ, UK*

A.N.G.　　A.N. GRAY *Forest Science Department, Oregon State University, Corvallis, OR 97331, USA*

P.J.G.　　P.J. GRUBB *Department of Plant Sciences, University of Cambridge, Downing Street, Cambridge CB2 3EA, UK*

E.O.G.　　E.O. GUERRANT JR *Berry Botanic Garden, 11505 SW Summerville Avenue, Portland, OR 97219, USA*

S.J.H.　　S.J. HALL *School of Biological Sciences, The Flinders University of South Australia, GPO Box 2100, Adelaide 5001, Australia*

A.H.　　A. HALLAM *School of Earth Sciences, University of Birmingham, Edgbaston, Birmingham B15 2TT, UK*

M.H.　　M. HASSALL *School of Environmental Sciences, University of East Anglia, Norwich NR4 7TJ, UK*

I.M.H.　　I.M. HEAD *Department of Fossil Fuels and Environmetal Geochemistry, University of Newcastle, Newcastle-upon-Tyne NE1 7RU, UK*

M.R.H.　　M.R. HEAL *Department of Chemistry, University of Edinburgh, West Mains Road, Edinburgh EH9 3JJ, UK*

J.B.H.　　J.B. HEALE *Division of Life Sciences, King's College London, University of London, Campden Hill Road, London W8 7AH, UK*

G.A.F.H.　　G.A.F. HENDRY *Biological Sciences, University of Dundee, Dundee DD1 4HN, UK*

M.O.H.　　M.O. HILL *ITE, Monks Wood, Abbots Ripton, Huntingdon PE17 2LS, UK*

A.R.H.　　A.R. HOELZEL *Department of Biological Sciences, University of Durham, South Road, Durham, DH1 3LE, UK*

J.J.H.　　J.J. HOPKINS *Joint Nature Conservation Committee, Monkstone House, Peterborough PE1 1JY, UK*

M.I.　　M. INGROUILLE *Department of Biology, Birkbeck College, University of London, Malet Street, London WC1E 7HX, UK*

J.I.　　J. IRVINE *Institute of Ecology and Resource Management, University of Edinburgh, Mayfield Road, Edinburgh EH9 3JU, UK*

S.K.J.　　S.K. JAIN *Department of Agronomy and Range Science, University of California at Davis, Davis, CA 95616, USA*

A.J.　　A. JENKINS *British Antarctic Survey, High Cross, Madingley Road, Cambridge CB3 0ET, UK*

G.D.J.　　G. DE JONG *Department of Plant Ecology and Evolutionary Biology, Universiteit of Utrecht, Padualaan 8, 3584 CH Utrecht, The Netherlands*

T.J.K.   **T.J. KAWECKI** *Zoology Institute, University of Basel, Rheinsprung 9, CH-4051 Basel, Switzerland*

J.K.   **J. KINDERLERER** *Department of Molecular Biology and Biotechnology, University of Sheffield, Sheffield S10 2TN, UK*

T.B.L.K.   **T.B.L. KIRKWOOD** *Department of Geriatric Medicine, University of Manchester, Oxford Road, Manchester M13 9PT, UK*

W.E.K.   **W.E. KUNIN** *Ecology and Evolution Research Group, School of Biology, University of Leeds, Leeds LS2 9JT, UK*

R.L.   **R. LAL** *School of Natural Resources, The Ohio State University, Columbus, OH 43210, USA*

J.L.   **J. LANCASTER** *Institute of Ecology and Resource Management, University of Edinburgh, Mayfield Road, Edinburgh EH9 3JU, UK*

J.D.Lz.   **J.D. LAZELL** *The Conservation Agency, 6 Swinburne Street, Jamestown, RI 02835, USA*

D.C.L.   **D.C. LEDGER** *Institute of Ecology and Resource Management, University of Edinburgh, Mayfield Road, Edinburgh EH9 3JU, UK*

J.D.L.   **J.D. LEWINS** *Director of Studies in Engineering and Management, Magdalene College, Magdalene Street, Cambridge CB3 0AG, UK*

R.I.L.S.   **R.I. LEWIS SMITH** *British Antarctic Survey, High Cross, Madingley Road, Cambridge CB3 0ET, UK*

J.Ly.   **J. LLOYD** *Max-Planck-Institut für Biogeochemie, Sophienstrasse 10, D-07743 Jena, Germany*

J.W.L.   **J.W. LLOYD** *School of Earth Sciences, University of Birmingham, Edgbaston, Birmingham B15 2TT, UK*

S.P.L.   **S.P. LONG** *Department of Biological Sciences, John Tabor Laboratories, University of Essex, Wivenhoe Park, Colchester CO4 3SQ, UK*

L.L.L.   **L.L. LOOPE** *US Geological Survey, Biological Resources Division, Pacific Islands Ecosystem Research Center, Haleakala National Park Field Station, PO Box 369, Makawao, HI 96768, USA*

W.L.   **W. LU** *The Conservation Agency, 6 Swinburne Street, Jamestown, RI 02835, USA*

A.B.M.   **A.B. MACKENZIE** *Scottish Universities Reactor Centre, East Kilbride, Glasgow G75 0QF, UK*

A.E.M.   **A.E. MAGURRAN** *School of Environmental and Evolutionary Biology, Bute Building, University of St Andrews, St Andrews KY16 9TS, UK*

A.M.M.   **A.M. MANNION** *Department of Geography, University of Reading, Whiteknights, Reading RG6 6AB, UK*

A.M.   **A. McDONALD** *Geography Department, University of Leeds, Woodhouse Lane, Leeds LS2 9JT, UK*

J.F.R.M.   **J.F.R. McILVEEN** *Environmental Science Department, Institute of Environmental and Natural Sciences, Lancaster University, Lancaster LA1 4YQ, UK*

L.R.M.   **L.R. McMAHAN** *The Berry Botanic Garden, 11505 SW Summerville Avenue, Portland, OR 97219, USA*

K.G.M.   **K.G. McNAUGHTON** *Environment Group, HortResearch, PO Box 23, Kerikeri, New Zealand*

G.F.M.   **G.F. MEDLEY** *Department of Biological Sciences, University of Warwick, Coventry CV4 7AL, UK*

J.M.   **J. MILBURN** [Deceased] *Department of Botany, University of New England, Armidale, New South Wales 2351, Australia*

J.B.M.   **J.B. MONCRIEFF** *Institute of Ecology and Resource Management, University of Edinburgh, Mayfield Road, Edinburgh EH9 3JU, UK*

P.D.M.   **P.D. MOORE** *Division of Life Sciences, King's College London, University of London, Campden Hill Road, London W8 7AH, UK*

J.I.L.M.   **J.I.L. MORISON** *Department of Biological Sciences, University of Essex, Wivenhoe Park, Colchester, CO4 3SQ, UK*

P.B.M.   **P.B. MOYLE** *Department of Wildlife, Fish, and Conservation Biology, University of California at Davis, Davis, CA 95616, USA*

M.O'C.   **M. O'CONNELL** *Palaeoenvironmental Research Unit, Department of Botany, National University of Ireland, Galway, Ireland*

P.O.   P. OLEJNICZAK *Institute of Environmental Biology, Jagiellonian University, Oleandry 2a, 30-063 Krakow, Poland*

I.O.   I. OLIVIERI *Institut des Sciences de l'Evolution, Universite Montpellier II, Place Eugene Bataillon, 34095 Montpellier, Cedex 05, France*

J.R.P.   J. R. PACKHAM *School of Applied Sciences, University of Wolverhampton, Wulfruna Street, Wolverhampton WV1 1SB, UK*

A.P.   A. PENTECOST *Division of Life Sciences, King's College London, University of London, Campden Hill Road, London W8 7AH, UK*

G.F.P.   G. F. PETERKEN *Beechwood House, St Briavels Common, Lydney GL15 6SL, UK*

J.K.P.   J. K. PIPER *Department of Biology, Bethel College, North Newton, KS 67117, USA*

G.B.R.   G. B. RABB *Species Survival Commission, Chicago Zoological Society, Brookfield, IL 60513, USA*

P.B.R.   P. B. RAINEY *Department of Plant Sciences, University of Oxford, South Parks Road, Oxford, OX1 3RB, UK*

D.J.R.   D. J. RANDALL *Department of Zoology, University of British Columbia, Vancouver, British Columbia V6T 1Z4, Canada*

P.G.R.   P. G. RISSER *Oregon State University, 646 Kerr Administration Building, Corvallis, OR 97331, USA*

M.L.R.   M. L. ROSENZWEIG *Department of Ecology and Evolutionary Biology, University of Arizona, Tucson, AZ 85721, USA*

G.R.   G. RUSSELL *Institute of Ecology and Resource Management, University of Edinburgh, West Mains Road, Edinburgh EH9 3JG, UK*

R.S.S.   R. S. SCORER *2 Stanton Road, London SW20 8RL, UK*

J.G.S.   J. G. SEVENSTER *Institute of Evolutionary and Ecological Sciences, University of Leiden, PO Box 9516, NL-2300 RA Leiden, The Netherlands*

B.S.   B. SHORROCKS *Ecology and Evolution Research Group, School of Biology, University of Leeds, Leeds LS2 9JT, UK*

H.S.   H. SIEVERING *Global Change and Environmental Quality Program, Geography and Environmental Sciences Department, University of Colorado at Denver, Box 172, Denver PO Box 173364, CO 80217, USA*

K.A.S.   K. A. SMITH *Institute of Ecology and Resource Management, University of Edinburgh, West Mains Road, Edinburgh EH9 3JG, UK*

R.H.S.   R. H. SMITH *Department of Biology, University of Leicester, University Road, Leicester LE1 7RH, UK*

T.A.S.   T. A. SPIES *USDA Forest Service, Pacific Northwest Forest Research Station, 3200 West Jefferson Way, Corvallis, OR 97331, USA*

J.S.S.   J. S. STATES *2 Canyon Shadows Road, Lander, WY 82520, USA*

S.C.S.   S. C. STEARNS *Zoology Institute, University of Basel, Rheinsprung 9, CH-4051 Basel, Switzerland*

J.H.T.   J. H. TALLIS *School of Biological Sciences, University of Manchester, Oxford Road, Manchester M13 9PT, UK*

K.C.T.   K. C. TAYLOR *Desert Research Institute, Water Resources Center, University and Community College System of Nevada, PO Box 60220, Reno, NV 89506, USA*

K.T.   K. THOMPSON *NERC Unit of Comparative Plant Ecology, Department of Animal and Plant Sciences, University of Sheffield, Sheffield S10 2TN, UK*

J.R.G.T.   J. R. G. TURNER *Ecology and Evolution Research Group, School of Biology, University of Leeds, Leeds LS2 9JT, UK*

P.R.V.G.   P. R. VAN GARDINGEN *Institute of Ecology and Resource Management, University of Edinburgh, West Mains Road, Edinburgh EH9 3JG, UK*

J.V.C.   J. VANDE CASTLE *Department of Biology, University of New Mexico, Albuquerque, NM 87131, USA*

Y.V.   Y. VASARI *Department of Ecology and Systematics, University of Helsinki, PO Box 7 (Unioninkatu 44), Fin-00014 University of Helsinki, Finland*

T.C.W.   **T.C. WHITMORE** *Department of Geography, University of Cambridge, Downing Place, Cambridge CB2 3EN, UK*

H.W.W.   **H.W. WHITTINGTON** *Department of Electrical Engineering, University of Edinburgh, Mayfield Road, Edinburgh EH9 3JL, UK*

A.J.W.   **A.J. WILLIS** *Department of Animal and Plant Sciences, University of Sheffield, Sheffield S10 2TN, UK*

S.N.W.   **S.N. WOOD** *Mathematical Institute, North Haugh, St Andrews KY16 9SS, UK*

S.R.J.W.   **S.R.J. WOODELL** *Wolfson College, Linton Road, Oxford OX2 6UD, UK*

F.W.   **F. WORSFORD** *The Transport Studies Group, University of Westminster, 35 Marylebone Road, London NW1 5LS, UK*

Preface

Following the successful launch of *The Encyclopedia of Ecology & Environmental Management* in 1998, we have been persuaded to prepare a couple of shorter and more focussed versions. This one, *Blackwell's Concise Encyclopedia of Environmental Management*, takes from the parent volume, edited versions of entries that are concerned with all aspects of management of the environment. A sister version does the same for ecology.

The aim has been to produce a concise version that meets the day-to-day needs of students, teachers and professionals working in this area. The entries culled from the full encyclopedia will, in general, be briefer than the originals, but there has still been an attempt, in many of the key terms, to go beyond the few-line definitions that are the hallmark of dictionaries to a more in-depth and critical appraisal, often with a historical commentary.

This concise version contains 1500 entries with extensive cross-referencing. Any relevant headword that is mentioned within the text of any other appears in SMALL CAPITALS. In addition, obviously related headwords are linked by *See also* at the end of entries. For brevity we have not included references, but there are a few figures and a series of helpful tables. Other conventions on hyphenation, alphabetical order, taxonomic nomenclature and abbreviations and acronyms are as in the parent work.

The initials of contributors are given at the end of each entry and their details are given on pp. vii–xii. The success of the *Encyclopedia* has been due to the joint efforts of these many contributors and this concise version also continues to owe much to them. I would also like to take this opportunity to record thanks to my secretary, Samantha Giles, and Blackwell's staff for excellent support in bringing this work into being. The success of our efforts is, of course, for users to determine and as with the *Encyclopedia* we would appreciate any comments, even negative ones, that might help us improve future editions.

PETER CALOW
Sheffield, 1999

A

abatement Reduction, lessening of POLLUTION, usually as a legislative requirement. [P.C.]

abiotic factors (physical factors) A descriptive collective term for components of the physical environment, for example TEMPERATURE, moisture and LIGHT. Distinguishes these features from BIOTIC FACTORS, which usually refers to other living organisms. [J.S.B.]

absorption spectrum A graph or chart showing how the absorption of RADIATION by a medium depends on the wavelength of the incident energy. Absorption is defined as the fraction of the incident energy that is absorbed. [J.G.]

abstraction Removal of WATER from natural supply: RIVERS, LAKES, ponds, groundwater. Usually controlled, often by licence, but there may also be some obligations in common law. [P.C.]

abundance The availability of a resource, or numbers in a population, often described in qualitative terms such as 'rare' or 'common'. Abundance may be used to describe the state of a species either in a restricted area of habitat or over its global distribution. [R.H.S.]

abyssal The bottom zone of the OCEAN at depths between about 4000 and 6000 m, constituting most of the DEEP SEA floor. Abyssal is also referred to as 'profundal'. [V.F.]

abyssal cones Important topographic features of the plains of the deep OCEAN. Abyssal cones are depositional features, composed of SEDIMENT derived from RIVERS. [V.F.]

acaricide A BIOCIDE intended to kill ticks and mites. *See also* INSECTICIDES; PESTICIDE. [P.C.]

acceptable risk In an environmental context, the perceived PROBABILITY that a process or substance may have an adverse EFFECT, but one that is deemed acceptable, usually because it is very low, by interested parties (e.g. politicians, policy-makers, regulators, public). *See also* RISK ASSESSMENT; RISK MANAGEMENT. [P.C.]

access to information (registers) Giving access to information on performance likely to influence the state of the environment. Is used as an instrument for environmental protection in both Europe and the USA. The rationale is that the information, once on public registers, is likely to influence the activities of pressure groups, customers and other interested parties such that the subjects are likely to try and anticipate this by altering their activities to avoid being placed on the registers or to present a more

acceptable record. *See also* MARKET INSTRUMENTS; TOXIC RELEASE INVENTORY. [P.C.]

accident In an environmental context, an undesirable, unexpected event that causes CONTAMINATION and possibly POLLUTION. [P.C.]

accreditation To make ENVIRONMENTAL MANAGEMENT SYSTEMS credible it is necessary to build in independent, third parties as verifiers of the audits. The verifiers have to be accredited. For this, they must be demonstrably competent in:
- environmental auditing methodologies;
- management information systems and processes;
- regulatory issues;
- environmental issues;
- relevant legislation and standards;
- relevant technical knowledge of the activities being verified.

See also ECOAUDIT. [P.C.]

accuracy/precision These terms commonly refer to how well a particular measurement has been made and are often used interchangeably, although strictly they do have slightly different meanings. Accuracy may be defined as 'the closeness of a measured or computed value to its true value', while precision may be defined as 'the closeness of repeated measurements of the same quantity'. [R.C.]

acid A substance that produces hydrogen ions in aqueous solution. Such protonic acids tend to be corrosive and are further classified as strong or weak. A strong acid (e.g. sulphuric, nitric and hydrochloric acids) is completely dissociated, whereas a weak acid (e.g. acetic, carbonic and citric acids) dissociates to form ions in aqueous solution. Also, an acid is a hydrogen ION donor. [M.C.G. & J.G.]

acid precipitation, impact on ecosystems The effect of acid precipitation is to reduce pH in the media that surround organisms. The consequences are complex and multifarious. Reduction in pH can have a direct effect, for example by causing imbalances in acid–base relationships in tissues and at membranes, and/or can also have indirect effects, for example by LEACHING calcium from soils and leading to the mobilization of metals such as aluminium in watercourses. [P.C.]

acid rain and mist RAIN is naturally acidic, containing carbonic acid formed by the solution of atmospheric CARBON DIOXIDE (CO_2), and has a pH of about 5.6. Acidic rain (lower pH) may be formed naturally from biogenic sources of sulphur-containing gases, such as dimethyl sulphide ($(CH_3)_2S$), which is released by marine PHYTOPLANKTON. These gases are oxidized to sulphur dioxide (SO_2), and ultimately to sulphuric acid (H_2SO_4), which is incorporated into cloud and raindrops. In polluted regions, anthropogenic EMISSIONS of sulphur and NITROGEN OXIDES from fossil fuel combustion are oxidized in the ATMOSPHERE to sulphuric and nitric acids, which cause widespread ACIDIFICATION of cloud and rainwater. [J.N.C.]

acidification Reduction in the pH of the environment, mainly due to human actions. [P.C.]

acronyms Alphanumeric abbreviations for programmes, procedures and principles. They are common in environmental policy and legislation. Examples include: BATNEEC; BOD; BPEO; EPA; LCA; QA; QC; RCC; RIVPACS; SAR; TIE; and UNCED. [P.C.]

act of God *See* ACT OF NATURE.

act of nature An occurrence, without the involvement of any human agency, that cannot be foreseen or prevented and usually has disastrous consequences for humans and/or the environment. Also called an act of God. [P.C.]

action level The level or concentration of a substance that triggers active management (avoidance, ameliorative or remedial measures) to safeguard public health and/or the environment. *See also* THRESHOLD. [P.C.]

activated charcoal Charcoal treated at high temperatures (*c.* 900°C) with an oxidizing gas (steam or carbon dioxide, CO_2) to greatly increase the surface area, up to $1500\,m^2g^{-1}$. [J.N.C.]

activated sludge Sludge from the ACTIVATED-SLUDGE PROCESS. [P.C.]

activated-sludge process The biological oxidation of SEWAGE to reduce the ORGANIC LOADING that raw sewage would otherwise impose on receiving water. The process involves aeration in tanks by agitators. Aerobic bacteria grow on the raw sewage, converting some of this to their own biomass with the rest being transformed to WASTE gases. The products are a suspension with reduced organic loading, and a SEDIMENT which consists of bacteria and protozoans. Part of the latter is recycled to seed the raw input, with the rest being disposed of on land, at sea or even by INCINERATION. [P.C.]

active ingredient In BIOCIDES, the component that kills the target organism. PESTICIDES are usually regulated primarily according to their active ingredients. [P.C.]

acute tests Testing, often referring to ECOTOXICOLOGY, for responses that are immediately debilitating; i.e. usually lethal over a short time-span (day(s)), and so involve relatively high concentrations of test substance. *Cf.* CHRONIC TESTS; LONG-TERM TESTS. *See also* PREDICTIVE ECOTOXICITY TESTS; SHORT-TERM TESTS. [P.C.]

adaptation to pollution POLLUTION represents

anthropogenic changes to environmental factors that cause STRESS to organisms. Populations usually show genetic heterogeneity and it is likely that different organisms show different responsiveness to the stress—as a result of physiological and/or morphological and/or behavioural differences. The POLLUTANT will therefore act as a selection pressure and possibly lead to the evolution of TOLERANCE. Thus plant strains sampled from metal spoil heaps are often more metal tolerant than strains of the same species from non-polluted soils. However, differing degrees of tolerance of organisms sampled from different populations, exposed to different levels of pollution, do not necessarily always signal genetic divergence. Exposure may induce the activation of genes that code for protection systems, such as METALLOTHIONEINS and HEAT-SHOCK PROTEINS, that are generally present irrespective of EXPOSURE. Such induction is often referred to as adaptability or acclimation. [P.C.]

additivity The phenomenon whereby the combined ecotoxicological EFFECT of a mixture of chemicals is equal to the sum of the effects of the individual components in isolation. [P.C.]

administrator In the USA, the head of the USEPA, or any office or employee of the Agency to whom authority has been delegated. *See also* REGULATORY AGENCIES. [P.C.]

advanced very-high-resolution radiometer (AVHRR) An imaging sensor used in environmental research. [P.J.C.]

adverse environmental effect The result of an action that is likely to be detrimental to the environment. [P.C.]

advisory committees on environment Bodies set up by local, national or international authorities to provide expert (usually scientific) judgement on environmental issues. The composition, method of appointment and powers of such committees are often, though not always, defined by legislation. There is often a requirement that advice must be sought by the authorities, but not necessarily taken. In Britain, examples that advise the Government are:

• Advisory Committee on Business and the Environment (ACBE);
• Advisory Committee on Hazardous Substances (ACHS);
• Advisory Committee on Pesticides (ACP);
• Advisory Committee on Releases to the Environment (ACRE);
• Advisory Group on Eco-management and Audit (AGEMA).
[P.C.]

aerial plankton Spores, bacteria and other microorganisms suspended and moving in the air. *See also* PLANKTON. [P.C.]

aerial (aircraft) spraying of pesticides *See* PESTICIDES AND SOIL CONTAMINATION.

aerobic decomposition The gradual disintegration of

dead organic matter by means of oxidation resulting from chemical processes or performed by organisms (detritivores and decomposers). Aerobic decomposition requires atmospheric OXYGEN and leads to the breakdown of complex organic molecules into CARBON DIOXIDE (CO_2), WATER and minerals. [P.O.]

aerosols The original definition of this term refers to suspended particles in the carrier medium, air. However, it is now customary to apply the term aerosols, or aerosol particles, more broadly to include deposits of particulate matter since the atmospheric aerosol is collected on filters on particle size-separating impactor plates. The word 'aerosol' covers a wide range of materials but should be distinguished from DUST, which is larger pieces of solid material (≥ 20–$30\,\mu m$ in diameter). [H.S. & J.N.C.]

afforestation The establishment of FOREST either by natural processes, i.e. during SUCCESSION, or by planting. *Cf.* DEFORESTATION. *See also* FORESTATION. [P.C.]

age class Grouping of the organisms within a POPULATION by age instead of by life stage (e.g. in the construction of a life table). [A.J.D.]

age structure The relative numbers of individuals within different AGE CLASSES in a POPULATION. [R.H.S.]

Agenda 21 Output of the UNCED, the so-called Earth Summit, held in Rio de Janeiro in June 1992. This reached a number of agreements, one of which was the Rio Declaration on Environment and Development which set out 27 principles for achieving SUSTAINABLE DEVELOPMENT. To support this general declaration the summit adopted Agenda 21, a comprehensive action plan for the pursuit of sustainable development into the 21st century. It contains 40 chapters of detailed recommendations aimed at all major players: international agencies; local and national governments; and non-governmental organizations (NGOs). A quinquennial review on progress was held in 1997. [P.C.]

Agent Orange *See* DIOXIN.

Agreement on Technical Barriers to Trade *See* GATT AND ENVIRONMENT.

agricultural meteorology A branch of METEOROLOGY, also known as agrometeorology, that is concerned with the study of all aspects of the links between the ATMOSPHERE and AGRICULTURE, where agriculture is usually interpreted in its widest form to include most forms of managed land use (i.e. including horticulture, animal husbandry, pisciculture and FORESTRY). The links are considered in both directions to include both the obvious effects of WEATHER on agriculture, and the less obvious but increasingly important effects of agriculture on the atmosphere (e.g. emission of gases from cultivated soils, change of surface reflectivity or roughness following clearance of forest for farming, evaporation of irrigation water). [J.I.L.M.]

agricultural pollution CONTAMINATION leading to adverse effects on ecological systems that arises from agricultural activities. Examples of these kinds of POLLUTION are wastes from farm animals, PESTICIDES, FERTILIZER treatment of CROPS and EMISSIONS from machinery. The term might also include the release of GENETICALLY MODIFIED ORGANISMS. Much of the release into surrounding ecosystems, both terrestrial and aquatic, will be diffuse and continuous (or semi-continuous) rather than from point sources, and so is difficult to control. [P.C.]

agricultural waste Any mixture of faeces, urine, bedding material, spoiled feed, etc. derived from livestock farming. [P.C.]

agriculture Although the word originally meant the act of cultivating fields, i.e. growing CROPS, it has now been extended to include all aspects of growing crops and raising livestock. Indeed, the definition is now flexible enough to include such contrasting activities as intensive animal production in feedlots or barns, ranching, horticulture and the complex small-scale subsistence farming which characterizes parts of the humid tropics. The common element is conscious management of a biological resource. [G.R.]

agrochemicals Chemicals used in AGRICULTURE; for example to enhance YIELD or to protect against pests. [P.C.]

agroecosystems Agricultural systems, particularly CROP plants and their weeds and associated human farming practices in the context of the wider semi-natural ECOSYSTEM. [G.A.F.H.]

air, chemical and physical properties Air is largely nitrogen (78% by volume) and OXYGEN (21%), with important but small concentrations of CARBON DIOXIDE (CO_2; 0.035%) and very low concentrations of several other gases (Table A1). The water vapour content is variable, with a fractional volume in the range 0.001–0.03 (*see* HUMIDITY). Common pollutant gases (*see* AIR POLLUTION) near ground level vary according to the presence of local sources

Table A1 The composition of air, based on the US Standard Atmosphere 1976, specified here for sea-level dry air.

Gas species	Molecular weight	Fractional volume
N_2	28.0134	0.78084
O_2	31.9988	0.209476
Ar	39.948	0.00934
CO_2	44.01	0.00035
Ne	20.183	0.00001818
He	4.003	0.00000524
Kr	83.80	0.00000114
Xe	131.30	0.000000087
CH_4	16.04	0.000002
H_2	2.016	0.0000005

Table A2 Temperature-dependent properties of air at a pressure of 101 kPa.

	Temperature (°C)					
	−5	0	10	20	30	45
ρ_a (kg m^{-3})	1.31	1.29	1.25	1.20	1.16	1.11
ρ_{as} (kg m^{-3})	1.31	1.29	1.24	1.19	1.14	1.01
k (mW m^{-1} K^{-1})	240	243	250	260	264	275
κ (mm^2 s^{-1})	18.3	18.9	20.2	22.2	22.8	24.9
υ (mm^2 s^{-1})	12.9	13.3	14.2	15.5	16.0	17.4
D_V (mm^2 s^{-1})	20.5	21.2	22.7	24.9	25.7	28.0
D_C (mm^2 s^{-1})	12.4	12.9	13.8	15.1	15.6	17.0

Symbols: ρ_a, density of dry air; ρ_{as}, density of water vapour-saturated air; k, thermal conductivity; κ, thermal diffusivity; υ, kinematic viscosity; D_V, diffusion coefficient of water in air; D_C, diffusion coefficient of CO_2 in air.

Table A3 Solubility of air and its main constituents in water. Volumes of dissolved gases (cm^3) contained in a kilogram of water saturated with air at 101 kPa.

	Temperature (°C)			
	0	10	20	30
Oxygen	10.2	7.9	6.4	5.3
Nitrogen, argon, etc.	19.0	15.0	12.3	10.4
Sum of above (air)	29.2	22.9	18.7	15.7

and the meteorological conditions. Concentrations that become damaging to plants are: OZONE 300 ppbv; nitrogen oxide (NO + NO$_2$) 30 µg m^{-3}; sulphur dioxide (SO$_2$) 30 µg m^{-3}. AEROSOLS, including DUST and pollens, are very variable. Values for the physical properties of air are often needed, for example in calculations of heat transfer and diffusion. Table A2 lists those that are temperature dependent. The specific heat of air at constant pressure is 1.01 J kg^{-1} K^{-1}. Air is sparingly soluble in cold water, and solubility declines with temperature (Table A3). The velocity of sound in air at sea level is 345 m s^{-1}. *See also* AIR QUALITY; ATMOSPHERIC CHEMISTRY; ATMOSPHERIC POLLUTION. [J.G.]

air mass A large body of air whose horizontal dimensions can be several hundred to several thousand kilometres in extent and in which at any vertical level the properties of TEMPERATURE and HUMIDITY are fairly uniform. Air masses are found over and near to the semi-permanent surface features of the atmospheric general circulation, for example subtropical high-pressure areas or snow-covered polar areas. [J.B.M.]

air pollution The existence of CONTAMINANTS in the air at levels that interfere with human health and/or ecological systems. [P.C.]

air-pollution control POLLUTION control pertaining to EMISSIONS into, and quality of, the ATMOSPHERE. *See also* AIR POLLUTION; ATMOSPHERIC POLLUTION. [P.C.]

air quality Description of the extent to which the ATMOSPHERE in a defined locale is contaminated and polluted. [P.C.]

air-quality standards Prescribed concentrations of substances in ambient ATMOSPHERE that cannot legally be exceeded during a given period in a specified location. *See also* AIR QUALITY. [P.C.]

aircraft pollution Consists of chemicals and noise. The principal chemical products of aircraft engine combustion are WATER vapour and CARBON DIOXIDE (CO$_2$). In addition, smaller amounts of HYDROCARBONS, CARBON MONOXIDE (CO), oxides of nitrogen (NO$_x$) and SMOKE particulates are produced. These potentially cause POLLUTION around airports but probably have more important impacts in flight. NO$_x$ EMISSIONS in supersonic flight in the STRATOSPHERE are likely to cause OZONE destruction. On the other hand, NOISE POLLUTION is most important around airports. The nuisance depends upon perceived noise levels and on the number of aircraft heard in a given period; an index combining these two quantities (the NNI—noise and number index) is used as an indicator of this nuisance. *See also* AIR POLLUTION; ATMOSPHERIC POLLUTION. [P.C.]

ALAP *See* AS LOW AS PRACTICABLE.

ALARA *See* AS LOW AS REASONABLY ACHIEVABLE.

ALARP (as low as reasonably practicable) *See* AS LOW AS PRACTICABLE.

albedo The shortwave (300–1500 nm) reflectance of a natural surface, also known as the reflection coefficient. [J.G.]

algal bloom Dense populations of free-floating algae, often imparting a distinctive colour and odour to the water body. BLOOMS occur in marine and fresh waters and result from a period of intense, often monospecific growth in response to favourable nutrition and light. Most freshwater blooms are caused by planktonic cyanobacteria belonging to the genera *Anabaena, Aphanizomenon* and *Microcystis*. Dinoflagellates of the genus *Gonyaulax* produce 'RED TIDES', often on a large scale. Huge blooms of oceanic coccolithophorid algae have been observed from space. Many blooms are toxic. They render the water unfit for drinking and unpleasant skin rashes may result from bathing. Some of the TOXINS are transported along the FOOD CHAIN. Poisoning from shellfish consumption is frequently associated with blooms of the algae *Gonyaulax* and *Prymnesium* in coastal waters. [A.P.]

algorithm A series of instructions for carrying out a specific computational task; it might be in the form of a flow diagram or in lines of computer code. [M.J.C.]

alien A non-indigenous organism; a species of plant or animal moved (typically by human agency) to a country outside its natural geographical range. [M.J.C.]

ALIs (annual limits on intake) *See* MAXIMUM PERMISSIBLE LEVEL.

allochthonous Describing organic matter not generated within an ecological COMMUNITY. [P.O.]

α-particle Particles of mass 4 amu (*see* ATOMIC MASS) and charge +2 (i.e. $^4_2$He nuclei), emitted during the radioactive decay of heavy, proton-rich nuclei. α-Particles typically have energies in the range 4–9 MeV. The α-particles emitted in the decay of a given RADIONUCLIDE generally all have a characteristic energy or group of energies. α-Particles cause intense ionization along straight-line paths in materials with which they interact, but have very limited penetrating power, with ranges of less than 0.1 mm in solids and only a few centimetres in gases. *See also* IONIZING RADIATION; SIEVERT. [A.B.M.]

alpine zone The alpine vegetation zone lies between the upper limit of tree growth and the snow line. Within the alpine zone vegetation communities vary depending on altitude, aspect, exposure, snow cover and water availability. [R.M.M.C.]

alternative energy/fuels Energy or fuels derived from non-traditional sources, such as solar, WIND, chemical feedstocks and wastes. [P.C.]

alternative hypothesis (H_1) The alternative to the NULL HYPOTHESIS, usually represented by H_1. Sometimes this is simply that the null hypothesis is not true, sometimes it is more precise. [B.S.]

alternative technology Technology designed to stand in place of the complex, often polluting production processes of the developed world. It is often intended primarily for use in developing countries. Hence it should be easy to construct, use and maintain. An example is the use of WIND POWER, rather than a diesel-powered motor, to pump water. Such technology will generally be less polluting than the usual system. [P.C.]

altitudinal zonation Vegetation shows a marked ZONATION with altitude because of changing TEMPERATURE and rainfall. In some ways the altitudinal zonation mirrors the latitudinal zonation (*see* LATITUDINAL GRADIENTS OF DIVERSITY) from the tropics to the polar regions, but the effects of both frost and the LIGHT regime are quite different between the tropics and other latitudes. [M.I.]

ambient Of, or relating to, surrounding environmental conditions. [P.C.]

Ames test A bacterial test for detecting point MUTATIONS. *See also* ECOTOXICITY; PREDICTIVE ECOTOXICITY TESTS. [P.C.]

Amoco Cadiz See ECOLOGICAL/ENVIRONMENTAL DISASTERS.

anadromous Describing a specific annual migratory pattern in fishes when they move from marine to freshwater environments. [R.C.]

anaerobic decomposition The partial disintegration of dead organic matter not involving atmospheric OXYGEN. The process yields less energy than its aerobic equivalent, and the products are only partially oxidized. [P.O.]

analysis of variance (ANOVA) A technique for comparing the difference between several SAMPLE means by analysing the VARIANCE in the total data. It is a parametric technique (*see* PARAMETRIC STATISTICS) and assumes that observations are normally distributed (*see* NORMAL DISTRIBUTION), with approximately equal variances in all samples. If these two conditions are not met they can frequently be obtained by TRANSFORMATION OF DATA. [B.S.]

ancient woodland/forest In Britain, WOODLAND which existed before either 1600 or 1700, depending on authority. Some ancient woodland has since been cleared and some survives in the modern landscape, having existed continuously since 1600. The sites and shapes of vanished ancient woods often survive in the modern field pattern with their original margin of mixed shrubs forming a hedge. All PRIMARY WOODLAND is ancient woodland, but ancient woodland also includes SECONDARY WOODLAND originating before 1600. The threshold date of 1600 is chosen to pre-date the main era of planting (so most ancient woods originated naturally) and to coincide with the general availability of maps (so there is a reasonable chance that individual woods can be proved to be ancient, or otherwise). [G.F.P.]

anemometer An instrument for measuring the speed of the WIND. [J.G.]

angiosperms, global diversity and conservation Flowering plants (angiosperms) are major components of the world's flora and its VEGETATION. Considered the culmination of evolution in the plant kingdom, they originated about 130 million years ago and evolved very rapidly, leading to an enormous progressive increase in plant DIVERSITY to the present day. The angiosperms are seed-producing vascular plants of extremely varied form; many are valuable as sources of food and other commodities. They are dominant in virtually all plant communities. [A.J.W.]

annual limits on intake (ALIs) *See* MAXIMUM PERMISSIBLE LEVEL.

anoxia (hypoxia) Environmental conditions with no (or low) OXYGEN. [P.C.]

Antarctic ozone hole The seasonal depletion of OZONE in a large area of the ATMOSPHERE over Antarctica. *See also* OZONE HOLE; STRATOSPHERIC CHEMISTRY. [P.C.]

Antarctica, ecology and conservation In biological terms, Antarctica comprises all land and associated ICE cover (including ice shelves attached to the land) south of latitude 60°S, but including the South Sandwich Islands (56–59°S) and Bouvetøya (54°S). Throughout this southern polar biome mean summer (December–February) air temperatures remain low, reaching 1–2°C only in the northernmost coastal areas. This, together with daily freezing and thawing cycles and almost daily drying and wetting cycles, impose severe physiological STRESS on terrestrial organisms, inhibiting metabolism, growth and reproduction, as well as the processes of colonization and community development.

By far the greatest diversity of species comprises cryptogams (mosses, liverworts, lichens, algae, cyanobacteria and fungi) and microarthropods (mites and springtails).

The simple, virtually pristine, terrestrial ecosystem is highly adapted to the stresses (*see* STRESS) imposed by the Antarctic environment. Its component communities are very fragile and sensitive to change and perturbation, for example climatic warming especially in summer, increasing UV-B resulting from OZONE depletion in spring, and a rapidly increasing population of fur seals which devastate vegetation in the maritime Antarctic. For these and other reasons, protection of the Antarctic environment has been foremost in the policy of the Antarctic Treaty since it came into force in 1961; indeed, the entire Treaty Area was designated a 'special conservation area'. Although lacking any strict legal conditions or any form of policing, such protection has been remarkably successful under the Agreed Measures for the Conservation of Antarctic Fauna and Flora. In 1991 this was superseded by the Protocol on Environmental Protection. [R.I.L.S.]

anthropomorphism Attributing human qualities, especially to animal behaviour and/or to the processes of nature. [P.C.]

antibiosis The production by microorganisms or plants of antimetabolites (antibiotics) that, in small amounts, are lethal or inhibiting to other organisms (usually bacteria or fungi). [P.C.]

antifouling Natural or artificial measures taken to prevent the growth of bacteria, plants and invertebrates on surfaces. Approaches suggested or used with success include the application of metals (copper, tributyltin), adjustment of surface wettability (e.g. by applying Teflon), incorporation of adsorbed enzyme molecules that are active against fouling, BIOLOGICAL CONTROL with predators or parasites of fouling organisms, periodic heating, electrical discharge, ultraviolet illumination, ultrasonic cleaning and various mechanical means. *See also* TRIBUTYLTIN (TBT) POLLUTION. [V.F.]

aphotic zone The region of the OCEAN and deep LAKES in which there is no LIGHT penetration and, hence, no PHOTOSYNTHESIS. [J.L.]

aquaculture Culturing aquatic organisms for commercial purposes, either in artificial systems—for example tanks or channels—or in nature. The latter might include cultures in completely open systems or in enclosures (e.g. cages). FISH FARMING is one form of aquaculture. Often EFFLUENTS from unconsumed food, wastes and pharmaceuticals can cause POLLUTION. [P.C.]

aquatic ecotoxicology *See* ECOTOXICOLOGY.

aquatic systems, conservation and restoration All aquatic ecosystems (LENTIC and LOTIC) can be considered as RENEWABLE RESOURCES and thus available or potentially available for industrial and/or non-consumptive purposes such as recreation. With the use of even a renewable resource there is the danger that the aquatic ECOSYSTEM will be changed or even destroyed.

Conservation and restoration of aquatic ecosystems has frequently been linked to the concept of ECOSYSTEM INTEGRITY. However, integrity is not an objective, quantifiable property and has four major, sometimes incompatible, themes:
1 ecosystem structure and/or process staying at predefined baseline levels;
2 a system permitted to change without human influence;
3 preservation of an organizing or self-correcting ability with an end state defined as normal or optimal; or
4 maintenance of qualities desired by society or components of society.
[R.W.D.]

aquifer A geological formation containing sufficient saturated permeable material to yield WATER to wells and springs in significant quantities. Aquifers are defined as unconfined if their upper surface is open to the atmosphere and confined, or artesian, if they are overlaid by impermeable layers. In confined aquifers the water pressure is greater than atmospheric pressure and if the confining layer is pierced by a well the pressure may be enough to force water to the land surface. Most of the world's major aquifers are in rocks of sedimentary origin, notably chalk, sandstone, coarse sand and gravel. [D.C.L.]

arboretum A collection of plants, in particular trees, shrubs and woody climbers, cultivated for scientific, conservation, educational and/or aesthetic purposes. The term can also embrace the institution/organization responsible for administering and maintaining such a collection. 'Botanical garden' describes a collection that is not restricted to ligneous (woody) plants, although in practice the distinction is sometimes blurred. [P.C.]

arboriculture The cultivation of woody plants, particularly trees, primarily for ornamental purposes in human-dominated settings (as opposed to SILVICULTURE in forests). [A.N.G. & G.A.F.H.]

Arctic Historically, the word Arctic refers to the region of the Earth below the stellar constellation of the Great Bear (Greek *Arktos*, bear). Climatically, the terrestrial Arctic can be considered to be that region of the Earth's land surface that is underlain by PERMAFROST or permanently frozen ground. Permafrost underlies approximately 20% of the Earth's land surface and occurs not only at high latitudes but also in some non-Arctic locations at high elevations and is the main limiting factor to the northward extension of trees (*see* TAIGA; TUNDRA). Geographically, the Arctic can be defined simply as the portion of the Earth's surface that lies north of the Arctic Circle (66°33'N). The Arctic can also be defined biogeographically on the basis of the species composition of the plant communities and as such is traditionally divided biogeographically into the low Arctic, with plant communities dominated by woody shrubs (e.g. *Alnus, Betula, Salix*), and the high Arctic, which is characterized by much of the land surface and SEA being covered by permanent ICE, with terrestrial vegetation limited to a thin discontinuous cover of diminutive flowering plants, mosses and lichens. At present, polar desert (see below) is found mainly in the northern Canadian archipelagos, the Queen Elizabeth Islands, Ellesmere Island, northern Greenland, Svalbard in Nordaustlandet, Kong Karls Land, the northern tip of Novaya Zemlya, Franz Josef Land, Cape Chelyuskin and Severnaya Zemlya. [R.M.M.C.]

arithmetic mean A measure of central tendency or average. *See also* MEAN. [B.S.]

artesian *See* AQUIFER.

artificial selection The deliberate choice of a select group of individuals to be used for breeding. The response to artificial selection is usually quite large, especially during the first generations of selection. [I.O.]

artificial substrate A material placed in the environment by an experimenter so that patterns of colonization and COMMUNITY development can be observed. [S.J.H.]

as low as practicable (ALAP) A regulatory principle that can be applied to control EXPOSURE to harmful substances. The exclusion of 'reasonably', as in 'as low as reasonably practicable' (ALARP) and AS LOW AS REASONABLY ACHIEVABLE, signals that the costs of the regulatory measure do not weigh too heavily. [P.C.]

as low as reasonably achievable (ALARA) A regulatory principle that can be applied to EXPOSURE to harmful substances. Inclusion of 'reasonably' (*cf.* AS LOW AS PRACTICABLE) signals that the costs of the proposed measure ought to be balanced against the benefits arising out of regulations. *See also* COST (RISK)–BENEFIT APPROACH; MAXIMUM PERMISSIBLE LEVEL. [P.C.]

as low as reasonably practicable (ALARP) *See* AS LOW AS PRACTICABLE.

asbestos The name given to a group of fibrous silicate minerals which, on account of excellent resistance to fire, heat and chemical attack, have been used in structural materials, brake linings, insulation and pipes. The commonest forms are chrysotile (white asbestos, $3MgO.2SiO_2.2H_2O$), crocidolite (blue asbestos, $Na_2O.Fe_2O_3.3FeO.8SiO_2.H_2O$) and amosite (brown asbestos, $(FeMg)SiO_3$). Asbestos is a human carcinogen, with inhaled small fibres of crocidolite in particular penetrating deep into the lungs, where their physical nature can give rise to mesothelioma and other diseases, often after lengthy latency periods of 20 years or more. Although uses are now severely curtailed and replacement programmes are common, major EMISSIONS of asbestos to the air can still occur from demolition works and LAND-FILL sites. [J.G.F.]

assemblage A general term for a collection of plants and/or animals, or the fossilized remains of these organisms in a geological SEDIMENT. Unlike the term 'COMMUNITY', it does not imply interrelationships between the organisms. [P.D.M.]

assimilative capacity The extent to which a system can take up, and (by implication) process, XENOBI-OTICS. [P.C.]

association Similar to CORRELATION, but a more general term. For example, it applies to the relationship between qualitative information in a CONTINGENCY TABLE. [B.S.]

Atlantic Ocean The warmest, saltiest, and second largest of the world's oceans and the first to be explored. The Atlantic Basin has an S-shape and stretches between Europe and Africa in the east and America in the west; its northern and southern boundaries are less clearly defined (the broadest definition extends from the Antarctic continent in the south to the Bering Straits in the north). The area, volume and mean depth of the Atlantic are $8.4 \times 10^7 km^2$, $3.23 \times 10^4 km^3$, and 3844 m, respectively, or $10.6 \times 10^7 km^2$, $3.51 \times 10^4 km^3$, and 3293 m, if its marginal seas are included. The deepest part of the Atlantic occurs in the Milwaukee Depth in the Puerto Rico Trench at 9219 m. The basin of the Atlantic can be separated into eastern and western troughs, symmetrically distributed on either side of the Mid-Atlantic Ridge. In contrast to the South Atlantic, which has one marginal SEA (i.e. the Weddell Sea), the North Atlantic has many marginal seas (i.e. MEDITERRANEAN SEA, Gulf of Mexico, NORTH SEA, BALTIC SEA, English Channel, Irish and Celtic Seas, NORWEGIAN SEA, Greenland Sea, Irminger Sea, Labrador Sea, Hudson Bay and Baffin Bay), some of which have a major influence on the circulation of the entire Atlantic. [V.F.]

atmosphere The mainly gaseous envelope overlying the solid and liquid surface of a planet. The Earth's atmosphere has mass equivalent to a 10-m-deep envelope of WATER, 90% of which is concentrated in the first 16 km above sea level. It consists almost entirely of air—a mixture of gases, many of which (with the important exception of water vapour) are kept in highly uniform proportions by stirring. In order of diminishing proportion the gases are: dinitrogen (N_2), dioxygen (O_2), argon (Ar), water vapour (H_2O; concentrated in the lowest few kilometres by efficient cloud formation and PRECIPITA-TION), CARBON DIOXIDE (CO_2), and hundreds of TRACE GASES such as OZONE (O_3). The Earth's atmosphere also contains very small amounts of condensed matter. In order of diminishing total mass they are cloud (localized suspensions of *c.* 10 μm scale water droplets and ICE crystals widespread in the TROPOSPHERE), precipitation (RAIN, hail and snow falling through and from thicker CLOUDS), and AEROSOL (the diffuse suspension of submicrometre scale particles and solution droplets in the troposphere and STRATOSPHERE). *See also* ATMOSPHERIC CHEMISTRY; ATMOSPHERIC POLLUTION. [J.F.R.M.]

atmospheric chemistry In the TROPOSPHERE, the chemical reactions by which trace substances released into the ATMOSPHERE from natural and anthropogenic sources are oxidized. [P.B.]

atmospheric circulation The patterns of air motion in the ATMOSPHERE, especially the TROPOSPHERE, after removing transient, localized distortions associated with individual WEATHER systems. [J.F.R.M.]

atmospheric pollution The addition of substances to the ATMOSPHERE that have a capacity to cause HARM to human health and/or ecological systems. It can involve the emission of chemicals from stacks, the emission of SMOKE and SOOT from chimneys, the emission of smoke, soot and chemicals from fire, explosions, leaks, etc. *See also* AIR POLLUTION; SMOG. [P.C.]

atomic absorption spectrometer Analytical equipment used to quantify the concentrations of dissolved metals. Sample solutions for analysis, containing the element of interest, are rapidly heated in a flame or a graphite furnace, to convert the element into individual atoms, which emit and absorb LIGHT of a specific wavelength. When light of the specific wavelength is shone through the heated gases, the amount of light absorbed is proportional to the concentration of element in the sample. [J.N.C.]

atomic mass The mass of an ISOTOPE of an element measured in atomic mass units (amu). In 1961 the amu was formally defined as $1/_{12}$ of the mass of ^{12}C carbon. The absolute mass of an amu is about 1.66×10^{-27} kg. Examples include: hydrogen, 1.008; LEAD, 207.19; thorium, 232.04. [J.G.]

atomic number The atomic number, Z, is the number of protons in the nucleus of an atom or the number of electrons associated with one atom. Examples include: for hydrogen, $Z = 1$; for LEAD $Z = 82$; for thorium $Z = 90$. [J.G.]

attenuation, light Diminution of light intensity with depth in water bodies due to absorption and scatter-

ing in the water column. Attenuation is expressed as the sum of the fraction of the radiant flux absorbed and the fraction scattered. Water is a poor absorber of visible RADIATION below about 560 nm wavelength, with minimal attenuance at about 475 nm. Thus, red light attenuates most rapidly in water whereas blue light penetrates deepest. Differences in colour between clean water (blue-green) and water containing DISSOLVED ORGANIC MATTER (yellow) are due to differential absorption of light by water molecules compared to organic substances. [V.F.]

aufwuchs See BENTHIC HABITAT CLASSIFICATION.

autecology The ECOLOGY of individual species as opposed to the ecology of whole communities. Autecology includes behavioural, physiological and population ecologies. [M.H.]

authorization Legal acceptance (usually in document form) of the release of EMISSIONS/EFFLUENTS of specified quality and quantity, usually with the aim of preventing POLLUTION. *See also* CONSENTS; POLLUTION PERMITS. [P.C.]

autochthonous Describing material originating in its present position; for example BIOMASS (leading to SEDIMENT) that is formed from PHOTOSYNTHESIS in a freshwater lake or river. *Cf.* ALLOCHTHONOUS. [P.C.]

automobile pollution *See* MOTOR VEHICLE POLLUTION.

autotroph Simply, an organism that can make its own food: the term is derived from the Greek *auto*, self, and *trophos*, feeder. Autotrophs can exploit simple inorganic compounds, using CARBON DIOXIDE (CO_2) or carbonates as the carbon source for building their organic constituents. Two categories of autotroph are defined by the energy source used in the synthesis of their organic requirements from inorganic carbon species.

1 Photoautotrophs: these use LIGHT energy, and comprise all photosynthetic organisms, including most terrestrial plants, algae and photosynthetic bacteria (*see also* PHOTOSYNTHESIS).

2 Chemoautotrophs: these comprise bacteria that obtain energy from the oxidation of simple inorganic or 1-C organic compounds and can use the energy released to assimilate CO_2 and transfer the energy into organic compounds. For example, *Thiobacillus* species can obtain their energy by oxidizing hydrogen sulphide or elemental sulphur to sulphuric acid. *Cf.* HETEROTROPH. [S.P.L.]

B

BACI (before–after/control–impact) A SAMPLING design used in RETROSPECTIVE ANALYSIS/MONITORING, involving replicate samples before and after DISTURBANCE in each of an undisturbed control and putatively impacted location. An impact due to the disturbance (e.g. effluent to river from a point source) will cause the difference in mean ABUNDANCE from before to after, in the impacted location, to differ from any natural change in the control.

However, there might still be natural temporal variations in the control and putatively impacted site that confound the interpretation. For example, following the release of an effluent from a pipe to a river, adult insects may arrive and lay eggs in the upstream, control location but not in the downstream location, purely by chance. As a result, BACI would suggest an apparent impact. Hence, the interpretation is complicated and any effect of the disturbance cannot be distinguished from the natural variation. Therefore, if there is an ENVIRONMENTAL IMPACT it is *necessary* to demonstrate differences between control and putatively impacted sites. But, in itself, this is not *sufficient* evidence of impact (*see also* PSEUDOREPLICATION).

A possible solution to these problems is to replicate the sampling, for example between control and impacted sites in separate RIVERS, but this is rarely possible or even desirable for impacted sites. So only the control sites might be replicated, and this leads to asymmetrical sampling designs for which some statistical procedures are available. *See also* BEFORE-AFTER STUDIES; STATISTICS. [P.C.]

background extinction rates *See* EXTINCTION MODELLING.

background level The concentration of a substance in the environment that is not attributable to a particular human activity. The term often refers to the concentration produced by NATURAL phenomena; i.e. of natural substances such as metals that can be added to by human activities. [P.C.]

backshore That part of the shore normally beyond the reach of the highest TIDES and subject only to very occasional inundation by saltwater. [B.W.F.]

bactericide A BIOCIDE used to control or destroy bacteria. [P.C.]

balance of nature The idea that there are tendencies in the natural world towards equilibria in populations, communities, ecosystems, etc. An extreme form of this is the notion that there is some kind of natural design or predetermined goal state—a notion rejected by most ecologists. A less extreme concept is that there are dynamic steady states brought about by BIOLOGICAL CONTROL systems of various kinds. *See also* GAIA. [P.C.]

Baltic Sea The largest brackish-water SEA in the world, lying between north and central Europe and including the Gulf of Bothnia, the Gulf of Finland, the Gulf of Riga, the Baltic proper, the Sound, the Belt Sea and the Kattegat (up to 57°N). Considered a young sea, it was formed during the last ice age, approximately 10000–15000 BP. It has a mean depth of only 55 m, and is characterized by a number of deep BASINS separated by shallow sills. The deepest basin is the Landsort Deep (459 m). The total area of the Baltic Sea is about 390000 km² and its volume is 20000 km³. The drainage area of the Baltic measures approximately 1650000 km². The surrounding countries engage in heavy industry and intensive agriculture, and sea traffic is considerable, including tankers, cargo vessels, large container ships and ferries. The Baltic is connected to the NORTH SEA through the Danish Straits (Great Belt, Little Belt) and the Sound. [V.F.]

bar A shingle or sand structure joined to solid coastline at both ends. Shingle bars may comprise several parallel ridges. A bar forms across an ESTUARY or a coastline indentation, and typically originates as a spit attached at one end which extends, eventually to link with solid coastline at the other end. [B.W.F.]

Barents Sea A marginal SEA of the ATLANTIC OCEAN and part of the polar BASIN around the ARCTIC. This high-latitude sea (i.e. above 70°N) has 3 months of continuous light in the summer and 3 months of continuous darkness in the winter. It is open to the NORWEGIAN SEA (and thereby the Atlantic) to the west. The Barents Sea has an unstable climate and is one of the most stormy seas in the world. Its location between the Atlantic and Arctic Oceans results in a number of interesting hydrographic features. One of the more prominent features is the polar FRONT which occurs at the boundary of cold Arctic and warm Atlantic waters and which is an area of unusually high productivity. [V.F.]

barometer An instrument for measuring atmospheric PRESSURE. [J.G.]

barrier island A shingle structure formed where a large mass of shingle accumulates offshore and is not connected to the mainland, often being separated from it by shallow LAGOONS. Frequently, such structures are associated with SAND DUNES, which may overlie the shingle, and with adjacent SALT MARSHES formed on the sheltered landward side. [B.W.F. & V.F.]

barrier reef A REEF adjacent to a landmass and separated from it by a LAGOON or channel of variable extent. Barrier reefs are not readily distinguishable from fringing reefs, though barrier reefs tend to be separated from the landmass by a greater distance and by a deeper water channel than fringing reefs. Barrier reefs are common throughout the CORAL REEF zones in all oceans. The largest barrier reef, extending nearly 200 km in length, is the Great Barrier Reef in Australia. [V.F.]

baseline data Data describing some original, or 'normal', state of a system—for example POPU-LATION DENSITY, population AGE STRUCTURE, species composition, energy flow—that can be used as standard/control against which changes are judged. This can often suffer from the problem of PSEUDOREPLICATION. [P.C.]

bases Substances that dissociate in WATER to yield hydroxyl ions, OH-. [J.G.]

basin A geographical area that is effectively enclosed, referring either to terrestrial or oceanic locations. In terrestrial situations it is typically a region that collects the precipitation falling upon it (*see* CATCH-MENT). [P.D.M.]

bathyal zone The bottom of the OCEAN between 200 m and about 4000 m depth, corresponding to the depth of the CONTINENTAL SLOPE and CONTI-NENTAL RISE. The bathyal zone occupies approximately 16% of the submerged ocean floor. [V.F.]

bathypelagic The oceanic water column between about 1000 and 4000 m depth, seaward of the SHELF-SLOPE BREAK. [V.F.]

BATNEEC *See* BEST AVAILABLE TECHNIQUES NOT ENTAILING EXCESSIVE COSTS.

battery A portable power supply, made from a set of electrolytic cells. A cell consists of two electrodes immersed in an electrolyte, one of which forms the positive pole (anode) and the other the negative pole (cathode). When the two poles are connected to an external circuit, current flows as a result of chemical reactions on the surface of the electrodes. Each cell produces a rather small voltage, but by connecting several cells together in series (i.e. the anode of one is connected to the cathode of another), a useful voltage is obtained. Batteries are specified by their voltage, their capacity (in ampere-hours (Ah)) and the type of storage cell from which they are composed.

The most common type of non-rechargeable battery until recently was the dry form of the Leclanché cell. The original Leclanché consisted of a positive electrode of carbon surrounded by manganese dioxide and carbon in a porous pot. The pot stood in the electrolyte, which was an ammonium chloride solution. The negative electrode was zinc.

Rechargeable cells are widely available, known as secondary cells. Batteries made of them are sometimes termed accumulators. Lead–acid batteries are the sort of rechargeable batteries used in motor cars.

Nickel–cadmium batteries have a nickel hydroxide cathode, cadmium anode and potassium hydroxide electrolyte, in steel containers. [J.G.]

beach A rather imprecise term used in a narrow sense to describe the layer of unconsolidated materials overlying harder geology occurring between the tidal limits (the shore). [B.W.F.]

becquerel (Bq) A measure of the RADIOACTIVITY present in a body; 1 unit represents 1 nuclear disintegration per second. Thus, when applied to a sheep which has been grazing on land on which radioactivity has fallen in rain, it is measured as the number of nuclear transformations per second per kilogram of flesh. Physically, it is a measure of the emission rate, or energy deposited in a recipient of the emission, and not of the biological effect on the sheep or on a person who ingests its flesh. This is an SI UNIT and supersedes the former unit, rem. [R.S.S.]

bedload The particles being moved along the bed of a RIVER or stream. [P.C.]

before–after studies A method of impact assessment that uses the state of the ENVIRONMENT and ecological systems within it as a STANDARD against which to judge the condition following development and/or release of EFFLUENTS/EMISSIONS. However, because ECOSYSTEMS are dynamic it cannot always be presumed that the properties of the system(s) before would have been like those after, even if there had been no impact. *See also* BACI. [P.C.]

benthic boundary layer The layer of water immediately above the SEA floor and extending upwards for a distance of 10 to several hundred metres from the bottom. It is the region above the bottom where flow is measurably slowed in comparison to the more vertically uniform mean velocity in overlying water. [V.F.]

benthic habitat classification Organisms associated with the substrate–water interface of LAKES, RIVERS, ESTUARIES and SEAS form the BENTHOS. The benthos can be either phytobenthos (plant) or zoobenthos (animal), both of which are subdivided into macro- (visible with the naked eye) or micro- (visible with a microscope). [R.W.D.]

benthic–pelagic coupling The functional linkage between benthic and PELAGIC subsystems. The supply of organic matter from the PLANKTON to the BENTHOS is balanced by MINERALIZATION of organic detritus by the benthic microbial community and release of dissolved metabolites to the overlying water. [S.J.H. & V.F.]

benthos Benthos refers to all the attached, creeping or

burrowing organisms that inhabit the bottom of RIVERS, LAKES and the SEA. The term is derived from Greek, meaning 'depth of the sea'. It includes plants and animals living on the SEDIMENT surface, on the surface of HARD SUBSTRATA or protruding from the bottom (EPIFAUNA and epiflora), as well as those living buried in the sediment column (infauna). The term DEMERSAL has also been used for organisms (especially fish) living on or near the bottom. [V.F.]

Bering Sea An extension of the North Pacific, the Bering Sea lies between the Aleutian Island Arc to the south (51°N) and the Bering Strait to the north (66°N) and between 157°W and 163°E. It is the second largest of the marginal seas with an area of $2.3 \times 10^6 \, \text{km}^2$, a volume of $3.4 \times 10^6 \, \text{km}^3$, an average depth of 1491 m and a maximum depth of 4096 m. It is unusual in having an extremely large CONTINENTAL SHELF. The southern Bering Sea maintains a series of FRONTS off the SHELF-SLOPE BREAK which divides the PELAGIC realm into several distinctive trophic webs. Owing to a lack of extensive lateral advection, the trophic webs remain distinct. *See also* PACIFIC OCEAN. [V.F.]

best available control technology (BACT) *See* BEST AVAILABLE TECHNIQUES NOT ENTAILING EXCESSIVE COSTS.

best available controls (BAC) *See* BEST AVAILABLE TECHNIQUES NOT ENTAILING EXCESSIVE COSTS.

best available techniques not entailing excessive costs (BATNEEC) Legislation controlling possible POLLUTION from EMISSIONS from industrial plants sometimes not only specifies standards to be achieved but also that they have to be done by the best available techniques—a precautionary device. BATNEEC is an important element of the UK ENVIRONMENTAL PROTECTION ACT 1990. 'Best' is interpreted as meaning 'most effective'; 'available' means procurable (not just in development) from anywhere in the world; 'technique' embraces both plant (technology) and how it is used, recognizing that a poorly skilled workforce may not realize the potential of the best technology, whereas a well-trained workforce may compensate for technology that is not the best available; 'excessive cost' can theoretically be interpreted in a number of ways, for example as environmental return, since the returns in protection may reduce increasingly as more and more is invested so there is a point where further investment is not worthwhile, or from the point of view of the financial position of the business. *See also* COST (RISK)–BENEFIT APPROACH. [P.C.]

best available techniques reference document (BREF) Guidance from the European Commission on best available techniques to be used in the context of integrated pollution prevention and control. *See also* INTEGRATED POLLUTION CONTROL. [P.C.]

best available technology (techniques) economically achievable (BATEA) *See* BEST AVAILABLE TECHNIQUES NOT ENTAILING EXCESSIVE COSTS.

best environmental option (BEO) An environmental management strategy, usually used in connection with INTEGRATED POLLUTION CONTROL, designed to regulate releases to give most benefit or least damage, irrespective of cost. It thus differs from BEST PRACTICABLE ENVIRONMENTAL OPTION, which provides most benefit or least damage at acceptable cost. The concept was first developed in the 12th Report of the ROYAL COMMISSION ON ENVIRONMENTAL POLLUTION. [P.C.]

best practicable environmental option (BPEO) Often in planning environmental protection measures more than one option is available. The BEST ENVIRONMENTAL OPTION (BEO) is the one that brings maximum gains. The best practicable environmental option is the one that brings the most gains in the most cost-effective manner. Thus under INTEGRATED POLLUTION CONTROL legislation in Britain, for certain substances and processes it is necessary to put technology and techniques in place that produce best effects across all media not entailing excessive costs (*see* BEST AVAILABLE TECHNIQUES NOT ENTAILING EXCESSIVE COSTS). Very often more than one option will be available. Each option can be judged in terms of the environmental effects it allows and its costs. BEO is the option that causes minimum impact. BPEO is the option that causes minimum impact without entailing excessive cost. *See also* BEST PRACTICABLE MEANS; COST (RISK)–BENEFIT APPROACH. [P.C.]

best practicable means (BPM) A strategy for the TECHNOLOGY-BASED CONTROL of release of CONTAMINANTS that emphasizes a pragmatic approach. It implies that while better EMISSION STANDARDS may be achievable, industry should not necessarily be required to implement them if this would not be practicable especially with respect to costs. *Cf.* BEST AVAILABLE TECHNIQUES NOT ENTAILING EXCESSIVE COSTS. *See also* BEST PRACTICABLE ENVIRONMENTAL OPTION; COST (RISK)–BENEFIT APPROACH. [P.C.]

β-particle Either a negatively charged electron (β⁻-particle) or a positively charged positron (β⁺-particle). β⁻-Particles are electrons emitted during radioactive decay of neutron-rich nuclei and typically have energies in the range 10 keV to 1 MeV. For a given RADIONUCLIDE, β⁻-particles have a continuous distribution of energies up to a defined maximum, since the decay energy is shared with a neutrino which is also emitted in the process. β⁻-Particles cause ionization in absorbers, but the specific ionization (amount of ionization per unit path length) is about 1000 times lower than that of α-PARTICLES of corresponding energy. β⁺-Particles are positrons emitted in the decay of proton-rich nuclides. *See also* RADIOACTIVITY. [A.B.M.]

Bhopal *See* ECOLOGICAL/ENVIRONMENTAL DISASTERS.

binomial classification The practice, due to Linnaeus, of describing taxa under a generic and a specific name (*see* LINNAEAN CLASSIFICATION). Thus, *Musca domestica* is the name of a fly, species *domestica*, belonging to the genus *Musca*. By convention, both names are italicized and the generic, but not the specific name has an initial capital. [L.M.C.]

binomial (sign) test A non-parametric test that may be used in lieu of the parametric paired *t* TEST to test for differences between matched observations, or to test for GOODNESS-OF-FIT. The principle of the test is very simple: the numbers of positive and negative signs among the differences between pairs of values are recorded. The NULL HYPOTHESIS that the numbers of positive and negative differences are equal is then tested. If the null hypothesis is true, then the sampling distribution of the signs of these distributions should follow a (positive) binomial distribution. [R.P.F.]

bioaccumulation The progressive increase in a substance—usually in an organism or part of an organism—because the rate of intake via the body surface (*see* BIOMAGNIFICATION) or in food (*see* BIOCONCENTRATION FACTOR) is greater than the output from active or passive removal processes. [P.C.]

bioactivation The metabolic conversion of a XENOBIOTIC to a more toxic derivative. [P.C.]

bioassays Methods of analysis that use living tissues or whole organisms or collections of organisms to make quantitative and/or qualitative measurements of the amounts or activity of substances. A bioassay is not synonymous with an ecotoxicity test. [P.C.]

bioavailability In ECOTOXICOLOGY, the extent to which a substance can be taken up into an organism from that in food or the surrounding environment. In TOXICOLOGY, the term is more precisely defined as the extent to which a substance to which the body is exposed (ingestion, inhalation, infection or skin contact) reaches the systemic circulation and the rate at which this occurs. [P.C.]

biochemical oxygen demand (BOD) A measure of OXYGEN absorption from a sealed sample of water over a fixed period, usually 5 days (BOD_5). It is therefore an index of ORGANIC LOADING and microbial activity and hence WATER QUALITY. A suitable dilution of sample with a mineral salt medium is prepared. A suitable inoculation can be added as well. The sample is then incubated at 20°C for a defined period in the dark, after which time the DISSOLVED OXYGEN is determined. The initial dilution of the sample should be judged to achieve a depletion of between 30 and 70% saturation level. A number of reservations can be made about the relevance of BOD as a measure of water quality— mismatched microbes, irrelevant incubation period, DILUTION EFFECTS, interference by algae—but it

continues to be used widely for this purpose. *Cf.* CHEMICAL OXYGEN DEMAND. *See also* SEWAGE POLLUTION. [P.C.]

biocide A generic term for any substance that kills (or inhibits) organisms. Examples of biocides include: BACTERICIDES (bacteria); FUNGICIDES (fungi and moulds); HERBICIDES (weeds); INSECTICIDES (insects); rodenticides (rodents); and PESTICIDES (pests in general). [P.C.]

biocoenosis A term used, most frequently in the East European literature, to denote biotic communities of populations living together in a physically defined space at the same time. *See also* COMMUNITY; ZOOCOENOSIS. [M.H.]

bioconcentration factor (BCF) The ratio of the concentration of a substance in an organism or tissue to the concentration in the surrounding environment at apparent equilibrium. Hence it expresses the extent to which the substance concentrates in the organism or tissue. However, it is sensitive to conditions both outside and inside the organism. *See also* BIOACCUMULATION; OCTANOL–WATER PARTITION COEFFICIENT. [P.C.]

biodegradation The processes of natural DECOMPOSITION/decay whereby synthetic and natural compounds are broken down to produce substances that can be used in biological renewal cycles. Thus in sewerage systems many synthetic chemicals are decomposed by microbial metabolism into CARBON DIOXIDE (CO_2), WATER, dinitrogen (N_2), phosphorus (P), etc. However, some synthetic compounds are not amenable to biodegradation (e.g. PLASTICS) and so can accumulate within ECOSYSTEMS. *See also* SEWAGE TREATMENT WORKS. [P.C.]

biodestructible Describing some artificial materials that are designed to be broken down by biological action. For example, some PLASTICS have starch included in the polymers. These are subject to microbial metabolism, so the large POLYMER is broken into smaller fragments. [P.C.]

biodeterioration Damage to materials (e.g. foodstuffs) caused by biological activity. [P.C.]

biodiversity The number and variety of taxa in ecological systems ranging from parts of communities to ECOSYSTEMS, regions and the BIOSPHERE. There is a deep concern that human activities are leading to species' losses, i.e. reduction in biodiversity. [P.C.]

biodiversity, economic value The protection of species brings constraints on economic development. For example, restrictions on the use of AGROCHEMICALS have implications for agricultural yields and also knock-on effects to employment in both the agricultural and chemicals sectors. At the same time there are possible economic returns from WILDLIFE in terms of food yield (e.g. from fish) and other resources such as pharmaceuticals and natural pest-control chemicals. More fundamentally, species support ecological processes that in turn provide ECOSYSTEM SERVICES to the human economy, such as clean air, clean water, good soil and so on. There are various ways of valuing these contributions to the economy (*see* ENVIRONMENTAL (ECO-LOGICAL) ECONOMICS), and of weighing these benefits derived from BIODIVERSITY with the costs associated with protecting it. *See also* COST (RISK)–BENEFIT APPROACH. [P.C.]

biodiversity gradients Life is more 'abundant' at the tropics than at the poles. This applies not only to the BIOMASS and number of individuals, but in many taxonomic groups to the number of species as well. The cause of this planetary 'biodiversity gradient' in SPECIES RICHNESS remains in doubt. [J.R.G.T.]

bioenergetics The study of energy flow through biological systems. It includes both the physiological studies of energy transfer during metabolic processes and ecological studies of the rates and efficiencies of energy transfer through organisms in different trophic levels. *See also* ECOLOGICAL ENERGETICS. [M.H.]

biofilm, in aquatic systems The organic layer that coats all underwater surfaces. It is a heterogeneous collection of largely heterotrophic bacteria, microfungi, protozoans and micrometazoans such as rotifers. It can also contain photosynthetic algae. There is usually a polysaccharide matrix. [P.C.]

biofouling Unwanted accumulation of BIOTA on water-covered surfaces or appliances (e.g. hulls of boats, pipes) that impedes their effectiveness. Algae/barnacle growths on ships are classical examples. The zebra mussel, *Dreissena polymorpha*, has been introduced into North American fresh waters from Europe. As an exotic species, the POPULATION GROWTH RATE is prolific and it has caused problems by fouling pipes. [P.C.]

biofuels Fuel/energy derived from extant BIOMASS (i.e. not fossil fuel). Examples are wood, bioethanol from sugar cane, and biogases from organic wastes. In principle, all biofuels represent RENEWABLE ENERGY sources. Historically, they have been the major source of energy for humans, but now supply less than 5% of the primary energy consumed by industrialized countries. [P.C.]

biogeochemical cycle Any of various natural cycles of elements, involving biological and geological compartments. *See also* CARBON CYCLE; NITROGEN CYCLE; PHOSPHORUS CYCLE; SULPHUR CYCLE. [P.C.]

biogeography Biogeography is concerned with the patterns of DISTRIBUTION of species over the face of the globe and understanding the origins and mechanisms which determine the distribution. Biogeography is also concerned with exploring the underlying changes (territorial expansions and contractions) that have taken place in the past or, increasingly, which may occur under CLIMATES of the future. [A.H. & G.A.F.H.]

bioindicator An organism or its metabolic system that is used to signal the presence of a CONTAMINANT and its effects. A bioindicator may be a microbe or metazoan; bacterium, fungus, plant or animal; a single-species or multi-species system. *See also* BIOMARKERS. [P.C.]

biological control The limitation of the abundance of living organisms by other living organisms. Biological control can refer to the naturally occurring regulation of plant or animal populations by herbivores, predators or diseases (natural biological control), or (more commonly) to the manipulation of these natural enemies by humans. Applied biological control is used as a means of reducing populations of PEST species, either on its own, or in combination with other control methods as part of an INTEGRATED PEST MANAGEMENT (INTEGRATED CONTROL) system. [S.G.C.]

biological invasions Expansion in the distribution of certain species of plants, animals and microorganisms which are transported by humans and often competitively favoured by the DISTURBANCE around human settlements. [L.L.L.]

biological monitoring Monitoring of biological organisms, species or ECOSYSTEMS is carried out with the aim of assessing the degree to which observations meet our expectations. This is usually conducted in the context of concern about loss of species, quality of HABITAT, increases in the levels of pollutants or some other problem. However, it is also important to monitor the effects of management carried out on reserves and other protected areas and to ensure that what we do is what we intended and is cost-effective.

There are several words in current usage with different shades of meaning in the context of MONITORING. These do not always have precise definitions and their meanings overlap to a certain extent. Biological recording is usually without motive, important and widely practised, whereas monitoring, strictly speaking, is conducted with clear objectives, a standardized procedure and clear rules for stopping (called termination by some people). Surveys are a one-off recording exercise whilst strictly speaking, SURVEILLANCE refers to repeated SURVEYS. CENSUS involves recording all individuals and usually information about RECRUITMENT (births) and MORTALITY (deaths). It not only applies to animals but also to plants with discrete individuals such as orchids and trees. [F.B.G.]

bioluminescence LIGHT emission, often as flashes and without sensible heat production, produced by bacteria, fungi, plants and animals at a wide range of frequencies from ultraviolet to the red end of the spectrum. [V.F.]

biomagnification The process whereby the concentration of a chemical in the tissues of organisms increases as the chemical moves up the FOOD CHAIN. It is the result of BIOACCUMULATION and bioconcentration. Hence, only small amounts of a toxic chemical may accumulate per head of plant-eating animals; but many of these are eaten by predators, which therefore accumulate more of the chemical per head. [P.C.]

biomanipulation The practice of manipulating the densities of species (usually top predators) to push a COMMUNITY towards a desired state. It is of particular interest for management of eutrophic LAKES where reductions in PHYTOPLANKTON abundance can improve water clarity and prevent the development of anoxic conditions. Lake biomanipulation theory predicts that increasing the abundance of piscivorous species (usually fish) will decrease plantivorous fish abundance, thereby increasing ZOOPLANKTON which in turn leads to a reduction in phytoplankton abundance. This chain of events is an example of a trophic cascade, if the reduction in phytoplankton density occurs through increased grazing pressure by zooplankton (*see also* TOP-DOWN CONTROLS). [S.J.H.]

biomarkers Effects in biological systems used to indicate the presence of CONTAMINATION. The effects are usually at molecular and cellular levels. Some would argue that effects can be physiological, behavioural or even at the level of population and community—but then biomarker studies become synonymous with ECOTOXICOLOGY. The effects should be relatively long-lasting and specific. They may involve induction of protective systems (e.g. METALLOTHIONEINS) or an indication of damage (e.g. enzyme inhibition). Clearly they signal EXPOSURE to a substance, but do not necessarily indicate an adverse ecological EFFECT. This is particularly true of the induction of protection mechanisms since these are part of homeostatic systems that by definition will prevent expression of adverse effects. The advantages of biomarkers over chemical assays is that they can potentially integrate conditions over time thus providing increased opportunity for picking up low-level contamination and/or episodic effects of contamination. *See also* BIOINDICATOR; EXPOSURE. [P.C.]

biomass The total mass of living material within a specified area at a given time. [P.D.M.]

biomes, major world Communities of plants and animals of characteristic composition, distributed over extensive areas or regions of the world constitute global biomes. Although over 250 000 flowering plant species have been described, no single species occurs worldwide. Each species has its limits of DISTRIBUTION. The great majority of plant species, indeed, have a very localized distribution. Despite this, it is possible to discern quite distinct patterns of similarity and dissimilarity in the composition of plant and animal communities.

Almost all biomes owe their origins to the distinctive CLIMATE of the region, particularly rainfall and temperature. Contemporary examples of FOREST biomes include the TROPICAL RAIN FORESTS, SUBTROPICAL dry forests, temperate deciduous

forests, subpolar or BOREAL conifer forests. Non-forest dominated biomes include open SAVANNAH, semi-arid SCRUB, dry DESERT and TUNDRA. Many biomes are of relatively recent origins reflecting both the evolution and expansion of particular plant families in the latter half of the Tertiary, for example GRASSLANDS, Asteraceae-rich drylands and the retreat of the forests with increasing global DROUGHT in the late Miocene. [G.A.F.H.]

biometeorology The study of the interactions between WEATHER and life. This is a multidisciplinary subject, drawing on CLIMATOLOGY, METEOROLOGY, biology, HYDROLOGY, physiology and medicine. Biometeorologists seek to record and understand the impact of weather on plants and animals, not only the more obvious and more extensively perceived effects (e.g. the influence of weather on the germination and establishment of CROPS, and the populations of insect pests) but also the more subtle and unexpected. These include the effect of weather on the incidence of heart attacks and suicides; the effect of sunspots on plant growth; human performance in extreme environments; the possible influence of negative ions on human well-being, and the design of cattle houses to provide shelter from heat stress. [J.G.]

biometrics The application of mathematical (usually statistical) techniques to biological systems. *See also* STATISTICS. [P.C.]

biomonitor Any system incorporating living organisms (ranging from microbes to vertebrates) that can be used to assess (often continuously) quality of the ENVIRONMENT. *See also* BIOPROBE; BIOSENSOR. [P.C.]

biophilia A term coined in 1979 by the biologist E.O. Wilson of Harvard University, who defined it in 1994 as 'the inborn affinity human beings have for other forms of life, an affiliation evoked, according to circumstance, by pleasure, or a sense of security, or awe, or even fascination blended with revulsion'. Wilson derives this idea from the fact that 'humanity is ultimately the product of biological evolution', and 'the diversity of life is the cradle and greatest natural heritage of the human species'. [J.D.Lz.]

bioprobe A form of BIOSENSOR located on a rod and used for taking measurements at specific points—like a pH or oxygen probe. *See also* BIOMONITOR. [P.C.]

bioremediation Remedying chemical POLLUTION using biological agents, usually microbes, with appropriate catabolic systems; for example using selected microbes to decompose oil after accidental spillage at sea. [P.C.]

biosensor A device that combines biological material and transducers, usually in intimate association, to signal the presence of a particular substance or group of substances. [P.C.]

biosphere All the organisms on the planet, and their environment, viewed as a system of interacting components. The biosphere may be regarded as a thin film on the planet's surface, consisting of all the organisms and the WATER, SOIL and air surrounding them. The biosphere thus includes parts of the ATMOSPHERE, the LITHOSPHERE and most of the HYDROSPHERE. [J.G.]

biosphere reserves Biosphere reserves are a worldwide system of designated protected areas and surrounding landscapes that attempt to integrate conservation, research, education and SUSTAINABLE DEVELOPMENT.

Biosphere reserves are designated by local or national governments, following guidelines of the Man and the Biosphere Programme (MAB) of the United Nations Economic, Scientific and Cultural Organization (UNESCO). The designation was established in 1971 in recognition of the need to ascertain global priorities for protecting biological DIVERSITY in an increasingly human-dominated landscape. As of 1995, 324 such reserves have been designated in more that 75 countries around the world. MAB's goal is to protect at least one representative area from each of the world's 193 biogeographic provinces, in a global system. [D.A.F.]

biota The total flora and fauna of a region. [S.R.J.W.]

biotechnology and genetically engineered organisms Manipulation of genetic systems by means other than selection and breeding and often with a view to commerical gain. *See also* GENETIC ENGINEERING; MOLECULAR ECOLOGY; TRANSGENIC ORGANISMS. [P.C.]

biotic factors Factors limiting the DISTRIBUTION of a species in space or time due to the effects of the animals, microorganisms and plants present. [P.J.G.]

biotic indices Biological criteria that are used to give information on ECOSYSTEM condition. Such indices have been used especially as indicators of riverwater quality. They use two observed characters of the effects of STRESS on communities: as POLLUTION stress increases the total number of species declines; moreover, as the extent of pollution stress increases, species tend to be selectively removed, with sensitive species (e.g. ephemeropterans) disappearing first and tolerant species (e.g. chironomids) last. Several indices are in general use in the UK: the Trent biotic index; the Chandler biotic score; and the Biological Monitoring Working Party (BMWP) scheme. A major weakness of all these indices is that the relative sensitivity of species is pollution specific. Sensitivity in the indices listed is largely by reference to ORGANIC POLLUTION and may not be appropriate for chemical pollution. *See also* DIVERSITY INDICES; RIVER INVERTEBRATE PREDICTION AND CLASSIFICATION SYSTEM. [P.C.]

biotope A region that is distinguished by particular environmental conditions and therefore a characteristic ASSEMBLAGE of organisms. *See also* HABITAT. [P.D.M.]

bioturbation Physical effect on SEDIMENT, by the activities of organisms in it. [P.C.]

biotype A specific type of plant or animal defined within a species; a group of individuals with similar genotypes. *Cf.* BIOTOPE. [P.O.]

black-box system Any complex system (cell, organism, POPULATION, ECOSYSTEM) about whose organization nothing is known except what can be deduced from inputs and outputs and relationships between them. [P.C.]

Black List Associated with environmental protection legislation, especially in Europe, are numerous LISTS of substances that are given some kind of priority in the way they are treated; for example, because of their potential to cause HARM, to bioaccumulate or to resist degradation. The European Community (EC) Existing Substances Regulation, for example, generates lists of priority substances on a regular basis for further more detailed RISK CHARACTERIZATION by the authorities.

Another good example of such lists is associated with the EC directive on POLLUTION caused by certain dangerous substances discharged into the aquatic environment. This established two lists for action: List I—sometimes referred to as the 'Black List'—contains a group of dangerous substances, pollution from which has to be eliminated; List II—sometimes referred to as the 'GREY LIST'—contains a group of substances for which it is necessary to reduce EMISSIONS to avoid pollution. [P.C.]

Black Sea A relatively ancient SEA, located between south-eastern Europe and Asia. Age estimates for the Black Sea vary from Precambrian to early Quaternary, with a Jurassic–Cretaceous age being favoured. It has an area of 461 000 km^2, a volume of 537 300 km^3 and a mean depth of 1197 m (including the Sea of Azov). During the Quaternary, the Black Sea experienced repeated changes in level and associated fluctuations in SALINITY as its connection with the Mediterranean was cut off and restored. It is an oval BASIN with a relatively thick crust (18–24 km) and a SEDIMENT cover 812 km thick. Sedimentation rates are of the order of 30 cm per thousand years. An important feature of the Black Sea is that, due to limited water exchange with the adjacent MEDITERRANEAN SEA, it is anoxic below about 200 m depth. Precipitation greatly exceeds evaporation so that the salinity is considerably less than that of the adjacent Mediterranean, as is species diversity of both planktonic and benthic organisms. A layer of relatively fresh water traps a body of normal-salinity water out of contact with the atmosphere or the open OCEAN. Black Sea waters are supersaturated with respect to calcium carbonate. The tidal range is only about 8–9 cm and much of the mixing is thus wind-driven. [V.F.]

blank A SAMPLE designed to detect the introduction of artefacts in measurement procedures. [P.C.]

bloom A sudden increase in density of algae in a water body, usually due to an excess of NUTRIENTS. *See also* ALGAL BLOOM. [P.C.]

blue-green algae toxins *See* CYANOBACTERIAL TOXINS.

BNFL *See* BRITISH NUCLEAR FUELS LIMITED.

BOD *See* BIOCHEMICAL OXYGEN DEMAND.

body burden The total amount of XENOBIOTIC in an organism at a given time. [P.C.]

body size *See* GROWTH.

bomb calorimeter A device for measuring the heat of combustion of fuels or BIOMASS. [J.G.]

boreal A term meaning 'northern', 'of the North' (from *Boreas*, Greek and Latin, (God of) the north wind; *boreus* and *borealis* adj., Latin). [Y.V.]

boreal forest Boreal forest, or TAIGA, is the world's largest vegetation formation, comprising coniferous forests that stretch around the Northern hemisphere interrupted only by the North Atlantic Ocean and the Bering Strait. It forms a 1000–2000 km broad zone between treeless TUNDRA in the north and either broad-leaved DECIDUOUS FORESTS (in oceanic areas) or dry GRASSLANDS and semi-deserts (in continental areas) in the south. Along the oceanic southern border of the boreal forests there is an intermediate hemiboreal zone with varying mixtures of coniferous and deciduous trees. The boreal forests proper begin in areas where the summers become too short (less than 120 days with temperatures higher than +10°C) and the winters too long (over 6 months) and severe for the broad-leaved deciduous trees. The northern boundary of the boreal forest follows approximately the +10°C ISOTHERM of the warmest month where also the winter becomes 8 months or longer. Because of orographic factors, boreal forests can occur in mountainous areas outside the zone of boreal coniferous forests. [Y.V.]

boundary layer WATER movements in RIVERS and streams are driven by gravitational gradients. The structure of this flow is mediated by friction induced by the channel boundary. The region where these frictional effects are felt is the boundary layer. In deep rivers it may occupy only a small proportion of total depth whereas in shallow rivers it may extend to the water surface. In turn it can be divided into component layers including a bed layer (closest to the bed, often a few millimetres thick, where there is often, but not always, LAMINAR FLOW), a logarithmic layer (not affected by the local roughness of the bed nor by the free stream-flow structure) and another layer that is influenced by the free-stream velocity. [P.C.]

brackish habitats Brackish waters and soils contain ionic solutes at higher concentrations than those of FRESH WATER or normal soil solutions but at considerably lower concentration than seawater. They originate by dilution of seawater with rain or groundwater, or by evaporation of water and con-

sequent enrichment with solutes in arid environments. [J.R.E.]

Braer *See* ECOLOGICAL/ENVIRONMENTAL DISASTERS.

British Nuclear Fuels Limited (BNFL) British Nuclear Fuels Limited operate a number of nuclear sites in the UK including four Magnox nuclear reactors and separate facilities for uranium enrichment, nuclear fuel production, nuclear fuel reprocessing and low-level solid RADIOACTIVE WASTE disposal. The Sellafield site, which is the location of the nuclear fuel reprocessing plant, also contained the now-defunct Calderhall NUCLEAR POWER-STATION and Windscale experimental piles. The authorized discharge of low-level liquid radioactive waste into the Irish Sea from Sellafield has been the focus of considerable attention in the context of marine environmental pollution. Radionuclides were also released to the environment from a fire in one of the Windscale experimental piles in 1957. *See also* WASTE DISPOSAL. [A.B.M.]

bryophytes A distantly co-related group of non-vascular terrestrial plants comprising the mosses and liverworts. The bryophytes are of ancient lineage, probably evolving directly from an algal ancestor at an early stage in land-plant evolution and possibly independent of the line which gave rise to vascular plants. Unlike vascular plants, the bryophytes have remained dependent on a close association with water for sexual reproduction. Unfortunately, because of their small size and relatively fine structure, bryophytes have not been readily recognized in the earliest fossil records. The majority of contemporary species are still found most commonly in continuously moist habitats (though there are a number of exceptions with extraordinarily high capacities for tolerance of desiccation). The bryophytes are classified into three taxa: the mosses (Musci), with about 9000 described species, the liverworts (Hepaticae), with about 8000 species, and a small and questionably related group of hornworts (Anthocerotae), of about 250 species. [G.A.F.H.]

BS 7750 A STANDARD produced by the British Standards Institution (BSI) on the elements of an ENVIRONMENTAL MANAGEMENT SYSTEM. COMPLIANCE enabled companies to carry the BSI mark and standard number on all documentation. It has now been replaced by standards produced by the International Organization for Standardization (ISO), under the designation ISO 14000. [P.C.]

bubble concept A concept used in POLLUTION control that involves drawing an imaginary dome-shaped boundary (the bubble) around a source of pollution (which can be a stack, plant, area or even geographical region) and putting an upper limit on the total amount of CONTAMINATION allowed into it. The idea, which has its origins in the USA, is that although the total level of CONTAMINANT is kept constant, increased emission from one plant can be balanced against reductions from another. A market can thus be created in options to release (*see* MARKET INSTRUMENTS). [P.C.]

buffer solution A solution that can resist changes in pH brought about by adding ACID or alkali. [J.G.]

buffer zone A buffer zone is a boundary area surrounding or adjacent to a core conservation area, such as a park or nature reserve (*see* BIOSPHERE RESERVES). Buffer zones are generally intermediate between core conservation areas and the surrounding landscape in several respects, including their ecological function, extent of human impact, and degree of protection. Buffer zones can be composed of successional habitat, such as second-growth or managed forests, abandoned agricultural lands, grazing or range land, or other areas that have been modified to some extent in composition, structure and ecological function. [D.A.F.]

C

C:N ratio In soils and BIOMASS, a close relationship exists between the ratios of the elements carbon and nitrogen. The C:N ratio in arable soils is often from 8:1 to 15:1, with a tendency for the ratio to be lower in arid climates and lower in subsoils. In biomass, the C:N ratio reflects the content of CELLULOSE and LIGNIN. For microorganisms the ratio is as low as 4:1 to 9:1, for leguminous plants it is 20:1 to 30:1, for straw residues it is 100:1 and for sawdust it is 400:1. Thus, the plant residues that become incorporated into the SOIL usually contain relatively little nitrogen in relation to the microbial population that they support. [J.G.]

calcicole A plant or organism limited to, or more abundant on, calcareous soils or in water of high calcium status (*cf.* CALCIFUGE). [J.R.E.]

calcifuge A plant or organism limited to, or more abundant on, soils or in water of low calcium status and usually of pH 5 or less (*cf.* CALCICOLE). [J.R.E.]

calibration Translation of units of measurement recorded by instrument or system into units of interest and/or operation for determining values or errors of instrument or system. Thus ATTENUATION of LIGHT at a particular wavelength is often used to measure concentration of a substrate with appropriate optical properties in metabolic reactions. Calibrations are carried out with standards of known concentration. Calibration can also result in a correction factor or factors that can subsequently be used to correct readings from the system. [P.C.]

calorific value The calorific value of a material is a measure of its energy content expressed in JOULES per unit mass. Hence, it is probably more properly termed a 'joule equivalent'. It is most frequently determined by combustion in a BOMB CALORIMETER, which monitors the rise in TEMPERATURE when a known mass of dried material is ignited in an oxygen-enriched atmosphere. The instrument is calibrated with benzoic acid of which the calorific content is accurately known. Estimating the calorific values of materials enables us to express different components of feeding and productivity equations in a common currency of energy units. *See also* ECOLOGICAL ENERGETICS. [M.H.]

canopy The upper stratum of a WOODLAND or FOREST, comprising trees receiving full daylight over all or part of their crowns. The canopy is uniform if it comprises trees of approximately the same heights, or irregular if it is a mixture of trees of different heights, including 'emergents', i.e. trees markedly taller than general canopy level. [G.F.P.]

carbon cycle The carbon cycle is one of the four key BIOGEOCHEMICAL CYCLES on Earth: carbon, nitrogen, sulphur and phosphorus. All these elements are cycled around the globe between different components (also known as reservoirs or compartments) by physical, chemical and biological processes. Carbon in particular is a key element in life on Earth, being a component of an enormous range of organic compounds, formed because of the stable, long-chain covalent bonding possibilities of the carbon atom. Elemental carbon is rare (diamonds, graphite) and the commonest carbon compounds are the oxidized forms of CARBON DIOXIDE (CO_2) and carbonate. The organic carbon compounds have been reduced by the action of organisms, for example in PHOTOSYNTHESIS. Carbon is exchanged between the major reservoirs of carbon: the ATMOSPHERE, the OCEANS and FRESH WATER (although the latter is only a very small component), the terrestrial BIOSPHERE, and the sediments and sedimentary rocks. On very long GEOLOGICAL TIME-SCALES, sedimentary rocks are exposed, allowing WEATHERING to return CO_2 to the atmosphere. However, the faster parts of the cycle are dominated by biological activity, removing carbon in the form of CO_2 from the atmosphere and from solution into living organisms (BIOMASS) during photosynthesis and releasing it during DECOMPOSITION (particularly the activity of microorganisms) as CO_2 and METHANE (CH_4). [J.I.L.M.]

carbon dioxide Carbon dioxide (CO_2), a colourless gas 1.5 times heavier than air, is produced when carbon is oxidized by ignition or during respiration. It is also produced from volcanoes and springs. Odourless, tasteless and non-toxic at the low concentrations generally found on Earth (0.03–0.05%), CO_2 is dangerous at the high concentrations sometimes found near volcanoes and springs (>20%) where it has a sharp taste and causes choking, asphyxiation and death. CO_2 is soluble in WATER (1 m³ gas dissolves in 1 m³ of water at 15°C) to form carbonic acid (H_2CO_3) with a pH of about 5.8.

CO_2 absorbs RADIATION in the infrared, with major absorption bands at 2.67, 2.77, 4.25 and 15 µm and lesser bands at 1.4, 1.6, 2.0, 4.8, 5.2, 5.4 and 10.4 µm. Consequently, it is an important

'GREENHOUSE GAS', and without it the temperatures at the surface of the Earth would be much lower than they are.

The concentration of CO_2 on Mars and Venus is very high (>90%), and presumed to have been derived from volcanic activity. On Earth, before the advent of PHOTOSYNTHESIS the CO_2 concentration may have also been high, and has usually been higher than present-day values. Concentrations of CO_2 have fluctuated considerably in more recent times, as can be seen by the analysis of gas bubbles in ice cores. Minimum concentrations of about 180 ppm by volume (ppmv) were reached 160 000 and 40 000 years ago. Over the last 200 years the concentration has increased from 280 to 355 ppmv as a result of combustion of fossil fuel and conversion of forested lands to AGRICULTURE, and is now rising by about 1.8 ppmv year^{-1}. Detailed measurements at remote sites worldwide show pronounced annual fluctuation in the atmospheric concentration, which falls when it is summer in the Northern hemisphere, the time of maximum global photosynthesis, and rises in winter.

Currently, about 2 Gt carbon is released as CO_2 to the ATMOSPHERE each year as a result of DEFORESTATION and 6.6 Gt from burning FOSSIL FUELS. About 4 Gt is taken up by 'sinks' such as OCEAN and forests, and the remainder appears in the atmosphere. The relative importance of these two sinks is controversial and may vary from year to year. *See also* CARBON CYCLE; PRIMARY PRODUCTIVITY. [J.G.]

carbon monoxide A highly flammable and toxic gas produced from incomplete combustion of carbon compounds. Carbon monoxide (CO) has an average ambient concentration of ~0.1 ppm by volume (ppmv) through atmospheric oxidation of METHANE (CH_4) and other natural HYDROCARBONS. Anthropogenic sources (principally car exhausts) account for about half of total global CO EMISSIONS. The major sink is complete oxidation to CO_2 by OH. CO is absorbed through the lungs and binds irreversibly to haemoglobin, causing drowsiness and response impairment. Urban levels of CO can exceed 10–20 ppmv, particularly inside vehicles, and the WHO has set limits of 9 ppmv and 27 ppmv for 8-hour and 1-hour means, respectively. *Cf.* CARBON DIOXIDE. [M.R.H.]

carbon tax Tax on FOSSIL FUELS, related to CARBON DIOXIDE-generating potential. A MARKET INSTRUMENT. [P.C.]

carcinogens, mutagens, teratogens (CMTs) Substances that can induce cancer, and/or MUTATIONS, and/or defects in development (sometimes also called reprotoxins). They are of considerable importance for individual organisms, but their ecological significance is open to question. Mutations in cells in the bodies of organisms, especially if they are somatic, and developmental abnormalities and cancers need

not have significant effects on the population as a whole. [P.C.]

carrying capacity (K) This term describes a DYNAMIC EQUILIBRIUM around which a POPULATION fluctuates. The exact nature of this relationship will vary between different organisms and habitats, although fundamentally it will be determined by basic demographic processes, such as NATALITY, as well as dynamic processes, such as competition and predation, which will interact with the surrounding physical environment to give the equilibrium density of a population. Carrying capacity is sometimes applied to a group of organisms rather than an individual population. These may consist of single-species groups or collections of similar species exploiting a common resource (e.g. insectivores). *Cf.* POPULATION GROWTH RATE. *See also* DENSITY DEPENDENCE; POPULATION DYNAMICS; POPULATION REGULATION. [R.C.]

carrying capacity, importance to conservation The maximum number of organisms of a given species that can be supported in a given habitat or geographic area, usually denoted as K (e.g. in the logistic equation) or as the K-value. CARRYING CAPACITY has a direct impact on the amount and quality of habitat that must be preserved to sustain a MINIMUM VIABLE POPULATION. The problem for managers of wildlife parks and nature reserves is compounded by the fact that carrying capacity and habitat requirements differ for different species. Furthermore, the size of reserves is often restricted by other practical considerations. It is often necessary to strike a compromise between the needs of neighbouring human communities and the minimal requirements of the most ENDANGERED SPECIES in the park. *See also* CONSERVATION BIOLOGY. [A.R.H.]

Carson, R. (1907–1964) Author of the influential bestseller *Silent Spring* (1967) that highlighted the blight of the environment by PESTICIDES. So captured the public imagination that it launched the popular environment movement. [P.C.]

caste The term 'caste' is used in biology to draw attention to differences among members of eusocial colonies. [N.R.F.]

casual species ALIEN species incapable of forming self-replacing populations and relying on continual reintroduction for persistence outside their native or naturalized ranges. [M.J.C.]

catadromous A pattern of migration in which adults living in FRESH WATER migrate to breeding sites in saltwater. Offspring move in the opposite direction. [P.O.]

catalyst A substance that increases the rate of a chemical reaction but is not itself altered chemically in the process. Finely divided metals and oxides at high temperature are often used as catalysts in chemistry. They work by providing a high surface area on which the reagents are adsorbed and therefore come together. In living cells, enzymes are the catalysts. They work by effecting the proper arrangement of the reacting molecules with respect to each other. [J.G.]

catalytic converter A term usually applied to the device for chemical transformation of POLLU-TANTS in vehicle exhausts. Two-way oxidation CATALYSTS oxidize unburnt fuel HYDROCARBONS and CARBON MONOXIDE (CO) to WATER and CARBON DIOXIDE (CO_2) but do not affect NITRO-GEN OXIDE (NO_x) emissions. Three-way catalytic converters contain a ceramic filter coated with a mixture of platinum, palladium and rhodium and also reduce NO_x to N_2. Operational mixture strength is regulated by an OXYGEN sensor in the exhaust manifold and electronic control of the engine. Unleaded petrol is required since LEAD poisons the catalyst. All new cars sold in the UK since 1993 have catalytic converters fitted. *See also* AIR POLLUTION; ATMOSPHERIC POLLUTION; MOTOR VEHICLE POLLUTION. [M.R.H.]

catch per unit effort Return from fishing, hunting and SAMPLING. Usually follows law of diminishing returns; for example number of species sampled from a community increases but at a reducing rate as sampling effort is increased. Hence catch per unit effort varies with effort. [P.C.]

catchment A geographical region within which hydrological conditions are such that water becomes concentrated in a particular location, either a BASIN or a single river by which the catchment is drained. The American term 'watershed' may be used as a synonym, but is employed rather differently in European literature where it implies a ridge separating catchments. [P.D.M.]

cellulose Cellulose is classified as a polysaccharide comprising linked monosaccharide units. It is a straight-chain natural POLYMER consisting of glucose units with average relative molecular mass of more than 500 000. Cellulose forms the main structural units of all plants and is the most abundant polysaccharide occurring in nature. Cellulose is the main constituent of cell walls of all higher plants, many algae and some fungi. [M.C.G.]

censuses Estimates of POPULATION SIZES. [P.C.]

CEQ *See* COUNCIL ON ENVIRONMENTAL QUALITY.

CERCLA (Comprehensive Environmental Response Compensation and Liability Act 1980) *See* SUPERFUND LEGISLATION; UNITED STATES LEGISLATION.

CEREs (Coalition of Environmentally Responsible Economies) *See* VALDEZ PRINCIPLES.

CFCs (chlorofluorocarbons) Synthetic substituted alkanes with one or more hydrogen atoms replaced by chlorine or fluorine, existing as gases or low-boiling liquids at normal temperatures and pressures. Chemically inert and non-toxic, CFCs are used as refrigerants, solvents, AEROSOL propellants and in blowing plastic foam, but are gradually being replaced by more reactive hydrochlorofluorocarbons (HCFCs) and hydrofluorocarbons (HFCs). They are important 'GREENHOUSE GASES', contributing about 10% to radiative forcing of the CLIMATE. CFCs accumulate in the TROPOSPHERE with lifetimes of tens to hundreds of years, and are transported to the STRATOSPHERE where they are photolysed and perturb the chemistry of OZONE. The largest contributors are CFC-11 ($CFCl_3$), CFC-12 (CF_2Cl_2) and CFC-113 ($CF_2ClCFCl_2$). Production and use of CFCs and other HALOCARBONS is now regulated under the 'Montreal Protocol', which seeks to prevent further depletion of stratospheric ozone and consequent increases in ultraviolet (UV)-B radiation at the Earth's surface. *See also* CLIMATE CHANGE; OZONE HOLE; OZONE LAYER. [J.N.C.]

chalk and limestone grassland Limestones are rocks composed mainly of calcium carbonate ($CaCO_3$), laid down in shallow seas. Chalk is a particularly pure form of limestone. The soils formed on these rocks are shallow, often with fragments of parent rock at or near the surface, and well drained. They are high in free calcium carbonate and have a high pH. They are also low in essential NUTRIENTS, especially nitrogen and phosphorus. Chalk and limestone grassland is found in warm areas with low rainfall, often on steep slopes, and is maintained by GRAZING animals, mainly sheep and rabbits. Frequently no species becomes really dominant and there is often an abundance of broad-leaved herbs, many deep rooted. Disturbance caused by grazing animals creates bare sites that are often colonized by annuals or short-lived perennials. [S.R.J.W.]

chaos Chaos is a term used to describe deterministic dynamic systems that are neither steady nor periodic, but which exhibit irregularity and complexity. Systems expressing chaotic dynamics display sensitive dependence on initial conditions. The sensitivity is exponential, meaning that as time goes on small errors in the solution (e.g. due to noise and computer round-off) grow exponentially. This means that short-term predictions may be made accurately, but it is not possible to make useful long-term predictions. Chaotic behaviour can be exhibited by deterministic equations and is called deterministic chaos. Chaotic behaviour exhibited by simple-looking equations was first described by the meteorologist Edward Lorenz in 1963. Since then, chaotic dynamics have been demonstrated in a wide variety of systems including fluids, plasmas, solid-state devices, circuits, lasers, mechanical devices, biology, chemistry, acoustics and celestial mechanics. [V.F.]

Charter for Sustainable Development Following the Brundtland Report *Our Common Future* from the World Commission on Environment and Development (1987), the International Chamber of Commerce established a task force of business representatives to create this Business Charter for Sustainable Development. It comprises 16 principles for environmental management which, for business, is a vitally important aspect of SUSTAINABLE DEVELOPMENT. It was formally launched in April 1991 at the Second World Industry Conference on Environmental Management.

1 *Corporate priority.* To recognize environmental management as among the highest corporate priorities and as a key determinant to sustainable development; to establish policies, programmes and practices for conducting operations in an environmentally sound manner.

2 *Integrated management.* To integrate these policies, programmes and practices fully into each business as an essential element of management in all its functions.

3 *Process of improvement.* To continue to improve corporate policies, programmes and environmental performance, taking into account technical developments, scientific understanding, consumer needs and community expectations, with legal regulations as a starting point; and to apply the same environmental criteria internationally.

4 *Employee education.* To educate, train and motivate employees to conduct their activities in an environmentally responsible manner.

5 *Prior assessment.* To assess ENVIRONMENTAL IMPACTS before starting a new activity or project and before decommissioning a facility or leaving a site.

6 *Products and services.* To develop and provide products or services that have no undue environmental impact and are safe in their intended use, that are efficient in their consumption of energy and natural resources, and that can be recycled, reused or disposed of safely.

7 *Customer advice.* To advise, and where relevant educate, customers, distributors and the public in the safe use, transportation, storage and disposal of products provided; and to apply similar considerations to the provision of services.

8 *Facilities and operations.* To develop, design and operate facilities and conduct activities taking into consideration the efficient use of energy and materials, the sustainable use of renewable resources, the minimization of adverse environmental impact and WASTE generation, and the safe and responsible disposal of residual wastes.

9 *Research.* To conduct or support research on the environmental impacts of raw materials, products, processes, EMISSIONS and wastes associated with the enterprise and on the means of minimizing such adverse impacts.

10 *Precautionary approach.* To modify the manufacture, marketing or use of products or services or the conduct of activities, consistent with scientific and technical understanding, to prevent serious or irreversible environmental degradation.

11 *Contractors and suppliers.* To promote the adoption of these principles by contractors acting on behalf of the enterprise, encouraging and, where appropriate, requiring improvements in their practices to make them consistent with those of the enterprise; and to encourage the wider adoption of these principles by suppliers.

12 *Emergency preparedness.* To develop and maintain, where significant HAZARDS exist, emergency preparedness plans in conjunction with the emergency services, relevant authorities and the local community, recognizing potential transboundary impacts.

13 *Transfer of technology.* To contribute to the transfer of environmentally sound technology and management methods throughout the industrial and public sectors.

14 *Contributing to the common effort.* To contribute to the development of public policy and to business, governmental and intergovernmental programmes and educational initiatives that will enhance environmental awareness and protection.

15 *Openness to concerns.* To foster openness and dialogue with employees and the public, anticipating and responding to their concerns about the potential hazards and impact of operations, products, wastes or services, including those of transboundary or global significance.

16 *Compliance and reporting.* To measure environmental performance; to conduct regular environmental audits and assessment of COMPLIANCE with company requirements, legal requirements and these principles; and periodically to provide appropriate information to the board of directors, shareholders, employees, the authorities and the public.

See also ENVIRONMENTAL MANAGEMENT SYSTEMS. [P.C.]

chelating agent The word 'chelate' is derived from the Greek *chela* meaning claw. A chelating agent or chelating ligand applies to a compound containing more than one atom with a lone pair of electrons that can be used to bind a metal ION, i.e. more than one OXYGEN, nitrogen or sulphur atom with a lone pair. The formation of chelate complexes can be used to provide a metal ion in a protected form, for example chelation enables the transport of metal ions across a membrane in biological systems. Additionally, WATER softening can be achieved by the chelation of Ca^{2+} ions. *See also* DETERGENTS. [M.C.G.]

chemical control Attempt to regulate, restrict or remove species populations (of pests) by use of toxic substances. *See also* PESTICIDE. [P.C.]

chemical monitoring Judging the quality of a WASTE stream, effluent/emission, receiving body, particular habitat by analysis of chemical composition, which may be done for one or many chemicals. *Cf.* BIOLOGICAL MONITORING. [P.C.]

chemical oxygen demand (COD) Amount of OXYGEN consumed in the complete oxidation of carbonaceous material in a WATER sample as carried out in a

STANDARD test, usually using potassium dichromate as oxidizing agent. *See also* BIOCHEMICAL OXYGEN DEMAND. [P.C.]

Chemical Release Inventory (CRI) List of pollution EMISSIONS from industrial plants in England and Wales controlled under INTEGRATED POLLUTION CONTROL (IPC). *See also* TOXIC RELEASE INVENTORY. [P.C.]

chemical time bomb The time-bomb analogy draws attention to conditions that are set now that might lead to a sudden and serious disaster in the future. Thus synthetic chemicals, especially organics, are known to accumulate in SEDIMENTS. Plausible scenarios can be imagined when changes in physico-chemical conditions in the surrounding medium, for example lowering pH due to ACIDIFICATION, can lead to release of these substances and therefore cause sudden and dramatic problems. [P.C.]

Chernobyl disaster Events at the water-cooled, graphite-moderated nuclear power reactor at Chernobyl in the Ukraine in April 1986 proved the most serious ACCIDENT in the history of the peaceful applications of nuclear power. The effects of the explosion and subsequent graphite fire caused the immediate deaths of over 30 fire-fighters and the widespread distribution of radioactive FISSION products over many parts of Europe. Although this led to restrictions on the use of agricultural land in many countries, these effects are generally minor compared to the local consequences in the Ukraine, Russia and Belorussia where there has been heavy CONTAMINATION, chiefly with caesium and strontium, causing local authorities to evacuate most agricultural settlements within 30 km of the plant. There is uncertainty about the direct effect of the RADIATION release on the local and wider populations of the former USSR. Ongoing international studies certainly record a substantial incidence of effects that might be attributable to IONIZING RADIATION but equally (and none the less real) to radiation phobia. Other consequences of the accident include the deterioration of the local diet due to the loss of food production and the disruption of distribution; and the shortage of electricity not only from the No. 4 reactor but from the other reactors on site, which have been closed for various periods since the accident. *See also* RADIATION POLLUTION. [J.D.L.]

chi-squared test (χ²) A non-parametric test that compares observed numbers, placed in categories, with those calculated (expected) on the basis of some hypothesis. [B.S.]

chlorinated hydrocarbons *See* ORGANOCHLORINES.

chlorinity Grams of chloride ions per 1000 g of seawater expressed as parts per thousand (‰). The constancy of the proportions of the major dissolved elements in seawater permits the use of chlorinity as an index of SALINITY. [V.F.]

chlorofluorocarbons *See* CFCs.

cholinesterase inhibitor Substance that inhibits the action of acetylcholinesterase (AChE) and causes hyperactivity in parasympathetic nerves. Includes carbamate and organophosphorous esters that are contained in many INSECTICIDES. *See also* PESTICIDE. [P.C.]

chronic tests Testing for responses that are not immediately debilitating, such as impairment of growth, reproduction, propensity for diseases including cancer. Therefore these tests are carried out at relatively low concentrations over long time-spans and hence at low concentrations *Cf.* ACUTE TESTS; SHORT-TERM TESTS. *See also* LONG-TERM TESTS; PREDICTIVE ECOTOXICITY TESTS. [P.C.]

circulation, oceanic OCEAN circulation can be subdivided into two components: surface circulation and thermohaline deep circulation. The major surface CURRENTS of the oceans are primarily WIND driven and thus closely follow the major wind systems. However, due to the rotation of the Earth, currents are deflected to the right in the Northern hemisphere (resulting in a tendency towards clockwise circulation patterns) and to the left in the Southern hemisphere (resulting in counterclockwise circulation patterns). Currents tend to be narrower, deeper and faster along the western edges of the oceans compared with those along the eastern edges. Western boundary currents transport substantial amounts of heat toward the poles, whereas eastern boundary currents are often associated with UPWELLING. Circulation patterns of deep water are controlled primarily by differences in density, which occur as a result of differences in SALINITY and TEMPERATURE. Deep water originates primarily at the poles. Owing to the high density of this very cold water, it sinks and flows toward the Equator. Originally high in OXYGEN, the deep water becomes gradually depleted in oxygen as it spreads across the ocean floor. The deep water is eventually returned to the surface by wind-driven mixing. [V.F.]

classification The process of arranging a set of objects in an order. The procedure is usually hierarchical. In the biological context there are two objectives. One is to produce a system allowing different types of organism to be referred to unambiguously. The other is to arrange them in an order that corresponds as nearly as possible to their evolutionary histories. [L.M.C.]

clay SOIL component consisting of mineral particles <2–4 μm, of low permeability and capable of being moulded when moist. [P.C.]

Clean Air Act *See* UNITED STATES LEGISLATION.

clean-up Action to move and remedy CONTAMINATION/POLLUTION. [P.C.]

Clean Water Act *See* UNITED STATES LEGISLATION.

clean(er) technology It is dubious if technology can ever be absolutely clean; invariably it uses up natural resources and generates WASTE. However, some options are likely to be better, i.e. cleaner, than others. This is the philosophy behind best available technology (BAT) and BEST PRACTICABLE ENVIRONMENTAL OPTION (BPEO). *See also* ENVIRONMENTAL INDUSTRIES SECTOR. [P.C.]

climate Climate is often regarded as 'average weather', i.e. a statistical description of the state of the ATMOSPHERE at any given location. The climate of an area can be described by its mean values of TEMPERATURE, rainfall, WIND speed or number of sunshine hours but it should also include some information on the extremes of the statistical distribution as it is often the extreme events that cause loss of life or economic hardship. Thus a climate description should mention, for example, the frequency of occurrence of hurricanes or DROUGHTS if relevant. To establish a proper statistical description of climate, WEATHER records for a reasonable length of time are required: a climatological average period is usually taken to be 30 years or so in length. [J.B.M.]

climate change Major changes in the Earth's energy balance and CLIMATE have occurred over geological time, and smaller changes are evident over the last few hundred years of recorded history. Climate change is not well understood as it involves many interacting factors, some of which are influenced by human activities but many others are natural.

It is the balance between incoming and outgoing RADIATION that determines the surface TEMPERATURE and essentially drives the climate system. The incoming radiation from the Sun varies because of changes in the luminosity of the Sun and variation in the Earth–Sun geometry. The outgoing radiation flux depends on the reflectance of the surface cover, and on the emission of thermal radiation from the surface which depends on the fourth power of surface temperature. Both the incoming and outgoing radiation streams are influenced by atmospheric composition. WATER vapour and volcanic SMOKE cause a reduction in the SOLAR RADIATION reaching the ground. Gases absorb radiation at certain wavelengths; many diatomic gases absorb thermal radiation and so contribute to the greenhouse effect.

Human activity may influence climate change in several ways. The release of the gases CARBON DIOXIDE (CO_2), METHANE (CH_4), nitrous oxide (N_2O) and CFCs enhances the greenhouse effect and is expected to cause GLOBAL WARMING. Changes in reflectance of the surface, brought about by changes in land use such as the replacement of forests by farmland, are thought to be significant. Release of AEROSOLS in fossil-fuel combustion may have a small effect.

Evidence for climate change in the past comes from various sources. Ice cores from the Antarctic and elsewhere contain a time series of gas concentrations, and associated oxygen isotope STRATIGRAPHY provides a record of temperatures. The geological record provides evidence for the ice ages when ICE covered a major part of the Earth. Over the last 10 000 years the record of pollens from PEAT bogs and lake sediments shows a warming until some 5000 years ago, followed by a cooling. History demonstrates that there have been recent changes, for example the depopulation of upland villages around AD 1700 as a result of a 'Little Ice Age'.

Evidence that climate change is presently occurring comes from the fact that glaciers everywhere in the world have been melting, and continue to melt. Another type of evidence comes from the data on temperature, collected from many sites over the world. This shows an increase of about 0.5°C since the year 1900. It also shows that most of the warmest years of the century have occurred since 1980.

The prediction that climate change will bring a warmer world is obtained by running general circulation models (GCMs) with a prescribed assumption ('scenario') about the rate at which CO_2 from anthropogenic sources will increase in the future. Such models take days or weeks to run on the largest computers, yet are still considered to lack critical detail about the behaviour of CLOUDS and the representation of canopy surface conductance to water vapour. The predictions are that a doubling of CO_2 will cause an increase in temperature of 1.5–4.5°C. Warming will not be uniform over the world, but more pronounced at high latitudes. Patterns of rainfall and storms cannot be predicted with much confidence.

Future climate change, if it occurs as fast as has been predicted, will have profound impacts on the BIOTA, affecting AGRICULTURE, FORESTRY and nature conservation. Although species are able to migrate (and certainly have done in the past), the rate of change may be too great for them to keep pace. OUTBREAKS of pests may be more common, especially insect pests at high latitudes. Sea level has been rising by 1–2 mm year^{-1} and will rise faster as the ice melts and as oceans undergo thermal expansion, posing problems for nations and people with low-lying ground.

The Intergovernmental Panel on Climate Change (IPCC) was established in 1988 with a mission to (i) assess the scientific information and (ii) formulate realistic response strategies for the management of climate change. *See also* GLOBAL WARMING; GREENHOUSE GASES. [J.G.]

climate zones The classification of the world into CLIMATE zones or regions, based partly on the mean annual rainfall and TEMPERATURE and also the soils and life forms of the VEGETATION. [J.G.]

climatology There are two meanings: (i) the climatology of a place is a description of the long-term CLIMATE there; and (ii) climatology is also the scientific study of the climate, by which is meant the long-term patterns in the WEATHER. [J.G.]

clone Genetically identical individuals, produced by mitotic cell division or physical division of viable plant parts (cuttings, rhizomes, grafted buds). [M.J.C.]

closed forest Stands of trees whose CANOPY cover is complete or nearly so. Individual tree crowns may not actually touch or overlap, but there are no gaps in the canopy into which a new tree may grow. [G.F.P.]

closed system A system is closed if there is no exchange of matter or energy with the outside world. The converse is an OPEN SYSTEM. ECOSYSTEMS are almost invariably open, because they depend on an external energy supply for their persistence. However, systems that are closed to external inputs of matter and which are open only to light are frequently constructed for experimental purposes; examples are aquatic microcosms and the Biosphere-2 experiment. Materially closed systems are particularly relevant to space travel (which necessitates them) and can serve as a model for the functioning of the BIOSPHERE. [M.O.H.]

cloud forest A kind of TROPICAL MONTANE FOREST. Hot moisture-laden lowland air rises up mountain slopes. As it rises it cools and at a certain altitude a flat-bottomed cloud layer is formed where the DEW POINT is reached. CLOUDS form and remain from mid-morning to evening, drastically reducing INSOLATION. The regular presence of the cloud layer produces a strong ALTITUDINAL ZONATION, a sharp discontinuity in the forest vegetation. [M.I.]

clouds Most commonly formed as a result of cooling of the air to below its dew-point TEMPERATURE by adiabatic expansion on rising to a greater height above the Earth's surface. This may be by convection (cumulus cloud) or at a frontal surface in a larger WEATHER system.

Theoretically, and in practice, cloud is formed when two masses of saturated or nearly saturated air, initially at different temperatures, are mixed to acquire an intermediate temperature, which must be below the DEW POINT of the mixture. However, this is uncommon except in aircraft condensation trails (contrails), some large industrial chimney plumes, fog thickening as a result of TURBULENCE in the WIND over rough ground and, occasionally, 'arctic smoke' (steaming fog) in very cold air over a warm WATER surface.

The edges of clouds are usually evaporating as a result of mixing with surrounding drier air. Therefore, the mixture acquires a changed temperature and a density which is different from that of the cloud or the clear air and as a consequence generates more eddies, which promote further mixing. The outer layer of a cumulus cloud can therefore usually be seen to be descending.

Larger areas of cloud may be evaporated as a result of adiabatic warming when the air subsides, as in an anticyclone.

The shapes produced by the condensation of cloud and evaporation are greatly influenced by fallout (RAIN, hail, snow or other PRECIPITATION), which forms streaks and descending air CURRENTS that evaporate the smaller droplets.

Condensation of cloud usually occurs if the air is cooled below its dew point; however, this requires the presence of condensation nuclei, which are almost always present in the air so that a significant degree of supersaturation is scarcely ever measured. The number of cloud droplets may be between 10 and 20 000 cm^{-3} of air, depending on the number of nuclei present.

Freezing to ICE crystals does not occur as soon as the air is cooled to below 0°C, and supersaturation with respect to ice often occurs because ice nuclei are uncommon. Supercooled water droplets in clouds are likely to remain unfrozen in the temperature range 0 to −39°C for long periods if no ice nuclei are present; however, if a few drops freeze, all the remaining drops may very soon freeze as a result of the multiplication of icy fragments emitted by droplets freezing on the outside first and shattering or squirting out fragments when the interior expands on freezing. Freezing becomes more likely as −40°C is approached and is usually spontaneous at or below that temperature. Before all the droplets become frozen, the freezing of supercooled droplets causes growth by condensation of the crystals and evaporation of the liquid droplets because the vapour PRESSURE over water exceeds that over ice. However, ACID salts on the droplets may reduce the freezing temperature to below the actual temperature, so that even at −90°C the cloud will have the optical properties of a cloud of spherical particles and not those of a cloud of ice particles, a special example being polar stratospheric clouds.

When cloud condensation nuclei are very plentiful and the initial number of nuclei is very large with the droplets being correspondingly small, unless the nuclei are hygroscopic salts SURFACE TENSION increases the interior pressure, which results in evaporation of the smaller droplets and growth by condensation of the largest. This begins a reformation of the drop-size spectrum and a reduction in the ALBEDO of the cloud. In regions where condensation nuclei are rare the number of droplets is smaller when the cloud first forms, as may be the case over some parts of the oceans. The exhaust from a ship, which is usually a profuse source of nuclei, causes a dramatic rise in the number, and reduction in size, of droplets and the ship's trail consists of cloud with a greatly increased albedo, i.e. a trail of much brighter white cloud. [R.S.S.]

Club of Rome Study Body established in 1965 by an international group of economists, scientists, technologists, politicians and others. The aim is to study the interaction of economic, scientific, biological and social aspects of humanity, with a view to predicting impacts of proposed and alternative policies on environment and the survival of humanity. *See also* ENVIRONMENTAL (ECOLOGICAL) ECONOMICS. [P.C.]

CMTs *See* CARCINOGENS, MUTAGENS, TERATOGENS.

coarse-particulate organic matter (CPOM) Plant DETRITUS in aquatic systems >1 mm in diameter. In fresh water will be of the form of decomposing leaves, needles and woody material. *Cf.* FINE-PARTICULATE ORGANIC MATTER (FPOM) (<1 mm but >0.45 μm) and DISSOLVED ORGANIC MATTER (DOM) (<0.45 μm). [P.C.]

coastal Referring to processes or features of the shallow portion of the OCEAN, generally overlying the CONTINENTAL SHELF, where CIRCULATION and other features are strongly influenced by the bordering land. Two features of particular importance in coastal areas are UPWELLING of deep nutrient-rich water and the formation of FRONTS (i.e. boundaries between horizontally juxtaposed water masses of dissimilar properties). [V.F.]

coastal lagoons *See* LAGOONS.

coastal wetlands The mixing of fresh and saline waters in low-lying, flat coastal areas leads to the development of a series of wetland vegetation types, depending upon climate, water-flow patterns, sedimentation, etc. Fine-particle deposition in temperate regions leads to the development of SALT MARSHES, consisting largely of herbaceous and dwarf shrub vegetation. In tropical and SUBTROPICAL regions, arboreal vegetation dominates the SUCCESSION, forming mangroves.

BEACH and REEF features can lead to the formation of LAGOONS, and where evaporation losses are considerable (as in the Carmargue of southern France) these can develop into highly saline lakes. [P.D.M.]

coastline lakes *See* LAKES, TYPES OF.

COD *See* CHEMICAL OXYGEN DEMAND.

coefficient of community The relation of the number of species common to two COMMUNITIES to the total number of species in these communities. The Jaccard coefficient or index of similarity is often used, expressed as a percentage:

$$IS_J = \frac{a}{a+b+c} \times 100$$

where *a* is number of species common to both communities, *b* is number of species unique to one community and *c* is number of species unique to the other. [A.J.W.]

coefficient of variation The sample STANDARD DEVIATION (*s*) is an estimate of the variation in a POPULATION (σ). If we wanted to compare the variation in mass of mice from several populations we could use the standard deviation. However, we could not compare the value of *s* for mass in mice and elephants, since the scale of the measurements are so different. One solution is to use the coefficient of

variation, $CV = s/\bar{x}$, usually expressed as a percentage by multiplying by 100. *See also* STATISTICS. [B.S.]

coliform count Test for purity of drinking waters, i.e. the number of coliform (i.e. gut organism) bacteria per 100 ml. *Escherichia coli* is used as an indicator. Though this species is not very pathogenic to humans, its presence indicates CONTAMINATION of water by faecal matter and hence the possibility of enteric disease. *See also* WATER QUALITY OBJECTIVE/STANDARD. [P.C.]

colloids Colloids are suspensions of very small particles in a fluid. Examples of colloids include starch in water, albumin and paint. Colloids are important in soil chemistry, where very small particles of HUMUS and CLAY are suspended in the soil solution; they provide an enormous surface area to which ions are adsorbed. [J.G.]

combined heat and power Productive use of heat generated from power production (e.g. in electricity generation) and, more generally, from INCINERATION. Some would count this as contributing to RECYCLING. Combined heat- and power-plants pipe hot water or steam to nearby industries, office blocks, institutions and housing. [P.C.]

command and control Use of law, in the form of specified prohibitions and CONSENTS that are monitored and infringement of which invites penalties, to protect the environment. *See also* REGULATORY INSTRUMENTS. [P.C.]

commercial fishing The commercial exploitation of fish accounts for roughly 5–10% of the protein consumed by the world's population. Approximately 86% of the total world fishery consists of marine species. Geographically, the major fisheries are concentrated in the waters overlying the continental shelves. The most important commercially exploited marine animals belong to four groups: bony and cartilaginous fish, marine mammals, molluscs and crustaceans. Fish are by far the most important group by mass, and commercial landings are dominated by herring, sardine and anchovy. As of 1987, these three groups accounted for 28% of the total world catch of fish and shellfish. The second largest group of commercial fish are the bottom-dwelling gadoids (i.e. cod, haddock, pollock and hake); the third largest group are the mackerels. Tuna are among the largest of the commercial fish species and the basis for the only major open ocean fishery. The introduction of modern fishing gear, including factory ships, larger nets and more accurate methods of locating fish, has led to overexploitation of many FISH STOCKS. The signs of overexploitation are normally a change in AGE STRUCTURE, a decline in average size of fish and an increase in effort needed to land the same amount of fish. Attempts to manage the fisheries by limiting the allowable catch through the enforcement of quotas have generally proved disappointing. Problems in setting effective quotas include the difficulty in selecting a reasonable catch itself, the problem of dealing with 'by catches' (i.e. fish recovered unintentionally with the species being fished) and the problem of ensuring accurate reporting of catches. Classic examples of overexploited fisheries include the Peruvian anchoveta, the catch of which peaked in the 1960s at about 10 million tonnes and which, exacerbated by a severe EL NIÑO, crashed in 1972 following at least a decade of OVERFISHING. The dramatic decline of the whale fishery was the direct result of overexploitation and of unsuccessful attempts at regulating this fishery. It has been estimated that the total SUSTAINABLE YIELD of the world fishery is approximately 100 million tonnes. Since current catches are in the range of 84 million tonnes, it is unlikely that the ocean can supply much more of the world's food. Potential areas for new fisheries development include Antarctic KRILL and possibly some continental-slope fish species. [V.F.]

Commission for Sustainable Development Set up by the United Nations after the UNCED to monitor progress in implementing agreements made at the conference. *See also* RIO SUMMIT. [P.C.]

common property resources Natural resources that are the property of no one. Open to abuse and overexploitation. *See also* THE COMMONS; TRAGEDY OF THE COMMONS. [P.C.]

commonness Can apply to a species that is locally abundant and/or has a wide geographical spread. *Cf.* RARITY, BIOLOGY OF. *See also* ABUNDANCE. [P.C.]

the Commons Major resources of the planet (ATMOSPHERE, WATER, SOIL) to which all have right of access and use, and which no one has a right to spoil. The concept was used more widely following a publication by Garrett Hardin in 1968. *See also* TRAGEDY OF THE COMMONS. [P.C.]

community The total living biotic component of an ECOSYSTEM, including plants, animals and microbes. The term (unlike 'assembly' or 'ASSEMBLAGE') implies interaction between the individuals and species in the form of competition, predation, mutualism, commensalism, etc. [P.D.M.]

community ecology Community ecology is the study of the interactions between populations of organisms, and between populations and the physical ENVIRONMENT, in a particular community, and the effects that those interactions have on the behaviour and structure of that competition. A community cannot simply be seen as the sum of its constituent species or populations, but has emergent properties that are not features of the component populations. The term, 'community' here encompasses a wide range of scales, and indeed one community can be described within another—thus a rotting tree stump may house a community of microorganisms, higher plants, and insects, whilst that stump might be part of a much larger community—a forest. *See also* ECOLOGY. [P.C.]

compensation depth The depth, in an aquatic ecosystem, at which ATTENUATION of LIGHT limits gross photosynthetic production so that it is equal to respiratory carbon consumption; or, alternatively, the depth at which the amount of OXYGEN produced in PHOTOSYNTHESIS equals the oxygen consumed in RESPIRATION. It may be defined for a single photosynthetic organism, for all photosynthetic organisms or for all producer and consumer organisms in the ecosystem. The basis of definition must be stated. [J.R.E. & V.F.]

compensation light intensity The light intensity at which OXYGEN evolved from a photosynthesizing organism equals that consumed in its RESPIRATION. [V.F.]

compensation point The compensation point for LIGHT is defined as the photosynthetically active radiant flux density at which gross PHOTOSYNTHESIS of a CANOPY (or a whole plant or plant organ) is equal to its gross RESPIRATION. At the compensation point the canopy, plant or organ is thus neither accumulating nor losing carbon, i.e. net photosynthetic carbon-fixation rate is zero. Light compensation point is widely variable, plants of open habitats having high values (5–10% full sunlight) and shade plants much lower values, down to 0.1% full sun or even less. [J.R.E.]

competent authorities In a European Union context, set up by member states to carry out certain functions with respect to European Commission legislation, for example in the context of chemical control legislation to receive, evaluate and make recommendations on premanufacture notifications and also to carry out RISK ASSESSMENTS of new and existing substances. Also referred to as rapporteurs. Usually will be a government department or agency. *See also* PREMANUFACTURE NOTICES. [P.C.]

complexity of ecosystems Strictly speaking, the term 'ECOSYSTEM complexity' should denote some integrated measure of the complexity of the biological COMMUNITY, together with its physical ENVIRONMENT. In practice, however, it is often taken to refer only to the biological community, the complexity of which often reflects that of the physical environment (*see* HABITAT STRUCTURE). The mean number of species in the system, the number of interactions between species or some combination of these and related measures can be taken as indices of complexity. As ecosystems become more mature they generally increase in structural and biological complexity (*see* SUCCESSION). Understanding the determinants of complexity and the relationship between this property and others such as the ecosystem stability remain a central goal for ecology. *See also* COMPLEXITY–STABILITY. [S.J.H.]

complexity–stability During the 1950s and 1960s, ecologists believed that increased complexity within a community would lead to increased stability. More recent models of communities suggest that stability tends to decrease as complexity increases. However, evidence from real communities indicates that the relationship between community complexity and stability varies with the precise nature of the community, with the way in which the community is perturbed and with the way in which stability is assessed. Ecologists have observed a general tendency for the existence of complex, dynamically fragile communities in stable environments (i.e. tropics) and the existence of simpler, dynamically robust communities in relatively variable environments (e.g. temperate regions). *See also* COMPLEXITY OF ECOSYSTEMS. [V.F.]

compliance Operating within the requirements of the law. In environmental terms this often means conforming with legally defined standards. [P.C.]

compost *See* COMPOSTING.

composting Biological breakdown of biological solids so as to stabilize them as humic substances (compost). [P.C.]

Comprehensive Environmental Response Compensation and Liability Act 1980 (CERCLA) *See* SUPERFUND LEGISLATION.

concentration–response The quantitative relationship between the concentrations of a TOXICANT to which a subject is exposed in the AMBIENT medium and the incidence or extent of an adverse EFFECT. *Cf.* DOSE–RESPONSE. [P.C.]

condition index (CI) Index of metabolic condition of an individual, usually in terms of mass per unit length. [P.C.]

confidence limit Confidence limits describe where we would expect a population parameter to lie in relation to a statistic estimated from a SAMPLE. For example, since the SAMPLING distribution of means (from samples of size $n \geq 30$) (*see* STANDARD ERROR) is a NORMAL DISTRIBUTION, we know that 95% of observed means will be within the interval $\mu \pm 1.96s/\sqrt{n}$, where $s/\sqrt{n}$ is the estimated standard error of the MEAN. Or, stated the other way round, we can be 95% confident that the interval $\bar{x} \pm 1.96s/\sqrt{n}$ will contain the population mean (μ). This interval is known as a confidence interval or more precisely, as the 95% confidence interval. The interval $\bar{x} \pm 2.58s/\sqrt{n}$ is known as the 99% confidence interval. Clearly, if the confidence interval is large we can place less reliability on the sample mean as an estimate of the population mean. [B.S.]

connectance Fraction of all possible pairs of species within a COMMUNITY that interact directly as feeder and food. In other words, the number of actual connections in a FOOD WEB divided by the total number of possible connections. [P.C.]

consents Same as AUTHORIZATION, but usually refer to effluent DISCHARGES to public sewer or receiving waters. *See also* POLLUTION PERMITS. [P.C.]

conservation biology Conservation biology is an emerging, interdisciplinary field that seeks to establish a scientific basis for the conservation and management of POPULATIONS, COMMUNITIES and ECOSYSTEMS. At the same time, conservation biology draws on the empirical observations and results of land management practices as primary source of information and insight. Consequently, conservation biology may be thought of as the interface between ECOLOGY and allied disciplines on one hand, and the practice of conservation management on the other. [D.A.F.]

constant-effort harvesting This type of HARVESTING is theoretically attractive as it involves natural FEEDBACK between the level of catch and the population of the harvested resource. The idea is that the amount of MORTALITY inflicted remains effectively constant. This can be done by setting, for example, a restriction on the amount of hunters or, in the case of fishing, the number of fishing vessels of a certain power. The operation of this constant amount of effort means that the catch will vary in proportion to the POPULATION SIZE. This makes an implicit assumption that catch is related to effort and population size by a simple linear relationship. The constant of proportionality is usually termed in fisheries as the catchability coefficient. [J.B.]

constant final yield This involves the idea of a population equilibrium in which the removals by HARVESTING (the YIELD) exactly equal the surplus that comes from the balance of births, deaths and growth in the population. This constant final yield can occur at all levels up to the MAXIMUM SUSTAINABLE YIELD, but not beyond it. In practice, this theoretical concept is useful, but as all resources are subject to environmental variation and, indeed, demographic variation such yields will tend to fluctuate around some characteristic average. *See also* SUSTAINABLE YIELD. [J.B.]

contaminant A non-natural substance in the natural environment, not necessarily causing HARM. *Cf.* POLLUTANT. [P.C.]

contaminated land Land which due to current or previous use has under or in it substances that are causing or might cause HARM to human health or the ENVIRONMENT. There is a divide between a precautionary approach, which would define contaminated land as that containing CONTAMINANTS, and a more pragmatic approach, which defines contaminated land as containing substances of a kind and/or quantity likely to cause harm. Treatment of CONTAMINATION can be costly and so this distinction may be important. It may also have implications for the extent of CLEAN-UP: to the limits of detection of contaminants, or to levels unlikely to cause problems in the context of the way land may be used (suitable for use). Problems with this latter approach are that requirements for use may change (e.g. especially as pressure is put on development of brown field sites), and not all implications of contamination for harm may be understood.

An expression that has been used in British legislation is 'contaminative use', i.e. any use of land (past or present) that may cause it to be contaminated. This obviated the need to demonstrate actual contamination, which depends upon available techniques. Using this as a legal basis for action proved controversial and, although included in British legislation, was never implemented.

In the UK these issues are the subject of the 19th Report of the ROYAL COMMISSION ON ENVIRONMENTAL POLLUTION. *See also* LAND RECLAMATION. [P.C.]

contamination Release of a by-product of human activity, chemical or physical. Contamination sometimes causes HARM to human health and/or the natural environment, but need not. *Cf.* POLLUTION. [P.C.]

contaminative processes *See* LAND REGISTERS.

contaminative use *See* CONTAMINATED LAND.

continental drift Alfred Wegener first put forward the revolutionary hypothesis of continental drift at the turn of the nineteenth/twentieth century. He proposed that several hundred million years ago the continents were united into one supercontinent that he called Pangaea, meaning all land. Late in the Mesozoic era it began to split up, with the opening of the Atlantic and Indian oceans, although the final severance of North America and Eurasia did not take place until as late as the Quaternary.

After initial sympathy from some German compatriots, a groundswell of opinion adverse to Wegener's hypothesis grew, and the general attitude to continental drift in the period between the two world wars was decidedly hostile, especially in North America. In particular, Wegener's failure to provide a mechanism plausible enough to satisfy the geophysicists was generally regarded as a telling point against his ideas. Within a few years in the 1960s there was a dramatic conversion of opinion to the new geological paradigm of PLATE TECTONICS, implying what was formerly called continental drift. The advent of plate tectonics marked a great advance in the earth sciences and forms the basis for present understanding of our planet. [A.H.]

continental front Continental fronts occur along the edges of continents as a result of wind-driven oceanic circulation. Divergent continental fronts form in association with CURRENTS that flow toward the Equator along the western coasts of continents. Owing to the Earth's rotation, the currents are driven away from shore and are thus associated with UPWELLING (e.g. Benguela Current, California Current, Peru Current). Convergent continental fronts are associated with currents flowing away from the Equator along the eastern coasts of continents. They are characterized by an accumulation of warm, nutrient-poor water (e.g. as occurs along the Great Barrier Reef). [V.F.]

continental margins The zones separating the emergent continents from the deep-sea bottom. [V.F.]

continental rise The part of the sea floor extending below the CONTINENTAL SLOPE and above the ABYSSAL plain, ranging to a depth of between 4000 and 5000 m. It is formed by the accumulation of SEDIMENT eroded from the continents and deposited at the base of the slope. [V.F.]

continental shelf A broad expanse of ocean bottom, representing the submerged edge of a continent. The continental shelf divides the open OCEAN from the inshore, or NERITIC, zone and accounts for about 7% of the sea floor. It extends from the line of permanent immersion to the depth (usually 200 m, but may be as deep as 700 m, e.g. around Antarctica) at which there is a marked increase in the slope. The width of the shelf averages 50 km, but it may be entirely absent (e.g. off Chile and south-western Alaska) or as wide as 1350 km (e.g. off the Arctic coast of Siberia). [V.F.]

continental slope The relatively steep downward slope extending seaward from the outer edge of the CONTINENTAL SHELF to the flat ocean floor. The continental slope usually extends to a depth of 2000–3000 m and varies in width between 20 and 100 km. It is usually covered by sediments of fine SILT and mud. [V.F.]

contingency table Most frequently a two-way table (at least two rows and two columns) in which qualitative information is displayed prior to analysis for ASSOCIATION. *See also* CHI-SQUARED TEST; STATISTICS. [B.S.]

contract (testing) laboratories Under contract to industry or regulators to make certain environmental measurements, for example contract ecotoxicological testing laboratories test NEW CHEMICALS according to regulatory GUIDELINES and generally are required to follow GOOD LABORATORY PRACTICE (GLP). [P.C.]

control action threshold (CAT) A term used in PEST CONTROL and defined as the pest density at which one should take action to prevent a pest outbreak. The CAT varies with the season, with the cost of the crop and of the preventive measures to be taken, and with the population densities of the natural enemies of the pest. [S.C.S.]

controlled waste *See* WASTE.

controlled waters In British law, those subject to protection under the ENVIRONMENTAL LAWS and including territorial waters, coastal and estuarine waters, surface fresh water and groundwater. [P.C.]

Convention on the International Trade in Endangered Species (CITES) *See* INTERNATIONAL CONSERVATION CONVENTIONS.

Convention on Wetlands of International Importance *See* INTERNATIONAL CONSERVATION CONVENTIONS.

coppice A WOODLAND managed by the practice of

coppicing. This involves cutting the tree at or near the ground and allowing it to sprout from the stump to generate a new crop of poles. The regrowth was traditionally cut again usually after 5–30 years, but both shorter and longer rotations have been recorded. Coppices usually included both coppiced trees (underwood) and timber trees (standards). [G.F.P.]

coral reefs Coral reefs are names for that group of cnidarians (belonging to the class Anthozoa) that secrete an external skeleton of calcium carbonate. They are found in shallow waters surrounding tropical landmasses. They are restricted to high SALINITY, silt-free waters warmer than 18°C, generally in a band that lies between the Tropic of Cancer and the Tropic of Capricorn. There are three types of coral reefs: atolls, BARRIER REEFS and fringing reefs. An atoll is a horseshoe or circular type of coral reef that grows around a subsided island (typically an oceanic volcanic SEAMOUNT) and encloses a shallow lagoon. In contrast to a barrier reef, an atoll has no central island extending above the sea surface. Fringing reefs do not have a lagoon separating the reef from its associated landmass. Atolls may be formed either by subsidence of an island surrounded by a fringing reef or by an increase in sea level following GLACIATION. [V.F.]

coral reefs, diversity and conservation CORAL REEFS are sites of extremely high biological DIVERSITY and may, in fact, be the most complex systems in the marine environment. There are many more species on a coral reef than in the surrounding water or sediments. Photosynthetic rates are an order of magnitude greater on the reef than in the surrounding waters due to rapid RECYCLING of NUTRIENTS, the fixation of nitrogen gas to nitrate (an inorganic source of nitrogen needed by photosynthetic organisms) by cyanobacteria associated with the reef, and an UPWELLING effect caused by the physical presence of the reef structure. The high productivity and habitat complexity of coral reefs support a rich variety of benthic algae, epifaunal and burrowing invertebrates (sometimes referred to as cryptofauna), a variety of crustaceans and fish. Bioerosion by the grazing and boring activities of cryptofaunal species may be the most important of the processes that act to break down coral reefs. Coral reefs are notable for the widespread coexistence of species with strongly overlapping resource requirements. Explanations for such coexistence remain controversial. Pacific reefs are more diverse than Atlantic reefs, i.e. there are 85% more coral species in the western Pacific, where corals are believed to have originated. Despite the high productivity, reef-building corals are highly adapted to low-nutrient environments and become stressed and eventually outcompeted if nutrient levels are in excess. Since corals are killed by minor deviations from optimal conditions, the climatic stability of coral-reef environments is evidenced by the persistence of reefs in the tropics for over 50 million years. Occasional environmental DISTURBANCE (e.g. hurricanes), as well as biological disturbances (e.g. predation and grazing), are believed to be important in maintaining diversity. However, recent population explosions of the coral-eating sea star, *Acanthaster planci*, have resulted in catastrophic mortality of reefs throughout the western Pacific. The cause of such population explosions is not completely understood, but may be partly human-induced. Bleaching of coral reefs occurs from the loss of the symbiotic zooxanthellae that live within the coral. Bleaching may occur as a result of increased water temperature or light-related effects. A particularly extensive bleaching episode (causing the death of at least 70% of the corals along the Pacific Central American coast) has been attributed to the EL NIÑO event of 1982–1983. Increased sedimentation from land RUN-OFF, dredging and in association with DEFORESTATION can damage corals by decreasing the amount of light available for PHOTOSYNTHESIS, by clogging the coral polyps and by preventing the settlement of coral larvae. Additional human-caused damage to coral reefs occurs from explosives used to kill fish and open channels, fishing with bleach and cyanide, shell collectors and tourism. *See also* CONSERVATION BIOLOGY. [V.F.]

correlation When two sets of measurements (often called x and y) are related or show ASSOCIATION they are said to be correlated. If one (y) increases when the other (x) increases they are said to be positively correlated. If one decreases when the other increases they are said to be negatively correlated. Both parametric (PRODUCT–MOMENT CORRELATION COEFFICIENT) and non-parametric (KENDALL'S RANK CORRELATION COEFFICIENT and SPEARMAN'S RANK CORRELATION COEFFICIENT) statistics are available. Remember that a correlation between two variables does not necessarily mean that one causes the other. It may be that the two variables are both effects of a common cause. [B.S.]

corridor A corridor is a linear patch of HABITAT, usually established or maintained to connect two or more adjacent habitat areas. Examples of corridors include HEDGEROWS, railroad and highway rights-of-way, forested shelter-belts, and GALLERY FORESTS along RIPARIAN zones. [D.A.F.]

cosms Artificial ECOSYSTEMS of various levels of complexity and scale. *See also* MACROCOSM; MESOCOSM; MICROCOSM. [P.C.]

cost recovery Legal process when potentially responsible parties (PRPs) that have contributed in some way to CONTAMINATION can be required to pay for CLEAN-UP, for example under SUPERFUND LEGISLATION in the USA. [P.C.]

cost recovery charging Part of the polluter-pays philosophy is that the cost of implementing environmental controls should be recovered from potential polluters. These include the costs for site inspection, the bureaucracy associated with CON-SENTS/AUTHORIZATION, substance MONITOR-ING and audit, etc. Increasingly, regulations try to recover these costs by charging those seeking consents/authorizations. *See also* COST RECOVERY. [P.C.]

cost (risk)–benefit approach Industry/technology bring benefits (i) in terms of products that improve health, food supply, welfare and create wealth. At the same time they carry risks (ii) for human health and the environment. This can be turned around: controlling industrial activities and outputs brings economic costs (iii) but can bring benefits (iv) of increased environmental protection and reduced risks to human health. Trying to balance these elements in coming to a view about the need for controls is generally described as cost (risk)–benefit analysis. However, note that this can refer to definition (i) versus definition (ii) or definition (iii) versus definition (iv) and this can sometimes mislead. *See also* ECOLOGICAL VALUATION; ENVI-RONMENTAL (ECOLOGICAL) ECONOMICS. [P.C.]

costs of resistance Resisting adverse effects from outside agents is often metabolically costly: escaping a predator requires increased activity; resisting parasitism or disease involves the deployment of active defence mechanisms; resisting chemical poisoning may require avoidance behaviour, active transport and excretion processes, detoxification and repair of damaged tissues. These can all be considered as costs of RESISTANCE. It is presumed that some costs trade off with other elements of fitness in the evolution of TOLERANCE. [P.C.]

Coulter Counter™ An electronic device used to estimate the BIOMASS of PLANKTON belonging to different SIZE categories. Biomass is thus estimated as the diameter of a sphere equivalent in volume to the original particle multiplied by the number of particles. [V.F.]

Council on Environmental Quality (CEQ) Set up by the US National Environmental Policy Act (NEPA) of 1969 to advise the President on environmental enforcement measures and objectives. [P.C.]

CPOM *See* COARSE-PARTICULATE ORGANIC MATTER.

cradle-to-grave analysis Assessment of ENVIRON-MENTAL IMPACT of product from raw materials to disposal. *See also* LIFE-CYCLE ASSESSMENT. [P.C.]

critical depth Depth at which the total photosynthetic PRODUCTION taking place in the water column is just balanced by the total respiratory losses of photosynthesizers in that same depth layer. *See also* COM-PENSATION DEPTH. [V.F.]

critical loads Quantitative estimate of EXPOSURE to one or more pollutants below which significant harmful effects on specified sensitive elements of the environment do not occur according to present knowledge. Usually refers to ATMOSPHERIC POL-LUTION (*Cf.* ENVIRONMENTAL QUALITY STAN-DARD). As usual there can be much debate about specifying appropriate sensitive elements of the environment and about the meaning of significant harmful effects. Also of relevance are the terms 'critical level' and 'target load'. A critical level is analogous to critical load but refers to a THRESHOLD of damage for gaseous pollutants acting upon species (usually vegetation). Target load is understood as the load determined by political agreement; it may be greater than the critical load and thus accepts a degree of damage or it may incorporate a safety factor and be less than the critical load. [P.C.]

crop Species used in AGRICULTURE and their YIELD; usually refers to plants (crop of maize, of rice; good crop from a harvest) but occasionally to animals (e.g. output/yield of fish farm in AQUACULTURE). [P.C.]

crust, Earth The solid outer portion of the Earth. Composed primarily of OXYGEN (46.60% by mass), silicon (27.72%), aluminium (8.13%), iron (5.00%), calcium (3.63%), sodium (2.83%), potassium (2.59%), magnesium (2.09%) and titanium (0.44%), which make up various silicate minerals. Crustal thickness and elastic properties vary widely and abruptly. Continental crust is lighter (average density $= 2.7\,\text{g cm}^{-3}$) and thicker (average thickness $= 50\,\text{km}$) than oceanic crust (average density $= 3.0\,\text{g cm}^{-3}$; average thickness $= 7\,\text{km}$). Beneath the oceans, the outermost layer of crust is composed of SEDIMENT deposits, weathered lavas and basaltic rocks. Continental crust has a relatively thin sedimentary top layer underlain by metamorphic rocks, thus forming two layers: the upper layer is rich in silicon and aluminium (called sial) and the lower layer is rich in silicon and magnesium (called sima). The crust beneath the oceans differs from that beneath the continents in that the former is generally thinner and lacks an upper layer rich in silicon and aluminium. New crust is generated at mid-ocean ridges and resorbed along SUBDUCTION zones (*see* PLATE TECTONICS). The oldest continental crust is nearly 4×10^9 years old, whereas the oldest oceanic crust is about 190 million years old. [V.F.]

cryopreservation The keeping of organisms, or their propagules, at low temperatures and hence extending their normal lifespans, usually for purposes of selective breeding and conservation. [P.C.]

cryptogamic soil crust Also called microbiotic SOIL crusts, these are delicate symbioses of cyanobacteria, lichens and mosses from a variety of taxa that inhabit arid and semi-arid ecosystems. Crusts perform several essential ecological functions: increase organic matter and available PHOSPHO-RUS, soil stability and water infiltration; provide favourable sites for the germination of vascular plants; and, most crucially, perform the major share of nitrogen fixation in desert ecosystems. [T.L.F.]

culling This term tends to be applied to the HARVEST-ING of large mammals, including marine mammals. [J.B.]

curie (Ci) A UNIT (now superseded) equal to the emission from 1 g of radium, which is equivalent to 3.7×10^{10} Bq. [R.S.S.]

currents Important agents of erosion on land and in the SEA. Ocean currents are driven by two forces: WIND drives horizontal surface WAVES, whereas density differences among water masses drive deep-water CIRCULATION and vertical exchange. [V.F.]

cyanobacterial toxins In nutrient-enriched fresh water or saltwater many blue-green algae (cyanobacteria) reproduce rapidly by vegetative cell division. The consequent high-density populations are described as BLOOMS and usually occur following EUTROPHICATION with phosphorus and nitrogen from agricultural FERTILIZERS or SEWAGE. When the cells die they may release TOXINS which poison fish, and birds or mammals drinking the water. The toxins include low relative molecular mass polypeptides, tertiary amines and alkaloids. Most are neurotoxins which cause respiratory distress and convulsions in animals. Some are suspected of causing liver failure in livestock and others are dermatogenic, causing skin inflammation in humans. In potable water supplies the toxins have been blamed for outbreaks of gastroenteritis. The cyanobacterium *Microcystis* occurs widely as blooms in rice paddy, and its toxin, a ring of seven amino acids, is believed to be the cause of a high incidence of primary liver cancer in rice-growing areas, where growth of cyanobacte-

ria is encouraged to take advantage of their nitrogen-fixing abilities. [J.R.E.]

cyclone A cyclone is a mass of air, ranging from a few metres to a few thousand kilometres in size, and often but not always extending from the Earth's surface up to the TROPOSPHERE, which is caused to rotate cyclonically by the convergence of air towards its centre and the upward divergence that must accompany it. The smallest are dust devils, waterspouts and tornadoes, with funnel CLOUDS ranging in width from a few metres to tens of metres at the surface. Small polar-air rotating storms range in size from a very few kilometres to tens or even hundreds of kilometres. Tropical cyclones, called hurricanes in the North Atlantic, the extreme western Pacific and some parts of the Indian Ocean but known as typhoons in the PACIFIC OCEAN, range in size from a few hundred kilometres to well over 1000 km. Large cyclones of temperate latitudes that travel into polar regions may occupy a width of up to 2000 or 3000 km and often have well-defined FRONTS, which are the boundaries between discrete AIR MASSES of different geographical origin and along which the main cloud and RAIN systems are aligned. These latter systems can be well represented in computer-based mathematical models, while the smaller systems are on too small a scale in both space and time to be adequately represented by the grid points of the model, which are of the order of 150 km spacing and 3 h time output (although the computed time interval may be as small as 20 min). [R.S.S.]

cyclonic Moving in a counterclockwise direction in the Northern hemisphere and in a clockwise direction in the Southern hemisphere. [V.F.]

D

dams, effects of The effects of a dam on a stream and its biota depends on the size of the dam, its location in the WATERSHED and how the impounded WATER is used. Most dams alter the hydrological regime of the stream below them, reducing both total stream flow and variability in flow, as well as altering water temperatures and clarity. Typically, seasonal peak flows are captured, reducing downstream processes that alter channels and flood RIPARIAN areas. This results in major changes in the riverine biota, often reducing biotic diversity because habitat diversity has been reduced. Dams block migrations of salmon, eels, lampreys and other DIADROMOUS fish, lowering their abundance by denying them access to upstream spawning and rearing areas. [P.B.M.]

Darwinism The theory of evolution by NATURAL SELECTION as elaborated by Charles Darwin (1809–1882). Darwin became convinced that, although distinct, species were not separately created by a divine hand but that transition occurred from one to another. This idea was by no means unique at the time, but it was strongly contested. Darwin's contribution was to provide a mechanism by which evolution could take place, namely natural selection. [L.M.C.]

data logger A programmable device for capturing data. Data loggers record signals from sensors over a period of time from seconds to weeks or even months whilst unattended, for subsequent inspection or downloading to a computer for further analysis. [J.G]

dating, radiocarbon The study of past environmental conditions (*see* PALAEOECOLOGY) demands the existence of a time-scale in which such studies can be set. It is necessary, therefore, to develop techniques of assigning dates to fossils or their matrices, usually sediments. Dating methods can be relative or absolute. Some of the most widely used absolute dating methods depend upon the predictability of radioactive decay in unstable isotopes. A number of such opportunities exist in rocks and sediments but their success requires the measurement of either the product of the decay or the residual ISOTOPE that remains undecayed. If the half-life of the isotope is known, the degree to which decay has proceeded can be calculated and hence the age inferred.

Potassium–argon dating uses the decay of the isotope ^{40}K into argon, ^{40}Ar. It is complicated by the fact that ^{40}K can decay into ^{40}Ca, which can also arise in other ways, but in situations where argon is retained in the rocks (as is often the case in rocks of volcanic origin) the method is a useful one. It has been extensively used in the study of human origins in the Pliocene/Pleistocene rocks of East Africa.

Uranium has many unstable isotopes with varying half-lives. As in the case of potassium–argon dating, it is the product of decay that is measured; in corals, for example, uranium is accumulated and subsequently decays to thorium and protactinium, which are retained in the coral skeleton and can be used to determine its age. Methods that measure end-products have the advantage that they are not limited in the time-scale over which they operate; the older the material, the greater the quantity of the decay product. Methods that measure the remnant of the isotope, on the other hand, are limited by the efficiency of detection of the declining resource and (depending upon the half-life of the isotope) can only be used over a defined time-scale. Such is the case with radiocarbon.

Radiocarbon dating is the most extensively used method for dating organic materials from the latter parts of the Pleistocene and the Holocene (in total approximately the last 40 000 years). It depends upon the decay of the radioactive carbon isotope ^{14}C into nitrogen atoms (from which they were originally generated in the atmosphere by cosmic bombardment with neutrons). The half-life of ^{14}C (the time taken for 50% of any given population of ^{14}C atoms to decay) is 5569 (±30) years. When an autotrophic organism dies, it no longer derives ^{14}C from the air so that the ratio of ^{14}C to the stable isotopes of carbon (^{12}C and ^{13}C) begins to decline. A comparison of the ratio of ^{14}C to the stable isotopes of carbon in a dead organism with that ratio in the atmosphere is a measure of the time elapsed since the organism died. Dates are conventionally given in years before present (BP), where 'present' is taken to be 1950. This datum was selected because the advent of above-ground nuclear testing at that time confused all subsequent radiocarbon production. The determination of age requires the estimation of the residual ^{14}C in a sample and this can be achieved either by observing the rate at which decay is taking place (β-PARTICLES are emitted) or, preferably, by direct measurement of the ^{14}C atoms using a cyclotron. Simply observing decay is less effective, particularly in older materials, since large samples are needed for analysis (because of low ^{14}C concentration) and decay may need to be logged over long periods if ^{14}C is scarce and emissions infrequent. The use of a cyclotron permits the use of smaller samples and is more time-efficient.

The use of radiocarbon dating depends upon the assumption that the rate of production of ^{14}C in the atmosphere is uniform over time; this is not the case. The CALIBRATION of the technique against items of known absolute age, such as the growth rings of trees, has shown that there is a deviation away from the true age that increases with time. A wood sample with a known age of 7000 years, for example, gives a radiocarbon date of approximately 6000 years. In addition, the calibration curve is not a simple one; there are 'wiggles' and 'plateaux' that can lead to considerable difficulties in the use of this dating method at particular points in history. At about 10 000 years ago, for example, there is a plateau in the calibration curve, which means that samples differing in age by several centuries at this time may give the same radiocarbon age. This is a particularly unfortunate period for such a plateau to occur since it was a time of rapid CLIMATE CHANGE at the opening of the Holocene, when palaeoecologists concerned with environmental reconstruction would much appreciate a fine-resolution dating method.

It has now become conventional to refer to dates derived from radiocarbon techniques as 'corrected' if subjected to adjustment by reference to the calibration curve, or 'uncorrected radiocarbon years' if not. Sometimes uncorrected dates are given as 'bp' rather than 'BP', but this convention is not universally accepted. Although we can regard radiocarbon dating as 'absolute', it can be seen that it still requires calibration. The truly absolute dating methods are those that require no such adjustments, such as the counting of annual growth rings in trees (dendrochronology), or the counting of annual laminations in lake sediments (varves) or in ICE cores. These are the most satisfactory dating techniques, but are available only for certain types of materials.

One further dating technique, which is becoming increasingly important for the study of events in the later part of the Pleistocene (the last 200 000 years), is amino acid racemization. This depends upon the L-isomer of amino acids (the form found in living proteins) reverting after the death of an organism to the D-isomer, with a decompositional half-life of approximately 15 000 years. Residual protein in bones and mollusc shells is often adequate for the provision of a date on this basis. [P.D.M. & V.F.]

day-degrees Product of the number of days and number of degrees (°C) by which the TEMPERATURE exceeds an arbitrary or predetermined THRESHOLD. [J.S.B.]

day number Day number is a chronology describing the number of days since the first day of January within a year: 1 January is defined as having a day number of 1. Day number is frequently confused with JULIAN DAY, which counts the number of days since noon on 1 January 4713 BC. *See also* TIME. [P.R.V.G.]

daylength The period of daylight between sunrise and sunset, which are defined as the times at which the true position of the centre of the solar disc passes over the horizon. Variation in daylength results from the Earth's rotation about its own axis, relative to the orbital motion of the Earth around the Sun. Daylength (N_d) at any location on Earth is a function of latitude (ϕ) and SOLAR DECLINATION (δ), which is itself a function of DAY NUMBER (all angles are given in degrees ($90° = \pi/2$ radians)):

$$N_d = \frac{2}{15} \cos^{-1}(-\tan\phi \tan\delta)$$

Several important observations follow from this equation. At the Equator, latitude (ϕ) is zero and daylength is always 12 h, independent of day number or solar declination. At the equinoxes, when solar declination (δ) is zero, daylength is independent of latitude and equal to 12 h. The precise dates of the equinoxes vary between years depending on the Sun–Earth geometry but are typically 21 March and 23 September. The longest and shortest days occur halfway between the equinoxes at the summer and winter solstices on about 21 June and 22 December. By convention, seasons and daylengths refer to the Northern hemisphere and should be reversed for the Southern hemisphere. The period of civil twilight is important for many biological processes and is defined as the interval between sunrise or sunset and when the centre of the solar disc passes 6° below the horizon. [P.R.V.G.]

DDT (dichlorodiphenyl-trichloroethane) DDT is a potent stomach and contact organochlorine INSECTICIDE, discovered in 1939, and considered a revolutionary development in PEST CONTROL. It was apparently much safer to humans than earlier insecticides and was widely used to control human lice and disease-transmitting insects in the Second World War. DDT was also used on a wide range of crops and on storage pests. However, it has been widely banned because of environmental PERSISTENCE and BIOACCUMULATION in animal body fats and the FOOD CHAIN, with concerns regarding reproduction in higher animals, notably thinning of egg-shells of raptorial birds. *See also* ORGANOCHLORINES; PESTICIDE. [K.D.]

dead zones Zones of reduced flow that retain water in a flowing-water body. If the bottom is 'rough', there will be many such zones, chiefly on the downstream side of large boulders where flow is reduced. The retained water in these zones is nevertheless progressively renewed by fluid exchange with the main flow. These areas can support an extensive PLANK-TON community. They also act as REFUGES for organisms and as temporary sinks for sediments under high flows. [P.C.]

debt for nature programmes These involve the purchase of a country's debt notes, which are discounted on the secondary market. These are presented to the debtor country in exchange for local currency in the amount of the face value of the debt, with the local currency being invested in conservation. [P.C.]

deciduous forest Forest whose trees reduce water loss by dropping their leaves during the unfavourable season of the year, which is winter in the case of summer-green deciduous forests. TROPICAL SEASONAL FORESTS occur in humid tropical climates with a pronounced DRY SEASON, during which some, many or all the trees drop their leaves. [J.R.P.]

decomposition Breakdown of chemicals to simpler products, i.e. nearer thermodynamic equilibrium. Often applied to breakdown of BIOMASS under physical and biological action. Complex organic systems are simplified, leading to a change in form (often from more to less organized) and ultimately the conversion of biomolecules to their inorganic constituents. Those organisms bringing about decomposition are known as decomposer organisms. They can involve bacteria, fungi and animals. Animal decomposers can effect decomposition by mechanical action (burrowing through SOIL and SEDIMENT) or by feeding processes. Those involved in decomposition by feeding are also known as DETRITUS-feeders, detritivores or detritophages. [P.C.]

deep sea The part of the marine environment that lies below the level of effective LIGHT penetration for PHYTOPLANKTON photosynthesis in the open OCEAN and below the depth of the continental shelves (greater than *c.* 200 m). It is sometimes referred to as the APHOTIC ZONE. [V.F.]

defoliant Substance causing loss of leaves from plants. *See also* BIOCIDE; HERBICIDE. [P.C.]

deforestation Deforestation, the removal of CLOSED FOREST or open WOODLAND, has been taking place all over the world for millennia. Commonly, deforestation is to create land for AGRICULTURE; if this is abandoned, shrublands and tree cover eventually re-establish unless the site has become very seriously eroded. The greatest tracts of remaining intact forest are the BOREAL conifer forests at high northern latitudes and the tropical moist forests that girdle the Equator (*see* TROPICAL RAIN FOREST). These last are currently undergoing massive and highly publicized deforestation, at a rate of about 0.9% per year during the decade 1980–1990. Peninsular Malaysia went from 74% to 40% forest cover in the 34 years from 1958 to 1990. The assault on tropical forests is thus the latest episode in mankind's continuing war on the world's natural vegetation

cover, more widely publicized due to modern communications and more rapid because of powerful modern machinery. What is unique to tropical moist forests is their phenomenal SPECIES RICHNESS in all groups of plants and animals. There is consequently a much higher probability of species extinction as the forest shrinks and becomes fragmented compared with what occurred in other parts of the world, for example in Britain where the substantial forest loss has led to negligible species loss. [T.C.W.]

Delaney Clause Former clause of the US Food, Drug and Cosmetic Act. States that food additives that cause cancer in humans or animals at any level shall be prohibited from use. This has been important from an environmental point of view since it suggests the principle that substances with carcinogenic properties should not be allowed into the environment at large, i.e. there are no safe THRESHOLD levels. [P.C.]

deme A local, randomly mating POPULATION, partially isolated from other such local populations; a basic unit of genetic population structure. [T.J.K.]

demersal Living on or near the bottom of a SEA or LAKE. *See also* BENTHIC HABITAT CLASSIFICATION. [P.O.]

demography The processes of birth, death, immigration and emigration that determine the size, FLUCTUATIONS and AGE STRUCTURE of populations. Also the study of these processes and their effects. *See also* POPULATION DYNAMICS. [A.J.D.]

density The number of individuals per unit area (terrestrial species) or per unit volume (aquatic or aerial species). Density is often used to quantify the quality or attractiveness of a HABITAT or a patch of habitat, for example prey density is a measure of food availability, while tree density might help to predict the attractiveness of an area for a tree-dwelling species. The factors that determine density have been a source of controversy. [R.H.S.]

density dependence Density dependence is where one or more demographic parameters (birth, death, immigration or emigration rates) is a function of POPULATION DENSITY, i.e. a change in population density allows prediction of a change in a demographic parameter. [R.H.S.]

density independence Density independence is the absence of a relationship between any demographic parameter and POPULATION DENSITY. [R.H.S.]

depuration Metabolic process that results in elimination of XENOBIOTIC material from organisms. *See also* DETOXIFICATION. [P.C.]

derelict land Land so damaged by industrial activity or other development that it is incapable of beneficial use without treatment. [P.C.]

desert Approximately 45% of the Earth's land surface is occupied by desert (which may be hot or cold), characterized by dry conditions and low BIOMASS and plant productivity. Despite having a PRIMARY PRODUCTIVITY rate of only about 0.3 kg m^{-2} year^{-1}, the deserts support about 13% of the world's human population.

Defining deserts in terms of PRECIPITATION is difficult because the TEMPERATURE conditions will determine evaporation rates and hence WATER availability in the SOIL. The United Nations Environmental Programme (UNEP) has devised an aridity index, calculated by dividing the annual precipitation by annual potential evaporation. On this basis, 10% of the Earth's surface can be regarded as dry (aridity index 0.50–0.65), 18% is semi-arid (0.2–0.5), 12% is arid (0.05–0.20) and 8% is hyper-arid (<0.05). [P.D.M.]

desertification The general reduction in the BIOMASS and productivity of the world's drylands that has become increasingly apparent over the past few decades has been termed 'desertification'. Many areas that were formerly capable of sustained AGRICULTURE and pastoralism have, as a consequence, been lost and widespread famines have periodically resulted. The role of human beings in the process of desertification has been widely stressed. [P.D.M.]

detergents Cleaning agents that are composed of: SURFACTANTS, wetting agents that provide a link between 'dirt' and WATER molecules; builders, sequestering agents that sequester 'hard' water ions so water becomes alkaline, which is necessary for removal of dirt; and a variety of brighteners, enzymes, perfumes, etc. Detergents are used as 'spreaders' in crop-spraying formulations, so that the droplets of spray do not run off the leaves. They tend to persist in the environment and have been linked with EUTROPHICATION of LAKES and RIVERS and implicated in endocrine disruption (*see* ENDOCRINE DISRUPTER). [P.C. & J.G.]

detoxification Metabolic reaction(s) that reduce(s) the possibility of XENOBIOTICS causing HARM within organisms. Often involves sequestering to reduce TOXICITY or increasing WATER solubility to facilitate excretion and/or reaction with other molecules leading to reduced toxicity. In medical TOXICOLOGY this term is used more strictly to describe treatment whereby toxicants are removed from intoxicated patients. [P.C.]

detritus Non-living organic matter. Usually refers to particulate matter and, because it persists longer, to that of plant rather than animal origin, for example leaf litter. However, the term can also be applied to animal materials such as faeces and can sometimes be used to describe soluble organic materials. [P.C.]

dew point The TEMPERATURE of a chilled solid surface at which dew begins to condense from the adjacent saturated WATER vapour. [J.F.R.M.]

diadromous Migrating between saltwater and FRESH WATER. *See also* ANADROMOUS; CATADROMOUS. [P.O.]

diapause Diapause is a condition of arrested GROWTH or reproductive development common in many organisms, particularly insects, that live in seasonally varying environments. [J.S.B.]

diel Referring to events or actions that occur with a 24-h periodicity, for example migrations of planktonic animals, changes in oceanic photosynthetic potential and changes in near-shore PLANKTON communities in response to the tidal cycle. Often used synonymously with the term 'DIURNAL' (i.e. diurnal TIDES have one high tide and one low tide each day). [V.F.]

dieldrin A non-systemic and persistent ORGANOCHLORINE insecticide, with high contact and stomach activity in most insects. First described in 1949, dieldrin was widely used until residue problems were confirmed in the 1970s. Dieldrin tends to partition into animal fats, concentrating in the FOOD CHAIN and resulting in poisoning levels in predators, which has hastened its withdrawal from most uses. It is still used to control locusts and tropical-disease vectors, and in timber preservation and similar uses in some countries. RESISTANCE to dieldrin has also appeared in some insects. *See also* CHEMICAL CONTROL; INSECTICIDES; PESTICIDE. [K.D.]

differential equations Differential equations are equations involving not only variables but also some of the derivatives of those variables with respect to each other. A typical ecological example might be the ordinary differential equation:

$$\frac{dN}{dt} = f(N)$$

to describe the way in which the rate of change of population abundance with time, dN/dt, is related to abundance, N, through the function $f()$. Another example is the partial differential equation:

$$\frac{\partial N}{\partial t} = rN + D\left(\frac{\partial^2 N}{\partial x^2} + \frac{\partial^2 N}{\partial y^2}\right)$$

for a population growing exponentially, subject to diffusive movement. Stochastic differential equations involve additional stochastic terms, but their use is complicated by theoretical difficulties associated with taking limits of differences of stochastic processes. *See also* POPULATION DYNAMICS. [S.N.W.]

diffuse sources CONTAMINATION of environment from a distributed area, for example from crop spraying, agricultural RUN-OFF in general. *Cf.* POINT SOURCE. [P.C.]

dilution effect An advantage of living in a group, whereby a member of a group dilutes the impact of an attack by a predator that can kill only one group member per successful attack. [P.O.]

dioxin Generic term for a family of chlorinated HYDROCARBONS including polychlorinated dibenzo-*p*-dioxins and furans. They are formed primarily during combustion of chlorinated organic materials (e.g. chlorinated solvents, PLASTICS), although vehicle EMISSIONS and coal burning are also sources. The different congeners have very different toxicities, with some being among the most toxic substances known, so that concentrations as low as 10^{-12} g m^{-3} in air, or less, need to be measured for effective monitoring of human health risks. [J.N.C.]

discharge Release of CONTAMINANT(S); usually EFFLUENTS to aquatic environment; usually from point sources. [P.C.]

dispersal Dispersal is the movement of individuals away from where they were produced and may be active or passive. [R.H.S.]

dispersion Dispersion is a statistical term meaning variation or spread and is not to be confused with DISPERSAL, which is a biological process. In ecology, dispersion usually refers to the spatial DISTRIBUTION of organisms. [R.H.S.]

disphotic zone The depth zone in the OCEAN between the EUPHOTIC ZONE and the APHOTIC ZONE, where there are small but measurable quantities of LIGHT. The amount of light is insufficient for PHOTOSYNTHESIS but is sufficient to elicit animal responses. The disphotic zone extends to a depth of about 1000 m. [V.F.]

dissolved organic matter (DOM) Dissolved molecules derived from degradation of dead organisms or excretion of molecules synthesized by organisms. In practice, DOM is defined arbitrarily to include all organic matter passing through a 0.45-µm filter. In the ocean, seasonal maximum values of DOM occur about 1 month after the phytoplankton BLOOM in temperate waters. DOM includes readily metabolizable compounds (such as glucose, amino acids, acetate) and refractory compounds (such as lignins, HUMIC ACIDS and proteins). [V.F. & P.C.]

dissolved oxygen (DO) OXYGEN in aquatic environments that is freely available to support RESPIRATION. [P.C.]

dissolved solids *See* DISSOLVED ORGANIC MATTER.

distribution Within ECOLOGY this term in used in two slightly different contexts. It can be used to describe the spatial distribution of the individuals in a POPULATION (*see* RANDOM DISTRIBUTION). It can also be used to describe the distribution of any set of measurements or observations (*see* PROBABILITY DISTRIBUTIONS). In some situations, a particular probability distribution can be used to describe the spatial distribution of individuals (*see* POISSON DISTRIBUTION). In this case the probability distribution attempts to describe the spatial distribution. *See also* DISPERSION; STATISTICS. [B.S.]

disturbance
1 Any process that destroys plant or animal BIOMASS (*sensu* Grime); effects of animals (GRAZING, trampling and burrowing), fire and bulldozer are all agencies of disturbance.
2 The creation of a seedbed by physical removal of vegetative cover, possibly accompanied by tillage

of the soil (e.g. break-up of the soil crust in arid ecosystems). Natural agencies of disturbance include landslide, hurricane, fire, flood, silt deposition, GLACIATION, etc. Digging animals (rabbits), tunnelling species (moles, earthworms) and colony-dwelling species (gophers) are important biotic agents of disturbance, creating open conditions for seedling establishment. In many ecosystems, the principal agents of disturbance are humans and their machines (agricultural cultivation, forest clearance, construction works, etc.).
3 The creation of microsites (safe sites) for RECRUITMENT of plant species, by whatever means (reduction of perennial plant cover, provision of bare soil or canopy gaps suitable for seedling establishment).
4 The creation of gaps in a forest canopy by removal or death of the dominant trees where sapling recruitment can occur (gap phase regeneration).

Disturbance creates space in previously closed communities and provides opportunities for establishment; thus disturbed communities are particularly susceptible to invasion by new species. [M.J.C. & K.T.]

diurnal Most terrestrial organisms are exposed to daily cycles of LIGHT and dark to which they become entrained, i.e. adapted. Many physiological (e.g. flowering) and behavioural (e.g. drosophilid eclosion) patterns are determined by specific periodic responses to such external cues. When a particular activity or response occurs during the light phase then it is described as diurnal (or circadian). Alternatively it may occur at dusk (crepuscular) or during the dark phase (nocturnal). [R.C.]

diversity The terms 'diversity', 'ecological diversity', 'species diversity', 'biological diversity' and 'BIODIVERSITY' all refer to the variety and ABUNDANCE of species at a specified place and time. Diversity is a concept that is intuitively easy to understand but remarkably difficult to quantify (*see* DIVERSITY INDICES). The reason for this is that diversity consists of not one but two components: SPECIES RICHNESS, i.e. number of species, and EQUITABILITY (sometimes termed 'evenness'), which is a measure of how equally abundant those species are. Communities with a large number of species are obviously more diverse than species-poor ones. However, high equitability, which occurs when species are equal or virtually equal in abundance, is also equated with high diversity. For example, a sample of 100 moths with 10 individuals in each of 10 species is considered more diverse than another which also has 100 moths and 10 species, but in which one of the species is represented by 91 individuals. These two components of diversity may be evaluated either separately (*see* EQUITABILITY; SPECIES RICHNESS) or jointly by means of various composite measures. [A.E.M.]

diversity, alpha, beta and gamma Three measures of

species DIVERSITY in space. The number of species at a single point in space and time is alpha diversity. It estimates how many species co-occur because they specialize on different interacting species. For example, differences in body size between species often lead to differences in which species consume them or which species they eat; so species of various body sizes often co-occur at a point and contribute to alpha diversity. Temporal differences can also contribute to alpha diversity because species may decline very slowly after their special season or year has passed.

As we sample areas larger than a point, additional habitats are included and diversity grows. The rate of growth is beta diversity. We have no standard formula to calculate beta diversity, but the most common uses the coefficients of the species–area relationship: $S = cA^z$, where S is the number of species and A is the area; c and z are constants.

The gamma diversity is the value of S in an area. It combines point diversity with the effect of having many habitats in space. [M.L.R.]

diversity indices Measures of species DIVERSITY play a central role in ECOLOGY and CONSERVATION BIOLOGY. Following the collection, sorting and species identification of samples from habitats, the ecologist is often left with large datasets including long lists of species and numbers of individuals of each species. A diversity index is technically a numerical expression or descriptive statistic that summarizes certain properties of such datasets and that can be used to allow comparisons to be made between the diversity of different groups of organisms within a COMMUNITY or between different communities themselves. Comparisons of this nature are useful in that they can potentially contribute to an understanding of processes that structure those communities. Diversity itself has two fundamental properties: (i) the number of different types of species in the sample or community; and (ii) the relative number of individuals in each species. The number of species is generally referred to as SPECIES RICHNESS (S). The relative abundance (p_i) or degree of dominance of individuals amongst species is usually referred to as evenness or EQUITABILITY. These two properties can be used to evaluate any component of biological diversity from the diversity of alleles for a particular genetic locus, to diversity of diet of predators, to the diversity of habitats in a landscape or of landscape types in a geographical region.

There are, in fact, three major groups of diversity index: (i) species-richness measures; (ii) SPECIES-ABUNDANCE MODELS with an associated diversity index; and (iii) indices based on proportional abundance of species that incorporate both properties of diversity (richness and relative abundance). The choice of appropriate index from the bewildering variety available depends on such factors as difficulty in appraisal of species abundance and the success in sampling and identifying all species present. [P.S.G.]

DNA banking Long-term storage of extracted genomic DNA, typically at −20 or −70°C in a buffered solution. Alternatively, cell lines derived from fibroblasts (from various tissues) are maintained in CRYO-PRESERVATION (under liquid nitrogen) from which cells can be cultured and DNA extracted. The latter is the more efficient method as it is a renewable source of DNA; however, tissue culture involves greater expense and initial effort than cold storage of extracted DNA. DNA banking can be used as a strategy towards the conservation and analysis of BIODIVERSITY, and to facilitate population genetic, phylogenetic and biomedical research. [A.R.H.]

DO *See* DISSOLVED OXYGEN.

DOM *See* DISSOLVED ORGANIC MATTER.

domestication Historical and evolutionary changes in plants and animals when brought under human household (Latin *domus*, home) care and uses. [S.K.J.]

dormancy Resting condition with relatively reduced metabolism that might involve the whole organism, as in higher plants and animals, or be confined to propagules, such as resting spores in fungi and bacteria, resting eggs in some animals, non-germinating seeds and non-growing buds in plants. Also referred to as hypobiosis. [P.C.]

dose–response The quantitative relationship between the amount of a TOXICANT administered or taken (usually by feeding or injection) or absorbed by a subject and the incidence or extent of adverse effects. *Cf.* CONCENTRATION–RESPONSE. [P.C.]

drainage Drainage is a network of underground pipes or surface ditches that moves surface and near-surface waters efficiently to adjacent streams. They are employed either where the WATER TABLE is near the surface or where permeability is low causing surface water ponding. Waterlogging or ponding restricts AGRICULTURE, industry and human occupancy. Cities have highly impermeable surfaces and complex drainage systems (sewerage) occur below city streets. Sewerage may be combined with sewers (WASTE flows) and are a significant determinant of WATER QUALITY in receiving streams.

In agricultural areas, tile-drains were used first but today drains are made from corrugated plastic pipes. To improve efficiency and to reduce silting the pipe circumference is expanded by an envelope of coarse material. The envelope may be natural (gravel, shells), organic (peat, flax, cocoa matting) or synthetic (fibreglass, rockwool, polypropylene/styrene grains). Drainage has significant environmental consequences because altered water conditions promote changes to vegetation communities. In some areas the drained water cannot flow by gravity and has to be pumped up to a higher level. Here, drainage forms a part of LAND RECLAMATION. [A.M.]

dredgings Muds removed from the bottom of water bodies by machine. Both the process of removal and subsequent dumping can disturb environments. [P.C.]

drift, freshwater When benthic organisms of streams or RIVERS enter the water column and are moved downstream, the phenomenon is known as drift. [R.W.D.]

drinking-water quality The quality of WATER delivered at the tap for the consumer. It should therefore be judged in terms of human consumer requirements for appearance, taste and safety. However, there are complications. Thus substances used in sterilization are, by definition, potentially toxic. Nevertheless, World Health Organization guidelines state that 'The potential consequences of microbial contamination are such that its control must always be of paramount importance and must never be compromised'. [P.C.]

drought Drought has no universally accepted definition, although it is normally recognized as a sustained and regionally extensive state of WATER deficiency. Frequently associated with famine and aridity, it should not be confused with either: famine can be caused by other natural and human agencies than drought; aridity is a permanent state whereas drought is ephemeral. Some regions of the Earth's surface are particularly prone to drought: sub-Saharan Africa (Sahel), Brazil's Nordest, the Midwest of the USA, southern Iberia and much of Australia. What characterizes such regions is the tendency for anomalous dry conditions to persist. However, with demand for water resources often finely tuned to its normal availability, few locations can be regarded as drought-proof. [M.B.]

drought and climate change There have been speculations as to whether GLOBAL WARMING and the greenhouse effect will increase DROUGHT frequency. Global warming implies increased evaporation within a strengthened hydrological cycle. The balance between the two opposing forces, and their seasonal phasing, suggests a complex spatial pattern of increased and diminished drought risk. Simulations by general circulation models reveal a tendency towards aggravated drought risk. This is due variously to the effect on evaporation demand outstripping the increase in moisture supply, altered SEASONALITY of soil moisture from a shortened snow season and a transient effect in which continental interiors warm up more rapidly than oceans. A further complicating factor is the influence of increased atmospheric CARBON DIOXIDE (CO_2)

concentration. Elevated CO_2 increases water use efficiency in many species so may assist by reducing the impact of drought. [M.B.]

dry mass The mass of a part of an organism, a whole organism or all the organisms from a given area after removal of its moisture by evaporation. It is used in preference to wet mass (i) because it, rather than wet mass, is the result of PRODUCTION, and (ii) because it is a more conserved quantity. [S.P.L.]

dry season A period of the year when PRECIPITATION is greatly reduced or absent. [P.D.M.]

dump Site used to dispose of solid wastes. Lack of controls are usually implied. [P.C.]

dumping at sea Transporting and disposal of domestic and/or industrial wastes in the open SEA, usually beyond COASTAL or tidal areas. Coming under increasing national and international controls. [P.C.]

dune An elevated landform produced by the activity of WIND upon sand. *See also* SAND DUNE. [P.D.M.]

dust Minute solids, light enough to be suspended in air (usually <25 μm); wind-blown soils; mechanically produced particles. [P.C.]

duty of care Legal requirement (either by statute or civil law liability) that a person takes all reasonable steps to avoid problems to human health and environment that might arise from an operation, and/or steps to ensure certain requirements are met with regard to how the operation is managed. Thus, the UK ENVIRONMENTAL PROTECTION ACT 1990 specifies a legally binding duty of care with respect to solid WASTE DISPOSAL. This requires the appropriate documentation of transfer notes to licensed operators, so that the fate of waste can be effectively tracked from factory gates to ultimate destination. [P.C.]

dynamic equilibrium A dynamic equilibrium occurs when some characteristic of a system is in an unchanging state, despite the fact that its constituent parts may be changing. [S.N.W.]

dynamically fragile If the dynamics that a system displays are very sensitive to parameter changes or small perturbations then the system is dynamically fragile. *Cf.* DYNAMICALLY ROBUST. [S.N.W.]

dynamically robust Dynamics that are fairly insensitive to parameter changes or perturbations are robust: the same patterns will occur for a relatively wide range of circumstances. *Cf.* DYNAMICALLY FRAGILE. [S.N.W.]

dystrophic A term applied to a shallow freshwater lake in which the presence of organic materials lends a dark brown colour to the water. Such LAKES are of low biological productivity and have poor light penetration. Cf. eutrophic and oligotrophic (*see* EUTROPHICATION). [P.D.M.]

E

EA (Environmental Agency) *See* ENVIRONMENTAL (PROTECTION) AGENCIES.

EC_{50} Statistically derived concentration of XENOBIOTIC that has a defined adverse EFFECT (often behavioural, e.g. 'dancing' movement in *Daphnia*) in 50% of an observed POPULATION over a prescribed time in defined conditions. Also referred to as median effective concentration. Can also refer to exposures in terms of dose (ED_{50}). *See also* MEDIAN EFFECTIVE CONCENTRATION/DOSE. [P.C.]

ecoaccident zones *See* RECLAMATION.

ecoarchitecture Design of buildings with an intention to make them more in keeping with their ecological surroundings and/or to minimize their impact, and/or that are based on ecological principles. An example of the latter is the ecohouse or autonomous house, which is supposed to simulate ECOSYSTEMS by creating autonomous cycles of materials, for example wastes are converted to fuel by anaerobic digestion for methane production; solar and wind energy is used for creating power, etc. [P.C.]

ecoaudit Business management tool involving a systematic, documented, regular and objective evaluation of the performance of the business, management systems within it and measures designed to protect the environment. It may involve an independent and expert body but can also be internal. It requires information upon which auditors can express opinion against prescribed standards and/or targets. The opinion of the auditors may or may not be made public. Ecoaudits are a key part of ENVIRONMENTAL MANAGEMENT SYSTEMS. [P.C.]

ecobalance Same as LIFE-CYCLE ASSESSMENT. [P.C.]

ecocline *See* ZONATION.

eco-controlling Way of making strategic choices about products and/or industrial production processes or about business options in a way that integrates economic and environmental considerations using a so-called 'ECO-RATIONAL PATH method'. [P.C.]

eco-efficiency More efficient use of materials and energy in order to reduce economic costs and ENVIRONMENTAL IMPACTS, i.e. 'more from less'. [P.C.]

ecofeminism *See* ENVIRONMENTAL ETHICS AND CONSERVATION.

ecofunds Finances made available on the basis of speculative investment from the private sector for industrial projects that will make a positive contribution to environmental protection, for example the development of CLEAN(ER) TECHNOLOGY. Stakes in these funds are often referred to as ecoshares. *See also* ETHICAL INVESTMENT; GREEN FUNDS. [P.C.]

ecolabel Label awarded to product deemed to have less ENVIRONMENTAL IMPACT per unit function, judged on the basis of a LIFE-CYCLE ASSESSMENT, than others designed to carry out the same or similar function. [P.C.]

ecological energetics Ecological energetics concerns the transfer of energy that occurs within ECOSYSTEMS measured at the level of the individual organism, populations, group of populations or TROPHIC LEVEL. [M.H.]

ecological/environmental disasters The word 'disaster' connotes large and sudden adverse effects; when applied to the environment it usually has consequences for both human health and ecological systems. The following is a list of some of the much publicized large-scale disasters:

• the release of DIOXINS after a major chemical explosion at Givandan's plant at Seveso in 1976, mainly affecting human health;

• *Amoco Cadiz*, a supertanker that ran aground off Brittany in March 1978 discharging >200000 tonnes of crude oil, causing the deaths of thousands of birds and extensive damage to marine life;

• leak of poisonous FUMES from Union Carbide's plant at Bhopal in 1984, mainly affecting human health;

• the explosion at the Soviet nuclear plant at Chernobyl in 1986, affecting both human health and ecological systems;

• a major industrial ACCIDENT at the Sandoz chemical plant in Basle, Switzerland, 1986 when the RUN-OFF from the water used in firefighting carried >13 tonnes of chemical into the River Rhine causing serious damage to flora and fauna and polluting the underlying AQUIFER;

• OIL SPILLS into Prince William Sound off Alaska from the *Exxon Valdez* in 1989, with immediate effect on the marine ecosystem;

• Saddam Hussein's deliberate oil releases in Kuwait during the Gulf War, with immediate effect on the marine ecosystem;

• oil spill from the *Braer* along the Shetland Island's southern coastline in 1993, with immediate effect on the marine ecosystem.

Cf. NATURAL DISASTERS. [P.C.]

ecological footprint The area of land functionally required to support a human community, which lies beyond the land occupied by that community, i.e. 'appropriate CARRYING CAPACITY'. [P.C.]

ecological indicator Organism(s) whose presence indicates occurrence of a particular set of conditions. *See also* BIOTIC INDICES. [P.C.]

ecological restoration Ecological restoration is the return of an ECOSYSTEM to an approximation of its structural and functional condition before damage occurred. Lost species cannot be merely replaced without ensuring that the system is functioning in a manner similar to its condition before DISTURBANCE. Similarly, restoring lost or damaged ecological functions while imposing a totally different structure (e.g. with exotic species) is not generally desirable either.

Some common failures of restoration projects are listed here.

1 Failure to set explicit goals. Vague generalities, such as 'restore wildlife habitat', are substituted for testable objectives. Even if explicit objectives are listed but fail to include both structural and functional components, only half of the explicitly stated goals are present.

2 Creation of a new habitat in a relatively natural system to replace a specific habitat destroyed by an airport taxiway, shopping mall or highway. Even if a habitat that is in plentiful supply is being destroyed to replace a lost habitat not in plentiful supply, some serious ecological and ethical questions still must be addressed about this procedure.

3 Restoration of a damaged site to replace 'in kind' habitat being destroyed by a development process. Sometimes the site is not actually restored. The project may be part of a mitigation agreement, but the destruction proceeds and the restoration never occurs.

4 Occurrence of unanticipated problems. Problems may make it impossible to follow original plans. Course corrections are made on site and without the same level of consultation that occurred when the project was originally endorsed. This on-site change may mean that biologists, hydrologists or others with necessary skills are absent and construction crews make decisions. For example, in one case, a contracting firm charged with constructing a wetland in mitigation for a lost wetland did so without consulting a hydrologist. The consulting firm was required to redo the project, but ecosystem functions were lost during the corrective period that occurred over a 2-year span.

5 Lack of MONITORING. No substantive monitoring is carried out of the progress and no monitoring of the site continues after the restoration has supposedly been completed. Thus, even if goals are explicitly stated, failure to determine whether they have been reached reduces the benefits of the goal-setting exercise.

6 Absence of reports. No reports are produced that can be reviewed by either regulatory agencies or restoration ecologists not on the project. Scientific review is an important quality-control or quality-assurance element that definitely should be present at all times.

7 Minimal staff. Regulatory agencies simply may not have the necessary staff to carry out SURVEILLANCE, and other groups in the area are not authorized to do so.

8 Denial of access. Regulatory agencies with appropriate staff may be denied access, or may have access delayed, when they wish to make on-site inspections. Competent professionals from academic organizations may also be denied access to the site. While the regulatory agencies do gain access, much valuable time has been lost through delays to legal tactics.

9 Uninformed public relations groups. Even if slides, photographs or videotapes are available for public relations, supporting data and/or measurable criteria to document any assertions about revegetation or wildlife restoration may not be a part of the presentation of a public relations group. Often public relations groups are not knowledgeable about ecological restoration and, therefore, are incapable of answering questions involving detailed evidence.

An exemplary ecological restoration project would be one in which all of these issues have been addressed adequately and substantial public involvement has been evident in the entire process from design through completion and follow-up. [J.C.]

ecological rucksack The total mass of material flow 'carried by' an item of economic consumption (product) in the course of its life cycle. *See also* LIFE-CYCLE ASSESSMENT. [P.C.]

ecological trusts *See* ETHICAL INVESTMENT.

ecological valuation Putting a money value on ecological entities. This is not intended to represent intrinsic value, but to be a quantitative indicator of social preferences, i.e. it is the value that people put on environmental entities. The methods fall into two categories: (i) revealed preferences, which use information from real expenditure (e.g. where households spend money on insulation to avoid ENVIRONMENTAL IMPACT) and/or market-places (e.g. fish or lumber); and (ii) contingent valuation, where market-research techniques are applied that try to discover what value people put on ecological systems for use (pastimes, sport) or simply to know that they exist. Somewhere between these extremes is the hedonic pricing method, which values non-marketed environmental resources from observed variations in the prices of marketed goods, such as property prices in different areas. Ecological values are used in cost–benefit analyses of environmental protection measures to compare benefits derived from controls with costs arising from what is controlled and/or the costs of controls themselves. *See* *also* ENVIRONMENTAL (ECOLOGICAL) ECONOMICS. [P.C.]

ecologism Use of ecological terms and concepts (often superficially and/or naively) in political/moral debate. Also refers to the terms that are used in that way. [P.C.]

ecology Heinrich Haeckel is usually attributed with originating the term from the Greek *oikos*, house or dwelling place. It began as a subject concerned predominantly with the ENVIRONMENT (Haeckel's 'house'), i.e. the study of the way that organisms are influenced by physicochemical conditions. However, as it has developed, it has become increasingly concerned with interactions between individuals, so that it is now probably best defined as that area of biology concerned with the study of collective groups of organisms. As such, it stands at the opposite end of the biological scheme of things from the study of cells and molecules.

The spheres of interest of ecology and ecologists therefore range from individual organisms, through populations, to communities and ECOSYSTEMS. Subdisciplines emphasize interests in different elements of these interactions: physiological ecology looks at the way physiology influences DISTRIBUTION and ABUNDANCE and is influenced by environment; behavioural ecology is concerned with the way behaviour responds to ecological challenges in both the short term and the longer (evolutionary) term; POPULATION ECOLOGY describes and explains distribution and abundance; COMMUNITY ECOLOGY describes and explains species associations; ecosystem ecology describes and explains FLUXES of energy and matter as with communities. The study of individuals to populations is sometimes referred to as AUTECOLOGY, whereas the study of communities and ecosystems is sometimes referred to as synecology. There are numerous other descriptions: functional ecology is physiological ecology but emphasizes an experimental and hypothesis-testing approach; trophic ecology studies feeding ecology; MOLECULAR ECOLOGY uses techniques from molecular biology to address ecological questions; ecological genetics tries to understand gene frequencies in terms of ecological processes, etc. And, of course, it can also be subdivided with respect to HABITAT (marine, freshwater, soil, littoral, benthic, etc.) and organisms (microbial, animal, plant, avian, fish, etc.).

Applied ecology involves using understanding from all these various aspects of ecology in the protection, conservation and management of ecological systems. [P.C.]

Eco-management and Audit Scheme (EMAS) European Union voluntary environmental management programme: applied on an industrial-site basis. *See also* ENVIRONMENTAL MANAGEMENT SYSTEMS. [P.C.]

ecomargin Ratio between an organization's actual ENVIRONMENTAL IMPACTS and those compatible with SUSTAINABLE DEVELOPMENT. The latter is almost impossible to measure so proxy measures are used, for example ratio of actual impacts and those minimal impacts that are technically feasible and/or required by law. Just as a firm cannot survive without a reasonable profit margin, it cannot survive in the long term without a low or minimum ecomargin. [P.C.]

economic injury level (EIL) A level of PEST abundance. Above this level it costs less to control the pest than is saved by PEST CONTROL. Below this level, pest control costs more than is saved. [P.O.]

economic instruments *See* REGULATORY INSTRUMENTS.

economic thresholds *See* INTEGRATED PEST MANAGEMENT.

ecopolitics Broadly, politics are about the implementation of policies that influence, to a greater or lesser degree, the creation of capital and its distribution. Ecopolitics attempts to base this on ecological principles and/or taking protection of the ENVIRONMENT as of paramount importance in developing the policies. Political parties have been formed to develop and implement these policies. The world's first Green Party was founded in New Zealand in 1972 and called the Values Party. The first green politicians to take seats in a legislature were in Switzerland; Swiss Greens won two seats in the Swiss Parliament in 1979. West German greens first won seats in the Bundestag in 1983. The British Green party, founded in 1973 as the People Party, was the first in Europe. In 1975 it changed its name to Ecology Party and in 1985 to the Green Party. *See also* ENVIRONMENTAL (ECOLOGICAL) ECONOMICS; GREEN(S); SUSTAINABLE DEVELOPMENT. [P.C.]

ecoprofile Another term for LIFE-CYCLE ASSESSMENT of manufactured products. [P.C.]

eco-rational path Outcome of ECO-CONTROLLING. [P.C.]

ecoregion A relatively homogeneous area in terms of geography, HYDROLOGY and land use. *See also* ECOSYSTEM INTEGRITY. [P.C.]

ecosabotage Disruption of activity/process by legal or illegal means to draw attention to its putative ADVERSE ENVIRONMENTAL EFFECTS. [P.C.]

ecoshares *See* ECOFUNDS.

ecosphere Same as BIOSPHERE. [P.C.]

ecosystem A functional ecological unit in which the biological, physical and chemical components of the ENVIRONMENT interact. This term focuses attention on the complex interplay between plants and animals and ABIOTIC FACTORS of their HABITAT. It is a much wider concept than the COMMUNITY with which it is sometimes confused. [A.J.W.]

ecosystem health It is relatively easy to know when people are ill; they develop disease-specific symptoms, feel off-colour and function abnormally. We can gauge the seriousness of this in terms of various general indicators such as body temperature and pulse rate, the extent to which normal function is impaired and also in terms of the likelihood of recovery. Increasingly, some scientists and policy-makers are describing the condition of ECOSYSTEMS in terms of states of health. Yet there are some important differences between human bodies and ecosystems. The latter are not as obviously and tightly organized as organisms. Where, for example, are the coordinating nerve centres of ecosystems? Individuals and species can be lost from ecosystems without apparently impairing normal function to an extent that cells, tissues and organs could not be lost from organisms. So ecological norms are not so easily defined as body norms; it is more difficult to identify the 'pulses' of ecosystems. Also it seems that their patterns of recovery after DISTURBANCE may not always be very predictable and the recovered systems may never be quite the same as the originals.

Ecosystem health is, of course, meant as an analogy between the human condition and that of ecosystems. Analogies are meant to use understanding in one area to help understanding in another. However, if the analogy is taken too literally, that ecosystems have similar properties to organisms, the analysis is not only unhelpful but misleading (*see* GAIA). If, on the other hand, the analogy is intended to draw attention to the similarities between the way we study human health and the condition of ecosystems, i.e. synthesizing observations on a variety of systems and using this in the light of previous experience to recognize symptoms of deterioration and diagnose possible causes, then it might be helpful. By using imagery that involves the human experience it is also helpful in promoting environmental protection needs amongst non-scientists. *See also* ECOLOGICAL RESTORATION; ECOSYSTEM MANAGEMENT. [P.C.]

ecosystem integrity The view that a number of key states (properties and processes) must be intact for an ECOSYSTEM to persist in a stable state. Under the Clean Water Act (*see* UNITED STATES LEGISLATION) the USEPA is required to 'evaluate, restore and maintain the physical and biological integrity of the Nation's waters'. The latter is judged in relation to the state of a suite of criteria of resident fish and bottom-dwelling invertebrates using baseline data obtained from reference sites within a defined ECOREGION. It is not based on first principles. As a concept it suffers similar problems to ECOSYSTEM HEALTH; and it suffers from the same shortcomings associated with RETROSPECTIVE ANALYSIS (MONITORING). [P.C.]

ecosystem management The science and art of directing human activities to sustain or restore the desired DIVERSITY and productivity of terrestrial and aquatic ecosystems in an area. The essence of ecosystem management (EM) lies in its systematic approach and its multiscale spatial and temporal views, not in the use of specific management practices. Implementation of EM requires many areas of expertise, including ECOLOGY, economics, sociology and politics. The term has been used at least since 1970 and came into widespread use in the late 1980s. [A.N.G. & T.A.S.]

ecosystem redundancy Removal of some species does not necessarily lead to the breakdown of function in an ECOSYSTEM. Hence it is presumed that their role is redundant (i.e. unneeded functional capacity) in 'normal' ecosystems. [P.C.]

ecosystem services Benefits that society obtains from properly functioning ECOSYSTEMS in terms of the supply of raw materials, food, clean water, clean atmosphere, etc. This is not to suggest that ecosystems are designed to provide these services, rather that humans have evolved in non-disturbed ecosystems and hence depend for their well-being on them. SUSTAINABLE DEVELOPMENT depends upon maintaining these services and environmental management should be directed towards this end. [P.C.]

ecoterrorism Threat or use of contrived ENVIRONMENTAL IMPACT/disaster to extort money and/or terms, or make political point. *See also* ECOSABOTAGE. [P.C.]

ecotope Term used in an evolutionary context to describe the full range of NICHE and HABITAT factors that affect a species and determine its survival. [B.W.F.]

ecotoxicity Capacity of chemicals to cause injury to ecological systems, i.e. populations and/or communities and/or ECOSYSTEMS. Expressed in terms of various indicators that can represent short-term/long-term, acute/chronic effects (e.g. LC_{50}, EC_{50}, IC_{50}, NOEC (NO OBSERVED EFFECT CONCENTRATION), LOEC (LOWEST OBSERVED EFFECT CONCENTRATION), MATC (MAXIMUM ACCEPTABLE TOXIC CONCENTRATION)). [P.C.]

ecotoxicity tests (predictive tests) *See* PREDICTIVE ECOTOXICITY TESTS.

ecotoxicology A subject area concerned with understanding where anthropogenic chemicals go in the environment (their FATE) and hence the extent to which ecological systems are exposed to them (EXPOSURE) and, in consequence, the ecological effects that they have (EFFECTS). It can be carried out retrospectively (are releases having effects?) and prospectively (are releases likely to have effects?). Retrospective analyses involve MONITORING programmes; prospective studies involve predictive tests. Ecotoxicology is therefore a multidisciplinary/interdisciplinary subject involving a combination of environmental chemistry, TOXICOLOGY and ecology. It is being used increasingly as a basis for environmental RISK ASSESSMENT in the development of environmental protection legislation. [P.C.]

ED_{50} *See* EC_{50}.

edaphic Edaphic factors are the physical, chemical and biotic characteristics of the SOIL that influence plant growth and distribution. The term is now rarely used but appears frequently in the earlier ecological literature. [J.R.E.]

education, environmental The branch of education that deals with teaching and learning about the relationships between living organisms and their non-living, natural and human-built ENVIRONMENT. This area of education primarily deals with the human role in ecological systems. In the broadest sense, environmental education allows human culture to flourish in diverse environmental conditions. It will include:

• raising general awareness of environmental issues and the need for a responsible approach to these issues;

• raising awareness on how the activities of individuals and other institutions/organizations operate in respect to the environment;

• imparting skills/knowledge to measure the environmental effects;

• imparting skills/knowledge to avoid or remediate our impacts on the environment;

• in all this, giving an awareness of the holistic context of environmental problems.

However, the term is usually meant to imply educational programmes that encourage wise decisions through an understanding of the evolutionary and ecological relationships of humans to their local environment. This might be done through courses, training programmes, media, magazines, books, etc. [S.J.B. & P.C.]

EEA *See* EUROPEAN ENVIRONMENT AGENCY.

effect

1 In an ecotoxicological context, adverse consequences of CONTAMINANT. May be expressed at one or more levels: molecular structure and processes; cellular structure and function; organismic survival, development, GROWTH and reproduction; POPULATION DYNAMICS; COMMUNITY structure; ECOSYSTEM function.

2 More generally, change ascribed to a cause. There may be one or more factors bringing about an effect. It is usually presumed that specific causes produce specific effects. However, effects in complex systems may be brought about by more than one kind of causal factor.

[P.C.]

effects register Literally implies listing of possible ecological effects (usually adverse) of emanations from an industrial process. However, most often involves lists of chemicals in those emanations that are known to be hazardous. Usually an integral part of an ENVIRONMENTAL MANAGEMENT SYSTEM. [P.C.]

effluents Waste release from point sources, usually as liquid into external environment. *Cf.* EMISSIONS. [P.C.]

EIA *See* ENVIRONMENTAL IMPACT ASSESSMENT.

EIL *See* ECONOMIC INJURY LEVEL.

EINECS *See* EUROPEAN INVENTORY OF EXISTING COMMERCIAL CHEMICAL SUBSTANCES.

EIONET (Environmental Information and Observation Network) *See* EUROPEAN ENVIRONMENT AGENCY.

EIS *See* ENVIRONMENTAL INDUSTRIES SECTOR.

El Niño Episodic climatic changes that include warming of the equatorial PACIFIC OCEAN and suppression of UPWELLING into the EUPHOTIC ZONE off the coast of Peru by intrusions of warm, nutrient-poor, surface water. The southward-flowing tongue of the equatorial countercurrent is a regular phenomenon in northern Peru and occurs every year in February or March. Periodically the current extends further south to >12°S and displaces the cold northward-flowing Peru current. El Niño is associated with a weakening of the TRADE WINDS, which occurs typically in cycles of 7 years and may be caused by global circulation anomalies that are in turn influenced by SOLAR RADIATION. The El Niño has been responsible for mass mortality of PLANKTON and fish, has led to starvation of seabirds and has contributed to the collapse of the Peruvian anchovy fishery.

El Niño (derivation: Christ boy-child, as it typically occurs around Christmas) was named by Spanish-speaking fishermen off Ecuador and Peru who correlated its occurrence (warm surface-water temperatures) with disastrous fishing conditions. The Australian Bureau of Meteorology (1988) definition is: 'the occasional warming of the usually cool surface waters of the eastern equatorial Pacific'. Over the past 40 years, nine El Niños have affected the South American continent.

The concept has gradually been extended to cover the whole of the Southern Ocean (*see* ENSO), and now beyond. El Niño now affects the entire Indo-Pacific oceanic region. However, in October 1997 there was an enormous incursion of El Niño driven air from the tropical Pacific into the Caribbean and North Atlantic, resulting in a 6-day reversal of the trade winds—to the south-west. In recent years there has been considerable interest in, and support for, the hypothesis that El Niño effects can explain the occurrence of DROUGHTS and also rainfall patterns in continents such as Australia. Australian rainfall patterns are strongly dependent on the fickle southerly incursions of tropical CYCLONES. Their genesis and frequency seem to be reduced by El Niño patterns, now generally monitored as a negative southern oscillation index (SOI). [J.M. & V.F.]

ELA *See* EXPERIMENTAL LAKE AREA.

electromagnetic pollution Electromagnetic RADIATION from electronic equipment, for example office equipment, is thought by some to lead to lethargy and to SICK BUILDING SYNDROME. A possibly more dangerous form is the extremely low frequency radiation produced by high-voltage power lines, alleged by some to cause epilepsy, through heart palpitations, and eye cancers. [P.C.]

ELINCS *See* EUROPEAN LIST OF NOTIFIED CHEMICAL SUBSTANCES. *See also* EUROPEAN INVENTORY OF EXISTING COMMERCIAL CHEMICAL SUBSTANCES.

elutriate test ECOTOXICITY test of aquatic SEDIMENT using a solution derived from it by elutriation. A slurry of sediment and WATER are mixed vigorously, then allowed to settle or filtered. The elutriate is then exposed to the test system. [P.C.]

EMAS *See* ECO-MANAGEMENT AND AUDIT SCHEME.

emission standards Amount of CONTAMINANT not to be exceeded in the DISCHARGE from a POINT SOURCE. Usually set to avoid POLLUTION, at least outside the MIXING ZONE. *See also* ENVIRONMENTAL QUALITY STANDARD. [P.C.]

emissions Waste release from point sources; usually refers to release into ATMOSPHERE through chimney stacks. *Cf.* EFFLUENTS. [P.C.]

EMS *See* ENVIRONMENTAL MANAGEMENT SYSTEMS.

end-of-pipe solution Removal of CONTAMINATION by treatment of EMISSIONS (*see* FLUE-GAS DESULPHURIZATION) and EFFLUENTS (e.g. by use of filters). [P.C.]

end-point Often used to refer to what is measured in ecotoxicological tests. These measurement end-points are presumed to relate to those aspects of ecological systems that are of interest, i.e. that we want to protect. These latter are sometimes referred to as assessment end-points. *See also* PREDICTIVE ECOTOXICITY TESTS. [P.C.]

endangered species Official designation is species that have 20% probability of becoming extinct in 20 years or 10 generations (US ENDANGERED SPECIES ACT). *See also* MINIMUM VIABLE POPULATION. [P.C.]

Endangered Species Act UNITED STATES LEGISLATION passed in 1973 to protect species in danger of becoming extinct in the wild. First of its kind, but many other nations now have similar legislation. *See also* ENDANGERED SPECIES. [P.C.]

endemic *See* EPIDEMIC.

endemic species An animal or plant that is native to a particular location and is restricted to that location in its DISTRIBUTION. An endemic species that is of ancient origin and has remained restricted because of problems of DISPERSAL is said to be a palaeo-endemic. One that has recently evolved and is restricted simply because it has had no time to disperse is a neoendemic. [P.D.M.]

endemism *See* ENDEMIC SPECIES.

endocrine disrupter TOXICANTS (POLLUTANTS) that impair reproduction and development by interfering with normal endocrine control. Tributyltin appears to have its effect by interfering with hormones that inhibit maleness in female molluscs. Many higher plants synthesize chemicals that interfere with the endocrine controls of animals (especially insects) that feed upon them. Many PESTICIDES are designed to have this specific effect.

Those endocrine disrupters that interfere with male systems by simulating vertebrate female hormones are called oestrogenic and those causing female disruption by simulating male hormones are called androgenic. Substances implicated have been pesticides, alkyphenols (used in cleaning products), POLYCHLORINATED BIPHENYLS, DIOXINS and by-products of the contraceptive pill. They can have adverse effects at very low concentrations. [P.C.]

endolithic Organisms living with rocks. [A.P.]

ENSO ENSO means EL NIÑO southern oscillation. [J.M.]

environment This word from the French *environer*, to encircle or surround, describes the supporting matrices of life: WATER, earth, ATMOSPHERE and CLIMATE. However, it projects two false impressions: one is that these matrices are separate from living things and the other is that they are designed to support life. On the first count, the chemical and physical compositions of the matrices that surround life are importantly influenced by the metabolism and behaviour of organisms. The composition of the atmosphere is crucially dependent on the gases that living things remove from it and add to it; the soils are largely dead plant materials that are importantly moulded by the microbes that decompose it and the animals that move through it; the quality of waters in the SEAS, LAKES and RIVERS depends to some extent on aeration by plants and a myriad of other transfers. So the environment of organisms can properly be said to consist not only of a dead but also a living matrix, i.e. other organisms as well.

On the second count, the adaptation of the environment to living things, the same criticisms apply as are levelled at the GAIA hypothesis. [P.C.]

Environment Act 1995 *See* ENVIRONMENTAL (PROTECTION) AGENCIES.

Environmental Action Programmes Series of strategic programmes adopted by the Commission (bureaucracy) of the European Union (EU) and playing an important part in defining policy used as a basis for legislation proposals put before the Council (law maker) of the EU. There have been five programmes. The first and second, adopted respectively in 1973 and 1977, included reference to prevention being better than cure and that polluters should pay. The third, adopted in 1982, shifted the emphasis from control to prevention. The fourth, adopted in 1987, emphasized effective implementation of legislation, increased public access to and dissemination of environmental information and the need for integration with other policies. The latest and fifth action programme, adopted in 1992 and reviewed in 1995, was entitled *Towards Sustainability* in line with UNCED. It emphasized more shared responsibility, less COMMAND AND CONTROL and the need for an integrated approach within economic sectors. *See also* ENVIRONMENTAL LAW; ENVIRONMENTAL (PROTECTION) POLICIES. [P.C.]

Environmental Agency (EA) *See* ENVIRONMENTAL (PROTECTION) AGENCIES.

environmental asset management Taking account of environmental commodities in general or particular environmental holdings in business practice. *See also* ENVIRONMENTAL ASSETS; ENVIRONMENTAL CAPITAL. [P.C.]

environmental assets Assets can mean general commodity from the environment, such as raw materials or sites for dumping waters, or particular holdings by companies, such as estates, forests, gardens, water bodies, etc. [P.C.]

environmental assurance bonding Proposed levy of an amount of money equal to the best estimate of the largest potential future environmental damage that might arise from a particular industrial process or product. This would be kept in an interest-bearing escrow account for a predetermined period. Portions of the bond (plus interest) would be returned if and when it could be demonstrated that the suspected worst-case damages had not occurred or would be less than anticipated. In the event of damages the bond would be used in REMEDIATION. The cost of the bond would define the price of the right to use the environmental resource in some specified way and would therefore be tradeable. *See also* REGULATORY INSTRUMENTS. [P.C.]

environmental burdens Concentration of XENOBIOTIC in an environmental compartment. *See also* CRITICAL LOADS. [P.C.]

environmental business charter Voluntary charters that by signing and implementing business organizations can demonstrate a commitment to environmental protection. Some of these are: Chemical Industries Responsible Care Programme; VALDEZ PRINCIPLES; International Chamber of Commerce (ICC) Business Charter for Sustainable Development (BCSD); and the Confederation of British Industry (CBI) Agenda for Voluntary Action. [P.C.]

environmental capital Natural resources potentially available for use by society (usually industry) and valued as such. Capital is usually thought of in terms of man-made measures, but total capital also includes natural, ENVIRONMENTAL ASSETS. It is argued by environmental (ecological) economists that these can be valued in money terms in the same way as man-made capital. *See also* ENVIRONMENTAL (ECOLOGICAL) ECONOMICS; SUSTAINABLE DEVELOPMENT. [P.C.]

environmental disclosures Disclosure is information made available to the public through the formal accounting procedures of a company. Environmental disclosure is information on the environmental performance of a company through the same route. *See also* ENVIRONMENTAL MANAGEMENT SYSTEMS. [P.C.]

environmental due diligence Exercise conducted by a purchaser, underwriter or lender in a wide range of commercial transactions, including public offering of shares, refinancing, asset purchase, share purchases or merger. The objectives are to ascertain what actual and/or potential environmental liabilities and risks they might be assuming as a consequence of the transaction and to quantify any liabilities found. It is therefore an external examination of the environmental implications of the operation of another company. [P.C.]

environmental (ecological) accountancy Applying accounting techniques and principles to assess the ENVIRONMENTAL IMPACT of businesses. It involves:
• identifying environmentally related costs and revenues within the accounting system;
• devising new forms of financial and non-financial accounting systems, information systems and control systems to encourage environmentally sensitive management;
• developing new forms of financial performance indicators that take environment into account;
• experimenting with ways sustainability can be assessed and incorporated into usual procedures.
See also ENVIRONMENTAL (ECOLOGICAL) ECONOMICS. [P.C.]

environmental (ecological) economics Economics is the study of how people use limited resources to supply their unlimited needs. It is therefore concerned with trade-offs and social preferences. It can be applied internationally to trade and its consequences (macroeconomics) or to small units such as businesses and households (microeconomics). It is concerned with judging value (social preferences) in market-places by reference to willingness to pay. Until recently, resources from the environment were considered external to these processes (as externalities); this included raw materials and space available for dumping WASTE. For a long time, however, economists have recognized that environmental resources are finite and hence should be taken into account in terms of competing human needs (e.g. Thomas Malthus in 1797 published *Essay on the Principles of Population* that made this point). Environmental entities should therefore be valued so that they can be taken into account in the overall scheme of human economics. This internalization is an important requirement in the defining of SUSTAINABLE DEVELOPMENT. Valuing environmental entities and taking these into account in the development of policies is referred to as environmental economics. Valuing ecological entities, such as HABITATS, ECOSYSTEMS and species, can be viewed as a subset of this and referred to as ecological economics.

Environmental valuation techniques involve the following.

1 Use of actual market-places where commodities are traded, such as might occur with fish and lumber.
2 Establishment of hypothetical market-places, for example when the values of entities traded are likely to be influenced by environment, such as house prices.
3 Use of sociological techniques, such as questionnaires, to gauge value that people might put on environmental entities. These are usually divided into assessments that involve values which people put on use of environmental entities and values which people put on existence of entities that they do not use. The former might involve use of local parks; the latter might involve entities such as the Antarctic that may never be visited.
4 Values might also be estimated from the costs of preventing HARM or the costs of REMEDIATION.

There are those who argue that valuation of ecological/environmental entities, no matter how it is done, is unethical. The economist's rejoinder is usually that the values given are not intrinsic values but simply measures of social preferences that can be taken into account in weighting the costs of environmental protection against potential benefits of what is being protected. [P.C.]

environmental ethics and conservation The field of moral philosophy that deals with human obligations and duties to non-human organisms and to the natural world. At the elementary level, environmental ethics is a simple extension of human ethical systems to other living beings. This extension may be based on utilitarian concepts of pleasure and pain, which can be used to extend moral regard to sentient animals. A further extension of human moral duties may be based on the thought that all life is worthy of moral regard. This biocentric extension of human morality affords limited rights to plants and other non-sentient organisms as well as sentient animals. Further still, ethical regard may involve abstract concepts of natural process and biological relationships. This evolutionary ecological, or ecocentric, concept of ethics assigns moral conditions to the actions of humans as they affect the natural environment.

Areas of ethical concern commonly treated as part of the emerging field of environmental ethics include animal rights, feminine critiques of ENVIRONMENTAL HARM (ecofeminism), radical ENVIRONMENTALISM and several schools of philosophical thought often called 'land ethics' after the work of Aldo Leopold. However, the inclusion of animal rights within the body of environmental ethics is not universally accepted because the emphasis on the moral treatment of individual animals seems to preclude ethical concern in the treatment of relationships such as species or process such as ECOSYSTEMS. The ecofeminist agenda ascribes the domination of nature to the same psychological and historical root as the domination of women. The radical environmentalist movement finds connections between the traditions of civil disobedience, abolitionist politics, anarchy and other political forms that seek rapid, radical and occasionally violent changes in society because of the perceived inadequacy of environmental protection and/or harmful environmental policies. Lastly, there are several philosophical approaches that attribute ethical concerns to the relationship of humans to biotic communities and evolutionary process. This last concept may be more than even a radical extension of human morality; it may represent an original level of moral discourse. *See also* CONSERVATION BIOLOGY. [S.J.B.]

environmental externality adders Surcharges to the prices of commodities, for example energy, in order to reflect the damage done to the environment in their production and use. Based on 1990 prices, the adders for various sources of electricity generation in the USA would be (US cents/kWh): coal (conventional), 0.058; oil (low sulphur), 0.0027; natural gas, 0.010; nuclear (including accidents and decommissioning), 2.910. *See also* ENVIRONMENTAL (ECOLOGICAL) ECONOMICS. [P.C.]

environmental harm Adverse change in one or more components of the physical, chemical and biological compartments of the environment, i.e. the EFFECT of POLLUTION. [P.C.]

environmental impact Having an EFFECT, usually harmful (*see* ENVIRONMENTAL HARM), on one or more of the physical, chemical and biological components of the environment. [P.C.]

environmental impact assessment (EIA) This is generally used to refer to the evaluation of effects likely to arise from a major project, such as the construction of a dam or a power-station. However, it would also apply to smaller projects, such as the construction of a new factory or of new plant within an existing industrial operation.

The EIA should supply decision-makers with an indication of the likely outcomes of their decisions. It should help selection between alternatives (methods and sites of construction) and lead to avoidance of unacceptable options. It is thus an anticipatory and participatory approach to environmental management.

Every EIA system is unique with respect to the project being proposed, its location and the environmental/ecological systems at risk. In general, though, they involve detailed SURVEYS of flora and fauna in the areas concerned with an assessment of how these might be impacted by the proposals. More often than not, this is done subjectively but, at least in principle, might be the subject of more rigorous modelling.

Occasionally, but not often, the EIA and its predictions might be subject to FEEDBACK from MONITORING either during or after the project. [P.C.]

environmental impairment insurance Contract transferring liability for environmental impairment to another party, the insurer, in consideration of a premium. The contract will usually have exclusions: payment of fines (implicitly), often (explicitly) the consequence of POLLUTION due to gradual release, cost of cleaning up the insurer's own site. [P.C.]

environmental impairment liability Legal responsibility for environmental impairment in the form of penalties, damages and REMEDIATION. Very often is strict, i.e. independent of wrongful intent or negligence, as compared with fault based. However, foreseeability is often a relevant criterion (those that are held liable should have reasonably been able to have anticipated the outcome) and it may be context dependent. Thus what is foreseeable now as a result of the state of science will be different from what was foreseeable 20 years ago, which has implications for retrospective action. *See also* ENVIRONMENTAL LAW. [P.C.]

environmental index Numerical indicator of ENVIRONMENTAL IMPACT from industrial process or product. For example, Rhône Poulenc calculate indices on a monthly basis for their major plants for impact on each of the major environmental compartments. The WASTE index calculates total output of toxic materials, SUSPENDED SOLIDS, total nitrogen, phosphorus and dissolved salts, together with an account of CHEMICAL OXYGEN DEMAND, each weighted by judgements of relative importance of impacts. These indices are used as FEEDBACKS on performance and as targets for future improvements. [P.C.]

environmental industries sector (EIS) Those industries that produce cleaner techniques and technologies for use in other production processes, for example filters that remove toxic substances from emission outlets, CATALYTIC CONVERTERS for transforming toxic products to less- or non-toxic outputs, probes that can measure pollutants and hence contribute to controls on polluting processes, the production of less hazardous raw materials such as water-based rather than organic solvent-based paints and lubricants. Sometimes, consultants needed in the provision of environmental services such as ECOAUDIT are described as being members of the EIS, but usually the term is restricted to the manufacturing sector.

Because of the pressure from environmental legislation, customers and other stakeholders for the use of cleaner techniques and technologies, it is thought that environmental industry is a rapidly growing business sector. [P.C.]

Environmental Information and Observation Network (EIONET) *See* EUROPEAN ENVIRONMENT AGENCY.

environmental law Laws and legal principles governing the behaviour of persons, businesses, government agencies and other public utilities to protect the ENVIRONMENT and the health of humans from possible adverse effects arising from the environment (not usually including the domestic environment and work-place). Environmental law can therefore encompass public health as well as conservation, POLLUTION control and land-use control.

There are two sources of environmental legislation: one is from statutes (hereafter referred to as statutory control) and the other from common law, essentially by case law in the courts. Statutory controls are involved in protecting the general interests of the State and granting powers through Parliament to the Government or its agencies whereby this can be achieved. A subset of common law is concerned with disputes between individuals and this, which will be referred to as civil law, is of environmental importance. It should also be said, though, that certain civil rights can be defined in statutes. Failure to respond to statutory controls can bring criminal proceedings, so some criminal law is defined in statute. Though of no consequence for environmental protection, some criminal law is established by common law, for example relating to murder. A further complication is that some transgression of civil law can also bring criminal prosecution. Finally, there is also law that governs the action of the Government and its agencies, and this is referred to as public or administrative law. [P.C.]

environmental limit standards (ELSs) *See* ENVIRONMENTAL LAW.

environmental management systems (EMS) Systems applied to business operations to control environmental effects. They usually entail: a systematic review of risks in an initial audit; the formulation of general policy aimed at controlling (usually reducing) risks; the development of procedures (techniques, technology and training) to effect this; methods of MONITORING and keeping records of achievements; and a system of auditing to ensure aims are being achieved. There may also be regular public statements that are generated by the EMS designed to keep the public informed on achievements. This system is formalized into various standards on environmental management systems (a British version, BS 7750, has been superseded by an international standard ISO 14001). An EC regulation (EEC 1863/93) allows voluntary participation by companies in the industrial sector in a community eco-management and audit scheme (EMAS).

See also ECOAUDIT; ECO-MANAGEMENT AND AUDIT SCHEME; ISO 14000. [P.C.]

environmental manual Document used by businesses with ENVIRONMENTAL MANAGEMENT SYSTEMS that collates the environmental policy, objectives and targets, and programme; specifies key roles and responsibilities of staff; describes the management system and how its elements fit together and interact; and provides direction to related documentation. In addition to covering normal procedures, it should also cover procedures under abnormal conditions and in the event of emergencies. [P.C.]

environmental (policy) statement Environmental policy statement is a statement (usually public) by a business of its approach to environmental protection in its operation. Frequently addresses very broad aspects of the organization's activities, but should be tailored to the nature of the organization. Often it will state commitments on reduction of WASTE and POLLUTION, efficient use of energy and resources, control of environmental effects of obtaining raw materials, on HABITATS and BIODIVERSITY and minimizing the environmental effects of new developments. An environmental statement, on the other hand, is a report (usually public and may be subject to formal VALIDATION) of achievements by business with respect to predetermined targets and of future interests. *See also* ENVIRONMENTAL MANAGEMENT SYSTEMS. [P.C.]

environmental politics Broad term for involvement of environmental issues in political processes. At one extreme it can involve the principles of environmental protection and respect as a basis for all political action (*see* ENVIRONMENTALISM; GREEN(S)). At the other extreme it simply means reference to environmental issues as part of a general political agenda. [P.C.]

environmental pressure (lobby) groups Groups that put pressure on policy-makers and industry, especially by influencing public opinion. Early examples in the UK were the Fog and Smoke Committee of 1880 and, a derivative, the Coal Smoke Abatement Society of 1899 formed to put pressure on the British Government to take action to prevent smogs by pressing for stricter implementation of existing law against the nuisance of black smoke EMISSIONS.

Now there are a number of national and international pressure groups with substantial following. Well known amongst these are Friends of the Earth (founded in the USA in 1969) and Greenpeace (founded in Canada in 1972). The World Wide Fund for Nature, initially founded as the World Wildlife Fund in 1961, though less confrontational, also plays a major role in lobbying for environmental protection. Also noteworthy in the UK are the Ramblers' Association, National Trust, Council for the Protection of Rural England, Royal Society for Nature Conservation and Royal Society for the Protection of Birds. *See also* GREEN(S). [P.C.]

environmental profile Analysis of businesses' actual and potential interaction with the ENVIRONMENT. [P.C.]

Environmental Protection Act (EPA) UK legislation to make provision for the improved control of POLLUTION from certain industrial and other processes, enacted 1990. Covers INTEGRATED POLLUTION CONTROL (IPC) and local authority AIR-POLLUTION CONTROL (LAAPC), WASTE, litter, radioactive substances, genetically modified organisms, nature conservation and a miscellany of other things. IPC was an innovation. [P.C.]

environmental (protection) agencies Regulatory/enforcement authorities given powers under governments to implement environmental protection legislation. Those for England and Wales (Environmental Agency, EA) and Scotland (Scottish Environmental Protection Agency, SEPA) were formed recently under the Environment Act 1995. The EA represents an amalgam of the National Rivers Authority (NRA), Her Majesty's Inspectorate of Pollution (HMIP) and waste regulation authorities. Similarly, SEPA was an amalgam of Her Majesty's Industrial Pollution Inspectorate (HMIPI), river purification authorities and waste regulation authorities. The USEPA was formed earlier, in 1970, by an Executive Order signed by President Nixon and bringing together the Federal Water Quality Administration from the Interior Department, the Pesticides Regulation Division from the Agriculture Department and the Office of Pesticide Research from the Department of Health Education and Welfare.

The underlying philosophy in the formation and operation of all these bodies is that INTEGRATED POLLUTION CONTROL requires integrated agencies to effect the control. The British and US agencies work in significantly different ways. The British agencies are only able to interpret legislation under guidance from government departments and secretaries of state. The USEPA can elaborate and extend legislation, within limits defined by legislation, by rule-making that is subject to scrutiny and challenge in the courts. *See also* REGULATORY AGENCIES. [P.C.]

environmental (protection) policies Set of principles, premises and presumptions that guide actions of government and other international bodies in developing measures and legislation on environmental protection. They involve a complex interaction between political philosophy, perception of public interest, lobbying and involvements and commitments at an international level. They are usually articulated in manifestos, consultation papers, white papers and action programmes. *See also* ENVIRONMENTAL ACTION PROGRAMMES. [P.C.]

environmental quality guideline Non-mandatory form of standard/objective. [P.C.]

environmental quality objective (EQO) In the UK, used to defined the state of environments in terms of ecological/human health goals, for example whether water is suitable for fish stocks, suitable for drinking, suitable for bathing. Elsewhere, often synonymous with ENVIRONMENTAL QUALITY STANDARD. Usually mandatory. *Cf.* ENVIRONMENTAL QUALITY GUIDELINE. [P.C.]

environmental quality standard (EQS) Concentration of a substance that should not be exceeded in an environment if HARM (to humans and/or ecosystems) is to be avoided. It is therefore based on the presumption that CONTAMINATION does not necessarily cause POLLUTION. EQSs are usually obtained by applying a safety margin to no-effect or low-effect concentrations identified in DOSE–RESPONSE toxicological and ecotoxicological studies. Sometimes used synonymously with ENVIRONMENTAL QUALITY OBJECTIVE (EQO). However, in the UK a distinction has been made. An EQO is the overall state to be aimed for in an aspect of the natural environment, for example water in a river such that fish can survive and breed. Hence an EQO is often expressed in qualitative not quantitative terms. An EQS is also different from a LIMIT VALUE (LV). The latter is the limit that must not be exceeded in an emission/effluent. It is designed to achieve EQSs and EQOs, but often also takes account of what can be achieved by a reliable technique. [P.C.]

environmental quality target State of the environment towards which management and control strategies are directed, for example a targeted ENVIRONMENTAL QUALITY STANDARD/OBJECTIVE. [P.C.]

environmental reporting Production and release of environmental statements by businesses, typically to shareholders, but also to employees and public. *See also* ENVIRONMENTAL (POLICY) STATEMENT. [P.C.]

environmental science Literally, scientific endeavour applied in describing and understanding the ENVIRONMENT. It has been equated with 'earth science', namely the study of the ATMOSPHERE, land, oceans and fresh waters and the biogeochemical FLUXES within them. The emphasis has been on the physics and chemistry of these processes, but increasingly the importance of biological/ecological systems is being recognized and the interface with human society is also clearly important, leading to interaction with social sciences and economics. This, then, is a broad multidisciplinary/interdisciplinary venture that plays an important part in understanding and hence mitigating our impact on natural systems and processes. [P.C.]

environmental tax Tax on commodities/products related to their actual or potential ENVIRONMENTAL IMPACTS. *See also* ENVIRONMENTAL (ECOLOGICAL) ECONOMICS; MARKET INSTRUMENTS. [P.C.]

environmental toxicology Study of how human health is impacted by toxic substances through environmental EXPOSURE (usually excluding home and work-place). Sometimes used more broadly and synonymously with ECOTOXICOLOGY. [P.C.]

environmental trustees In the UK, body controlling funds from a rebate out of a LANDFILL levy on WASTE. Industry can opt to pay levy into these funds instead of as tax, and funds can be used by the trust to enhance local environmental amenities. [P.C.]

environmental utilization space or ecospace The capacity of the BIOSPHERE'S environmental functions to support human economic activities, sometimes defined at a national or PER CAPITA level according to a 'global fair shares' principle. [P.C.]

environmental valuation *See* ENVIRONMENTAL (ECOLOGICAL) ECONOMICS; SUSTAINABLE DEVELOPMENT. [P.C.]

environmental verifier Person/organization accredited to scrutinize and confirm company environmental statements. *See also* ENVIRONMENTAL MANAGEMENT SYSTEMS; ENVIRONMENTAL (POLICY) STATEMENT. [P.C.]

environmentalism Ideology that protection of, and respect for, environment should influence all that we do and that this is (usually) in contrast to the industrially driven, capitalist western societies. *See also* ENVIRONMENTAL ETHICS AND CONSERVATION. [P.C.]

environmentally friendly Shorthand for any action, industrial process or product that has, or is intended to have, reduced impact on the environment. Some would say that no industrial process or product can be without some impact, so it is better to refer to one as friendlier (more friendly) than others. [P.C.]

environmentally sensitive area Area designated under law as being particularly desirable to conserve, protect or enhance, for example by the adoption of particular agricultural methods. *See also* SITE OF SPECIAL SCIENTIFIC INTEREST. [P.C.]

ephemeral habitats Habitats that are transitory or short-lived. Strictly speaking, ephemeral means lasting only a day (from the Greek, *ephemeros*). In ecology, habitats are described as ephemeral for species whose generation time is longer than the typical duration of that habitat, for example fungi or fruits are ephemeral habitats for fruit flies, though they are long-lived habitats for many microorganisms. [R.H.S.]

epibenthic Living on the surface of (usually) the SEA bottom (although strictly it could also refer to freshwater systems). The term 'epibenthic' may include PELAGIC species that live in association with the sea floor. Sometimes used synonymously with EPIFAUNA. [V.F.]

epibiont An organism of restricted RANGE whose DISTRIBUTION has contracted from a formerly more extensive range. [P.D.M.]

epidemic An increase in the number of cases of a disease per unit time (incidence) above that expected in a defined population over a period less than the life expectancy of the HOST. Disease may be continuously present in a host population when it is referred to as endemic. An endemic infection may show a pattern of recurrent epidemics. A global epidemic is referred to as a pandemic. [G.F.M.]

epidemiology The study of patterns of disease (infectious and non-infectious) and health states in populations. Can be applied to both human and wildlife populations. [G.F.M.]

epifauna Animals that live on the bottom of aquatic environments (benthic fauna) and on the substrate surface, as opposed to living within the substrate (infauna) or resident in burrows. [J.L.]

epilimnion *See* LAKE STRATIFICATION.

epiphyte An organism that grows upon the surface of a plant, using its HOST only for support. [P.D.M.]

episodic pollution EMISSIONS and EFFLUENTS that come in bursts, for example from STORMWATER DISCHARGES, RUN-OFF after storms, accidental spills and emissions. They can be characterized by their duration, amplitude (peak concentration) and frequency. [P.C.]

epizootic An EPIDEMIC in a non-human animal population. [G.F.M.]

EQO *See* ENVIRONMENTAL QUALITY OBJECTIVE.

EQS *See* ENVIRONMENTAL QUALITY STANDARD.

equitability In no ecological community are all species equally common. Instead, some species will be very abundant, others moderately common, with the remainder infrequent or rare. Equitability (sometimes also termed 'evenness') is a measure of the extent to which species are equally represented in a community. For example, if one species is dominant and the others rare (as might occur, for instance, when only one species of moss thrives in the shaded conditions of a conifer plantation) then equitability is low. On the other hand, when the ABUNDANCES of species are almost equal (e.g. in certain bird communities) equitability is high. [A.E.M.]

erosion and topsoil loss Loss of topsoil as a result of physical removal by WIND and WATER, and physical, chemical and biological changes. It is a natural process but its intensity has been increased by human activities. For example, removal of natural VEGETATION for agricultural purposes exposes soil to increased action of wind and water. Worldwide, it has been estimated that >25 million tonnes of material are removed each year from topsoil by excessive erosion. [P.C.]

ERS *See* EUROPEAN REMOTE SENSING (ERS) SATELLITE.

essential elements There are 17 elements essential for plant GROWTH. From the air and water, carbon, hydrogen and OXYGEN are derived. From the SOIL the following are obtained: nitrogen, phosphorus, potassium, calcium, magnesium, sulphur and, in trace quantities, iron, manganese, boron, molybdenum, zinc, chlorine and cobalt. The last seven are termed 'MICRONUTRIENTS' or 'TRACE ELEMENTS'. A few other elements are apparently needed as micronutrients by some plant or animal species: sodium, fluorine, iodine, silicon, strontium and barium. [J.G.]

estimated (predicted) environmental concentration Predicted concentration of XENOBIOTIC in an environmental compartment based on information on patterns and amounts of production, use and disposal, and physicochemical properties of the chemicals. *See also* PREDICTED ENVIRONMENTAL CONCENTRATION. [P.C.]

estuary A semi-enclosed body of water that has a free connection with the open SEA and within which seawater is diluted measurably with FRESH WATER derived from land drainage. [V.F.]

ethical investment Provides investors with investment opportunities that do not compromise their ethics, for example with respect to avoiding oppressive regimes, businesses connected with tobacco, alcohol, weapons, etc. Green or ecological trusts selectively invest in businesses that minimize their ENVIRONMENTAL IMPACTS. [P.C.]

EU/EC environmental protection The Treaty of Rome (EEC Treaty) established the European Economic Community (EEC) in 1957 and was about a common trading market. However, harmonization of national laws to prevent trade barriers (Article 100 EEC) was used as a basis for justifying laws relating to environmental protection. Article 235 (EEC) relating to general and residual powers was also used as a justification for environmental protection (e.g. a directive on wild birds was legitimized on this basis in 1979). The Single European Act (SEA; came into force 1986) amended the EEC Treaty by introducing explicit environmental law-making powers in Articles 130r, 130s and 130t. It also introduced Article 100a, which requires that the issuing of legislation for the approximation of measures within member states with respect to the functioning of the internal market will take as a base a high level of protection concerning the environment. The Treaty on European Union (TU) extended environmental responsibility further. It was signed in Maastricht in February 1992, but not formally ratified by all member states and adopted until November 1993, and consists of two segments. The first, on common provisions, stands alone. The second amended the EEC Treaty in detail and renamed it the Treaty Establishing the European Community (EC Treaty). The second segment introduced a modification to Article 2 (EC Treaty) that stated that the community will promote 'a harmonious and balanced development of economic activities, sustainable and noninflationary growth respecting the environment'. This is taken further by the Treaty of Amsterdam, adopted in 1997, but at the time of writing, not formally ratified by all member states. It also introduced the PRECAUTIONARY PRINCIPLE as a major consideration into Article 130.

The TU created the European Union (EU). This rests on three pillars: common foreign and security policy; home affairs and justice policy; all policies previously carried out under the terms of the EEC Treaty. The first two pillars were new. The last one is as redefined in the amended EC Treaty. It remains correct, therefore, to refer to the latter as EC policy. At the same time, since the EC is part of the European Union, it also remains correct to refer to the EU. The Treaty of Rome, on the other hand, initially created the European Economic Community and this was explicitly replaced in the TU by European Community, so EEC is no longer appropriate. One last complication: the European Commission, an institution of the EC/EU, is also sometimes abbreviated to EC, but more often to CEC.

The legal instruments that are formed under the treaties are directives, which have to be implemented by member states through their own legislation, and regulations that apply directly. These are formulated by the European Commission, the bureaucracy of the EU, but can only be adopted by the Council (composing heads of state but with an Environment Council comprising environment ministers). The European Parliament also has a voice and can block certain kinds of legislation.

There are now hundreds of pieces of legislation that have an influence on environmental protection covering water, WASTE, air, harmful substances, RADIOACTIVITY, WILDLIFE and countryside, noise, impact assessment and provision of environmental information. It includes not only COMMAND AND CONTROL instruments but also financial and economic instruments and makes some provision for voluntary activities. *See also* ENVIRONMENTAL (PROTECTION) POLICIES. [P.C.]

eulittoral zone Generally also called the LITTORAL ZONE (although sometimes classified as a subdivision of this zone) or INTERTIDAL ZONE. [V.F.]

euphotic zone Also called the photic or epipelagic zone. Refers to the lighted part of the OCEAN in which PRIMARY PRODUCTIVITY occurs. It extends from the surface to the depth at which PHOTOSYNTHESIS is no longer possible due to a lack of LIGHT. [V.F.]

European Environment Agency (EEA) Created under European Community (EC) legislation to collect, collate and disseminate information relating to the quality of the environment, the pressures on the environment and its sensitivities to these pressures. It is required to establish an Environmental Information and Observation Network (EIONET). It currently has no regulatory or enforcement functions,

cf. ENVIRONMENTAL (PROTECTION) AGENCIES. It is located in Copenhagen, Denmark. [P.C.]

European Environmental Bureau Federation of about 150 environmental non-governmental organizations. It is located in Brussels. [P.C.]

European Inventory of Existing Commercial Chemical Substances (EINECS) Listing of all commercial chemicals on the market in Europe to 18 September 1981 amounting to *c.* 100000 chemical substances. It is required under European Community (EC) law. Chemicals on the list are designated as existing substances. Chemicals not on the list are new substances. Manufacturers of new substances must submit a NOTIFICATION of properties influencing environmental HAZARDS associated with the substance, on which basis it can be packaged, classified and labelled in a standard way. Substances on EINECS, under separate legislation, are prioritized according to likely environmental effects and then subject to RISK ASSESSMENT as a possible product for RISK MANAGEMENT. [P.C.]

European List of Notified Chemical Substances (ELINCS) A list of chemical substances notified under European Community (EC) new substances legislation. *See also* EUROPEAN INVENTORY OF EXISTING COMMERCIAL CHEMICAL SUBSTANCES. [P.C.]

European Remote Sensing (ERS) satellite A REMOTE SENSING satellite. The first European Remote Sensing satellite (ERS-1) has a Sun-synchronous polar orbit with an altitude of 780 km and a 3-day repeat cycle. It was launched in July 1991 and carries three sensors: a C band SYNTHETIC APERTURE RADAR (SAR) that produces images of the Earth's surface independently of solar illumination/atmospheric conditions with a spatial resolution of 30 m; a radar altimeter that measures the height of the satellite above the Earth to an accuracy of ±2 cm; and the Along-Track Scanning Radiometer that measures and maps sea-surface temperature to an accuracy of ±0.5°C. ERS-2 was launched in April 1995. [P.J.C.]

eury- From the Greek *eurus* meaning wide. Applied as prefix meaning wide range of tolerance for some environmental factors, for example eurybathic for hydrostatic PRESSURE, eurythermal for TEMPERATURE, euryhaline for SALINITY. *Cf.* STENO-. [P.C. & V.F.]

eutrophic *See* EUTROPHICATION.

eutrophication Biological effects of an increase in plant NUTRIENTS (usually nitrogen and phosphorus, but sometimes silicon, potassium, calcium, iron or manganese) on aquatic systems. The term 'eutrophic' was first used by Weber, a German botanist, at the turn of the century to describe the conditions that determine the plant community in the initial stages of raised peat bogs. He subsequently described the nutrient stages that control vegetation changes as leading from 'eutrophe' to 'mesotrophe' and then 'oligotrophe'. These three terms were used in LIMNOLOGY shortly after by the Swedish botanist Naumann to describe freshwater-lake types containing low (oligotrophic), moderate (mesotrophic) and high (eutrophic) concentrations of phosphorus, nitrogen and calcium, though precise levels were never specified. Indeed, there is still a lack of precision in the definition of these terms, possibly because the trophic nature of water bodies varies considerably from system to system.

The sequence of changes in LAKES subject to eutrophication involve increases in plant biomas and changes in the OXYGEN regime, largely resulting from the accumulation and decay of plant DETRITUS and oxygen consumption of microbial decomposers. Both suspended and settled particulate matter increase, leading to the attenuation of light and ultimately reduced PHOTOSYNTHESIS and plant BIOMASS. All these changes have knock-on effects to the species composition of aquatic flora and fauna at all levels.

Eutrophication may be due to the natural effects of in-filling and SUCCESSION slowly affecting lake morphometry and to the effects of accelerated nutrient enrichment from human sources, largely from SEWAGE inputs. *See also* ORGANIC POLLUTION. [P.C.]

evenness *See* EQUITABILITY.

ex *situ* genetic reserves Conservation of species (and often subspecies) is increasingly focused on botanic gardens, germplasm centres, microbial culture and gene library collections. Together with zoos, they constitute *ex situ* as opposed to *in situ* conservation (*see IN SITU* GENETIC RESERVES), the latter more the provenance of nature reserves or natural habitats protected by conservation legislation. The concept of *ex situ* conservation is particularly well established in botanic gardens worldwide, with about 1000 institutions (as a conservative estimate) currently active in *ex situ* plant conservation. [G.A.F.H.]

exceedance In an environmental context, the violation of environmental protection standards by exceeding authorized (consented) levels. [P.C.]

exclosure An exclosure is any area from which animals are excluded. Exclosures are typically used to prevent the entry of GRAZING mammals (wild or domesticated) into an area that is protected for scientific or ecological management purposes. Experimental exclosures are used in GRASSLAND, SAVANNAH and FOREST research to study effects of grazing or browsing on VEGETATION development and SUCCESSION. [D.A.F.]

exclusive economic zone An area of territorial waters over which a coastal country assumes authority for controlling resources and POLLUTION and in which exploitation by other countries is officially banned. [V.F.]

existing chemicals Inventories of chemicals known to be in existence for commercial purposes prior to arbitrarily specified dates for legal purposes. Under US Toxic Substances Control Act (TSCA) this was December 1979 and amounts to *c.* 70 000 chemicals. For the European Community (EC), the date was September 1981 and amounts to *c.* 100 000 chemicals. This latter list is called the EUROPEAN INVENTORY OF EXISTING COMMERCIAL CHEMICAL SUBSTANCES (EINECS). Chemicals on these LISTS are subject to prioritization followed by RISK ASSESSMENT and possibly RISK MANAGEMENT. Any chemicals not on the lists are described as NEW CHEMICALS. [P.C.]

existing substances *See* EUROPEAN INVENTORY OF EXISTING COMMERCIAL CHEMICAL SUBSTANCES.

exotic and invasive species Species of plants and animals that have been transported, with human aid, beyond the limits of their native GEOGRAPHIC RANGES and which continue to expand their distributions by displacing species indigenous to the invaded areas. Other terms (e.g. introduced, immigrant, non-indigenous, ALIEN) are commonly used to describe such species, which may have been transported intentionally or inadvertently. BIOLOGICAL INVASION is not an entirely new phenomenon; it has occurred through the ages, but in recent decades has been accelerated by orders of magnitude. Invasive species are often competitively favoured during range expansion by the DISTURBANCE caused by human activities but are frequently able to persist and thrive in their newly occupied habitats, often in natural disturbance niches of these habitats or in artificial ECOSYSTEMS. [L.L.L.]

experimental lake area (ELA) Area containing a number of lake basins in north-western Ontario, Canada that have been subjected to comprehensive manipulation to explore ECOSYSTEM responses to EUTROPHICATION, ACIDIFICATION and POLLUTION. For example, one interesting study involved the gradual acidification of Lake 223 from pH 6.8 to 5.0 between 1976 and 1983. The manipulation was carried out after a 2-year period of baseline studies. Primary production and phytoplankton diversity remained unchanged, but several species replacements occurred. Some fish populations, including young lake trout, increased slightly in intermediate stages of the experiment. However, recruitment failed at pH levels near 5.6 due to appreciable changes in benthic production. [P.C.]

expert judgement Basing decisions about environmental protection and/or conservation measures on the views of persons whose qualifications and/or experience enable them to assess and interpret complex evidence. An expert witness is a person testifying in legal proceedings who, on the basis of qualification and/or experience, is allowed to use hearsay, assumptions and hypothetical questions;

cf. a lay witness who is allowed to testify only on the basis of facts within their personal knowledge. [P.C.]

expert system Software involving methods of solving problems and carrying out tasks by means of an information base containing rules and data based on human experience and previously encountered problems. [P.C.]

expert witness *See* EXPERT JUDGEMENT.

explanatory variable The x-axis in a regression analysis or analysis of covariance, or the factors in an ANALYSIS OF VARIANCE. Combinations of continuous explanatory variables and categorical explanatory variables (factors) are used in GENERALIZED LINEAR MODELS to partition variation in the RESPONSE VARIABLE, and hence to form a view on the relative importance of the different explanatory variables in causing variation in the response variable. Formerly known as independent variables. *See also* STATISTICS. [M.J.C.]

exponential growth Unlimited population growth or population growth with no competition for resources. Exponential growth is only possible in the short term while conditions for population increase are favourable and effectively constant, for example during the log phase of bacterial population growth. Characterized by a constant average rate of increase per individual or POPULATION GROWTH RATE *r* (also known as the INTRINSIC RATE OF INCREASE). [R.H.S.]

export of pollution Provocative phrase sometimes used to describe transport of chemicals and radioactive wastes from one nation to another. [P.C.]

exposure The contact concentration and/or intensity of exposure between a chemical or physical agent and a biological system. For chemicals, depends upon FATE. [P.C.]

extinction crisis, current global A total of about 490 animal extinctions and 580 plant extinctions have been recorded globally since 1600. The number of extinctions has increased dramatically in the last 100 years. There has been a preponderance of extinctions on islands compared to continents. For example, 75% of recorded animal extinctions since 1600 have been of species inhabiting islands, even though islands support a small fraction of the number of animal species found on continents. The apparent decline in extinctions in the last 30 years to 1990 is at least partly due to the time-lag between extinction events and their detection and recording. A number of species are likely to have become extinct recently without yet having been recorded as such. It is also possible that conservation efforts over the last 30 years have slowed the rate of extinctions.

While it is difficult to estimate the absolute values of current and future extinction rates, there is little doubt that we are in the midst of a MASS EXTINCTION event of a magnitude matched only by five

other such events in geological time. The current mass extinction event is unique because it is the product of the impact of a single species rather than the result of environmental change. [M.A.B.]

extinction modelling Extinction modelling is the process of building conceptual, statistical and mathematical models to summarize our understanding of the dynamics of extinction and to predict patterns of extinction. The likelihood of extinction of species has been estimated by developing statistical models of local extinction (extirpation) based on species characteristics. Some factors important to mammals and birds include POPULATION SIZE and range, body size, social structure and the ability to use disturbed habitat.

Extinction risks for individual species may be estimated by developing dynamic mathematical models that include stochastic elements representing sources of UNCERTAINTY, a process known as population viability analysis. It may be used to explore how management activities influence the systematic decline or PROBABILITY of extinction of a species. The probability of extinction is usually estimated by MONTE CARLO SIMULATION of the factors that govern the chances of persistence of the species including demographic parameters (survivorships and fecundities), density-dependent regulation, environmental variation, spatial correlation of environmental variation, DISPERSAL, changes in the status of habitat and the impact of infrequent, catastrophic events such as fire. Appropriate model structure depends on consideration of the ecology of the species, data availability and requirements, and an understanding of management needs. *See also* ENDANGERED SPECIES; EXTINCTION CRISIS, CURRENT GLOBAL; MASS EXTINCTION. [M.A.B.]

extractive reserves Extractive reserves (ERs) are designated conservation areas in which natural resource extraction is carried out complementary to the objective of conserving biological diversity and the natural resource base. Today, many parks, reserves and other established protected areas worldwide include some form of resource extraction and consumption.

Extraction of products can include anything from the natural resource base of the reserve: wildlife for meat or other products; plants for food and medicines; wood used as lumber for building, pulp for paper or as raw material for other products; many non-wood forest products such as flowers, fruits, nuts and leaves; or water for domestic and industrial use. [F.W.B.]

exudates Dissolved metabolites (i.e amino acids short-chain ACIDS, glycerol, carbohydrates and polysaccharides) released by PHYTOPLANKTON. [V.F.]

Exxon Valdez *See* ECOLOGICAL/ENVIRONMENTAL DISASTERS.

F

F test A statistical procedure that tests the NULL HYPOTHESIS (H_0) that two SAMPLE variances are from POPULATIONS with equal variances (H_0: $\sigma_1^2 = \sigma_2^2$). One VARIANCE is divided by the other to produce a ratio that will equal one if the two variances are equal. This ratio (the variance ratio) has been called F, in honour of R.A. Fisher, an English statistical biologist. [B.S.]

FAO (Food and Agriculture Organization) *See* UNITED NATIONS PROGRAMMES AND BODIES.

farming practices, sustainable Agricultural activities that:

1 maintain and enhance the quality and productivity of the SOIL;

2 conserve soil, WATER, energy, natural resources, species diversity, genetic diversity and WILDLIFE habitat;

3 maintain and enhance the quality of surface water and groundwater;

4 protect the health and safety of persons involved directly in AGRICULTURE as well as consumers;

5 promote the well-being of animals;

6 maintain the economic viability of farming. [J.K.P.]

farmland and farming communities, conservation Activities that protect agricultural soils and adjacent NATURAL areas from loss via erosion, CONTAMINATION or development. Protection of human communities supported by AGRICULTURE involves maintaining the economic viability of farming while preserving the integrity and self-sufficiency of agriculturally based communities. A variety of life and culture is maintained by preserving the agricultural practices and CROP varieties specific to local areas. [J.K.P.]

fate The destiny of a XENOBIOTIC in the environment. It is influenced by transport, transformation and degradation. *See also* PREDICTED ENVIRONMENTAL CONCENTRATION. [P.C.]

feedback Information regarding a control mechanism or controlled system that enables actual performance to be compared with target performance. Performance can then be adjusted either positively or negatively, corresponding to, respectively, either positive or NEGATIVE FEEDBACK. Feedback can involve physical feedback loops, as with thermostats, reflex responses and management systems. Alternatively, feedback can be apparent, for example when liquid escapes from a leaking tank the rate of outflow reduces as volume reduces, giving the impression that there is feedback control on rate of loss, but there is no feedback hardware here. [P.C.]

femtoplankton Planktonic organisms of size in the range 0.02–$0.2\,\mu m$, i.e. viruses. [V.F.]

fen A RHEOTROPHIC wetland ecosystem, dominated by herbaceous plants, in which the WATER TABLE approximately coincides with the soil surface during the drier times of year. [P.D.M.]

feral Living in a wild or NATURAL state. Used especially for domesticated animals and plants that become wild. [P.C.]

fertilizers Materials added to the SOIL to increase the productivity of farmland or forest by supplying chemical elements that are at suboptimal levels for plant growth. Fertilizers can be classed as inorganic (salts such as ammonium nitrate, NH_4NO_3) or organic (based on carbon compounds). Manures are complex organic fertilizers derived from plant residues or animal excreta.

Fertilizers normally contain nitrogen, phosphorus and potassium compounds but may also contain sulphur, calcium and occasionally MICRONUTRIENTS. Lime, which is used to adjust the soil pH to increase the availability of nutrients and increase the effectiveness of rooting, is sometimes classed as a fertilizer.

Fertilizer usage is quoted either as the mass of fertilizer or of nutrients per unit area. In 1996, fertilizer consumption ranged from $20\,kg\,ha^{-1}$ of cropped land in Africa to $200\,kg\,ha^{-1}$ in the European Union. However, these figures hide variation from less than $1\,kg\,ha^{-1}$ in some African countries to more than $400\,kg\,ha^{-1}$ in the intensively farmed countries of western Europe. Phosphorus (P) and potassium (K) in fertilizer can be quoted either as the elemental form or as the P_2O_5 or K_2O equivalent. Elemental P and K can be calculated from the P_2O_5 and K_2O equivalents by multiplying by 0.83 and 0.44 respectively. [G.R.]

field A term often used to describe NATURAL sites or systems, for example field experiments are carried out in the open as opposed to in laboratories. [P.C.]

fine-particulate organic matter (FPOM) Plant detritus in aquatic systems between *c.* $0.45\,\mu m$ and 1 mm. *Cf.* COARSE-PARTICULATE ORGANIC MATTER. [P.C.]

fish, diversity and conservation strategies Fish are the most numerous of the vertebrates, a reflection of their antiquity and the extent and variety of habitats they occupy. Although estimates vary, there are probably around 24 000 species, the majority of which (14 500; 62%) are marine. Most are torpedo-shaped; however, round, flat and even angular body forms exist. Some attain sexual maturity when only 2–3 cm in length (e.g. the world's smallest commercially exploited fish, the Philippine goby, *Mistichthys luzonensis*), while others, such as the whale shark (*Rhincodon typus*), can attain lengths in excess of 20 m.

Fish DIVERSITY is now recognized to be diminishing at an unprecedented rate, losses being greatest in fresh waters where fish are the most threatened group of vertebrates after the amphibians. It is estimated that 20% of the world's freshwater fish fauna is extinct or in danger of extinction, and that in Mediterranean climates this figure may be as high as 65%.

Although the causes differ from one biogeographical area to another, losses of fish diversity have largely resulted from habitat degradation, species introductions and overexploitation. Habitat degradation, widely regarded as the single greatest threat to fish diversity, arises not only from changes in land use (e.g. DEFORESTATION) but also as a result of POLLUTION and EUTROPHICATION, changes in hydrological regimes and global CLIMATE CHANGE. Habitat destruction causes reductions in species ranges, increasing the vulnerability of populations to extinction by other causes, while pollutants can affect populations by reducing food intake, growth and reproductive success.

Fish introductions, accidental or for fisheries or AQUACULTURE development, have been widespread, resulting in habitat destruction and extinction of local species or populations through competition or predation. Problems are particularly apparent in fresh waters.

The conservation of aquatic BIODIVERSITY remains comparatively neglected and there has been less effort on the conservation of fish than any other vertebrate group. Traditionally, fish have been regarded from a largely utilitarian point of view, as a resource to exploit to the maximum for their food potential, a situation that has few parallels among terrestrial vertebrates. Fish are further disadvantaged by being largely invisible, and by being generally perceived as cold, wet and slimy: hence, the emotionally loaded publicity campaigns employed to save other threatened vertebrates are unlikely to be effective. [M.C.M.B.]

fish farming The culture of fish (often used broadly to include both fish and molluscs!), in indoor/outdoor tanks or enclosures in natural water bodies, for human consumption. *See also* AQUACULTURE. [P.C.]

fish kill Observed MORTALITY, usually extensive, in natural fish populations signalling POLLUTION from known, suspected or unknown causes. [P.C.]

fish stocks The standing stock is the total mass of fish present at a given time in a fishery. Understanding the dynamics of fish stocks is a primary goal of fisheries biology and includes study of the rates at which fish grow, die and reproduce. Fish stocks may be estimated by analysis of commercial fish catches, by scientific sampling of fish populations, or by extrapolating from estimates of PRIMARY PRODUCTIVITY. Fisheries managers attempt to estimate the MAXIMUM SUSTAINABLE YIELD, i.e. the largest number of fish that can be harvested year after year without diminishing the stocks. Stock RECRUITMENT models are fisheries models that predict the amount of juvenile recruitment as a function of the parent stock. [V.F.]

fisheries, conservation and management Fisheries biologists have long realized the need to manage the commercial exploitation of aquatic and marine resources. This need for the conservation of marine fish stocks has been recognized by the international community, and this has led to the formation of advisory and legislative bodies, for example the International Council for the Exploration of the Sea (ICES). Such organizations have implemented a number of control measures, for example EXCLUSIVE ECONOMIC ZONES (EEZ) and total allowable catches (TAC).

Fisheries management encompasses four basic objectives: (i) to maximize annual YIELD from the resource; (ii) to prevent stock collapse; (iii) to maximize economic functions (i.e. profit); and (iv) to achieve a socio-economic balance (i.e. employment). The three principal means of achieving these objectives are:

1 Control of fishing effort, either indirectly by imposing quotas or closed seasons, or directly by effort control.
2 Controlling the age or size at which fish are first caught by having tighter control on the mesh sizes used or by excluding fishing vessels from fish nursery areas or known juvenile habitats.
3 Measures to enhance either stock or habitat. [C.W.B.]

fixed-quota harvesting A HARVESTING strategy in which harvesting activity is regulated by a fixed catch level. This catch level is usually set below the maximum that can be sustained and thus, in theory, should mean that the resource is protected from severe exploitation. The main problem with this type of harvesting is that it does not involve any natural FEEDBACK between the POPULATION SIZE and the level of harvesting. Thus, if for any reason, the population falls below the level at which its natural surplus is less than the fixed quota, then the decline will continue. [J.B.]

fjord A narrow, deep, steep-walled inlet, formed either by the submergence of a glaciated mountainous coast or by entrance of the OCEAN into a deeply excavated glacial trough after the glacier melts. [V.F.]

flagship species Popular, and usually charismatic, species that provide a symbol and focus for conservation awareness and action, for example the panda and dolphins. *See also* CONSERVATION BIOLOGY. [P.C.]

flocculation The formation of clots or aggregates of CLAY minerals. [V.F.]

floods Flows of WATER on areas of land not normally covered with water and which cause or threaten to cause damage. [A.M.]

Floras Floras are publications giving a taxonomic (systematic) treatment of plants of a particular geographical area, which may be a country, region or smaller area. Floras may cover one or several major plant groups; most include vascular plants only. Treatment may be general but more detailed for small areas, with full descriptions of taxa and information, for example on habitat, distribution and ecology. Many Floras have keys for identification; not all are illustrated. [A.J.W.]

fluctuations Variations over time, for example in the size of a POPULATION or in environmental variables such as temperature, salinity, pH, etc. [V.F.]

flue gas The gases vented by a chimney to the ATMOSPHERE in static fossil-fuel combustion. The major POLLUTANT flue gases are sulphur dioxide (SO_2) and NITROGEN OXIDES (NO and NO_2), which are precursors to acid deposition (*see* ACID RAIN AND MIST). FLUE-GAS DESULPHURIZATION (FGD) systems can achieve 90% reductions in SO_2 by spraying a slurry of lime into the flue gas to absorb and oxidize SO_2 to calcium sulphate. Flue-gas denitrification (FGN) is less efficient and relies on burner redesign or injection of urea or ammonia into the combustion zone to effect chemical conversion of NO to N_2. [M.R.H]

flue-gas denitrification (FGN) *See* FLUE GAS.

flue-gas desulphurization (FGD) A system for removing sulphur dioxide (SO_2) from gas emitted from a chimney after combustion in the burner that it is venting. SO_2 is absorbed by a limestone slurry spray to form calcium sulphite, which is then oxidized to calcium sulphate, which, together with WATER, forms gypsum ($CaSO_4.2H_2O$). Removal of SO_2 from the EMISSIONS of coal-fired power-stations makes a positive contribution to reducing acid rain (*see* ACID RAIN AND MIST). The main disadvantages are: (i) that considerable quantities of limestone are needed; and (ii) that not all the gypsum produced may be used efficiently, so creating difficulties with storage and problems from possible leachates. [P.C.]

fluxes Rates of transfer; for example, of carbon or energy in FOOD CHAINS, or of elements in BIOGEOCHEMICAL CYCLES. [P.C.]

fly ash The residue produced after burning pulverized fuel, for example coal in power-stations, or rubbish in incinerators. Although very efficiently removed from exhaust gases by electrostatic precipitators, pulverized fuel ash (PFA) is found ubiquitously as an AEROSOL in the ATMOSPHERE, and in RAIN, and may be transported for hundreds of kilometres from its source. PFA particles are characterized microscopically as spherical siliceous particles with diameters in the range 0.1–10 μm. Fly ash removed from exhaust gases by precipitators is often used as LANDFILL, or for LAND RECLAMATION at coastal sites. [J.N.C.]

fly tipping The illegal disposal of solid WASTE in an unauthorized manner and location. [P.C.]

fodder Dried, cured plant material (e.g. hay and straw) used as feed for animals. [P.C.]

Food and Agriculture Organization (FAO) *See* UNITED NATIONS PROGRAMMES AND BODIES.

food chain A series of organisms linked by their feeding relationships. Each link in the chain feeds on, and obtains energy from, the preceding link and provides food and energy for the following link. The number of links in the chain is limited: for example primary producer → herbivore → primary carnivore → secondary carnivore. [M.H.]

food web Food webs are ways of describing the structure of ecological communities, and the trophic interactions which occur between the component units of a COMMUNITY. They illustrate that FOOD CHAINS are not isolated sequences but are interconnected with each other; for example, some animals feed on both plant and animal material and are therefore intermediate between primary and secondary consumer levels. Other animals may change their feeding habits as they get older. Thus, it is apparent that comprehensive food webs of real communities can become very complex. Even so, patterns can be discerned, even in very complex food webs, due to the common constraints of energy flow, population dynamics and the structural design of animals. The explanation and prediction of food-web patterns is fundamental to understanding the processes at work in an ECOSYSTEM. [M.H.]

foraminiferan Any member of an order (Foraminifera) of planktonic or benthic protozoans that (usually) secrete a calcareous test and possess pseudopodia. They range in size from about 30 μm to a few millimetres and feed on bacteria, PHYTOPLANKTON or small ZOOPLANKTON. There are approximately 40 known PELAGIC species and 4000 benthic species. [V.F.]

foreshore The portion of the shore lying between the normal high- and low-water marks; the INTERTIDAL ZONE. [V.F.]

forest Nowadays, this term usually refers to a large area of tree-covered land, but including other habitats in a matrix of trees. However, in Britain, it originally referred to unclaimed land beyond the bounds of farmland and habitation (cf. 'foreign', possibly from the same root). This land was commonly wooded, but not necessarily so. By the medieval period the term had been appropriated to describe large tracts of open land, including WOODLAND, subject to a particular form of law (i.e. Forest Law), which constituted the Crown hunting grounds and a source of fresh venison. Each forest was administered by a hierarchy of officials. Some medieval forests survive as forests (e.g. New Forest, Forest of Dean), whereas others survive in name only. Other ancient well-wooded tracts were also 'forests', though they were never Crown land (e.g. Forest of Arden, Leicester Forest). In the 20th century a forest has become the basic unit of administration of land managed by the Forestry Commission, much of which has been planted with Sitka spruce (*Picea sitchensis*) and other introduced conifers. Accordingly, 'forest' (and 'FORESTRY') has come to connote extensive plantations managed primarily for timber, whereas woodland has come to denote native tree cover, managed traditionally or not managed at all. The original usage to describe open land as well as tree-covered land (e.g. Dartmoor and Exmoor Forests) survives in the modern 'deer forests' of the Scottish Highlands, most of which are virtually devoid of trees. [G.F.P.]

forest fragmentation *See* FRAGMENTATION OF HABITATS AND CONSERVATION.

forestation The creation of FOREST conditions on an area of land which has not been forested for a long time, normally decades or centuries. [J.F.B.]

forestry Forestry concerns the interaction of trees, woodlands or forests with people. It comprises both practice and theory—the management of forest resources for a specific purpose and the scientific study of forest ECOSYSTEMS, including all aspects of their management. The terms 'woodland' and 'forest' refer primarily to smaller and larger areas of tree-dominated land respectively, although they can also refer to specific types of forest cover. [J.F.B.]

forestry practices Activities used to create or maintain desired FOREST conditions and products. [A.N.G.]

fossil fuels HYDROCARBON energy sources derived from fossil organic materials: coal, oil and natural gas. *See also* ACID PRECIPITATION, IMPACT ON ECOSYSTEMS; ACID RAIN AND MIST. [P.C.]

FPOM *See* FINE-PARTICULATE ORGANIC MATTER.

fragmentation of habitats and conservation Fragmentation of natural systems is a pervasive ecological phenomenon and a central problem in conservation and restoration ecology. As forested landscapes become fragmented, changes occur in the physical environment of forests, the ability of organisms to migrate and disperse across the landscape, and the spatial and temporal dynamics of DISTURBANCE. With increased spatial DISPERSION of suitable or accessible HABITAT, populations of some species may experience reduced success in dispersing to, or colonizing, new sites. Populations may also decline as habitat area is reduced and may become increasingly vulnerable to local extinction due to genetic, demographic or environmental stochasticity. Finally,

fragmentation may favour some groups of species over others, resulting in changes in biotic composition of the forested landscape.

Consequently, fragmentation is a central issue in the conservation and management of parks and protected areas. By virtue of their fragmentation, many protected ECOSYSTEMS become modified remnants of once large and more continuous systems. There is growing concern that over time, fragmentation will cause degradation of the ecological characteristics of many protected areas. [D.A.F.]

fresh water WATER with no significant amount of dissolved salts or minerals. It generally contains $<1000\,mg\,l^{-1}$ of dissolved solids. *Cf.* SEA. [P.C.]

front

1 Relating to WEATHER; *see* FRONTAL SYSTEM.

2 A boundary between horizontally juxtaposed WATER masses of dissimilar properties where CIRCULATION and mixing change abruptly. Fronts can be classified into six general types: (i) river plume fronts; (ii) UPWELLING fronts; (iii) shallow sea fronts; (iv) shelf break fronts; (v) fronts at the edge of major western boundary CURRENTS; and (vi) fronts of planetary scale, removed from major OCEAN boundaries. The first four types are COASTAL phenomena, whereas the last two types are open-ocean phenomena. Fronts act to concentrate NUTRIENTS and PLANKTON, and are thus sites of high productivity. [V.F.]

frontal system A front is a transition zone between two AIR MASSES of different densities and usually temperatures. It may also be distinguished by a PRESSURE trough, major discontinuity, and change in the WIND direction. The frontal system is the pattern of fronts as illustrated on summary WEATHER charts. [P.C.]

fuelwood Wood was the first energy resource for humankind, and is still used as the prime energy supply for cooking and heating by the majority of the world's population. Probably half of all the wood harvested is used as fuelwood. [J.G.]

fugacity The tendency for a substance to transfer from one environmental medium to another. It is analogous to chemical potential—the tendency of a chemical to escape from a phase. The concept is used in models that predict the environmental FATE of CONTAMINANTS. [P.C.]

fugacity models Predictions of EXPOSURE to CONTAMINANTS that model the partition of substances between environmental compartments on the basis of the FUGACITY of chemicals—essentially a chemical's partial pressure that can be viewed as an escaping tendency or pressure. It has units of pressure and can usually be related linearly to concentration. *See also* MACKAY FATE MODELS. [P.C.]

fugitive emissions Uncontrolled and unwanted releases of CONTAMINANTS to the environment through leaks. [P.C.]

fumes Airborne, suffocating POLLUTANTS; they may be gaseous and/or suspensions of solids and/or vapours. [P.C.]

fungi, diversity Membership in the kingdom Fungi is generally assigned to organisms which are heterotrophic (i.e. those which cannot independently synthesize a nutritional energy source), nucleated, usually filamentous, and typically reproduce by sexual and asexual spores. As thus defined, fungi constitute an extremely diverse, polyphyletic assemblage of over 100 000 species classified in the phyla Zygomycota, Ascomycota and Basidiomycota. This definition is often extended to include fungal-like protists such as the aquatic moulds (Chytridiomycota and Oomycota) and the slime moulds (Myxomycota and Acrasiomycota). [J.S.S.]

fungicides PESTICIDES designed to eradicate or control fungal pathogens on plants, animals and materials derived from organic sources. Fungicides have to cope with a wide range of pathogenic fungi. The latter can be classified according to the mode of infection.

1 Airborne infections, involving:
 (a) motile spores that are water-dependent at infection stage, e.g. downy mildews;
 (b) spores that move passively through water and mycelia that live under the cuticle (e.g. botrytis);
 (c) spores that are not directly dependent on water and mycelia that live under the cuticle or deeper (e.g. powdery mildews and rusts).

2 Internal and external seedborne infections of many kinds.

3 Soilborne infections (e.g. club root, damping off).

The first agricultural fungicide to be formulated may have been the mixture of copper sulphate and lime (Bordeaux mixture) used for control of downy mildew of vines from 1885. By the turn of the century, lime sulphur was being used on fruit trees and copper sulphate for control of potato blight. Organomercury seed dressings were introduced in 1913 to control a range of seedborne diseases, but it was not until 1934 that the first of the modern organic chemical fungicides, thiram (a non-systemic dithiocarbamate fungicide), was introduced. These novel compounds had a predominantly contact action; i.e. if plant surfaces are treated, the fungicide protects against the germination of fungal spores arriving after treatment.

Systemic fungicides appeared in the 1960s. These compounds act against internal fungal mycelia and haustoria. They attack already established diseases or offer protection from attack. They are not as subject to degradation as external protectants. The older protective compounds have tended to be generally non-specific, but most modern fungicides are rather more target- and site-specific (such as attacking single receptors or enzymes), and many of these are systemic in action. Systemic fungicides applied to roots or seed may be translocated to protect other parts of the plant from airborne infections.

In practice, most CROPS are subjected to simultaneous attacks by pathogens, and mixtures of two or more compounds, including systemic and contact materials, are often employed. Such mixtures of types of fungicide help to reduce the risk of RESISTANCE to fungicides, which is otherwise a major problem in the maintenance of established products, and in the development of new products. Plant breeding for disease resistance is an equally important technique in managing fungal diseases.

Many fungicides can be used very safely for the control of fungal diseases on animals because of their specificity of action, and in the control of fungal attacks on many materials derived from organic sources.

The earlier multiple-site protectants such as organomercurials and copper sulphate are more generally toxic to animals, and the organomercurials have been banned in a number of countries. As many modern fungicides tend to be very target specific, they tend to have low TOXICITY to other organisms. [K.D.]

fynbos A flora unique to the southern and southwestern coastal region of South Africa, consisting of over 8500 species, of which almost one-fifth are endemic. The almost treeless VEGETATION (*fynbos* is Afrikaans for fine bush) characteristically consists of tough, fine-leaved bushy plants. [G.A.F.H.]

G

Gaia In Greek mythology, Gaia, or Gaea, is the goddess of the Earth. The name has been used by James Lovelock for his theory that the planet operates as a self-regulatory system—a superorganism—to ensure that life is maintained. This does not necessarily mean that human life will be maintained.

A major problem with the Gaia theory is that it presumes that the activities of species are somehow coordinated for the common good, whereas Darwinian selection favours species that behave selfishly! Moreover, life on the planet does not appear to be as tightly coordinated and integrated as the cells, tissues and organs are within an organism. [P.C.]

Galapagos Islands A group of islands in the PACIFIC OCEAN lying on the Equator at about 90°W, some 1000km from the coast of South America. The islands are volcanic in origin, with a maximum age of 5 million years. They belong to Ecuador and have both Spanish and English names, the latter used in relation to their significance in the history of evolutionary theory.

The endemic fauna and flora of the Galapagos Islands served in part as inspiration for Darwin's theory of evolution by NATURAL SELECTION after Darwin had visited the Islands on his expedition with HMS *Beagle* in 1835. For example, the pattern of carapace of the tortoises varies between islands, suggesting that they have diverged from one another. Perhaps the most famous example is that of Darwin's finches, which consist of 13 endemic species on the Galapagos Islands and one on Cocos Island, lying between the Galapagos and Panama. They display a pattern of adaptation on the islands, occupying niches that, on the neighbouring continent, are filled by species in other families. They are the classic example of insular adaptive radiation. An international biological research station has been established to support the study and conservation of the Islands' fauna and flora [I.M.C.]

gallery forest A type of FOREST vegetation found along the stream and river banks within dry SAVANNAH grasslands. GRAZING and an annual rainfall of less than 1500mm excludes forest from the grassy plains of the savannah, but beside the watercourses the moist soils support forest. [M.I.]

γ-rays Photons of electromagnetic RADIATION which are emitted during de-excitation of product nuclides in radioactive decay. The energies of γ-rays (typically in the range 10keV to 50MeV) are characteristic of the nuclide undergoing decay. They are highly penetrating, requiring 10cm of LEAD to provide effective shielding, but have low linear energy transfer (LET) rates. γ-Rays interact with matter by: (i) the photoelectric effect, in which the PHOTON imparts all of its energy to an electron; (ii) Compton scattering, in which the photon imparts some of its energy to an electron and is scattered with a reduced energy; or (iii) pair production, in which the photon is converted into a positron–electron pair. [A.B.M.]

gas chromatography A technique used for the determination of chemical components in a wide range of environmental samples. An inert carrier gas transports the sample through a column containing an immobilized medium (referred to as the stationary phase). Separation and identification of components is achieved through differences in migration rates and known retention times within the column. The stationary phase may be a solid with a large surface area (gas–solid chromatography). However, many compounds remain permanently adsorbed on solid media, requiring the use of a liquid stationary phase (gas–liquid chromatography). Samples are introduced into the carrier gas stream as a discrete 'plug' of vapour by means of a gas sampling valve or injection system. Non-gaseous samples are vaporized. In gas–liquid chromatography the stationary phase may be held either (i) on a finely ground inert solid (packed column), or (ii) as a sub-micrometre thick coating within a narrow capillary column.

Methods of detecting the elution of compounds from the column include:
1 pyrolysis in a hydrogen–air flame (flame ionization detector);
2 changes in the thermal conductivity of the gas stream (thermal conductivity detector);
3 ionization of the gas stream using β-radiation (electron capture detector).
[I.J.D.]

gas emissions Gas EMISSIONS associated with ECOSYSTEM processes lead to large-scale cycling of the elements between the ATMOSPHERE and terrestrial and oceanic biota. These phenomena are components of the BIOGEOCHEMICAL CYCLES, via which substances in the natural environment are transported and transformed on a global scale. The major global cycles are of carbon, sulphur, nitrogen and WATER. Human interventions have led to perturbations in these global cycles through industrial processes, energy use and in the terrestrial sphere through land-use change. The impacts of gas emissions on ecosystems are presently great, and potentially even greater in future. [W.N.A.]

GATT and environment Of the three international economic institutions proposed following the Second World War, only two—the International Bank for Reconstruction and Development (World Bank) and International Monetary Fund—were formally established. The third, the International Trade Organization (ITO), was only realized as a General Agreement on Tariffs and Trade (GATT). GATT came into force in 1948 with the objective of reducing tariffs and other barriers to, and eliminating discrimination in, international trade. By 1991, 103 states were formal Contracting Parties (CPs) to GATT, including the 24 industrialized countries that comprise the OECD and account for 75% of world trade. Another 29 states were applying GATT on a *de facto* basis.

GATT's rules are principally aimed at obtaining non-discriminatory treatment:
• of products, whether produced domestically or imported, or consumed domestically or exported; and
• of countries, specifically GATT CPs.

In general, domestic laws and regulations that treat like products equally, irrespective of their country of origin and destination, will not contravene GATT rules. Unequal treatment is likely to do so. GATT rules are amended, or their scope enlarged, by periodic 'Rounds' of negotiations.

The GATT rules do not mention the ENVIRONMENT, although they do allow exceptions to be made where 'necessary to protect human, animal or plant life or health', or 'relating to the conservation of exhaustible resources'. The environment is specifically acknowledged in the Agreement on Technical Barriers to Trade, concluded in 1979 as part of the Tokyo Round and accepted by 38 countries by 1991, as one of the considerations that can justify the setting of product standards higher than international norms.

Permitting general unilateral action for environmental reasons would, however, increase protectionism, encroach on national sovereignty and deny the exploitation of legitimate competitive advantage. Moreover, not only would such action almost certainly not be the most efficient way to address an environmental problem, it could even be counterproductive.

Environmentalists contend that the GATT rules amount to a serious obstacle to the attainment of SUSTAINABLE DEVELOPMENT. They also point out that the rules may also run counter to the trade measures envisaged for the enforcement of various international environmental agreements, such as the Montreal Protocol to protect the OZONE LAYER. They argue that GATT should be reformed specifically to allow environmental protection to take

precedence over the promotion of international trade. [P.C.]

Geiger counter An IONIZING RADIATION detector, also called Geiger–Müller counter, which consists of a glass tube filled with an inert gas, and fitted with a central anode and cathode concentric with the walls. Geiger counters are used as basic radiation monitors and for analysis of β-emitting RADIONUCLIDES. [A.B.M.]

gelbstoff A German word meaning 'yellow substance', used as a name for poorly identified, dissolved organic compounds found in water and usually considered to consist at least in part of humic and fulvic compounds. [V.F.]

gene The functional unit of heredity; a hereditary determinant that behaves as a unit of inheritance occupying one (usually) contiguous region of a chromosome and which can mutate to various allelic forms. [V.F.]

generalized linear models (GLIM or GLM) Models that extend conventional parametric statistical analyses by allowing the user to specify non-normal errors and non-identity link functions. They are especially useful in environmental work for dealing with count data (e.g. log-linear models for CONTINGENCY TABLES), proportion data (e.g. logistic analysis of mortality data), binary response variables (e.g. dead or alive, infected or not, male or female, etc.) and the analysis of survival data (e.g. age at death, using exponential or Weibull errors). The general term used to describe residual variation in GLM is deviance; this is analogous to the familiar error SUM OF SQUARES used in regression and ANALYSIS OF VARIANCE. The models are called linear models because they are linear in their parameters and in their error term. It does *not* mean that they are restricted to describing linear relationships between the RESPONSE VARIABLE and the EXPLANATORY VARIABLES. [M.J.C.]

genetic engineering Manipulation of the genome, usually DNA, with various techniques. It allows artificial manipulation of genetic VARIABILITY within species and even the combination of genetic materials across species. *See also* TRANSGENIC ORGANISMS. [P.C.]

genetic fingerprinting A method used to quantify genetic differences among individuals, populations or species. A pattern, or so-called 'fingerprint', is obtained by enzymatically cleaving a protein or nucleic acid and subjecting the digest to two-dimensional chromatography or electrophoresis. [V.F.]

genetically modified organism (GMO) Organism whose genome is modified by direct manipulation, not by breeding. When such organisms are used as constituents of food, the food is referred to as GM food. *See* TRANSGENIC ORGANISMS. [P.C.]

genotoxic A broad term that usually describes a CONTAMINANT that has a measurable/observable

EFFECT on DNA and/or chromosome structures. Genotoxicity can be measured by a variety of techniques based on determinations of MUTATIONS, DNA damage/repair or chromosomal aberrations. [P.C.]

geographic information systems (GIS) in conservation The use of computer hardware and software tools for the acquisition, management, analysis and display of resource data for conservation. These data, for example, can include elevation, soil or vegetation types, road or river networks, as well as image data acquired from aircraft- and satellite-based cameras or sensors. The actual input data will depend on what conservation information is required. These diverse data are integrated within a common framework of the GIS by relating and referencing the data by their spatial location. The integration of these data permits evaluation, modelling, statistical analy-

sis and visual display. GIS analysis can display the results of past, current and future outcomes of different conservation practices, providing information to assist in resource management planning and decisions. [J.V.C.]

geographic range The extent of the global DISTRIBUTION of a species. [P.C.]

geological time-scales The age of the solar system is believed to be 4.7×10^9 years, and the oldest terrestrial rocks are dated at 4.0×10^9 years. Geologists use a hierarchical chronology for the time-span from the origin of fossils to the present day, in which the largest unit is the era. There are only four eras covering the fossil record of life: Cenozoic, $0–65 \times 10^6$ years ago; Mesozoic, $65–245 \times 10^6$ years ago; Palaeozoic $245–540 \times 10^6$ years ago; and Protozoic, $0.540–2.7 \times 10^9$ years ago. The eras are divided into periods, which are themselves divided into epochs.

Table G1 The geological time-scale covering the Cenozoic, Mesozoic and Palaeozoic eras.

Era	Period	Epoch	Age (years ×10⁶)	Events and noteworthy fossils (dates ×10⁶ BP)
Cenozoic	Quaternary	Holocene	0	*Homo sapiens* 0.4, Iron Age 0.003, Atomic Age 0.00005
		Pleistocene	1.6	*Homo erectus* 0.5–1.6, *Homo habilis* 2
	Neogene*	Pliocene	5.2	*Australopithecus* 2.3–4
		Miocene	23	
	Palaeogene*	Oligocene	34	Tree-dwelling primate
		Eocene	53	
		Palaeocene	65	**Mass extinction 65**
Mesozoic	Cretaceous	Late	95	North America, Eurasia, India, Africa, Antarctic/Australia, South America, North America separate
		Early	135	Flowering plants, including herbaceous habit
	Jurassic	Late	152	*Archaeopteryx*
		Middle	180	Coccoliths
		Early	205	**Mass extinction 208**
	Triassic	Late	230	Dinosaurs
		Middle	240	Cycadales
		Early	250	**Mass extinction 245**
Palaeozoic	Permian	Late	260	Reptiles
		Early	300	
	Carboniferous	Silesian	325	Coal formation, winged insects
		Dinantian	355	Amphibia
	Devonian	Late	375	**Mass extinction 367**
		Middle	390	Secondary xylem, tree ferns, 'age of fishes'
		Early	410	Tall vascular plants
	Silurian			Small vascular plants on land
			438	**Mass extinction 439**
	Ordovician			Land plants with spores and cuticles, probable bryophytes
				Corals, first vertebrates
			510	**Mass extinction**
	Cambrian		570	Arthropoda, Echinodermata, Hemichordata, Chordata

* These two units are commonly combined as a single period, the Tertiary.

Table G1 depicts the time-scale spanning the Ceno-zoic, Mesozoic and Palaeozoic eras, with some of the most important events. [J.G.]

geometric mean The back-transformed MEAN of loga-rithmically transformed observations. The formula for calculating the geometric mean (GM) is:

$$GM = antilog\left(\frac{\sum \log x}{n}\right)$$

where x is each observation in the SAMPLE, n is the number of observations in the sample, and the Greek symbol Σ (capital sigma) is the mathematical notation for 'sum of'. [B.S.]

geometric series Also called a geometric progression, a series of terms in which each term is a constant mul-tiple of the preceding term. The general form of a geometric series is $a, ar, ar^2, ar^3, \ldots, ar^n$, where a is a constant and the sequence has n terms. [B.S.]

geostationary satellite (GEOSAT) A satellite that remains stationary relative to the Equator. The orbit of a geostationary satellite is synchronous with that of the Equator at an altitude of around 36 000 km. A scanning RADIOMETER on board provides meteo-rological images of the entire Earth disc every half hour in 3–4 wavebands. Examples of these satellites are the Geostationary Operational Environmental Satellites (GOES) of the NATIONAL OCEANIC AND ATMOSPHERIC ADMINISTRATION (NOAA), and Meteosat of the European Space Agency (ESA). [P.J.C.]

GIS *See* GEOGRAPHIC INFORMATION SYSTEMS (GIS) IN CONSERVATION.

glaciation
1 The processes and the results of erosion and depo-sition arising from the presence of an ICE mass on a landscape.
2 The term glaciation may also refer to geological periods during which a large part of the Northern hemisphere was covered with an ice sheet (also called ice ages). Glaciation in this sense refers to ice cover of extensive parts of the landscape associated with climatic oscillation. The last 700 000 years have been dominated by major ice ages with an approxi-mate 100 000-year cycle interrupted by relatively short interglacials such as we are currently enjoying. [V.F. & P.C.]

glass Any disordered, non-crystalline solid; i.e. one whose constituent atoms have no long-range ordered pattern. A glass is formed when a solid com-pound such as silica is heated above its melting point and then rapidly cooled. A glass does not have a sharp melting point but tends to soften over a range of temperatures. Common glass, or soda glass, is used for windows and bottles and is produced when a mixture of sodium carbonate (Na_2CO_3) and calcium oxide (CaO) is added to the silica melt. The properties of a glass can be altered by varying the additive compounds. For example, borosilicate glass (B_2O_3 added to silica) is tougher than soda glass and

expands and contracts little over a wide temperature range, making it useful for laboratory ware and cooking utensils. The addition of potassium monox-ide (K_2O) and lead monoxide (PbO) to the silica melt results in an especially tough glass with high melting point, which can be ground with precision to pro-duce optical glasses and contact lenses. The addition of the PbO produces a denser glass with a higher refractive index.

A further type of glass, termed bioglass, in which the additives are sodium monoxide (Na_2O), calcium oxide (CaO) and phosphorus pentoxide (P_2O_5), is compatible with bone and is used as a coating on surgical implants.

Melted glass can also be drawn into fibres which may be spun into threads and woven into fabrics. The main use of these fibres, in conjunction with resins, is in the production of strong, corrosion-resistant structures, for example boat superstruc-tures, car bodies. [M.C.G.]

GLIM *See* GENERALIZED LINEAR MODELS.

GLM *See* GENERALIZED LINEAR MODELS.

global databases Global meteorological, oceanogra-phic and geophysical data; now widely available, either over the Internet or on archived media such as tapes and CD-ROMs. [J.Ly.]

Global Environmental Facility (GEF) A fund, estab-lished in 1991 and administered by the World Bank and United Nations Development Programme, to promote environmental and conservation projects in developing countries. *See also* UNITED NATIONS PROGRAMMES AND BODIES. [P.C.]

global warming CLIMATE warming on a global scale, usually attributed to an enhanced greenhouse effect. There is no doubt that the TEMPERATURE of the Earth has increased since the end of the 19th century, by 0.3–0.6°C. A trend can be seen in the record from meteorological stations in both the Northern and Southern hemispheres (Fig. G1). It is known from historical records that sea levels have risen and that glaciers are receding. There is also no doubt that the atmospheric concentration of CARBON DIOXIDE (CO_2) has increased over the last century (it was 280 ppm and is now 360 ppm), and that the concentrations of other GREENHOUSE GASES have been increasing over the past few decades. This observed rise in the concentration of greenhouse gases is believed to be the underlying cause of recent global warming. The link between these two phenomena is explored by mathematical models of the energy balance of the Earth's surface in relation to the optical properties of the ATMOS-PHERE. Generally, in such models, any overall increase in the concentration of greenhouse gases causes an increase in the global temperature. Quan-titative predictions of the extent of this effect need very elaborate global circulation models (GCMs) that run on supercomputers. Long-term change in the surface air temperatures following a doubling in

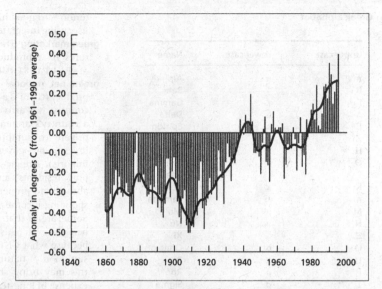

Fig. G1 Combined land, air and sea surface temperatures relative to 1961–1990 averages. (Data from IPCC (1996) *Climate Change 1995: The Science of Climate Change.* Cambridge University Press, Cambridge.)

the CO_2 concentration is predicted to be between 1.5 and 4.5°C, with the 'best' estimate being 2.5°C. There is evidence that vegetation in the Northern hemisphere is already responding to global warming. The spring 'drawdown' of CO_2 caused by photosynthesis is occurring earlier, and so is the spring 'greening' as seen from satellite-borne sensors. [J.G.]

gnotobiotic Describing a culture, COSM or laboratory animal(s) (e.g. used in TOXICITY/ECOTOXICITY tests) in which the exact composition of organisms is known, including, in principle, all associated microbiota. The word derives from the Greek *gnosis*, knowledge, and *bios*, life. [P.C.]

good laboratory practice (GLP) A formalized process under which laboratory studies on ECOTOXICITY are carried out to ensure reliability and REPEATABILITY of results. This is essential in tests that are used in a legal context, where results might be open to challenge. Standardization of procedures should therefore avoid duplication, ensure mutual recognition and reduce the numbers of animals involved. The procedures for GLP involve following standard protocols and keeping thorough and accurate records of observation. They also involve appropriate training and MONITORING by independent observers (*see* QUALITY ASSURANCE AND QUALITY CONTROL). The principles of GLP were originally laid down by the OECD. [P.C.]

goodness-of-fit The extent to which an observed and expected frequency DISTRIBUTION coincide. It is frequently assessed using non-parametric tests (*see* NON-PARAMETRIC STATISTICS) such as a CHI-SQUARED TEST or a *G* test. *See also* STATISTICS. [B.S.]

gradient The rate of change of a characteristic over distance. [A.J.W.]

gradients of species richness It is evident that some habitats are richer in species than others, and it has also been observed that low latitudes and low altitudes tend to support richer floras and faunas than high latitudes and high altitudes. In the case of bird species, for example, there are 603 species breeding in Costa Rica, 472 in Guatemala, 286 in California and 222 in Alaska. There is thus a latitudinal GRADIENT in RICHNESS from the tropics to the Arctic. Similar gradients can be observed in different types of organism. Among mammals, for example, Costa Rica has 140 species and Alaska has 40. Florida has approximately 180 species of tree, while the boreal regions of Canada have only 20–30 species. [P.D.M.]

grasslands BIOMES dominated by herbaceous species in which grasses (Poaceae) or sedges (Cyperaceae) are abundant, accompanied by forbs, which account for the highest proportion of plant species found in grasslands, with sometimes scattered shrubs and trees. Grasslands can be classified as natural, semi-natural and artificial. [J.J.H.]

grazing The consumption of the above-ground parts of plants by animals. [G.A.F.H.]

grazing practices Managing the GRAZING of wild plant communities by domesticated animals is one of the oldest human professions. Land chosen for this usage is typically among the least productive biologically; arid and semi-arid rangelands are often too marginal for AGRICULTURE, FORESTRY or other commodity extraction uses. Grazing by livestock (primarily cattle, sheep and goats) is the most widespread ecological influence in many dryland ecosystems; for example, approximately 70% of western North America, including DESERTS, shrub-STEPPE, FORESTS and alpine TUNDRA, is grazed by livestock. [T.L.F.]

Greek alphabet

Upper case	Lower case	Name
A	α	Alpha
B	β	Beta
Γ	γ	Gamma
Δ	δ	Delta
E	ε	Epsilon
Z	ζ	Zeta
H	η	Eta
Θ	θ	Theta
I	ι	Iota
K	κ	Kappa
Λ	λ	Lambda
M	μ	Mu
N	ν	Nu
Ξ	ξ	Xi
O	ο	Omicron
Π	π	Pi
P	ρ	Rho
Σ	σ	Sigma
T	τ	Tau
Y	υ	Upsilon
Φ	φ	Phi
X	χ	Chi
Ψ	ψ	Psi
Ω	ω	Omega

Green Alliance An independent, non-profit-making organization in the UK which aims to raise the prominence of the environment on the agendas of all key policy-making institutions. *See also* ENVIRONMENTAL PRESSURE (LOBBY) GROUPS. [P.C.]

green consumerism The use of criteria relating to ENVIRONMENTAL IMPACTS in making choices about the purchase of goods. It emerged as an important instrument in the 1980s. *See also* ECOLABEL. [P.C.]

green funds Money invested in the financial markets not only on the basis of potential financial returns but also on the basis of the environmental (more generally ethical) credentials of companies. These investment products can cover unit trusts, pension funds, personal equity plans (PEPs), investment trusts and venture capital funds. Like other shares, green shares are best bought during bear markets, but there is evidence that they tend to outperform in bull markets and underperform in bear markets (possibly because markets tend to sell off high-grade stock in times of uncertainty), and seem to be attractive for investors interested in long-term capital gains. [P.C.]

green logistics Logistics is the spatial or geographical aspect of the flows of materials and products from manufacturers to markets and vice versa. Green logistics refers to devising distribution systems that minimize ENVIRONMENTAL IMPACT. A major cri-terion is to maximize distribution for minimum fuel use, using integrated strategies. [P.C.]

green marketing The use of good environmental features of a product to promote its sales. *See also* MARKET INSTRUMENTS. [P.C.]

green net national product (gNNP) Gross domestic product (GDP) is a measure of economic activity in a country. It is arrived at by adding the total value of a country's annual output of goods and services = private consumption + change in building-stock + investment + government expenditure + (exports − imports). The gross national product (GNP) is GDP plus residents' incomes from economic activity abroad and property held abroad minus the corresponding incomes of non-residents in the country. Some argue that these indices of economic well-being are at odds with environmental well-being because what GNP measures is a result of the consumption of natural resources, natural capital, and this may bring short-term gains but only at the expense of long-term prospects; it is not sustainable. GDP and GNP are not good indicators of a sustainable economy. They require also to take into account losses of natural capital to give a green net national product. [P.C.]

green tourism Tourism is travelling for pleasure. It is one of the world's largest businesses; for example, in Europe it accounts for *c.* 5% of gross domestic product (GDP) overall, *c.* 5% of export earnings and *c.* 6% of total jobs, with obvious centres such as the Mediterranean Basin. The impact on the environment thus results from travel to and from countries, and from activities that cause physical damage to sites and create wastes; this impact can be enormous. Green tourism, also referred to as 'sustainable tourism' (and, sometimes, 'ecotourism', although this can sometimes mean travel to view ecologically interesting sites), is a recognition of the problem and strives to ameliorate or reduce the impact.

Such action could include:
• development of international and national management plans for centres;
• staggering of holidays;
• practical guides for the industry and for the tourists themselves;
• development of codes of conduct.

This is not just altruism on the part of the industry or the tourist centres: degradation of the environment can itself destroy the business and lead to the search for undisturbed centres, so spreading the problem. [P.C.]

green trusts *See* ETHICAL INVESTMENT.

greenhouse effect *See* GREENHOUSE GASES.

greenhouse gases Gases that contribute to GLOBAL WARMING by absorbing long-wave energy emitted from the Earth's surface—the so-called 'greenhouse effect'. The most widely discussed greenhouse gases are CARBON DIOXIDE (CO_2), METHANE (CH_4), nitrous oxide (N_2O) and the various CFCs, all of which have increased in the last hundred years or so as a result of human activities. WATER vapour is also a greenhouse gas, though often overlooked, and so is OZONE. These gases differ enormously in their effectiveness as greenhouse gases, and various methods have been devised to express this effectiveness, based upon spectroscopic data. The relative molecular forcing is the effectiveness per molecule of the gas, relative to the effectiveness of CO_2. A more useful index is the global warming potential (GWP), which takes into account the fact that some TRACE GASES persist for longer periods in the ATMOSPHERE than others. GWP is the warming that would result from the instantaneous release of 1 kg of the gas relative to that from the simultaneous release of 1 kg CO_2, integrated over a stated period of time (Table G2).

Although CO_2 is a relatively weak greenhouse gas per molecule or per unit mass, the total EMISSIONS of CO_2 from fossil-fuel burning and DEFORESTATION far exceed those of the other gases, and so the calculated warming resulting from one year's emissions, integrated over 100 years, shows CO_2 to be dominant (Table G3). [J.G.]

Green(s) A term usually used to describe those associated with green (environmental/ecological) political parties or groups (*see* ECOPOLITICS), but it may be used more broadly to describe anyone who embraces ENVIRONMENTALISM. [P.C.]

Greenwich mean time (GMT) *See* TIME.

Grey List A list of potentially hazardous chemicals drawn up under EC Framework Directive 76/464/EEC. Formally known as List II. [P.C.]

Table G2 The global warming potentials (GWPs) of greenhouse gases, integrated over 20, 100 and 500 years, and the approximate lifetimes.

Gas	Lifetime (years)	GWP_{20}	GWP_{100}	GWP_{500}
CO_2	10	1	1	1
CH_4	10	63	21	9
N_2O	150	270	290	190
CFC-11	60	4500	3500	1500
CFC-12	130	7100	7300	4500

Table G3 Estimated contributions made to global warming by the main greenhouse gases, given the current rate of emissions, calculated from the global warming potentials with a 100-year integration time. (Tg = 10^{12} g.)

Gas	Current man-made emissions (Tg year^{-1})	Contribution to warming as a percentage of total warming
CO_2	26000	61
CH_4	300	15
N_2O	6	4
CFC-11	0.3	2
CFC-12	0.4	7

grey literature Literature not generally available through normal bookselling channels, and so difficult to identify and obtain. It includes reports, technical notes and specifications, conference proceedings, proposals, supplementary publications, data compilations, etc. A considerable amount of environmental information is conveyed in this way. Publications issued by pressure groups are often of this kind. Often grey literature does not have an international standard book number (ISBN) or an international standard serial number (ISSN). [P.C.]

gross primary production (GPP) The process of energy, matter or carbon accumulation by the AUTOTROPHS in a community. Its rate, gross primary productivity (P_g or G), equals the sum of net primary productivity and RESPIRATION by the autotrophs. Essentially, gross primary productivity by plants, or other photoautotrophs, represents the rate of total transformation of light energy into chemical energy. In practice, it is estimated for terrestrial plants by correcting net primary productivity with estimates of respiratory losses, most commonly determined from the rate of CARBON DIOXIDE (CO_2) emission in darkness and the assumption that the rate during daylight hours will equal that during the dark. In PHYTOPLANKTON, gross primary productivity may be estimated by feeding $^{14}CO_2$ or $H^{14}CO_3^-$ over a short time period so that the radioactive label is assimilated in PHOTOSYNTHESIS, but does not have sufficient time to enter pools of respiratory substrates. [S.P.L.]

groundwater *See* HYDROGEOLOGY.

groundwater pollution CONTAMINATION of groundwater to an extent that is likely to cause HARM to human health (if the groundwater is used as source of drinking water) and the environment. *See also* POLLUTION. [P.C.]

Groundwork Trust An organization that assists people from all sectors in the UK to improve their local environment through partnerships that involve business, local government and voluntary organizations. [P.C.]

growth The net increase in size or mass of an organism. [V.F.]

guidelines Usually, documents that supplement legislation. Thus the European Commission produces technical guidance documents that facilitate interpretation of RISK ASSESSMENT and management procedures for existing and new substances; the OECD produces guidelines on how to carry out ecotoxicological tests; and the USEPA produces guidelines on risk assessment. Guidelines do not normally have the same legal force as legislation. [P.C.]

Gulf Stream The clockwise OCEAN current carrying warm water from the Gulf of Mexico across the Atlantic to the British Isles and Scandinavia. The Gulf Stream separates the relatively warm, saline water of the Sargasso Sea from the colder, fresher waters near the coast of North America. It is the dominant GYRE in the North Atlantic and transports between 75 and 115 million m³s⁻¹ of seawater northwards, extending down to the sea floor in most regions. Maximum velocities in the main axis reach 4–5 knots. The Gulf Stream consists of three segments.

1 The Florida Current, which flows between Cuba and Florida. It has an average speed of 5 km h⁻¹ and carries 20–40 million m³s⁻¹.

2 The Gulf Stream proper, which reaches its greatest volume off Chesapeake Bay, equal to 70 million m³s⁻¹, varies in width between 50 and 150 km (averaging 80 km) and travels at a speed of 5–12 km h⁻¹ with an average depth of 500 m.

3 The North Atlantic Current, which represents the north-eastern Gulf Stream and is slower and less definite. It brings warm water as far north as the NORWEGIAN SEA and ARCTIC, and has a significant influence on the CLIMATE of the British Isles and Scandinavia.

[V.F.]

guyot A flat-topped submerged mountain that is an extinct volcano. In the past, guyots stood above sea level, but were truncated by waves and have sunk to various depths. [V.F.]

gymnosperms, global diversity and conservation The gymnosperms are an ancient group of seed-producing trees whose origins go back at least to the Late Devonian some 400 million years ago. (In contrast the flowering plants, or angiosperms, only appear in the fossil record around 130 million years ago; *see* ANGIOSPERMS, GLOBAL DIVERSITY AND CONSERVATION.) The distinction between the gymnosperms and angiosperms lies in the reproductive organs and fertilization processes. In the gymnosperms the seeds are naked (covered only by an often paper-thin integument) and borne on a megasporophyll (the cone) which does not entirely enclose the developing seeds (gymno- derives from the Greek γυμνος, naked). In angiosperms (angio-, αγγειον, vessel) the megasporophyll (the carpel) entirely surrounds the seed. Unlike angiosperms, double fertilization does not occur in gymnosperms thus no true endosperm is formed. The structure of gymnosperm wood is also distinctly different from angiosperms, the gymnosperm water-conducting xylem is composed only of tracheids (though vessels are present in the Gnetales) and the phloem lacks companion cells.

Gymnosperms were particularly abundant in the Carboniferous period and are a significant component of coal deposits. By the Jurassic period, around 200 million years ago, they had reached their greatest DIVERSITY and their most widespread, almost global, distribution. Their history thereafter has been one of geographical retreat and MASS EXTINCTIONS.

Some 600 species are all that remains of a once globally dominant group; these present-day species include the pines, cypresses, cedars, junipers, spruces, firs, larches and yews, many of which are immensely valuable for their timber and other products. A few conifers attain remarkable sizes and ages; specimens of *Sequoia sempervirens* may exceed 100 m in height and have over 2000 growth rings, while 5000-year-old examples of *Pinus longaeva* are known. Most conifers are trees, but a small number are bushy and a few (Australasian) species form heather-like shrubs.

What we see today is a once widespread, even ecologically dominant ancient order undergoing a prolonged evolutionary decline, if not into extinction then at least into evolutionary obscurity. A considerable effort has been made, particularly in the last two decades, to undertake a comprehensive programme of conservation of gymnosperms. In part this has been stimulated by the pharmaceutical value of gymnosperm products, such as taxol (used in cancer treatment) and ephedrine (used in treating respiratory disorders), but also because of the all too visible effecs of logging, particularly in North America. [G.A.F.H.]

gyre A circular or spiral form, usually applied to a very large semi-closed current system, in an open ocean BASIN. The major ocean gyres are centred in SUBTROPICAL high-pressure regions (i.e. 30°N and 30°S). The gyres circulate clockwise in the North Atlantic and North Pacific Oceans and counterclockwise in the South Atlantic, South Pacific and Indian Oceans. [V.F.]

H

habit

1 The regular performance of a particular activity acquired by an animal as a result of learning. In contrast to a conditioned reflex a habit does not require an external stimulus.

2 The characteristic form or mode of growth of an animal or plant. [P.O.]

habitat The ecological term 'habitat' refers to a place where a species normally lives, often described in terms of physical features such as TOPOGRAPHY and SOIL moisture and by associated dominant forms (e.g. intertidal rock pools or mesquite woodland). [S.K.J. & P.C.]

habitat destruction and alteration, global HABITAT destruction is probably the most important cause of BIODIVERSITY loss. The world's habitats have been so significantly modified by humans that very few can be considered not to bear the mark of human action. Some estimates suggest that more than 70% of the Earth's land surface, other than rock, ice and barren land, is either dominated by human action or at least partially disturbed. Even that which is considered 'undisturbed' is probably subject to some impact.

These anthropogenic impacts take two main forms:

1 conversion of one habitat type to another (e.g. for AGRICULTURE or for dwellings);

2 modification of conditions within a habitat (e.g. managing natural FORESTS).

Habitat loss is, therefore, a major cause of biodiversity loss, though surprisingly little information is available on the extent of habitat loss worldwide. [P.C.]

habitat structure The term HABITAT structure, or 'architecture', refers to the physical structure of the ENVIRONMENT that individuals inhabit. [S.J.H.]

hadal Of, or pertaining to the biogeographic region of the deep OCEAN. The hadal zone lies directly below the ABYSSAL zone and encompasses all marine habitat below about 6000 m. [S.J.H.]

halocarbons Chemical compounds of carbon and one or more halogens (fluorine, chlorine, bromine, iodine). The term usually refers to small molecules which are gases or liquids at normal temperatures and pressures. They are widely used as solvents, dry-cleaning and degreasing agents. Although CFCs are non-toxic, other halocarbons are cumulative TOXINS (e.g. carbon tetrachloride, chloroform). Methyl bromide is used agriculturally as a seed fumigant. Concern over the effects of chlorine and bromine on OZONE concentrations in the stratosphere, and over the role of halocarbons as GREENHOUSE GASES, has led to international controls on their production and use, defined by the MONTREAL PROTOCOL. [J.N.C.]

haptobenthos *See* BENTHIC HABITAT CLASSIFICATION; WITHIN-STREAM/RIVER HABITAT CLASSIFICATION.

hard substrata Those substrata that present a surface to which an organism must attach or into which it must bore. [V.F.]

harm An adverse EFFECT on individuals or an ecological system (populations, communities, ecosystems). For individuals, the adverse effects are judged in terms of probability of dying, health, development, growth, reproduction, etc. For populations, adverse effects are judged in terms of reduction in density over time. For communities and ecosystems, adverse effects are judged in terms of diversity, energy and matter processing. Often specified in the aim in ENVIRONMENTAL LAW, but rarely defined very precisely. [P.C.]

harmonic mean The reciprocal of the MEAN of reciprocals. The formula for calculating the harmonic mean (H) is:

$$\frac{1}{H} = \frac{1}{n} \sum \frac{1}{x}$$

where x is each observation in the SAMPLE, n is the number of observations in the sample, and the Greek symbol Σ (capital sigma) is the mathematical notation for 'sum of'. *Cf.* GEOMETRIC MEAN. *See also* STATISTICS. [B.S.]

harmonized electronic dataset (HEDSET) A system for collecting information on chemicals, under the EXISTING CHEMICALS legislation of the European Union. [P.C.]

harvest method A technique for measuring productivity, usually the net primary productivity of herbaceous terrestrial vegetation, for example, grasslands. Sample areas are selected, normally by a randomized block sampling design, and harvested at intervals through the growing season. Harvests are made by clipping the vegetation to ground level. BIOMASS (B) in the harvested material is separated from the dead material (D), and DRY MASS determined. The technique is most suited to annual crops and wild annuals. [S.P.L.]

harvesting The exploitation of a renewable natural resource, including FORESTRY, fisheries, game ranching and AGRICULTURE, although in agriculture a large number of other factors enter into the assessment of the process. [J.B.]

hazard A measure of the potential of a substance or process to cause HARM to human health and the environment. As far as chemicals are concerned, hazards are assessed from results of TOXICITY and ECOTOXICITY tests. This is sometimes referred to as HAZARD IDENTIFICATION. Cf. risk (*see* RISK ASSESSMENT). *See also* ECOTOXICOLOGY. [P.C.]

hazard identification Assessment of potential to cause HARM from results of TOXICITY and/or ECOTOXICITY tests. *See also* HAZARD. [P.C.]

hazardous substance A substance that, due to its intrinsic properties, has the potential to cause HARM to human health and ecological systems given appropriate circumstances. *See also* HAZARD IDENTIFICATION. [P.C.]

hazardous waste *See* WASTE.

heat-shock protein (hsp) Any of a subset of stress proteins, induced in what was originally referred to as a heat-shock response—because it occurred in response to exposure to elevated temperatures—but is now known to be induced by a variety of stressors; these include: HEAVY METALS; XENOBIOTICS; ANOXIA; SALINITY; and teratogens. Most are referred to by their apparent relative molecular mass on polyacrylamide gels, for example hsp 90, hsp 70, hsp 58. They are used as BIOMARKERS of STRESS. *See also* METALLOTHIONEINS; MIXED-FUNCTION OXIDASE. [P.C.]

heathland This term is generally used to denote areas of land dominated by dwarf shrubs, usually of the family Ericaceae. Traditionally, it has been applied to the lowland regions of western Europe in which the heather, *Calluna vulgaris*, is the dominant plant, but its use has extended to related habitats of acidic soil and low vegetation; thus terms such as grass-heath and lichen-heath have evolved. The similar physiognomy, and sometimes shared species, of some Mediterranean vegetation types has led to the application of the term heath to these regions also. [P.D.M.]

heavy-metal pollution CONTAMINATION by substances described as HEAVY METALS to an extent that HARM is caused to human health and/or ecological systems. The term 'heavy metal' has been used loosely in this context. *See also* TRIBUTYLTIN (TBT) POLLUTION. [P.C.]

heavy metals A widely used but rather poorly defined term commonly adopted for the metals associated with environmental POLLUTION. It is often incorrectly taken to be synonymous with 'toxic metals' (such as the biologically non-essential metals LEAD (Pb), cadmium (Cd) and MERCURY (Hg)) and, even less satisfactorily, with 'trace metals' (i.e. metals present at concentrations of less than $100\,mg\,kg^{-1}$ in the Earth's CRUST, which include those, such as zinc and copper, that are biologically essential).

One definition of the term 'heavy metals' is that it covers the block of elements in the PERIODIC TABLE bounded at its corners by titanium (Ti, period 4, group 4), hafnium (Hf, period 6, group 4), arsenic (As, period 4, group 15) and bismuth (Bi, period 6, group 15), with relative densities (the loose origin of the term) ranging from $4.5\,g\,cm^{-3}$ for titanium to $22.5\,g\,cm^{-3}$ for osmium. This enables the inclusion of environmentally and toxicologically important metalloids like arsenic and selenium, and excludes metals which are certainly not 'heavy', on the basis of relative density, like aluminium and beryllium, but are associated with toxic effects. The major drawback of the term 'heavy metals', however, is that it encompasses a heterogeneous array of elements with diverse chemical and biological properties.

It is particularly important to distinguish those elements which are unequivocally essential, and can give rise to deficiency problems, in animals (including, most probably, humans)—for example cobalt (Co), chromium (Cr), copper (Cu), iron (Fe), manganese (Mn), selenium (Se) and zinc (Zn)—and plants—for example Cu, Fe, Mn, molybdenum (Mo) and Zn—from those which are non-essential—for example cadmium, mercury and lead. All elements are potentially toxic in high concentrations, although additional major controlling factors of TOXICITY (and benefit) are duration of EXPOSURE, chemical form, route of absorption, synergism or antagonism of other agents, and biological individuality.

The most important anthropogenic releases of heavy metals to air, water and soils are from mining, agriculture, fossil-fuel combustion, metallurgical, electronic and chemical industries, and WASTE DISPOSAL. [J.G.F.]

hedgerow A row of shrubs and saplings forming a boundary or barrier; a type of managed natural fencing. Hedgerows act as harbours for natural vegetation and animal life. They have been subject to widespread destruction as a consequence of the mechanization of AGRICULTURE—leading to ecological impoverishment of the English countryside. [P.C.]

HEDSET *See* HARMONIZED ELECTRONIC DATASET.

Her Majesty's Industrial Pollution Inspectorate (HMIPI) *See* ENVIRONMENTAL (PROTECTION) AGENCIES.

Her Majesty's Inspectorate of Pollution (HMIP) *See* ENVIRONMENTAL (PROTECTION) AGENCIES.

herbaria Collections of dried, pressed plants, mounted on sheets, labelled and stored for reference. [A.J.W.]

herbicide A BIOCIDE that kills weeds, i.e. unwanted plants. Herbicides can operate selectively or non-selectively. They are sometimes known as DEFO-LIANTS. [P.C.]

heterotroph An organism requiring a supply of organic material from its ENVIRONMENT as food. [M.H.]

hibernation A state of greatly reduced metabolic activity employed by certain mammals as a way of surviving adverse winter conditions. [P.C.]

HMIP (Her Majesty's Inspectorate of Pollution) *See* ENVIRONMENTAL (PROTECTION) AGENCIES.

HMIPI (Her Majesty's Industrial Pollution Inspectorate) *See* ENVIRONMENTAL (PROTECTION) AGENCIES.

home range Individuals of most animal species spend their lives within a circumscribed area which can be thought of as their home range. Home range has a temporal as well as a spatial dimension, often changing on a seasonal basis (some migratory species inhabit different geographical regions at different times of year) or with shifts in resource distribution. [C.J.B.]

homeorhesis The maintenance of a pattern of change—as in development—despite environmental disturbances. It is equivalent to HOMEOSTASIS but is concerned with a dynamic rather than a static condition. [P.C.]

homeostasis The tendency of a system (organism, POPULATION, COMMUNITY or ECOSYSTEM) to change its properties in a way that minimizes the impact of outside factors. Homeostasis is shown at the level of the community or ecosystem where early-successional plants quickly restore the canopy COVER in gaps caused by DISTURBANCE ('scab-formers') and minimize potentially degenerative effects such as soil erosion. *See also* GAIA. [P.J.G.]

homing The ability of some animals to navigate over long distances to find their way back to a home area (e.g. a nest or breeding site). [R.H.S.]

horizontal resistance *See* MULTIPLE RESISTANCE TO PESTICIDES.

hormesis Phenomenon in which benefits (e.g. to survival, growth, reproduction) appear to be derived from EXPOSURE to small doses/concentrations of substances that are toxic at larger dose/concentrations. [P.C.]

host A living organism that acts as a 'medium' for the growth and development of another organism. [R.C.]

humic acid A general term for a wide variety of organic compounds resulting from DECOMPOSITION of vegetable material. Such compounds impart acidity and a dark coloration to waters containing them. [P.C.]

humidity The WATER content of the air, expressed as a partial pressure, concentration, or percentage saturation. [J.G.]

humification The microbial DECOMPOSITION of organic matter in soil involves the progressive breakdown of complex molecules into simpler, more soluble ones. HUMIC ACID is a component of these

breakdown products and its production is termed humification. [P.D.M.]

humus The natural organic product of DECOMPOSITION of plant material in the SOIL. It is colloidal, composed largely of humic groups—aromatic structures, including polyphenols and polyquinones, which are the products of decomposition, synthesis and polymerization. The compounds vary in relative molecular mass from a few hundred to a few thousand, and are dark in colour. They are very resistant to attack ('recalcitrant') and they form a substantial stock of the world's soil carbon. Examples are fulvic acid, HUMIC ACID and humin. Humus also contains non-humic groups, such as polysaccharides from higher plants and polyuronides from microorganisms, that tend to stick soil particles together and give soil some of its structure.

Humus COLLOIDS are negatively charged (especially so at high pH) and usually constitute a large part of the soil's cation exchange capacity. [J.G.]

hydric Means wet. *Cf.* XERIC. [P.C.]

hydrocarbons An extremely large class of organic compounds composed of the elements carbon and hydrogen only. Hydrocarbons divide into three categories.

1 Aliphatic: open chains of carbon atoms, e.g. ethane (C_2H_6) and ethene (C_2H_4).

2 Cyclic: at least one closed ring of carbon atoms, e.g. cyclohexane (c-C_6H_{12}).

3 Aromatic: a special class of cyclic hydrocarbons specifically containing six-membered rings in which carbon bonds are intermediate between single and double bonds, e.g. benzene (C_6H_6).

Hydrocarbons up to C_4 are gases at ambient temperatures but liquid hydrocarbons from C_5 to C_{12} also have significant vapour pressures. The most widespread natural and anthropogenic hydrocarbons fall within these categories and, together with their many functional group derivations, are generically classified as VOLATILE ORGANIC COMPOUNDS (VOCs). The bulk of hydrocarbon release to the environment is through VOCs to the ATMOSPHERE.

An important class of hydrocarbons is POLYCYCLIC AROMATIC HYDROCARBONS (PAHs) consisting of fused benzene rings, for example naphthalene (two rings), anthracene and phenanthrene (three rings), pyrene and benz[a]anthracene (four rings) and benzo[a]pyrene (five rings). (*See also* PAH POLLUTION.)

Petroleum hydrocarbons constitute a major POLLUTANT to coastal marine systems and it is estimated that more than 3 Mt are discharged annually. The main sources are oil transportation, municipal and industrial wastes, and RUN-OFF. Natural sources (marine seeps and sediment erosion) comprise only a small component (0.25 Mt annually). Atmospheric deposition to the marine environment is similarly small (0.3 Mt annually), although evidence suggests this is increasing. The relative rates of hydrocarbon evaporation to atmosphere, dissolution and COLLOID formation, partitioning to suspended particulates, and microbial and photochemical degradation, all affect the FATE of aqueous hydrocarbon discharge. Degradation processes generally act more rapidly on lighter molecular mass components, while PAHs are more persistent.

The most flexible and discriminative technique for analysis of hydrocarbons is GAS CHROMATOGRAPHY coupled with flame ionization and/or mass spectrometric detection. Gaseous samples are concentrated on to a capillary column by trapping to an adsorbent and thermal desorption and liquid samples by solvent extraction or headspace analysis. Detection limits of ppt or lower are achieved. [M.C.G. & M.R.H.]

hydrodynamics A branch of fluid mechanics dealing with WATER in motion. The mathematical theory of the motion of ideal, inviscid fluids. [V.F.]

hydrogeology Hydrogeology is the study of WATER in the ground. It relates to both the saturated zone in the ground, in which all of the void space (porosity) is filled with water, and the unsaturated zone, in which the voids are only partially filled with water. The water is referred to as groundwater. Most groundwater is derived from PRECIPITATION directly as infiltration, or indirectly via a RUN-OFF mechanism, and therefore forms part of the hydrological cycle (*see* WATER (HYDROLOGICAL) CYCLE). When water infiltrates into the ground some will be taken up by plant use (evapotranspiration) and the remainder will flow to depth (recharge), through the unsaturated ground. Where significant recharge occurs the ground becomes saturated, a hydraulic head gradient is created, and under suitable topographical and geological conditions groundwater flow will occur. The groundwater will eventually DISCHARGE to a spring, a river, a lake, or the SEA, having moved through the ground via either a primary porosity (intergranular), or secondary porosity (fracture and/or fissure) route, or probably a combination of both. The movement or flow transmission through the ground is controlled by the resistance to flow in the ground, which reflects the porosity and is termed the hydraulic conductivity, and the hydraulic head that exists between recharge and discharge points. The flow is three-dimensional within area-limiting boundaries such as a river, a recharge mound divide, or a marked geological change. [J.W.L.]

hydrograph A graph of DISCHARGE (*y*-axis) against time (*x*-axis) in rivers and streams. Also FLUCTUATIONS of water levels with time in water. [P.C.]

hydrographics The arrangement and movement of bodies of WATER, such as CURRENTS and water masses. Hydrography is the science and art of studying, surveying and mapping SEAS, LAKES, RIVERS and other waters, including study of their physical features, TIDES, currents, etc. [V.F.]

hydrology The study of WATER, both the quantity and the chemicals and SEDIMENT which it carries, as it moves through the land phase of the hydrological cycle (*see* WATER (HYDROLOGICAL) CYCLE). [J.H.C.G.]

hydroponics The practice of growing plants without soil in which the roots are suspended in WATER or supported by inert material such as lava rock and covered in water. [R.M.M.C.]

hydrosphere The part of the Earth covered by liquid or frozen WATER. *See also* ATMOSPHERE; BIOSPHERE; LITHOSPHERE. [J.H.C.G.]

hydrothermal vent A place on the OCEAN bed, on or near to a mid-ocean ridge, from which water heated by molten rock issues. This is often rich in dissolved sulphides, which are oxidized by chemosynthetic bacteria in the fixation of CARBON DIOXIDE (CO_2) and synthesis of organic compounds. Near to the vents there are animal communities that utilize these compounds and may even live symbiotically with the bacteria. [P.C.]

hypolimnion *See* LAKE STRATIFICATION.

hyporheic *See* BENTHIC HABITAT CLASSIFICATION.

hyporheic fauna *See* WITHIN-STREAM/RIVER HABITAT CLASSIFICATION.

hyporheos *See* BENTHIC HABITAT CLASSIFICATION; WITHIN-STREAM/RIVER HABITAT CLASSIFICATION.

I

IBI *See* INDEX OF BIOTIC INTEGRITY.

IBP *See* INTERNATIONAL BIOLOGICAL PRO-GRAMME.

IC$_{50}$ Statistically derived concentration of a XENO-BIOTIC that inhibits some metabolic property (e.g. growth) in 50% of an observed population over a prescribed time in defined conditions. Also expressed in terms of dose, ID$_{50}$. *See also* EC$_{50}$; LC$_{50}$; MEDIAN TIMES TO EFFECT; PREDICTIVE ECO-TOXICITY TESTS. [P.C.]

ice The solid phase of WATER, stable at temperatures below 273.15 K at atmospheric pressure. It has the unusual property of being less dense than the liquid phase, a result of the open crystal structure caused by hydrogen bonding. The strength of the hydrogen bonds accounts for the abnormally high melting temperature, compared with that for the hydrides of heavier elements in the same group as OXYGEN. Only 2.3% of the Earth's water is in the solid form, but this accounts for 99% of the FRESH WATER. [A.J.]

ice ages *See* GLACIATION.

ice-core projects In some locations, the amount of snow that falls in an average year exceeds the amount of snow that melts in an average year. The snow that does not melt is compressed by subsequent snow fall and forms a layered sedimentary sequence of ICE, which contains PRECIPITATION and associated atmospheric particulates. Atmospheric gases are entrapped in the ice at a depth of 50–90 m when the pore spaces are sufficiently compressed that they are no longer interconnected, thus ceasing the exchange of gases. Specialized drilling equipment is used to recover individual ice cores, which are typically 5–20 cm in diameter and up to 6 m long. By recovering adjoining cores in a single hole, a continuous sampling of the ice is obtained. The chemical, physical and isotopic characteristics of the ice, particulates and gases are used to determine the environmental conditions when the material was entrapped in the ice. Ice-core records can have higher temporal resolution than other long palaeo-climate records, which permits investigation of rapid or short duration changes in CLIMATE.

Recent polar projects include the Vostok ice core from Antarctica, which has provided a 225 000-year record of atmospheric gases and temperature, and the companion GRIP (Greenland Ice core project) and GISP (Greenland Icesheet Project 2) projects in Greenland, which have provided a high temporal resolution record of the last 80 000 years. Ice cores have also been used to develop records for low-latitude high-elevation sites. Environmental records from ice cores have played a key role in enhancing our understanding of what the Earth's climate has been and what it might become. [K.C.T.]

ice sheets The largest bodies of ICE on the planet, sometimes covering entire continents. The term is generally applied to ice masses greater than 50 000 km^2 in extent. At present there are two ice sheets on the Earth, one in Greenland and the other in Antarctica. The latter is by far the largest, containing 30 million km^3 of ice, compared with a more modest 2.6 million km^3 in Greenland. If all this ice were to melt, global sea level would rise by 70 m. The thickest ice (4.8 km) is found in Antarctica, where the mass of the ice sheet depresses the underlying bedrock by up to 1 km. Parts of the Antarctic ice sheet rest on bedrock that would be up to 2 km below sea level even after removal of the ice load. These areas are regarded as being the most sensitive to environmental change. [A.J.]

icebergs Floating ICE calved from a glacier or ICE SHEET that terminates in the SEA or less commonly a lake. [A.J.]

ICM *See* INTEGRATED CATCHMENT MANAGEMENT.

IGBP (International Geosphere–Biosphere Programme) An international programme that coordinates research into BIOSPHERE dynamics with the stated goal 'to describe and understand the interactive physical, chemical and biological processes that regulate the total Earth system, the unique environment that it provides for life, the changes that are occurring in the system, and the manner in which they are influenced by human actions'. The IGBP was instituted by ICSU (International Council of Scientific Unions) in 1986 as an open-ended programme and the science plan of the programme as a whole was published in 1988. The IGBP secretariat is located at the Royal Swedish Academy of Sciences.

The programme comprises a set of linked 'core projects'. Each core project has a broadly similar structure with a staffed project office and with a science plan that divides the research into broad foci and specific activities. Ecology permeates the entire IGBP and is especially prominent in the Global Change and Terrestrial Ecosystems (GCTE) core project. GCTE's aim is to be able to predict effects of changes in CLIMATE and land use on terrestrial ecosystems and their feedbacks into the climate system. GCTE has four foci on ecosystem physiology, ecosystem structure, agriculture, forestry and soils, and ecological complexity.

In common with the other core projects GCTE does not fund research directly, but achieves its aims through facilitating meetings and identifying gaps. It engages the support of individual scientists who are nationally funded and who elect to contribute their research to the project.

In addition to the thematic core projects, IGBP has three cross-cutting 'framework' activities for data and information (DIS), global analysis (GAIM) and training and developing country involvement (START). Close ties are maintained with the World Climate Research Programme and the Human Dimensions of Global Environment Change Programme. Starting in 1995 a system of transects has been developed, initially five in number and around 1000 km long. Study sites are to be located along the gradients, which will serve the needs of several core and cross-cutting projects. [M.B.]

ILO (International Labour Organization) See UNITED NATIONS PROGRAMMES AND BODIES.

IMO (International Maritime Organization) See UNITED NATIONS PROGRAMMES AND BODIES.

imposex Imposition of male sexual organs on the female. Can occur in marine gastropods as a result of POLLUTION from tributyltin contained in ANTIFOULING paints. [P.C.]

***in situ* bioassays** Biological monitors that are either planted out in the environment to be monitored or in close proximity such that continuous or semi-continuous samples can be taken from it. Thus fish fitted with appropriate sensors can be caged and immersed in the habitat to be monitored or they can be housed in tanks on the bank through which water from the habitat to be monitored is run. [P.C.]

***in situ* genetic reserves** Contemporary (and much favoured) practices in the conservation of genetic resources include the protection and management of animals and plants in their natural habitats (*in situ* reserves) as opposed to protection in zoos and botanic gardens (*see EX SITU* GENETIC RESERVES), often far removed from the natural habitats.

In situ conservation of plants through control of land use, with or without the status of reserve, is an important aspect of plant conservation practices. However, the effectiveness of these controlled areas varies considerably even between neighbouring countries. In Poland, over 90% of threatened plant species are present in reserves. In the UK, the figure is about 75% but in southern Europe declines to less than 20%. In Norway, until recently, the figure was even lower. In the UK, as elsewhere, *in situ* conservation is often most effective in areas of little value to agriculture and forestry (e.g. mountain tops, tidal marshes). [G.A.F.H.]

incineration The controlled burning of usually solid, but sometimes liquid or gaseous, combustive wastes to produce gases and solid residues containing little or no combustible materials. Burning solids has four distinct objectives:

1 volume reduction (depending upon composition, volume reductions can be >90% and mass reductions >70%);

2 stabilization, for example incinerated output (ash) is considerably more inert than the input of mixed municipal solid WASTE;

3 recovery of energy; and

4 sanitation.

The key factors for high levels of combustion and destruction of organics are TEMPERATURE (high), RESIDENCE TIME (long) and TURBULENCE (high). The majority of municipal solid waste incinerators have a furnace with a moving grate design. The moving grate keeps waste moving through the furnace. Primary air for combustion is pumped through the grate; secondary air is introduced over the fire to ensure good combustion in the gas phase (e.g. of DIOXINS). Alternative designs are fluidized bed incinerators. The combustion chamber contains a fluidized bed, created by air forced through a bed of inert material such as sand. This hot fluidized bed ensures a high level of combustion and benefits from having no moving parts. Emissions need to be cleaned (dust filtered; acid gases removed; NO_x gases removed; dioxins removed by maintaining high temperatures). The bottom ash is cooled, usually exposed to a magnet to recover ferrous metal, and then disposed of together with the FLY ASH and residues from gas cleaning. Bottom ash is usually dumped in LANDFILLS. [P.C.]

index of biotic integrity (IBI) Attempt to quantify divergences from 'normality' in ECOSYSTEMS (ecosystem harm/disturbances) by measuring a number of attributes of populations and species, in particular: fish and/or macroinvertebrate SPECIES RICHNESS; ratios of native versus non-native species; trophic composition; overall ABUNDANCE and condition. Relatively disturbed sites are compared with IBIs from undisturbed sites in the region. Though multifactorial, this index suffers from similar problems to other BIOTIC INDICES. [P.C.]

indicator species This can be used as a general term to indicate species that may be indicative of a COMMUNITY or set of environmental conditions or, very precisely, to refer to species objectively defined as indicators of a phytosociological class, for example sea pink (*Armeria maritima*) for sea cliffs, salad burnet (*Sanguisorba minor*) for chalk grassland and bluebell (*Hyacinthoides non-scriptus*) for oceanic oak woods. The former approach is widely encountered in many areas of biology and is then based on the experience of the person talking or writing or their collective field experience. In the more objective case, the indicator species are derived by some statistical or multivariate technique to specially derive such groupings.

Presence of tolerant species or absence of sensitive species can signal environmental STRESS from natural or human causes. There are two potential problems with this approach.

1 Specificity: organisms that are sensitive/tolerant to one stressor may not respond similarly to others so their presence/absence may not provide an indication of stress.

2 Generality: organisms showing general sensitivity/TOLERANCE do not give sufficiently precise information about environmental conditions.

[F.B.G. & P.C.]

industrial ecosystem Designing industrial operations on the basis of natural ecosystems; resources are shared and WASTE recycled, for example spare heat from one factory is sold or bartered with another. Important features of industrial ecosystems are:
- compatibility with natural systems;
- maximum internal REUSE of materials and energy;
- selection of processes with reusable waste;
- extensive interconnection among companies and industries;
- sustainable rates of natural resource use;
- waste intensity matched to natural process cycle capacity.

[P.C.]

industrial melanism Many animals, especially insects, have melanic or black colour forms. Industrial MELANISM is a term used to describe the situation in which there is a correlation between the frequency of these forms within populations of a species and some measure of the level of AIR POLLUTION or industrial development. [P.M.B.]

infochemicals The involvement of chemicals in conveying information in intraspecific and interspecific interactions between organisms is widespread. Examples can be found in interactions among and between vertebrates, invertebrates, plants and microorganisms in the same or different trophic levels.

Infochemicals can be further classified according to the interaction they mediate. Two criteria are important: (i) whether the interaction mediated by the infochemical is between two individuals from the same species (pheromones) or (ii) between individuals from different species (allelochemicals). In both cases, three subclasses can be distinguished, depending on whether the emitter, the receiver or both benefit from the infochemical (Table I1). [M.D.]

infrared gas analyser (IRGA) Infrared gas analysers measure the density (moles per unit volume) of gas components such as CARBON DIOXIDE (CO_2) and WATER vapour. Heteroatomic gases absorb RADIATION in characteristic wavebands, particularly in the infrared region of the spectrum. Infrared gas analysers for CO_2 are routinely used in biological applications to measure rates of PHOTOSYNTHESIS

Table I1 Definitions of infochemical classes.

Infochemical
A chemical that, in the natural context, conveys information in an interaction between two individuals, evoking in the receiver a behavioural or physiological response

Pheromone
An infochemical that is pertinent to the biology of an organism (1) and that evokes in a receiving organism of the *same* species (organism 2) a behavioural response that is adaptively favourable to:
  organism 1 but not to organism 2: (+,–) pheromone
  organism 2 but not to organism 1: (–,+) pheromone
  organism 1 and 2: (+,+) pheromone

Allelochemical
An infochemical that is pertinent to the biology of an organism (1) and that evokes in a receiving organism of a *different* species (organism 2) a behavioural response that is adaptively favourable to:
  organism 1 but not to organism 2: allomone
  organism 2 but not to organism 1: kairomone
  organism 1 and 2: synomone

---

and RESPIRATION; infrared analysers for water vapour are used to estimate TRANSPIRATION rates of plants. Rapid-response CO_2 and water vapour infrared gas analysers are used as part of eddy covariance systems used to estimate FLUXES of CO_2 and water vapour above communities of vegetation. Industrial applications of infrared gas analysers for process control and environmental monitoring cover a wide range of gases including HYDROCARBONS. Analysers are designed to measure the density of gas either on an absolute scale or as a differential relative to a reference gas of known composition.

Infrared gas analysers are designed as either dispersive (DIR) or non-dispersive (NDIR) instruments. DIR analysers are based around a gas cell in the optical path of a scanning spectrometer, allowing determination of the composition of complex gas mixtures. NDIR analysers measure the transmission of broad-band infrared radiation through an optical cell. NDIR measurements are made specific for one or two selected gases using a combination of optical filters and/or gas-filled detectors, although all NDIR analysers retain some degree of cross-sensitivity between interfering gases such as CO_2 and water vapour. NDIR analysers are used in most ecological applications since they tend to be more robust and can be made field portable. DIR analysers are reserved for analytical applications where their cost, larger size and complexity are considered acceptable. [P.R.V.G.]

insecticides The problem of insect pests has an ancient history, with classical Greek, Roman and biblical references. Until 1939 the insecticides available were often very poisonous, such as arsenic and nicotine; safer natural products such as derris and pyrethrum, which were difficult to produce in quantity, lacked persistency and potency and were not stable in light. The discovery of the insecticidal properties of DDT in 1939 was revolutionary, changing the view of researchers that such useful and apparently safer materials could be synthesized on a large scale. DDT was welcomed as a major breakthrough that saved millions of lives by preserving food CROPS and stocks and protecting humans and livestock from parasites and disease-carrying insects. Since that discovery, a very large range of insecticides have been found, mostly within a few main classes of compounds: organophosphates (*see* ORGANOPHOSPHORUS PESTICIDES), ORGANOCHLORINES (including DDT), carbamates and pyrethroids; other groups include organotins, acylureas, formamides and growth regulators (including pheromone attractants).

The TOXICITY of insecticides to other animal life has always been of concern, but particularly attracted attention in the 1960s with the publication of *Silent Spring* by Rachel Carson. It became evident that although a number of insecticides were immediately highly toxic, others were less directly toxic but accumulated in the environment, while yet others, notably some organophosphates and organochlorines, accumulated in animal fats and thus were concentrated in higher levels of organism in the FOOD CHAIN.

Such concerns have led to the withdrawal or banning of a number of compounds in all or some sectors of the market, and there is increased emphasis on discovering analogues and new chemical groups of greater selectivity. For example, the synthetic pyrethroids, first introduced in 1976, have rapidly made an impact as more selective insecticides with reduced environmental PERSISTENCE, although they are not as effective soil-acting materials as members of the other chemical groups; however, more recent analogues are showing greater soil activity.

The non-agricultural uses of insecticides may be as important as the agricultural uses. They are important not only in human health, helping to control diseases such as malaria, sleeping sickness, typhus and yellow fever that are carried by insect vectors, but also in the preservation of organic materials, such as wood and clothing, from insect attack. [K.D.]

insects, diversity and conservation Insects eclipse all other forms of life by sheer numbers and DIVERSITY, constituting about three-quarters of all animal species. They belong to phylum Arthropoda and share the features of an exoskeleton composed of chitin and sclerotin, and appendages divided into segments separated by joints. Insects constitute class Insecta. They differ from all other arthropods by having three specialized body segments (head, thorax and abdomen), three pairs of appendages (six legs) on the thorax and a single pair of antennae on the head. Insects often have one or two pairs of wings on the thorax in addition to their legs.

The number of insect species described exceeds 750 000; a reasonable estimate of the total number is about 10 million. Being small has not only conferred success but also difficulty in being recognized. The huge gap between described and existing insect species imposes difficulties for insect conservation. Emphasis on discovery and description is the avenue of the future. The conservation of insects' incredible genetic diversity must overcome the traditional bias towards charismatic megavertebrates and against pests (only a few species of insects). It is essential to increase public recognition of insects' ecological services to society in terms of food supply, silk and wax production, medicine, POLLINATION, biocontrol, energy recycling and DECOMPOSITION, in addition to the awareness of nature's worth. [W.L.]

insolation Exposure to SOLAR RADIATION. [J.G.]

integrated catchment management (ICM) River management based on the understanding that a river system cannot be divided into stretches—there is a continuum of interaction throughout the system—and cannot be isolated from surrounding land. The quantity of water in a river is influenced by the surrounds (by RUN-OFF) and influences the surrounds (by flooding). Moreover, there is a continuum between riverwaters and lateral groundwaters. Thus management of WATER QUALITY has to be carried out in an integrated way, with all these factors in mind. Integrated CATCHMENT models try to capture this complexity and are used, for example, to simulate the input of run-off and its effects on water quality. [P.C.]

integrated conservation strategies Integrated conservation strategies are plans created to conserve species, particularly plants, using all available resources to meet a goal, such as species recovery. [E.O.G. & L.R.M.]

integrated environmental management Control of business operations to minimize ENVIRONMENTAL IMPACT by reference to the whole operation, including personnel, and the interactions within it. An alternative is to address isolated issues, such as 'bolting on' CLEAN-UP systems to the 'end of pipe'. An integrated approach, on the other hand, would involve managing the whole process, including the actions of personnel (e.g. through training) and even the design of the product to minimize WASTE and EMISSIONS. Integrated environmental management ought, therefore, to be more cost-effective in the long term, especially since it should also take account of the fact that business operations are complex integrated systems. [P.C.]

integrated pest management (integrated control) Use of different methods in combination to suppress

PEST populations below their economic THRESH-OLD. Techniques to be used are selected rationally with an emphasis on their economic and ENVIRON-MENTAL IMPACT. Most successful integrated pest management (IPM) schemes combine chemical and BIOLOGICAL CONTROL with additional methods. [J.S.B.]

integrated pollution control (IPC) It follows from the laws of thermodynamics and conservation of matter that substances removed from one WASTE stream are likely to turn up in others, albeit in transformed states. A consequence of this is that POLLUTION from one environmental compartment may be shifted to another; removing pollutants from chimney EMISSIONS may create solids that need disposal in LANDFILL or that leach into natural waters. An integrated approach to pollution control recognizes this and, while trying to remove emissions in the first place, attempts to find the optimum solution for dealing with unavoidable emissions. This is generally done with respect to principles of best (practicable) environmental options (B(P)EO) and best available technology (BAT). IPC is now a central feature of UK environmental pollution legislation since the ENVIRONMENTAL PROTECTION ACT 1990, but in Europe has its roots in an EC Council Directive (87/217/EEC) on the prevention and reduction of pollution by ASBESTOS, which requires emission for all environmental compartments to be taken into account. Integrated pollution prevention and control (IPPC) has now been adopted as a European Union measure (a Directive adopted in 1995). *See also* BEST AVAILABLE TECHNIQUES NOT ENTAILING EXCESSIVE COSTS; BEST AVAILABLE TECHNIQUES REFERENCE DOCUMENT; BEST PRACTICABLE ENVIRONMENTAL OPTION. [P.C.]

integrated pollution prevention and control (IPPC) *See* INTEGRATED POLLUTION CONTROL.

integrated waste management There is a variety of management options in terms of dealing with solid WASTE: source reduction, REUSE, RECYCLING, COMPOSTING, INCINERATION (possibly with energy recovery), LANDFILL. For complex waste, such as municipal solid waste, no one of these options may be suitable for all components. Thus integrated waste management refers to the complementary use of a variety of waste management options to optimize the overall result. [P.C.]

Intergovernmental Panel on Climate Change (IPCC) A group of scientists convened in 1988 to review and summarize the literature on CLIMATE CHANGE and present policy options. [J.G.]

International Biological Programme (IBP) One of the first attempts to study ecosystems on a world scale through international cooperation. It was initiated by the International Council of Scientific Unions and extended from 1964 to 1974, involving some 40 countries. The sections were: productivity of terrestrial communities, production processes on land and water, conservation of terrestrial communities, productivity of freshwater communities, productivity of marine communities, human adaptability and the use and management of biological resources. [J.G.]

International Code of Botanical Nomenclature The code is an agreed set of rules and recommendations that govern the scientific naming of plants and fungi. [M.I.]

International Code of Zoological Nomenclature (ICZN) These are the regulations governing the scientific naming of animals. They are drawn up and supervised by the International Commission on Zoological Nomenclature (ICZN). [P.C.]

international conservation conventions These are agreements that are concerned with the protection of species or natural areas involving two or more nations.
• Convention on International Trade in Endangered Species of Wild Fauna and Flora (CITES). Multilateral, signed in 1973. Designed to control commercial trade in species in danger of extinction.
• Convention on Wetlands of International Importance. Often referred to as Ramsar after the Iranian town in which it was formulated in 1971. It was the first multinational convention. It remains the only one that is concerned with protection of one general type of ecosystem.
• UN Convention on Biological Diversity. Adopted in 1992 at the Earth Summit (*see* RIO SUMMIT). Deals comprehensively with the protection of natural areas, species and genetic material for the purposes of global SUSTAINABLE DEVELOPMENT.
• Man and the Biosphere Programme (MAB). International, not legally binding, agreement with UNESCO (*see* UNITED NATIONS PROGRAMMES AND BODIES) with the aim of establishing an international network of reserves (BIOSPHERE RESERVES) for the purpose of studying human effects on natural systems.
[P.C.]

international environmental law *See* ENVIRONMENTAL LAW.

International Geosphere–Biosphere Programme *See* IGBP.

International Labour Organization (ILO) *See* UNITED NATIONS PROGRAMMES AND BODIES.

International Maritime Organization (IMO) *See* UNITED NATIONS PROGRAMMES AND BODIES.

International Monetary Fund *See* GATT AND ENVIRONMENT.

International Organization for Standardization (ISO) *See* BS 7750; ISO 14 000.

international organizations and programmes associated with environmental protection *See* UNITED NATIONS PROGRAMMES AND BODIES.

International Species Information System (ISIS) Organizes and facilitates sharing of basic information on animals in zoos and other facilities worldwide.

Involves more than 400 institutions in more than 50 countries and has a total inventory of >720 000 organisms. Developed microcomputer-based programs (VORTEX and SPARKS) for population management. [P.C.]

International Union for the Conservation of Nature and Nature Resources *See* IUCN.

International Whaling Commission (IWC) This body was set up shortly after the Second World War to regulate the WHALING industry. [J.B.]

interstitial The water-filled spaces between the individual particles that comprise aquatic sediments or terrestrial soils form the interstitial habitat, and interstitial organisms are those that can move between the particles without displacing them. [R.S.K.B.]

interstitial water *See* POREWATER.

intertidal zone The shoreward fringe of the seabed between the highest and lowest extent of the TIDES. The intertidal zone is characterized by widely varying physical conditions and, particularly on ROCKY SHORES, by vertical zonation of the dominant species. [V.F.]

intrinsic bioremediation Stated simply: selfpurification. This involves encouraging a system's own capacity to clean-up CONTAMINATION and POLLUTION. For example, soils often have the capacity to degrade organic CONTAMINANTS through the action of indigenous microbes, but rates might be enhanced by appropriate management. Thus toluene contamination of soils in industrial sites is subject to microbial degradation, but this can be enhanced by good aeration of the soil since the process appears to be aerobic. *See also* REMEDIATION. [P.C.]

intrinsic rate of increase The POPULATION GROWTH RATE, *r*. The intrinsic rate of increase is an instantaneous rate and represents the average rate of increase per individual (female) in a population, normally in the absence of crowding effects and shortage of resources; *r* is also known as the innate capacity for increase and may be calculated from age-specific birth and death rates. [R.H.S.]

introduction and reintroduction Introduction and reintroduction are emerging as important elements in conservation strategies for rare and ENDANGERED SPECIES. Although traditional conservation prescriptions rely primarily on preservation and management of naturally occurring populations in their native habitats, populations of many species have become so seriously affected by human activities as to require more direct intervention. However, in responsible hands introduction and reintroduction are always practised as elements of overall strategies based ultimately on the recovery and return to natural POPULATION DYNAMICS *in situ*.

The primary circumstance driving the need for introduction and reintroduction is the continued high rate of destruction of natural habitats worldwide. On every continent and in every major BIOME, the remaining inventory of unaltered native HABITAT dwindles with every passing year. Many species are declining in the number, size and distribution of populations as these major changes take place on the global landscape. Parks and other protected areas are becoming surrounded by anthropogenic landscapes and hence ecologically isolated from other components of their larger ECOSYSTEM. As a result, it can no longer be assumed that protected and other natural areas will be large or numerous enough, or distributed in the correct locations, to ensure the survival of all, or even a majority, of species on Earth. Introduction and reintroduction are among the measures that can be used when populations are reduced or extirpated from their native habitat under these circumstances. [D.A.F.]

ion An ion is formed from an atom by loss of one or more electrons making it positively charged (cation), or by gain of one or more electrons making it negatively charged (anion). [M.C.G.]

ionizing radiation Ionizing RADIATION is the name that is collectively applied to high-energy electromagnetic and particulate radiations that deposit their energy in matter mainly by interactions with electrons, resulting in ionization and breaking of chemical bonds. The energy of ionizing radiation is normally expressed in units of electron volts (eV), where $1\,eV = 1.6 \times 10^{-19}$ J. A number of types of ionizing radiation arise from radioactive decay of unstable nuclei, including α-radiation (particles of mass 4 amu (atomic mass unit) and charge +2, with energies normally in the range 4–9 MeV), β-radiation (β^--particles are electrons and β^+-particles are positrons, with energies normally in the range 10 keV to 4 MeV) and γ-radiation (photons of electromagnetic radiation with energies normally in the range 5 keV to 7 MeV). X-rays also constitute a form of ionizing radiation and can be produced by two distinct processes. 'Characteristic X-rays' are photons of electromagnetic radiation, with energies in the approximate range 1–150 keV, which originate from rearrangements of electrons in atoms following the creation of a vacancy in an inner shell. Such inner-shell vacancies are produced when accelerated electrons, or other types of radiation (e.g. γ-photons), interact with matter. The X-rays produced in this way have discrete energies that are characteristic of the atom from which they were emitted. Alternatively, X-rays known as bremsstrahlung can be produced by deceleration of an electron in the electromagnetic field of a nucleus. Bremsstrahlung energy spectra have a continuous distribution extending from the energy of the electron, which can be as high as 100 MeV, down to zero. Neutrons are not inherently ionizing but give rise to ionization as a secondary effect via neutron capture or other reactions with nuclei, resulting in the emission of ionizing radiation. Additional forms of ionizing radiation, such as protons, deuterons and other high-energy charged particles generally occur only in special experimental facilities and are not encountered in the environment.

Ionizing radiation presents a potential health hazard to living organisms as a result of bond breaking in biological tissue. Such effects are classed as: (i) somatic effects, which involve health detriment to the exposed individual; or (ii) genetic effects, which involve damage to the offspring of the exposed individual. Dose limits for exposure to radiation from industrial sources are recommended by the International Commission for Radiological Protection (ICRP) and the present limit for members of the general public is 1 mSv year^{-1}, while the limit for occupational exposure of workers is 5 mSv year^{-1}. [A.B.M.]

IPC *See* INTEGRATED POLLUTION CONTROL.

IPCC *See* INTERGOVERNMENTAL PANEL ON CLIMATE CHANGE.

IPPC (integrated pollution prevention and control) *See* INTEGRATED POLLUTION CONTROL.

IRGA *See* INFRARED GAS ANALYSER.

irrigation On a world scale plant growth is frequently limited by the supply of WATER, a fact known to early civilizations, who introduced irrigation to enhance agricultural production. Irrigation methods vary from place to place. Water can be stored using large dams to provide an essentially constant flow of water that is conveyed by canals, conduits and furrows to perennial CROPS, as in the case of the Aswan High Dam in Lake Nasser, Egypt. Irrigation in Israel utilizes water from Lake Kinneret (Sea of Galilee) and the coastal AQUIFER that feeds into a nationwide pressurized supply to sprinklers and drip systems covering much of the cultivated land area. In Saudia Arabia, 'fossil' water is pumped from great depths and sprayed on the land using single-centre pivot systems that provide highly productive circular fields on which is grown crops such as cereals and alfalfa. High-technology scheduling of irrigation, such as that used for high-value crops in California USA, depends on the sensing of the water requirement, based on data from a network of weather stations, and the computer control of pumps and valves to deliver the required quantity of water each day. Irrigation is not only used in dry climates; it is commonly used in the humid tropics to grow rice and in north-west Europe in dry summer periods and in DROUGHT years. [J.G.]

island biogeographic theory in conservation Island biogeographic theory (*see* ISLAND BIOGEOGRAPHY) has been adapted to the management of nature reserves, which are in effect islands located in oceans of ALIEN habitat. In theory, a single large nature reserve would conserve more species than a number of small ones of the same total area. Large nature reserves may also be needed to maintain viable populations of key species, such as predators. However, a number of small islands, spanning a range of habitat types, may in fact accommodate more species than a single large one and small islands may help contain the spread of EPIDEMICS. These considerations have led to the SLOSS (single large or several small) controversy. If the source area is lost then the DIVERSITY of nature reserves will dwindle, since immigration will not be able to counterbalance the inevitable extinctions. [A.E.M.]

island biogeography The theory of island biogeography was first proposed by Robert MacArthur and Edward Wilson in 1967. This is an equilibrium theory based on the observation that there is a constant relationship between the area of the world's islands and the number of species contained therein. The SPECIES RICHNESS of an island is the result of a balance between the rate of immigration of species to the island and the rate of extinction on the island. The resulting equilibrium is dynamic in so far as species are continually arriving and continually becoming extinct, though as time progresses the rates of arrival and extinction diminish. This theory involves a stochastic DYNAMIC EQUILIBRIUM that operates over long time-scales. It also considers island size and distance from the mainland. [A.M.M.]

ISO (International Standards Organization) *See* BS 7750; ISO 14000.

ISO 14000 The International Standards Organization (ISO) has developed a series of standards, under the designation ISO 14000, that establish a framework for businesses to manage the present and potential future effects of their operations and their products on the environment. The core is ISO 14001, which defines a model ENVIRONMENTAL MANAGEMENT SYSTEM (EMS). A specification of the elements of an EMS should be in place to manage environmental matters effectively. It provides a basis whereby a company's EMS can be reviewed by a third party and a determination made on COMPLIANCE. In the event of satisfactory compliance a registration is issued that states that the STANDARD has been met and this can be displayed by the company. However, the specification does not set a standard for what a company's performance should be. These only establish what management system should be in place for a company to meet its specified performance standards and improve upon them. ISO standards are voluntary and applicable to companies of all sizes. ISO 14001 is compatible with EMAS (ECO-MANAGEMENT AND AUDIT SCHEME). [P.C.]

isotope Atoms of the same element that differ in their MASS NUMBER are termed 'isotopes'. Isotopes may be stable or unstable. *See also* RADIOACTIVITY. [J.G.]

IUCN (International Union for the Conservation of Nature and Nature Resources) Now renamed the World Conservation Union, although it still goes by the abbreviation IUCN. Created in 1948, it is a multinational body that compiles lists of rare species and protected natural areas. It also provides advice/expertise to national governments. *See also* CONSERVATION BIOLOGY. [P.C.]

IUCN Red (Data) Book *See* RED (DATA) BOOK.

J

joule (J) SI UNIT of energy, work and heat, defined as the work done when a force of 1 N acts through 1 m. Relation to other units: $1\,\mathrm{erg} = 10^{-7}\,\mathrm{J}$; $1\,\mathrm{eV} = 1.602 \times 10^{-19}\,\mathrm{J}$; $1\,\mathrm{calorie} = 4.18\,\mathrm{J}$; $1\,\mathrm{Btu} = 1055\,\mathrm{J}$. [J.G.]

Julian day Julian day is a chronology based on the Julian era with the epoch defined at noon on 1 January 4713 BC. The Julian day is frequently confused with that of DAY NUMBER, which counts the number of days from 1 January within a year. [P.R.V.G.]

K

Kendall's rank correlation coefficient (τ) A non-parametric statistic that summarizes the degree of CORRELATION between two sets of observations (x and y). The correlation coefficient (τ) varies between +1 (perfect positive correlation), through 0 (no correlation) to −1 (perfect negative correlation). The two variables need not follow a NORMAL DISTRIBUTION. [B.S.]

key organisms A term sometimes used by those involved in environmental management and conservation, which might refer to: importance in dynamics and structure of communities (e.g. as in KEYSTONE SPECIES); important representative of, for example, trophic groups in COMMUNITY; particularly sensitive species in terms of STRESS and/or DISTURBANCE and/or POLLUTION. None of these criteria is exclusive of the others, so that all might be intended. [P.C.]

keystone species A keystone species is one upon which many other species in an ecosystem depend and the loss of which could result in a cascade of local extinctions. The keystone species may supply a vital food resource, as for example in the case of a plant with energy-rich seeds on which many animals rely for food. Or it may be a predatory species that holds in check the populations of certain herbivores which would otherwise overgraze, reduce primary production potential and lead to the loss of other herbivorous animals, together perhaps with certain specific parasites and predators. Conservation biologists should be particularly anxious to identify and give special attention to such keystone species. [P.D.M.]

kick sampling *See* SAMPLING METHODOLOGY/ DEVICES.

kilogram (kg) SI UNIT of mass. The international prototype kilogram is at the Bureau International des Poids et Mesures, Sèvres, near Paris. Relation to other units: $1\,g = 10^{-3}\,kg$; $1\,lb = 0.453\,kg$. [J.G.]

Kolmogorov–Smirnov two-sample test A non-parametric test that examines differences between two distributions, rather than using ranks and comparing medians as in the MANN–WHITNEY *U* TEST. [B.S.]

krill Derived from Norwegian *kril* (young fish) but now used as a common term for euphausids: PELAGIC, marine shrimps distributed globally. Key animal in Antarctic marine ecosystem because of its great abundance and its position in the FOOD WEB between the microalgae upon which it feeds and the large vertebrate predators, whales, seals and penguins, that feed on it. Now exploited by fisheries that lead to a range of end-products for human and animal consumption. [P.C.]

krummholz Trees growing at (or just above) the TREE LINE on mountain slopes that exhibit a prostrate growth form, pruned by WIND and ice-blast. [M.J.C.]

Kruskal–Wallis test This is the non-parametric equivalent of a one-way ANALYSIS OF VARIANCE. However, it is used to compare several medians rather than several means. The procedure is very similar to the MANN–WHITNEY *U* TEST. [B.S.]

kurtosis A statistic that measures one type of departure from a NORMAL DISTRIBUTION. Kurtosis is the 'peakedness' of the distribution. A leptokurtic distribution has more observations in the centre and tails, relative to a normal distribution. A platykurtic distribution has less in the centre and tails, relative to a normal distribution. An extreme platykurtic distribution would be a bimodal distribution. *See also* STATISTICS. [B.S.]

L

lagoons A lagoon is a shallow body of coastal brackish or saltwater that is semi-isolated from the open SEA by some form of natural barrier. The term is used to describe two rather different types of environment: coastal lagoons and those impounded by CORAL REEFS.

Coastal lagoons, which occupy 13% of the world's coastline, are virtually tideless, pond- or lake-like bodies of coastal saline or brackish WATER that are partially isolated from the adjacent sea by a sedimentary barrier, but which nevertheless receive an influx of water from that sea. Characteristically, coastal lagoons are floored by soft sediments, fringed by reed beds, mangroves or salt-marsh vegetation, and support dense beds of submerged macrophytes such as seagrasses, pondweeds or *Ruppia*.

The second environment to which the word 'lagoon' is applied is associated with coral reefs; coral here replaces the unconsolidated sedimentary barrier of the coastal lagoon. Circular atoll reefs enclose the 'lagoon' within their perimeter, whilst BARRIER REEFS are separated from the mainland by an equivalent although less isolated body of water. Indeed, barrier-reef lagoons are virtually sheltered stretches of coastal sea. However, atoll lagoons are distinctive in being floored by coral sand that supports submerged beds of seagrasses and fringing MANGROVE swamps just as the coastal lagoons of similar latitudes. The similarity between the two types of lagoon is nevertheless purely physiographic, since the atoll lagoon fauna is that typical of coral reefs in general and not related in any way to those of coastal lagoons. [R.S.K.B.]

lake stratification Two layers of WATER in a lake at different temperatures tend to remain static, with the denser, cooler, water lying beneath the less dense warmer water. Energy must be expended to mix the two layers and such a temperature-layered lake shows thermal resistance to mixing. The amount of energy needed to mix two layers of water at different temperatures increases as the temperature difference increases, particularly at high temperatures.

In climates cold enough for ICE formation the water column will be at a uniform temperature of approximately 4°C after ice melt in spring. Wind action on the lake surface will move surface water downwind, with a compensatory upwind movement of deeper water. As a result of these contrary water movements, mixing will occur since thermal resistance is low. The whole lake water will thus be circulated and mixed by the WIND and will gradually increase in temperature as a result of SOLAR RADIATION. As spring progresses, more heat enters the lake bringing the surface water temperature to a level substantially higher than that of the lower waters so that thermal resistance to mixing will be too great to be overcome by the wind. The lake is thus stratified into two principal regions, an upper circulating warmer region (epilimnion) and a lower, cooler, more-or-less stationary layer (hypolimnion). Little heat is transmitted to the hypolimnion, which thus remains at the temperature it had at the time of stratification. Between the epilimnion and hypolimnion there is a transitional layer (metalimnion or THERMOCLINE), in which there is a steep change of temperature with depth (as high as $3°C\,m^{-1}$). The metalimnion is not only a boundary between water masses of different temperatures but also a barrier to free movement between the contents of the epilimnion and the hypolimnion because of density differences.

As summer progresses, the rate of heat income to the lake decreases resulting in cooling of the epilimnion which thus sinks and erodes the metalimnion. With the epilimnion cooling while the hypolimnion remains at a constant temperature, the thermal resistance to mixing decreases gradually; eventually resistance to mixing is overcome by winds and the whole lake once again mixes and circulates. Thus until the water temperature of the whole lake drops to 4°C, the water temperature will be uniform from top to bottom.

If heat loss from the water surface is such that the surface freezes, the lake will remain insulated under a layer of ice for the rest of the winter. Such LAKES show inverse stratification, with the surface ice and water immediately below at 0°C. Beneath this layer there is a gradual increase of water temperature to the winter maximum somewhere between 0 and 4°C. The following spring, heat income increases, the ice melts and the lake again mixes and circulates. Such a lake showing two periods of total circulation or mixing (turnover) per year and two periods of stratification or stagnation is termed 'dimictic'.

At the time of circulation, most lakes are mixed completely from top to bottom and are termed 'holomictic'; however, some lakes have a permanently stagnant water layer at the bottom and are termed 'meromictic'. Meromixis occurs because the energy available from the wind at the water surface is insufficient to overcome the resistance to mixing.

At high latitudes and at high elevations in lower latitudes, the climate may never permit the water temperature to rise above 4°C. Thus, lakes will never attain summer stratification and are termed 'cold thereimictic'. In climates where the difference between summer and winter is relatively slight and the winter temperatures not much below 4°C (as in many oceanic temperate regions), lakes never develop ice cover and circulate throughout the winter; these are termed 'cheimomictic'.

Shallow tropical lakes, particularly if they are in windy climates and at high elevations (where nocturnal heat loss is greater than at low elevations), circulate freely most of the time, with stratification occurring only under unusually calm conditions. Polymixis similar to this is also frequently found in small ponds in temperate latitudes which may, under very warm and calm weather conditions, stratify daily and circulate every night. [R.W.D.]

lakes A hole or BASIN containing a volume of WATER that is relatively large compared with its annual inflow and outflow. Lake basins can be small with EPHEMERAL water levels, such as temporary rain-fed rock pools, or extremely large and long-lived, such as Lake Baikal which contains 20% of the world's FRESH WATER and has had a continuous lacustrine history for at least 65 million years. [J.L.]

lakes, types of Of whatever origin, LAKES may be either 'open' with WATER losses from outlets or seepage, or 'closed' where the only water losses occur through evaporation.

Tectonic lakes are produced by some form of earth movement other than volcanic.

Volcanic lakes are formed in the craters of volcanoes, sometimes from a single cone when they are usually relatively small and circular in shape, or from multiple craters in which case the lakes are large and irregularly shaped.

Landslide lakes are formed when debris from rockfalls, mudflows or any other landslide block the course of running water and a lake, often transitory, collects behind the landslide dam.

Glacial lakes are formed by the action of ICE. A lake can be formed at the foot of a glacier (proglacial), by the moraine, by ice scour or by retreat up a valley (cirque). Kettle lakes are formed by the deposition of large blocks of ice covered in mud and/or gravel when the main ice sheet retreats and tend to be shallow and ephemeral.

Solution lakes are formed by the percolation of water through soluble rocks either on the surface or underground; in the latter case, collapse of the chambers results in surficial depressions. Limestone is one of the commonest soluble rocks involved, but solution lakes also occur in sodium chloride

(NaCl), calcium sulphate ($CaSO_4$), ferric hydroxide and aluminium hydroxide bearing rocks and consequently have high total dissolved solids and high conductivity.

Fluviatile lakes are formed by the erosion and/or deposition of sediments by running water. A waterfall has the erosive power to excavate a depression and if the river subsequently changes course the remaining basin forms a plunge or evorsion lake. Eddies in a river or stream can produce a pool, which can either be isolated seasonally or permanently.

RIVERS also deposit SEDIMENT that can form dams, either blocking the main watercourse to form a fluviatile lake or more commonly blocking the tributary valleys to form a lateral lake. In the lower reaches of rivers, particularly where there is a wide flood plain, meandering of rivers can produce oxbow lakes. In large rivers, sediments tend to be deposited in the marginal zones, forming levees where water can accumulate to form lakes.

Wind-formed lakes are formed either by the deposition of wind-borne material such as sand damming a valley or in the parallel valleys produced between SAND DUNES (slacks). Wind erosion can produce deflation basins that fill with water.

Coastline lakes are formed by the deposition of a sediment BAR (tombolo) across an indentation or irregularity in the coast of either the sea or a large lake or between the coast and an island.

Organic-accumulation lakes are formed by the accumulation of less readily decomposable parts of organisms (usually plant in origin but animal material, e.g. coral, can have the same effect), which act as a dam or form a ring around the basin.

Meteoric lakes occur when a meteor strikes the surface and forms a crater, partially from the impact itself but also frequently as a result of the explosion of the water and gases in the rocks due to the intense heat produced by the impact. Since the pressure of this explosion is equal in all directions, craters are usually circular and the floor of the crater consists of crushed or fused rocks.

Lakes produced by animals such as beavers (*Castor*) are well known. Humans have produced artificial lakes (reservoirs) by building dams since 2000 BC (in Egypt and Sri Lanka); lakes are also formed in disused quarries, clay pits and peat excavations. [R.W.D.]

Lamarckian inheritance Inheritance of acquired characters. We now know that it is virtually impossible for acquired TRAITS to become incorporated in the genetic material for two reasons. First, information flows from the genes to the phenotype rather than in the opposite direction (the 'central dogma' of Francis Crick) and, more importantly, environmental effects on the phenotype cannot cause purposive or directed changes in the genes. [L.M.C.]

laminar flow Flow of any fluid in which the lines of flow (as revealed by injecting a tracer, such as smoke, dye or particles) are parallel. Laminar flow tends to occur at low flow rates. The tendency for laminar flow to break up into chaotic motion (turbulent flow) is measured by the REYNOLDS NUMBER:

$$Re = ud/v$$

where u is the speed of the fluid, d is the characteristic dimension of the surface and v is the kinematic VISCOSITY of the fluid. [J.G.]

land contamination *See* CONTAMINATED LAND; LAND RECLAMATION.

land decontamination *See* LAND RECLAMATION.

land drainage *See* DRAINAGE.

land reclamation The term used for any activity by which land is brought back into some sort of beneficial use. It can include full restoration, where the area is returned to the pre-existing land use, rehabilitation, in which this end-point is only partly achieved, or replacement, in which something new is created. Remediation is often used as a synonym for RECLAMATION although the emphasis is more on the operations involved. Since it is ecosystems that are always damaged there is now considerable interest in what is called 'ecological restoration', in which the specific aim is to restore ecological structures and functions, normally of the ECOSYSTEM that existed immediately before degradation occurred but sometimes of the original indigenous ecosystem. [A.D.B.]

land registers Lists of actually or potentially CONTAMINATED LAND intended to guide the need for CLEAN-UP, the possibilities for development, the decisions of investors, purchasers, etc. Because it is never possible to prove zero contamination on a site (evaluation in the wrong place or for the wrong substance; improving analytical techniques might expose contamination where it was previously undetectable), it is usually not wise to compile lists on the basis of actual contamination. Instead, potential contamination, for example identified as a result of contaminative proccesses that might have occurred historically on the site, is more reliably defined. Though helpful to some, these registers are frowned on by others because of the possible effects on land prices, i.e. so-called land blight. [P.C.]

land rehabilitation *See* LAND RECLAMATION.

land remediation *See* LAND RECLAMATION.

land replacement *See* LAND RECLAMATION.

land restoration *See* LAND RECLAMATION.

landfill WASTE DISPOSAL method that involves dumping WASTE below or on the surface (and sometimes in the sea to create more land, as in Hong Kong). It essentially involves long-term storage of inert materials and relatively uncontrolled DECOMPOSITION of biodegradable waste. It stands alone as the only waste disposal method that can deal with all materials in the solid waste stream and so there will always be a place for it. The outputs from landfill involve gases and LEACHATE emissions, both of which can be polluting and dangerous, and so some containment and control of releases is required. One extreme of this is complete containment with not only impervious lining to floor and sides but also capping. This dry containment has been described as long-term storage, since it slows down biological decomposition processes that depend crucially on the availability of water. This also means that it reduces the initial production of landfill gas. Decomposition will, of course, ultimately occur but possibly at a time in the future when the site is in a poorer state of repair and management. An alternative, therefore, is to admit water to accelerate decomposition and gas production at an early stage when the outputs can be more easily managed. This is tantamount to operating the site as a large bioreactor. A problem with this is that understanding of the process is rudimentary, which means that management cannot be too precise. The bioreactions are likely to vary depending on the quality of the waste and also local climatic conditions. In both systems, leachates are contained until leaks ultimately occur or are removed in a controlled way. It is presumed that bioreaction will remove organic pollutants. However, the understanding of this process is again rudimentary and inorganic pollutants such as HEAVY METALS will remain a problem. So there is a need to monitor, and probably treat, controlled releases. [P.C.]

landfill sites *See* LANDFILL.

landrace A CROP cultivar or animal breed that has been improved by traditional agriculturalists, but has not been influenced by modern breeding practices. [P.C.]

landscape architecture *See* LANDSCAPE ECOLOGY.

landscape ecology The study of the interactions between the temporal and spatial aspects of a landscape and its flora, fauna and cultural components. This covers the academic side of the subject, which focuses on the large-scale pattern of landscape elements and their function, but not the applied work of the professional landscape ecologist, which is more practical and site based. At both scales it involves the study of habitats where the effect of people is a major influence, such as public open space, cemeteries, allotments, town parks, precincts, industrial areas, intensively cultivated regions, construction sites, roads and gardens. Knowledge of these habitats lags far behind that of more natural communities as the powerful anthropogenic influences in operation have rendered them unattractive to ecologists, who find the high proportion of exotics and mixtures of planted and spontaneous vegetation bewildering. In addition to studying these habitat patches much of the work of a landscape ecologist is involved with habitat creation and how to set about greening cities. [O.L.G.]

Langmuir circulation A pattern of water CIRCULATION that occurs when WIND blows steadily across the surface of relatively calm seas and which is characterized by vortices (several metres in diameter) that revolve around vertical axes, causing UPWELLING and downwelling of water. The vortices, or cells, tend to be regularly spaced and are often arranged in staggered parallel rows with their long axes parallel to the wind. The alternating areas of divergence and convergence tend to cause aggregations of PLANKTON, which can enhance nutrient regeneration. Langmuir cells provide an important mechanism for transporting heat, momentum and matter from the water surface to layers a few centimetres deep. *See also* LAKES. [V.F.]

larva A discrete stage in the life cycle of many species. [V.F.]

latitudinal gradients of diversity Perhaps the most striking pattern in BIOGEOGRAPHY is the dramatic increase in the DIVERSITY of BIOTA between the poles and the Equator. Although there are conspicuous exceptions to the general rule, for example penguins are much more diverse at high latitudes and most species of salamanders and voles occur in temperate zones, the vast majority of taxa from all the major habitats show the same qualitative trend. This increase in diversity towards the tropics is apparent when either wide geographic regions are considered or when small communities are examined. For example, TROPICAL RAIN FORESTS contain 40–100 species of tree per hectare compared with deciduous forests in the USA (10–30 species) or coniferous forests in northern Canada (1–5 species). Also, many species groups are only found in the tropics, for example New World fruit bats and the Indo-Pacific giant clam. [S.J.H.]

law of constant final yield Farmers have long known that sowing more seed does not lead to increased YIELDS at harvest. Above a relatively low THRESHOLD seed density, final yield is independent of seeding density; the higher the seed density, the lower the SIZE and fecundity of the adult plants. [M.J.C.]

LC$_{50}$ Statistically derived concentration of XENOBIOTIC that is lethal to 50% of an observed population over a prescribed time in defined conditions. Also referred to as MEDIAN LETHAL CONCENTRATION. Also expressed in terms of dose (LD$_{50}$). Common indicator of ECOTOXICITY because when deaths are normally distributed with respect to concentration most of the population will be affected at this concentration and so it can be defined with greatest confidence. *See also* EC$_{50}$; IC$_{50}$; PREDICTIVE ECOTOXICITY TESTS. [P.C.]

LCA *See* LIFE-CYCLE ASSESSMENT.

LCI *See* LIFE-CYCLE INVENTORY.

leachate Liquid that seeps through WASTE and hence contains CONTAMINANTS; may therefore lead to hazardous substances entering surface water, groundwater or SOIL. *See also* FATE; LANDFILL; LEACHING; LYSIMETER. [P.C.]

leaching Removal by water of soluble components from SOIL or WASTE tip. The output is called a LEACHATE. [P.C.]

lead (Pb) A heavy, malleable bluish-grey METAL (ATOMIC NUMBER=82; relative ATOMIC MASS= 207.19; melting point=327.5°C; boiling point= 1740°C) that is a trace constituent (13 mg kg^{-1}) of the Earth's CRUST. Found in galena ore (PbS), lead has had many uses, including lead–acid BATTERIES, solders, cable sheathing, piping, roofing, pigments (e.g. 'white lead', 2PbCO$_3$.Pb(OH)$_2$) and chemicals (e.g. lead arsenate PESTICIDE, PbHAsO$_4$), anti-knock petrol additives (e.g. tetraethyl lead (C$_2$H$_5$)$_4$Pb), etc. As a result of these uses and major releases from the mining and smelting of lead and the combustion of FOSSIL FUELS, lead has been widely distributed throughout all phases of the environment. As a biologically non-essential and toxic metal, lead has therefore been one of the most intensively studied elements in terms of its environmental distribution, behaviour and impact upon health.

The deleterious effects of lead upon human health have been known since Roman times, when it was used not only in plumbing and pottery but also, in the form of lead acetate, as a sweetener in wine. Today, effects are recognized as ranging from non-specific symptoms such as moodiness and irritability, through severe abdominal pains and anaemia, to peripheral nerve involvement, paralysis of fingers, hands and wrists, and brain damage. Rather more controversial, although fairly widely accepted now, has been the claim that lead exposure of young children in particular can result in behavioural problems and intelligence deficits. Children absorb ingested lead rather more readily than adults. Once absorbed via the gut or, if inhaled, via the lungs, lead is carried on the surface of red blood cells, which bring it into contact with soft tissues, including the brain, before ultimately being stored in bones and teeth. Certainly, subtle biochemical effects such as inhibition of the enzyme δ-aminolaevulinic acid dehydratase can be observed at blood lead concentrations of about 5 µg dl^{-1}, not untypical of the Western world today. Further effects, for example inhibition of the biosynthesis of haem and fetal TOXICITY (lead can cross the placenta, the blood–brain barrier is more permeable and there is less bone to act as a storage site), occur as concentrations increase to ~40 µg dl^{-1}, which is generally considered a benchmark for clinical signs of lead toxicity, eventually resulting in encephalopathy at ~100 µg dl^{-1}. The toxic mode of action of organolead compounds, which can be absorbed through the skin as well as the lungs, is rather different. For example, tetraethyl lead (C$_2$H$_5$)$_4$Pb is converted in the liver to (C$_2$H$_5$)$_3$Pb$^+$, which attacks the central nervous system. In addition to anthropogenic emissions of organolead compounds during the manufacture and use of tetraalkyl lead petrol additives, there is evidence for some natural alkylation (methylation) of inorganic lead in the environment.

Despite the ongoing debate about the existence and/or importance of subclinical effects of lead upon human health, regulatory bodies in many countries have taken strong measures to reduce exposure of the public to lead. These include reduction and/or elimination of lead additives from petrol; the removal, or the imposition of strict limits upon the use, of lead compounds in paints; the banning of lead-soldered cans and the introduction of more stringent limits upon the lead content of food; and measures to reduce the lead content of water in susceptible areas that have lead pipes and tanks, lead-soldered copper pipes, etc. [J.G.F.]

least significant difference (LSD) The smallest difference between any two means that will allow them to be significantly different from each other. Calculated as part of an a posteriori test, after an ANALYSIS OF VARIANCE. [B.S.]

least squares method The method of least squares was discovered independently by two mathematicians, K.F. Gauss and A.-M. Legendre, about 200 years ago. It is used widely as a method for minimizing the residual variation when fitting a relationship or function to a set of observations. For example, when we fit a straight-line function to a set of paired observations (x and y) we are in fact splitting each 'observed y' into two components, a 'fitted y' reflecting the underlying straight line and a 'residual' reflecting the random departure from the straight line. [B.S.]

lek A traditional mating ground where adult males defend very small territories devoid of obvious resources to which females move for the purpose of mating. [J.C.D.]

lentic Still water system, i.e. ponds and LAKES. *Cf.* LOTIC. [P.C.]

Leopold, A. (1886–1948) In an influential essay, 'The Land Ethic', expressed the need for humanity to treat nature as something to which we belong, not as a commodity to be exploited. [P.C.]

life-cycle assessment (LCA) Commercial products have life cycles: from raw materials through production to use and ultimate disposal. It is myopic to consider environmental effects at just one point in this sequence because it might ignore more important effects at others. A more sound approach is to consider effects across all stages of a life cycle 'from cradle to grave' (*see* CRADLE-TO-GRAVE ANALYSIS). The four main stages of an LCA are as follows.
1 Initial phase: defining the problem and establishing an inventory of important elements, i.e. LIFE-CYCLE INVENTORY (LCI).
2 Inventory phase: detailed description of raw material and energy inputs used at all points and the EMISSIONS/EFFLUENTS and solid WASTE outputs.

3 Impact assessment phase: relating inventoried inputs and outputs to real-world environmental problems.
4 Improvement phase: using information collected in the other phases to improve overall environmental importance.

Major challenges are to incorporate potential POLLUTION impacts and to find ways of representing and judging the relative merits of input and output effects of different components. Also of considerable importance is defining the boundaries of the study, which otherwise can extend indefinitely. Thus, a particular product might use wood as raw material: does the LCA stop at the forest or take into account the fuel used to run the lumber operation, the construction of the equipment such as saws, etc.? A rule of thumb is that if effects are likely to be less than 5% of the total they can be ignored, although knowing that this is the case is not straightforward, especially before the LCA is done.

LCA is used in establishing ECOLABEL criteria. [P.C.]

life-cycle inventory (LCI) Inventory of use of RESOURCES (including energy) and creation of polluting WASTE along the life cycle of a product from raw materials, through manufacture and use, to disposal. *See also* LIFE-CYCLE ASSESSMENT. [P.C.]

lifespan Measure of the duration of life, used variously to describe either the maximum or average duration of life in a population or the duration of life of an individual organism. [T.B.L.K.]

light Electromagnetic RADIATION in the wavelength range 400–700 nm, where the human eye is most sensitive. Often the adjacent wavelength ranges, ULTRAVIOLET RADIATION on the shortwave side and infrared radiation on the longwave side, are included and the terms 'ultraviolet light' and 'infrared light' are often used but not recommended. To specify the range 400–700 nm the term 'visible light' can be used. It is also called photosynthetically active radiation (PAR), since it is the most important spectral band for plant PHOTOSYNTHESIS. A common misconception is that 'infrared radiation' is synonymous with 'heat radiation'. All daylight, including visible light, is heat radiation from the Sun, while infrared laser radiation is not heat radiation (although things absorbing infrared laser radiation will be heated by it). [L.O.B.]

lightning When WATER vapour is forced high in the ATMOSPHERE by powerful updrafts, it forms ICE particles that collide with each other and with water droplets. Electrical charge separation by friction occurs and a thundercloud is formed. Typically, a thundercloud is several kilometres in diameter and stores tens to hundreds of coulombs, corresponding to a voltage of around 10^8 V: under such conditions lightning occurs. Although about 80% of lightning strokes are cloud to cloud (sheet lightning), most is known about cloud-to-ground lightning. [H.W.W.]

lignin Lignins are polymeric natural products arising from an enzyme-initiated polymerization of three primary precursors: *trans*-coniferyl 1, transinapyl 2 and *trans*-*p*-couramyl 3 alcohols. They are intimately associated with, and bonded to, hemicelluloses in plant cell walls and give wood its characteristic strength. Lignin is resistant to bacterial decay but is attacked by some fungi. [J.G.]

limit of detection (LOD) No CONTAMINATION detected within the limits of the analytical procedure. *See also* LIMIT OF QUANTIFICATION. [P.C.]

limit of quantification (LOQ) CONTAMINATION detected but at levels too small to quantify within the limits of the analytical procedure. *See also* LIMIT OF DETECTION. [P.C.]

limit value Limit concentrations or absolute amounts of CONTAMINANTS set to protect the environment and which must not be exceeded in EMISSIONS. Usually refer to end-of-pipe or end-of-stack levels. *Cf.* ENVIRONMENTAL QUALITY STANDARD. [P.C.]

limits of tolerance Maximum level (dose, concentration) of a STRESS that an organism can tolerate. Injurious effects are initially sublethal, affecting development and reproduction, then increasingly lethal. Measurable stresses include TOXICANTS (PESTICIDES), low temperatures and desiccation. Tolerance is usually normally distributed within a population, producing a characteristic sigmoidal DOSE–RESPONSE curve. An appropriate data transformation analysis (probit) is used to estimate doses required to kill a given proportion of a population; LD_{50} is the dose/concentration of an insecticide required to kill 50% of a target population. [J.S.B.]

limnology Derived from the Greek *limnos* meaning SWAMP, lake or MARSH, the word 'limnology' was used originally to define the study of LAKES. Limnology was later expanded to include all inland waters (fresh and salt) contained within continental boundaries including standing (LENTIC) ecosystems such as lakes and ponds and running (LOTIC) waters (springs, streams, creeks, RIVERS). Brackish waters in river estuaries are also included in limnology as are ephemeral (temporary) water bodies such as pools, tree holes, etc. Limnology is the study of the functional relationships and productivity of inland waters and the effects of the physical, chemical and biotic environment on their communities. It includes disciplines such as geology, chemistry, physics, biology and ecology. In recent usage, limnology has been defined by some authors to include only the study of fresh waters excluding saline and brackish waters. [R.W.D.]

lindane An organochlorine INSECTICIDE first reported in 1935; the generic name of >99% pure γ-hexachlorocyclohexane (gamma-HCH). It is ingested, with some contact and soil fumigant activity, and is active on soil-dwelling and PHYTOPHAGOUS insects, public-health pests and animal ectoparasites. It was used, along with DDT, to kill human lice without apparent ill effects during the Second World War. However, it is very persistent in the environment, building up in the FOOD CHAIN and affecting a wide range of higher animals. It may be carcinogenic in some species. Although use is now restricted, the degradation characteristics of lindane mean that disappearance in the environment has been slow. *See also* BIOCIDE. [K.D.]

Linnaean classification The system of CLASSIFICATION of organisms devised by the Swedish polymath Carl von Linné or Carolus Linnaeus (1707–1778) and originally presented in his *Systema Naturae*. The position in the system of a new species is determined using a set of characters chosen for their discriminatory value. A feature of outstanding importance, which Linnaeus established in his *Species Plantarum*, is the binomial, consisting of a generic and a specific name, as a unique identifier for each species. [L.M.C.]

lists Within European Union (EU), US and UK legislation there are numerous lists of hazardous substances. These are usually compiled on the basis of HAZARD assessments. Examples are the EU BLACK and GREY LISTS of substances dangerous to the aquatic environment. The UK has a similar RED LIST. There are ENDANGERED SPECIES lists (in US federal legislation) and lists of violating facilities compiled by the USEPA. There are also many and various other environmental data lists. [P.C.]

lithosphere This is simply defined as the Earth's CRUST, although this definition does not indicate the wide diversity of materials that are present. Specifically, it refers to the rocks and ICE that cover the surface of the Earth. [E.A.F.]

littoral zone

1 For LAKES, the edge, sometimes defined imprecisely as the extent to which SAMPLING is possible before water overflows the boots, and sometimes more precisely as the area in which PHOTOSYNTHESIS is possible by benthic primary producers. *See also* WITHIN-LAKE HABITAT CLASSIFICATION.

2 For the seas, also called the eulittoral or INTERTIDAL ZONE. The limits of this zone are sometimes considered to lie between mean high-water and mean low-water levels. Alternatively, the zone may be considered to extend from the level of the highest spring high tide to the lowest spring low tide. Additionally, the supralittoral zone (splash or SPRAY ZONE) may be used to refer to those levels on the shore only submerged during spring high TIDES. [V.F.]

Local Agenda 21 Initiative developed by local governments in the UK; Chapter 28 of AGENDA 21 encourages them to define their own SUSTAINABLE DEVELOPMENT strategies. [P.C.]

LOD *See* LIMIT OF DETECTION.

LOEC *See* LOWEST OBSERVED EFFECT CONCENTRATION.

log normal distribution One of the four commonly used SPECIES-ABUNDANCE MODELS (distributions). [B.S.]

logarithmic wind profile Measurements of the velocity of any viscous fluid close to a boundary reveals that the layers of fluid closest to the boundary move more slowly than layers further from the boundary because of the effects of surface friction. The fluid velocity at the boundary is at rest relative to the boundary; fluid velocity increases asymptotically with distance from the boundary. The same principle applies to measurements of horizontal WIND speed made within a few metres of the Earth's surface. Wind speed increases exponentially with height and the relationship between wind speed and the logarithm of height can be described by a straight line. The slope of this line and its intercept are important measures of the degree of TURBULENCE in the air and the aerodynamic roughness of the ground surface respectively. [J.B.M.]

Long-Term Ecological Research Program (LTER) Programme in the USA that was initiated in the 1970s by the National Science Foundation. It focused on examining ecological processes and problems with temporal or spatial scales that could not be addressed by more traditional research projects with shorter time horizons. It now involves 18 sites that range from the Arctic/Antarctica to temperate and tropical. [P.C.]

long-term tests TOXICITY/ECOTOXICITY tests that are carried out over periods of time that are long relative to the LIFESPAN of the organism. Thus 1 day would be short term for a vertebrate but long term for a microbe. [P.C.]

longevity The length of life. [A.J.D.]

LOQ *See* LIMIT OF QUANTIFICATION.

lotic Running waters, such as RIVERS and streams. *See also* LIMNOLOGY. [J.L.]

lowest observed effect concentration (LOEC) The lowest concentration of chemical in an ECOTOXIC-ITY test series to cause a statistically significant difference in an observed variable (EFFECT) from control. Clearly, this will depend upon the concentration intervals used in the experimental series, i.e. there could be lower unobserved effect concentrations between the LOEC and the NO OBSERVED EFFECT CONCENTRATION (NOEC). This is why the term 'observed' is used. LOECs should always be reported with the NOEC. [P.C.]

LSD *See* LEAST SIGNIFICANT DIFFERENCE.

LT$_{50}$ *See* MEDIAN TIMES TO EFFECT.

LTER *See* LONG-TERM ECOLOGICAL RESEARCH PROGRAM.

lysimeter Experimental system consisting of a block of soil to which an aqueous liquid of known quality is added and from which the routes and rates of loss, by percolation, evapotranspiration and RUN-OFF, can be budgeted. The quality of percolate is often tested ecotoxicologically. Amongst other things, it may be used to test the potential of chemicals sprayed on land and LANDFILL materials to contaminate and pollute ground and surface waters. *See also* LEACHATE. [P.C.]

M

MAB (Man and the Biosphere Programme) *See* INTER-NATIONAL CONSERVATION CONVENTIONS.

Mackay fate models A series of models that predict where chemicals go in the environment and to what extent, on the basis of EMISSIONS and FUGACITY of chemical. They vary in complexity from a simple equilibrium distribution of a conservative chemical to steady-state and time-varying descriptions of reactive components. *See also* EXPOSURE; FATE. [P.C.]

macrocosm Large, isolated and controlled multispecies system, often outdoors, used for experimental ecology and ECOTOXICITY testing. Some attempt has been made at being more precise in specifying size of system for which the term applies, but the separation of macrocosm from MESOCOSM is not sharp and probably not really helpful. *See also* COSMS; MICROCOSM. [P.C.]

macrofauna

1 Generally, fauna in SAMPLES that are visible unaided by lens.

2 More specifically, the extraction of animals from marine sediments almost invariably requires the use of sieves and hence the mesh size of the sieve used determines the SIZE of animal retained—the macrofauna are defined as those benthic animals retained by a 0.5-mm mesh and, by extension, the same term is often used for animals of the same size from other benthic habitats (*cf.* MEIOFAUNA; MICROFAUNA). [R.S.K.B]

macronutrients These are the elements (other than carbon, hydrogen and OXYGEN) required by living organisms in substantial amounts: nitrogen, phosphorus, potassium, calcium, magnesium, sulphur and chlorine (*cf.* MICRONUTRIENTS). [K.A.S.]

malathion A non-systemic organophosphorous IN-SECTICIDE and ACARICIDE of diminished TOXI-CITY to mammals compared with earlier chemicals of the type. Malathion is the generic name for $C_{10}H_{19}O_6PS_2$. It has a wide range of agricultural and horticultural CROP uses and additionally is used to control animal ectoparasites, flies, household insects, human lice and mosquitoes. It is dangerous to the aquatic environment, so considerable care is needed with use near water. It has short to moderate PERSISTENCE in the environment. Excessive doses lead to poisoning and chromosome abnormalities in mammals, including humans. [K.D.]

Man and the Biosphere Programme (MAB) *See* INTER-NATIONAL CONSERVATION CONVENTIONS.

mangrove The word can be applied either to the plant belonging to a group of trees that dominate tropical intertidal forests or to the forest habitat itself. Some ecologists prefer to use the term 'mangal' specifically for the habitat in which mangrove plants grow rather than for the plants themselves. [P.D.M.]

Mann–Whitney *U* test (Wilcoxon rank sum test) This is the non-parametric equivalent of the $z(d)$ TEST or t TEST. However, it is used to compare two medians, rather than two means, and is suitable for unmatched observations). [B.S.]

manometer An instrument for measuring the PRES-SURE of a gas relative to that of the atmosphere or some other reference. [J.G.]

mantle, Earth's The largest layer of the Earth, the mantle has a volume of $898 \times 10^9 km^3$. It lies between the CRUST and the core from 40 to 3500km depth. The mantle consists of dense rock $(4.5 g cm^{-3})$. The upper part of the mantle, or athenosphere, is partially molten and flows plastically, whereas the lower mantle is rigid. The LITHOSPHERE includes the crust and the uppermost part of the mantle above the athenosphere. The mantle provides the source for new crust that forms along the MIDOCEANIC RIDGES. Convective movements occurring within the mantle, due to escaping heat from deep within the Earth, result in movement of the lithospheric plates and thus the movement of the continents and formation of ocean BASINS. [V.F.]

mariculture The artificial cultivation of marine species. [V.F.]

marine ecology *See* ECOLOGY.

marine snow Amorphous particulate matter derived from living organisms. It is formed from mucus released by large planktonic filter feeders, which produces flakes. The flakes become colonized by bacteria and their flagellate and ciliate grazers. Sinking of this material, especially in dense concentration, looks like a snowfall. [V.F.]

maritime climate A CLIMATE typical of coastal areas and characterized by relatively little seasonal change, with warm moist winters and cool summers. [V.F.]

market instruments A way of using consumer choice to effect environmental protection. Information on the relative environmental 'friendliness' of a product is fed into the market-place, either as information (labels) or by differential application of taxes. The latter are referred to as economic instruments. *See also* ECOLABEL; REGULATORY INSTRUMENTS. [P.C.]

marsh This term causes confusion in wetland nomenclature because it is used in very different senses in different parts of the world. In North America, the expression is equivalent to the European term 'SWAMP' and is discussed under that entry in this encyclopedia. In Europe, 'marsh' is used to refer to ecosystems with periodically waterlogged mineral soils but with little or no PEAT formation. The soils often take the form of groundwater gleys and the vegetation, which is usually herbaceous, is characteristically capable of tolerating waterlogging. [P.D.M.]

mass balance Accumulation of total mass in a system is equal to the difference between input and output. May also apply to a particular substance, and will apply to elements. Based on the principle of conservation of mass. [P.C.]

mass extinction Mass extinctions are substantial BIODIVERSITY losses that are global in extent, taxonomically broad and rapid relative to the average persistence times of species in the taxa involved. Five major mass extinction events have been identified for marine invertebrates, the group for which the fossil record is relatively extensive, reliable and well studied. Terrestrial vertebrates and plants exhibit perturbations that correlate approximately with the major mass extinctions detected in the oceans. The magnitude and timing of land-based and marine extinctions is still controversial. The five mass extinctions differed from one another and each one affected different taxonomic groups differently (see Table M1). [M.A.B.]

mass number Mass number (*A*) is the integer nearest to the ATOMIC MASS of an element (equal to the number of protons plus neutrons). [J.G.]

mass spectrometer Mass spectrometry is used for the identification of chemical elements and compounds

Table M1 Extinction rates among marine invertebrates during the five major mass extinction events. (After Jablonski, D. (1995) Extinctions in the fossil record. In: *Extinction Rates* (eds J.H. Lawton & R.M. May), pp. 25–44. Oxford University Press, Oxford; by permission of Oxford University Press.)

Mass extinction event	Families lost (%)	Genera lost (%)	Species lost (%)
1 (439 mya)	26	60	85
2 (367 mya)	22	57	83
3 (245 mya)	51	82	95
4 (208 mya)	22	53	80
5 (65 mya)	16	47	76

mya, million years ago.

on the basis of their charge to mass (*e*:*m*) ratio. Gaseous atoms or molecules of the analyte are bombarded by high-energy electrons to produce positively charged ions. These ions are accelerated and focused into a beam by an electromagnetic field. The ions pass through a further magnetic field that deflects their path according to their *e*:*m* ratio. The beam impacts on a photographic detector plate allowing accurate and precise identification of ions with different *e*:*m* ratios: ions with higher ratios are deflected further. A wide range of *e*:*m* ratios can be measured by altering the strength of the deflecting magnetic field. Mass spectra are produced by varying the magnetic field so that ions of progressively higher masses strike the detector. The electron ionization step is a high-energy process that often leads to fragmentation of molecules, which means that compounds are usually identified by examination of their fragment ions. An example of the use of mass spectrometry in ecology is in the measurement of the isotopic abundance of soil gases. The measurement of ^{15}N in nitrous oxide (N_2O) and ^{13}C in METHANE (CH_4) and CARBON DIOXIDE (CO_2) can be used to determine the sources and metabolic pathways by which these gases are formed. [I.J.B.]

MATC *See* MAXIMUM ACCEPTABLE TOXICANT CONCENTRATION.

matter flux Matter flux is one of two fundamental processes that occur in the BIOSPHERE, the other being energy flux. Alternative descriptions for matter FLUXES include BIOGEOCHEMICAL CYCLES and nutrient transfers. Matter fluxes occur continually as elements and compounds are exchanged between the abiotic (non-living) and biotic (living or dead organic matter) components of the biosphere and the ATMOSPHERE. They can be classified as gaseous, sedimentary or hydrological depending on the dominant milieu in which the exchange occurs. For example, carbon, OXYGEN and nitrogen all have important atmospheric pools and many exchanges of these elements occur either in the atmosphere or at the boundary between the atmosphere and the biosphere. Consequently, they can be described as gaseous biogeochemical cycles. Metal and phosphorus fluxes occur predominantly in the biosphere with little if any involvement of the atmosphere and comprise exchanges between rocks, soils and biota. They are sedimentary biogeochemical cycles, whilst fluxes of hydrogen and oxygen are components of the hydrological cycle (*see* WATER (HYDROLOGICAL) CYCLE). [A.M.M.]

maximum acceptable toxicant concentration (MATC) Hypothetical THRESHOLD, somewhere between NO OBSERVED EFFECT CONCENTRATION and LOWEST OBSERVED EFFECT CONCENTRATION. [P.C.]

maximum likelihood methods Maximum likelihood is the most general method of making a statistical estimate; it is an alternative to the LEAST SQUARES

METHOD. Given a model (M) and some data (D), the likelihood of a given value of an estimated parameter (V) is the PROBABILITY of the data given the model and that value of the parameter, $P(D: V,M)$. The probability of the data is thus considered as a function of the parameter. The probability of all possible datasets must add up to 1, but when the data are held constant and the parameter is varied the different values of $P(D: V,M)$ do not have to add to 1; they are called likelihoods to distinguish them from probabilities. The maximum likelihood method chooses that value V that maximizes the probability that the observed data would have occurred. [S.C.S.]

maximum permissible level Maximum permissible concentrations of CONTAMINANTS in environmental materials are normally set by national regulatory bodies at levels that are estimated to give an acceptable degree of risk to public health. In addition to concentration limits, annual limits on intake (ALIs) may be defined for contaminants. Releases of RADIOACTIVE WASTE are also subject to the ALARA principle, which is that human RADIATION exposure or RADIONUCLIDE intake resulting from any waste DISCHARGE must not only be within limits but must also be AS LOW AS REASONABLY ACHIEVABLE (ALARA). The corresponding philosophy for non-radioactive pollutants is that waste releases must be within limits and their effects must be minimized by employing the BEST AVAILABLE TECHNIQUES NOT ENTAILING EXCESSIVE COSTS (BATNEEC). [A.B.M.]

maximum sustainable yield This key concept is largely theoretical but has a sensible underlying idea. A population's ability to sustain a harvest is limited: that limit is the maximum sustainable yield (MSY). [J.B.]

mean This is the most common MEASURE OF CENTRAL TENDENCY or average, familiar to most people. It is calculated by summing all the individual observations in a SAMPLE and dividing this sum by the number of observations in the sample. The formula for calculating the mean ($\bar{x}$ or x-bar) is therefore:

$$\bar{x} = \frac{\sum x}{n}$$

where x is each observation in the sample, n is the number of observations in the sample and the Greek symbol Σ (capital sigma) is the mathematical notation for 'sum of'. [B.S.]

measure of central tendency (average) A single number that is representative of all the numbers in a set of observations. Three types of average are commonly used: the MEAN, the MEDIAN and the MODE. When the observations follow a symmetrical DISTRIBUTION then the mean, median and mode have the same value. In a non-symmetrical

(skewed) distribution the mean is moved towards the extended tail of the distribution. [B.S.]

measurement end-point *See* END-POINT.

median effective concentration/dose Statistically derived concentration (dose) expected to produce an EFFECT (lethality, inhibition, other effect) in 50% of the population. *See also* EC$_{50}$; IC$_{50}$; LC$_{50}$; PREDICTIVE ECOTOXICITY TESTS. [P.C.]

median lethal concentration (MLC) Same as LC$_{50}$. *See also* PREDICTIVE ECOTOXICITY TESTS. [P.C.]

median (second quartile) This MEASURE OF CENTRAL TENDENCY or average is calculated as the middle observation in a SAMPLE of observations that have been placed in numerical order. Therefore the median divides a set of observations into two halves. In the following sample of seven observations or measurements:

2, 3, 3, 5, 9, 15, 16

the median value is 5. [B.S.]

median times to effect Times for 50% of test population to manifest the adverse EFFECT(s) under consideration at a specified concentration of TOXICANT. Might be in terms of lethality (LT$_{50}$), or inhibition (IT$_{50}$), or any other effect END-POINT (ET$_{50}$). *See also* PREDICTIVE ECOTOXICITY TESTS. [P.C.]

Mediterranean Sea The SEA between Europe, Asia Minor and Africa. The area of the Mediterranean (including the BLACK SEA) is 3.02 million km², the average depth is 1450 m and the maximum depth is 5097 m. It is completely surrounded by land except for a narrow passage to the North Atlantic through the Strait of Gibraltar and to the Black Sea through the Bosporus. The Mediterranean is divided into a number of smaller seas (e.g. Adriatic, Aegean, etc.) and contains numerous small islands. The CONTINENTAL SHELVES are relatively narrow (less than 40 km on average) and the CONTINENTAL SLOPES are steep with many submarine canyons. Despite the fact that three major rivers empty into the Mediterranean, the Rhône, the Nile and the Po, evaporation generally exceeds PRECIPITATION, causing vertical mixing as dense, saline surface water sinks. The SALINITY of deep water is between 38.4 and 39.0‰. Nutrient concentrations in the Mediterranean are low relative to the North Atlantic and TIDES are primarily semi-diurnal. [V.F.]

megaplankton ZOOPLANKTON of between 20 and 200 cm in size. All are metazoans. [V.F.]

meiobenthic fauna *See* BENTHOS.

meiofauna The extraction of animals from marine sediments almost invariably requires the use of sieves and hence the mesh size of the sieve adopted determines the SIZE of animal retained. The meiofauna are defined as those multicellular benthic animals that pass through the 0.5-mm mesh used to collect the MACROFAUNA and, by extension, the same term is often used for animals of the same size from other benthic marine habitats, although it is not used in respect of the PLANKTON or terrestrially. [R.S.K.B.]

melanism Many animals, especially species of moths and other insects, exhibit melanic forms that are black or dark in colour due to the deposition of melanin pigment in the cuticle or skin. [P.M.B.]

mercury (Hg) A heavy, silver-white METAL (ATOMIC NUMBER = 80; relative ATOMIC MASS = 200.59; melting point = −39°C; boiling point = 357°C), mercury is an ultratrace constituent (0.08 mg kg⁻¹) of the Earth's CRUST. Found in cinnabar (HgS) and in association with lead–zinc–silver ores, it is the only metal that is liquid (quicksilver) at normal temperatures and is used in chlor-alkali production, electrical BATTERIES and CATALYSTS. The high volatility of this non-essential element renders it extremely dangerous, inhaled mercury vapour being capable of passing the blood–brain barrier and, with its great affinity for the SH groups of enzymes, severely affecting the central nervous system. The best-known case of industrial mercurialism was that of the 'mad hatters' in the 19th century, who used mercuric nitrate in the manufacture of felt. Inorganic mercury salts can also damage the kidneys. Released to the environment from volcanoes, mining, fossil-fuel combustion, the use of mercury compounds and the discharge of mercury-containing wastes, mercury is not greatly taken up by plants but can undergo methylation to highly toxic ORGANOMERCURY compounds, which are found in fish. [J.G.F.]

merolimnic fauna *See* DRIFT, FRESHWATER.

meromictic lakes *See* LAKE STRATIFICATION; LAKES.

meroplankton Organisms that spend part of their life cycle in the water column, usually the eggs and LARVAE of benthic or nektonic adults. *See also* PELAGIC. [V.F.]

mesocosm As MACROCOSM, but 'medium sized' and often indoors. [P.C.]

mesopelagic The part of the OCEAN water column extending from the bottom of the epipelagic zone (*c.* 200–300 m) to about 1000 m depth. It corresponds approximately with the dysphotic (twilight) zone and is located seaward of the SHELF-SLOPE BREAK. [V.F.]

mesoplankton ZOOPLANKTON species that are between 0.2 and 20 mm in size. [V.F.]

metal A dense substance having a metallic lustre, being a good conductor of heat and electricity, ductile and malleable. With the exception of mercury, metals are solid at room temperature. [J.G.]

metalimnion *See* LAKE STRATIFICATION; LAKES.

metallothioneins Low relative molecular mass proteins rich in cysteinyl residues. They have affinity for certain metals that bind to sulphydryl groups. Synthesis is induced by the presence of cadmium, zinc, copper, MERCURY or gold in the diet or ambient medium. They are thought to play a protective role in organisms as a sink for toxic metals and as part of 'normal physiology' in transport and storage of essential metals. Sometimes abbreviated as MT. *See also* HEAT-SHOCK PROTEIN; PROTECTIVE PROTEINS. [P.C.]

metapopulations The DISTRIBUTION of a species is often more or less fragmented, most obviously by being confined to isolated patches of suitable habitat. An assemblage of such separate populations can itself be treated as an entity with its own emergent properties: a metapopulation. The crucial feature of its dynamics is the balance between the rate of extinction of the local populations of which it is made and the rate at which empty habitat patches are recolonized by individuals or propagules migrating from the extant populations. [J.R.G.T.]

meteorology Originally the science of things aloft (from the Greek), it has come to mean the science of the physical nature of the lower ATMOSPHERE, especially the behaviour and forecasting of WEATHER systems. *See also* MICROMETEOROLOGY. [J.F.R.M.]

methane The simplest hydrocarbon, methane (CH_4) exists as a gas at normal temperatures and pressures (boiling point −164°C); it is also known as coal gas, marsh gas and fire damp and is the major constituent of domestic 'natural gas'. It is found as a fossil fuel, often associated with oil and coal, where it may form an explosion hazard in coal mines and is actively vented to the atmosphere. It is also produced by microbes in waterlogged soils and LANDFILL sites (METHANOGENESIS) and by insects (e.g. TERMITES) and animals (especially ruminants). Natural sources account for about 160 Mt of the estimated annual EMISSIONS of 540 Mt. CH_4 is a 'greenhouse gas', contributing about 20% to the radiative forcing of the atmosphere. Concentrations in the atmosphere were 1.71 ppm by volume (ppmv) in 1992 and are currently rising by about 0.8% per year. Preindustrial concentrations (i.e. prior to 1800) were around 0.7 ppmv. The steady increase in CH_4 concentrations was interrupted in 1991 and 1992, but data from 1993 indicate a resumption of the upward trend. [J.N.C.]

methanogenesis The production of METHANE (CH_4) from an organic substrate occurs via the following pathways.

1 By the action of microbes in anaerobic conditions in SOIL. The largest global methane sources are natural WETLANDS (*c.* 25%) and flood-irrigated AGRICULTURE, notably rice paddies (*c.* 12%). Large quantities of methane are also generated in LANDFILL sites, where buried organic waste is converted by microbes to methane, which may escape into the ATMOSPHERE or be tapped as a source of fuel.

2 By the action of microbes in the gut of animals.

3 By the chemical transformation of organic matter

at high temperatures and pressures in the earth, leading to the formation of natural gas, oil and coal. [J.N.C.]

metre (m) SI UNIT of length, originally conceived as 10^{-7} of the distance on the Earth's surface from the North Pole to the Equator; now defined as the distance that LIGHT travels in $1/299\,792\,458$ of a second. Relation to obsolete units: $1\,m = 39.3701$ inches; 1 yard $= 0.914\,m$. [J.G.]

MFO *See* MIXED-FUNCTION OXIDASE.

microbial ecology The science that specifically examines the relationships between microorganisms and their biotic and abiotic environments. [V.F.]

microbial loop This refers to the regeneration of NUTRIENTS and their return to the FOOD CHAIN that is mediated by bacteria and protozoans. Bacteria can utilize both particulate DETRITUS (faecal pellets, dead organisms) and DISSOLVED ORGANIC MATTER (excretory products and microbial EXU-DATES). The bacteria are in turn fed upon by protozoans, which are fed upon by higher trophic levels (e.g. copepods). Of the total PHYTOPLANKTON production converted to dissolved organic matter, 10–50% is consumed by bacterioplankton. Much of this material is cycled through the microbial loop. The microbial loop occurs, but is less well understood, in the BENTHOS where dominant bacterial grazers are probably flagellated protozoans and where ciliates feed on larger phytobenthos and flagellates. *See also* BENTHIC–PELAGIC COUPLING. [V.F.]

microclimate The CLIMATE in small places, usually considered over a spatial scale of a few centimetres or metres and over short periods of time (hours). [J.G.]

microcosm As MACROCOSM, but 'small' and usually indoors, in laboratories. [P.C.]

microfauna The extraction of animals from marine sediments almost invariably requires the use of sieves and hence the mesh size of the sieve used determines the SIZE of organism retained. The microfauna are defined as those benthic 'protozoans' (more correctly the animal-like protists) that pass through a 0.5-mm mesh and, by extension, the same term is often used for heterotrophic protists from other benthic habitats, although it is not used in respect of the PLANKTON. The microfauna are therefore distinguished from the MEIOFAUNA not on the basis of size but by the kingdom (Protista) to which they belong; their ecology is essentially the same as that of the meiofauna. Ciliates and flagellates dominate this fauna. [R.S.K.B.]

microflora (symbionts) Usually refers to microscopic algae and possibly also bacteria and fungi. *Cf.* MICROFAUNA. [P.C.]

microhabitat Precise physical location of a species. For example, epilithic algae and benthic invertebrates live on submerged stones and pebbles, their HABITAT. However, the algae live on the upper sur-faces, where they are exposed to light needed for PHOTOSYNTHESIS, and the invertebrates often occur on lower surfaces, where they obtain shelter from water movements and predators. Thus upper surfaces are the microhabitats of algae and lower surfaces the microhabitats of benthic invertebrates. [P.C.]

micrometeorology Micrometeorology is the branch of METEOROLOGY concerned with the lowest layers of the ATMOSPHERE at heights within a few tens of metres of the surface and the interaction of this surface BOUNDARY LAYER with Earth's surface. Essentially it is concerned with the layer of the atmosphere with which we are most familiar, which we breathe and live in, and in which our crops grow. It is the study of how the surface and the atmosphere interact through the exchange of heat, moisture and other properties such as CARBON DIOXIDE (CO_2) or air pollutants. [J.B.M.]

micronutrients These are elements required by living organisms only in small amounts (*cf.* MACRONU-TRIENTS). The great majority, for example boron, manganese, copper, zinc and molybdenum in plants and fluorine, manganese, cobalt, copper, zinc, selenium and iodine in animals, are trace elements; iron is also an essential micronutrient even though it is very abundant in the LITHOSPHERE. Below the micronutrient concentration range where normal growth occurs, plants and animals exhibit deficiency symptoms and in severe cases may die. [K.A.S. & J.R.E.]

microtine cycles The enormous changes in population abundance characteristic of certain small rodents, particularly voles and lemmings, that lead to regular population explosions and crashes. The cycles occur with a fairly regular periodicity of between 2 and 5 years, but may vary widely in amplitude. Factors that have been proposed to explain the cycles include weather, food, predators, parasites, hormonal changes and behavioural changes. Despite intensive study, no clear explanation for the occurrence of these cycles has been found. [V.F.]

middle infralittoral zone *See* WITHIN-LAKE HABITAT CLASSIFICATION.

midoceanic ridge The longest mountain chain on Earth, extending through the ATLANTIC, Indian, Antarctic and South Pacific oceans, the NORWE-GIAN SEA and the Arctic Basin to a distance of more than 56 000 km. The midocean ridges are areas in which new crustal material is forming as regions of the Earth's outer shell move apart. The midocean ridges extend to a height of 1–3 km above the sea floor and are generally more than 1500 km wide. They are roughly symmetrical, lie generally parallel to the CONTINENTAL MARGINS, are cut transversely by faults and exhibit high seismic activity and high heat flow, especially near the axial regions. The middle part of the ridges contain a rift valley, a deep notch or cleft in the ridge crest. [V.F.]

Minamata Classic case of environmental POLLUTION that affected human health. Minamata is a town on the west coast of Kyushu Island, Japan where methyl mercury contaminants of fish, the staple diet of the local population, caused severe disablement (numbness and seizures) and death. The source was a PVC plant that discharged an effluent containing both inorganic and organic mercury. The inorganic form was converted by fish into methyl mercury. [P.C.]

mine drainage These waters often emerge at low pH and rich in HEAVY METALS. Water ACIDIFICATION is due to the oxidation of pyrite (Fe_2S) and other sulphides exposed by the mining activities. H^+ is generated from sulphides in a series of complex reactions. The oxidation process is catalysed by bacteria that use pyrite as a source of energy. The extremely ACID conditions generated at the site lead to high dissolution of minerals, including heavy metals. Acid mine drainage is neutralized downstream of the source; as this happens FLOCCULATION and PRECIPITATION, especially of iron hydroxides, occur that are themselves damaging to the BENTHOS. Potentially toxic metals may be remobilized from such deposits if there is a subsequent drop in pH, for example during periods of high flow. *See also* POLLUTION. [P.C.]

mineral nutrients Those NUTRIENTS that originate mainly by WEATHERING of minerals in the SOIL, including the MACRONUTRIENTS nitrogen, phosphorus, potassium, calcium, magnesium and sulphur, and the MICRONUTRIENTS iron, manganese, boron, molybdenum, zinc, chlorine and cobalt. Of these, nitrogen comes partly from the ATMOSPHERE but is still regarded as a mineral nutrient. The term is synonymous with 'inorganic nutrient'. All of these nutrients are found in the soil, and the study of their behaviour in relation to the very complex chemical and physical environment of the soil is a large part of the discipline of soil science. [J.G.]

mineralization The natural process whereby MINERAL NUTRIENTS such as nitrogen, sulphur and phosphorus are released from immobile organic forms in the SOIL and thus become available as inorganic ions for uptake by plants. [J.G.]

minimum viable population (MVP) This is a popular concept in CONSERVATION BIOLOGY and is defined as the threshold POPULATION SIZE below which rapid extinction is virtually guaranteed. Clearly, in general, smaller populations will be more vulnerable than larger ones, although it has not been established, either theoretically or empirically, that there is some critical population size below which the vulnerability to extinction increases suddenly. It is perhaps more useful to estimate extinction probability as a function of time for different population sizes than to identify some specific MVP. [P.C.]

mire This term has been used in a variety of ways,

some specific and many broad and general. Over the past 30 years it has been used increasingly of PEAT-forming habitats and ecosystems and has proved a most valuable general term in this area. [P.D.M.]

mitigation, compensatory Compensatory mitigation is a political/legal concept that presumes the destruction of natural habitats or populations can adequately be offset by actions elsewhere. Examples include the creation of artificial wetlands to compensate for the destruction of natural wetlands and attempts to translocate affected populations to another site. The degree to which an artificially created habitat or population is ecologically equivalent to, and adequately performs the same ECOSYSTEM functions as, the naturally occurring ones destroyed in the process is a matter of active debate and may differ significantly from site to site and species to species. [E.O.G. & L.R.M.]

mixed-function oxidase (MFO) Mixed-function oxidases (or monooxygenases) are a group of enzymes that catalyse the conversion of lipophilic substrates (organic xenobiotics) to more polar, i.e. water-soluble, products. They occur in smooth endoplasmic reticulum. They require OXYGEN, NADPH and a cytochrome P450 isozyme; they are inducible. MFO activity is used as a BIOMARKER. [P.C.]

mixing zone Body of water (or air) immediately next to DISCHARGE in which dilution is taking place and hence in which the concentration of a CONTAMINANT may exceed the maximum allowable level. Usually defined by the regulatory authority. [P.C.]

MLC *See* MEDIAN LETHAL CONCENTRATION.

mode This MEASURE OF CENTRAL TENDENCY or average is simply the value of the most common observation. It is the 'peak' of the DISTRIBUTION. [B.S.]

model A simplified representation of the real world that aids understanding. In environmental sciences, models of the real world are usually constructed from equations but they can be made in physical structures as well. [B.S.]

Moh scale of hardness The Moh scale of hardness is based on a ranked list of minerals, such that each one can be scratched by the one below: 1, talc; 2, gypsum; 3, calcite; 4, fluorite; 5, apatite; 6, orthoclase; 7, quartz; 8, topaz; 9, corundum; 10, diamond. [J.G.]

mole (mol) SI UNIT for the amount of a substance based on the Avagadro number (6.022×10^{23}) of particles it contains, whether atoms, molecules, ions or photons. For example, 1 mol of the pure ISOTOPE ^{12}C contains 6.022×10^{23} atoms and has a mass of 12 g, whereas 1 mol of $^{12}CO_2$ has a mass of 44 g. [J.G.]

molecular ecology Molecular ecology is a generic term loosely applied to ecological studies that employ the tools of molecular biology. 'Molecular ecology' might suggest the existence of a branch of ecology devoted to the study of organisms and their ENVI-

RONMENT at a molecular level. Unfortunately, ecology is not yet so advanced and most studies in molecular ecology, with a few notable exceptions, use molecular biology primarily as a source of genetic markers. [P.B.R.]

monitoring Continuous or regular assessment of the quality of EMISSIONS or EFFLUENTS, or sources that lead to these, or specific places in the environment possibly subjected to them. For the latter, this can involve both chemical and biological assessment. [P.C.]

monoculture The agricultural, arboricultural and horticultural practice of cultivating one plant species, often a single cultivar, in one location. [G.A.F.H.]

monsoon forest Tropical and SUBTROPICAL forests of certain areas, such as northern India and Burma, are supplied with rainfall during a wet season as a result of monsoon rains penetrating the continent as warm, moist winds blow from the ocean. During the wet season growth is lush, but in the following DRY SEASON the forest may suffer drought. During the drought many trees lose their leaves, thus avoiding excessive transpiration. The SEASONALITY of these forests distinguishes them from the consistently wet TROPICAL RAIN FORESTS, where there is no significant interruption to water supply.

Many of the trees of monsoon forests are of great value as sources of hardwood timber, such as teak (*Tectona grandis*). This has led to intensive exploitation of this vegetation type. [P.D.M.]

montane forests High-elevation forests are those forests below the TIMBER LINE (subalpine) but at least 1000 m (3280 feet) above sea level. These elevations apply generally, although higher elevations are required at lower latitudes before montane forests can occur. [P.M.S.A. & G.P.B.]

Monte Carlo simulation Method used to explore UNCERTAINTY in mathematical simulation models. It involves an iterative process in which model parameter values are selected at random from a specified frequency distribution. Output values, following simulation runs, are used to determine the PROBABILITY of occurrence of particular values, given the uncertainty in the parameter. *See also* RISK ASSESSMENT. [P.C.]

Montreal protocol UN instrument, developed under the auspices of the UNEP, on control of substances that deplete the OZONE LAYER. Adopted in 1987 and revised in 1990, it provides for the successive phasing out of CFCs and other specified substances likely to deplete the ozone layer. *See also* UNITED NATIONS PROGRAMMES AND BODIES. [P.C.]

moorland Upland areas of heather-dominated vegetation in north-western Europe are termed 'moorland'. The floristic distinction between HEATHLAND and moorland is imprecise. Generally, the wetter moorlands are richer in species of *Vaccinium*, *Trichophorum* and *Eriophorum*. As in the case of heath-

lands the soils are acid, but the higher levels of precipitation in the uplands lead to the development of thicker layers of peaty material at the surface of the soil. In the wettest types of moorland the vegetation merges into blanket bog. [P.D.M.]

mor A surface HUMUS horizon that forms beneath conifers and open HEATHLAND and MOORLAND in temperate climates. It is acid, low in most microbinal activities (not of fungi) and consists of several separated layers in various degrees of decomposition. [P.C.]

morbidity Any departure from a state of physiological (and/or psychological in people) well-being. Synonymous with sickness, illness or ill health. It is more difficult to measure than MORTALITY but can be done, for example in terms of proportion of population 'ill', frequency of periods of illness, duration of illness. [P.C.]

mortality At its most simplistic level, mortality describes the number of individuals dying in a particular population. Most frequently it is expressed as a relative value or rate of change. A relative measure describes the proportion of individuals dying relative to the whole population, while a rate describes the pattern of mortality over time. These values are often combined to describe the proportional rate of mortality at key life stages (e.g. juvenile mortality). Mortality and its underlying causes are major factors in the regulation, DISTRIBUTION and ABUNDANCE of natural populations. [R.C.]

mortality rate The proportion of a population dying in each time interval, equivalent to the average PROBABILITY of an individual dying in that time interval. [A.J.D.]

motor vehicle pollution No other mechanical product has made the same impact on the average person as the motor vehicle, especially the private car. Motor vehicle growth really became noticeable in the years following the Second World War and in many ways was a visible manifestation of the greater economic prosperity among wide sections of society. For example, according to the Washington-based World Watch Institute, in 1950 there were 53 million cars in the world. By the late 1980s this figure had increased to over 423 million. If commercial vehicles, such as trucks, buses and coaches, are added the figure rises to over 550 million. It is predicted, on current trends, that this figure will double by the year 2010.

The picture has been mirrored in Britain. In 1950 there were just under 4 million motor vehicles on the roads. Each year since then the number of motor vehicles has steadily increased. In 1996 official Department of Transport statistics revealed that there were over 25.6 million vehicles on Britain's roads, a 540% increase since 1950. It is predicted that the motor vehicle population will rise by 50% by the year 2015.

In addition to the environmental problems caused

by growing road traffic congestion and noise, especially in urban areas, and land used for road building, motor vehicles are responsible for producing a significant amount of pollutants at both a global and regional level. For example, the safe disposal of old motor vehicles, millions of used tyres, old BATTERIES and used oil will litter and contaminate the landscape if not properly controlled and recycled.

At the same time, the millions of road vehicles in daily use pollute the ATMOSPHERE with potential health and environmental risk. Motor vehicles only harness 10–20% of the potential energy in their fuel; the rest is converted to heat and exhaust pollutants. It is this aspect of motor vehicles where most official, media and public attention has focused. And with good reason.

It is now generally accepted that the EMISSIONS generated by fossil fuel (petrol and diesel)-powered motor vehicles have become a major source of ENVIRONMENTAL IMPACT, especially poor AIR QUALITY. Much AIR POLLUTION is produced by the combustion of FOSSIL FUELS. Motor vehicle exhaust emissions generate CARBON DIOXIDE (CO_2), CARBON MONOXIDE (CO), NITROGEN OXIDES (NO_x), sulphur dioxides (SO_x), HYDROCARBONS (HC) and particulate matter (PM10s). These pollutants are harmful and have a deleterious effect on society. Motor vehicles are responsible for about 85% of CO pollution, NO_x is a major contributor to acid rain (see ACID RAIN AND MIST) and CO_2 is one of the main gaseous pollutants from motor vehicles and the largest single contributor to GLOBAL WARMING.

In western Europe, motor vehicles are responsible for more than 80% of all CO emissions, 51% of NO_x, 45% of HC, 8% of particulates and 3% of SO_x. According to the European Union (EU) 1992 White Paper *The Future Development of the Common Market Transport Policy*, there has been a substantial increase over the last two decades in the number of transport-related pollutants, the most important of these being CO_2. The White Paper pointed out that between 1971 and 1989 CO_2 emissions from motor vehicles within the EU had increased by 76%. These findings are echoed in official British figures. [F.W.]

mud *See* MUDFLAT.

mudflat 'Mud' is not a precise concept: it generally denotes any ground that is soft and wet. Likewise 'mudflat' is applied to any TIDAL FLAT that does not have the usual clean appearance of sand. In practice, this means that appreciable quantities of SILT (particles 0.002–0.06mm diameter) are present even though the major sedimentary component may still be sand (0.06–2.0mm diameter) or even gravel (2–60mm diameter). 'Sandy mud' and 'muddy sand' are terms often used to indicate muddy sediments dominated by silts or sands, respectively. [R.S.K.B.]

mull A surface HUMUS that forms in deciduous forests. It is neutral or alkaline. It provides generally favourable conditions for decomposition and in consequence it is well mixed. [P.C.]

multiple resistance to pesticides Also called multiresistance, this occurs when organisms evolve RESISTANCE to several pesticides. For example, *kdr*, a gene that helps confer resistance to DDT, also contributes to resistance to pyrethroids. [D.A.B.]

multispecies (eco)toxicity tests Systems for assessing and/or predicting the ecological effects of substances or EFFLUENTS involving more than one species. They can range in size or complexity from two-species interactions, to collections of several species in indoor/outdoor enclosures, to samples of multi-species systems either extracted from nature or isolated *in situ*. They can be small scale (*see* MICROCOSM), medium scale (*see* MESOCOSM) or large scale (*see* MACROCOSM). Claimed by some to be more ecologically relevant, since they incorporate between-species interactions that, by definition, are not a feature of single-species studies. However, the isolates may not be representative and isolation can destabilize the dynamics of the interacting populations. Moreover, the maintenance and deployment of multispecies systems is usually more time-consuming and costly than single-species ones. *See also* PREDICTIVE ECOTOXICITY TESTS. [P.C.]

mutagen A mutagen is any agent, such as IONIZING RADIATION, that can cause MUTATION of the genetic material of living organisms. *See also* SIEVERT. [A.B.M.]

mutation Any spontaneous, random change, large or small, in the genome. However, a distinction is sometimes made between a point mutation (impact on a single gene or even base substitution) and a macromutation (change with major, usually obvious visible, effect on the phenotype). Random mutation is intended to imply non-directional with respect to the course of evolution. [P.C.]

MVP *See* MINIMUM VIABLE POPULATION.

mycelium The fungi are characterized by a life cycle in which their dispersed propagules (spores) germinate on a favourable substratum by formation of a germ tube, which develops into a radiating system of filamentous, branching, tubular threads termed 'hyphae', producing a three-dimensional network collectively known as the mycelium (representing the thallus). [J.B.H.]

mycorrhiza A long-lived association of a fungal MYCELIUM and plant roots that results in readily observable morphological complexes. The association is an example of a symbiotic relationship, i.e. coexistence of different species for at least part of their life cycle. More importantly, it is also mutualistic, with both partners deriving direct benefit (e.g. an exchange of NUTRIENTS and/or metabolites), although in some cases a controlled, weak parasitism may also be involved. In general, the partners survive better together, i.e. they are more 'fit' as dual organisms than when apart. The main benefit to the fungus as a heterotrophic organism is a supply of organic carbon, mainly in the form of hexose sugars that are obtained by selectively increased plant cell permeability (probably directed by the fungus), and which are then converted to sugar alcohols, for example arabitol, mannitol, etc. For the autotrophic plant partner, there is an increase in root branching and root surface area, resulting in more effective utilization of a given volume of SOIL, the mycorrhizal fungus taking up selected soil nutrients (especially phosphorus- and nitrogen-containing compounds) and water more effectively than non-mycorrhizal roots. In other cases, such as orchids, the seed may only germinate if the appropriate fungal partner is present and the plant derives its carbon requirements from the fungus (as also for monotropoid mycorrhizae). [J.B.H.]

N

NASA (National Aeronautics and Space Administration) The US organization responsible for conducting space research and exploration, and for supporting many associated research programmes of universities and other independent organizations. It has pursued exemplary cooperation with the WORLD METEOROLOGICAL ORGANIZATION both directly and through other national meteorological services to provide extensive routine observations by satellite. Used for research and data-gathering in the meteorological, oceanographic and terrestrial fields, these satellite observations have enormously extended human knowledge. [R.S.S.]

natality (fecundity) A measure of the production of offspring in a population. [R.C.]

National Oceanic and Atmospheric Administration (NOAA) Satellite The name of the satellite carrying the ADVANCED VERY-HIGH-RESOLUTION RADIOMETER (AVHRR) sensor. The US National Oceanic and Atmospheric Administration has operated several generations of meteorological satellites. These have a Sun-synchronous polar orbit and an altitude of 833 km. The even-numbered satellites (e.g. NOAA 12) cross the Equator at 7.30 a.m. (0730 hours) and 7.30 p.m. (1930 hours), and the odd-numbered satellites (e.g. NOAA 13) cross the Equator at 2.30 p.m. (1430 hours) and 2.30 a.m. (0230 hours). For environmental applications the most useful have been NOAA 6 (1979) onwards as these have carried the AVHRR. [P.J.C.]

National Priority List (NPL) *See* SUPERFUND LEGISLATION.

National Rivers Authority (NRA) *See* ENVIRONMENTAL (PROTECTION) AGENCIES.

native and naturalized species Native species are those that have evolved in place or have become established independently of human activity. Naturalized species were brought to a place by human activity, either intentionally or not, and have subsequently established self-sustaining populations. [E.O.G. & L.R.M.]

Natura 2000 The collective name for sites in Europe that are subject to legislation on the conservation of natural habitats and wild fauna and flora. Provides for the establishment of a coherent network of designated sites on land and at sea, including special areas of conservation (SACs). The overall aim is the conservation of BIODIVERSITY by protecting habitats. [P.C.]

natural Literally, of nature. The term usually implies a situation in which there has been no modification by humans: for example, a natural landscape, a natural community. But there is another view, namely that humans are also 'of nature', being products of evolution, so 'natural' should not exclude humans and the consequences of their actions. Clearly, it is a difficult term to pin down unambiguously to the satisfaction of all. [P.C.]

natural disasters Upheavals leading to impacts on human society and/or ecological systems and/or the abiotic environment by phenomena that are not attributable to human causes. Examples include earthquakes, volcanoes, storms, tornadoes, hurricanes, FLOODS, forest fires, DROUGHT and meteorite impacts. *Cf.* ECOLOGICAL/ENVIRONMENTAL DISASTERS. [P.C.]

natural resource accounting and green gross domestic produce (GDP) Alternative systems of national accounting and performance measures, which incorporate ecological and human welfare considerations. *See also* ENVIRONMENTAL (ECOLOGICAL) ECONOMICS; GREEN NET NATIONAL PRODUCT. [P.C.]

natural selection A process involving differences between individuals in their rates of survival or reproduction, leading to some types of organism being represented more than others in the next generation. The process of natural selection is generally held to explain most if not all evolutionary change. [J.R.G.T.]

nature versus nurture Shorthand for the relative involvement of, respectively, heredity (genetics) and ENVIRONMENT in the control and development of TRAITS. It is usually applied to the human condition, concerning which there have been heated debates on the relative involvement of these elements in determining such things as intelligence and criminality. From quantitative genetics we know that the variation in all traits can be ascribed to genotype, environment and genotype × environment components. It is the relative importance of these that varies from trait to trait, and from species to species. [P.C.]

Nearctic faunal region North America north of the tropics comprises the Nearctic region. [A.H.]

necromass Dead organic matter accumulated in a COMMUNITY. Unlike BIOMASS, necromass is incapable of transforming energy into new biomass.

Necromass provides a source of energy to detritivores and decomposers. It consists of dead bodies, including dead wood that is part of living trees, and faeces. [P.O.]

negative feedback The coupling of an output process to an input process in such a way that the output process is inhibited. For example, high birth rate leads to high population, which leads to crowding and reduced birth rate, thus tending to reduce population growth (in this example birth rate is the input process and population increase the output process). Negative feedbacks tend to be stabilizing, although this is not always the case if the FEEDBACK is delayed. [S.N.W.]

nekton Pelagic animals whose swimming abilities permit them to move actively through the water column and to move against CURRENTS. [V.F.]

Neotropical The biogeographical region which comprises the tropics and subtropics of the New World (in contradistinction to palaeotropical, i.e. of the Old World tropics). [W.G.C.]

neritic Referring to inshore waters between mean low water to 200 m in depth that overlie CONTINENTAL SHELVES (i.e. the zone landward of the SHELF-SLOPE BREAK). The neritic zone is characterized not by a fixed depth but by the fact that it is euphotic and thus an area in which PHOTOSYNTHESIS can occur. [V.F.]

net photosynthetic rate (NPR) The difference between gross PHOTOSYNTHESIS (gain) and RESPIRATION (loss). The plant grows when NPR > 0 and loses mass when NPR < 0 (e.g. in prolonged darkness). [M.J.C.]

net primary production (NPP) The process of energy, matter or carbon accumulation net of respiratory losses by the AUTOTROPHS of a community. Its rate, net primary productivity (P_n or N), equals the difference between gross primary productivity and RESPIRATION by the autotrophs. Although the term applies to all autotrophs it is most commonly used in the context of photosynthetic organisms. The term net primary production has often been used synonymously with 'net primary productivity'. However, by precedence, net primary productivity should be used to describe the rate of net primary production, whereas PRODUCTION is the process itself. [S.P.L.]

net radiometer A type of RADIOMETER that measures the difference between the energy transferred by RADIATION of all wavelengths to the Earth's surface and that which is reflected at or emitted by the surface. A net radiometer is usually a thermopile device, in which the imbalance in the radiation incident on an upward facing plate and a downward facing plate results in a TEMPERATURE difference between them. [J.B.M.]

neuston Planktonic organisms of the PELAGIC zone that live at or very near the surface. [V.F.]

neutron probe An instrument for measuring soil water content. The neutron probe provides nondestructive, accurate measurements of changes in soil water content with depth. A probe containing a radioactive source of high-energy fast neutrons is lowered down an access tube permanently installed in the soil. The fast neutrons collide with hydrogen atoms in the soil and in the water, and lose energy. These slow neutrons are sampled by a detector also housed in the probe. Because the strength of the signal is a measure of the number of hydrogen atoms in both the soil and the water, the soil must be calibrated. This is best done by gravimetric sampling close to the site under study. The water content is determined from the difference between wet and oven-dry mass, over a range of moisture contents. Any long-term drifts in the instrument CALIBRATION are removed by calculating soil moisture content with respect to a water STANDARD. The sampling volume of a neutron probe is a sphere around the source, with 95% of the signal being the result of interactions within a radius of some 300 mm. [J.H.C.G.]

new chemicals Chemicals, produced commercially, that are not listed on the inventories of EXISTING CHEMICALS. These are subject to a NOTIFICATION procedure leading to RISK ASSESSMENT and possibly RISK MANAGEMENT. [P.C.]

new forestry Forest practices designed to retain more ECOSYSTEM complexity than is found in traditionally managed forests while also removing commodities (usually wood). [A.N.G.]

new substances *See* EUROPEAN INVENTORY OF EXISTING COMMERCIAL CHEMICAL SUBSTANCES.

newton (N) The SI UNIT of force, defined as the force required to give 1 kg an acceleration of 1 m s^{-2}. Its relation to the obsolete British unit is: 1 N = 0.225 lb. [J.G.]

niche This term is often used loosely by both ecologists and laymen, but defining the niche concept formally is rather complicated. An old interpretation considers it to be the functional role or 'occupation' of a species in a COMMUNITY. Presently, the generally used concept is that of the 'Hutchinsonian niche', which is defined as the requirements that the ENVIRONMENT has to meet to allow the persistence of (a POPULATION of) a species. [J.G.S.]

NIMBY *See* NOT IN MY BACK YARD.

NIMTO *See* NOT IN MY TERM OF OFFICE.

nitrate pollution Run-off from agricultural land that has been worked with chemical fertilizer, or from AGRICULTURAL WASTE, which can be rich in nitrates. Such POLLUTION is a major cause of EUTROPHICATION in receiving waters. The CONTAMINATION of groundwater with nitrates is an important problem in Europe and North America. Groundwater is extensively used as a source of drinking water, and nitrates can cause problems for human health—not because they are toxic in themselves but in the mouth can be transformed by bacterial action to nitrites, which can induce methaemoglobinaemia (a reduction in oxygen-carrying capacity of the blood) especially in infants. According to WHO, water becomes unpotable when nitrates exceed 45 mg l⁻¹. The European Union has issued a directive requiring any area where nitrates exceed 50 mg l⁻¹ in surface or groundwater to be declared a vulnerable area in which compulsory restrictions on farming must be applied. [P.C.]

nitrogen cycle The movement of nitrogen between the ATMOSPHERE, the BIOSPHERE and the HYDROSPHERE, and the associated transformations between different chemical forms. The Earth's atmosphere contains about 10^{15} t of nitrogen, as the relatively inert gas dinitrogen (N_2). This quantity is nearly 10 times greater than that contained in the oceans and in sediments. Biological nitrogen fixation, the conversion of atmospheric N_2 to ammonia by organisms, is the main natural mechanism for transfer of N to the biosphere (c. 150 Tg N year⁻¹) and hydrosphere (c. 40 Tg N year⁻¹). Industrial fixation is another major source. The ammonia is either used directly, or converted to urea, ammonium nitrate or ammonium phosphates, for fertilizer use. [K.A.S.]

nitrogen oxides Gases formed from nitrogen and OXYGEN, including nitrous oxide (N_2O), nitric oxide (NO) and nitrogen dioxide (NO_2). N_2O is inert in the TROPOSPHERE, but is decomposed in the STRATOSPHERE. NO and NO_2 are collectively known as NO_x and are formed at high temperatures from the direct combination of atmospheric oxygen and nitrogen, as well as from the combustion of nitrogen in fuel. Worldwide, estimates of NO_x EMISSIONS vary between 80 and 230 Mt per year (expressed as NO_2), predominantly from anthropogenic sources. NO_x reacts in air to form nitric acid (HNO_3), a component of acid rain (see ACID RAIN AND MIST), and nitrate aerosols. It is a major constituent of PHOTOCHEMICAL SMOG, with OZONE and PEROXYACETYL NITRATE (PAN). NO_x affects plant growth at concentrations above 15 ppb by volume (ppbv) and NO_2 may cause breathing problems to humans above 100 ppbv. Deposition of the gases from the ATMOSPHERE, and as nitrate in rain, contributes to EUTROPHICATION. *See also* MOTOR VEHICLE POLLUTION. [J.N.C.]

no observed effect concentration (NOEC) In an ECOTOXICITY test series, the highest concentration of a chemical to show no statistically significant difference from the control in an observed variable (the EFFECT). The NOEC clearly will depend upon the concentration intervals used; i.e. there could be a higher unobserved no effect concentration between the NOEC and the LOWEST OBSERVED EFFECT CONCENTRATION (LOEC). Moreover, proving a negative is always tenuous. It is for these reasons that the term 'observed' is used. NOECs should always be reported with LOECs. *See also* PREDICTIVE ECOTOXICITY TESTS. [P.C.]

NOEC *See* NO OBSERVED EFFECT CONCENTRATION.

noise pollution Sound, including vibration, that is socially or medically undesirable. Excessive noise could also have an impact on ecological systems, for example by scaring wildlife, but this is not well documented. What constitutes noise POLLUTION is complex as not only the physical properties of the sound have to be taken into account, but also the psychological responses of those exposed to the noise. Environmental controls on noise and vibration most usually refer to conditions at the site boundary and beyond. Conditions within factories are usually subject to 'conditions at work' legislation. [P.C.]

nominal concentration In an ECOTOXICITY test, the concentration of chemical calculated from how solutions are made up; i.e. from the extent of dilution of an original concentrate. It contrasts with the actual concentration, which is measured at some time during the test. The two often differ, for example due to error or chemical 'sticking' to glassware. *See also* PREDICTIVE ECOTOXICITY TESTS. [P.C.]

non-indigenous species A species occurring outside its NATURAL geographical range; also known as an ALIEN species, in contrast to a native species (*see* NATIVE AND NATURALIZED SPECIES). [M.J.C.]

non-parametric statistics Statistical tests are frequently classified into parametric and non-parametric tests. Non-parametric ones do not require quantitative information/observations to follow a NORMAL DISTRIBUTION and to have similar VARIABILITY (homogeneous variances). Non-parametric tests can be carried out on qualitative information, i.e. ranked information or information in categories. Examples of non-parametric tests/techniques are Mann–Whitney tests (*see* MANN–WHITNEY *U* TEST), KENDALL'S RANK CORRELATION COEFFICIENT, SPEARMAN'S RANK CORRELATION COEFFICIENT, KRUSKAL-WALLIS TEST and the BINOMIAL (SIGN) TEST. [B.S.]

non-point source pollution *See* DIFFUSE SOURCES.

non-renewable resources Resources, such as minerals or FOSSIL FUELS, that are replaced only on geological time-scales, or species of organisms which, once extinct, cannot be replaced. *Cf.* RENEWABLE RESOURCE. [P.C.]

normal distribution A continuous PROBABILITY DISTRIBUTION that is symmetrical, unimodal and bell-shaped. For all normal distributions, the following percentages of observations lie within the indicated number of standard deviations, either side of the mean:

68.26% of observations within the $\mu \pm \sigma$

95.44% of observations within the $\mu \pm 2\sigma$

99.73% of observations within the $\mu \pm 3\sigma$

More conveniently:

95% of all observations lie within the $\mu \pm 1.960\sigma$

99% of all observations lie within the $\mu \pm 2.576\sigma$

[B.S.]

North Sea The largest marginal SEA of the Atlantic; a shallow marine region on the European CONTINENTAL SHELF, formed by the flooding of a landmass. This epicontinental sea extends northwards to 62°N and includes the Skagerrak, with a southern limit extending east from Cape Skagen, roughly at 57°N to the English Channel and its approach east of 5°W. It is surrounded by the British Isles, Norway, Denmark, Germany, Holland and Belgium. It has a mean depth of about 90 m and a maximum depth of 725 m in the Norwegian Trench.

The North Sea covers an area of 5.8×10^5 km² and has a volume of 50 000 km³. The surface SALINITY increases towards the north and west; in the central North Sea salinity ranges between 34.8 and 35.1‰, whereas along the German shore the salinity ranges from 29‰ (in summer) to 32‰ (in winter). CIRCULATION is counterclockwise in the upper layer but irregular at the bottom. Approximately 90% of the water inflow enters between the Shetland and Orkney Islands. The TIDES are primarily semidiurnal, and tidal height decreases towards the east. The North Sea is one of the world's most productive fishing areas and is rich in oil, gas and minerals. [V.F.]

North Sea Conference This began in 1984 to address marine pollution of the NORTH SEA on an international level. The third conference was held in 1990 and the fourth in 1997. Each produced a ministerial declaration applied to the protection of the coastal waters of the nine North Sea states (Belgium, Denmark, Germany, France, The Netherlands, Norway, Sweden, Switzerland and the UK). The European Union (EU) also participates and there are observers from the PARIS COMMISSION (PARCOM) and the International Maritime Organization (IMO). [P.C.]

Norwegian Sea A large intercontinental SEA, constituting the transition of the north-east Atlantic to the ARCTIC. It lies between 62°N and 70°N. In the north-east it passes into the BARENTS SEA, in the west into the Greenland Sea, in the south into the NORTH SEA, and in the south-west into the main ATLANTIC OCEAN. Oxygen saturation in the Norwegian Sea is high due to active vertical mixing. Sediments consist largely of foraminiferal and diatomaceous oozes in the deeper parts of the Norwegian Basin, and volcanic sediments in the west, around Iceland. [V.F.]

not in my back yard (NIMBY) A phrase characterizing the position of individuals or bodies who agree to developments that have ADVERSE ENVIRONMENTAL EFFECTS as long as such developments are not in close proximity. A variant is NIABY: not in anybody's back yard! *See also* NOT IN MY TERM OF OFFICE. [P.C.]

not in my term of office (NIMTO) A phrase describing politicians or other officials who only oppose a locally unpopular development—usually one with ADVERSE ENVIRONMENTAL EFFECTS—if it coincides with their term of office. *See also* NOT IN MY BACK YARD. [P.C.]

notification A dossier of physicochemical and ECOTOXICITY information on substances given by a producer/importer to a regulatory authority as required by legislation—or the act of submitting such information. [P.C.]

notification of new chemicals The supply of information relevant to human health and environmental quality, concerning synthetic chemicals designated as new, prior to AUTHORIZATION for the manufacture or marketing of such chemicals. The information covers the physicochemical properties of the substances and their TOXICITY and ECOTOXICITY. In the USA the latter is usually obtained from QUANTITATIVE STRUCTURE–ACTIVITY RELATIONSHIP (QSAR) analysis, whereas in the European Union actual testing is required according to defined procedures. The level of details required in the NOTIFICATION depends upon the intended volume of production. [P.C.]

NO$_x$ emissions Emissions of various NITROGEN OXIDES, for example from fossil fuel-powered power-stations and automobiles. These compounds participate in PHOTOCHEMICAL SMOG. *See also* MOTOR VEHICLE POLLUTION. [P.C.]

NPL (National Priority List) *See* SUPERFUND LEGISLATION.

NRA (National Rivers Authority) *See* ENVIRONMENTAL (PROTECTION) AGENCIES.

nuclear fission Nuclear fission refers to a process in which the nucleus of an atom is split into two or more major fragments accompanied by the emission of small charged particles and intense electromagnetic RADIATION known as γ-RAYS and, usually, some neutrons. The release of neutrons in induced neutron fission implies the possibility of a self-sustaining chain reaction. The fragments are themselves radioactive and will decay with characteristic half-lives through a sequence of daughter products until ultimately becoming a stable ISOTOPE.

The fission process can release significant quantities of energy (*see* NUCLEAR POWER-STATIONS), principally in the kinetic energy of the fission fragments, which manifests itself as heat as the fragments are slowed down in the fuel of a reactor, but also in the environmentally significant energies of the associated α-, β- and γ-radiation. The latter is the most penetrating and generally calls for the greatest care in shielding a nuclear reactor. [J.D.L.]

nuclear power-stations The chief type of nuclear power-station in use worldwide today is the pressurized water reactor (PWR). This was developed initially in the USA as an offshoot of the necessarily compact nuclear-powered submarine programme and has led to power-stations—each generating some 3000 MW thermal power, converted to, say,

1000 MW of electrical power—in many developed and developing countries. A variant, which has not achieved the dominance of the PWR, is the boiling water reactor (BWR). Obsolescent types include gas-cooled reactors.

The history of nuclear reactors, however, started with the use of graphite rather than water as the moderator, or slowing-down element, and some countries, notably the UK and France, pursued the development of graphite reactors for some decades before converting to the PWR. Graphite is less efficient as a moderator and consequently such power-stations are larger for the same capacity than either PWR or BWR stations, at least in the 'nuclear island' if not in the ancillary equipment or conventional islands of turbines, generators, etc. Therefore, one can say that the compactness is essential to the economy of producing more from less, but represents a larger risk from the greater power density.

A large amount of energy is released from the NUCLEAR FISSION process. The complete fission of 1 kg of uranium per day will serve to fuel a plant producing about 1 GW thermal power or some 300 MW electrical power. The vastly greater quantities of coal or oil needed to generate equivalent amounts of power impose ENVIRONMENTAL BURDENS in the extraction and transport of fuel to the power-station, and in the products of combustion. Like most other producers of electricity, the thermal stages of nuclear power-plants create the need to dispose of waste heat to the environment on substantial scales, as warmed water or air.

The processing of the fuel after use in a reactor involves dealing with intensely radioactive products, even allowing for the usual minimum delay of, say, 90 days to allow for natural decay. There is international controversy over whether reprocessing should take place immediately, whether only after centuries of decay, or perhaps never at all, with the disposal of used fuel elements directly in underground (or undersea) sites. Generally, the UK and France (more equivocally Germany) have undertaken reprocessing, whereby not only are the active fission products concentrated to make for easier storage but the unused uranium and, more tendentiously, the created plutonium, are available for reuse. This reuse with uranium as a mixed oxide fuel (MOX) has already been demonstrated commercially; it may be the most satisfactory way of disposing of the large quantities of 'spare' plutonium resulting from scaling down of the superpowers' weapons programmes.

The storage and/or disposal of the radioactive products, principally from the fuel, has engendered much controversy, a prime example of the 'NIMBY' approach—NOT IN MY BACK YARD. Most countries have encountered political opposition when they have sought to establish a disposal site. Ideally, perhaps, there should be no measurable release of activity. But this is an ideal that must be matched against the risks associated with other treatments of the material, with other forms of electricity production or, indeed, with the consequences of not producing electricity. To search for disposal facilities 'guaranteeing' no release for, say, 10^5 years is unrealistic; no one could accept a 'proof' of such a claim. Perhaps some realism can be brought to bear if it is recognized that underground disposal would be nullified by the probable consequences of the next ice age, due within some 20 000 years, in which it is expected that the top kilometre of Europe will be removed and deposited in the Atlantic. [J.D.L.]

nuclear winter A term coined to express the effect of the increased SMOKE and DUST burden in the ATMOSPHERE which would result from the explosion of thermonuclear devices at the surface and in the air as a result of a nuclear war. The effect of the smoke and dust has been modelled by computer simulation and it is expected that the ATTENUATION of sunlight would be such as to reduce the normal levels of daylight to levels more typical of present dusk or dawn, or midwinter. The reduction in SOLAR RADIATION would result in widespread cooling of the Earth's surface. [J.B.M.]

nuisance species Non-indigenous species, usually introduced as a result of human activity, that threaten the density and/or abundance of native species. [P.C.]

null hypothesis (H_0) The hypothesis that forms the basis of a statistical test. A neutral, or null, hypothesis is one proposing no difference, and is usually symbolized by H_0. For example, when carrying out a t TEST, the null hypothesis is that the two SAMPLE means ($\bar{x}_1$ and $\bar{x}_2$) are from populations with the same means (H_0: $\bar{\mu}_1 = \bar{\mu}_2$); i.e. if the sample means are different it is only due to chance. Similarly, when carrying out an F TEST, the null hypothesis is that the two sample variances (s_1^2 and s_2^2) are from populations with the same variances (H_0: $\sigma_1^2 = \sigma_2^2$); i.e. if the sample variances are different it is only due to chance. There is always an ALTERNATIVE HYPOTHESIS to H_0. [B.S.]

Nusselt number A non-dimensional quantity, commonly used in environmental engineering, that expresses the rate of heat transfer to or from an object. [J.G.]

nutrient budget The nutrient budget, or the nutrient balance, is an attempt to account quantitatively for the inputs ('income') of NUTRIENTS to an ECOSYSTEM, and the losses. In natural ecosystems, income is from RAIN, wet and dry deposition, nitrogen fixation and WEATHERING of rocks. Losses are by LEACHING and RUN-OFF, and by volatilization during fire and denitrification. [J.G.]

nutrients Raw materials needed for life. [P.C.]

O

ocean The vast body of WATER covering 70.8% of the surface of the globe, or any one of its principal divisions: the Antarctic, ATLANTIC, Arctic, Indian and PACIFIC OCEANS. The average depth of the ocean is 3729 m and the deepest parts are 11 022 m from the ocean surface. The total area of the world ocean is $3.62 \times 10^8 \text{ km}^2$, and its volume is $1.35 \times 10^9 \text{ km}^3$. The ocean is believed to have formed between 4400 and 3000 million years ago. All known phyla originated in the ocean. [V.F.]

octanol–water partition coefficient (K_{ow}) The ratio of the concentrations of a chemical in n-octanol (C_o) and WATER (C_w) at equilibrium; i.e. K_{ow} (sometimes P or P_{ow}) = C_o/C_w, measured in a standard way. The higher the value of K_{ow} the more hydrophobic and lipophilic is a chemical, and this correlates positively with its BIOACCUMULATION potential and non-specific TOXICITY in some animals. *See also* ECO-TOXICOLOGY. [P.C.]

OECD (Organization for Economic Cooperation and Development) A 'club' of some 20 member countries that gathers information and promotes cooperation with a view to promoting economic development. It collects and collates data on environmental degradation and spending on environmental protection as well as promoting a number of cooperative ventures aimed at environmental protection. Of particular importance are:

• Guidelines for Testing Chemicals, which seek standardization in ecotoxicological procedures;
• Principles of GOOD LABORATORY PRACTICE.

The OECD is also coordinating a High Production Volume (HPV) programme, in which member countries are now investigating in a coordinated way the risks associated with chemicals produced at high volumes. This may lead to recommendations on risk reduction.

Recommendations and decisions of the OECD are not mandatory, but they have had a major influence on the development of environmental protection measures in member countries and the European Union. [P.C.]

oil smoke plume Any system of continuous combustion produces a plume of its gaseous combustion products. These are primarily WATER vapour and CARBON DIOXIDE (CO_2) from the burning of HYDROCARBONS, with an admixture of sulphur dioxide (SO_2) according to the amount of sulphur present in the fuel, together with a few other components peculiar to the source including compounds of chlorine. Oxides of nitrogen (NO_x) may be present, primarily nitric oxide (NO) which, within an hour or two, becomes oxidized in the ATMOSPHERE to nitrogen dioxide (NO_2) if there are normal amounts of OZONE (O_3) present. [R.S.S.]

oil spills Spills of crude oil from tanker accidents account for around 12% of the 3.2 Mt of PETROLEUM hydrocarbons released to the OCEANS every year. This is about one-third of the quantity entering the SEAS from sources such as atmospheric fallout and other inputs associated with the transportation of crude oil such as washings from tanks. Oil spills from tankers, in contrast to other sources of crude oil in the marine environment, produce locally very high levels of crude oil. It is this factor, coupled with the emotive images of oiled seabirds and mammals, that raises most public awareness of oil POLLUTION. Oil spills not only cause acute effects, such as oiling and poisoning of marine birds, mammals and invertebrates, but also have less tangible long-term effects such as changes in population structure of an ecosystem and reductions in reproductive success. Concomitant with this, damage to commercial fisheries and tourism may also occur.

As soon as oil has been spilled there are a number of natural mechanisms that come into play to dissipate an oil slick. These include spreading, evaporation, dissolution, emulsification, degradation by microorganisms and photo-oxidation. Quantitatively the most important mechanisms are evaporation and BIODEGRADATION. The most effective means of removing oil pollution rapidly is by enclosing the slick with inflatable booms and removing the oil from the water surface. This is not often feasible due to remote location or prevailing weather conditions at a spill site. When oil is beached it is much more difficult to clean up and, until recently, REMEDIATION involved physical removal with mechanical diggers and high-pressure water. The relatively successful use of BIOREMEDIATION in the wake of the *Exxon Valdez* spill in March 1989, has demonstrated that a further weapon is now available for the effective removal of oil pollution from contaminated BEACHES. *See also* ECOLOGICAL/ENVIRONMENTAL DISASTERS. [I.M.H.]

oligotrophic *See* EUTROPHICATION.

ombrogenous Describing peatland that has developed under conditions where the sole input of water (and therefore nutrient elements) is derived from precipitation falling directly upon it. [P.D.M.]

ombrophilous Describing habitats, vegetation or individual species that require a water source (and therefore nutrient element source) that is solely derived from direct precipitation; literally, 'rain-loving'. [P.D.M.]

omnivore An animal that feeds on both animal and vegetable matter. [P.O.]

one-tailed test In the NORMAL DISTRIBUTION 95% of observations are found to one side of $\mu \pm 1.65\sigma$ (where μ is the MEAN and σ is the STANDARD DEVIATION) and the other 5% of observations are found in the remaining tail of the distribution. When we carry out a $z(d)$ TEST to examine the difference between two means, and we have a priori reasons to expect a value of the test statistic above or below $z = 0$ (one mean should be larger), we use the 5% level of significance that corresponds to $z = 1.65$. This is a one-tailed test, and corresponds to a NULL HYPOTHESIS (H_0): $\bar{x}_1 = \bar{x}_2$ and an ALTERNATIVE HYPOTHESIS (H_1): $\bar{x}_1 > \bar{x}_2$. Any statistical test that uses the PROBABILITY in one tail of a distribution is therefore a one-tailed test. The alternative is to use the value of the test statistic that cuts off a total of 5% in both tails. For the normal distribution this would correspond to $z = 1.96$. Using this value as the 5% significance point would imply a TWO-TAILED TEST. [B.S.]

ooze, calcareous and siliceous A SEDIMENT containing 30% or more FORAMINIFERAN or radiolarian skeletons. [V.F.]

open canopy Stands of trees in woodlands and forests in which the density of trees in the upper stratum is low enough to allow significant gaps to be present between the crowns of neighbouring trees. Collectively, a stand has an open CANOPY if the crowns of trees in the tallest stratum cover less than about 50% of the crown by vertical projection. Open canopies form naturally after non-catastrophic fires, windthrow, drought and disease, and by silvicultural thinning. [G.F.P.]

open system An open system is commonly used to describe a physical system in which energy and matter can enter and leave without restriction. The definition can, however, also be applied to biological systems. In a physical sense the BIOSPHERE is an open system when radiant energy is considered but closed when geochemical cycles (e.g. carbon) are considered. In the same sense a biological system may be either open or closed. The key process that determines this is migration. When individuals move between suitable HABITAT patches then the system may be described as open. For each species this process will occur on different scales. Most functional natural communities are open and consist of a number of interacting subpopulations or compartments. [R.C.]

opportunistic species Species that can successfully exploit new resources as and when they arise. [T.J.K.]

optimal harvest This idea involves a consideration of economic factors as well as the purely biological. The simple idea of a MAXIMUM SUSTAINABLE YIELD (MSY) is a purely biological concept. It may well be that the level of harvest which achieves, for example, maximum profit, may be greater or less than the MSY. Indeed, in certain situations it may be optimal, in the sense that profits are maximized, for a population to be driven to extinction. This occurs when the SUSTAINABLE YIELD is relatively small compared to the size of the stock. In such a situation, the yield is lower than that which can be obtained in market interest rates and hence it becomes attractive to overexploit the resource and turn it into money which can earn interest. *See also* FISHERIES, CONSERVATION AND MANAGEMENT; HARVESTING. [J.B.]

optimum pollution This concept stems from the recognition that it is often necessary to compromise between the benefits of POLLUTION control — in terms of human health and the environment — and the costs of the restrictions — in terms of lost social benefits to health, food production and general welfare. Thus many pesticides pollute; but they bring benefits to food production that may be crucial in the developing world.

The ROYAL COMMISSION ON ENVIRONMENTAL POLLUTION, in a report published in 1972, describes the concept as 'unavoidably troublesome'. The Sixteenth Report (1992) comments:

> ... the concept of 'optimum' is 'coherent'
> (only) in the context of the analysis of a whole
> range of public decisions in which the harm
> caused by a certain amount of pollution needs
> to be compared with the harm which would be
> caused if *resources* were directed from other
> important purposes, not connected with
> pollution.

So optimality arguments are certainly difficult; objectively defining costs and benefits is intellectually challenging, and does not always lead to comfortable conclusions. But these trade-offs have to be kept in the public mind; it is important to realize that pollution control has to be paid for and that very often difficult decisions have to be made about the appropriateness of alternative products or courses of action. *Cf.* PRECAUTIONARY PRINCIPLE. [P.C.]

organic farming AGRICULTURE that avoids, as far as possible, chemical support through FERTILIZERS and BIOCIDES. *See also* FARMING PRACTICES, SUSTAINABLE. [P.C.]

organic loading The addition of abnormal amounts of dead organic matter to the environment — usually to a watercourse. For example, the addition of SEWAGE to a river. *See also* BIOCHEMICAL OXYGEN DEMAND. [P.C.]

organic pollution Usually means CONTAMINATION

from WASTES derived from living things that causes adverse effects on human health and/or ecological systems (*see also* SEWAGE POLLUTION). Can sometimes be intended as POLLUTION from organic chemicals. [P.C.]

Organization for Economic Cooperation and Development *See* OECD.

organochlorine pesticides *See* INSECTICIDES.

organochlorines Organic compounds containing one or more chlorine atoms. The first commercially produced organochlorine was carbon tetrachloride (1907), and other industrial solvents including 1,1,1-trichloroethane followed in the 1920s. These compounds display a range of toxic and carcinogenic properties; for example, carbon tetrachloride causes extensive damage to the liver whilst chloroform causes kidney damage and induces cancer in rats and mice. The toxic properties of polychlorinated compounds led to their widespread use as pesticides and herbicides; examples include DDT (dichlorodiphenyl-trichloroethane); and 2,4-D (2,4-dichlorophenoxyacetic acid). An awareness of the toxic effects of these chemicals on other organisms has led to imposed limitations on their use. *See also* PERSISTANT ORGANIC POLLUTANTS; VOLATILE ORGANIC COMPOUND. [M.C.G.]

organometal pollution A few metals and metalloids are capable of forming compounds with organic moieties via metal–carbon bonds to form organometal compounds. Of special relevance in the aquatic environment are compounds involving MERCURY (Hg), LEAD (Pb) and tin (Sn). However, the production of synthetic organometals is at an early stage, and there is considerable scope for the formation of new molecules, so possible future environmental problems from these compounds cannot be ruled out.

A common form of organolead is alkyl lead, used as a petrol additive to increase octane rating. The most toxic forms of alkyl lead degrade rapidly in the environment. Methyl mercuric compounds are the most common forms of mercury in the aquatic environment, deriving from methylation of inorganic mercury in solution. They are highly toxic, being 4–30 times more toxic than inorganic forms, and highly bioaccumulative. A wide variety of organotin compounds are used in industrial processes (e.g. for stabilization of PVC, GLASS strengthening and various catalytic reactions, and in BIOCIDES). Tributyltin (TBT) has been used extensively in antibiofouling paints for boats and caused POLLUTION of the marine environment, which has been studied extensively. Many fish and crustaceans are sensitive to TBT, with lethal thresholds in the low microgram per litre range and chronic effects at submicrogram per litre levels. Molluscs are particularly sensitive to TBT, with sublethal effects at levels of low to subnanograms per litre. *See also* IMPOSEX; TRIBUTYLTIN (TBT) POLLUTION. [P.C.]

organophosphorus pesticides Organophosphorus pesticides form a very large group of AGROCHEMICALS, mostly insecticidal compounds, stemming from research in the 1930s that showed that esters of monofluorophosphoric acid were very toxic. The first useful insecticide, parathion was to be developed in 1944:

The success of this chemical stimulated agrochemical companies to look further at phosphorus-based pesticides. There are now about 250 such compounds in use in the world.

The compounds exhibit a very wide range of selectivity, stability and PERSISTENCE, and may be used as contact, soil-active and plant systemic INSECTICIDES (i.e. can move within plants). They are used in most of the major arable CROPS such as cotton, rice, maize, soybean and small-grain cereals, and horticultural crops such as soft fruit and vegetables. Products such as dichlorvos find important application as agents for control of ecto- and endoparasites in livestock.

Organophosphorus pesticides vary considerably in their TOXICITY to higher animals; the earliest analogues were extremely toxic, but now the LD_{50} (rat) ranges from $5\,mg\,kg^{-1}$ body mass for parathion up to $5000\,mg\,kg^{-1}$ for tetrachlorvinphos, and many of the earlier products have been withdrawn from use. The search for even more selective materials continues.

Organophosphorus insecticides are relatively unstable in biological systems compared with organochlorine insecticides, so are generally not persistent. However, varying sublethal effects have been noted in birds, fish and some mammals, including humans. Teratogenic effects, with some indication of potential mutagenicity, has been noted for certain compounds, such as diazinon and parathion, and possibly MALATHION.

Organophosphorus insecticides phosphorylate the hydroxyl group of acetylcholine hydrolase (acetylcholinesterase), which controls the functioning of acetylcholine, a chemical transmitter of nerve impulses in the insect nervous system, as well as in vertebrates. They also affect cholinergic neuromuscular functions in mammals. Death in mammals is mainly due to paralysis of the respiratory mechanism; it is not so certain what is the cause of insect death.

Organophosphorus insecticides can be classified according to their practical application.

1 Soluble in WATER, rapidly hydrolysed. Contact insecticides; for example mevinphos, tetrachlorvinphos.

2 Soluble in oils, moderate or high stability. Persistent contact insecticides, moving into plant foliage but not systemic; for example diazinon, malathion, trichlorphon.

3 Able to enter plants and translocate; moderate to high stability. Systemic insecticides; for example dimethoate, phorate, disulfuron.

4 High vapour pressure. Fumigants; for example dichlorvos.

5 Effective in soils; for example bromophos, chlorfenvinphos.
[K.D.]

Oriental faunal region The Oriental faunal region essentially consists of tropical Asia and closely associated continental islands including Indonesia, Taiwan and the Philippines. [A.H.]

oscillations Regular fluctuations through a fixed cycle above and below some mean value. *See also* POPULATION DYNAMICS. [V.F.]

osmosis Diffusion of a solvent through a semipermeable membrane into a more concentrated solution. The osmotic pressure is the pressure that must be applied to oppose the osmotic flow. The osmotic potential, ψ_s, is the tendency of a solution or solid to attract solvent through a semi-permeable membrane, on a scale where pure water at sea level = 0, and with the sign convention that solutions are negative. [J.G.]

outbreaks

1 Outbreaks are (small) EPIDEMICS of infectious disease localized in time and space. The term is usually used to describe an increase in MORBIDITY and MORTALITY due to an endemic infection. Outbreaks may often occur by chance.

2 Can also refer to PEST species.
[G.F.M.]

outwelling The outflow of NUTRIENTS from an ESTUARY or SALT MARSH system to shelf waters. [V.F.]

overfishing The practice of HARVESTING fish in quantities greater than can be replaced by RECRUITMENT to the population. *See also* FISHERIES, CONSERVATION AND MANAGEMENT. [P.C.]

overgrazing GRAZING by domestic or wild animals can provide a management tool both for habitat conservation and for economic gain. When the consumption rate of the grazer is matched by the primary production of the vegetation, or where the grazers feed only seasonally on a particular area, an equilibrium can be maintained. If, however, the population of herbivores exceeds the CARRYING CAPACITY of the system (i.e. if the food demand in the long term is greater than the primary productivity), then overgrazing results and the plant BIOMASS of the ecosystem goes into decline.

In addition to a general loss of biomass in such a situation, overgrazing will also result in compositional changes in the flora. Species of plants that are more attractive to the grazer will be removed first and other, less attractive species will increase in abundance as a result of reduced competition. The types of plant favoured in the early stages of overgrazing will be those that are unpalatable, either because of their chemical composition or as a result of structural features. Spiny plants may prove more difficult for some animals; dense, fibrous species may offer poorer rewards; rosette species with leaves flattened close to the soil surface may prove more difficult to graze. A grassland or range manager with experience of vegetation responses should be able to detect overgrazing in its early stages and reduce stock density to prevent undue damage. [P.D.M.]

oxygen (O) A gaseous element (ATOMIC NUMBER = 8; relative ATOMIC MASS = 15.9994) and the most abundant element in the Earth's CRUST (49.2% by mass). In the free elemental state oxygen is a colourless, diatomic gas (dioxygen, O_2; melting point = −218.4°C; boiling point = −183.0°C) and constitutes 20.9% by volume of the ATMOSPHERE. It is a powerful oxidant and is essential for combustion and in RESPIRATION of plants and animals to release energy. The non-equilibrium mixture of oxygen and oxidizable material on the Earth is maintained by release of oxygen through PHOTOSYNTHESIS. An important allotrope of oxygen is OZONE (O_3), which absorbs solar ULTRAVIOLET RADIATION and prevents it reaching the Earth's surface. [M.R.H.]

oxygen sag The fall and recovery in DISSOLVED OXYGEN downstream of a major source of organic effluent, such as a SEWAGE works, brewery or paper mill. *See also* BIOCHEMICAL OXYGEN DEMAND. [P.C.]

ozone A gaseous allotrope of OXYGEN with formula O_3 and boiling point −112°C. It is a very powerful oxidizing agent, sparingly soluble in WATER, and is used industrially for water sterilization. In the STRATOSPHERE, ozone is formed by photolysis of molecular oxygen, and it absorbs ULTRAVIOLET RADIATION (UV-B) in the OZONE LAYER, thereby protecting life on Earth. Several synthetic chemicals, notably CFCs, perturb the chemistry of the stratosphere and can destroy ozone, leading to large increases in the transmission of UV-B radiation, particularly in polar regions in winter.

In the TROPOSPHERE, ozone occurs naturally, both from transport from the stratosphere, and from reactions of NITROGEN OXIDES (NO_x). Background concentrations in the Northern hemisphere have doubled in the past century as a result of pollutant EMISSIONS, rising from 15 ppb by volume (ppbv) to around 30 ppbv. Ozone is a minor GREENHOUSE GAS, but is important in controlling the rates of oxidation and removal of many other TRACE GASES in the ATMOSPHERE. Large concentrations, over

50 ppbv, are formed by reactions of sunlight with pollutant nitrogen oxides and HYDROCARBONS. Ozone is a major component of PHOTOCHEMICAL SMOG, and is toxic to plants. For long-term EXPOSURE, some plants show effects at concentrations as low as 40 ppbv, and visible injury to leaves of sensitive species can be observed after several hours' exposure to 60 ppbv. Ozone is also toxic to animals. The UK threshold limit value (TLV) for people at work is 100 ppbv over 7 h. [J.N.C.]

ozone hole Thinning of stratospheric OZONE (O_3) over the Antarctic is a climatological feature, but since the late 1970s severe depletion has occurred each year in September and October, forming the ozone hole. Ozone depletion is most severe between altitudes of 16 and 22 km where the Antarctic lower STRATOSPHERE is extremely cold. On the surfaces of frozen cloud particles, chemical reactions take place which transfer chlorine from inactive to active species. Ozone is then catalytically destroyed, predominantly by the following cycle:

$$ClO + ClO + M \rightarrow Cl_2O_2 + M$$

$$Cl_2O_2 + h\nu + M \rightarrow 2Cl + O_2 + M$$

$$2Cl + 2O_3 \rightarrow 2ClO + 2O_2$$

where M is any molecule and $h\nu$ is a PHOTON. The chlorine is largely produced from anthropogenic CFCs. [J.A.]

ozone layer Approximately 90% of atmospheric OZONE (O_3) occurs in the ozone layer, in the STRATOSPHERE 10–50 km above the Earth's surface. Ozone absorbs ULTRAVIOLET RADIATION, thereby protecting the BIOSPHERE from its harmful effects. It is formed naturally by the action of sunlight on OXYGEN molecules. [J.A.]

P

P : B ratio The rate of energy or matter accumulation per unit BIOMASS per unit time; i.e. the ratio of productivity to biomass. Because biomass may increase over the period of measurement of net primary productivity the mean or average biomass for the period is used to calculate $P:B$. [S.P.L. & M.H.]

P : R ratio The ratio of PRODUCTION rates (P), which represent the 'benefits' of energy transfer in terms of formation of new somatic and reproductive tissues, to RESPIRATION (R), which represents the energy 'costs' of metabolism and activity. This is an ecological cost/benefit statistic indicating how efficiently a particular trophic unit is able to accumulate BIOMASS from the energy it assimilates from the TROPHIC LEVEL below. [M.H.]

pachycaul Thick-stemmed plant. *See also* ALPINE ZONE. [P.C.]

Pacific Ocean The oldest, deepest and largest of the major ocean BASINS. The Pacific, so named by Ferdinand Magellan (1480–1521), covers an area of 1.7×10^8 km² or 1.8×10^8 km² including its marginal seas (i.e. more than one-third of the Earth's surface). The volume and average depth of the Pacific are 7.0×10^8 km³ and 4188 m, respectively, or 7.1×10^8 km³ and 3940 m, if its marginal seas are included. The greatest depth of the Pacific is 11 022 m, in the Mariana Trench. The most striking features of the Pacific Ocean TOPOGRAPHY are the great island arcs that lie along its northern and western sides (e.g. Aleutian, Japanese and Philippine archipelagos), many of which are active volcanoes. The Pacific is surrounded by young mountain ranges, particularly along its eastern side, which inhibit the inflow of sediment and fresh water from land. Approximately 36.2% of the Pacific Ocean floor is covered by calcareous ooze, 14.7% by siliceous ooze, and 49.1% by red clay. [V.F.]

PAH *See* POLYCYCLIC AROMATIC HYDROCARBONS.

PAH pollution The introduction by humans, directly or indirectly, of POLYCYCLIC AROMATIC HYDROCARBONS (PAH) to the environment resulting in deleterious effects such as: hazards to human health (e.g. some PAH are carcinogenic, some are very acutely toxic); hindrance of activities such as fishing (e.g. fish may develop lesions or other toxic effects); impairment of the quality for use of environmental resources (e.g. PAH-polluted water would not be suitable for drinking); and reduction in amenities such as recreation (e.g. tourists may be deterred from using beaches contaminated with PAH-containing oil and grease). PAH are produced naturally by microorganisms and plants, by natural burning of forests and prairies, and by volcanic activity. However, the main sources of PAH to the environment are from anthropogenic activities such as:

- combustion of wood and FOSSIL FUELS;
- sludge EFFLUENTS or OIL SPILLS;
- coke production in the iron and steel industry;
- catalytic cracking in the PETROLEUM industry;
- carbon black;
- coal-tar pitch;
- asphalt hot road mix processes;
- heating and power generation;
- controlled refuse INCINERATION.

PAH do not generally occur as single substances but in combination, and the profile of PAH can provide information on the sources of CONTAMINATION. Photo-oxidation is the major DECOMPOSITION process by which PAH are degraded, BIODEGRADATION by microorganisms being a secondary reduction mechanism. Biodegradation is primarily an aerobic process, and PAH become increasingly refractory under reducing conditions (e.g. when buried in sediments). PAH released to the ATMOSPHERE become associated with AEROSOLS of various sizes and types. PAH enter the OCEAN mainly from marine transportation and river and urban RUN-OFF, and because of their hydrophobic nature, become rapidly associated with particulate material and concentrated in sediments. Decomposition of PAH in aquatic environments is influenced by oxygen concentration, temperature, salinity, hydrodynamics, PAH concentration, organic matter concentration, microbial composition and BIOTURBATION by infaunal invertebrates. *See also* MOTOR VEHICLE POLLUTION. [V.F.]

paired-sample *t* test (or *t* test for matched pairs) A specific form of the *t* TEST is used when you have matched observations. [B.S.]

Palaearctic faunal region The Palaearctic vertebrate fauna occupies a region that essentially corresponds to Eurasia north of the tropics. [A.H.]

palaeoclimatic reconstruction Palaeoclimatic reconstruction is normally based on proxy evidence for past CLIMATE CHANGE rather than on instrumental readings, largely because reliable instrumental measurements are only available from the earlier part of the 18th century onwards and then only at a very limited number of locations worldwide until the 20th century. Evidence for past climate change may be gleaned from historical sources but, generally, such sources are at best patchy with respect to both spatial and temporal distribution. Most long-term palaeoclimatic reconstructions are, therefore, based on indirect or proxy evidence that may be biological, isotopic, physical or geomorphological.

Biological evidence for past climate change is contained mainly in the fossil record. Both macro- and microfossils of animals and plants have been used to track and quantify palaeoclimate change through time. For example, severe climatic deterioration at the end of the Younger Dryas stadial in Ireland led to the extinction of the giant Irish deer (*Megaloceros giganteus*), the remains of which (usually male and with antlers) are frequently found at the transition from Allerød to Younger Dryas sediments (*c.* 10 600 cal. BC (radiocarbon-calibrated (sidereal) years BC)). Extinction can be attributed with confidence to a severe climatic downturn for which there is abundant supporting evidence.

Fossil pollen data, in the form of pollen diagrams, are an important source of evidence of past vegetation distribution patterns which, to varying degrees, are under the control of climate. Several pollen records from south-eastern France, extending back to the penultimate GLACIATION (*c.* 180000 BP), provide a record of climate change in terrestrial habitats situated in mid-northern latitudes.

Deep ocean cores, drilled from the 1960s onwards, have provided long and continuous records of palaeoclimate change, in some instances extending back to the early Quaternary, i.e. 2 million years. Changes in $\delta^{18}O$, as recorded in the testae of benthic FORAMINIFERANS, reflect primarily the degree of glaciation rather than variation in ocean temperature which, in deep waters, varies by less than 2°C between glacial and interglacial cycles. During interglacials, $\delta^{18}O$ values are typically depressed from *c.* −1‰ to less than −2‰ because of the release of large volumes of WATER from the ICE SHEETS that are 'light' with respect to ^{18}O ($\delta^{18}O$ values normally less than −30‰). During glacial periods, ^{18}O values increase due to the cessation of 'light' meltwater input. Consistency in the pattern of movement of the $\delta^{18}O$ curve in ocean cores from various parts of the world has led to the recognition of oxygen isotope stages (OIS), with odd/even-numbered stages representing periods with low/high $\delta^{18}O$ values (warm/cold periods), respectively. The more or less regular cyclicity of warm/cold periods, that these studies have demonstrated, has played an important part in the acceptance of the Croll–Milankovitch theory of astronomical forcing. This theory proposes that cyclical changes in the precession of the equinoxes, the Earth's tilt and the eccentricity of its orbit, underlies long-term climate change during the Quaternary.

In addition to isotopic studies, changes in species composition (foraminifera and diatoms) and physical and chemical composition of ocean cores—for example the presence of iceberg-rafted sand and calcium carbonate ($CaCO_3$) concentration—have also provided important indicators of palaeoclimate change. From these and other investigations, it has become clear that ocean CIRCULATION patterns *per se* and, in particular the North Atlantic deep water circulation system, play a major role in heat transfer from lower to upper latitudes in the North Atlantic region so that when it is shut down, as happened during the Younger Dryas stadial, a major climatic deterioration ensued. Ice cores have also been used, especially the Vostok core drilled in Antarctica during the early 1980s. [M.O'C.]

palaeoecology Palaeoecology is the study of the ecology of past communities and past environments. It involves the reconstruction of the conditions and the flora and fauna of the past on the basis of a wide range of evidence, some biological, some geological. It is dependent upon the existence and survival of 'fossil' evidence of such past communities and conditions upon which the palaeoecologist can operate. [P.D.M.]

palaeolimnology The study of lake history based on the analysis of lake sediments. [R.W.B.]

palsa mire A tundra MIRE type, whose name is derived from Finnish, found only within climates where the average air temperature remains at or below 0°C for more than 200 days in the year, roughly corresponding to the southerly limit of discontinuous PERMAFROST. Palsa mires are often associated with northerly aapa mires, being found mainly on the flatter regions. The mire consists of elevated mounds, often 50m or more in diameter and several metres in height, consisting of a core of frozen SILT and PEAT, with a peat and vegetation cover over their summits. These palsa hummocks are interspersed with pools of similar area, many of which become infilled by vegetation to form extensive wet lawns. [P.D.M.]

paludification The process by which soils become waterlogged and PEAT formation commences and/or spreads. [P.D.M.]

palynology Palynology is the study of pollen grains of flowering plants and gymnosperms and of spores from pteridophytes, bryophytes, algae and fungi. Such work can involve studies of structure, development, taxonomy, evolution, dispersal, preservation and STRATIGRAPHY. The applications of the studies are many, including allergies, forensic science and PALAEOECOLOGY. [P.D.M.]

pampas The extensive areas of temperate GRASSLANDS in South America. [A.M.M.]

Paracelsus' principle The principle that any chemical can be toxic at a high enough concentration. It was recognized by the Swiss physician Philippus Paracelsus (1493–1541), who pioneered the medical use of chemicals. This principle of TOXICOLOGY is also applicable for ECOTOXICOLOGY. [P.C.]

parameters The summary measurements or characteristics of a POPULATION. These are represented by Greek letters, for example, the MEAN (μ) and the VARIANCE (σ^2). *See also* STATISTICS. [B.S.]

parametric statistics Statistical tests are frequently classified into parametric and non-parametric tests. Parametric tests are older and require quantitative information/observations to follow a NORMAL DISTRIBUTION and to have similar VARIABILITY (homogeneous variances). Parametric tests cannot be carried out on qualitative information, i.e. ranked information or information in categories. If the underlying conditions are met then parametric tests are usually more powerful (*see* STATISTICAL POWER). Examples of parametric tests/techniques are *t* TEST, PRODUCT–MOMENT CORRELATION COEFFICIENT and ANALYSIS OF VARIANCE. *Cf.* NON-PARAMETRIC STATISTICS. [B.S.]

páramo Humid arctic/alpine meadows and SCRUB, occurring in the Andes and kept moist by mist. [P.C.]

parasite An organism that interacts with another organism (the HOST) to reduce the fitness (survival and/or reproduction) of the host, and increase the fitness of the parasite, such that the parasite does not have to kill the host in order to derive the benefit (although the host may die as a result of the interaction). The term parasite is traditionally used for macroparasites, although increasingly it is used to include microparasites. [G.F.M.]

parasitoid Any insect whose larvae develop by feeding on the bodies of other arthropods, usually insects. [H.C.J.G.]

Paris Commission (PARCOM) The body responsible for the implementation of the Paris Convention for the Protection of the Marine Environment for the northeast Atlantic. All countries bordering on this area are signatory. It prepares controls on specific substances through binding 'Decisions' and non-binding 'Recommendations'. The Convention contains general provisions to reduce POLLUTION from land-based sources and offshore installations and to ban all types of DUMPING AT SEA. It recognizes the need for MONITORING and assessment as a basis for decisions. *See also* UNITED NATIONS PROGRAMMES AND BODIES. [P.C.]

parsimony There is an infinite number of hypotheses that might be suggested by a particular set of data. Scientists and philosophers rely on the principle of simplicity (parsimony) to pick the simplest hypothesis; the hypothesis that explains the data in the most economical manner. Simplicity, economy and parsimony all refer to the same general concept. [D.R.B.]

particulate organic matter (POM) Dead organic material (DETRITUS) either suspended in the water column or settled on the substratum of aquatic habitats. It may be divided into COARSE-PARTICULATE ORGANIC MATTER (CPOM), such as leaf fragments, and FINE-PARTICULATE ORGANIC MATTER (FPOM), such as sediments. *Cf.* DISSOLVED ORGANIC MATTER. [P.C.]

partition coefficient The ratio of the equilibrium concentrations of a substance distributed between two phases in contact with each other (often symbolized as K or P). [P.C.]

parts per billion *See* PPB.

parts per million *See* PPM.

pascal (Pa) The SI UNIT of PRESSURE (i.e. force per unit of area). $1\,Pa = 1\,Nm^{-2}$. Relationship with old units: $1\,Pa = 0.01$ millibar $= 0.02089$ pound force per square foot. Atmospheric pressure is about $10^5\,Pa$. [J.G.]

pasture GRAZING land that is managed to provide appropriate YIELD in terms of quantity and sometimes quality of herbs and grasses. *See also* AGRICULTURE. [P.C.]

pathogen A medical (human and veterinary) term for PARASITE, especially one associated with a high degree of MORBIDITY or MORTALITY. [G.F.M.]

PCB *See* POLYCHLORINATED BIPHENYLS.

peat An unconsolidated, stratified organic material derived largely from undecomposed or partially decomposed vegetation. It varies in its degree of DECOMPOSITION (HUMIFICATION) depending upon the nature of its content and the degree of waterlogging at the time of and since its formation. Peats formed under very wet conditions grow more quickly and are less decomposed than those formed under drier conditions. This offers some opportunity for the use of peat humification in long peat profiles as a proxy climate indicator.

Peat derived from *Sphagnum* mosses is usually poorly humified and consists of complete moss stems and leaves. In other types of peats, roots often predominate, forming a fibrous matrix. Peat may also contain wood fragments, fruits, seeds, leaves and stems, together with chitinous remains of fungi and the exoskeletons of insects and arachnids, such as mites. The analysis of peat contents provides a means of reconstructing the local vegetational and environmental history of a MIRE. The presence of smaller fossils, such as pollen, and fine dust particles of siliceous phytoliths or volcanic tephra offer additional opportunities for the use of peat profiles in historical monitoring of the environment (*see* PALAEOCLIMATIC RECONSTRUCTION).

Peat has a high water-retaining capacity (often 95% of its mass consists of water) and it also has efficient cation-exchange properties. It is therefore much in demand as a soil conditioner in horticulture, and this has resulted in extensive draining of mires for peat extraction. The high organic content of peat also makes it valuable as an energy resource and it is widely used for fuelling powerstations in Ireland and in Russia. [P.D.M.]

peatlands Areas occupied by peat-forming vegetation (*see* MIRE; PEAT). [P.D.M.]

PEC *See* PREDICTED ENVIRONMENTAL CONCENTRATION.

pedology The study of SOIL in all its aspects. [S.R.J.W.]

pedosphere The upper part of the Earth's CRUST that is occupied by soils. [E.A.F.]

pelagic Living in the water column (for marine organisms), seaward of the SHELF-SLOPE BREAK. [V.F.]

per capita Latin: literally, according to heads. [R.C.]

percentile Any of the 99 actual or notional points that divide a DISTRIBUTION or set of observations into 100 equal parts. *See also* QUARTILE. [B.S.]

periodic table A table of all known elements arranged in order of increasing ATOMIC NUMBER. The arrangement is such that elements in the same vertical columns (called groups or families) have similar chemical properties. This is because they have the same arrangement of outermost electrons. The horizontal rows of elements in the table are called periods. [M.C.G.]

periphyton A term sometimes applied to the community of bacteria and algae that occurs in the littoral or benthic zones of LAKES, and found attached to natural substrates such as larger plants (epiphyton), stones and rocks (epilithon), and sand grains (epipsammon). It also includes communities of motile algae that live on and beneath mud surfaces (the epipelon). [R.W.B.]

permafrost A naturally occurring earth material whose temperature has been below 0°C for several years regardless of the state of any moisture that might be present. The ground may be almost any kind of material including bedrock, CLAY, gravel, sand, SILT or organic SOIL. Dry permafrost has little excess ICE and is associated with inorganic substrates, whereas wet permafrost is found in finegrain soils. Continuous permafrost covers about 7.64 million km² of the Northern hemisphere.

The depth of permafrost can reach 1000 m, with temperatures as low as −12°C. Above the permafrost the seasonally thawing soil is called the active layer. This is the biologically active area of the ground available for plant roots and soil flora and fauna. In many areas of the ARCTIC the active layer may be only 20–40 cm thick, while in northern Yakutia, only *c.* 11 cm of the SOIL PROFILE thaws each summer.

The presence of permafrost, in addition to contributing to the thermal dynamics of the soil, also controls HYDROLOGY in that it impedes drainage. Areas of discontinuous permafrost on the southern boundary of the Arctic are particularly sensitive to CLIMATE warming. Active layer detachment from the permafrost on slopes can lead to great DISTURBANCE at the landscape level. Permafrost contains and covers large amounts of the greenhouse gas METHANE. [T.V.C.]

peroxyacetyl nitrate (PAN) A photochemical oxidant gas, formula $CH_3CO.O_2NO_2$, formed in polluted air by the action of sunlight on a mixture of HYDROCARBONS and NITROGEN OXIDES (NO_x), and associated with the formation of OZONE (O_3) and PHOTOCHEMICAL SMOG. The highest concentrations are found in urban areas with high traffic densities, in warm, sunny weather. PAN is thermally unstable, but at the low temperatures found high in the TROPOSPHERE and in polar regions, PAN may be transported for many hundreds of kilometres to act as a source of POLLUTANT NO_x. It is a powerful lacrimator, and causes characteristic bronzing of plant leaves at high concentrations (>10 ppb by volume). [J.N.C.]

persistence The capacity of a commercial chemical to endure, without change, in environmental compartments. *Cf.* BIODEGRADATION. [P.C.]

persistent organic pollutants (POPs) Organic chemicals that, because of their resistance to natural destruction, can last for long periods in the environment and accumulate. They are toxic and/or ecotoxic. It is further often required as part of the definition that they are capable of regional or global transport in the ATMOSPHERE and/or HYDROSPHERE. They include DDT, aldrin, DIELDRIN, endrin, chlordane, heptachlor, hexachlorobenzene, mirex, toxaphene, POLYCHLORINATED BIPHENYLS (PCBs), DIOXINS and furans. They are under consideration for international regulation through the United Nations. [P.C.]

pest An animal (or, occasionally, a plant) that consumes and/or damages living or dead plant materials (less usually animal materials) intended for human consumption or use; for example, animals that consume CROPS, animal feeds or stored products. Such pests are effectively competitors with humans. [P.C.]

pest control Attempts to eradicate or reduce densities of pests to levels where they are no longer effective competitors with humans. Control can be by chemical means (PESTICIDE) or biological means (*see* BIOLOGICAL CONTROL), or a combination of these (*see* INTEGRATED PEST MANAGEMENT). [P.C.]

pesticide A substance that kills PESTS. Pesticides can be specific or non-specific. [P.C.]

pesticide formulation A particular PESTICIDE-containing product designed for sale. It generally consists of a complex mixture of ACTIVE INGREDIENT(S), carrier(s) and adjuvant(s). These are put together in such a way that the product is effective for the purpose claimed. [P.C.]

pesticide treadmill The seemingly endless search for new PESTICIDES that is required to counter the development of pest RESISTANCE to existing pesticides. PESTS can, potentially, adapt (i.e. develop resistance) to any excessively used pesticide. This can necessitate the design of different pesticides against which there is no initial resistance. But pest resistance against these NEW CHEMICALS can potentially evolve. [P.C.]

pesticides and soil contamination PESTICIDES—HERBICIDES, FUNGICIDES, INSECTICIDES and molluscicides—are used extensively to increase plant productivity by regulating unwanted biotic interference, and in control of human and animal diseases. The application of pesticides almost inevitably involves contact with the soil surface, particularly where drifting of the pesticide occurs through aerial applications or where AEROSOLS and fine dusts remain airborne for extended periods. The development of SURFACTANTS, the control over aerial (aircraft) spraying, advice on suitable weather conditions for applications, and an awareness of the toxic effects of pesticides have combined to greatly reduce the unintentional targeting of pesticides in AGRICULTURE, horticulture and FORESTRY.

Once in the SOIL, pesticides are removed from the degradative processes of photochemistry. Persistence thereafter is a function of temperature, rainfall, soil pH, soil structure and aeration, activity of microbial and other biotic degradative agencies as well as the chemical composition, solubility and stability of the pesticide molecule. The widespread application of organochlorine insecticides between 1948 and 1968 has left a legacy of persistent and toxic compounds in the BIOSPHERE, including the soil. The average time for 95% disappearance of DDT, DIELDRIN and LINDANE from the soil is 10, 8 and 6.5 years, respectively. The relative insolubility of DDT in the soil and its slow release into water bodies meant that it took 7 years from 1977 to achieve a two-fold reduction in DDT in Lake Michigan—despite the ban on the agricultural use of DDT in the USA in 1973. The discovery of persistent POLYCHLORINATED BIPHENYLS, originally formulated as pesticides, in soils led to the evacuation of one town in Missouri 10 years after the original CONTAMINATION. Legislation, at least in western Europe and North America, today controls the use of persistent organic pesticides, such that most are degraded in the soil within weeks of application. However, inorganic pesticides based on toxic metals (e.g. copper, arsenic and MERCURY)—such as Bordeaux mixture—may leave a toxic residue which persists, under suitable soil conditions, for decades. [G.A.F.H.]

petroleum A mixture of aromatic and aliphatic HYDROCARBONS and non-hydrocarbon compounds such as carbazoles, thiophenes, furans and phenols, that is produced in deep subsurface sediments and can be extracted in a liquid (crude oils) or gaseous form (natural gas). It is widely believed that petroleum is formed originally from biologically produced organic matter deposited in aquatic sediments. Petroleum can be released to the environment as a result of human activities (oil extraction and transport) and from natural sources such as naturally occurring hydrocarbon seeps where petroleum-bearing rock strata have been exposed near the surface of the Earth or the sea floor.

Since petroleum is produced by natural processes and petroleum hydrocarbons have been present in the environment for many millennia, low levels of petroleum hydrocarbons do not constitute a serious threat to the environment. It is only when uncontrolled release of large quantities of petroleum occurs that serious environmental problems may ensue.

The aliphatic components and many of the aromatic components of petroleum are readily dissipated in the environment by evaporation and BIODEGRADATION—hydrocarbon-degrading microorganisms are all but ubiquitous. Some components of petroleum, generally those not readily removed by natural processes, are highly toxic. These include compounds like dibenzofurans and POLYCYCLIC AROMATIC HYDROCARBONS (PAHs). PAHs are lipophilic and can accumulate in animal tissues; they are subject to BIOMAGNIFICATION in food chains. In addition, oxygenase enzymes present in the liver can partially oxidize PAHs to form hydroxylated derivatives that are highly mutagenic. *See also* MOTOR VEHICLE POLLUTION. [I.M.H.]

pH A logarithmic scale indicating the activity (or, approximately, the concentration) of hydrogen ions in solution:

$$pH = -\log_{10}[H^+]$$

where $[H^+]$ is the concentration of H^+ in moles per litre. [K.A.S.]

phosphorus cycle The movement of phosphorus (P) between the BIOSPHERE, LITHOSPHERE and HYDROSPHERE, and the associated transformations between its different chemical forms, from the release of P from its main reservoir in apatites (complex calcium phosphates) and other minerals to the ultimate formation of new minerals. Weathering converts some P into exchangeable phosphate anions, which are absorbed by plants and pass into the biological cycle. The uptake is often promoted by the association between roots and mycorrhizal fungi. P is present in all living organisms, for example in DNA and phospholipids. Organic residues returned to the SOIL (and aquatic sediments) are mineralized by microorganisms, releasing phosphate again for return to the biological cycle or PRECIPITATION as insoluble phosphates of iron, aluminium or manganese (ACID conditions) or of calcium (alkaline conditions). P is often the limiting nutrient in aquatic ecosystems, and increased supply can result in ALGAL BLOOMS and other problems. *See also* EUTROPHICATION. [K.A.S.]

photic zone The uppermost zone of a water body in which the penetration of LIGHT is sufficient for PHOTOSYNTHESIS to exceed RESPIRATION. [J.L.]

photochemical smog Atmospheric haze. It appears to be initiated by nitrogen dioxide (NO_2), especially from motor vehicle EMISSIONS. Visible or ultraviolet (UV) energy of sunlight converts NO_2 to nitric oxides and free OXYGEN atoms (O). The latter combine with molecular oxygen (O_2) to form OZONE (O_3), which causes a variety of reactions to take place with HYDROCARBONS and certain other organic compounds. The low-volatility organic products contribute to the haze of small droplets that constitutes the SMOG. The phenomenon was first recognized in Los Angeles, but now occurs in urban conurbations worldwide. Clearly this kind of smog is likely to be most intense when the sunlight intensity is greatest, i.e. early afternoon. It contrasts with smog, which is most intensive in early morning. *See also* AIR POLLUTION; ATMOSPHERIC POLLUTION; MOTOR VEHICLE POLLUTION. [P.C.]

photon A quantum of LIGHT or other electromagnetic RADIATION. [L.O.B.]

photoperiod The length of the day (*see* DAYLENGTH); or the length of the LIGHT period in experimental studies. [J.G.]

photosynthesis Photosynthesis is the process in which LIGHT energy is used to reduce CARBON DIOXIDE (CO_2) to sugars and other carbohydrates and in which molecular OXYGEN (O_2) is evolved. It is central to all life, in that photosynthesis ultimately produces all sources of food. Past photosynthetic activity also produced the present oxygen-rich atmosphere, and the oil, gas and hydrocarbon-rich sediments.

The basic photosynthetic process takes place in all green higher plant and algal cells, within organelles termed chloroplasts, which have the necessary pigments (chlorophylls) to absorb and utilize light energy. A similar process also occurs in the cyanobacteria and in photosynthetic bacteria. The term photosynthesis is also used generally to indicate the uptake of CO_2 by plants, which involves the diffusion of CO_2 from the atmosphere into the leaves through the stomatal pores, and into the photosynthetic cells. Because of this diffusion, photosynthesis is intimately linked with TRANSPIRATION—the loss of WATER by evaporation from cells in the leaf, and diffusion of the water vapour out through the pores into their air. [J.I.L.M.]

physical constants See Table P1. For physical properties of water and air, *see* WATER and AIR, CHEMICAL AND PHYSICAL PROPERTIES. [J.G.]

physical factor Any non-living, non-chemical factor that influences biological processes. Physical factors include: heat, LIGHT, electricity, magnetism, RADIATION, gravity and PRESSURE. *Cf.* BIOTIC FACTORS. [P.C.]

physiological ecology Physiological ECOLOGY has traditionally been concerned with explaining distributions in terms of the interaction between physiological processes and physical and chemical conditions; for example, how TEMPERATURE influences RESPIRATION; how chemical quality of the environment influences the *internal milieu* of organisms; explaining the evolution of physiological adaptations in terms of environmental conditions.

Table P1 Physical constants.

Name	Symbol	Numerical value
Acceleration due to gravity on Earth	g	$9.8067\,\mathrm{m\,s^{-2}}$
Avogadro constant	L or N_A	$6.022 \times 10^{23}\,\mathrm{mol^{-1}}$
Molar gas constant	R	$8.3145\,\mathrm{J\,K^{-1}\,mol^{-1}}$
Gravitational constant	G	$6.67 \times 10^{-11}\,\mathrm{N\,m^2\,kg^{-2}}$
Planck constant	h	$6.6261 \times 10^{-34}\,\mathrm{J\,s^{-1}}$
Speed of light	c	$2.998 \times 10^8\,\mathrm{m\,s^{-1}}$
Stefan–Boltzmann constant	σ	$5.6705 \times 10^{-8}\,\mathrm{W\,m^{-2}\,K^{-4}}$
Molar volume of ideal gas at 0°C 100 kPa		$2.27106 \times 10^{-2}\,\mathrm{m^3\,mol^{-1}}$
Molecular mass of air	M_a	$28.96 \times 10^{-3}\,\mathrm{kg\,mol^{-1}}$

Exploring these issues has relied upon a comparative approach that has analysed divergences between related organisms in different environments (e.g. contrasting physiologies of organisms in different zones on the seashore) or the convergence between unrelated organisms in similar environments (e.g. the evolution of anaerobic metabolism in endoparasites).

Recently, physiological ecology has become more concerned with issues of POPULATION DYNAMICS: explaining how physiological processes influence POPULATION SIZE changes through time; i.e. by influencing growth rates and hence time to breeding, reproductive output and survival probability; explaining how different physiologies and the dynamics that are associated with them are favoured under different ecological circumstances so leading to physiological and life-cycle adaptations. Exploring these issues has relied on an interaction between the development of theoretical models and the design of experiments to test the hypotheses incorporated into the models and the predictions that emerge from them. [P.C.]

physiological time Physical TIME is invariant. However, whereas 1 minute is a long time with respect to the physiological processes and total LIFESPAN of a bacterium, it is a short time in the physiological processes and total lifespan of an elephant. Physiological time probably scales with body mass in the same way as metabolic rate. [P.C.]

phytobenthos *See* BENTHIC HABITAT CLASSIFICATION.

phytochrome A protein pigment present in trace quantities in the leaves, stems and seeds of green plants, which changes its form depending on the ratio of red to far-red LIGHT. [J.G.]

phytogeography The study of the geographical DISTRIBUTION of plants on the Earth's surface. [A.M.M.]

phytophagous Feeding on plants. [G.A.F.H.]

phytoplankton The collective name for groups of algae and bacteria that are adapted to living suspended in the open waters of marine and freshwater environments. [R.W.B.]

phytotelmata Phytotelmata are small water bodies that occur in or on plants. Good examples are water-filled tree holes and the water contained in pitcher plants. [S.J.H.]

PIC *See* PRIOR INFORMED CONSENT.

picoplankton PLANKTON, mostly bacteria, measuring 0.2–2.0 μm in size. [V.F.]

PICT *See* POLLUTION-INDUCED COMMUNITY TOLERANCE.

planetary boundary layer The turbulent layer of the ATMOSPHERE closest to the ground (often called the atmospheric BOUNDARY LAYER) that is influenced by processes at the Earth's surface, such as friction, heating and cooling, on time-scales less than a day. The height of the layer can vary widely. Over land the layer is typically 1–2 km deep in the afternoon, while at night it can be less than 100 m deep. Over the oceans it displays little DIURNAL variation and is typically about 0.5 km deep. Above the planetary boundary layer lies the free atmosphere, where TURBULENCE is weak, intermittent or absent and which is little affected by processes at the ground. [K.G.M.]

plankton The term plankton refers to very small, mainly microscopic organisms—bacteria (bacterioplankton), algae and cyanobacteria (PHYTOPLANKTON) or animals (ZOOPLANKTON)—that live suspended in the open water of freshwater and marine environments. [R.W.B.]

plant toxins Toxic compounds are widespread throughout most plant groups, including angiosperms, gymnosperms, pteridophytes and bryophytes. Of the 10 000 or so characterized terpenoids, 8000 phenolic compounds and several thousand alkaloids, probably the majority induce toxic responses, at least *in vitro*. Whether this toxic effect is the natural function has only been confirmed for a few hundred compounds. Even fewer TOXINS are known, with certainty, to confer a significant ecological benefit to the producer. However, intuitively and logically it is most likely that the majority of plant toxins function in the control of herbivory—ranging from the GRAZING of large mammals and larvae of moths to the FEEDING of aphids. Plant toxins also act as a potent defence against fungal, bacterial and viral challenge. The major plant toxins may be classified, for convenience, into three groups, based on structural affinities (Table P2). [G.A.F.H.]

plantation A term used in FORESTRY to distinguish areas of deliberately planted trees from FORESTS which are natural or have regenerated after clear-felling (or burning) without further human intervention. [G.A.F.H.]

plastics Synthetic polymers that can be moulded into shape by using heat and/or pressure. Plastics are derived from petrochemicals, are often cheap to make and form compared to metals, and have good thermal and electrical insulating properties. They are relatively inert, and are strong relative to their mass.

Plastics form a large fraction of domestic refuse, and they are non-degradable by microorganisms and light. Moreover, they are not easily recycled. Thus

Table P2 The major groups of plant toxins.

Group or generic name	Structure based on	Chemical example	Mode or type of action	Plant source
Phenolic	Phenylpropenoic acid	Coumarins	Haemolysis	*Melilotus alba*
	Gallic acid	Tannins	Indigestion	Nuts/bark of trees
	Naphthaquinone	Juglone	Antifungal	*Juglans nigra*
	Anthraquinone	Hypericin	Photosensitivity	*Hypericum* spp.
	Flavonol	Kaempferol	Allelopathic	Widespread
	Iso-flavone	Rotenone	Respiration inhibitor	Legumes
Terpenoid	Monoterpene	Pinene	On insect antennae	*Pinus* spp.
	Sesquiterpene	Gossypol	Taste repellent	*Gossypium barbadense*
	Diterpene	Rhodojaponin	Taste repellent	*Rhododendron* spp.
	Steroid	Progesterone	Mammal infertility	*Tulipa* bulbs
	Saponin	Digitonin	Haemolysis	*Digitalis* spp.
Nitrogen-based	Non-protein amino acid	Dihydroxyphenyl alanine	Insect cuticle assembly	*Mucuna* spp.
	Cyanoglycoside	Hydrogen cyanide	Respiration inhibitor	*Lotus corniculatus*
	Pyrrolidine alkaloid	Atropine	Vasodilation	*Atropa belladonna*
	Indole alkaloid	Hordenine	Taste repellent	*Phalaris* spp.
	Diterpene alkaloid	Aconitine	Respiratory inhibitor	*Aconitum* spp.
	Protein	Trypsin inhibitor	Inhibits digestion	*Glycine max*

they pose a formidable environmental problem. Attempts to produce plastics that are biodegradable or photodegradable are being made, but the bulk of plastics used today do not have these properties and have to be buried in LANDFILL sites or incinerated.

Chemicals added to the plastic polymers to improve the properties of the finished plastic may enter the FOOD CHAIN. Plasticizers such as phthalates are not polymerized and may be volatile, leachable and biologically active, and so are a potential HAZARD when plastics containing such compounds are used for food wrapping or water pipes. [J.G.]

plate tectonics The process by which lithospheric plates are moved across the Earth's surface to collide (i.e. at SUBDUCTION zones), slide by one another (i.e. to form transform faults), or move away from each other (i.e. at divergence zones) to produce the topographic configuration of the Earth. [V.F.]

playas Shallow, circular basins of alluvial fans in plains and DESERT landscapes, they are also known as bajadas. Fine-textured SOIL and accumulation of salts make playa lakes a poorly drained habitat; precipitation provides ephemeral water inflow, with each of the playas and its WATERSHED developing vegetation in a CLOSED SYSTEM. Over 20 000 playas are found on the southern High Plains in Texas and New Mexico, with an average size of 6.3 ha but high variance in size. [S.K.J.]

plume A continuous stream of fluid emerging from a localized source and penetrating and mixing with an AMBIENT fluid under the influence of initial momentum and/or buoyancy. Mixing with ambient fluid causes the plume to diverge away from its source and dilutes the momentum and buoyancy of the plume, and any POLLUTANT it contains. In natural and artificial ATMOSPHERE plumes, the mixing is effected by TURBULENCE within and around the plume, and the ambient air is almost always turbulent as well. Usually the temperature and momentum of the plume become indistinguishable from those of its surroundings at a relatively short distance from the point of injection, whereas the presence of a pollutant may be visible or chemically distinguishable to a much greater distance. For example, the main radioactive plume from Chernobyl was detectable several thousand kilometres from its source. A plume which is not effectively continuous with its origin is known as a puff, and mixes even more rapidly with its surroundings on account of its larger surface to volume ratio. [J.F.R.M.]

PM10s *See* MOTOR VEHICLE POLLUTION.

PMN *See* PREMANUFACTURE NOTICES.

PNEC *See* PREDICTED NO EFFECT CONCENTRATION.

point source An identifiable, discrete origin of CONTAMINATION or POLLUTION, such as the outlet of a pipe or chimney stack. *Cf.* DIFFUSE SOURCES. *See also* PLUME. [P.C.]

Poisson distribution A discrete PROBABILITY DISTRI-

BUTION that describes situations where rare observations (e.g. individuals in a sampling unit) follow a RANDOM DISTRIBUTION in either space or time. The terms of the Poisson distribution, or Poisson series, can be calculated from:

$$P_{(x)} = e^{-m} \frac{m^x}{x!}$$

where $P_{(x)}$ is the probability of observing a certain number of individuals in a sampling unit, e is the base of natural logarithms (2.7183), m is the mean number of individuals per sampling unit and $x!$ is x factorial $(4! = 4 \times 3 \times 2 \times 1 = 24$, etc. and $0! = 1)$. [B.S.]

pollard A tree whose top has been cut off well above the ground and which has sprouted again from the stump. [G.F.P.]

pollen analysis The extraction, identification and quantitative assessment of fossil pollen grains in stratified lake sediments or PEAT deposits as a means of reconstructing the past history of vegetation in a region. [P.D.M.]

pollination Pollination is the process of transferring pollen from anthers to receptive stigma in the flowers of seed plants. [W.E.K. & J.Cr.]

pollutant A substance that in the environment has an adverse EFFECT on human health and/or ecological systems. [P.C.]

polluter pays principle (PPP) The 'polluter pays principle' (PPP) is at the heart of environmental legislation in both the UK and the rest of the European Union (EU). It is one of the most widely advocated and, because of its appeal to equity, widely accepted principles in environmental policy and legislation. But there are some sources of ambiguity that, in practice, mean PPP has not been as widely and consistently applied as it might.

Pays for what? This question can elicit a whole hierarchy of possible answers, which can include:

1 for the administration involved, for example in producing CONSENTS and AUTHORIZATIONS;

2 for costs of monitoring COMPLIANCE;

3 for costs of REMEDIATION following an illegal incident;

4 for costs of remediation of damage caused even when EMISSIONS are at a level deemed acceptable by public authorities.

PPP is taken as far as 1 and 2 in the UK issuance of authorizations, and 3 now has a statutory basis in UK and EU legislation. Moreover, the spectre of 4, as a very strict definition of liability for WASTE, has been raised in the EU proposals on civil liability for waste and general liability for environmental damage and is applied in the SUPERFUND LEGISLATION. The latter US instrument also raises the question of whether PPP should be applied retrospectively.

Who are the polluters? The answer to this question is not always as obvious as it seems. For example, it has been argued that since it is the community at large, rather than specific dischargers, that benefits from enforcement activities, the community should pay the costs. The counterargument is, of course, that most of the costs can be passed back anyway via product prices to the community at large and in so doing provide more effective signals on environmental hazards. More serious questions can, nevertheless, be raised about the costs of establishing standards in the first place and of maintaining public registers. And there are, of course, the thorny questions about how jointly and severally the liabilities might be shared amongst managers, directors, lenders, insurers, etc. *See also* ENVIRONMENTAL ACTION PROGRAMMES; ENVIRONMENTAL (PROTECTION) POLICIES; UNITED NATIONS PROGRAMMES AND BODIES. [P.C.]

pollution The release of a by-product of human activity—chemical or physical—that causes HARM to human health and/or the natural environment; CONTAMINATION causing adverse effects. [P.C.]

pollution avoidance Measures taken to prevent POLLUTION either from ACCIDENTS or over the long term. It is based on the doctrine that prevention is better than cure. *See also* POLLUTION PREVENTION PRINCIPLE. [P.C.]

pollution-induced community tolerance (PICT) This is an ecotoxicological method based upon the premise that pollutants will act as SELECTION PRESSURES excluding sensitive and favouring more tolerant forms. This selection can operate between genotypes within species and between species in communities. Hence, communities that have been exposed to a POLLUTANT should show more TOLERANCE to it than communities that have not. The approach is applicable generally, but has largely been used on periphytic algae. Empirical evidence suggests that the community response is relatively pollutant specific. [P.C.]

pollution permits AUTHORIZATIONS, CONSENTS and licences that, normally, are issued by a regulatory agency to allow the release of potentially harmful substances into the environment. [P.C.]

pollution prevention principle (PPP) The principle that it is best to avoid POLLUTION in the first place rather than rely on REMEDIATION; i.e. what is repaired is rarely as good as the original, and the costs of repair may be considerable. [P.C.]

pollution quotas Rights to release specified quantities of potentially polluting substances, issued usually by regulatory authorities, and generally set so that overall releases to the environment are below thresholds that cause harmful effects (so the term 'pollution' is something of a misnomer in this context). Such quotas may be tradeable. [P.C.]

polychlorinated biphenyls (PCB) Polychlorinated organic compounds containing two benzene rings linked by a single bond between ring carbons, also known as polychlorobiphenyl compounds. In total there are 209 PCB compounds. They were first produced on a commercial basis (in 1929) for use in printing inks and paints, as softeners in PLASTICS and insulators in transformers. They are highly toxic to wildlife, and bioaccumulate and persist in the environment, especially in SEDIMENTS, for long periods. [M.C.G.]

polycyclic aromatic hydrocarbons (PAH) Non-polar, generally planar, organic compounds, composed of two or more fused benzene or other aromatic rings. They are of environmental concern because of their widespread distribution, PERSISTENCE, potential to bioaccumulate, acute TOXICITY, mutagenicity and carcinogenicity. In humans, exposure to PAH occurs from inhalation of tobacco smoke (by both active and passive smoking) and polluted air, and from ingestion of various vegetables (containing naturally produced PAH), fried and smoked foods, and contaminated seafood and water. [V.F.]

polymer The product of a polymerization reaction, i.e. a chemical reaction in which two or more (usually many) identical molecules join together to form a material with new physical and chemical properties. [J.G.]

POM *See* PARTICULATE ORGANIC MATTER.

poorly (sparingly) water soluble Describing toxicants or other materials, usually organic, that do not dissolve readily in WATER and hence create difficulties for presenting in TOXICITY/ECOTOXICITY tests. In these cases it is not uncommon to read reports where toxic concentrations exceed the solubility of the substance. Here, test animals may have been exposed to much lower than expected concentrations with most of the chemical being on the bottom of the test vessel. This can be overcome, to some extent, by adding small amounts of relatively low-toxicity solvents such as acetone, which are miscible with water and which can maintain high concentrations of the chemical in solution. These are known as carriers. [P.C.]

POPs *See* PERSISTENT ORGANIC POLLUTANTS.

population

1 In ecology, a group of organisms of the same species, present in one place at one time. This definition is not always so simple to put into practice because the 'place' occupied by a population is not clear-cut. A population may extend over a large area, with limited interaction (e.g. occasional mating) between individuals in different parts of the population. POPULATION DYNAMICS nowadays stresses the METAPOPULATION concept, where local populations form part of a larger, regional population.

2 In STATISTICS, a term referring to all the observations that could be made on a particular item. The summary measurements of populations (PARAMETERS) are represented by Greek letters, for example, the MEAN (μ) and the VARIANCE (σ^2). [R.H.S & B.S.]

population density The local ABUNDANCE of a species expressed quantitatively as numbers per unit area or numbers per unit volume. [R.H.S.]

population dynamics The variations in time and space of the sizes and densities of populations. [V.F.]

population ecology The study of the relationships of populations of organisms with the members of the POPULATION, with other populations and with external environmental factors. [R.H.S.]

population explosion *See* POPULATION (HUMAN), GLOBAL PROJECTIONS AND IMPACTS.

population genetics The branch of genetics concerned with the occurrence, patterns and changes of genetic variation in natural populations. [G.D.J.]

population growth rate The number of individuals present at a particular time unit, divided by the number of individuals present one time unit earlier. [G.D.J.]

population (human), global projections and impacts The world's human population was *c.* 3.6 billion in 1970, passed 5 billion in the mid-1980s, and 6 billion in the mid-1990s. UN projections up to 2150 give a range of estimates. On the medium projection (considered most probable), world population will increase to 10 billion in 2050, levelling off at around 11.6 billion in 2150. The low projection is based on the presumption that births will fall globally below replacement—this predicts that population will peak in 2050 and then fall. The high projection presumes that there will be a global average of 2.2 children per woman worldwide, so the world population will continue to rise indefinitely (12.5 billion by 2050 and 20.8 billion by 2150). This corresponds to a modest increase in PER CAPITA birth rate from 2.2 to 2.5.

More than 95% of the growth in population is taking place in developing countries. The consequences, in terms of demand for resources—not least of which will be living space—and the generation of wastes, are likely to be enormous, putting particular emphasis on the search for sustainable methods of economic and social development.

Since T. Malthus, there has been much speculation about the CARRYING CAPACITY of the Earth in terms of human population, but this still remains a matter for speculation. [P.C.]

population regulation Regulation implies a tendency for a POPULATION to decrease if numbers are above a certain level, or conversely to increase if numbers are low. In other words, if population regulation occurs, POPULATION SIZE is controlled by density-dependent variation in birth, death, immigration or emigration rates. Density-independent factors, such as climatic variation or random catastrophic MORTALITY, operate at a significant level in many natural populations and may obscure patterns of population regulation. Field evidence for population regulation has been hard to find in animal populations but is more common in plant populations. It

is now recognized that population regulation may occur at different scales and that detection of population regulation requires study at the appropriate spatial scale. [R.H.S.]

population size The total number of individuals in a POPULATION. [P.C.]

porewater The WATER that surrounds the solid particles in SEDIMENT and SOIL, also referred to as INTERSTITIAL water. It is thought to be an important source of exposure to toxicants for sediment (soil)-dwelling organisms. [P.C.]

potentially responsible parties (PRPs) *See* COST RECOVERY.

power transmission lines Electricity transmission is predominantly overhead because this is much cheaper (up to 20 times) than the equivalent underground cable option. Bare METAL conductors (lines) of aluminium, with a steel core for strength, are normally used, suspended from lattice towers (pylons), generally constructed from angled sections of galvanized steel. The conductors are suspended from cross-arms on the towers, using strings of insulating GLASS or ceramic discs. [H.W.W.]

PP *See* PRECAUTIONARY PRINCIPLE; PRIMARY PRODUCTIVITY.

ppb (parts per billion) A UNIT of measurement of concentration, used especially in describing the concentrations of substances occurring in trace amounts, for example certain environmental pollutants. For example, 1 ppb = 1 part in $10^9 \equiv 1\,\mu g\,kg^{-1}$ (by mass) or $1\,\mu g\,l^{-1}$ (by volume; sometimes ppbv). Note that ppb was formerly used in the UK to mean parts per million million (i.e. 10^{12}), but US usage is now generally accepted. Where there is the possibility of doubt the unit should be defined as mass per unit mass, or mass per unit volume. [P.C.]

ppm (parts per million) A UNIT of measurement of concentration used especially in describing the concentrations of substances occurring in minute amounts. 1 ppm = 1 part in $10^6 \equiv 1\,mg\,kg^{-1}$ (by mass) or $1\,mg\,l^{-1}$ (by volume; sometimes ppmv). [P.C.]

PPP *See* POLLUTER PAYS PRINCIPLE; POLLUTION PREVENTION PRINCIPLE.

prairie The plains GRASSLANDS of North America, named from the French word for meadow. [J.J.H.]

precautionary principle (PP) This principle is used to justify the imposition of controls to protect the environment where there is incomplete understanding of the relationship between human actions/products and their effects on the environment, yet there is a perception of likely major problems. It has its roots in the German *VORSORGEPRINZIP*.

Precaution and scientific RISK ASSESSMENT are different responses to uncertainties about human impacts on the environment. An extreme version of the precautionary principle argues that we should always presume the worst, i.e. that there will be a significant environmental EFFECT from a CONTAMINANT or development, and the onus to prove otherwise should be with those who stand to gain from what is being proposed. The problem is that this sets science an impossible task—we can never be sure that there will be no effect (this is both a matter of logic and practicality)—so taken to extreme this could be a recipe for no new developments. Risk assessment, on the other hand, uses scientific analysis of likely exposures and effects to calculate the probabilities that adverse effects will occur. The onus is then with society and its representatives in the form of government, COMPETENT AUTHORITIES, regulators, etc., to take decisions about the tolerability of risks; this is usually done, implicitly if not explicitly, by reference to the benefits that derive from what is being considered for control.

The distinction between the precautionary and scientific approaches need not be presented quite so sharply as this; there are other less extreme interpretations of precaution. For example, one interpretation is that precaution simply implies the need for anticipation and prevention, which could be completely compatible with using scientific risk assessment to anticipate and prevent. Precaution, it could be interpreted, is anticipation that goes beyond the strict requirements of demonstrating causation in developing preventative measures.

Another situation in which precaution is applied is in recognition of either the shakiness of science and/or the perceived seriousness of the potential problems that might arise if the science were wrong. So UNCERTAINTY margins are often built into risk assessments as application or safety factors. But even here it is worth noting that these factors are not rationally defined; if they were we would not need to apply the precautionary principle for we would then be applying margins on the basis of scientific understanding and hence demonstrating our confidence in it. [P.C.]

precipitation
1 WATER in liquid or solid form, falling to earth under gravity as RAIN, snow or hail.
2 The coagulation and agglomeration of suspended particles (usually solids in water) to a size where the rate of gravitational settling becomes greater than the rate at which TURBULENCE maintains suspension in the fluid.
[J.N.C.]

predicted environmental concentration (PEC) The concentration of any particular substance that is anticipated to occur in the environment. It is usually derived from FATE models, which take into account levels and patterns of production, use and disposal, and physicochemical properties of the substances that influence the ways they are likely to partition between environmental compartments, and how likely they are to be transformed or degraded. *See also* EXPOSURE; MACKAY FATE MODELS. [P.C.]

predicted no effect concentration (PNEC) The concentration of a substance at and below which no ecological EFFECT is expected. It is used to set limits (e.g. ENVIRONMENTAL QUALITY STANDARDS) by regulators. However, proving negatives and guaranteeing no effects is notoriously risky, so the PNEC is better understood as the level below which effects are unlikely. [P.C.]

predictive ecotoxicity tests The use of test systems to attempt to predict the likely effects of substances on ecological systems and to determine probable no EFFECT levels (*see* ENVIRONMENTAL QUALITY STANDARD). The test systems can involve single species or many species; within species they may involve organismic or physiological/biochemical effects. They can be carried out at high concentration over short periods (acute) or lower concentrations over longer periods (chronic). Some are standardized, routine tests, while others may be specific to a particular problem and/or site (Table P3). They can

Table P3 Types of tests and a crude indication of their frequency of use. (From Calow, P. (ed.) (1993) *Handbook of Ecotoxicology*, Vol. 1. Blackwell Scientific Publications, Oxford.)	Time (*re* generation time)	Short, i.e. acute		Long, i.e. chronic
	Form	Quantal		Continuous
	When measured (*re* exposure)	During	After	During
	Level of biological organization			
	Suborganismic (molecules and cells)	Common	None	?
	Single-species	Very common*	Some	Common
	Multispecies	Uncommon	?	Reasonably common

* Some short-term, subchronic (sublethal) tests attempt to assess chronic effects by concentrating on sensitive stages, e.g. sensitive (usually early) life-stage tests.

be carried out under laboratory conditions or in field or near-field situations. In any event it is important that all relevant variables are controllable so that the link between dose/concentration of substance and effect can be defined as precisely as possible. [P.C.]

premanufacture notices Under the US Toxic Substances Control Act all NEW CHEMICALS must undergo premanufacturing NOTIFICATION (PMN) review. Notices must contain specified information on the properties of the chemicals that enables the USEPA, among other bodies, to assess ECOTOXI-CITY. [P.C.]

prescribed burns and fire management Prescribed fire is the skilful application of fire under known conditions of fuel, weather and TOPOGRAPHY to achieve resource management objectives. It includes fire ignited by managers, and fires ignited by natural sources, such as LIGHTNING, that are managed after ignition by daily monitoring. The use of fire is based on principles of fire ecology, so that the application of fire will meet land management goals. [J.K.A.]

prescribed processes Industrial processes identified for special attention under environmental protection legislation. In the UK these include industrial operations, as defined under the ENVIRONMENTAL PROTECTION ACT 1990, that are subject to INTEGRATED POLLUTION CONTROL. The UK list is a successor to scheduled processes defined under the earlier pollution prevention legislation. It includes some of the most polluting industrial processes; for example fuel and power, WASTE DISPOSAL, and metal and chemical industries. It is extended by EC Integrated Pollution Prevention and Control legislation. [P.C.]

pressure Force per unit area. The SI UNIT of pressure is the PASCAL (symbol: Pa), equal to 1 NEWTON of force distributed over 1 square METRE; i.e. 1 Pa = 1 N m^{-2}. Relation to old units: 1 bar = 0.1 MPa; 1 pound per square inch = 6.984 kPa; 1 atm = 0.101 MPa; 1 mmHg (torr) = 0.133 kPa. [J.G.]

pressure, atmospheric The force per unit area exerted on a body or surface by the ATMOSPHERE. The rate at which PRESSURE and density of the atmosphere change with altitude is seen in Table P4. [J.G.]

primary effects of pollution The direct metabolic effects of POLLUTION on an organism, or the consequential effects on that organism, such as impaired survival, growth, or reproduction. *Cf.* SECONDARY EFFECTS OF POLLUTION. [P.C.]

primary productivity (PP) The rate at which BIOMASS is produced per unit surface area of land or ocean by plants or chemoautotrophs. Where biomass may be described by its chemical energy, DRY MASS or carbon. 'Primary' indicates that this is the first step in the energy flow through an ECOSYSTEM; 'productivity' indicates the rate of manufacture or output. Primary productivity is often, but incorrectly, used as a synonym of net primary productivity. [S.P.L.]

primary woodland Woodland occupying a site which

Table P4 Pressure and density of the Earth's atmosphere at various altitudes. (From NOAA/NASA (1976) *US Standard Atmosphere*. Government Printing Office, Washington, D.C.)

Altitude (m)	Pressure (MPa)	Density (kg m^{-3})
0	0.101	1.225
500	0.0954	1.167
1 000	0.0898	1.112
1 500	0.0846	1.058
2 000	0.0795	1.006
2 500	0.0746	0.957
3 000	0.0701	0.909
3 500	0.0657	0.863
4 000	0.0617	0.819
5 000	0.0540	0.736
6 000	0.0472	0.660
7 000	0.0411	0.590
8 000	0.0356	0.525
9 000	0.0308	0.467
10 000	0.0265	0.413

has remained wooded throughout the period since the original FORESTS of a region were fragmented. [G.F.P.]

prior informed consent (PIC) A procedure established by UNEP and FAO where before allowing export of hazardous substances for the first time to a country, the exporting state is required to provide a suite of information, including identity, precautions necessary, summary of restrictions and reasons for them, to appropriate authorities in the country of destination. [P.C.]

prioritization of chemicals Given the large number of existing commercial chemical substances it would not be possible to carry out an exhaustive assessment of the environmental risks associated with most of them. One approach is to find out what is known about them and to identify those in need of most urgent attention. This is referred to as prioritization. In fact many priority LISTS have been compiled on this basis for regulatory purposes. Criteria used include production levels, HAZARD IDENTIFICATION, indicators of PERSISTENCE and BIOACCUMULATION. These can be used to identify priority substances in at least two non-mutually exclusive ways: decision trees and scoring systems.

Decision trees classify on the basis of levels of TOXICITY, persistence, bioaccumulation and production. They therefore generate lists without ratings. Scoring, on the other hand, ascribes quantities to levels of response and production and can therefore rank priorities, but this can give a false impression that the process is more precise than it is. A very common difficulty in all these procedures is lack of adequate data. Some systems exclude substances in which this is the case (with the risk of excluding important substances) whereas others use worse-case default values (with the risk of including unimportant substances). Above all, it is important that the system favoured is simple to use and transparent. [P.C.]

probability The chance of an event or measurement being observed. Probability is measured on a scale of 0 (impossible) to 1 (absolutely certain). For example, the probability, p, of getting a 'head' when you spin an unbiased coin is $p = 0.5$ (or $p = 1/2$, or $p = 50\%$). Probabilities can be calculated in two ways: a priori (before the event) and a posteriori (after the event). Before spinning the coin (a priori) we can imagine that the probability will be $1/2$ since there are two sides to the coin and we are only interested in one of them (heads). We exclude the possibility of the coin landing on its edge! After spinning the coin several times (a posteriori) we could estimate the probability by dividing the number of 'heads' actually observed by the total number of spins. The accuracy of this estimate will depend upon the total number of spins (n). For example, if by chance we get one more 'head' than we expect when $n = 10$ then $p = 60\%$, but if $n = 100$, $p = 51\%$. [B.S.]

probability distribution A theoretical or observed distribution of probabilities or frequencies. Theoretical distributions use a priori probabilities, while observed distributions use a posteriori probabilities (*see* PROBABILITY). Some people restrict the term 'probability distribution' to the theoretical, while using the term 'frequency distribution' for the observed. However, both can be used and interpreted in the same way. [B.S.]

product–moment correlation coefficient (*r*) A PARA-METRIC STATISTIC that summarizes the degree of CORRELATION between two sets of observations (x and y). The correlation coefficient (r) varies between +1 (perfect positive correlation), through 0 (no correlation), to −1 (perfect negative correlation). Both variables should approximately follow a NORMAL DISTRIBUTION, and are assumed to be measured with error. This is in contrast to some types of regression analysis (*see* REGRESSION ANALYSIS, LINEAR), in which only the y variable (dependent variable) is considered to follow a normal distribution and to be measured with error. [B.S.]

product stewardship The responsible design, production and marketing of products, together with after-sales care, that takes into account possible HARM to humans and impact on the environment. It should obviously include LIFE-CYCLE ASSESSMENT as an integral part. [P.C.]

production Sometimes a distinction is made between the process generating new BIOMASS and the output of new biomass. Some refer to the process as production and the output as productivity. Occasionally the reverse senses are intended. Usually, however, the two terms are used interchangeably. [P.C.]

productivity *See* PRODUCTION.

produktlinienalyse (PLA) A form of LIFE-CYCLE ASSESSMENT, pioneered in Germany, that takes a broad qualitative approach in describing adverse effects of products, including social and economic aspects, from cradle to grave. It completely avoids aggregation of the inventory data, which makes it somewhat difficult to interpret. [P.C.]

profile A cross-sectional view of a HABITAT or of a sedimentary deposit. [P.D.M.]

profundal *See* ABYSSAL; WITHIN-LAKE HABITAT CLASSIFICATION.

prohibition notice A legal device, served by a regulator, requiring the cessation of a practice that is deemed to be adversely affecting the environment and contravening legislation. [P.C.]

protective proteins A generic term for proteins that provide defence against abiotic stressors such as HEAVY METALS (*see also* METALLOTHIONEINS) or excessive heat (*see also* HEAT-SHOCK PROTEIN). [P.C.]

psammon A term used to describe the communities of microscopic flora, mainly unicellular algae, and associated fauna which inhabit the INTERSTITIAL spaces between sand grains on a seashore or lakeshore. [B.W.F.]

pseudoreplication For statistical purposes in making comparisons between situations it is necessary to make more than one observation per situation to consider if the variation of observations within a situation is more or less than that between situations. So observations are replicated, and it is presumed that the SAMPLING is carried out such that the replicates are independent. When they are not truly independent, pseudoreplication is said to have been effected with the likelihood of underestimating VARIANCE within situations. There are three cases all common in survey work.

1 Spatial: 'upstream/downstream' comparisons around, for example, an effluent outlet pipe often involve comparisons of means from replicate samples taken either side of the POINT SOURCE. But this is not true replication because the replicates are nested within each site. Here, true replication would involve making observations on a number of similar 'upstream/downstream' sites.

2 Temporal: samples are often taken through time at the same place to test for 'before and after treatment'. But samples taken through time from the same place are likely to be correlated and therefore not independent. Again, true replication would involve comparison across a number of similar treatment situations.

3 Sacrificial: this occurs when researchers do have a number of the replicates per treament but then inappropriately analyse units nested within experimental systems or ignore replicates by pooling data. [P.C.]

psychrometer An instrument for measuring atmospheric water vapour pressure from the TEMPERA-TURE recorded on a dry and wet bulb thermometer. [J.G.]

pteridophytes, global diversity and conservation The ferns and their allies, or pteridophytes, as presently constituted, are not a natural grouping but represent, today, the end-points of several distinct evolutionary lines of non-seed-forming vascular plants.

The clubmosses and quillworts are cosmopolitan in distribution though many are highly intolerant of POLLUTION.

The horsetails also once constituted one of the dominant tree groups of the Carboniferous, but are today reduced to the single, largely herbaceous genus *Equisetum*. The 30 extant species are today cosmopolitan, and can become weeds of economic significance in wet soils.

The true ferns today comprise four distantly related orders totalling some 10 000 species. Most present-day ferns are herbaceous although a small number form trees, notably the 20 m high, palmlike members of *Cyathea*. Although widespread, ferns are relatively scarce in arid zones and have their greatest concentration in the moist tropics; around 12% of the world's fern flora is thought to be located in Papua New Guinea.

Many ferns (and their allies) have now been recognized as rare or threatened, at least within the well-studied western European flora. Five per cent of plant species enjoying statutory protection in Great Britain are ferns. [G.A.F.H.]

pulp-mill pollution Pollution caused by effluent from pulp mills. Pulp is the raw material for paper, usually obtained from trees by either physical means (grinding the wood to separate the fibres) and/or chemical means (use of sulphite, sulphate or soda processes to dissolve lignins and release the CELLULOSE fibres). Consequently the effluent can have a high BIOCHEMICAL OXYGEN DEMAND, and contain SUSPENDED SOLIDS with a mix of hazardous chemicals. [P.C.]

pycnocline A zone in the water column within which the rate of change of density of seawater with increasing depth reaches a maximum. [V.F.]

Q

Q_{10} A measure of the TEMPERATURE sensitivity of a chemical reaction or any other process. [J.Ly.]

QA *See* QUALITY ASSURANCE AND QUALITY CONTROL.

QC *See* QUALITY ASSURANCE AND QUALITY CONTROL.

QSAR *See* QUANTITATIVE STRUCTURE–ACTIVITY RELATIONSHIP.

quadrat A small area, delimited by a frame, used to study the DISTRIBUTION and ABUNDANCE of species, commonly of VEGETATION but also fauna. [A.J.W.]

quality assurance (QA) and quality control (QC) In ECOTOXICOLOGY/TOXICOLOGY, quality control may refer to procedures incorporated in protocols to reduce the possibility of error. Quality assurance can refer to the independent VALIDATION of the quality-control systems and their operation. Both QA and QC are required by GOOD LABORATORY PRACTICE. [P.C.]

quantitative structure–activity relationship (QSAR) An equation, often derived by regression analysis, that relates environmental EFFECT and FATE properties of chemicals to measures and indices of their physicochemical and structural properties. For example,

with chemicals that cause non-specific narcosis there is often a good correlation between TOXICITY and OCTANOL–WATER PARTITION COEFFICIENT. Hence the latter can be used as a predictor of the former. This is therefore a short-cut technique that avoids the use of toxicity tests. More complex toxicological effects require more complex equations, which may not provide reliable predictions. *See also* ECOTOXICITY; ECOTOXICOLOGY; EXISTING CHEMICALS; NEW CHEMICALS; STRUCTURE–ACTIVITY RELATIONSHIP. [P.C.]

quantum sensor A sensor (transducer) for LIGHT or other electromagnetic RADIATION (e.g. ULTRAVIOLET RADIATION) that is almost equally sensitive to all photons (quanta) within its spectral sensitivity range. [L.M.C.]

quartile Any of the three points that divide a DISTRIBUTION or set of observations into quarters, or four equal parts. The first quartile (Q1, or lower quartile) has 25% of observations below it. The second quartile is the median (Q2, or middle quartile) and the third quartile (Q3, or upper quartile) has 75% of observations below it. Some rounding is necessary when the number of observations is not exactly divisible by 4. *See also* MEDIAN (SECOND QUARTILE); PERCENTILE. [B.S.]

R

radar (remote sensing) A microwave remote sensor used to derive images of the Earth's surface. The radar senses the terrain to the side of the aircraft or satellite track. It does this by pulsing out electromagnetic RADIATION of long (up to radio) wavelengths and recording first the strength of the pulse return to the sensor, to detect objects, and second the time it takes for the pulse to return, to give the range of the objects from the sensor. (The name 'radar' is the ACRONYM of these functions: radio detection and ranging.) These pulses are emitted at right angles to the direction of travel and pulse lines can be built up to form an image. A SYNTHETIC APERTURE RADAR (SAR) is the commonly used radar for environmental applications. [P.J.C.]

radiation Radiation is the transfer of energy by rapid oscillations of electromagnetic fields. Electromagnetic radiation travels in straight lines at very high speed $(3.0 \times 10^8 \, \text{m s}^{-1})$, and is characterized by its wavelength, flux density and direction. In normal conditions, most of the radiant transfer of energy in the BIOSPHERE is in the waveband 0.2–100 μm, this being a small part of the electromagnetic spectrum. [J.G.]

radiation dose For ACCIDENTS, such as that at Chernobyl in 1986, the personal risk is expressed in terms of detrimental effects, and long-term effects which are regarded as stochastic, which have been accurately observed at Hiroshima and Nagasaki. The setting of dose limits for civil purposes involves assumptions about the equivalence of a dose received instantaneously and the same dose over a long period at a lower intensity.

The absorbed dose, measured in energy per unit of body mass (J kg^{-1}), depends also on the type of RADIATION (α-, β-, γ-, X-), and the organ or tissue irradiated. This is allowed for by the use of weighting factors from which the PROBABILITY of detriment is computed, and may include hereditary and age effects which are particularly relevant in respect of length of loss of life in the case of fatal cancers. [R.S.S.]

radiation laws Physical laws for electromagnetic RADIATION. Several of them (Wien's radiation law, Rayleigh's radiation law, Stefan–Bolzmann's law and Wien's displacement law) can be regarded as special cases or derivations of the more general Planck's radiation law, which states that the heat radiation from a black body of absolute temperature T and unit surface is given by:

$$\text{d}E = 8\pi h v^3/c^3/[\exp(hv/kT) - 1]\text{d}v$$

where v is the frequency (LIGHT velocity divided by wavelength), $\text{d}E$ is the energy radiated in the frequency interval $\text{d}v$, h is the Planck constant $(6.626176 \times 10^{-34} \, \text{J s})$, and k is Boltzmann's constant $(1.380662 \times 10^{-23} \, \text{J K}^{-1})$. The law may be stated in several other mathematical forms.

Other important laws concerning electromagnetic radiation are Einstein's law, which states that in a photochemical reaction one PHOTON interacts with exactly one molecule, and Kirchhoff's radiation law, which states that the spectral emissivity of a certain surface at a certain frequency is equal to the spectral absorptivity at that frequency. Although not having a specific name, the relation (derived by Max Planck) that the energy of a photon is proportional to the frequency (the proportionality factor being Planck's constant) is another important radiation law. The frequency is the velocity of propagation divided by the wavelength. [L.O.B.]

radiation pollution IONIZING RADIATION consists of 'fast-flying' particles or waves that come naturally from the nuclei of unstable atoms or from nuclear facilities. Human beings and ecological systems are exposed daily to a certain amount of low-level radiation, or background radiation. Humans may also be exposed to radiation from medical uses. There may also be EXPOSURE due to accidental releases from the nuclear industry. [P.C.]

radical In chemistry, the term radical formerly referred to a group of atoms which maintained its identity in reactions involving the rest of the molecule. Now the term radical or free radical is applied to species which have one or more free valencies. Thus, the atom at the centre of the radical does not have its full complement of electrons and so radicals are often reactive species. Examples of radicals include single atoms (e.g. •Cl, •Br) and those formed by the rupture of chemical bonds in organic compounds; for example, peroxides (ROOR) decompose on heating to give a pair of radicals (2R–O•). Radicals formed from chlorinated compounds in the ATMOSPHERE are important in the depletion of OZONE. Radicals are also industrial CATALYSTS in polymerization reactions. Radicals have a wide range of stabilities; examples of more transient free radicals include •C_2H_5 and •OH. [M.C.G.]

radioactive fallout Radioactive fallout, mainly from atmospheric testing of nuclear weapons in the 1950s and 1960s, has resulted in worldwide low-level radioactive CONTAMINATION. Maximum atmospheric releases of radionuclides from weapons tests occurred in 1963, after which inputs were much smaller following the introduction of the atmospheric test-ban treaty. Weapons tests from 1954 to 1970, involving fission of some 10^{28} atoms of uranium or plutonium, released approximately 7.8×10^5 TBq of ^{137}Cs, 1.3×10^6 TBq of ^{90}Sr, 8.9×10^2 TBq of ^{239,240}Pu and 2.1×10^2 TBq of ^{238}Pu to the ATMOSPHERE. In 1964 the atmospheric burn-up of a US satellite, containing a system for nuclear auxiliary power (SNAP), released 6.3×10^2 TBq (1 kg) of ^{238}Pu, giving a composite ^{238}Pu/^{239,240}Pu activity ratio for fallout (weapons testing plus SNAP) of about 0.05 in the Northern hemisphere. Inventories of fallout radionuclides in soils depend upon rain-fall, with values for the UK in 1977 being 3.7×10^3 Bq m^{-2} of ^{137}Cs, 1.3×10^3 Bq m^{-2} of ^{90}Sr and 68 Bq m^{-2} of ^{239,240}Pu per metre of rainfall.

Significant radioactive fallout also occurred as a result of the Chernobyl reactor disaster in April 1986 (*see* CHERNOBYL DISASTER), when about 2×10^{18} Bq of volatile fission and activation products, including about 4×10^{16} Bq of ^{137}Cs, were released to the atmosphere. Chernobyl fallout had a ^{134}Cs/^{137}Cs activity ratio of about 0.5, distinguishing it from weapons-testing fallout, which did not contain ^{134}Cs. The Chernobyl release of radionuclides from a POINT SOURCE resulted in significantly higher contamination levels throughout much of Europe and Scandinavia than those from weapons-testing fallout. Weapons-testing and Chernobyl-fallout radionuclides provide useful chronological markers in accumulating sediments. *See also* RADIATION POLLUTION; RADIONUCLIDE. [A.B.M.]

radioactive waste Radioactive WASTE is classified as high-, intermediate- or low-level depending upon the activity of RADIONUCLIDES present. Intermediate- and high-level radioactive wastes arise mainly from the nuclear industry in the form of spent fuel rods, highly irradiated reactor components and reprocessing wastes. The nuclear industry is also the dominant producer of low-level radioactive waste, but smaller quantities arise from other sources including hospitals, universities and industrial facilities. Selective concentration of natural decay series radionuclides generates radioactive waste in some non-nuclear industries (e.g. oil extraction, coal combustion and metal refining). Radium- or tritium-containing wastes can also occur in the environment from the disposal of manufactured luminescent materials.

Gaseous and liquid low-level radioactive wastes are disposed of by authorized discharges to the environment, with the aim of dispersion in the atmosphere or aquatic environment to give dilution to levels that present a negligible radiological HAZARD. Solid low-level wastes are disposed of by burial in near-surface engineered repositories.

Designs for intermediate- and high-level waste repositories are based upon the concept of isolating the radionuclides for a sufficient length of time to allow the activity to decay to a non-hazardous level. In such designs, it is envisaged that the engineered section of the repository (known as the near field) will contain a series of barriers which will, for an extended period of time, prevent ingress of groundwater and subsequent releases of radionuclides. A typical design of this type would be to place the vitrified waste in a stainless-steel container which would be surrounded by bentonite clay and concrete. Upon the eventual failure of the near-field barriers, radionuclides will migrate through the host rock (known as the far field) and the rock type and repository depth would be selected to give long-term stability and a low rate of radionuclide migration. [A.B.M.]

radioactivity Radioactivity is a spontaneous process in which an unstable nucleus undergoes a transition to produce a new nucleus of lower internal energy plus radiation. One such transition is called a decay or disintegration, and the number of decay events per unit time is called the activity (A). The SI UNIT of activity is the BECQUEREL (Bq), which is a decay rate of one disintegration per second. The former unit of activity, the CURIE (Ci), corresponds to a decay rate of 3.7×10^{10} disintegrations per second (the activity of 1 g of ^{226}Ra). The main radioactive decay processes are as follows.

• α-Decay: emission of an α-PARTICLE (mass 4 amu, charge +2), giving a product nuclide two places to the left in the PERIODIC TABLE.

• β$^-$-Decay: emission of a β$^-$-particle (i.e. an electron) and a neutrino (V), giving a product nuclide one place to the right in the periodic table.

• β$^+$-Decay: emission of a β$^+$-particle (i.e. a positron) and a neutrino, giving a product nuclide one place to the left in the periodic table.

• γ-Emission: de-excitation of a nucleus by emission of photons of electromagnetic radiation known as γ-radiation or γ-rays.

• Electron capture: capture of a 1s electron by the nucleus, giving a product one place to the left in the periodic table.

• Spontaneous nuclear fission: splitting of the nucleus into two lighter nuclei.
[A.B.M.]

radiometer A sensor for measuring the flux radiation in W m^{-2}. [J.G.]

radionuclide A radionuclide is a nuclide which has an unstable combination of neutrons and protons in its nucleus and spontaneously undergoes radioactive decay to produce a new nuclide of lower energy plus RADIATION. [A.B.M.]

radiotelemetry *See* TELEMETRY.

radon (Rn) A radioactive gaseous element (ATOMIC NUMBER = 86; relative ATOMIC MASS = 222; melting point = −71°C; boiling point = −62°C) that is chemically inert and has known isotopes from ^{211}Rn to ^{224}Rn. It occurs naturally in the uranium and thorium decay series as ^{219}Rn ($t_{1/2}$ = 3.96 s), ^{220}Rn (sometimes called thoron) ($t_{1/2}$ = 55.6 s) and ^{222}Rn ($t_{1/2}$ = 3.825 days). Of the natural isotopes, only ^{222}Rn lives for a sufficient length of time to allow significant environmental transport. Movement of ^{222}Rn in groundwater and soil gas can result in its accumulation in mines and buildings, causing increased radiation EXPOSURE to humans and other organisms, and raised incidences of lung cancer. [A.B.M.]

rain WATER droplets falling under gravity from CLOUDS to the Earth's surface, as the liquid phase of PRECIPITATION. [J.N.C.]

rain forest Any FOREST in either tropical or temperate latitudes that receives particularly high levels of rainfall and whose structure and composition is determined by the high HUMIDITY of the environment. [P.D.M.]

raised bog A domed MIRE found in temperate regions. The central dome of PEAT is surrounded by lower-lying wetland habitats through which groundwater flows. The main cupola of peat can extend over several square kilometres and can be elevated in excess of 6 m above the groundwater table. [P.D.M.]

RAMSAR *See* INTERNATIONAL CONSERVATION CONVENTIONS.

random distribution A term used to describe the spatial DISTRIBUTION of the individuals in a POPULATION. When individuals in a population follow a random distribution, the VARIANCE (s^2) of individuals per SAMPLE is equal to the MEAN number ($\bar{x}$) of individuals per sample ($s^2 = \bar{x}$). This is frequently summarized by saying that the variance to mean ratio is equal to 1 ($s^2/\bar{x} = 1$). [B.S.]

random sample This is an unbiased subset of a POPULATION under investigation and is required for many statistical tests. [C.D.]

range management The utilization of extensive areas of GRASSLANDS for pastoral purposes in both temperate and tropical areas demands careful management to avoid possible destructive effects (*see* OVERGRAZING). Range management has traditionally been applied to the control of stock density of domestic animals, usually cattle or sheep, to ensure the continued productivity of the ecosystem. [P.D.M.]

rarity, biology of Rare species have low ABUNDANCE, or small ranges, or frequently both. Rarity is highly scale-dependent, both temporally and spatially, and may frequently have one apparent cause at the large scale (e.g. climatic restriction) and another at a smaller scale (e.g. soil type). Naturalists, ecologists and conservationists pay particular attention to rare species because they are more likely to become extinct and because they are considered to be of higher value. [K.T. & F.B.G.]

reclamation Reclamation is defined by the National Research Council (1992) as a 'process designed to adapt a wild or NATURAL resource to serve a utilitarian human purpose, putting a natural resource to a new or altered use—often used to refer to processes that destroy native ecosystems and convert them to agricultural or urban uses.' Regrettably, the term 'reclamation' is often used interchangeably with the term 'ecological restoration', which aims to return a damaged ECOSYSTEM to a former natural condition. The terms 'reclamation' and 'creation' imply putting a landscape to a new or altered use to serve a particular human purpose. 'Preservation', of course, is the maintenance of the integrity of a natural system.

'Mitigation', another term commonly used in conjunction with ecosystem damage, is simply the intent to alleviate any or all detrimental effects arising from a given action. Reality may not always follow intention, however. For example, mitigation for filling in a wetland in order to build an airport taxiway may involve restoring a nearby, or even somewhat distant, wetland that had been filled in for some other reason, or it could involve creating a wetland on an adjacent area that was formerly upland vegetation. Before human society and REGULATORY AGENCIES appreciated the ecological importance of WETLANDS, they were often reclaimed for housing developments (e.g. Fort Lauderdale, Florida), filled in for agricultural purposes, or filled in for an airport taxiway or highway. [J.C.]

recreation ecology The branch of ecology concerned with the impact of recreational and leisure activities on natural populations and the environment. [P.D.M.]

recruitment The addition of individuals to a POPULATION. [A.J.D.]

recycling The processing of materials so they are available for REUSE by living organisms, manufacturing industries, etc. All matter cycles in nature (*see* BIOGEOCHEMICAL CYCLE) and so, by definition, is renewable. But such transformations are not always reversible; moreover they require energy and may lead to POLLUTION. So the recycling of human wastes requires care to optimize environmental protection. The most effective form of recycling from this point of view is usually reuse. Other forms of recycling involve reuse of materials but not necessarily in their original form. Direct recycling involves the reconversion of materials into a similar functional form; for example, pulp from WASTE paper being made into new paper. Indirect recycling involves conversion to a different functional form; for example, pulp from waste paper being made into packaging board. This term might even be applied to INCINERATION when heat is recovered and used productively (*see* COMBINED HEAT AND POWER). [P.C.]

Red (Data) Book A catalogue, published by the IUCN, listing species that are rare or in danger of becoming extinct locally or nationally. [P.C.]

Red List A list of 23 dangerous substances designated under the UK ENVIRONMENTAL PROTECTION ACT 1990 as chemicals whose DISCHARGE to water should be minimized by application of the BATNEEC (BEST AVAILABLE TECHNIQUES NOT ENTAILING EXCESSIVE COSTS) principle. Discharge CONSENTS are required for these substances. [P.C.]

red tide Red, brown or yellowish discoloration of COASTAL waters during ALGAL BLOOMS of dinoflagellate PHYTOPLANKTON, due to high concentrations of accessory pigments other than chlorophyll *a*. Some Dinophyceae produce potent TOXINS that can cause illness or death of marine organisms and/or humans. [J.L.]

redox potential (Eh) Redox potential is a measure of the ability of an electron carrier to act as a reducing (addition of electrons) or oxidizing (removal of electrons) agent.

$$Eh = E_0 - 59\,(a/n)pH$$

Where E_0 is the standard potential at equal activities of reduced and oxidized species, *a* is the number of protons transferred, and *n* is the number of electrons involved in the reaction. [R.M.M.C.]

reed-bed purifiers Artificially constructed WETLANDS created for the sole purpose of wastewater or stormwater treatment. During the last decade, they have been put into operation as a means of low-cost treatment applicable to urban and industrial areas across the world. [A.D.]

reef An off-shore consolidated rock, often presenting a hazard to navigation. *See also* CORAL REEFS. [V.F.]

reforestation The replacement of FOREST cover which has been removed either recently or in the past. [J.R.P.]

refugia Populations of animals and plants that survive in HABITATS of limited area in regions which would not otherwise support such organisms or communities. A refugium typically constitutes the flora and fauna of an ENVIRONMENT or COMMUNITY that was once widespread but is now considerably diminished in area. [G.A.F.H.]

region of compliance Part of an ecosystem in which COMPLIANCE with an environmental STANDARD is required and/or exists; for example, outside the MIXING ZONE. [P.C.]

register of effects LISTS of potential ENVIRONMENTAL IMPACTS compiled as part of an ENVIRONMENTAL MANAGEMENT SYSTEM and taking into account all aspects of an operation from 'cradle to grave', including past activities that might

have led to, for example, land CONTAMINATION, and considering normal, abnormal and accidental situations. In practice, the register usually consists of lists of potentially polluting EMISSIONS (potential causes of POLLUTION) rather that actual effects on ecological systems. This is not surprising given the complexity of making precise linkages between complex business operations and complex ecological processes, especially at a global level. [P.C.]

registers, environmental
1 Under environmental (protection) legislation, any of various LISTS of environmental information that are open to public scrutiny. Such registers are usually compiled by authorities as a statutory requirement.
2 In the context of ENVIRONMENTAL MANAGEMENT SYSTEMS, any of various lists of applicable legislation and possible adverse environmental effects.
[P.C.]

regression analysis, linear Linear regression analysis is a technique that fits a straight-line relationship (a regression line) to a set of paired observations, using the simple straight-line equation $y = a \pm bx$. The quantity *a* denotes the point that the regression line crosses the *y*-axis (the *y* intercept) and the quantity *b* is the slope (steepness) of the regression line. If *b* is positive then increasing *x* means increasing *y*. If *b* is negative then increasing *x* means decreasing *y*. [B.S.]

regulated-escapement harvesting A form of HARVESTING that aims to ensure that the number of adults escaping harvest is sufficient to provide (potentially) satisfactory RECRUITMENT of young to the population. [J.B.]

regulated-percentage harvesting This is an uncommon term, but basically it refers to the simple idea of having a constant level of MORTALITY inflicted on the harvested population. It is closely related to CONSTANT-EFFORT HARVESTING, and is also an implicit part of the analysis that is involved in density-dependence models where a fixed fishing mortality is applied. Theoretically it is an attractive mechanism as long as the percentage harvest taken is below the maximum percentage that the stock can bear. [J.B.]

regulating factors MORTALITY (or FECUNDITY-reducing) factors which act in a density-dependent manner, such that the percentage dying increases with POPULATION DENSITY (or the proportion of realized fecundity declines with increasing population density), and this DENSITY DEPENDENCE is responsible, in interaction with density-independent factors, for determining the equilibrium POPULATION SIZE. All regulation factors are density dependent, but not all density-dependent factors are regulating. [M.J.C.]

regulator An organism that can maintain some aspect of its physiology (e.g. body temperature) constant despite different and changing properties of the external ENVIRONMENT. [V.F.]

regulatory agencies Organizations empowered by governments to implement and enforce environmental legislation. The US Environmental Protection Agency (USEPA) was assembled from components of various federal agencies in 1970 in pursuance of an Executive Order signed by President Nixon. The Environment Agency for England and Wales (sometimes referred to as 'Agency' or EA), and the Scottish Environmental Protection Agency (SEPA) were formed by an Act of Parliament in 1995, again by combining existing bodies. In the case of the former the principal bodies subsumed were the National Rivers Authority (NRA) and Her Majesty's Inspectorate of Pollution (HMIP), while for the latter it was mainly elements of the River Purification Authorities and Her Majesty's Industrial Pollution Inspectorate (HMIPI). [P.C.]

regulatory instruments Methods used by REGULA-TORY AGENCIES to protect the environment. They can include COMMAND AND CONTROL and economic/market instruments (*see* MARKET IN-STRUMENTS). [P.C.]

regulatory organizations/authorities *See* ENVIRON-MENTAL (PROTECTION) AGENCIES; REGULA-TORY AGENCIES.

relict A surviving fragment of a plant or animal POPU-LATION or ASSEMBLAGE that was formerly more diversified (a phylogenetic, evolutionary or taxonomic relict) or more widely distributed (a geographical relict). [J.H.T.]

remediation The process of putting right (i.e. remedying) the effects of POLLUTION, or attempts to do so. [P.C.]

remote sensing The gathering/recording of information about a population, ecosystem, area, phenomenon, etc., using any device that is not in physical contact with the subject—for example, by radio, visually by camera, or by satellite imaging. [P.C.]

renewable energy Energy from sources that are not depleted by the process, for example solar, wind and waves. Cf. non-renewable sources: FOSSIL FUELS. [P.C.]

renewable resource A resource that is produced by natural ecosystems at rates that can potentially balance rates of removal. Examples of renewable resources include lumber, fish and game. [P.C.]

repeatability The closeness of agreement between successive observations employing the same method, test material and laboratory. For example, closeness of results from repeated ECOTOXICITY tests of a single substance. [P.C.]

reproducibility The closeness of agreement between observations from different laboratories carrying out the same method with the same test material. For example, the closeness of results from different laboratories using the same ECOTOXICITY test (identical protocols) on the same test substance.

Reproducibility is assessed by RING TESTS. [P.C.]

reprotoxins *See* CARCINOGENS, MUTAGENS, TER-ATOGENS.

residence time The period of time for which an entity remains within an ecological unit of interest. For instance, the time for which a food particle or molecule remains within the gut; or for which an organism, nutrient or WATER molecule remains within a stretch of river or within a lake or pond; or the time for which a molecule of a POLLUTANT remains in the ATMOSPHERE. [P.C.]

resilience A measure of COMMUNITY or POPULA-TION stability which has many definitions. The most frequently used is the speed of recovery of a community after a DISTURBANCE from a local equilibrium. This means that a highly resilient community will return very rapidly to local equilibrium. Definitions of resilience are often confused with those of RESIS-TANCE. [C.D.]

resistance
1 The ability of an organism to show insensitivity or reduced sensitivity to a chemical that normally causes adverse effects. Resistance and TOLERANCE have often been used synonymously.
2 A measure of COMMUNITY or POPULATION sta-bility that has many different definitions. One defini-tion is that resistance is a measure of the amount of change which can be applied to a system before it is disturbed from its equilibrium. By this definition, systems with high resistance will not move from a local equilibrium when exposed to change. An extension to this definition is to use resistance as a measure of the change of state variables within a system in response to a change in a variable. Resistance and RESILIENCE are often confused. [P.C. & C.D.]

respiration Respiration is the oxidation of food by organisms to release energy in the form of adenosine triphosphate (ATP). [D.J.R. & J.I.L.M.]

response variable The y variable in statistical analysis; the response (measurement or count) for which we aim to understand the relative importance of various EXPLANATORY VARIABLES in causing variation. Formerly known as the dependent variable. [M.J.C.]

restoration ecology *See* ECOLOGICAL RESTORA-TION.

retrospective analysis (monitoring) It is often neces-sary to consider if human activity is having an adverse EFFECT on ecological systems. This might be a concern at particular sites that are exposed to regular EMISSIONS of EFFLUENTS or following accidental releases; or it might apply to assessing the general quality of systems subject to possible impacts from a wide range of activities. These are all retro-spective analyses: i.e analyses performed after the human activity has occurred.

In general we are rarely able to predict, from first

principles, what sorts of ecological ASSEMBLAGES should occur in particular habitats if undisturbed, so retrospective analysis is often based upon comparisons between putatively undisturbed and putatively disturbed systems; i.e. systems separated in space (e.g. upstream vs. downstream comparisons) or time (before vs. after comparisons). Hence, it is usually not straightforward to separate VARIABILITY due to a specific cause (POLLUTANT) from natural variability. How, given that ecosystems are so variable through space and time, can we be sure that the control site would have exhibited ecological characteristics similar to those of the putatively disturbed site had there been no DISTURBANCE? Even carefully designed and replicated SAMPLING programmes cannot completely remove these uncertainties. Therefore, observations and MONITORING should be associated with experimental analysis. For example, does SEDIMENT from the contaminated site have appropriate ecotoxicological properties? Can these properties be removed by stripping out the contaminant? And so on.

Other techniques plant out organisms as *IN SITU* BIOASSAYS. This method has the virtue that initial conditions can be made constant in the control and exposed systems; but it can be open to criticisms of artificiality. Often, especially in general SURVEYS concerned with assessing quality, detailed comparisons are not made; instead, effects are judged in terms of the presence or absence of INDICATOR SPECIES or species complexes that, on the basis of past experience (sometimes captured formally in empirical models), are generally expected to be present in clean or polluted conditions. This is the BIOINDICATOR (biotic index) approach, which itself suffers from a number of problems. *Cf.* PREDICTIVE ECOTOXICITY TESTS. *See also* BIOTIC INDICES; BIOMONITOR. [P.C.]

reuse A form of RECYCLING of WASTE that involves using the object or material again, for the function originally intended. Returned bottles, reused as bottles, are good examples. *See also* WASTE DISPOSAL. [P.C.]

Reynolds number *(Re)* A dimensionless quantity named after the 19th century scientist, Sir Osborne Reynolds. Fluid mechanics uses the Reynolds number to define whether the flow of fluid is laminar or turbulent. Theoretically, the Reynolds number is defined as the ratio between inertial forces and viscous forces (inertial forces are those associated with the mean motion of the fluid; viscous forces are those associated with frictional shear stress). Mathematically, the Reynolds number is defined as:

$$Re = du/v$$

where d is a characteristic length scale, u is the velocity of the fluid and v is the kinematic VISCOSITY of the fluid. Most atmospheric flows tend to be turbulent because the magnitude of v is of the order of $10^{-5}\,m^2\,s^{-1}$ and the magnitude of u is of the order of 0.1–$10\,m\,s^{-1}$. [D.D.B.]

rheophilous Describing a wetland habitat, vegetation or an individual species that demands a flow of WATER to supply its mineral nutrient requirements; literally 'flow-loving'. [P.D.M.]

rheotrophic Describing a wetland ecosystem that receives at least part of its nutrient input through a flow of groundwater; literally 'fed by the flow'. [P.D.M.]

rhizobenthos *See* BENTHIC HABITAT CLASSIFICATION; WITHIN-STREAM/RIVER HABITAT CLASSIFICATION.

rhizosphere The rhizosphere is the narrow zone (*c.* 1–2 mm) of SOIL immediately surrounding the actively growing root, in which the plant has a direct influence on the soil MICROFLORA (and to some extent also, the MICROFAUNA). [J.B.H.]

richness The number of species present at a particular place and time. No assumptions are made about the relative ABUNDANCES (or EQUITABILITY) of these species. [A.E.M.]

Richter scale A measure of seismic activity devised by C. Richter in 1935 at the California Institute of Technology. It measures how much energy is released by ground movement from the centre of a seismic shock. It is logarithmic, so a 6.0 earthquake is 10 times more powerful than a 5.0. The highest ever recording is 8.9. [P.C.]

riffles, in streams *See* WITHIN-STREAM/RIVER HABITAT CLASSIFICATION.

ring test A means of assessing between-laboratory variation in a TOXICITY/ECOTOXICITY test. Single substances are tested according to standard GUIDELINES/protocols, and the results from different laboratories are compared and contrasted. Such procedures are important in the standardization of tests, to ensure that different laboratories achieve the same results for the same test compounds. They are also essential for scientific and legal credibility. [P.C.]

Rio Summit The name commonly given to the UN Conference on Environment and Development (UNCED), held in 1992 in Rio de Janeiro, Brazil. *See also* SUSTAINABLE DEVELOPMENT. [P.C.]

riparian Pertaining to the bank(s) of a natural watercourse. [P.C.]

riparian rights The rights of landowners with respect to water on or bordering their land; for example, the right to prevent upstream water from being diverted or misused. [P.C.] ·

risk assessment In an environmental context, this involves predicting the extent to which the potential of a substance or process to cause HARM is realized under normal and/or abnormal and/or emergency/ACCIDENT conditions. For hazardous chemicals, therefore, this involves a combination of HAZARD assessment (potential to cause harm) with likely

FATE of chemicals in the environment and hence EXPOSURE of ecological systems. For industrial processes, risk assessment involves a combination of assessing the potential to cause problems (as a result of ENVIRONMENTAL IMPACT and/or likelihood of litigation) with an assessment of the likelihood of those problems being manifested, which depends upon how the system is operated and managed. Ideally, this should lead to calculation of an explicit probability of a particular magnitude of EFFECT and frequency of occurrence. But often this is not possible in environmental risk assessment due to:
• a lack of understanding of all the complex interactions;
• imprecise definition of the targets one is trying to protect.
So, risk indicators are often used instead. [P.C.]

risk characterization A step in the process of RISK ASSESSMENT. Thus in European Community (EC) legislation concerning existing and new substances, risk characterization involves comparing PREDICTED ENVIRONMENTAL CONCENTRATIONS (PEC) with PREDICTED NO EFFECT CONCENTRATIONS (PNEC)—a so-called RISK QUOTIENT. [P.C.]

risk communication The exchange of information on likely impairment of human health and/or environment, between risk assessors, risk managers, the public, media, interest group, etc. [P.C.]

risk management In an environmental context, the formulation and enactment of instruments that are intended to control or reduce risks to human health and the well-being of ecological systems from processes and substances. The instruments can involve regulatory (COMMAND AND CONTROL) action; economic incentives, either by direct means (e.g. applying taxes or levies) or by indirect means (by providing appropriate information on performance to customers and stakeholders); and voluntary agreements. [P.C.]

risk perception The awareness or impression of a risk to health or the environment adopted by the public and/or media and/or pressure groups. It may or may not relate to scientific RISK ASSESSMENT, but it is important in influencing policy-makers and regulators and hence is often a driving force in RISK MANAGEMENT. [P.C.]

risk phrases Standard phrases used as labels of substances to identify potential health and environmental hazards (so something of a misnomer; *cf.* RISK ASSESSMENT). Risk phrases are required, for example, by European Community (EC) Directive 67/548/EEC. This includes such phrases as: 'very toxic to aquatic organisms'; 'toxic to aquatic organisms'; 'harmful to aquatic organisms'; and 'may cause long-term adverse effects in aquatic environment'. The choice of label depends upon ECOTOXICITY criteria. [P.C.]

risk quotient (RQ) Used in assessment of NEW CHEMI-CALS and EXISTING CHEMICALS as an indicator of risk (*see* RISK ASSESSMENT). Involves comparing environmental concentrations (PREDICTED ENVIRONMENTAL CONCENTRATIONS, PECs) with threshold concentrations below which no effect is expected (PREDICTED NO EFFECT CONCENTRATIONS, PNECs). So when PEC/PNEC is less than 1, the likelihood of adverse effects is low; when it is greater than 1, an adverse effect is possible and RISK MANAGEMENT is invited. [P.C.]

river continuum concept RIVERS flow, and there are bound to be changes in ecological structure and function from source (springs) to finish (ultimately the SEA). Because of the likelihood of shading from surrounding vegetation, heterotrophic processes often dominate in the upper reaches, whereas primary PRODUCTION becomes more important in the middle reaches. Because of SEDIMENT loading causing shading, heterotrophic processes are likely to become dominant again in the lower reaches. Hence there is a shift in the major sources of energy inputs along the length of a river. Moreover, the energetics of the ecosystems in any one stretch are influenced by the energetics of upstream stretches—for example by import of production and washed-out DETRITUS—and in turn influence the energetics of downstream stretches (by export). Hence there is a longitudinal continuum of ECOSYSTEM processes and COMMUNITY structure.

That such a longitudinal SUCCESSION of processes and hence community compositions exists in rivers seems almost beyond doubt. But the river continuum concept (RCC) goes further than this to suggest that there will be general and predictable shifts in these properties. However, such longitudinal patterns can easily be disturbed by POLLUTION, land management and also, potentially, by local discontinuities in natural features such as geology and sediments. Moreover, flowing-water systems are temporally very dynamic, a consequence of VARIABILITY in physical conditions, especially flow rates. This, in combination with variability in other physical features, is likely to lead to patchiness in susceptibility to scouring by spate, which could result in unpredictable patchiness in the distribution of ecological features compared with the smooth transitions predicted by the RCC. [P.C.]

river invertebrate prediction and classification system (RIVPACS) A model for assessing riverwater quality. The model was constructed empirically from an initial survey of 'clean sites'. It is based on kick samples of benthic invertebrates obtained in a specified way over a specific time. Multivariate discriminant analysis sought CORRELATION between a minimum number of physicochemical variables and taxa present. Then for a particular site the model predicts expected taxa from observations on the same physicochemical variables, and this prediction can be used as a yardstick for the taxa that are actually collected from the site. The extent of divergence between expected and observed is supposed to give an index of river quality. This kind of approach avoids PSEUDOREPLICATION but is based on correlation analysis, and so until the mechanistic basis of the correlation is defined a divergence from the expected cannot be ascribed with certainty to any particular cause. [P.C.]

river purification authorities *See* ENVIRONMENTAL (PROTECTION) AGENCIES.

rivers Rivers are the natural channels which carry WATER from the land surface to the oceans. [A.M.]

rivers and streams, types of A number of classification schemes have been developed to distinguish the different sections along the course of a river, with changes in the BIOTA classified with reference to the physical changes of the river.

A river arising in a mountainous region can be divided into three sections.

1 An upper (or mountain) course with a V-shaped valley in which the water flows fast enough to carry stones.

2 A middle (or foothill) course where the valley is broader in section with stable sides and less prone to erosion, and the water velocity is still fast enough to carry sand and mud in suspension.

3 A lower (or plain) course with a broad, shallow valley and a water velocity slow enough to deposit sediments.

An alternative classification system, originally designed for European rivers, divides the river into two sections.

1 Rhithron—the region extending from the source to the point where the mean monthly water temperature rises to 20°C, the OXYGEN concentration is always high, the water velocity is fast and turbulent, and the bed is composed of rocks, stones or gravel with a fauna that is cold stenothermic and contains no PLANKTON.

2 Potamon—the region of the river where the mean monthly water temperature rises to over 20°C, occasional oxygen deficiencies occur, the water velocity is slow and the substratum consists of either mud or sand with a fauna that is either eurythermic or warm stenothermic and does contain plankton.

In areas outside western Europe, the mean monthly water temperature cut-off point between rhithron and potamon must be adjusted according to the geographic and climatic differences.

A stream or river system consists of a pattern of tributaries joining one another and coalescing to form the main river. Tributaries can be arranged into a hierarchy. First-order streams have no tributaries, but when two first-order streams meet they form a second-order stream. When two second-order streams meet they form a third-order stream and so on. Comparing streams in different orders, there are 3–4 times as many streams, each of less than half the

length and draining a little more than one-fifth the drainage area in each successive order. [R.W.D.]

RIVPACS *See* RIVER INVERTEBRATE PREDICTION AND CLASSIFICATION SYSTEM.

road run-off Aqueous drainage from roadways following RAIN or snow/ice-melt. Such RUN-OFF is often loaded with organic and inorganic CONTAMINANTS, derived from motor vehicles, from the road materials themselves, or from materials used to grit the road, particularly for de-icing. *See also* MOTOR VEHICLE POLLUTION. [P.C.]

rocky shores Usually refers to the marine environment, but occasionally can refer to LAKES when there are rocky outcrops on the shoreline. In general, marine rocky shores are the most densely populated and most biologically diverse of all intertidal shores. They are characterized by prominent vertical zonation of the dominant species. Horizontal ZONATION also occurs, with the degree of wave exposure having a major influence of the types of species present. [V.F.]

roentgen The earliest unit used to measure EXPOSURE to RADIATION, named after W. Roentgen, the discoverer of X-RAYS. It preceded the discovery of RADIOACTIVITY, and is applicable only to X-rays and γ-RAYS. Hence it is now superseded by the SI UNIT of exposure, coulomb per kilogram. One roentgen produces 1 esu of electric charge in 1 cm^3 of air at normal temperature and pressure. [R.S.S.]

round robin test The same as RING TEST. [P.C.]

Royal Commission on Environmental Pollution (RCEP) A UK standing body constituted on 20 February 1970 'to advise on matters both national and international, concerning the POLLUTION of the environment; on the adequacy of research in this field; and on the future possibilities of danger to the environment'. Appointments to the Commission are by Royal Warrant, on the advice of the Prime Minister. The Commission is therefore an independent body, not constrained by government departmental boundaries. The Commission has no specific or restricted task. It is authorized to inquire into any matter on which it thinks advice is needed, and also to inquire into any issues within its terms of reference that are referred to it by any Secretaries of State or Ministers. It has written reports on such matters as toxic pollution, INCINERATION and traffic problems. It has been enormously influential in the development of UK government policies. [P.C.]

rule making The USEPA has powers to interpret and implement and, to some extent, extend legislation by developing formal statements. These are subject to public scrutiny and challenge in the courts. [P.C.]

run-off The fraction of the PRECIPITATION falling on a land area that leaves it as surface or subsurface WATER flow. [D.C.L.]

Rylands versus Fletcher A ruling in British private or TORT law that has implications for environmental protection. The ruling arose out of a case reported in 1865 and involved the following:

> . . . that the person for his own purposes brings on to his land and collects and keeps there anything likely to do mischief if it escapes, must keep it in at his peril, and if he does not do so, is *prima facie* answerable for all the damage which is the natural consequence of its escape.

This therefore involves an important legal principle: that liability for POLLUTION is strict, i.e. it applies even if there was no intent to do HARM. In principle the implications for environmental protection that follow from this are wide ranging; in practice, however, a number of restrictions placed on the interpretation of the principle in the courts has constrained its effects. One recent development arose out of a decision of the House of Lords in the case of Cambridge Water Co. vs. Eastern Counties Leather in favour of the latter party (ECL), overturning an earlier decision of the Court of Appeal. The facts were that ECL has operated a tannery in such a way as to allow the escape of significant quantities of organochlorine solvent into the groundwater through spillages. This ceased in 1976 but damage to Cambridge Water Company's (CWC's) borehole was discovered only in the 1980s. The House of Lords reasoned that damages in private nuisance or under Rylands vs. Fletcher depend upon foreseeability and that this, despite a previous ruling to the contrary by the Court of Appeal, was not a reasonable interpretation here.

The significance of the ruling is that the highest court in the UK appears to put a barrier in the way of development of strict (i.e. no fault) liability for environmental damage. Nevertheless, strict civil liability for environmental damage embodied in the principle is being considered for application throughout the European Union and forms the basis of Superfund legislation in the USA. Indeed, the decision from the House of Lords on the ECL case actually stated that if strict liability is to be developed within this context it is more appropriate for Parliament to carry out this change than the Courts. [P.C.]

S

SACs (special areas of conservation) *See* NATURA 2000.

safety (safe) level In an environmental context this implies a level of CONTAMINATION that has zero effect. But logically it is impossible to prove a negative—some effect on a hitherto untested physiological system or individual species, process or ecosystem might arise. So this concept is scientifically not very useful. It is better to specify probabilities of effects, with the term 'safe level' used to indicate a low probability of effect. [P.C.]

salinity Salinity is the extent of dissolved salts in waters or soils. SALINIZATION is the process whereby soils accumulate salts over time. Seawater contains about $33\,g\,l^{-1}$ of dissolved salts, made up as follows (all units $mg\,l^{-1}$): sodium, 10600; magnesium, 1300; calcium, 400; potassium, 380; chlorine, 19000; bromine, 65; sulphur, 900; carbon, 28, and many other elements at trace levels. Rainwater contains $10–15\,mg\,l^{-1}$ of dissolved salts.

Salinity of waters and soils is often assessed by measuring the electrical conductivity using a conductivity cell. SOIL is mixed with distilled water to make a paste for these measurements. The conductivity is measured in millisiemens per centimetre $(mS\,cm^{-1})$. [J.G.]

salinization An increase in the salt concentration of the soils (or waters) of a habitat, usually resulting from human activity. [P.D.M.]

salt flat A flat, saline area in a DESERT created by the evaporation of a former lake (playa). [P.D.M.]

salt marsh A term used to describe the habitat, vegetation and fauna associated with the accretion of fine sediments (mud to fine sand) between high neap- and high spring-tide levels. [B.W.F.]

salt pan A shallow, isolated depression formed in a SALT MARSH and typically devoid of vascular plants. It may form from natural slight depressions of the salt-marsh surface, or from the damming of small tributary creeks. In high-level pans, SALINITY levels tend to be high through evaporation at low tide, but rainwater may accumulate during extended low-tide periods and reduce salinity levels. [B.W.F.]

SAM *See* STANDARDIZED AQUATIC MICROCOSMS.

sample A statistical term that refers to a subset or selection of all the observations that could be made on a particular item. The summary measurements of samples (STATISTICS) are therefore estimates of population PARAMETERS. They are represented by Roman letters, for example the MEAN $(\bar{x})$ and the VARIANCE (s^2). *See also* POPULATION. [B.S.]

sampling In almost all ecological studies it will be impossible to account for every individual in a POPULATION. Therefore it is necessary to examine a subgroup of the total population and extrapolate from this to the whole population. The process by which the subgroup of the population is selected is sampling. There are several steps in the development of a sampling strategy.

Choice of sample unit. A sampling unit may either be defined arbitrarily, such as a QUADRAT or pit-fall trap, or be defined naturally, such as a leaf or individual.

Number of sample units. This is nearly always determined by the amount of labour available. However, it is possible to calculate the number of sample units required to produce an accurate estimate of the population size. In general, more sample units will be preferred: as the number of sample units increases the ACCURACY of the population estimate improves.

Positioning of sample units. An unbiased estimate of a population is only possible if the sample units are representative of the total population. The easiest way of achieving this is for each sample unit to contain a RANDOM SAMPLE of the population.

Timing of sampling. Most populations will be affected by season, time of day and local weather conditions. It is very important that timing is taken into account either by sampling strategy or by later analysis. [C.D.]

sampling methodology/devices It is rarely possible to count all the species in a COMMUNITY or record all the individuals in a POPULATION. Ecologists try to obtain representative samples that give indicators of these measures, for example in terms of numbers of species per unit space/volume, or numbers/ BIOMASS of individuals per unit space/volume.

One important distinction is that between relative estimates of ecological quantities (relative ABUNDANCE of species or life stages within species to other life stages/species) and absolute estimates of ecological quantities (expressed relative to area, volume, habitat). It is therefore possible to identify broad classes of techniques that have potential applicability with respect to the two kinds of estimates. In general, those appropriate for relative estimates will not be applicable for absolute ones. On

Table S1 Information that can be obtained from different sampling methods.

Sampling method	Relative abundance	Absolute abundance
Effort-based	Y	N
Time-based	Y	N
Traps	Y	S
Space-limited	Y	Y
Volume-limited	Y	Y
Habitat-limited	S	Y
Artificial substrates	S	Y
Mark–release–recapture	N	Y

Y, yes; N, no; S, some situations.

the other hand, those which are useful for absolute measures can generally be used to provide relative estimates, though the effort required would generally be prohibitive. Table S1 summarizes this classification. [P.C.]

sand dune A term used to describe a mound or hill of sand formed where wind-blown sand accretes (aeolian deposition), typically around surface obstacles, often vegetation. [B.W.F.]

sandy shores Sandy shores can be categorized along a continuum from dissipative to reflective. Dissipative BEACHES experience strong wave action, have fine particles and a gentle slope, are very eroded, and most of the wave energy is dissipated in a broad surf zone. Reflective beaches tend to experience little wave action, have coarse SEDIMENT and a steep slope, are depositional, and wave energy is reflected off the beach face. [V.F.]

saprobien system An early biotic index of WATER QUALITY that recognized four stages in the oxidation of organic matter in freshwater systems: polysaprobic; α-mesosaprobic; β-mesosaprobic; and oligosaprobic. Each stage was identified by the presence/absence of INDICATOR SPECIES. The system was elaborated in the 1950s to take into account the relative ABUNDANCE of organisms in a SAMPLE. The saprobien system has been used widely in continental Europe but has not been taken very seriously in the UK or North America. [P.C.]

satellite remote sensing Satellites carry a range of remote-sensing devices for the production of images of the Earth and its ATMOSPHERE. [P.J.C.]

savannah Tropical vegetation, dominated by grasses, but with various amounts of intermixed tall bushes and/or trees. [P.C.]

SBS *See* SICK BUILDING SYNDROME.

scheduled process A process that is listed and subject to environmental legislation. In the UK such processes used to come under the provision of the Alkali, etc. Work Regulation Act 1906; this was superseded by the ENVIRONMENTAL PROTECTION ACT 1990. *See also* PRESCRIBED PROCESSES. [P.C.]

scope for growth (SFG) The difference between an organism's energy intake and output; i.e. that energy, equivalent to the PRODUCTION term in the energy budget, that is potentially available for somatic production (i.e. GROWTH proper) and reproduction. Because both of these processes potentially influence population RECRUITMENT, this physiological organismic measure is sometimes used as a surrogate for possible population effects. [P.C.]

scoping A preliminary, low-cost environmental assessment of a business (*see* ECOAUDIT), or product (*see* LIFE-CYCLE ASSESSMENT) or impact of development (*see* ENVIRONMENTAL IMPACT ASSESSMENT). [P.C.]

Scottish Environmental Protection Agency (SEPA) *See* ENVIRONMENTAL (PROTECTION) AGENCIES.

scrap Material (usually metals) discarded from manufacturing or products that have reached the end of their useful life. They may be suitable for reprocessing or RECYCLING. [P.C.]

scrub Communities dominated by shrubs or bushes which are intermediate between FOREST and GRASSLAND, often forming an intermediate zone between them. [J.R.P.]

sea A term often used synonymously with OCEAN or in reference to a subdivision of an ocean, or a very large enclosed body of (usually salt) water. Sea may also describe waves generated or sustained by winds within their fetch or a portion of the ocean where waves are being generated by wind. [V.F.]

sea-level changes Alterations in the level of oceanic waters with respect to the neighbouring landmasses. Such changes are caused by the accumulation (causing levels to fall) and melting (causing levels to rise) of glaciers. Sea level is believed to have risen by about 100 m since the melting of the Pleistocene glaciers, approximately 10 000 years ago. It has been estimated that the world mean sea level has been rising at about 1.2–1.5 mm year^{-1} during the first half of the 20th century. [V.F.]

seamount A submerged, isolated, volcanic mountain that rises from the sea floor and may reach a height of 900 m or more. [V.F.]

season Any of the four equal periods, marked by the equinoxes and solstices, into which the year is divided. Because the Earth rotates and its axis is inclined in relation to the Sun, and because it revolves around the Sun in an elliptical orbit, the distribution of solar energy over the Earth's surface varies and results in changes of season. At the spring and autumn equinoxes the Equator receives maximum SOLAR RADIATION, whereas at the winter (22 December) and summer (22 June) solstices, the Sun is vertical over the Tropic of Cancer (Northern hemisphere) or the Tropic of Capricorn (Southern hemisphere).

At the summer solstice the days are at their longest and temperatures are high in the north, whereas in the south the reverse is true. When winter prevails, the Sun's rays have to pass through more of the Earth's ATMOSPHERE, as they are oblique, and solar radiation is consequently less. The pattern of seasonal change is repeated annually. Local conditions, particularly TOPOGRAPHY, proximity to oceans, and altitude, will modify seasonal variations, but ultimately the position of the Sun controls the seasons. [S.R.J.W.]

seasonality The nature and degree of climatic (or other) changes associated with changes in SEASON. [S.R.J.W.]

second

1 The SI UNIT of time-interval (symbol: *s*), equal to $^1/_{60}$ of a minute. It is defined in terms of the resonance vibration of the caesium-133 atom, the interval occupied by 9 192 631 770 cycles.

2 A unit of angular measure (symbol: ") equal to $^1/_{60}$ of a minute of arc. [J.G.]

secondary effects of pollution Effects of POLLUTION caused not by a direct impact on survival, development, reproduction, etc., of organisms but via an ecological interaction; for example, the reduction or extinction of a food source; the weakening of a competitor; or the reduction of predation pressure by selective impairment of predators. [P.C.]

secondary forest FOREST (either temperate or tropical) which has regenerated following human clearance. [P.D.M.]

secondary productivity Productivity is the rate at which an individual population, or other ecological unit belonging to the same TROPHIC LEVEL, accumulates BIOMASS or energy by the production of new somatic and/or reproductive tissues. Productivity of AUTOTROPHS is PRIMARY PRODUCTIVITY, and productivity of HETEROTROPHS is referred to as secondary productivity, whether the heterotrophs are members of the grazing or decomposer food webs. [M.H.]

secondary woodland WOODLAND occupying a site which has at some time been artificially cleared of woodland, but which has reverted to woodland by natural SUCCESSION or by planting. [G.F.P.]

sediment A general term for unconsolidated deposits of either minerogenic or organic origin. The minerogenic deposits are divisible into three groups: (i) sorted, or stratified; (ii) unsorted, or non-stratified mechanical sediments (clastic sediments); and (iii) chemical (non-clastic) sediments.

Biogenic sediments, of mainly organic origin, are divided into two main groups. AUTOCHTHONOUS sediments are formed mainly *in situ*, of material originating from the mother ecosystem. ALLOCHTHONOUS sediments consist partly of transported material. [Y.V.]

sediment toxicity Many TOXICANTS, both inorganic and organic, will adsorb on to dead organic particles, and hence accumulate within aquatic SEDIMENTS and SOILS. Sediment so contaminated may be toxic to the organisms dependent upon it. There is a complex chemical relationship between toxicants adsorbed on to sediment particles and the WATER between particles (so-called POREWATER). ECOTOXICITY tests designed to study sediment TOXICITY can involve samples of whole sediment and/or samples of extracted porewater (e.g. by centrifugation, elutriation). [P.C.]

seed bank Seed banks are repositories of dormant seeds found either *in situ* in nature, for example soil seed banks, or maintained artificially *ex situ* as a conservation tool or for economic uses such as crop breeding. Seed banks of both kinds result from the ability of the seeds of many species to survive long periods of DORMANCY, from several years to many decades. [E.O.G. & L.R.M.]

selection Usually shorthand for NATURAL SELECTION, though can also be used for ARTIFICIAL SELECTION. [P.C.]

selfish genes The selfish gene concept was popularized by R. Dawkins in his book *The Selfish Gene* (1976), in which he developed the argument that an organism is a gene's way of making more genes. [V.F.]

semi-natural vegetation Genuinely virgin, untouched COMMUNITIES are uncommon, but there is much semi-natural vegetation in which there has been minimal DISTURBANCE, thus allowing the continued existence of natural communities in a relatively unchanged form. The term is also frequently employed for communities, such as traditional hay meadows, which owe many of their characteristic properties to the way in which they have been regulated by humans, often very consistently and over long periods. [J.R.P.]

sensitivity analysis Any form of analysis that quantifies the change of one variable in response to changes in another. [H.C.]

sentinel species Species that are used as indicators of environmental conditions. Such species are usually immobile, and include attached algae, lichens, angiosperms and sedentary/sessile animals such as mussels and enclosed (caged) animals. Various attributes can be used as indicators: for example, uptake of a particular substance; biochemical, cellular and physiological responses; population responses. *See also* BIOMARKERS; BIOMONITOR; RETROSPECTIVE ANALYSIS (MONITORING). [P.C.]

SEPA (Scottish Environmental Protection Agency) *See* ENVIRONMENTAL (PROTECTION) AGENCIES.

serpentine soil Serpentine (serpentinite) is an ultra-basic rock dominated by the magnesium silicate minerals, antigorite and chrysotile. [E.A.F.]

set-aside Land taken out of AGRICULTURE, usually by financial inducement (e.g. subsidies) to prevent overproduction. Such land may be allowed to return to a natural state. *See also* FARMING PRACTICES, SUSTAINABLE. [P.C.]

Seveso Directive A legal instrument of the European

Union (Directive 85/201/EEC as amended by 87/216/EEC and 88/610/EEC; substantially amended in Directive 96/82/EC) on major ACCIDENTS attributable to certain industrial activities. Its common name is after the major accident at Seveso, Italy, in 1976, which prompted the legislation. It requires manufacturers using certain dangerous substances above specified THRESHOLD quantities to limit any possible adverse consequences for humans and the environment and to report major accidents. Specifically, manufacturers have to produce: a safety report and on-site emergency plans; a COMPETENT AUTHORITY must produce an official emergency plan; the public must be informed of safety measures and of the correct behaviour in the event of accident. [P.C.]

sewage A dilute mixture of domestic WASTE, industrial (trade) waste, infiltration from the subsoil, and in a greater or lesser extent, RUN-OFF of surface water. Its composition is extremely complex and varies considerably depending on the amount of water used per head of population, the degree of infiltration of subsoil water and the nature and proportion of trade EFFLUENTS present. [A.D.]

sewage fungus A visible, plumose slimy growth of heterotrophic organisms found in organically polluted waters. The organisms are usually bacteria and/or protozoans but sometimes microfungi are present. [P.C.]

sewage pollution POLLUTION from human excretion and defecation. Also, pollution from SEWAGE TREATMENT WORKS, which may be of domestic and/or industrial origin. [P.C.]

sewage sludge Sludge resulting from treatment of raw SEWAGE. *See also* SEWAGE TREATMENT WORKS. [P.C.]

sewage treatment works A place that treats WASTE water (containing SEWAGE) from domestic and industrial sources. It is essentially concerned with the reduction of ORGANIC LOADING that would arise if raw sewage were allowed directly into watercourses. The main objective of sewage treatment is to reduce the strength (concentration of POLLUTANTS) of sewage to a sufficient degree to be safely discharged to natural waters without causing a nuisance or offence. For practical purposes, the impurities can be divided into three groups: (i) substances suspended in the liquid; (ii) substances dissolved in the liquid; and (iii) extremely fine, colloidal substances. There are several stages in the treatment process.

Primary treatment involves physical screening to remove large SUSPENDED SOLIDS, and sedimentation to allow as much suspended organic solids as possible to settle.

Secondary treatment involves biological oxidation, either in percolating filters or in an ACTIVATED-SLUDGE PROCESS. This is usually followed by sedimentation, and most treatment stops at this point.

Tertiary treatment involves microstraining with special filters, and possibly reverse OSMOSIS. It may also employ other systems designed to facilitate physical settlement. [P.C. & A.D.]

shelf-slope break A line demarcating a change from the gentle CONTINENTAL SHELF to the much steeper depth gradient of the CONTINENTAL SLOPE. [V.F.]

shelterwood system The practice in FORESTRY of HARVESTING maturing trees on two or more occasions to allow natural regeneration of seedlings from the remaining standing trees. [G.A.F.H.]

Sherwood number A non-dimensional quantity, commonly used in environmental engineering, that expresses the rate of mass transfer to or from an object. [J.G.]

shifting cultivation The practice of bringing into AGRICULTURE previously uncultivated land for several seasons followed by abandonment as part of a human nomadic culture. It is increasingly recognized that the traditional shifting cultivation practised by indigenous peoples, particularly in the tropics, represents a sustainable form of agriculture that is well adapted to natural and seminatural ecosystems, most notably in RAIN FORESTS. [G.A.F.H.]

shingle beach A BEACH made up wholly or in large measure of pebbles (SEDIMENT size 2–200 mm). [B.W.F.]

short-term tests TOXICITY/ECOTOXICITY tests carried out over periods of time that are short relative to the LIFESPAN of the organism. Thus a day may be a short span for toxicologists but not for microbes. *Cf.* CHRONIC TESTS; LONG-TERM TESTS. *See also* ACUTE TESTS. [P.C.]

SI units (Système International d'Unités) A system of units for use in science and engineering, consisting of seven base quantities, two supplementary units, and many derived units. The base units are given in Table S2.

The supplementary units are (i) the radian (symbol: rad; the plane angle between two radii of a circle which cut off on the circumference an arc equal in length to the radius); and (ii) the steradian (symbol: sr; the solid angle which, having its vertex

Table S2 The seven SI base quantities, with their corresponding units and symbols.

Physical quantity	Name of unit	Symbol
Length	metre	m
Mass	kilogram	kg
Time	second	s
Electric current	ampere	A
Thermodynamic temperature	kelvin	K
Luminous intensity	candela	\cd
Amount of substance	mole	mol

Table S3 Some SI derived quantities and their units.

Derived quantity	Unit name	Unit symbol	Base units
Area	square metre		m^2
Volume	cubic metre		m^3
Density	kilogram per cubic metre		$kg\,m^{-3}$
Frequency	hertz	Hz	s^{-1}
Concentration	mole per cubic metre		$mol\,m^{-3}$
Velocity	metre per second		$m\,s^{-1}$
Acceleration	metre per second per second		$m\,s^{-2}$
Force	newton	N	$m\,kg\,s^{-2}$
Pressure, stress	pascal	Pa	$N\,m^{-2}$
Viscosity (dynamic)	pascal second		$Pa\,s$
Viscosity (kinematic)	squared metre per second		$m^2\,s^{-1}$
Energy, work, heat	joule	J	$N\,m$
Power	watt	W	$J\,s^{-1}$
Electric charge	coulomb	C	$A\,s$
Potential difference	volt	V	$W\,A^{-1}$
Electrical resistance	ohm	Ω	$V\,A^{-1}$
Electrical conductance	siemens	S	Ω^{-1}
Capacitance	farad	F	$C\,V^{-1}$
Radioactivity	becquerel	Bq	s^{-1}
Irradiance, heat flux density	watt per square metre		$W\,m^{-2}$
Heat capacity, entropy	joule per kelvin		$J\,K^{-1}$
Thermal conductivity	watt per metre kelvin		$W\,m^{-1}\,K^{-1}$
Molar heat capacity	joule per mole kelvin		$J\,mol^{-1}\,K^{-1}$

at the centre of a sphere, cuts off an area of the surface of the sphere equal to that of a square with sides equal to the radius of the sphere).

There are many derived units. Some of the more useful are given in Table S3.

When quantities are very small or large in relation to the base unit, they may be indicated by prefixes, as given in Table S4. For example, $1\,Mg = 10^6\,g = 1\,000\,000\,g$. Prefixes that are not multiples of 3 (h, da, d, c,) are usually not necessary and should be avoided.

Current practice is that SI units are in use in all journals, but that exceptions are sometimes allowed. Chemists and soil scientists persist with eq (equivalents); Gt, or billion tonnes, is often preferred to the SI unit petagram Pg; and the litre is commonly used instead of dm^3. In forestry, the hectare (ha) is still more widely understood than multiples of m^2. Other non-SI units that are commonly allowed are minute (min), hour (h), day (d) and degree (°). *See* UNIT for other non-SI units. [J.G.]

sick building syndrome (SBS) A condition associated with buildings in which a significant number of occupants (usually >20%) report illness perceived as being due to the internal working environment. The symptoms may include irritation to sensitive surfaces, drying of mucous membranes and skin, headaches, coughs, nausea and faintness. SBS has been attributed to lack of ventilation, building materials and even mites. [P.C.]

sievert (Sv) The SI UNIT of dose equivalent, used to measure the biological effect of IONIZING RADIA-

Table S4 Prefixes used with SI units.

Factor	Name	Symbol
10^{18}	exa-	E
10^{15}	peta-	P
10^{12}	tera-	T
10^9	giga-	G
10^6	mega-	M
10^3	kilo-	k
10^2	hecto-	h
10	deca-	da
10^{-1}	deci-	d
10^{-2}	centi-	c
10^{-3}	milli-	m
10^{-6}	micro-	μ
10^{-9}	nano-	n
10^{-12}	pico-	p
10^{-15}	femto-	f
10^{-18}	atto-	a

TION. The dose equivalent (in sieverts) is obtained by multiplying the dose (in grays) by a quality factor (Table S5), which accounts for the different linear energy transfer (LET) values of different types of RADIATION. The effective dose equivalent is used to evaluate the EXPOSURE of individual organs or groups of organs to ionizing radiation and is determined by multiplying the dose equivalent (in sieverts) by a weighting factor for the organ concerned (Table S6). For irradiation of more than one organ,

Table S5 Quality factors for different types of ionizing radiation.

Type of radiation	Quality factor
X-rays	1
γ-radiation	1
β-radiation	1
Protons	1
Neutrons	20
α-particles	20

Table S6 Weighting factors for calculating effective dose equivalent for different organs.

Organ	Weighting factor
Gonads	0.25
Breast	0.15
Red bone marrow	0.12
Lung	0.12
Thyroid	0.03
Bone (excluding marrow)	0.03
Whole body	1.0

the total effective dose equivalent is calculated as the sum of the values for the individual organs. The committed dose equivalent is the dose equivalent summed over a 50-year period, taken to be a working lifetime. The collective dose equivalent is used to estimate the collective dose to a population, and is obtained by multiplying the average individual dose equivalent by the number in the population. The former SI unit of dose equivalent was the rem (10^{-2} Sv). *See also* RADIOACTIVITY; RADIONUCLIDE. [A.B.M.]

silt A wet mixture of particles (size range 4–60 µm) found in aquatic environments and sewers, and intermediate between CLAY and mud. [P.C.]

silviculture The scientific principles and techniques of controlling, protecting and restoring the regeneration, composition and growth of natural FOREST vegetation and its PLANTATION analogues. It is often also referred to as FORESTRY PRACTICES. [P.M.S.A. & G.P.B.]

similarity coefficient A numerical measure, calculated from multivariate attribute data, of the similarity of two objects. Several well-known similarity coefficients increase from 0, when there is no resemblance, to 1, when there is identity.

In ecological contexts, the objects are often samples or quadrats and the attributes are species abundances. Let x_{ip}, x_{jp} be the abundances of species p in objects i, j. A popular similarity measure for such objects is Czekanowski's coefficient, defined as:

$$s_{ij} = \frac{2\sum_p \min(x_{ip}, x_{jp})}{\sum_p (x_{ip} + x_{jp})}$$

which is equal to 0 when there are no species in common, and to 1 when all species are present in equal abundance. [M.O.H.]

site of special scientific interest (SSSI) Any site designated by nature conservation bodies in Britain as a representative example of British habitats. Each site is seen as 'an integral part of a national series' established with the aim of 'maintaining the present diversity of wild animals and plants in Great Britain'. The selection is on scientific grounds rather than to enhance amenity or provide recreation. Powers for establishing these sites were created by the Wildlife and Countryside Act 1981. Owners and occupiers of SSSIs must seek permission to carry out any potentially damaging operation. [P.C.]

size When applied to an organism, means its dimensions. These are often expressed as length, but can be expressed in mass, volume or energy. [P.C.]

skewness A statistic that measures one type of departure from a NORMAL DISTRIBUTION. It is another name for asymmetry. In skewness, one tail of the distribution is drawn out more than the other. Distributions are skewed to the right or the left depending upon whether the right or left tail is drawn out. In ecological data, distributions skewed to the right are very common. [B.S.]

slack (dune slack) A low-lying, flat area situated amongst SAND DUNES. [B.W.F.]

slash and burn A traditional agricultural system employed by certain nomadic groups. An area is cleared by burning, cultivated for short periods and then abandoned as crop yields fall. Also known as SHIFTING CULTIVATION, it is best suited to low POPULATION DENSITIES. [P.C.]

smog Fog containing air pollutants (e.g. SMOKE, sulphur dioxide (SO_2), unburnt HYDROCARBONS and NITROGEN OXIDES (NO_x)), usually trapped near the ground by temperature inversion. *Cf.* PHOTOCHEMICAL SMOG. [P.C.]

smoke A suspension of fine particles in a gas, usually derived from incomplete combustion or chemical reaction. The particles are usually <2 µm in diameter and are largely of carbon. Smoke may also contain silica, fluoride, aluminium, LEAD, ACIDS, BASES and organic compounds such as phenols. [P.C.]

soft substrata Substrata consisting of sedimentary mineral grains and small organic particles derived from dead and decaying plants and animals. Most of the sea floor, and thus most of the Earth's surface, is covered by marine soft SEDIMENT. Soft substrata are characterized by grain size, sorting and mineral composition. [V.F.]

soil The term 'soil' means different things to different people. To the soil scientist, soil is the profile that is exposed when a pit is dug into the surface of the

Earth (*see* SOIL PROFILE). To the agriculturist and horticulturist, soil is a medium for plant growth, and when carefully tended will produce good crops. To many others, soil is dirt; hence the term soiled. [E.A.F.]

soil profile A SOIL profile is a vertical face that is exposed when a pit is dug into the surface of the Earth. It is generally about 1 m wide, and extends down to the relatively unaltered material, which may occur at a depth that varies from <50 cm to >5 m. This vertical face usually displays a unique type of banding; the bands are known as horizons, of which there are a very large number. The specific nature of a soil profile is determined by the influence of the parent material, CLIMATE, organisms, TOPOGRAPHY and time. [E.A.F.]

soil–vegetation–atmosphere transfer scheme (SVATS) The path of WATER from SOIL through the plant to the ATMOSPHERE can be regarded as a hydrodynamic flow through the various plant tissues, and this paradigm is the basis for the usual soil–vegetation–atmosphere transfer scheme. [J.G.]

solar altitude (α) The term solar altitude or solar angle describes the elevation of the Sun in the sky (celestial sphere) relative to an observer, as the angle between the plane of the observer's celestial horizon and a line from the observer to centre of the Sun. It is symbolized by α. The solar zenith angle, θ_z, the complement of solar altitude (i.e. $90 - \alpha°$), is defined as the angle between the local zenith and the line joining the observer and centre of the Sun. The zenith is defined as the point on the celestial sphere directly above the observer.

Solar altitude can be calculated as a function of latitude (ϕ, north positive), hour angle (ω) and SOLAR DECLINATION (δ), where δ is a function of DAY NUMBER (d_n):

$$\sin\alpha = \cos\theta_z = \sin\delta\sin\phi + \cos\delta\cos\phi\cos\omega$$

The hour angle (ω) is calculated with 24 h equalling 360° or 2π radians, morning positive and solar noon zero. The hour angle changes by 15° or $\pi/12$ rad h^{-1} such that $\omega = 15(12 - h)$ degrees, or $\omega = \pi/12(12 - h)$ radians, where h is the true solar TIME or local apparent time.

Solar altitude and SOLAR AZIMUTH angles together describe the location of the Sun in the celestial sphere and are used in calculations of the energy balance of plants, animals and human artefacts. [P.R.V.G.]

solar azimuth (ψ) Solar azimuth describes the position of the Sun in the sky (celestial sphere) relative to the observer's location, in terms of its angle east or west of a line running north–south on the celestial horizon. Solar azimuth angles are defined with south zero and east positive, and vary between ±180° or ±π rad. Solar azimuth can be calculated for any combination of latitude (ϕ), SOLAR DECLINATION (δ) and SOLAR ALTITUDE (α) using the following equation, where solar declination is a function of DAY NUMBER and solar altitude is a function of true solar TIME:

$$\psi = \pm\cos^{-1}\left[\frac{\sin\alpha\sin\phi - \sin\delta}{\cos\alpha\cos\phi}\right]$$

The two solutions to this equation result from the symmetrical distribution of solar altitude around true solar noon, with positive values of azimuth (easterly) occurring before noon. [P.R.V.G.]

solar declination (δ) Solar declination in the equatorial system of solar geometry is the angle between a plane defined by the Earth's equator and a line joining the centres of the Earth and the Sun. Solar declination varies annually by ±23.5° resulting from the geometry between Earth's axis of rotation and its orbit around the Sun. Values for solar declination can be obtained from tables (Astronomic Almanac), from diagrams or by calculation (equations 1 and 2).

The value of solar declination (δ) measured in degrees can be computed with high accuracy using equation 1:

$$\delta = \frac{180}{\pi}(0.006918 - 0.399912\cos\Gamma + 0.070257\sin\Gamma$$
$$- 0.006758\cos2\Gamma + 0.000907\sin2\Gamma$$
$$- 0.002697\cos3\Gamma + 0.00148\sin3\Gamma) \tag{1}$$

where Γ is the day angle calculated from DAY NUMBER (d_n) as $\Gamma = 360(d_n - 1)/365$ degrees or $\Gamma = 2\pi(d_n - 1)/365$ radians.

An alternative equation, more suited to manual calculation, gives adequate results for many applications:

$$\delta = 23.45\sin\left[\frac{360}{365}(d_n + 284)\right] \tag{2}$$

[P.R.V.G.]

solar power Energy from sunlight harnessed to generate electricity and/or to provide heating for water and space. *See also* RENEWABLE RESOURCE. [P.C.]

solar radiation The term 'solar radiation' is restricted to electromagnetic RADIATION emanating from the Sun, although the Sun also radiates charged particles (usually referred to as the solar wind) and neutrinos. Most of the energy of this radiation is in the wavelength range 280 nm–4 mm, but the shorter wavelength components (γ-radiation, of wavelength <0.01 nm; X-RAYS, of wavelength 0.01–50 nm; and ultraviolet-C radiation, of wavelength 50–280 nm — these wavelength limits are not universally agreed conventions) are sufficiently intense at the top of the Earth's ATMOSPHERE that they would kill unprotected organisms. Fortunately, all these shorter wavelength components are completely absorbed by the atmosphere. The Sun also radiates radiowaves of a wavelength exceeding 4 μm. [L.O.B.]

solarimeter An instrument for measuring the total

energy RADIATION from the Sun, integrated over all wavelengths. [L.O.B.]

sonde (radiosonde) A free-flying balloon-borne package of sensors used to measure near-vertical profiles of PRESSURE, TEMPERATURE, relative HUMIDITY and WIND through the TROPOSPHERE and into the low STRATOSPHERE, for WEATHER observation and forecasting. [J.F.R.M.]

soot Finely divided carbon particles, capable of adhering together, that are left in flues when FOSSIL FUELS are incompletely burnt. [P.C.]

spawning The deposition or production of eggs or young, usually in large numbers. [V.F.]

Spearman's rank correlation coefficient (r_s) A NON-PARAMETRIC STATISTIC that summarizes the degree of CORRELATION between two sets of observations (x and y). The correlation coefficient (r_s) varies between +1 (perfect positive correlation), through 0 (no correlation), to −1 (perfect negative correlation). The two variables need not follow a NORMAL DISTRIBUTION; it is only necessary that they can be ranked. [B.S.]

species-abundance models In no COMMUNITY are all species equally abundant. Usually a few species are very common and many species are rare. Data on species ABUNDANCE can be depicted as species rank/abundance plots, showing the number of species falling into different abundance classes or ranks. In addition to these graphs, species abundance data can frequently be described by one or more of a family of mathematical distributions. [B.S. & P.S.G.]

species-level diversity, global Despite widespread interest in biological DIVERSITY, estimates of how many species inhabit the Earth are surprisingly vague. Larger organisms are relatively well studied and it is known, for instance, that there are about 9000 species of birds, 20000 species of fish and 225000 species of plants (from mosses to angiosperms). Other groups, such as marine MACROFAUNA, fungi and particularly the insects, have only begun to be catalogued. It is, however, evident that insects are by far the most speciose taxon on Earth. At present about 1 million species of insects have been recorded. The total number of 'known' species (across all taxa) is of the order of 1.8 million. Yet, estimates based on the number of beetles in the canopies of certain tropical trees hint at much higher totals, and it has been suggested that there could be as many as 30 million tropical arthropod species. This extrapolation assumes that there are approximately 160 species of canopy beetle per tropical tree species, that beetles represent about 40% of arthropod species, that for every two insect species in the canopy there is at least one existing elsewhere on the tree, and that there are about 50000 different species of tropical tree. Each step in the logic is fraught by uncertainty, and slight shifts in, for instance, the estimate of the proportion of the

fauna specialized on a given tree species can cause the overall total to rise (to above 100 million) or fall (to below 10 million) dramatically. The most conservative estimate puts the global total of invertebrates (and hence the overall species catalogue) at 3 million.

Suggestions that other poorly studied groups, such as marine molluscs, crustaceans, polychaete worms and other benthic macrofauna may contribute another 10 million species worldwide (as opposed to the 200000 already recorded) are open to debate. It is, however, notable that marine systems contain only about 15% of recorded species but have over 2.5 times as many phyla as terrestrial systems so may actually be much richer depositories of diversity than commonly assumed. The diversity of the microbial world is harder to quantify. Much of it is uncharted, and objective measures of microbial diversity have yet to be produced. [A.E.M.]

species richness The total number of species present in a COMMUNITY. It is the simplest measure of the taxonomic variety of a community, but is not on its own an adequate measure of species DIVERSITY because it does not take account of the relative ABUNDANCES of different species. For example, if two communities were both comprised of 10 species and 100 individuals, and in one there was 1 individual of each of 9 species and 99 individuals of the 10th species, but in the other community 10 individuals of each of 10 species, then both communities would have the same species richness (10). The second one would, however, be a much more diverse community. For this reason most indices of species diversity have both species richness and EQUITABILITY components. [M.H.]

Species Survival Commission (SSC) A body formed in 1949 to provide leadership to species conservation efforts internationally. It is the largest and most active of the six volunteer Commissions of IUCN. At the end of 1997, the SSC network encompassed 7000 volunteer member scientists, field researchers, government officials and conservation leaders from 169 countries. SSC members provide technical and scientific counsel for BIODIVERSITY conservation projects throughout the world and serve as resources to governments, international conventions and conservation organizations.

The SSC's goal is to conserve biological DIVERSITY by developing and executing programmes to save, restore and manage wisely species and their habitats. Toward this goal, the SSC:

• develops and promotes conservation Action Plans, which prioritize steps necessary to ensure the survival of selected species and habitats;

• provides technical information about biological diversity to international treaties, such as the Convention on International Trade in Endangered Species (CITES);

• formulates policy and procedural recommendations on a variety of issues such as sustainable use of wild species, reintroduction of plants and animals to their native habitats, and assessment of the risk of extinction for individual species.

The SSC works primarily through its 109 Specialist Groups, most of which represent particular plant or animal groups that are threatened with extinction, or are of importance to human welfare. A few groups deal with cross-cutting species conservation issues, such as veterinary medicine, CAPTIVE BREEDING, reintroduction of species, invasive species and sustainable use of WILDLIFE. A special task force is investigating the global decline in amphibian populations. *See also* INTERNATIONAL CONSERVATION CONVENTIONS; UNITED NATIONS PROGRAMMES AND BODIES. [G.B.R.]

specific humidity The mass of WATER per mass of moist air. *See also* HUMIDITY. [J.G.]

spectroradiometer An instrument used to measure the spectral distribution of electromagnetic RADIATION (usually in $Wm^{-2}nm^{-1}sr^{-1}$): variations, ultraviolet; visible/PAR (photosynthetically active radiation); solar infrared; thermal infrared. [J.A.C.]

spirals of matter BIOTA remove chemical elements from the environment but return them to the environment at a later time. This leads to nutrient cycling (*see* BIOGEOCHEMICAL CYCLE). In a flowing-water system (river/stream) a nutrient released at one point will be taken up by biota downstream. So matter here is said to spiral rather than cycle. [P.C.]

spit A shingle or sand structure which extends from a point on the solid coastline and remains unattached at its growing point. [B.W.F.]

spray zone (splash zone) The zone above high tide that is kept moist by breaking waves. [V.F.]

stability, communities The tendency of a COMMUNITY to return to its original state after a DISTURBANCE or to resist such disturbance. [V.F.]

standard
1 A requirement in legislation that if breached or contravened is likely to invite prosecution. *See also* ENVIRONMENTAL QUALITY OBJECTIVE; ENVIRONMENTAL QUALITY STANDARD.
2 An exact value, physical entity or abstract definition established by an authority and/or custom and practice as a reference, yardstick, model or rule in measurement procedures, in establishing practices or procedures, or in evaluating and auditing activity. [P.C.]

standard deviation A measure of variation. In a SAMPLE it is represented by the Roman letter *s*, and is an estimate of the POPULATION standard deviation, represented by the Greek letter sigma (σ). It is the square root of the VARIANCE. *See also* STATISTICS. [B.S.]

standard error (of the mean) If we take a SAMPLE of observations from a POPULATION, the sample MEAN ($\bar{x}$) will be an estimate of the population mean (μ). However, it is unlikely that $\bar{x} = \mu$ because

just by chance the sample we have taken may contain a non-representative collection of observations. If we repeatedly take a large number of samples, of size *n*, from a population, the sample means will themselves form a DISTRIBUTION. This SAMPLING distribution of means will be normally distributed, with its mean (the grand mean of means) = μ. This result is called the central limit theorem. The variation in this sampling distribution of means can be measured by a STANDARD DEVIATION which, to distinguish it from the standard deviation of a sampling distribution of single observations, is called the standard error (SE) of the mean.

The SE will be influenced by two things: (i) the size of the sample (*n*) — smaller samples will result in more variation in the sampling distribution of means (larger SE); and (ii) the variation in the population (σ) — larger σ will give larger SE. In fact, the precise relationship, worked out by statisticians, is:

$$SE = \frac{\sigma}{\sqrt{n}}$$

In practice σ will be unknown, so we estimate the SE using the formula:

$$SE = \frac{s}{\sqrt{n}}$$

In addition to the sample mean, other sample statistics have SEs but their calculation is frequently much more complex. [B.S.]

standard overcast sky A specification of the brightness of a densely overcast sky, in which the sky is brightest at the zenith and falls to one-third of this value at the horizon. [J.G.]

standardized aquatic microcosms (SAM) Multispecies ECOTOXICITY test systems with standardized initial conditions, monitoring and test procedures. *See also* COSMS; MICROCOSM. [P.C.]

standards organizations There are a large number of standards organizations and their work covers a wide range of subjects. This work is relevant in environmental protection and CHEMICAL CONTROL in that it ensures standardization in methods and methodology of measurement and ecotoxicological tests, and hence facilitates the mutual acceptance of information and classifications between interested parties on an international, national and local scale.

The major players can be organized in a geographical hierarchy, from international — involving the OECD and the International Standards Organization (ISO) — to regional — involving the Comité Européen de Normalisation (CEN) in Europe and the American Society for Testing and Materials (ASTM) in the USA — and, finally, to a national level. Some of the national standards organizations are listed in Box S1. [P.C.]

standing crop The mass of VEGETATION in a given area at one particular time. [P.D.M.]

Box S1 Standards institutions

AFNOR (France): Association Français de normalisation

BSI (UK): British Standards Institute

DIN (Germany): Deutsches Institut für Normung e. V.

ELOT (Greece): Hellenic Organisation for Standardisation

IBN (Belgium): Institut belge de normalisation (Belgisch Instituut voor Normalisatie)

DS (Denmark): Dansk Standardiseringrad

NNI (The Netherlands): Nederlands Normalisatie Instituut

IIRS (Ireland): Institute for Industrial Research and Standards

Luxembourg: Inspection du travail et des mines

UNI (Italy): Ente nazionale italiano di unificazione

CEI (Italy): Comitato elettrotecnico italiano

Box S2 State of the environment reports: some examples

World
• *Environmental Data Report 1991/92*, 3rd edn. United Nations Environment Programme/Basil Blackwell, Oxford.
• *The World Environment 1972–1992, Two Decades of Challenge.* (1992) (Eds M.K. Tolba & O.A. El-Kholy), 884 pp. Chapman & Hall, London (for United Nations Environment Programme).

OECD
• *The State of the Environment 1991.* OECD Publication Service, Paris.

Europe
• *The State of the Environment in the European Community.* (1992) (Accompanying the Fifth Action Pro-Programme: *A New Strategy for the Environment and Sustainable Development.*)
• *Forest Condition in Europe.* (1992) Executive Report, International Cooperation Programme on Assessment and Monitoring of Air Pollution Effects on Forests. UNECE and CEC.
• *Europe's Environment.* The Dobris Assessment. (1995) European Environment Agency, Copenhagen.

UK national
• *The UK Environment.* (1992) HMSO, London.

UK regional
• *The Scottish Environment Statistics*, No. 3. (1991) Government Statistics Service, Edinburgh.
• *Environment Digest for Wales*, No. 6. (1991) Government Statistical Services, Cardiff.

---

state of environment reports Reports providing data on physical, chemical and biological indicators of environmental quality. There is, in fact, a whole hierarchy of reports carrying such information, ranging from a global perspective (UNEP reports) to a Europe-wide assessment (European Union reports) to national levels (e.g. UK Department of the Environment reports) right down to regional and local levels. See Box S2.

Two points continue to emerge from these reports. First, there are few indications of grounds for congratulation or complacency—the environment, particularly at the global level, continues to deteriorate. Second, however, in many respects the data on which these conclusions are based are not ones in which too much confidence can always be placed. Too often they are not extensive (either geographically or temporally) or reliable enough. Most agree that more effort should be devoted to the problems of collection and interpretation of environmental BASELINE DATA. There is particular need for reliable, long-term measurements of key environmental indicators at key sites.

The EUROPEAN ENVIRONMENT AGENCY, set up under Regulation 1210/90 of the European Community (EC) and now based in Copenhagen, is likely to play an increasingly important part in preparing reports on the state of the environment in the European Union (EU). Its remit is to provide the EU and its member states with 'objective, reliable and comparable information at European level' as a base for environmental protection measures, to assess the results of such measures and 'to ensure that the public is properly informed about the state of the environment'. [P.C.]

statistical power Statisticians frequently refer to the power of a statistical test. It is the PROBABILITY of rejecting the NULL HYPOTHESIS (H_0) when it is incorrect and the ALTERNATIVE HYPOTHESIS (H_1) is correct. That is, it is the probability of reaching the correct conclusion. Three things affect the power of a test.

1 The difference between the null hypothesis and the alternative hypothesis—it would be easier to distinguish between $H_0 = 0$ and $H_1 = 100$, than between $H_0 = 0$ and $H_1 = 0.01$.

2 The SAMPLE size—increasing the sample size increases the power of a test.

3 The test used—different statistical methods, testing approximately the same hypothesis, may differ greatly in their power. In general, parametric tests (*see* PARAMETRIC STATISTICS) have greater power than non-parametric tests (*see* NON-PARAMETRIC STATISTICS), when the assumptions of the parametric test are met. [B.S.]

statistical tables Tables that show the critical values of test STATISTICS for varying levels of PROBABILITY.

Such test statistics include Fisher's F, z, t, χ^2, Mann–Whitney U, and Wilcoxon's T. The probability level in the table is related to the area, in the tail of the PROBABILITY DISTRIBUTION, outside a particular value of the test statistic (*see* NORMAL DISTRIBUTION). For some test statistics (e.g. χ^2) this area is only in one tail of the DISTRIBUTION (ONE-TAILED TEST). In other test statistics (e.g. F and t) it can be in one tail or both tails (TWO-TAILED TEST). [B.S.]

statistics The summary measurements or characteristics of a SAMPLE. These are represented by Roman letters; for example, the MEAN ($\bar{x}$) and the VARIANCE (s^2). [B.S.]

statutory water quality objectives (SWQO) Legally defined standards—in terms of concentrations of substances—that must not be exceeded as a result of effluent DISCHARGE outside a MIXING ZONE. Such objectives are usually set to avoid POLLUTION outside the mixing zone. *See also* ENVIRONMENTAL QUALITY OBJECTIVE; ENVIRONMENTAL QUALITY STANDARD. [P.C.]

the steady-state economy A human economy characterized by constant population, capital stocks and rate of material/energy throughput. [P.C.]

steno- A prefix denoting narrow, particularly a narrow range of tolerance for some environmental factor; for example, stenobathic for PRESSURE, stenothermal for TEMPERATURE, stenohaline for SALINITY. It is from the Greek *stenos* narrow. *Cf.* EURY-. [P.C.]

steppe Natural GRASSLANDS of Eurasia, extending in a broad zone from Ukraine in the west to Manchuria in the east. [J.J.H.]

sterile male technique (sterile insect technique, SIT) A method for controlling insect pests by releasing sterilized males in large numbers. Females mate with sterilized males and the eggs they produce are infertile. [D.A.B.]

Stevenson screen A ventilated, wooden box used to screen thermometers from PRECIPITATION and solar and terrestrial RADIATION, and hence standardize the measurement of shaded air TEMPERATURE near the surface. [J.F.R.M.]

stormwater discharge Discharge from a device on a combined or partially separate sewerage system, for relieving system of flows in excess of a selected rate in the event of a storm. The excess is discharged, possibly after removal of gross solids, to a convenient receiving water and can be highly polluting. *See also* SEWAGE POLLUTION; SEWAGE TREATMENT WORKS. [P.C.]

strandline (driftline) The line of debris left at a high-tide mark, comprising natural (mostly dead seaweed) and materials of human origin. [B.W.F.]

stratigraphy Stratigraphy is the study of the development and succession of stratified horizons in rocks. [P.D.M.]

stratosphere The atmospheric layer bounded below by the tropopause (10–15 km above sea level), and

above by the stratopause (about 50 km above sea level), and containing 10–30% of the mass of the Earth's ATMOSPHERE. Although deformed by WEATHER systems in the underlying TROPOSPHERE, it plays little direct role in them, and contains almost no cloud except for rare mother-of-pearl CLOUDS and diffuse polar ICE clouds. Much commercial air traffic uses the low stratosphere, and the protective OZONE maximum is maintained in the middle stratosphere by complex photochemistry and gentle air motion. *See also* STRATOSPHERIC CHEMISTRY. [J.F.R.M.]

stratospheric chemistry The term refers principally to the chemical processes that determine the concentration of OZONE in the STRATOSPHERE. It also refers to the reactions that oxidize and decompose trace substances released into the ATMOSPHERE from natural and anthropogenic sources. If these are stable enough to escape oxidation in the TROPOSPHERE, they find their way across the tropopause into the stratosphere and are oxidized there (*see* TROPOSPHERIC CHEMISTRY). [P.B.]

stress The term 'stress' implies an adverse EFFECT, but its precise definition has been somewhat elusive, largely because it is both level- and subject-dependent. It is level-dependent because an adverse response to some environmental variables at, say, a molecular or cellular level may not become manifest at an organismic/population level due to HOMEOSTASIS. It is subject-dependent because there may be genetic VARIANCE for stress responses between individuals in a population, and certainly between species.

Some would restrict stress—by analogy to its definition in physics—to the environmental variables that lead to the response in biological systems—the response being referred to as 'strain'. But this is not general, and in biology the word 'stress' is used both for the cause of a response and the response itself.

Similarly, some ecologists would restrict the definition of stress to environmental factors that impair production processes—growth and reproduction—with the term 'disturbance' applied to factors that impair survival. But again this is not general. Stress is usually employed to describe impairment in general.

The concept of stress has been criticized as being unmeasurable, and as drawing an unreal distinction between favourable and unfavourable environments (the argument being that all environments are unfavourable, because the struggle for existence goes on everywhere). [P.C.]

stress proteins *See* HEAT-SHOCK PROTEIN.

structure–activity relationship (SAR) The relationship between the structural properties of chemicals and their toxicological/ecotoxicological effects. Determination of this relationship provides some basis for predicting the likely effects of chemicals for which toxicological/ecotoxicological observations are lacking. When these relationships are made quantitative, usually by regression techniques, they are referred to as QUANTITATIVE STRUCTURE–ACTIVITY RELATIONSHIPS (QSARs). This technique applies almost exclusively to organic molecules and is most successful, as far as predicting effects is concerned, for non-polar compounds that have non-specific narcotic effects.

The technique has its roots in the development of drugs such as anaesthetics and antiseptics. Pioneering work was carried out by C. Hansch and colleagues in the 1960s. The general form of a QSAR equation is:

$$C = \alpha + \beta_1 \pi_1 + \beta_2 \pi_2, \text{ etc.}$$

Where C = concentration to produce a particular biological response; α and β terms are constants; and π terms are chemical descriptors that might be obtained either by calculation or observation.

For biological effects QSARs the most important molecular properties are those that relate to solubility in aqueous and lipid components of organisms, since they determine transport to and interaction with active sites. If the mode of action is specific, particular steric and electronic factors can be important.

With more than 100 000 artificial chemicals in use and several thousand additional ones being produced annually SAR/QSAR techniques provide the possibility of saving time and effort on ecotoxicological tests. [P.C.]

subacute/subchronic tests Referring to TOXICITY/ECOTOXICITY tests that are applied at concentrations of chemicals intermediate between the concentrations that are usually applied in acute and CHRONIC TESTS (hence the term subacute), over periods of time that are intermediate between those usually employed for chronic and ACUTE TESTS (hence the term subchronic). Sometimes a subchronic test is distinguished from a subacute test on the basis of its lasting for a much longer time. But all these terms are somewhat imprecise and demand careful usage. *See also* PREDICTIVE ECOTOXICITY TESTS. [P.C.]

subduction The process by which the Earth's outer shell is consumed by descending into the mantle. A subduction zone is an inclined plane descending away from a TRENCH, separating a sinking oceanic plate from an overriding plate. It is a region of high seismic activity. [V.F.]

sublittoral zone The depth zone on the shore below the level of mean low tide (or alternatively from the depth of spring low tide; *see* LITTORAL ZONE) and extending to a depth of 200 m. Also known as the subtidal zone. The vast majority of the sublittoral zone of the OCEAN consists of soft SEDIMENT. Rocky sublittoral zones, kelp forests and CORAL REEFS represent other types of sublittoral habitat, but all occur in restricted areas at relatively shallow depths. [V.F.]

submarine canyon A deep TRENCH cutting through the CONTINENTAL SHELF or slope. Such features are believed to form as a result of erosion by submarine CURRENTS coursing down the CONTINENTAL SLOPES. [V.F.]

submergence marsh The lower part of a SALT MARSH which is subject to (often extended) daily periods of submersion (immersion) at all TIDES, and where the key environmental factors are associated with periods of submersion (immersion). [B.W.F.]

suborganismic tests TOXICITY/ECOTOXICITY tests that involve observations at a level below that of the whole organism; i.e. on physiology, anatomy and functioning of organ systems and tissues; cellular structure and processing; or molecular composition and reactions. The extent to which changes at these levels translate into effects at population, community and ecosystem levels is problematic. *See also* PREDICTIVE ECOTOXICITY TESTS. [P.C.]

substrate/substratum
1 The material acted upon in a biochemical reaction.
2 The material to which organisms attach and with which they interact to a greater or lesser extent. Sometimes the substrate is used simply as a physical anchor (e.g. rocks for barnacles), whereas in other cases the substrate provides a nutrient source (e.g. SOIL for plants).
[P.C.]

subtropical The subtropical zones lie mainly polewards of 30°N and 30°S between the tropics and temperate zones. [S.R.J.W.]

succession Directional change in VEGETATION (or in COMMUNITIES of animals or microorganisms). [P.J.G.]

sulphur cycle The movement of sulphur (S) between the LITHOSPHERE (the dominant reservoir) and the ATMOSPHERE, HYDROSPHERE and BIOSPHERE, and the associated transformations between different chemical forms. Natural release of S into the atmosphere, as sulphur dioxide (SO_2), occurs by volcanic action and by BIOMASS burning (about 30 Tg S year^{-1}). Fossil-fuel burning and smelting of METAL sulphide ores are major anthropogenic sources of SO_2 (80 Tg S year^{-1}). [K.A.S.]

sum of products An analogous term to SUM OF SQUARES. When observations consist of paired measurements (x and y), the 'sum of products':

$$= \sum (\bar{x} - x)(\bar{y} - y)$$

Like 'sum of squares' (*see* VARIANCE) there is an equivalent, but more convenient formula:

$$\text{Sum of products} = \sum xy - \left(\sum x\right)\left(\sum y\right)/n$$

where x and y are each paired observations in the SAMPLE, n is the number of paired observations in the sample, and the Greek symbol Σ (capital sigma) is the mathematical notation for 'sum of'. When the 'sum of products' is divided by its degrees of freedom we obtain the covariance. [B.S.]

sum of squares The squared deviations of observations about a MEAN. For example, in the numerator of the formula for the VARIANCE, the 'sum of squares' = $\Sigma(\bar{x}-x)^2$. It has the important property that it can be partitioned or summed. *See also* ANALYSIS OF VARIANCE; REGRESSION ANALYSIS, LINEAR. [B.S.]

sunspot cycles Sunspots are local disturbances on the solar surface, seen as dark spots when an image of the Sun is projected on to a screen. The intensity of sunspots varies on an 11-year cycle causing small variations in the energy flux to the Earth, and associated changes in the magnetosphere and ionosphere. Some people believe that these cycles influence the growth of plants and the behaviour of animals, but the effect is very small if it exists at all. [J.G.]

superfund legislation UNITED STATES LEGISLATION concerned with polluted sites. The legislation is formally designated as the Comprehensive Environmental Response Compensation and Liability Act (CERCLA, or Superfund) 1980, and the Superfund Amendments and Reauthorisation Act 1986 (SARA).

CERCLA was enacted in 1980 to address actual or threatened releases from sites containing hazardous substances. It arose as a direct result of the emergency that occurred in August 1978 when chemicals that had been buried for a long time were discovered seeping out of the ground and into homes in the Love Canal area of Niagara Falls (New York State). Remedial work at the site and relocation of some 200 families cost the State in excess of $30 million; there was no federal programme to provide assistance. Owners and operators of facilities where hazardous substances and wastes are stored, treated or disposed of were required to notify, by 9 June 1981, USEPA of quantities and types of hazardous substances and wastes, and any known suspected or likely releases of these to the environment. USEPA used this information to formulate the original National Priority List (NPL), an inventory of contaminated sites requiring CLEAN-UP. USEPA revises this List from time to time. Currently the NPL has more than 1000 sites requiring immediate remedial attention.

CERCLA gives the federal government power to deal with hazardous substances either by removal or remedial action. It established a substantial billion-dollar trust fund. This is intended to pay for action only on an interim basis or in instances where no party can be held responsible. The primary aim of CERCLA is to require parties connected with a contaminated site, or with the hazardous substances it contains, to pay for the cost of clean-up. Cost estimates for clean-up of the thousand or so waste sites is in the billion dollar range. It is anticipated that responsible parties, rather than the superfund, will bear much of this expense.

CERCLA imposes strict liability upon any party that owned the site from which the actual or threatened release is taking place; which generated, transported or disposed of the substances at the site; or which operated the site. Liability is joint and several among all such parties. It is no defence that the party's actions may have been lawful—indeed, allowed by permits. Responsible parties are not only responsible for remedial and removal costs but also for damage to natural resources. The President may also issue administrative orders to responsible parties obliging them to take protective measures. SARA added an 'innocent landowner' defence to deal with problems faced by lending institutions and others.

In addition to the amendments to CERCLA, SARA contains a self-contained law that addresses emergency planning and community right-to-know. Amongst other things this requires companies to:
• work with community groups to define how various parties should respond to emergencies involving chemicals;
• notify local groups if an extremely hazardous chemical is released into the environment;
• produce an annual inventory of toxic chemicals that each facility routinely releases into the environment, including data on the average volume of the chemical on hand and the quantity and method of EMISSIONS.
This last provision has reputedly had a significant effect on POLLUTION AVOIDANCE. *See also* TOXIC RELEASE INVENTORY. [P.C.]

supply-side ecology An investigative approach to examining factors that influence local POPULATION DYNAMICS and COMMUNITY composition and structure, which stresses the importance of the supply of colonists or RECRUITMENT (often involving physical transport processes) from a regional pool. [P.S.G.]

surface tension The tension that exists in the surface of a liquid as a result of the tendency of molecules to cling to each other. As a result of surface tension liquids behave as if they have a skin. Surface-tension phenomena enable small insects to walk on water, they cause liquids to exist as droplets rather than thin films, and they cause water to rise inside capillaries. Surface tension in water is reduced by the addition of DETERGENTS, also known as wetting agents because they enable water to exist as films instead of droplets on surfaces. [J.G.]

surfactants Substances, also known as surface-active agents or wetting agents, that are the major ACTIVE INGREDIENTS of DETERGENTS. They reduce the SURFACE TENSION of liquids. Surfactants can be anionic, cationic or non-ionic, and they include both soaps and synthetic materials from PETROLEUM as well as natural oils (e.g. from coconut). Large quantities are disposed of down drains, but are often effectively degraded in SEWAGE treatment. Some are ecotoxic. [P.C.]

surveillance Repeated, standardized measurement of ecological variables at a site or sites to investigate possible trends in time. *Cf.* MONITORING; RETROSPECTIVE ANALYSIS (MONITORING); SURVEYS. [P.C.]

surveys Chemical and/or biological SAMPLING programmes to establish a pattern of spatial variation at one point in time. *Cf.* MONITORING; RETROSPECTIVE ANALYSIS (MONITORING); SURVEILLANCE. *See also* BIOLOGICAL MONITORING. [P.C.]

survival of the fittest *See* NATURAL SELECTION.

survival rate The proportion of the organisms at one age or stage remaining alive at the beginning of the next. [A.J.D.]

survivorship curve A graph of the numbers of an organism against time or age. [A.J.D.]

suspended solids Non-living organic particles occurring in the water column of flowing waters, LAKES or the marine environment, and maintained in suspension by physical forces. Unless filtered out by filter-feeding organisms, or decomposed by attached microbes, such particles ultimately sink to form SEDIMENTS. Suspended solids are defined experimentally as the DRY MASS of solid obtained by filtering a known volume of water through a filter with specifed pore size, and are measured in milligrams per litre. *See also* PARTICULATE ORGANIC MATTER. [P.C.]

sustainability *See* SUSTAINABLE DEVELOPMENT.

sustainable city A city designed to last; i.e. one in which infrastructure and social organization are such as to create lasting opportunities for its inhabitants in terms of employment and recreation while minimizing the effects on the environment. [P.C.]

sustainable demand Demand made by customers on business—and hence ultimately by business on environmental resources for raw materials and the reception of WASTE—that is compatible with the principles of SUSTAINABLE DEVELOPMENT. [P.C.]

sustainable development According to *Our Common Future* (1987), the report that emerged from the World Commission on Environment and Development set up by the UN in 1987, sustainable development is 'Development that meets the needs of the present generation without compromising the ability of future generations to meet their own needs'. It is neither an obvious logical necessity, nor a principle that is tried and tested. Indeed, it provides much room for interpretation, which is why many pages have been written on it and almost as many clarifying definitions have been offered in place of that given above. It is in reality a statement of faith that we can live in some kind of balance with our environment.

The sustainable development idea makes a number of assertions:

1 that development is about meeting human needs, implying not only wealth but also welfare—the emphasis is on *our* needs, the approach is frankly anthropocentric;

2 that we are talking about the needs of everyone in all parts of the world (intragenerational equity) and through time (intergenerational equity);

3 that our response to satisfying these needs can be increased—development implies improvement/progress, certainly not regression—without necessarily impairing our surroundings to such an extent that development will ultimately cease or be reversed;

4 'without compromising' nevertheless recognizes that there will be limitations on how this can be achieved.

So how is this to be understood? Presume that the servicing of needs depends upon wealth. Not all are happy with this materialistic orientation; but a major result of the sustainable development debate is not only an embracing of the link between needs and traditional economic activities, but the fact that social and ecological elements must be factored in as well. So overall wealth (C_T) is made up of the traditional economic capital (C_M), social capital (C_S) in the form of education, technology, medicine, etc., and natural capital (C_N) in the form of environmental and ecological entities. The sustainable development idea goes further and recognizes a delicate and complex interaction between these components. Thus, increasing C_M uses up resources and pollutes thereby having a negative impact on C_N; but by providing resources it enhances C_S and so might indirectly benefit C_N by providing people with the 'comfort' they need to worry about environment. It might also have beneficial effects on C_N by providing cleaner technology and methods of REMEDIATION.

As already noted, there are those who object to this economics representation of the problem—as if a sustainable life can be achieved in an economic vacuum. Yet life and living are fundamentally about using and optimizing the use of limited resources of time, effort and raw materials so there can be no escape from economics, whatever the currency. There are, nevertheless, various ways that the balance between the elements of the economy can be understood:

1 C_T can be maintained or enhanced only if C_N is protected—no negative effects allowed;

2 C_N can be subdivided into renewable (C_{NR}) and non-renewable (C_{NNR}) natural capital—OXYGEN, CARBON DIOXIDE and OZONE are renewable components of the environment but species are not—and C_T can only be maintained or increased if C_{NNR} is protected;

3 increases in C_T will inevitably involve negative effects on C_N, both the renewable and non-renewable components, but that the system can be optimized in some way to minimize the effects on non-renewables and to maximize the EFFICIENCY

of use of renewables, which will lead to a maintained or increasing C_T;

4 C_T can only be maintained at the expense of negative effects on C_N—but this should not be a concern because increasing levels of C_M and C_S will enable compensation for further loss of C_N. For example, loss of a non-renewable energy source could be compensated by a development in technology that replaces it. (It would be hard to apply similar reasoning to species extinction, but some might argue that such losses are compensated by the benefits achieved in terms of social welfare.)

These approaches, which need not be as sharply distinct as they are presented, move from what might be described as the 'deep green' and idealistic, to the 'light green' and pragmatic, and finally to the 'non-green'.

Ever since *Our Common Future*, there has never been the view that development entails no change in our surroundings, and some have even admitted that 'Every ecosystem everywhere cannot be preserved intact'. Just how much, if any, change is acceptable for our long-term well-being as a species is open to question and debate. *See also* ENVIRONMENTAL (ECOLOGICAL) ECONOMICS. [P.C.]

sustainable yield Removing resources from the environment (HARVESTING) at a rate which allows balanced replacement by natural processes. [P.C.]

swamp The definition of this type of WETLAND varies in different parts of the world, but one important characteristic is that the SEDIMENT surface normally remains below the WATER TABLE throughout the year. [P.D.M.]

SWQO *See* STATUTORY WATER QUALITY OBJECTIVES.

synthetic aperture radar (SAR) A specific type of imaging RADAR in which the effective length of the antenna has been enlarged synthetically in order to increase the spatial resolution of the imagery. SARs are carried by aircraft and several satellites, notably EUROPEAN REMOTE SENSING (ERS) SATELLITE, Fuyo, Almaz and the Space Shuttle. [P.J.C.]

systems ecology The application of systems theory to ecological processes and entities; i.e. an approach based on the premise that these need to be studied and represented as integrated wholes. The study should be 'top down', because study of parts alone (i.e. reductionism) misses the all-important interactive components. Such an approach has involved the application of control theory, information theory, black-box analysis, etc. [P.C.]

T

t test This is the small SAMPLE (either n_1 or $n_2 < 30$) version of the $z(d)$ TEST. Basically, the formula for the test is the same, except that we treat the result as t rather than $z(d)$. We also make a combined estimate of the VARIANCE. That is:

$$d = \frac{\bar{x}_1 - \bar{x}_2}{\sqrt{\left(\frac{s_1^2}{n_1} + \frac{s_2^2}{n_2}\right)}} \text{ becomes}$$

$$t = \frac{\bar{x}_1 - \bar{x}_2}{s_c \sqrt{\left(\frac{1}{n_1} + \frac{1}{n_2}\right)}}$$

where $\bar{x}_1$ and $\bar{x}_2$ are the sample means, s_c is the combined estimate of the sample STANDARD DEVIATION and n_1 and n_2 are sample sizes. The combined estimate of the variance is calculated using the formula:

$$s_c^2 = \frac{\left[\sum x_1^2 - \left(\sum x_1\right)^2 / n_1\right] + \left[\sum x_2^2 - \left(\sum x_2\right)^2 / n_2\right]}{n_1 + n_2 - 2}$$

where the terms in square brackets are the SUM OF SQUARES for each sample, and n_1 and n_2 are the sample sizes. Sometimes the above two formulae are shown combined to give:

$$t = \frac{(\bar{x}_1 - \bar{x}_2)}{\sqrt{\left[\frac{(n_1 - 1)s_1^2 + (n_2 - 1)s_2^2}{(n_1 + n_2 - 2)}\right]\left(\frac{n_1 + n_2}{n_1 n_2}\right)}}$$

The DISTRIBUTION of the test statistic we call t was discovered by W.S. Gossett (1876–1937), a statistician working for the Guinness brewery in Dublin, who published his findings under the *nom de plume* of 'Student'. Consequently this test is often called Student's t test. Gossett found that when sample size was small ($n < 30$) the relationship between $z(d)$ and the area under the curve (PROBABILITY) changed. The smaller the value of n, the more the relationship changed (in tables of t, n is replaced by degrees of freedom (v)). Instead of 5% of the distribution being outside $z(d) = \pm 1.96$, with $v = 25$, 5% was now outside $z(d) = \pm 2.06$ and with $v = 5$, 5% was outside $z(d) = \pm 2.57$. To avoid confusion, he replaced $z(d)$ with the new symbol t. Therefore, if the above test formula gives, for example, $t \geq 2.06$ with $v = 25$ (degrees of freedom in the test

$= n_1 + n_2 - 2$), the NULL HYPOTHESIS is rejected and the difference between the two means is said to be significant at the 5% level. The t test above is only used if the two sample variances (s_1^2 and s_2^2) are approximately equal, and this equality is determined using the F TEST.

If the two sample variances are very different, and therefore you cannot make a combined estimate of the variance, the formula for the $z(d)$ test is used but the degrees of freedom (taken to the nearest whole number) are calculated as:

$$\frac{1}{v} = \frac{u^2}{n_1 - 1} + \frac{(1-u)^2}{n_2 - 1} \text{ with}$$

$$u = \frac{s_1^2 / n_1}{(s_1^2 / n_1) + (s_2^2 / n_2)}$$

[B.S.]

taiga A Russian term denoting a marshy, Siberian WOODLAND and often used to denote the circumpolar BOREAL FOREST. However, it is also used to describe the ecotone zone between the boreal forest and the Arctic TUNDRA. This transition zone is marked by more open woodland sometimes confined to areas along river courses where the PERMAFROST zone is deeper in the SOIL and permits root development to a depth sufficient to support tree growth. Such open arctic-fringe forest is also described as lichen woodland. [R.M.M.C.]

tailings Fine-grained WASTE from mining, and processing of ore, usually following washing. Can be polluting. [P.C.]

taxonomic categories Biologists recognize a hierarchy of taxonomic categories that expresses the relatedness between organisms. Groups of organisms showing a few major features in common can be subdivided into groups showing these plus other features, etc. Linnaeus thought that this represented a scale of order imprinted on nature by God and specified a series of categories arranged hierarchically to define it, viz:

Kingdom
  Class
    Order
      Genus
        Species
Moving down the series, the categories contain more

and more characters in common. Through the years many additional categories have come to be used, but the system is still based on the Linnean hierarchy, although this is now viewed as an outcome of evolutionary processes. Most modern biologists recognize the following categories:

Kingdom
  Phylum (usually Division in botany)
    Class
      Order
        Family
          Genus
            Species

Each category can be subdivided further. Thus at the level of order we can have: superorder, order, suborder, infraorder. [P.C.]

taxonomy Taxonomy is the theory and practice of describing the DIVERSITY of ⁄organisms and of ordering this diversity into a system of words, called CLASSIFICATIONS, that convey information concerning kinds of relationships among organisms. [D.R.B.]

TBT *See* TRIBUTYLTIN (TBT) POLLUTION.

technology-based control Legal control of quality of EMISSIONS/EFFLUENTS that refers not (just) to chemical characteristics but also requires the use of specific techniques/technology or makes reference to the use of best available techniques. *See also* BEST AVAILABLE TECHNIQUES NOT ENTAILING EXCESSIVE COSTS; OPTIMUM POLLUTION. [P.C.]

tectonic Applies to the dynamics of the Earth's CRUST and their consequences: warping, folding and faulting. *See also* PLATE TECTONICS. [P.C.]

telemetry The automatic transmission of data from remote sites. [J.H.C.G.]

temperate grassland Grass- (Poaceae) or sedge- (Cyperaceae) dominated vegetation found in temperate climatic zones. [J.J.H.]

temperate rain forest Temperate forests vary considerably with climate, and those occurring in exceptionally wet conditions are sometimes referred to as temperate rain forests. [P.D.M.]

temperature Temperature is a property of a body or region of space which can be sensed subjectively as relative hotness. It is a measure of the average kinetic energy status of the molecules or atoms making up the system. If there is a temperature difference between two bodies then heat will flow between them. Temperature can only be measured by observing the behaviour of another substance which varies predictably with temperature, for example the expansion of MERCURY or the electromotive force produced by a thermocouple. Temperature scales are based either on arbitrary points of observable reference such as the freezing point or boiling point of WATER (Celsius scale) or on an absolute scale in which the so-called thermodynamic temperature is a function of the energy

possessed by matter (Kelvin scale). *See also* THERMOMETRY. [J.B.M.]

TEQM *See* TOTAL ENVIRONMENTAL QUALITY MANAGEMENT.

termites Eusocial and polymorphic species of the insect order Isoptera, living in large family groups composed of reproductive (winged) forms together with numerous apterous, sterile soldiers and workers. Approximately 2600 species have been described in 280 genera and six families.

Termites are an important indicator group for biogeographical and ecological analysis and MONITORING. This is attributable to their taxonomic tractability, ecological diversification, relatively sedentary habit, the fact that individuals are present throughout the year, their functional importance in ecosystems and their measurable response to disturbance. *See also* INSECTS, DIVERSITY AND CONSERVATION. [D.E.B. & P.E.]

terrigenous Referring to OCEAN sediments composed of debris from land erosion. [V.F.]

test guideline/protocol Specific, and often very detailed, instructions on how TOXICITY and ECOTOXICITY testing should be executed and updated. Required by GOOD LABORATORY PRACTICE (GLP). Standards organizations, especially the OECD, play a key role in ensuring international standardization of tests so that there is mutual acceptance of data generated from them. This facilitates international control of POLLUTION and also helps to reduce animal testing. [P.C.]

thermal imaging A technique providing a visual representation of the incident thermal RADIATION field. [J.A.C.]

thermal pollution Heat release into the environment as a by-product of human activity and having a harmful EFFECT on ecosystems. For example, direct thermal POLLUTION of waters may occur at powerstations where more than 50% of the heat content of the fuel may end up as WASTE heat that is removed by the cooling waters and is ultimately released into RIVERS. This can raise the TEMPERATURE of waters to an extent that favours exotic species. It also reduces DISSOLVED OXYGEN causing metabolic STRESS. [P.C.]

thermal stratification An important feature of water bodies that results when differences in TEMPERATURE occur between the surface water layers and deeper layers. [V.F.]

thermocline That portion of the water column where TEMPERATURE changes most rapidly with each unit change in depth. [V.F.]

thermometry Thermometry is the measurement of TEMPERATURE. This is achieved by using one of several types of sensor.

Mercury-in-glass thermometers are still widespread, being relatively cheap and readable to 0.1°C or 0.5°C, depending on their specification, and are available as maximum–minimum thermometers.

Thermocouples are the most widely used temperature sensor in experimental work, as they are easy to construct, very cheap, small, and produce an electrical signal which can be recorded on a data logger. They consist of wires of different metals, twisted or welded together to make a thermojunction, and depend on the thermoelectric effect (the tendency of electrons to migrate from one METAL to another, at a rate that is a non-linear function of temperature). A thermocouple circuit consists of two thermojunctions, one kept at a reference junction and the other is used to sense temperature. A thermocouple circuit produces very small signals which require a sensitive microvoltmeter to measure (a copper–constantan thermocouple pair produces about 40 μV per degree Celsius of temperature difference; for accurate work it is essential to calibrate thermocouples, as the composition of the metals may vary somewhat from batch to batch).

Platinum resistance thermometers (PRTs) are coiled lengths of platinum wire. The sensor exploits the effect of temperature on electric resistance. Platinum is chemically non-reactive and so the sensors are durable and stable over a long time. Instruments supplied as laboratory standards claim an ACCURACY of 0.002°C, and in the field an inexpensive PRT is likely to have an accuracy of 0.01°C.

The thermistor, like the PRT, is a resistance thermometer, but is made of a bead of semi-conductor material. Thermistors have been widely used in environmental science and form the basis for most hand-held electronic thermometers. Integrated circuit sensors are also available, consisting of a semi-conductor diode with trimmed resistors, set up during manufacture so that the signal in millivolts is conveniently equal to degrees Celsius.

Infrared thermometers are now widely available and are excellent for measuring the temperature of natural surfaces. They calculate the temperature from the measured thermal RADIATION emitted by a surface and are usually accurate to within 1°C. The viewing angle may be quite narrow (2°), enabling, for example, the temperature of a leaf to be found very conveniently. [J.G.]

therophyte A plant life form that survives unfavourable conditions (usually DROUGHT) as a seed. [P.D.M.]

thorn scrub Sparse shrub vegetation characteristic of semi-arid areas which is usually deciduous and richly provided with thorns, thus reducing its palatability to large herbivores. [P.D.M.]

threshold In environmental parlance, the divide between when an EFFECT does and does not take place. For example, in ECOTOXICOLOGY, the concentration above which an adverse effect is observed and below which it is not. Cf. a graded increase from zero level (e.g. concentration) upwards. *See also* ACTION LEVEL; PREDICTED NO EFFECT CONCENTRATION. [P.C.]

tidal energy Energy from the ebb and flow of TIDES. Can use barrages with conventional turbines positioned so that the incoming and outgoing tides generate power, and floating devices in which wave-driven paddles and floats generate the power. [P.C.]

tidal flat Tidal flats are the gently sloping or effectively level expanses of marine SEDIMENT that may be exposed by low TIDES. They form the feeding grounds of shorebirds and wildfowl, and of many fish, including juvenile flat-fish. [R.S.K.B.]

tides The periodic movement of WATER resulting from gravitational attraction between the Earth, Sun and Moon. Tidal range is greatest during spring tides and is least during neap tides. [V.F.]

tiered tests TOXICITY/ECOTOXICITY tests that involve increasing levels of detail according either to the results from lower-level tests (e.g. that signal high toxicity/ecotoxicity) or in terms of increasing production and/or marketing and/or importation levels. [P.C.]

timber line The border between the outmost wood stands and the treeless vegetation of the polar regions, mountains and arid areas. [Y.V.]

time Time is a fundamental physical quantity describing the duration of events as a dimension, or the sequence of a number of events. The SI UNIT for time is the SECOND (s) which is defined relative to the frequency of transition between two levels of the ground state of a ^{133}Cs atom. Most other common units of time are defined with reference to the second.

Systems describing time were originally based on the DIURNAL cycle of the Earth's rotation around it's own axis and the seasonal cycle resulting from the orbit of the Earth around the Sun.

True solar time or local apparent time is based upon the apparent motion of the Sun across the sky. Solar noon is defined for any locality as the time when the Sun reaches its highest point or solar angle. This point is known as the local meridian. The period between two meridians is defined as 1 day. The length of the solar day varies by up to 16 minutes during the year because of the position of the Earth in orbit around the Sun. The variation in length of the solar day is described by the equation of time often published as part of ephemeris tables (e.g. Nautical and Astronomical Almanacs). In many biological applications, true solar time must be calculated from local standard time making allowances for longitude, the equation of time and daylight saving. The mean solar day length averaged over a year is used by convention for most purposes. Mean solar time is defined relative to the movement of a hypothetical sun travelling across the sky at the same rate throughout the year. Sidereal time is defined using fixed stars as a reference, with a 'sidereal day' being the period required for the Earth to rotate once relative to a fixed star. The length of a sidereal day is approximately 4 min shorter than the mean solar day. Ephemeris time is based upon the annual revolution of the Earth around the Sun, removing the difference associated with the variation in the speed of rotation of the Earth about its axis.

Standard time was developed from mean solar time to avoid complications for travel and communications associated with communities using their own local solar time. The Earth was divided into 24 standard time zones, each separated by 15° longitude. True solar time differs from standard time by 4 minutes for each degree of longitude east or west of the meridian for the time zone. The reference standard time zone is located at the 0° meridian of longitude that passes through the Royal Greenwich Observatory in England. The local mean solar time at the Greenwich meridian is referred to as Greenwich Mean Time (GMT) or Universal Time (UT). Standard time zones are described by their distance east or west of Greenwich but are sometimes modified for political or geographical reasons. Daylight saving is a system where clocks are set 1 or 2 hours forward during the summer months, resulting in an additional period of daylight in the evening.

The GEOLOGICAL TIME-SCALE is a record of the Earth's history defined relative to major geological episodes. Divisions of geological time are based on changes in the fossil record in geological strata. [P.R.V.G.]

time-domain reflectometry A technique originally used to detect the properties of electrical transmission lines. Time-domain reflectometry (TDR) has recently been used to measure WATER content and electrical conductivity of soils. A step voltage is applied to steel pins embedded in the SOIL. The timing and attenuation of the reflected signal as displayed on an oscilloscope relate to the dielectric (K) and conductivity of the soil, respectively. Water has a high dielectric ($K = 80$) compared to other soil components, air ($K = 1$) and soil grains ($K = 3 - 5$), thus allowing empirical CALIBRATIONS of volumetric water content using the measured dielectric constant. [J.I.]

time-lags The effect of many processes is not immediate, and these are said to be 'time-lagged'. [S.N.W.]

tolerance The reduced response to a TOXICANT, BIOCIDE or POLLUTANT as a result of repeated EXPOSURE. This may occur within individuals as a result of physiological acclimation/acclimatization — for example as a result of induction of protective, metabolic systems such as melallothioneins or MIXED-FUNCTION OXIDASES (MFOs). It may also occur by selection of more tolerant genotypes. *See also* ADAPTATION TO POLLUTION; COSTS OF RESISTANCE; RESISTANCE. [P.C.]

top-down controls Important influence on COMMUNITY structure and possibly function from upper trophic levels. Thus removal of a predator releases

pressure on prey which has knock-on effects for its competitors and the species populations that form its food. *See also* SYSTEMS ECOLOGY. [P.C.]

top species The species at the ends of FOOD CHAINS, i.e. the pinnacles of trophic pyramids. [P.C.]

topogenous Used of a MIRE that owes its development to the concentration of water in a region by drainage from a CATCHMENT. [P.D.M.]

topography The surface features of the Earth, including the relief, the terrain, the VEGETATION, the SOILS and all the features within the landscape. It is not synonymous with relief alone. [P.J.C.]

topology The branch of mathematics concerned with properties of objects that are not distorted by stretching, etc. [M.J.C.]

tort Literally, a crooked act. A breach of civil law relating to rights. It has implications for environmental protection from remedies it affords under nuisance, negligence, trespass, RYLANDS VERSUS FLETCHER, and certain RIPARIAN RIGHTS. *See also* ENVIRONMENTAL LAW. [P.C.]

total environmental quality management (TEQM) One way of representing business activities is in terms of an input–output system that transforms raw materials and energy into products and services. However, this is only a partial representation. An alternative is to consider a business as a way of transforming information from customers into actions that meet customer requirements. The major contributions of this total quality management (TQM) approach have been to recognize the primacy of the customer (unless a business is responding positively to appropriate signals from customers, it will cease to survive), to recognize that customer information inputs impinge on all elements of management, and to suggest, therefore, that these inputs should be central to business affairs.

TQM also translates this relationship between external customer and business to internal affairs with internal customer–supplier philosophy between divisions, department, teams, etc. But, the information flows between external customer and business must still remain of prime importance, because it is on the extent to which responses to these are successful that bottom-line profitability will depend.

Environmental consideration can similarly be placed at the heart of business affairs, i.e. with information flowing from the sources of environmental pressure to all elements of business practice as indicated above. This is because of the following.

1 Customers are taking environmental considerations more and more into account in exercising consumer choice. Moveover, REGULATORY AGENCIES are making increasing use of this to effect environmental protection by requiring more and more information on environmental performance to be made public—for example by labels, in inventories, registers, public audit statements, and so on. Therefore, environmental thinking will play an

increasingly prominent role in the information flows from customer to business. Not only do traditional customers need to be taken into account, but the views of other stakeholders, such as investors and insurers, will also be of importance. Again, because of the pervasiveness of environmental issues in all managment sectors, these flows of information, from customer and stakeholders to company, should be taken into account by all elements of management.

2 As with all company legislation, environmental legislation has to be taken seriously, for failing to comply can bring bad publicity (negative information flows in 1), penalties and possible threats of shut-down. However, the influence of environmental legislation is different from most other kinds of legislation, again because of its pervasiveness. Just as environmental issues impinge on all elements of business practice, so environmental legislation is also likely to impinge on all elements of business practice.

TQM puts the external customer at the centre of business practice and recognizes the primacy of information flows from customer to management schemes. TEQM similarly puts the environment at the centre of business practice and recognizes the primacy of information flows from sources of environmental pressure to all elements of business practice. *See also* ENVIRONMENTAL MANAGEMENT SYSTEMS. [P.C.]

toxic bloom One possible outcome of EUTROPHICATION is the appearance of toxic algae, i.e. those algae, most usually blue-greens, capable of excreting substances that are toxic to wildlife and/or domestic animals and/or humans. [P.C.]

toxic release inventory (TRI) This is required by the US Superfund Amendments and Reauthorisation Act (SARA). Companies report their stocks of dangerous chemicals, of specified types and exceeding certain specified quantities, to the environmental protection agency (EPA). The EPA is bound to keep all these data, the so-called toxic release inventory (TRI), easily accessible to the public and media as data-based information. It is claimed that the compilation of the TRI has in itself caused cleaner practices in industry. *See also* CHEMICAL RELEASE INVENTORY; LISTS. [P.C.]

Toxic Substances Control Act (TSCA) *See* UNITED STATES LEGISLATION.

toxic units Investigations on the TOXICITY/ECOTOXICITY of mixtures have usually been made with SHORT-TERM TESTS in which CONCENTRATION–RESPONSE curves are obtained from individual chemicals and then compared with the curve for the mixture. LC_{50}s are used to measure the definitive responses because they represent equilibrium conditions. Say the LC_{50} for chemical X is $10\,mg\,l^{-1}$ and for chemical Y is $2\,mg\,l^{-1}$ and that the LC_{50} for the mixture is obtained when the concentration of

$X = 5\,mg\,l^{-1}$ $Y = 1\,mg\,l^{-1}$, then the combined action is additive (*see* TOXICITY OF MIXTURES). If the LC_{50} for a given chemical and test system is given a value of 1 toxic unit (TU) as in the example, the mixtures contained 0.5 TU of X and 0.5 TU of Y, i.e. the combined toxicity was 1 TU. *See also* TOXICITY EQUIVALENCY FACTOR. [P.C.]

toxicant Artificially produced substances that have poisonous effects on humans or wildlife. They may be produced as intended poisons, i.e. BIOCIDES, or they may be produced for other reasons but have toxic/ecotoxic effects. *Cf.* TOXINS. *See also* PARACELSUS' PRINCIPLE. [P.C.]

toxicity The extent of adverse effects on living organisms caused by the substance under consideration. Restricted to effects on individuals, for example impaired survival as judged by LC_{50}/LD_{50}. Should be contrasted with ECOTOXICITY—concerned with ecological systems not just individuals—but often used as shorthand for it. [P.C.]

toxicity equivalency factor (TEF) Factor used to estimate the TOXICITY of a complex mixture of toxicants, most commonly for a mixture of chlorinated dibenzo-*p*-dioxins, furans and biphenyls. In the latter the equivalency factor is based on relative toxicity to 2,3,7,8-tetrachlorodibenzeno-*p*-dioxin (TEF = 1). *See also* ECOTOXICITY TESTS. [P.C.]

toxicity identification evaluation (TIE) Systematic and sequential ecotoxicological analysis of complex chemical mixtures arising as EFFLUENTS from industrial processes with a view to defining the TOXICITY (ECOTOXICITY) of the components. They involve a combination of sophisticated chemistry and ecotoxicity. They can be used in the context of reducing toxicity of effluents, i.e. in toxicity reduction evaluations (TREs). [P.C.]

toxicity of mixtures Refers to the combined EFFECT of two or more chemicals on test systems. Chemicals might combine in a number of ways with respect to toxic effects: (i) additively, when the total effect is equal to the sum of known individual effects; (ii) synergistically when the combined effect is greater than the additive effects; and (iii) antagonistically, when the combined effect is less than the additive effects. [P.C.]

toxicology The science dealing with the effects of poisons (TOXICANTS) on individual organisms (often with humans in mind) (*cf.* ECOTOXICOLOGY). It covers both the routes of EXPOSURE and the mechanisms of the effects and provides a scientific basis for managing risks from toxicants. [P.C.]

toxins Natural poisons produced by organisms, for example plant poisons, snake and spider venoms, and antibiotics. They are usually produced as intended poisons. *Cf.* TOXICANT. [P.C.]

toxkits 'Off-the-shelf' TOXICITY/ECOTOXICITY tests, which usually involve organisms that are derived from resting cysts (e.g. *Artemia*, the brine shrimp, and rotifers) so that no elaborate culturing system is needed. The kits usually provide simplified means of exposing the organisms and recording effects. *See also* PREDICTIVE ECOTOXICITY TESTS. [P.C.]

trace element Eight elements—OXYGEN, silicon, aluminium, iron, calcium, sodium, potassium and magnesium—make up nearly 99% of the Earth's CRUST. The remaining elements of the PERIODIC TABLE constitute the trace elements. Occasionally, a trace element may be found in considerable quantities, for example in an ore deposit or mine spoil, but generally their concentrations are low, from <1 mg kg^{-1} to a few hundred mg kg^{-1}. [K.A.S.]

trace gases A trace gas is one which is found in very low quantities ('trace quantities') in the ATMOSPHERE. [J.G.]

trade winds The WIND system, occupying most of the tropics, which blows from the SUBTROPICAL highs toward the equatorial lows. Trade winds are from the north-east in the Northern hemisphere and from the south-east in the Southern hemisphere. Trade winds produce a strong equatorial drift of westward-moving water. [V.F.]

tragedy of the commons This is the title of a classic, though much disputed, paper by Garret Hardin published in 1968. The argument is as follows:

> There is an area of common land on which herders graze cattle. Each herder will seek to graze as many cattle as possible and eventually the carrying capacity is reached. This should result in stability. However, since the positive consequences of adding an additional head go to the herder owning the animal, whereas negative consequences are felt by all herders, the result is net gain to the individual who increases herd size. This 'inherent logic of the commons remorselessly generates tragedy'

Later the metaphor was developed as an example of the Prisoner's dilemma. Consider two users of a water supply who also pollute that supply. The formal analysis shows that it is in the interests of each user to pollute, because the returns from so doing exceed those from not so doing, whatever the other does.

If one accepts this argument, use of commons, whether a local river or the global atmosphere, has to be subject to some kind of control which means that they cannot be treated as freely available commons. Some would argue that this is the ultimate tragedy of the common. *See also* GAME THEORY; SUSTAINABLE DEVELOPMENT. [P.C.]

trait Character, usually presumed to be under genetic control and hence open to SELECTION. It can be 'simple' (e.g. eye colour), part of a complex (e.g. life-history feature) or a complex (e.g. semelparous life history). [P.C.]

trajectory The path in a phase plane graph. [B.S.]

tramp species Animal (usually bird) species found on most tropical and subtropical oceanic islands. These animals often live in habitats created directly or indi-

rectly by human settlement. *See also* DISTRIBUTION. [M.J.C.]

transboundary effects Environmental effects across state boundaries, for example due to active transport (road, rail or air) or substances, of passive transport in the atmosphere, rivers or sea. *See also* ACID RAIN AND MIST; EXPORT OF POLLUTION; PRIOR INFORMED CONSENT. [P.C.]

transect A line along which the DISTRIBUTION of the VEGETATION or fauna of an area is investigated. Transects are frequently used in zoned vegetation. [A.J.W.]

transformation of data There are three reasons why the original observations recorded by an ecologist need to be transformed or converted into more suitable units. These are:

1 for visual convenience in a graph;

2 to convert a curved relationship into a more convenient straight line; and

3 because the original data is unsuitable for PARAMETRIC STATISTICS.

There are three common transformations.

1 Logarithmic: each observation (x) is transformed to logarithms (usually base 10). Therefore the transformed data = $\log(x)$. Data skewed to the right are made more symmetrical and the variance is less dependent upon the mean. If there are zero observations then replace x with $\log(x + 1)$.

2 Square root: each observation is transformed to its square root. Therefore the transformed data = $\sqrt{(x)}$. This is frequently used when the observations are whole number counts, for example the number of insects on a leaf. This reduces the CORRELATION between the variance and the mean. If there are zero counts, then replace x with $\sqrt{(x + 0.5)}$.

3 Arcsine or angular: used when observations are proportions. In this case the data cannot be normally distributed because it is confined by 0 and 1. The transformed data = $\sin^{-1}[\sqrt{(x)}]$. [B.S.]

transgenic organisms Transgenic organisms are organisms which have been modified by the insertion of 'foreign' nucleic acid to allow the expression of a new TRAIT or phenotype which would not normally be observed for that organism. A more formal definition, paraphrased below, is given in *The Regulation and Control of the Deliberate Release of Genetically Modified Organisms*—DoE/ACRE Guidance Note 1 (1993) to the Genetically Modified Organism (Deliberate Release) Regulations 1992, UK Department of the Environment, London.

> Transgenic organisms are those in which a new combination of genetic material has been introduced so that the combination could not occur naturally and within which the introduced material will be heritable. This may include integration of the genetic material within the genome of the host organism. The usual method would involve the insertion by

any method into a virus, bacterial plasmid or other vector system of a nucleic acid molecule which has been produced 'artificially' outside that vector. Transgenic organisms may also be produced using the techniques of micro-injection, macro-injection, micro-encapsulation or other methods which insert the genetic material directly, or even the fusion or hybridisation of two or more cells to form cells which have new combinations of heritable material. The definition includes the possibility of self-cloning, where nucleic acid is removed from a cell or organism and then re-inserted into the same cell type or into phylogenetically closely related species. [J.K.]

transition mire This term is used of RHEOTROPHIC mires in which the flow of water is slow and the mineral nutrient content of the water is poor, leading to the development of an acidophilous vegetation intermediate between poor FEN and ombrotrophic bog. [P.D.M.]

transpiration Loss of WATER from the plant surface by evaporation through the stomata. [J.G.]

transplant experiments The transfer of individuals, or samples of populations or communities, from one place to another Usually done to investigate the importance of the physical/geographical location in characteristics being observed. [P.C.]

tree line The limit of isolated bigger or smaller FOREST stands and single trees towards treeless vegetation in polar regions, on high mountains and in arid continental regions. *See also* TIMBER LINE. [Y.V.]

trench Deep and sinuous depressions in the OCEAN floor, usually seaward of a CONTINENTAL MARGIN or a volcanic island arc, where the oceanic crust is destroyed as it is subducted downward to the mantle. [V.F.]

tributyltin (TBT) pollution Tributyltin is an organo-metallic substance used in ANTIFOULING paints. It can cause ecological effects at low to sub-nanogram quantities per litre, for example IMPOSEX in gastropods. It is therefore considered to be one of the most toxic kinds of compounds in the aquatic environment. Its use is now strictly controlled in most places. [P.C.]

troglobitic Cave-dwelling species. [P.C.]

trophic level A trophic level is a position in a FOOD CHAIN determined by the number of energy transfer steps to that level. Thus, in complex natural communities all organisms which obtain their food from living plants by feeding the same number of steps away from the plants along food chains, form a trophic level within that GRAZING food-web COMMUNITY. Similarly for the dead plants and the decomposer FOOD WEB. Green plants form the first trophic level of the primary producers, herbivores form the second trophic level, carnivores feeding on the herbivores the third trophic level, and secondary carnivores which feed on them the fourth trophic level. [M.H.]

tropical montane forest Above about 1200–1500 m the composition of the tropical FOREST changes. Various kinds of tropical montane forest can be recognized. The most common kind is broad-leaved. Microphyllous or needle-leaved coniferous or ericaceous forest is another kind, and in some places bamboo forest is present. [M.I.]

tropical rain forest The term 'tropical rain forest' was coined by the German plant geographer A.F.W. Schimper in 1898. The lowland equatorial forests are located mainly in South America (about 50% of the world's tropical RAIN FOREST is found in this region), south-east Asia (about 30%) and central Africa (20%). The vegetation is typically dominated by evergreen trees whose buds lack scales or any protection against DROUGHT or cold. Mean annual precipitation usually exceeds 2000 mm and may be greater than 4000 mm. Temperature shows little seasonal fluctuation and usually lies around 26–30°C. [P.D.M.]

tropical seasonal forest Rainfall is relatively uniformly distributed throughout the year in many equatorial regions, as in south-east Asia generally, and also in much of Brazil. But other areas have an uneven rainfall pattern, such as southern Nigeria, coastal Zaire and parts of Central America. The incidence of distinct dry and wet seasons, particularly as one moves away from the equatorial regions and into the monsoon zone (*see* MONSOON FOREST), leads to new selective pressures on plant and animal species. Seasonal tropical forests may still be dominated by evergreen species of tree, or by species that shed all or a large proportion of their leaves as the DRY SEASON develops. Buds may also be protected by coverings in such species. Climbers and epiphytes are still present, but are less abundant than in the more open of the equatorial RAIN FORESTS and become less frequent with the increasing severity of the dry season. [P.D.M.]

troposphere The WEATHER-filled part of the ATMOSPHERE, bounded below by the Earth's surface and above by the tropopause (10–15 km above sea level), and containing 70–90% of its mass (the larger in low latitudes) and almost all of its WATER vapour and cloud. It is continually disturbed by a wide variety of types of weather system, and has typically steep TEMPERATURE lapse rates associated with widespread convection.

The lowest few hundred metres (the atmospheric BOUNDARY LAYER) is directly affected by the underlying surface through friction, surface shape, heating and cooling. [J.F.R.M.]

tropospheric chemistry The chemical processes occurring in the TROPOSPHERE by which trace substances released into the ATMOSPHERE from natural and anthropogenic sources are oxidized. [P.B.]

TSCA (Toxic Substances Control Act) *See* UNITED STATES LEGISLATION.

tsunami Also called a seismic sea wave. A very large sea wave, with a long period (several minutes to several hours), caused by a submarine earthquake, volcanic eruption, etc. In the open OCEAN, tsunamis may travel for thousands of kilometres at velocities of 700–900 km h^{-1}. When they reach the coast, their height may reach 30–70 m and they can therefore cause great damage in coastal areas. [V.F.]

tundra In origin from Finnish or Lappish *tunturi* meaning a treeless hill which has been absorbed via Russian to describe the dwarf shrub, herb and moss vegetation that exists in polar regions too cold to support tree growth. The treeless nature is due in part to the presence of PERMAFROST sufficiently near the soil surface which restricts the depth of soil available for tree root development and necessary to support full-grown trees. Exceptions to the exclusion of trees from permafrost zones are the black spruce of North America (*Picea mariana*) and the dahurian larch of north-eastern Siberia (*Larix dahurica*). Both these species are able to extend shallow root systems over a soil ICE horizon and thus support substantial trees in permafrost areas. [R.M.M.C.]

turbidity Reduced transparency of either ATMOSPHERE (caused by absorption and scattering of RADIATION by solid or liquid particles in suspension) or liquid (caused by scattering of LIGHT by suspended particles). [P.C.]

turbulence The chaotic and seemingly random motion of fluid parcels is known as turbulence. [D.D.B.]

two-tailed test In the NORMAL DISTRIBUTION 95% of observations are contained within $\mu \pm 1.96\sigma$ and the remaining 5% of observations are equally divided between the two tails of the distribution, 2.5% in each tail. When we carry out a $z(d)$ TEST to examine the difference between two means, and we have no a priori reason to expect a value of the test statistic above or below $z = 0$ (either MEAN could be larger), we use the 5% level of significance that corresponds to $z = 1.96$. This is a two-tailed test and corresponds to a NULL HYPOTHESIS of $H_0 : \bar{x}_1 = \bar{x}_2$ and an ALTERNATIVE HYPOTHESIS of $H_1 : \bar{x}_1 \neq \bar{x}_2$. Any statistical test that uses the PROBABILITY in both tails of a distribution is therefore a two-tailed test. The alternative is to use the value of the test statistic that cuts off 5% in just one tail. For the normal distribution this would correspond to $z = 1.65$. Using this value as the 5% significance point would imply a ONE-TAILED TEST. [B.S.]

type 1 error The rejection of a NULL HYPOTHESIS when it is actually true. For example, if we use a *t* TEST to examine the difference between the means of two samples (null hypothesis that they come from populations with the same MEAN: $\mu_1 = \mu_2$) and conclude that they are significantly different when they are not (i.e. conclude that $\mu_1 \neq \mu_2$ when in fact $\mu_1 = \mu_2$). The PROBABILITY of making such a type 1 error, with a *t* test, would be $\alpha = 0.05$ if we accept the 5% level of significance. [B.S.]

type 2 error The acceptance of a NULL HYPOTHESIS when it is actually false. For example, if we use a *t* TEST to examine the difference between the means of two samples (null hypothesis that they come from populations with the same MEAN: $\mu_1 = \mu_2$) and conclude that they are not significantly different when they are (i.e. conclude that $\mu_1 = \mu_2$ when in fact $\mu_1 \neq \mu_2$).

Scientists are often more worried about type 1 than type 2 errors; making false claims about treatments. However, a situation where there might be a concern about type 2 errors is in accepting no difference between polluted and non-polluted sites when in fact they exist. [B.S. & P.C.]

U

ultraviolet radiation Electromagnetic RADIATION in the wavelength interval between X-RAYS and visible LIGHT, i.e. from c. 100 nm to 400 nm (these limits are not universally agreed upon; some scientists set the lower limit at 5 nm or even lower, or the upper limit at 380 nm). UV radiation is subdivided in different ways depending on the discipline. A convenient subdivision for most purposes is: (i) vacuum UV, wavelength less than 180 nm; (ii) UV-C, 180–280 nm; (iii) UV-B, 280–320 nm; and (iv) UV-A, 320–400 nm. Thus defined, the biological effects of UV-A, are similar to those of visible light, and this radiation is only very weakly absorbed by the ATMOSPHERE. UV-B is partly absorbed by OZONE (but hardly by any other constituents) in the atmosphere, and its intensity at ground level is strongly dependent on the ozone content. UV-C does not penetrate at all to ground level. Vacuum UV is so strongly absorbed by air and WATER that evacuated equipment is needed for experimentation with it.

UV radiation has a number of beneficial as well as deleterious effects on the human body. Best known among the former is the production of vitamin D, which requires UV-B radiation. UV-B also ameliorates skin tuberculosis and a number of other diseases. Excessive amounts produce erythema and increase the risk of skin cancer. Although the immediate effect of UV-B is more dramatic than that of UV-A, the risk from the latter is not negligible. It penetrates deeper and affects more cells than does UV-B. UV-B has a negative effect on the immune system, and in contrast to erythema and skin cancer that affect mostly light (Caucasian-type) skin, all human races are subject to immune suppression by UV-B.

UV radiation can also damage the eyes. As in the skin, UV radiation of longer wavelength penetrates deeper. UV-C radiation damages only the cornea and the conjunctiva. A painful inflammation develops within a few hours of EXPOSURE. The main effect of UV-B is in the lens, where it causes cataract, which may result in blindness. Even small amounts of UV-B probably accelerate the ageing and yellowing of the lens. UV-A penetrates to the vitreous body. In infants, significant amounts of both UV-A and UV-B may penetrate to the retina, which calls for special caution. Also in the eye, cancer may develop as a result of exposure to UV radiation.

Health protection GUIDELINES have been issued by the International Radiation Protection Association (IRPA) and the International Non-Ionizing Radiation Committee (INIRC). The basic exposure limit for both general public and occupational exposure to UV radiation incident within 8 hours on the skin or eye is 30 effective Jm^{-2}. This effective exposure is calculated by weighting the spectral exposure values (in Jm^{-2}) for each wavelength by a dimensionless HAZARD (relative spectral effectiveness) function and integrating over all wavelengths.

More important than medical effects may be UV radiation effects on other biological systems, such as PHYTOPLANKTON and terrestrial plant communities. The stratospheric ozone depletion has caused concern about the consequences that increases in such effects may have on a global scale. [L.O.B.]

UNCED (United Nations Conference on Environment and Development) The United Nations Conference on Environment and Development was held in Rio de Janeiro in 1992 and is commonly known as the Earth Summit. It was a follow-up to the World Commission on Environment and Development that first promoted the concept of SUSTAINABLE DEVELOPMENT. The main products of the Earth Summit were as follows.

AGENDA 21 — a comprehensive ·programme of actions needed throughout the world to achieve a more sustainable pattern of development for the 21st century.

Climate Change Convention — an agreement between countries about how to protect the diversity of species and habitats in the world.

Statement of Principles — for the management, conservation and sustainable development of all the world's forests.

International machinery has also been established to follow-up these agreements.

• A new UN Commission on Sustainable Development (CSD) was set up to monitor progress on Agenda 21.

• Each of the conventions will have a conference of parties to monitor progress against commitments and review the need for further advice.

• The CSD will monitor implementation of the forest principles.

See also UNITED NATIONS PROGRAMMES AND BODIES. [P.C.]

uncertainty Lack of understanding or control of situations due to: (i) ignorance; (ii) poor experimental design and/or sloppy observation; and/or (iii) stochasticity in the process being studied. [P.C.]

understorey The shrubs and young trees found beneath the trees in woods and FORESTS. [J.R.P.]

unit Quantity or dimension adopted as a standard for measurement. The scientific community has adopted SI UNITS (Système International d'Unités) as the standard. [J.G.]

United Nations programmes and bodies The United Nations (UN) was established in 1945 to maintain international peace and security and to achieve international cooperation in solving international problems of an economic, social, cultural or humanitarian character. It has spawned a number of programmes and bodies.

Food and Agriculture Organization (FAO). Established in 1945, the main purpose of the FAO is to raise levels of nutrition and standards of living of all peoples and to secure improvements in the efficiency of production and distribution of all food and agricultural products.

International Labour Organization (ILO). This was initially established in 1919 under the Peace Treaty of Versailles alongside the League of Nations, and became a specialized body of the UN in 1946. Its main purpose is to promote social progress *inter alia* by adequate protection for the life and health of workers in all occupations; it is therefore largely concerned with the working environment.

International Maritime Organization (IMO). Established in 1978 as the *International Maritime Consultation Organization* (IMCO) it was renamed as IMO in 1982. It aims to facilitate cooperation among governments on technical matters affecting international shipping, and including special responsibilities for safety of life at sea and for the protection of the marine environment through prevention of POLLUTION at sea.

United Nations Environment Programme (UNEP). This is a programme, not an agency. Its main aim is to continuously review the world environmental situation, to develop and recommend policies on the protection and improvement of the environment, to promote international cooperation at all levels in the field of the environment, and to catalyse environmental work in and outside the UN system.

World Health Organization (WHO). This was established in 1946 to promote the attainment by all peoples of the highest possible level of health.

Other United Nations organizations. Another UN organization of relevance is the UN Educational, Scientific and Cultural Organization (UNESCO), established in 1945 and in which the Intergovernmental Oceanographic Commission (IOC) and the Man and the Biosphere Programme (MAB) pay some attention to pollution by chemicals. The UN Industrial Development Organization (UNIDO), established in 1966, encourages and assists developing countries to promote and accelerate their industrializations. Its provisions include hazardous WASTE management, or waste reutilization. Attention is also paid to the safety implications of pesticides. The World Bank, established in 1944, gives loans for large-scale development programmes, but these should take account of ENVIRONMENTAL IMPACT and the potential for chemical pollution. [P.C.]

United States legislation There are five main areas of US federal legislation covering:

1 controls on substances (Toxic Substances Control Act, TSCA, and the Federal Insecticide, Fungicide and Rodenticide Act, FIFRA);

2 controls on environmental quality (the Clean Air Act, CAA, and the Clean Water Act, CWA);

3 controls on current intentional dumping of wastes (the Resource Conservation and Recovery Act, RCRA);

4 powers to address previously CONTAMINATED LAND (Comprehensive Environmental Response Compensation and Liability Act, CERCLA or Superfund, and the Superfund Amendments and Reauthorization Act, SARA);

5 controls on the movements of hazardous materials (Hazardous Materials Transportation Act, HMTA).

Both TSCA and FIFRA require labelling of dangerous substances. RISK MANAGEMENT is done on the basis of RISK ASSESSMENT procedures but (in both TSCA and FIFRA) tempered with a need to balance environmental risks from the product against benefits derived from it in economic and social terms.

Both CWA and CAA define POLLUTION in terms of alterations to the ambient quality—chemical, physical and biological. Both recognize the need for the control of especially dangerous substances and both identify 'priority lists'. Regulation is largely through emission controls (that in CAA may be tradeable) based on ENVIRONMENTAL QUALITY STANDARDS and available technology—with some account of cost of implementation being taken into account. But the Pollution Prevention Act is now putting more emphasis on reduction at source.

RCRA has set up a cradle-to-grave tracking system for WASTE. CERCLA/SARA, in addressing earlier CONTAMINATION, impose strict liability that is joint and several. The Superfund provisions also introduces provisions to guard against major ACCIDENTS and to keep the public informed of potential dangers.

Finally, HMTA makes provision for controlling substances in transit, both nationally and internationally, by requiring appropriate documentation.

Both RCRA and CERCLA are concerned with protection of the soil and in this sense also complement the habitat orientated provisions of CWA and CAA. There is also a series of acts that seek to protect nature (Wildlife and Wilderness Acts). These cover ENDANGERED SPECIES, marine mammals and fish and WILDLIFE. *See also* ENVI-

RONMENTAL LAW; ENVIRONMENTAL (PROTEC-
TION) AGENCIES. [P.C.]

upstream–downstream comparison Comparison of
the BIOTA above and below an effluent stream emp-
tying into a stream or RIVER. Upstream is used as a
comparator for deviations from normality downstream, i.e. it is presumed that the downstream
system would be like the upstream in the absence of
STRESS—but this need not be so. *Cf.* BACI. *See also*
MONITORING. [P.C.]

upwelling Process by which deep, cold, nutrient-laden
water is brought to the surface, usually by diverging
equatorial CURRENTS or COASTAL currents that
pull water away from the coast. The nutrient-
rich waters generally promote PHYTOPLANKTON
growth which in turn supports rich ZOOPLANKTON
and fish populations. [V.F.]

urban reclamation *See* RECLAMATION.

**USEPA (United States Environmental Protection
Agency)** *See* ENVIRONMENTAL (PROTECTION)
AGENCIES.

UV-A *See* ULTRAVIOLET RADIATION.

UV-B *See* ULTRAVIOLET RADIATION.

UV-C *See* ULTRAVIOLET RADIATION.

V

Valdez principles Principles developed following the *Exxon Valdez* disaster by CEREs—the Coalition of Environmentally Responsible Economies (Box V1). Businesses are invited to sign publicly to show commitment to environmental protection. [P.C.]

validation A term applied to BIOASSAYS and ECO-TOXICITY tests. Implies checking their ability to yield 'true' assessments, but the pursuit of truth is elusive in science. Instead, it generally involves checking the sensitivity of one measure of an environmental signal against another. *See also* RING TEST. [P.C.]

variability Changes in ecological properties and processes through space and time. Also refers to changes in results from experiments carried out simultaneously (replicability), or at different times in the same laboratory (REPEATABILITY), or at different laboratories (REPRODUCIBILITY). It can be measured as a COEFFICIENT OF VARIATION. *See also* POPULATION DYNAMICS. [P.C.]

variance A measure of variation. In a SAMPLE it is represented by the Roman letter s^2, and is an estimate of the POPULATION variance represented by the Greek letter sigma-squared (σ^2). It is the square

---

Box V1 The Valdez principles

1 *Protection of the biosphere.* We will minimize and strive to eliminate the release of any pollutant that may cause environmental damage to the air, water, or Earth or its inhabitants. We will safeguard habitats in rivers, lakes, wetlands, coastal zones and oceans and will minimize contributing to the greenhouse effect, depletion of the ozone layer, acid rain or smog.

2 *Sustainable use of natural resources.* We will make sustainable use of renewable natural resources such as water, soils and forests. We will conserve non-renewable natural resources through efficient use and careful planning. We will protect wildlife habitat, open spaces and wilderness while preserving biodiversity.

3 *Reduction of disposal of waste.* We will minimize the creation of waste, especially hazardous waste, and wherever possible recycle materials. We will dispose of all wastes through safe and responsible methods.

4 *Wise use of energy.* We will make every effort to use environmentally safe and sustainable energy sources to meet our needs. We will maximize the energy efficiency of products we produce or sell.

5 *Risk reduction.* We will minimize the environmental, health and safety risks to our employees and the communities in which we operate by employing safe technologies and operating procedures and by being constantly prepared for emergencies.

6 *Marketing of safe products and services.* We will sell products or services that minimize adverse environmental impacts and that are safe as consumers commonly use them. We will inform consumers of the environmental impacts of our products and services.

7 *Damage compensation.* We will take responsibility for any harm we cause to the environment by making every effort to fully restore the environment and to compensate those persons who are adversely affected.

8 *Disclosure.* We will disclose to our employees and to the public incidents relating to our operations that cause environmental harm or pose health or safety hazards. We will disclose potential environmental, health or safety hazards posed by our operations, and we will not take any action against employees who report any condition that creates a danger to the environment or poses a health and safety hazard.

9 *Environmental directors and managers.* At least one member of the board of directors will be a person qualified to represent environmental interests. We will commit management resources to implement these principles, including the funding of an office of vice president for environmental affairs or equivalent executive position, reporting directly to the chief executive officer (CEO), to monitor and report upon our implementation efforts.

10 *Assessment and annual audit.* We will conduct and make public an annual self-evaluation of our progress in implementing these principles and in complying with all applicable laws and regulations throughout our worldwide operations. We will work toward the timely creation of independent environmental audit procedures which we will complete annually and make available to the public.

of the STANDARD DEVIATION. The formula for calculating the sample variance is:

$$s^2 = \frac{\sum (\bar{x} - x)^2}{n-1}$$

Where $\bar{x}$ is the sample MEAN, x is each observation in the sample, n is the number of observations in the sample, and the Greek symbol Σ (capital sigma) is the mathematical notation for 'sum of'. [B.S.]

vector, mathematical A quantity having both size and direction as opposed to a scalar quantity that has size only. [B.S.]

vector, parasites Parasites must transmit between definitive hosts and if a second species acts to convey the PARASITE between hosts, it is known as a vector species. [G.F.M.]

vegetation The sum total of plants in the broadest sense (tracheophytes, bryophytes and algae) at a site, by convention including certain symbiotic fungi (mutualistic mycorrhizae and mycorrhizae parasitized by orchids and a few other specialized plants) but not the fungi parasitic or saprophytic on the plants. [P.J.G.]

vehicle emissions *See* MOTOR VEHICLE POLLUTION.

veld The temperate GRASSLANDS of the eastern area of the southern part of Africa. [P.D.M.]

vernal pools Seasonally wet, shallow pools, commonly found in the Central Valley and surrounding lower foothill regions of the coastal and Sierra Nevada ranges in California. [S.K.J.]

viscosity The property of a fluid to resist motion within itself, arising from the intermolecular forces between layers as the fluid flows over a surface. [J.G.]

vitamins Organic compounds that are essential for heterotrophs only in minute quantities, but which they cannot synthesize themselves. Vitamins, or derivatives from them, normally have a coenzyme function. [P.C.]

VOC *See* VOLATILE ORGANIC COMPOUND.

volatile organic compound (VOC) Volatile organic compounds evaporate readily and have adverse effects on human health and the environment. Examples of VOCs include ethylene, propylene, benzene, styrene and acetone. *See also* HYDROCARBONS. [P.C.]

volcanic gases A volcanic eruption reduces the pressure on gases which are enclosed in rock cavities and these are often released explosively. WATER vapour (H_2O), CARBON DIOXIDE (CO_2) and sulphur dioxide (SO_2) are the most common. Sulphur is often also present as the element and is quickly oxidized on exposure to the ATMOSPHERE at temperatures commonly observed in eruptions (700–1200°C).

All these gases are present in the PLUME after an eruption, but large quantities of fine DUST are also commonly emitted and are carried up into the STRATOSPHERE by the buoyancy of the plume (Mt. Pinatubo was a spectacular example of dust at high temperature, and Sakura-jima in Kyushu is a continuous source of these components, while Stromboli emits primarily SO_2 and is therefore called a solfatara). [R.S.S.]

Vorsorgeprinzip One of the several principles of German environmental policy that roughly translates into the PRECAUTIONARY PRINCIPLE. It was first enunciated by the German Federal Government in 1976, and became more widely used in the rest of Europe in the 1980s. It raises the need to act against risks that are not yet understood or have not yet been proved, and can also include the need to act in the absence of risk, as in maintaining an environmental resource undisturbed. The other principles of action include the principle of proportionality of administrative actions and the prohibition of excessive actions. Action taken under *Vorsorgeprinzip* thus requires a balancing of risks, and costs and benefits. [P.C.]

W

WAF *See* WATER ACCOMMODATED FRACTION.

waste That for which there is no further use. But this is very much in the eye of the beholder. Thus metal that is SCRAP to one group may form the raw material of another; discarded food materials can form the useful basis of compost; all organic wastes can be used as a source of heat energy. As far as the law is concerned, waste is usually identified relative to the views of the producer rather than user. Wastes can be classified by source (household, industrial, clinical), form (liquid, solid, slurries, etc.) and legal definitions (controlled, special, etc.) *See also* WASTE DISPOSAL. [P.C.]

waste disposal Options for dealing with WASTE. In principle this should only be considered once recovery, REUSE or RECYCLING options are exhausted. This can involve LANDFILL, treatment (biological, chemical and physical), fixation (encapsulation in a variety of matrices), deep underground disposal, DUMPING AT SEA, or INCINERATION. Waste disposal is usually subject under the law to a DUTY OF CARE whereby all those in the chain leading from source, through collection and transport, to ultimate sink are required to adhere to the regulations, thus ensuring the safe handling of waste at all times and enabling the route and disposal of the waste to be tracked. [P.C.]

waste minimization Attempts to reduce losses of WASTE by effective management, increased efficiency and attending to FUGITIVE EMISSIONS. So-called win–win management: environment gains through reduced impact; business gains by increased efficiency and hence ultimately profits. [P.C.]

waste regulation authorities *See* ENVIRONMENTAL (PROTECTION) AGENCIES.

water A widely distributed compound (H_2O) essential for life. Water differs from similar small molecules (e.g. ammonia (NH_3), METHANE (CH_4), nitrogen dioxide (NO_2)) in being a liquid as opposed to a gas at 'normal' temperatures because the H_2O molecule is strongly polarized, making the molecules cling together through weak hydrogen bonding. [J.G.]

water accommodated fraction (WAF) That fraction of a complex mixture of chemicals (e.g. from oils) that is present in the aqueous phase following a period of mixing. Sometimes referred to as a water soluble fraction (WSF), but WAF is preferred as it is often the case that stable microemulsions of finely dispersed droplets can exist, that do not represent true solutions. WAF is used in ecotoxicological tests of oils. As WAFs form naturally after OIL SPILLS, it is claimed they cause the most important ecological problems. [P.C.]

Water Acts Series of Acts (1989 and 1991) of the UK Parliament establishing controls over the quality of waters from the tap and in the environment, largely for England and Wales. Amongst other things, these privatized the water industry and established the National Rivers Authority (NRA) as the regulatory body for England and Wales. They have now been supplemented by the Environment Act 1995. *See also* ENVIRONMENTAL LAW. [P.C.]

water (hydrological) cycle It was the English astronomer Edmund Halley who, in 1691, first wrote about the natural cycle of evaporation, condensation and rainfall. On the Earth's surface, 97% of the WATER is in the oceans, and most of the remainder is in the ice caps. Only a tiny fraction of the total is in the ATMOSPHERE at any time (Table W1). Each day about $1200\,km^3$ of WATER evaporates from the oceans and $190\,km^3$ is lost from the terrestrial surface by evapotranspiration. Around $1000\,km^3$ falls on the SEA as RAIN and other PRECIPITATION, and $300\,km^3$ falls over the land. A flow of some $110\,km^3$ is returned to the sea via RIVERS, groundwater and meltwater.

In practice there are numerous short circuits to this cycle. Water, having fallen on to the Earth's surface, may travel back into the atmosphere through any of a number of different pathways. On land, some of the precipitation will be intercepted by the vegetation and evaporated directly back into the atmosphere. Unless the SOIL is saturated, when overland flow may be generated, the precipitation reaching the ground enters the soil, and is either taken up by plants and evaporated as TRANSPIRATION, or drains through the soil to reach rivers and then the oceans, either directly or via groundwater.

Average residence times for the different phases of the hydrological cycle vary from a few days, for the atmospheric phase, to sometimes more than hundreds of years for groundwater. The size of the global water reservoirs and fluxes is given in Table W1. [J.H.C.G. & J.G.]

water quality The wholesomeness of WATER to drink, its appearance, its odour, the abundance of fish and other living things within it have all formed part of a subjective assessment of what is meant by 'water

Table W1 Global water reservoirs and fluxes. (After Ward, R.C. & Robinson, M. (1990) *Principles of Hydrology*. McGraw-Hill, Maidenhead. Reproduced with the kind permission of McGraw-Hill Publishing Company.)

	Values (km³ × 10³)	Percentage of reservoir
Global reservoir		
Ocean	1350000	97.403
Atmosphere	13	0.001
Land	35978	2.596
Terrestrial reservoir		
Rivers	2	0.006
Freshwater lakes	100	0.278
Inland seas	105	0.292
Soil water	70	0.195
Groundwater	8200	22.792
Ice caps/glaciers	27500	76.436
Biota	1	0.003
Annual flux		
Evaporation		
Ocean	425.0	
Land	71.0	
Total	496.0	
Precipitation		
Ocean	385.0	
Land	111.0	
Total	496.0	
Run-off to oceans		
Rivers	27.0	
Groundwater	12.0	
Glacial meltwater	2.5	
Total	41.5	

quality'. In this sense the concept is a management test rather than having an objective meaning. Neither is 'water quality' synonymous with water chemistry for this can vary, even in uncontaminated systems.

It is impossible to say what water quality should be in any particular circumstances without setting some target that is related to use. Such targets are implicitly biological: safe for drinking; suitable for fish; supporting wildlife in general; suitable for recreation, etc. Water chemistry is important in enabling these biological targets to be met; because chemical measures have proved useful in SURVEIL-LANCE since they are relatively easy to monitor. However, if water chemistry had no biological impact it would have little intrinsic importance in management. Hence, biological criteria are also important. [P.C.]

water quality objective/standard (WQO/WQS) In UK law, WQO is the target for WATER QUALITY in a stretch of river, for example to supply fisheries, ABSTRACTION for drinking, etc. WQS is a quantitative concentration below which the defined environmental/ecological objectives are likely to be achieved. Elsewhere there is a tendency to use WQO and WQS interchangeably to refer to standards. *See also* ENVIRONMENTAL QUALITY OBJECTIVE; ENVIRONMENTAL QUALITY STANDARD. [P.C.]

water soluble fraction (WSF) *See* WATER ACCOMMODATED FRACTION.

water table The WATER table is the upper envelope of the subsurface zone which is saturated with water, it separates groundwater from the SOIL moisture in the unsaturated zone above. [J.H.C.G.]

watershed Drainage BASIN. *See also* CATCHMENT. [P.C.]

watt (W) The SI UNIT of power, equal to 1 JOULE of energy per SECOND (Js^{-1}). Its relation to obsolete units are: 1 horsepower = 0.745 kW; 1 cheval-vapeur = 0.735 kW. [J.G.]

wave power Using energy in the waves on seawater to generate electricity. This is a renewable power source. [P.C.]

weather Weather represents the state of the ATMOSPHERE at a particular instant of time and includes a description of its significant features such as anticyclones, fronts and depressions and their progression in time. [J.B.M.]

weathering Destruction or partial destruction of rock by thermal, chemical and mechanical processes. [V.F.]

weed (i) A plant where I don't want it; (ii) a plant whose virtues have yet to be discovered; (iii) a plant in the wrong place; (iv) a plant which is the target of HERBICIDE application; (v) a plant for whose removal or destruction someone is willing to pay money or expend effort. [M.J.C.]

Wentworth scale A geometric grading scheme for expressing sedimentary grain diameters. [V.F.]

wetlands A broad term for a wide range of habitats characterized by their abundant WATER supply. The Ramsar Convention (an international meeting concerned with wetland conservation, held in Iran in 1971) defined wetlands as:

Areas of marsh, fen, peatland or water, whether natural or artificial, permanent or temporary, with water that is static or flowing, fresh, brackish or salt, including areas of marine water the depth of which at low tide does not exceed six metres.

[P.D.M.]

whaling Although whales have been hunted by mankind since prehistoric times, the term whaling usually refers to modern commercial catching of whales using tethered, barbed harpoons, which sometimes carry an explosive tip. The INTERNATIONAL WHALING COMMISSION (IWC), the inter-government regulatory body for whaling established in 1946, has introduced progressively stricter restrictions on whaling since the 1960s, culminating in a general ban on commercial whaling from 1986

Table W2 The Beaufort scale.

Beaufort number	Descriptor	Speed (m s⁻¹)	Specification
0	Calm	0–0.2	Smoke rises vertically
1	Light air	0.3–1.5	Smoke drifts, but wind-vanes unresponsive
2	Light breeze	1.6–3.3	Wind felt on face, wind-vanes respond, leaves rustle
3	Gentle breeze	3.4–5.4	Wind extends light flag, leaves and small twigs in motion
4	Moderate breeze	5.5–7.9	Raises dust and loose paper, small branches in motion
5	Fresh breeze	8.0–10.7	Crested wavelets form on inland waters, small trees sway
6	Strong breeze	10.8–13.8	Large branches sway, umbrellas used with difficulty, whistling of overhead telegraph lines heard
7	Near gale	13.9–17.1	Whole trees in motion, difficulty walking against the wind
8	Gale	17.2–20.7	Twigs break from trees
9	Strong gale	20.8–24.4	Slight structural damage to roofs
10	Storm	24.5–28.4	Trees uprooted, structural damage widespread
11	Violent storm	28.5–32.6	Widespread damage
12	Hurricane	32.7 and over	

onwards. The IWC has recently been developing scientific approaches to the management of whaling which would eventually enable whale populations to be harvested on a sustainable basis. Although previous approaches to sustainable management of whaling have proven unworkable, the Revised Management Procedure, approved by the IWC in 1994, is considered by most experts to be sound. It will not be implemented until other outstanding issues, such as enforcement of regulations, are resolved. As an additional safety measure, the IWC in 1994 designated most of the Southern Ocean south of 40°S as a sanctuary for whales in which whaling is not permitted. [J.G.C.]

WHO (World Health Organization) *See* UNITED NATIONS PROGRAMMES AND BODIES.

wildlife In principle, wildlife refers to all the indigenous flora and fauna in nature. In practice, its use often intends only animal life. [P.C.]

win–win management *See* WASTE MINIMIZATION.

wind The ATMOSPHERE in motion. Wind is important for several reasons: (i) because of the catastrophic damage it does to buildings and other structures; (ii) because of its indirect and direct effects on plants, both at macroscopic and microscopic scales; (iii) because of its effect on heat loss from buildings, people and crops; and (iv) as a medium for DISPERSAL of pollens, spores, seeds and pollutants. Wind is strong enough in many parts of the world to have potential as an energy supply. Wind speed is measured with an ANEMOMETER, and direction is measured with a wind-vane. The wind speed is found to increase with height above the ground in a logarithmic manner, depending on the aerodynamic roughness of the land cover. At meteorological stations the wind speed is measured well above the ground (10 m). The Beaufort scale (Table W2) describes the wind in a way that relates to everyday experience. [J.G.]

wind-break A barrier or line of trees (shelterbelt)

Table W3 Table of wind-chill equivalent temperatures.

Actual temperature (°C)	Wind speed (m s⁻¹)			
	Calm	5	10	15
0	−1	−2	−7	−11
−5	−4	−9	−13	−16
−10	−9	−13	−19	−25
−15	−13	−19	−26	−33
−20	−18	−26	−34	−42
−30	−28	37	−50	
−40	−37	−50		

designed to reduce the speed of the WIND to benefit crops or livestock. [J.G.]

wind-chill The extent to which a human feels cold depends not only on the air TEMPERATURE but also on the WIND speed. Heat loss from the body surface involves convective transfer of heat, which is a function of wind speed as well as air temperature. It has proved useful to have a scale of wind-chill that encompasses wind and temperature, and enables people engaged in outdoor pursuits to be advised about the chilling effect of the WEATHER (Table W3). [J.G.]

wind power The use of WIND vanes to harness energy from the wind in driving electrical turbines. *See also* RENEWABLE RESOURCE. [P.C.]

wind tunnel A construction for making a controlled flow of air over an experimental object. [J.G.]

within-lake habitat classification In LAKES the substrate from the shore down to the deepest parts of the water exhibit a series of zones.

1 Epilittoral—entirely above the water, uninfluenced even by spray.

2 Supralittoral—entirely above the water but affected by the spray.

3 Littoral—from the edge of the water to the point of light penetration where PRIMARY

PRODUCTIVITY equals RESPIRATION (COMPEN-SATION POINT). The littoral is subdivided into:

(a) eulittoral—between the highest and lowest seasonal levels;

(b) upper infralittoral—with emergent rooted vegetation (rhizobenthos);

(c) middle infralittoral—with floating leaves on the rooted vegetation;

(d) lower infralittoral—with submerged rooted vegetation.

Typically, the rhizobenthos forms concentric rings within the LITTORAL ZONE with one group replacing the next as the water depth changes. In the littoral zone the primary producers are of two types: rhizobenthic and haptobenthic, made up of aquatic macrophytic spermatophytes and phytobenthic algae.

4 The region in the deeper waters which has no rooted vegetation is the profundal where respiration exceeds PRODUCTION, while the transition zone between the littoral and profundal zones is the littoriprofundal.

5 The open water zone is termed the limnetic (or PELAGIC) zone and is equivalent to the EUPHOTIC ZONE, where respiration equals PHOTOSYNTHESIS and the compensation point is usually approximated as 1% of full sunlight.

The profundal community thus depends on the littoral and limnetic zones for its energy sources since respiration exceeds production. While the biotic diversity is not high, the profundal community is of importance in trapping NUTRIENTS and chemical cycling.

Physically, the air–water interface consists of a monomolecular layer of proteins or lipoproteins derived from decomposing plant material which is an important source of food, as well as support, and for entrapping of organisms subsequently used for food. The biological community at the air–water interface is the pleuston which is divided into the macropleuston, which has an upper dry surface and a lower wet surface, and the micropleuston which is associated with either the undersurface (hypomicropleuston) when it is totally wet, or the upper surface (epimicropleuston) when it is totally dry.

Organisms which permanently inhabit the air–water interface are termed eupleuston compared to organisms which only temporarily inhabit this habitat which are termed pseudopleuston. [R.W.D.]

within-stream/river habitat classification There are two major habitat types:

1 in riffles (or rapids) the water is shallow with water velocities high enough to keep the bottom clear of SILT and mud;

2 in pools the water is deeper with velocities low enough that silt and other loose materials can settle on the bottom.

The hyporheos consists of the interstices between the particles composing the substrate forming a middle zone between the surface waters of the stream and the groundwater (AQUIFER) below. There is also a pleuston community associated with the water–air interface of streams but this is never as well developed as in LAKES. *See also* RIVER CONTINUUM CONCEPT. [R.W.D.]

wood-pasture A semi-cultural type of vegetation with a mosaic of alternating patches of open meadows and small copses of deciduous trees and shrubs. [Y.V.]

woodland Tree-covered land and associated habitats in a matrix of trees. Now usually associated in Britain with small woods consisting mainly of native trees, and with traditional or other non-intensive forms of management in which timber-growing is only one of many objects of management (*cf.* FOREST). In other English-speaking countries, woodland labels open-canopied forest in Australia, but is uncertain in its connotations in North America. [G.F.P.]

World Bank *See* GATT AND ENVIRONMENT.

World Conservation Union *See* IUCN.

World Conservation Union's Commission on National Parks and Protected Areas *See* EXTRACTIVE RESERVES.

World Health Organization (WHO) *See* UNITED NATIONS PROGRAMMES AND BODIES.

World Meteorological Organization (WMO) The WMO is a specialized agency of the UN located in Geneva. Its programmes include World Weather Watch, World Climate Programme, Global Climate Observation System (and its GCOS Data System), and it also has an Education and Training Programme. It has a page on the World Wide Web which documents many of its programmes: http:/www.wmo.ch/. *See also* METEOROLOGY. [J.G.]

World Weather Watch (WWW) *See* METEOROLOGY.

WQO/WQS *See* WATER QUALITY OBJECTIVE/ STANDARD.

WSF (water soluble fraction) *See* WATER ACCOMMODATED FRACTION.

WWW (World Weather Watch) *See* METEOROLOGY.

X

X-rays (X-radiation) Electromagnetic radiation in the wavelength range between γ-radiation and ULTRAVIOLET RADIATION, i.e. from approximately 0.001 nm to approximately 50 nm (some scientists set the upper limit as low as 5 nm). [L.O.B.]

xenobiotic A foreign substance in a biological system, i.e. a substance not naturally produced and not normally a component of a specified biological system. Usually applied to manufactured chemicals. *See also* ECOTOXICOLOGY; TOXICANT; TOXINS. [P.C.]

xeric Dry or lacking in moisture (*cf.* HYDRIC meaning wet). [R.M.M.C.]

Y

yield Return, usually expressed in mass or energy, of natural resources (e.g. fish, lumber) from an area or volume of the environment (*see also* SUSTAINABLE YIELD). Can also refer to a CROP. [P.C.]

Z

z(d) test A procedure that most commonly tests whether the difference observed between two sample MEANS is simply due to chance or is real (NULL HYPOTHESIS, $H_0: \bar{x}_1 = \bar{x}_2$, ALTERNATIVE HYPOTHESIS, $H_1: \bar{x}_1 \neq \bar{x}_2$) for both sample sizes ≥30 (*see* ONE-TAILED TEST and TWO-TAILED TEST). The formula for the test is:

$$z(d) = \frac{\bar{x}_1 - \bar{x}_2}{\sqrt{\left(\frac{s_1^2}{n_1} + \frac{s_2^2}{n_2}\right)}}$$

where $\bar{x}_1$ and $\bar{x}_2$ are the sample means, s_1^2 and s_2^2 are the sample variances and n_1 and n_2 are the sample sizes. In effect, the result of the test is a standardized normal deviate, because we are dividing an observed difference $\bar{x}_1 - \bar{x}_2$ (which is an estimate of $\bar{\mu}_1 - \bar{\mu}_2$) by its STANDARD ERROR. That is, we are dividing by the STANDARD DEVIATION of the sampling DISTRIBUTION of the quantity $\bar{x}_1 - \bar{x}_2$. Since this sampling distribution is normally distributed we can use this standardized normal deviate or z-score to test the null hypothesis ($H_0: \bar{x}_1 = \bar{x}_2$). A $z(d) \geq 1.96$ is only compatible with H_0 5% of the time. Therefore if $z(d) \geq 1.96$ we reject H_0 and accept H_1. Such a difference between two means is said to be a significant difference, or significant at the 5% level, or that the PROBABILITY of obtaining this value of $z(d)$, by chance, is $P < 0.05$. If $z(d) \geq 2.58$ we reject H_0 and accept H_1. However, such a difference between two means is now said to be a very significant difference, or significant at the 1% level, or that the probability of obtaining this value of $z(d)$, by chance, is $P < 0.01$. [B.S.]

zebra mussel (*Dreissena polymorpha*) *See* BIOFOULING; EXOTIC AND INVASIVE SPECIES.

zero emissions Discharges containing no CONTAMINATION. This is unrealistic on at least two grounds: (i) a technological society could not persist on this basis; and (ii) what is 'zero' depends upon the ability to measure it, 'detection limit' is a more apt descriptor. [P.C.]

zonation A type of pattern in which zones or bands of communities (coenocline) or ecosystems (ecocline) form a GRADIENT across the landscape. [B.W.F.]

zoo Abbreviation for zoological garden or park. These have evolved from menageries, as displays of exotic animals, to centres of education, conservation and some research. They are referred to by some as 'modern arks'. [P.C.]

zoocoenosis A term used most frequently in the east European literature to denote the animal component of a BIOCOENOSIS. It is thus equivalent to an animal COMMUNITY within an ECOSYSTEM. [M.H.]

zoogeography The scientific study of the geographic DISTRIBUTION of animals. [A.H.]

zooplankton The animal component of the PLANKTON that live free-swimming or suspended in the water column of marine, freshwater LENTIC and, to a lesser extent, LOTIC systems (where they are called potamoplankton). [J.L.]